SENSATION & PERCEPTION
SECOND EDITION

SENSATION AND PERCEPTION
SECOND EDITION

Stanley Coren
University of British Columbia

Clare Porac
University of Victoria

Lawrence M. Ward
University of British Columbia

Harcourt Brace Jovanovich, Publishers
and its subsidiary, Academic Press
San Diego New York Chicago Austin Washington, D.C.
London Sydney Tokyo Toronto

Requests for permission to make copies of any part of the work should be mailed to: Permissions, Harcourt Brace Jovanovich, Publishers, Orlando, Florida 32887

ISBN: 0-15-579634-8
Library of Congress Catalog Card Number: 83-73183

Printed in the United States of America

Contents

Preface

The Blue Jay, as we clearly see,
Is so much like the green Bay tree
That one might say the only clue
Lies in their difference of hue,
And if you have a color sense,
You'll see at once this difference.*
—R. W. Wood 1917

The jay

The bay

The woodcut above provides a somewhat frivolous example of the way one form of sensory information can tell us how objects in our world are similar or different. In a more serious vein, we all realize that without our senses, our experiences would be incredibly limited. Consider the impossible problem of explaining the

difference between the color blue and the color green to a person who has been blind since birth. Or how would you explain to a person who has no taste buds how the taste of chocolate and vanilla differ from each other? Such aspects of the world will never exist for these individuals. For the blind person, salt and pepper differ only in taste. For the person with no ability to taste, salt and pepper differ only in color. For those of us who have senses of sight, hearing, taste, touch, and smell, our world is a continuous flow of changing percepts. Each

*From *How To Tell the Birds from the Flowers and Other Wood-Cuts* by Robert William Wood, reprint of the original edition, Dodd, Mead and Company, New York, 1917.

new sensation carries with it information about our world.

This book provides an introduction to the study of sensation and perception. Revised substantially since the first edition, it contains more than 40 percent new material. These changes reflect many of the recent findings that have emerged, or coalesced into meaningful patterns, since the completion of the first edition. We have also added several chapters and reorganized or amalgamated materials from some chapters that appeared in the first edition. On the other hand, we have retained all those features that instructors felt made the first edition such a useful teaching tool. For instance, concrete examples are used throughout the book in order to make the subject matter come alive for students. Whenever possible, common or natural instances of perceptual phenomena are described during the discussion of the concepts underlying them. Each chapter is preceded by an outline that serves as a preview to its contents. These outlines also provide a structure that can guide students as they review the chapters.

Although terms are defined at the time of their introduction in the text, a glossary has now been provided at the end of each chapter as well. Any item printed in boldface in the text is also listed in the chapter glossary. Students will find that these glossaries serve as a succinct review and chapter summary. They can also be used for self-testing and study purposes.

One special feature of our book is the inclusion of 80 Demonstration Boxes. Each box describes a simple demonstration that students can conduct for themselves, using stimuli provided in the box or materials found in most homes and dormitory rooms. These demonstrations allow the students to actually experience many of the perceptual phenomena described in the text. Although most demonstrations require only a few moments of preparation, we feel this is time well spent in improving understanding of the concepts under discussion and in maintaining student interest. Of course, the demonstrations may be performed in class if the instructor desires. In this case, they may also serve as the focal point for a lecture or for classroom discussion.

The book is designed to survey the broad range of topics generally included under the heading "sensation and perception." Because a single author can only know a limited portion of the literature in so vast a field, we decided to adopt a team approach in order to present a more complete and balanced picture. In this spirit, this volume has been a truly collaborative effort. While each of us had primary responsibility for specific chapters, all three authors made comments, suggestions, and contributions to every chapter. In addition, each chapter of the final draft has been reviewed by all of us and rewritten in order to provide a uniform tone and flow throughout the book.

No single theory of perception is championed. This is partly because we often hold divergent opinions about how any particular perceptual problem should be approached. In general, we have attempted to be as eclectic as we could, since we felt that nearly every alternative viewpoint of a problem contained some kernel of truth.

The topics in this book were selected on the basis of our experience in teaching our own courses; therefore, much of the material has already been class tested. We have included three chapters, "Attention and Search," "Speech," and "Individual Differences," that are not often seen in sensation and perception textbooks. These areas have attracted a good deal of experimental work in recent years, and they are sufficiently relevant to many issues in perception that we felt students should be aware of their existence.

In order to keep the book a manageable size, we have occasionally been selective in our coverage. Our first priority has been to cover the central concepts of each topic in enough detail to make the material clear and coherent. To include all the topics ever classified as part of the field of sensation and perception would require a "grocery list" of concepts and terms, each treated superficially. Such an alternative was unacceptable to us.

Each chapter has been written so that it is relatively self-contained and independent of the other chapters. When material from other places in the book is used in a discussion, the location of that information is always cited in the text. This has been done to provide the instructor with maximum flexibility as far as the sequence of chapter presentation is concerned, thus permitting the instructor to impress his or her orientation upon the material. We have chosen a sequence of chapter presentation based on ascension from more physiologically based processes to higher level cognitive processes. Another approach would be to organize the course around specific sensory systems by having students read the chapters in the sequence:

Systems reading sequence

(Introduction and methods)
    Chapter 1: Sensation and Perception
    Chapter 2: Psychophysics
(Chemical and mechanical senses)
    Chapter 5: The Chemical and Mechanical Senses
    Chapter 9: Taste, Smell, Touch, and Pain
(Audition)
    Chapter 4: The Auditory System
    Chapter 8: Auditory Qualities
    Chapter 13: Speech

(Vision)
    Chapter 3: The Visual System
    Chapter 6: Brightness
    Chapter 7: Color
    Chapter 10: Space
    Chapter 12: Form
    Chapter 14: The Constancies
    Chapter 15: Attention and Search
    Chapter 11: Time and Motion
(Perceptual plasticity)
    Chapter 16: Development
    Chapter 17: Learning and Experience
    Chapter 18: Individual Differences

A semester course with an emphasis on *perception* might simply omit Chapters 3, 4, and 5, while one with an emphasis on *sensation* might omit Chapters 14, 15, 17, and 18. The point is that each individual unit is relatively complete and independent, and the organization of the course thus remains in the hands of the instructor who will actually teach it.

In our attempts to collect and interpret the information for this book, we have been assisted at various stages by some of our colleagues, including R. Corteen, R. Lakowski, R. Hare, and R. Tees, all of the University of British Columbia, and J. Kess of the University of Victoria. In addition, J. Antes of the University of North Dakota, F. Bagrash of California State University at Fullerton, T. Bourbon of Stephen F. Austin State University, D. Czech of Marquette University, L. Elfner of Florida State University, G. Hawkes of Virginia Commonwealth University, and S. Schwartz of Kean College of New Jersey read the entire manuscript and provided useful comments and criticism. A special appreciation goes to K. Wright, who updated and organized the glossaries and was a mainstay in the final manuscript preparation. We have also been assisted by two very capable typists, S. Louie and L. Spellacy. Our research assistants, M. Blum, E. Cheung, S. Goldsmith,

H. Henderson, B. Kovar, and W. Wong provided support in terms of duplicating, library work, and all the small but necessary chores that eat up innumerable hours of a textbook writer's time. We would also like to thank our editors and the production team at Academic Press for their careful work and enthusiastic support.

Finally, the reader might notice that there is no dedication page. This is not to say that we do not wish to dedicate the book to anyone. It reflects the fact that there are too many people who have been important in our personal and professional lives to list on any single page (no matter how small the print). Perhaps it is best to simply dedicate this book to all those researchers who have provided the knowledge that we have attempted to organize and review between these covers, and to all those researchers who will provide further insights into sensation and perception for future authors to collate, review, digest, wonder at, and learn from.

S.C.
C.P.
L.M.W.

Sensation and Perception

Sensation, Perception, Cognition, and
Information Processing
The Plan of the Book

CAN YOU ANSWER THE FOLLOWING questions? What color is the sky? Which is warmer—fire or ice? Which tastes sweeter—sugar or vinegar? Which has a stronger smell—burning wood or burning rubber? Which sounds louder—a chirping bird or the crack of a rifle? Such questions probably seem trivial, and the answers obvious. Perhaps we should phrase the questions differently. How do you know what color the sky is? How do you know how hot fire is relative to ice? How do you know that sugar is sweet? Again, you might feel that the answers are obvious. You can see the color of the sky, you can feel the temperature of the flame and an ice cube, and you can taste the sweetness of sugar—in other words, the answers come through your senses.

Let us push our questioning one step further. How do you know anything about your world? You might say that you learn from books, television, radio, films, lectures, and the actual exploration of places. But how do you obtain the information from these sources? Again, the answer is through your senses. In fact, without your senses of vision, hearing, touch, taste, and smell, your brain—the organ that is responsible for your conscious experience—would be an eternal prisoner in the solitary confinement of your skull. You would live in total silence and darkness. All would be a tasteless, colorless, feelingless, floating void. Without your senses, the world would simply not exist for you. The philosopher Thomas Hobbes recognized this fact in 1651 when he wrote, "There is no conception in man's mind which hath not at first, totally or by parts, been begotten upon the organs of sense." The Greek philosopher Protagoras was actually stating the same thing around 450 B.C. when he said, "Man is nothing but a bundle of sensations."

You may protest that this is a rather extreme viewpoint. Certainly, much of what we know about the world does not arrive through our eyes, ears, nose, and other sense organs. We have complex scientific instruments, such as telescopes that tell us about the size and the shape of the universe by analyzing images too faint for the human eye to see. We have sonar to trace out the shape of the sea bottom, which may be hidden from our eyes by a hundred feet of water. We have spectrographs to tell us about the exact chemical composition of many substances, compared with the crude chemical sensitivity of our noses and tongues. While such pieces of apparatus exist and measure phenomena not directly available to our senses, the fact remains that it is the perception of the scientist that constitutes the subject matter of every science. It is the eye of the scientist that presses against the telescope or examines the photograph of the distant star. It is the ear of the scientist that listens to the sound of sonar tracing out the size and distance of objects. While the tongue of the scientist does not taste the chemical composition of some unknown substance, the scientist's eye, aided by the spectrograph, provides the data for analysis. In reality, the only data that reach the mind of the scientist come not from instruments but from the scientist's senses. The instrument may be perfectly accurate, yet if the scientist misreads a dial or does not see a critical shift in a measurement device, the obtained information is wrong, and the resulting picture of the world is in error. The minds of the scientist, the nonscientist, our pet dog sniffing about the world, and a fish swimming about in a bowl—in fact, the minds of all living, thinking organisms—are prisoners that must rely on information smuggled into them by the senses. Your world is what your senses tell you it is. The limitations of your senses set the boundaries of your conscious existence.

Because our knowledge of the world depends on our senses, it is important to know how our senses function. It is also important to know how well the world that is created by our senses corresponds to external reality. At this point, you are probably smiling to yourself and thinking, "Here comes another academic discourse that will attempt to make something that is quite obvious appear to be complex." You may be saying to yourself, "I see my desk in front of me because it is there. I feel my chair pressing against my back because it is there. I hear my phone ringing because it contains a bell that makes sounds. What could be more obvious?" Such faith in your senses is a vital part of existence. It causes you to jump out of the way of an apparently oncoming car, thus preserving your life. It provides the basic data that cause you to step back from a deep hole, thus avoiding a fall and serious bodily harm.

Such faith in our senses is built into the very fabric of our lives. As the old saying goes, "Seeing is believing." Long before the birth of Christ, Lucretius stated this article of faith when he asked, "What can give us surer knowledge than our senses? With what else can we distinguish the true form from the false?" Perhaps the most striking example of this faith is found in our courts of law, where people's lives and fortunes rest solely on the testimony of the eyes and ears of witnesses. While a lawyer might argue that a witness is corrupt or lying, or even that his or her memory has failed, no lawyer would have the audacity to suggest that a client should be set free because the only available evidence was based on what the witnesses saw or heard. Certainly no sane person would charge the eye or ear with perjury!

The philosophical position that perception is an immediate, almost godlike knowledge of external reality has been championed not only by popular sentiment but also by philosophers of the stature of Immanual Kant (1724–1804). Unfortunately, it is wrong. Look at the drawings in Figure 1-1. Clearly, they are all composed of outlined forms on various backgrounds. De-

spite what your senses tell you, A, B, and C are all perfect squares. Despite the evidence of your senses, D is a perfect circle, and despite the evidence of your senses, the lines in E are both straight and the lines marked X and Y in F are both the same length.

The ease with which we use our senses, seeing apparently through the simple act of opening our eyes, or touching apparently by merely pressing our skin against an object, masks the fact that perception is an extremely sophisticated activity of the brain. Perception calls upon stores of memory data. It requires subtle classifications, comparisons, and myriad decisions before any of the data in our senses become our conscious awareness of what is "out there." Contrary to what you may think, the eyes do not see. There are many individuals who have perfectly functioning eyes yet have no sensory impressions. They cannot perceive because they have injuries in those parts of the brain that receive and interpret messages from the eyes. As Epicharmus said 450 years before the birth of Christ, "The mind sees and the mind hears. The rest is blind and deaf."

"So what?" you mutter to yourself, "So, sometimes we make errors in our perceptions; the real point is that the senses simply carry a picture of the outside world to the brain. The picture in the brain represents our percept. Of course, if we mess up the brain we will distort or destroy perception." Again, this answer is too simple. If we look outside and see a car, are we to believe that there is a picture of a car somewhere in our brains? If we notice that a traffic light is green, are we to believe that some part of the brain has turned green? And suppose that there were such images in the brain, carried without distortion from the senses, would this help us to see? Certainly, images in the brain would only be of value if there were some other eyes in the head, which

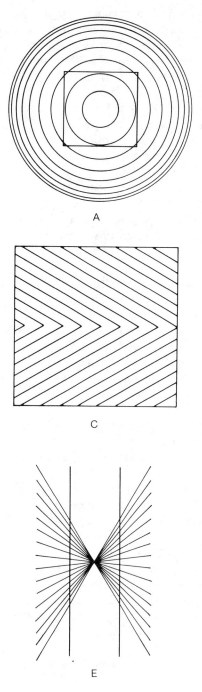

A

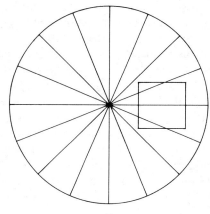

B

C

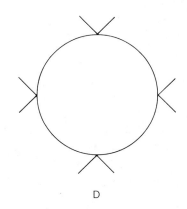

D

E

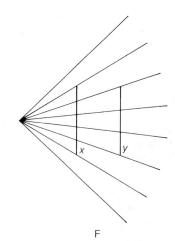

F

Figure 1-1. Some instances in which the senses tell lies.

would look at these pictures and interpret them. If this were the case, we would be left with the question of how these internal eyes see. Thus, we would eventually be forced to set up an endless chain of pictures and eyes and pictures and eyes, because the question of who is perceiving the percept, and how, still remains.

If we are to understand perception we must consider it in its natural context. Sensation and perception are the first of many complex processes that occur when an individual initiates a behavior. No clear line exists between perception and many other behavioral activities. No perception gives direct knowledge of the outside world; rather, such knowledge of the outside world is the end product of many processes. The wet-looking black spot on the edge of a desk could be the place where ink was spilled. Of course, this percept could be wrong. The ink may be dry, or the spot might not be there at all. The desk that is seen and touched might not really exist. We might be dreaming, drugged, or hallucinating. Too extreme, you say? Consider the following example that actually happened to one of the authors. One night he walked across the floor of his darkened home. In the dim gloominess of the night, he saw his dog resting on the floor, clearly asleep. When he bent to touch the dog, he found that it was a footstool. He stepped back, somewhat startled at his stupidity, only to bump against the cold corner of a marble-topped coffee table. When he reached back to steady himself, he found that the corner of the table was, in fact, his dog's cold nose. Each of these perceptions, dog, stool, table, and dog again, seemed to represent reality. Yet, sensory data are not always reliable. Sometimes they can be degraded or not completely available. There seems to be no sudden break between perceiving or sensing an object and guessing its identity. In some respects, one can say that all perception of objects requires some guessing. Sensory stimulation provides the data for our hypotheses about the nature of the external world, and it is these hypotheses that form our perceptions of the world.

Many human behaviors have been affected by the fallible and often erroneous nature of our percepts. For example, the most elegant of the classic Greek buildings, the Parthenon, is bent. The straight, clean lines, which bring a sense of simple elegant grandeur, are actually an illusion. If we schematically represent the east wall of the building as it appears, it is square (as shown in Figure 1-2A). Actually, the Parthenon was built in a totally distorted fashion in order to offset a series of optical illusions. There is a common visual distortion in which we find that placing angles above a line (much like the roof is placed over the architrave) causes the line to appear slightly bowed. One form of this illusion is shown in Figure 1-2B. If the Parthenon had been built physically square, it would appear to sag as a result of this visual distortion. This is shown in an exaggerated manner in Figure 1-2C. The sagging does not appear because the building has been altered to compensate for the distortion. Figure 1-2D illustrates what an undistorted view of the Parthenon would look like. The upward curvature is more than 6 cm on the east and west walls and almost 11 cm on the longer north and south sides.

The vertical features of the Parthenon (such as the columns) were inclined inward in order to correct for a second optical illusion in which the features of rising objects appear to fall outward at the top. Thus, if we projected all the columns of the Parthenon upward, they would meet at a point about a mile above the building. Furthermore, the corner columns were increased in thickness because it was found that when these columns were seen against the sky, they appeared to be thinner than those seen against the darker background formed by the interior wall.

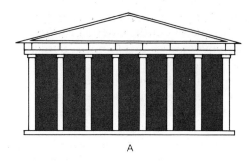

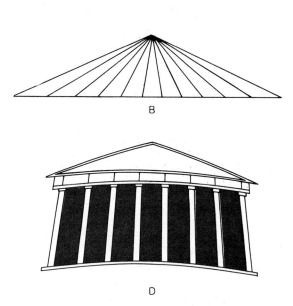

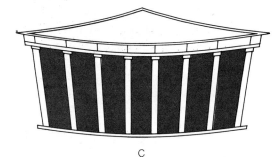

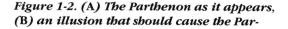

Figure 1-2. (A) The Parthenon as it appears, (B) an illusion that should cause the Parthenon to appear as (C), and (D) the way the Parthenon is built to offset the illusion.

These corrections were consciously made by the Greek architects. To quote one of them, Vitruvius, writing around 30 B.C.: "For the sight follows gracious contours, and unless we flatter its pleasure by proportionate alterations of these parts (so that by adjustment we offset the amount to which it suffers illusions) an uncouth and ungracious aspect will be presented to the spectators." In other words, the Parthenon appears to be square, with elegant straight lines, because it has been consciously distorted to offset perceptual distortions. If it were geometrically square, it would not be perceptually square.

It is amazing to discover how much our conscious experience of the world can differ from physical reality. While some perceptual distortions are only slight deviations from the physical reality, others can be quite complex and surprising, such as that shown in Demonstration Box 1-1.

Such distortions, in the form of disagreements between percept and reality, are quite common. We call them **illusions**, and they occur in predictable circumstances for normal observers. The term *illusion* is derived from the Latin root *illudere*, meaning "to mock." In a sense, illusions mock us for our blind reliance on the validity of our sensory impressions. Every sensory modality is subject to these distortions, illusions, and systematic errors that misrepresent the outside environment in our consciousness. There are illusions of touch, taste, and hearing, as well as visual illusions. Virtually any aspect of perception can be subject to such errors. For instance,

---

Demonstration Box 1-1. Gears and circles

The pattern shown in this box should be viewed in motion. Move the book around so the motion resembles that which you would make if you were swirling coffee around in a cup without using a spoon. Notice that the six sets of concentric circles seem to show radial regions of light and dark that appear to move in the direction you are swirling. They look as though they were covered by a liquid surface tending to swirl with the stimulus movement.

A second effect has to do with the center circle that seems to have gearlike teeth. As you swirl the array, the center gear seems to rotate, but in a direction *opposite* to that of the movement of the outer circles. Some observers see it moving in a jerky, step-like manner from one rotary position to another while other observers see a smooth rotation. Of course, there is no *physical* movement within the circles, and the geared center circle is also unchanging, despite your conscious impression to the contrary.

---

such basic and apparently simple qualities as the brightness of an object, or its color, may be perceptually misrepresented, as shown in Demonstration Box 1-2.

Many perceptual errors are merely amusing, such as that in Demonstration Box 1-1, or thought provoking, as in Demonstration Box 1-2. Others may lead to some embarrassment or annoyance, such as might have been felt by the artisan who created the picture frame shown as Figure 1-3*A*. While his workmanship is faultless, the final product is flawed by the prominent wood grain. Despite the fact that the picture is perfectly rectangular, it appears to be distorted. Unfortunately, some perceptual errors or illusions are quite serious. Figure 1-3*B* shows a surgeon probing for a bullet. She is using a fluoroscope, which presents the out-

line of the patient's ribs. We have positioned her probe so that it is exactly on line with the bullet lodged below the rib. As you can see, it appears that she will miss and pass too far below the bullet, even though the probe is angled perfectly. Figure 1-3*C* shows an even more disastrous occurrence of an illusion. It represents a radar screen with various flight regions marked across its face. The two oblique streaks represent jet aircraft approaching the control region, both flying at about 950 kilometers per hour. This information is the same as an air traffic controller might use. From it he might conclude that if these two aircraft continue in the same direction they will pass each other with a safe distance between them. At the moment represented here, however, these aircraft are traveling on a direct line. If they

---

Demonstration Box 1-2. A subjective color grid

The figure in this box consists of a series of thinly spaced diagonal black lines alternating with white spaces. Study this figure for a couple of seconds, and you will begin to see faint, almost pastel streaks of orange-red and other streaks of blue-green. For many observers, these streaks tend to run vertically up and down the figure crossing both white and black lines, while for others they seem to form a random, almost fishnetlike pattern over the grid. These colors are not present in the stimulus; hence they are *subjective*, or *illusory*, colors.

---

are both flying at the same altitude, they will very likely collide. This example illustrates how important discrepancies between perception and reality can be. It becomes important for us, therefore, to know how our perceptions arise, how much we can rely on them, under what circumstances they are most fallible, and under what conditions our perceptions most accurately present a picture of the world. An exploration of these questions is the purpose of this book.

SENSATION, PERCEPTION, COGNITION, AND INFORMATION PROCESSING

The study of perception is diverse. Partly this is a result of the length of time that perceptual problems have been studied. The Greek philosophers, the pre-Renaissance thinkers, the Arabic scholars, the Latin scholastics, the early British empiricists, the German physicists, and the German physicians who founded both physiology and psychology considered issues in sensation and perception as basic questions.

The first English textbook on psychology, written by Alexander Bain in 1855, was titled *The Senses and the Intellect*. The most extensive coverage was reserved for sensory and perceptual functions. The major portion of both the theorizing and the empirical work produced by Wilhelm Wundt, who often is credited with the founding of experimental psychology, was oriented toward sensation and perception. In addition to the diversity caused by a long and varied history, perception has been affected by many "schools" of thought. Each has its own major theoretical viewpoint and its own particular set of methodological techniques. Thus we encounter psychophysicists, gestaltists, functionalists, analytic introspectionists, transactionalists, sensory physiologists, sensory-tonic theorists, "new look" psychologists, and efferent theorists, to name but a few. There are even theorists (such as some behaviorists) who deny the existence of, or at least deny our ability to study, the conscious event we call perception. Despite this chorus of diverse voices and viewpoints, there seems to be a consensus about the important aspects of perceptual study.

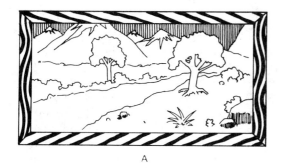

A

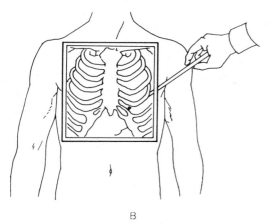

B

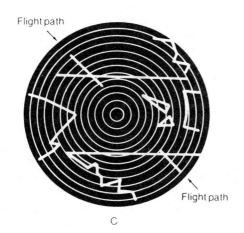

C

Figure 1-3. Some perceptual distortions in common situations.

Before we look at the major areas of emphasis in the study of the perceptual process, let us first offer a disclaimer. We recognize that it is difficult, perhaps impossible, and most certainly unwise to attempt to draw sharp lines separating one field of inquiry from another. Certain problem areas, or orientations, however, characterize groups of investigators, and these seem to be definable. The study of **sensation**, or *sensory processes*, is concerned with the first contact between the organism and the environment. Thus, someone studying sensation might look at the way in which electromagnetic radiation (light) is registered by the eye. This investigator would look at the physical structure of the sense organ and would attempt to establish how sensory experiences are related to physical stimulation and physiological functioning. Such studies tend to focus on less complex (although not less complicated) aspects of our conscious experience. For instance, these investigators might study how we perceive brightness, loudness, or color; however, the nature of the object having a given brightness, sound, or color would not make much difference to them.

Someone who is interested in the study of **perception** is interested in our conscious experience of objects and object relationships. For instance, the sensory question might be, "How bright does the target appear to be?" while the perceptual questions would be: "Do you recognize what that object is?", "Where is it?", "How far away is it?", or "How large is it?" In a more global sense, those who study perception are interested in how we form a conscious representation of the outside environment and the accuracy of that representation. For those of you who have difficulty in drawing a hard and fast line between the concepts of perception and sensation, rest easy. Since Thomas Reid introduced the distinction in 1785, some investigators have championed its use, while others have totally ignored the difference, choosing to treat sensation and perception as a unitary problem.

Cognition is a term used to define a very active field of inquiry in contemporary psychology. The word itself is quite old, probably first introduced by St. Thomas Aquinas (1225–1274). He divided the study of behavior into two broad categories. One he labeled *cognition*, meaning how we know the world, and the other he labeled *affect*, which was meant to encompass feelings and emotions. Today's definition of cognition is equally broad as that of Aquinas. While many investigators use the term to refer to memory, association, concept formation, language, and problem solving (all of which simply take the act of perception for granted), other investigators include the processes of attention and the conscious representation and interpretation of stimuli as part of the cognitive process. In other words, cognition tends to be somewhere between the areas that were traditionally called *perception* and *learning*, and it incorporates elements of both. The similarity between many of the problems studied by cognitive psychologists and those studied by perceptual psychologists is best seen by the fact that both often publish in the same journals and on similar topics.

Information processing—a relatively new term—is a recent attempt to avoid making distinctions between sensation, perception, and cognition. Information processing describes behavior by assuming that the way in which observers process information includes a *registration*, or sensory, phase, an *interpretation*, or perceptual phase, and a *memoric*, or cognitive, phase. Looking at the entire scheme, the global term *information processing* seems appropriate. Actually, information processing should be viewed as an approach rather than as a separate subdiscipline. It relies on a **levels-of-processing analysis** in which each stage of sensory processing, from the first registration of the stimulus on the receptor to the final

representation entered into memory, is systematically analyzed.

None of these labels should be taken as representing inflexible, or completely separate, areas of study. At a recent professional meeting, one well-known psychologist lamented, "When I first started doing research, people said I studied perception. After a while, they said I studied cognition. Now they say that I am studying human information processing. I don't know what is going on—I've been studying the same set of problems for the last ten years!"

In this book, we address the problem of how people build a conscious picture of their environment through the use of information reaching their senses. We shall follow the lead of many contemporary theorists (for example, Coren and Girgus, 1978; Uttal, 1981) and try to use data from all levels of the perceptual process in order to give an integrated picture of this complex and intriguing process. After all, the label we apply to our approach is considerably less important than the answer itself.

THE PLAN OF THE BOOK

The orientation of this book is implicit rather than explicit. While theories are introduced and discussed in the various chapters, no all-encompassing theoretical orientation has been adopted. We have chosen to be "militantly eclectic" in our orientation. Thus, this book is primarily concerned with perceptual and sensory *processes*. In general, the presentation of the material follows a levels-of-processing approach, extending from the more basic sensory processes through the more clearly perceptual processes that have strong cognitive influences.

The individual chapters are relatively self-contained. We begin by explaining how sensations and perceptions are measured (Chapter 2). This chapter presents the basic psychophysical techniques of measurement and tries to orient you toward some of the issues and approaches that will appear later in the book. Chapters 3—5 present the physiological basis of perception by describing the functions of the sensory receptors themselves. Without knowledge of how the eye, ear, or any of the other senses work at the physiological level, we can never have a full picture of how perception is achieved. Chapters 6—9 deal with the basic sensory responses, including, among others, the sensory qualities of brightness, color, loudness, touch, and taste. Chapters 10—15 deal with those problems that have traditionally been treated as part of classical perception. They discuss our perceptual representation of space, time, motion, form, and size. Some of the more cognitive aspects of perception are introduced in Chapters 13 and 15 that deal with the issues of speech perception and attention. The last three chapters (Chapters 16—18) deal with perceptual diversity, which includes many of the factors that make the perceptual experience of one individual different from that of another. These factors include the changes that occur in the developing individual because of the normal aging process, life history, experience, learning, and personality factors, to name a few.

Each chapter includes a series of *Demonstration Boxes*. These are experimental demonstrations that you can perform for yourself, using materials that are easily found around a house or living quarters. The demonstrations illustrate many aspects of the perceptual process. Quite often they demonstrate concepts that are quite difficult to put into words but that, when experienced, are immediately understandable. We encourage you to try these demonstrations as they are an integral part of the book. In the same way that perception involves interaction with the world, these demonstrations allow you to interact with your senses in a controlled manner and to gain insight into yourself.

We hope that this book will provide you with some understanding of the limits and the abilities of your senses. This knowledge should expand your comprehension of many behavioral phenomena that depend upon perception as a first step. Perception seems to be the final judge of the truth or the falsity of everything we encounter as part of our human experience. How often have you heard the phrases, "Seeing is believing" and "I didn't believe it until I saw it with my own two eyes"? Yet you have already seen in this chapter that such faith in the truthfulness of our conscious percepts is often misplaced. In 500 B.C. Parmenides considered the way in which perception can deceive us. He summarized his feelings when he said, "The eyes and ears are bad witnesses when they are at the service of minds that do not understand their language." In this book we shall try to teach you their language.

GLOSSARY

The following definitions are specific to this book.

Cognition   The process of knowing, incorporating both perception and learning.

Illusions   Distortions or incongruences between percept and reality.

Information processing   The processes by which stimuli are registered in the receptors, identified and stored in memory.

Levels-of-processing analysis   Analysis of the contribution of each stage of processing to the final percept, beginning with the receptor and ending with cognitive mechanisms.

Perception   The conscious experience of objects and object relationships.

Sensation   Simple conscious experience associated with a stimulus.

2

Psychophysics

THE OCEAN LINER GLIDES SLOWLY through the thick stormy night. Somewhere in the distance is New York harbor. With the visibility near zero, the captain is forced to rely solely on the ship's radar system for information about the position of obstacles impeding the passage of the ship. The ship is in a heavily traveled trade route, and the crew must continually be alert for possible collisions with other ships. The radar operator is watching his screen intently. He is searching for a radar "echo" caused by the presence of another ship nearby. Actually, he is also wrestling with a basic sensory-perceptual problem, that of **detection**. He is trying to answer the question, "Is there anything there?"

He is sure he sees an echo. Now the question becomes, "What is it?" Is it an echo from another ship or just a "ghost," a false echo often encountered in stormy weather? The radar operator is facing a second basic problem: **recognition**. We normally solve the detection and recognition problems quickly and automatically, since we generally encounter stimuli that are so strong and provide so much information that they pose little problem for us. The complex nature of detection and recognition only emerges in the context of a difficult or degraded stimulus situation.

The echo turns out to be just a "ghost," and the order is given to maintain the previous heading (compass direction). The helmsman has been given the bearing and now holds the ship's direction so that the compass needle always points to the correct place on the dial. At this moment, he is asking himself, "Has the needle drifted slightly toward the north?" If so, he must compensate by turning the wheel so that the needle moves back to the desired compass point. He is continually concerned with the problem of whether the compass needle is centered on the desired heading. This task also evokes an important perceptual process called **discrimination**. "Is this stimulus different from that one?" is the general discrimination question.

Finally, through the clearing weather the entrance to New York harbor appears. The ship is taken in tow by a tugboat and maneuvered toward its berth at the dock. The captain of the tugboat peers from his bridge, carefully judging the distance between the ship and the concrete wall of the pier. He must continually ask himself, "How far does the ship appear to be from the pier?" Such questions are part of another sensory problem, "How much of X is there?" This is the problem of **scaling**.

These four problems—*detection, recognition, discrimination*, and *scaling*—are the central concerns of the area of perceptual psychology called *psychophysics*. Psychophysics owes its name and origin to Gustav Theodor Fechner (1801–1887), a physicist and philosopher who set out to determine the relationship between the magnitude of a sensation registered in the mind and the magnitude of the physical stimulus that gave rise to it. Hence, the name psychophysics (from the Greek roots *psyche*, or mind, and *physike*, which refers to naturally occurring phenomena). Fechner not only established the philosophical rationale for studying the relationship between sensations and physical stimuli, but he also developed many of the experimental methods still in use today. These methods of collecting and analyzing data are employed in every aspect of the study of perception and many other areas of psychology, including social, personality, and clinical psychology (Baird and Noma, 1978; Grossberg and Grant, 1978).

DETECTION

The basic task for any sensory system is to detect the presence of energy changes in the environment. Energy changes may take the form of electromagnetic (light), mechanical (sound, touch, movement, muscle tension), chemical (tastes, smells), or thermal stimulation. The problem of detection is centered around the problem of how much of such a stimulus (relative to a zero energy level) is necessary for an individual to say that the stimulus is heard, tasted, smelled, or felt. Classically, this minimal amount of energy has been called the **absolute threshold**. In 1860, Fechner defined a threshold stimulus as one that "lifted the sensation or sensory difference over the threshold of consciousness." The idea is that below some critical value of the stimulus, a person would not be expected to detect a stimulus. As soon as this threshold value is exceeded, however, we would expect the observer to always detect its presence.

We can represent this relationship by a graph on which we plot the percentage of time an observer would be expected to detect the presence of a stimulus (values along the *ordinate*, or vertical axis) against stimulus magnitude (values along the *abscissa*, or horizontal axis). This has been done in Figure 2-1 using

arbitrary values for stimulus intensity. Notice that the percentage of time that the stimulus is detected takes a sudden step up from 0 to 100 percent when the stimulus reaches a value of 3.5. The absolute threshold is thus 3.5.

Method of limits

How do we measure absolute thresholds? Let us conduct a relatively simple but typical experiment to measure the threshold of hearing. In this experiment, an observer sits in a soundproof room wearing headphones. The experimenter presents a faint undetectable tone of a particular and constant frequency and, in steps, gradually increases its intensity until the observer reports, "I hear it." On alternate trials the experimenter starts with a tone that can easily be heard and decreases the intensity until the observer reports, "I no longer hear it." This method of determining a threshold is called the **method of limits**. Kraepelin gave it that name in 1891, because a stimulus series always ends when the observer reaches a limit or a point of change in his judgments. The two modes of presenting (increasing or decreasing) the stimulus are usually called ascending or descending stimulus series. A sample of the kind of data such an experiment might generate is shown in Table 2-1.

The first thing we notice about the data in Table 2-1 is that the "absolute threshold" for hearing is not a fixed value as we first proposed but appears to vary from trial to trial. For instance, on trial 6 the observer could no longer detect the stimulus when we presented a tone with an intensity of 8; on trial 4, a stimulus intensity of only 5 was detected. Such data indicate that the "absolute threshold" is anything but absolute. It seems that the threshold varies from measurement to measurement, or moment to moment. As early as 1888, Joseph

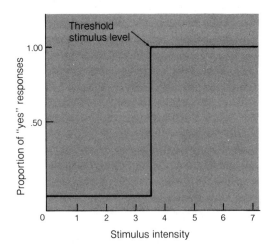

Figure 2-1 Absolute threshold.

Table 2-1. Determination of the absolute threshold of hearing by the method of limits

Sound intensity (scale units)	Trials					
	↑ 1	↓ 2	↑ 3	↓ 4	↑ 5	↓ 6
16						+
15						+
14		+				+
13		+				+
12		+		+		+
11		+		+		+
10		+		+		+
9		+		+		+
8		+	+	+	+	−
7		−	−	+	+	
6	+ᵃ	−	−	+	−	
5	−ᵇ		−	+	−	
4	−		−	−	−	
3	−		−	−	−	
2	−		−	−	−	
1			−			
Threshold for series	5.5	7.5	7.5	4.5	6.5	8.5

Computations

$$\text{Mean descending threshold} = \frac{7.5 + 4.5 + 8.5}{3} = 6.8$$

$$\text{Mean ascending threshold} = \frac{5.5 + 7.5 + 6.5}{3} = 6.5$$

Mean absolute threshold = 6.65 sound units

a. "I hear it."
b. "I don't hear it."

Jastrow speculated on the reason for this variability in the threshold over time. He theorized that lapses of attention, slight fatigue, and other psychological changes could cause the obtained fluctuations of the threshold. Demonstration Box 2-1 shows how you can experience this threshold variability for yourself.

We can compute an estimate of the average absolute threshold from the tabled data simply by taking the average stimulus intensity at which a response shifted either from an "I hear it" to an "I don't hear it," or from an "I don't hear it" to an "I hear it." This gives us a threshold value of 6.65 intensity units. These computations are shown at the bottom of the table. Table 2-1 also shows that there is a slight difference in the threshold value depending on whether it was computed from an ascending

---

Demonstration Box 2-1. The variability of the threshold

For this demonstration you will need a wrist watch or an alarm clock that ticks. Place the clock on a table and move across the room so that you can no longer hear the ticking. If the tick is faint, you may accomplish this merely by moving your head away some distance. Now gradually move toward the clock. Note that by doing this, you are actually performing a method of limits experiment since the sound level steadily increases as you approach the watch. At some distance from the watch you will just begin to hear the source of the sound. This is your momentary threshold. Now hold this position for a few moments and you will notice that occasionally the sound will fade and you may have to step forward to reach threshold, while at other times it may get noticeably louder and you may be able to step back farther and still hear it. These changes are a result of your changing threshold sensitivity.

---

or a descending series of stimuli. Such differences may arise from observers continuing to report "yes" in a descending series and "no" in an ascending series, a tendency called the **error of perseveration**. It is also possible to have an **error of anticipation**. Here an observer feels that she has said "yes" too often and decides that it is time to say "no," even though she still faintly hears the tone. To balance out such possible constant errors we use alternating ascending and descending stimulus series, and we begin the series of the same kind at different stimulus intensities.

The method of limits has been modified to produce a different method for measuring absolute thresholds called the **staircase method**. Here the experimenter attempts to mark the absolute threshold by changing the direction of the steps whenever the observer changes her response. Thus, we might increase the intensity of a tone, step by step, until the observer reports that she hears it, and then start to decrease it one step at a time from that level until it is no longer heard, and then again start to increase it by steps. Notice that in this way the value of the test stimulus flips back and forth around the threshold value. The advantage of this procedure is that it allows the experimenter to "track" the threshold, even if sensitivity is continually changing, such as after the administration of some drugs, or adaptation to different background stimuli (Békésy, 1947; Jesteadt, 1980).

Why does the threshold seem to vary from moment to moment? First, we must recognize that we have been assuming that the only stimulus present is the stimulus we are asking our observer to detect. This is quite false. A constantly present and ever changing background of stimulation exists for any signal that we present to the observer. If you place both your hands over your ears to block out the room noises, you will hear a sound that one observer poetically called "the sound of waves from a distant sea" and another, somewhat less poetically, "the faint hissing of radio static." Similarly, if you sit in a completely lightproof room in absolute darkness, you do not see complete blackness. Your visual field appears to be filled with a grayish mist (which has been termed "cortical grey") and occasionally you can even see momentary bright pinpoint flashes here and there. Any stimulus that we ask an observer to detect must force itself through this spontaneously generated fluctuating background. It is as if every stimulus to be detected is superimposed on a background of noise generated within the observer.

As this *endogenous*, or internal, noise level changes, so does our measured threshold, in the same way that a person standing in a noisy crowd must talk louder in order to be heard. Some experimenters have introduced experimentally controlled background noise in order to achieve more constant conditions than would be possible if they simply relied on the constancy of internally generated noise. Under such circumstances, the experimenter has a better idea of the noise level with which the stimulus is competing. In fact, many of the experiments we will discuss have employed a controlled background noise level. By *noise* we mean any background stimulus other than the one to be detected. Of course, if we define "noise" in this way we may have visual, chemical, mechanical, and thermal, as well as auditory noise.

Method of constant stimuli

Discussion of another method will allow us to see more clearly the nature of the threshold. This method is preferred when the absolute threshold must be measured precisely, but it is more time consuming to use because it requires so many stimulus presentations and reponses. Suppose we take a set of stimuli ranging from clearly imperceptible to clearly perceptible and present them, one at a time, to our observer. We present each stimulus many times in a prearranged irregular order. The observer is simply required to respond "yes" when she detects the stimulus and "no" when she does not. This procedure is called the **method of constant stimuli**, a name derived from the fact that a fixed or constant set of stimuli is chosen beforehand and presented a fixed or constant number of times to each

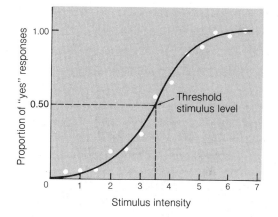

Figure 2-2 Typical data from the method of constant stimuli in detection.

observer. Some typical data obtained with this method are presented graphically in Figure 2-2.

We see in the figure that as the stimulus energy increases, the relative number of times the observer says "yes" (meaning the stimulus was perceived) gradually increases. It is not the single jump that we might have predicted from the definition of absolute threshold illustrated in Figure 2-1. These S-shaped curves, called *ogives*, are obtained commonly with the method of constant stimuli in all sensory systems.

What does the "proportion of yes responses" indicate in such experiments? One basic assumption made by psychophysicists is that any type of behavior, such as saying "yes, I see it," has some *strength*. The strengths of various behaviors can be represented by numbers, which indicate their relative magnitudes. The measure that has found most favor among contemporary workers in the field is a numerical estimate of the likelihood that the particular response in question will occur. We shall call this likelihood the *response probability*. We can estimate the response probability for detecting the stimulus, or more exactly for saying "yes, I see it," by using the formula

$$p(Yes) = \frac{\text{Number of "Yes" Responses}}{\text{Number "Yes" + Number "No"}}$$

The data in Figure 2-2 make it clear that the probability that an observer will detect a stimulus is not an "all or none" affair (as in Figure 2-1), but rather it changes gradually as the stimulus intensity increases. Then where is the absolute threshold? Here, as in many places, we must make a somewhat arbitrary decision. The point usually taken as the absolute threshold is that value where the probability of saying "yes" is the same as the probability of saying "no". This is simply the stimulus intensity that the subject claims she detected 50 percent of the time. In Figure 2-2 we have indicated this threshold value by dotted lines. The threshold is about 3.5 energy units for this observer.

Here are some examples of approximate sensory threshold values as measured by these methods. The visual system is so sensitive that a candle flame can be seen from a distance of more than 48 km on a dark clear night. In the auditory system, we can detect the ticking of a wristwatch in a quiet room at a distance of 6 m. Increases in auditory sensitivity beyond this point would allow us to hear the sound of air molecules colliding. As for our other senses, we can taste one teaspoon of sugar dissolved in 7½ liters of water and smell one drop of perfume diffused through the volume of an average three-room apartment (Galanter, 1962).

Signal detection theory

Some of you may have been bothered by one aspect of the psychophysical measurement techniques we have been discussing. We are supposedly studying an observer's sensory ca-
pacities, yet we have not been talking about the probability that an observer *detects* a stimulus, but rather the probability that he says "yes, I hear (or see, or whatever) it." We can imagine that if an observer feels that this is a "test" of some sort, where it would be good for him to appear to be quite sensitive, he might say "yes" on almost every trial. What is to prevent this from happening? Although we might argue that people are basically honest and would not lie about whether or not they heard a stimulus, this is not the sort of guarantee upon which scientists would like to rest their conclusions. We are not criticizing the reliability of observers in psychophysical experiments, for most are quite sincere and honest. Rather, we are pointing out that at the very low stimulus energies used in most detection experiments, an observer may be unsure about whether a sensation has been experienced. This may result in being unsure about whether or not to respond "yes" on any particular trial. Thus, on some trials a "guess" response is made. Therefore, in order to assess sensory capacities accurately, we must take into account the observer's decision-making behavior.

Experimenters became aware of this problem early in the history of psychophysics. They first attempted to cope with it by inserting **catch trials**, which were trials in which no stimulus was presented. They reasoned that if observers were honest in reporting what was detected, they would respond "no" on these catch trials. If the "yes" response came too frequently, the observer was warned by the experimenter. Alternatively, an attempt was made to adjust the calculated threshold to account for the guesses, or the data were simply discarded. Over many experiments, however, it became clear that the observers were not trying to fool anyone. Somehow their behavior was reasonable, although it was not clear what they were doing.

If we now change our classical absolute threshold experiment so that we can study not only the observer's ability to detect a stimulus when it is there, but also his guessing behavior as reflected in a "yes" response when no signal is present, we have entered the domain of **signal detection theory** (see Baird and Noma, 1978; Egan, 1975; Green and Swets, 1966). It is a mathematical, theoretical system, which recognizes that the observer is not merely a passive receiver of stimuli but is also engaged in the process of deciding whether or not he is confident enough that the stimulus was present to say, "Yes, I detected it."

For the purposes of the following discussion we shall list all the possible behaviors in a new type of detection experiment and give them names. Table 2-2 is a schematic representation of the standard signal detection experiment. There are two types of "stimulus" presentations (at the left of the table). A *signal absent* presentation is like a classical catch trial in which no stimulus is presented and the observer sees or hears only the noise generated by the sensory system. *Signal present* is a trial in which the experimenter actually presents the target stimulus (which is, of course, superimposed on the endogenous noise in the sensory system). There are also two possible responses in the experiment (at the top of the table). "Yes" indicates that the observer thinks a stimulus was presented on a particular trial (that is, signal present), and "no" indicates that the observer thinks the signal was absent. The

combination of two possible stimulus presentations and two possible responses leads to four possible outcomes on a given trial (the four cells of the table). When the signal was present and the response was "yes," the observer has made a **hit**. But if the observer responded "yes" when the signal was absent, then a **false alarm** has been made. The other cells are called **misses** and **correct negatives**. The relationships between these responses will depend not only on the nature of the signal but also on the decision processes occurring within the observer.

Consider a typical experiment as an example. Suppose that we wanted to measure an observer's ability to detect a tone. The tone for a given experiment will be constant in intensity and frequency. After a ready signal, the observer is required to respond by pushing one button to indicate "yes, the signal tone was detected" and a different button to signify "no" when it was not. Let us also consider some different experimental conditions that might be introduced. The first is one in which the signal was presented on 50 percent of the trials, and no signal was presented for the remaining 50 percent. A typical set of data for one observer, expressing the proportion of the trials that the observer reported that the signal was present or absent, is shown in Table 2-3.

Notice that on 25 percent of the trials when no signal was present, the observer responded, "Yes, the signal was present." Why should the observer report that a signal was heard when

Table 2-2. Outcomes of a signal detection experiment

Signal	Response	
	Yes	No
Present	Hit	Miss
Absent	False alarm	Correct negative

Table 2-3. Stimulus present 50 percent of the time

Signal	Response	
	Yes	No
Present	0.75	0.25
Absent	0.25	0.75

no signal was presented? First, clearly the observer is not always sure whether or not he heard the signal. Thus, many nonsensory aspects of the situation might influence his pattern of responding. Consider the effect of his expectations. For instance, if the observer knows that the signal is given on almost every trial, he might find himself responding "yes" to even the faintest or most ambiguous of sensations (perhaps even generated by endogenous noise in his own nervous system). This is sensible behavior because, if the stimulus occurs most of the time, on these "doubtful" trials he will quite often be correct. If the signal rarely occurs, however, he would be less tempted by ambiguous, faint sensations, and might want to wait until he experienced a clear sensation before saying "yes." If our description of what the observer is doing is correct, then we should be able to change the observer's response pattern by changing his expectations, even though his sensitivity remains the same. Typical results from the same observer are presented in Table 2-4. In one case the signal was present on 90 percent of the trials and in the other on only 10 percent of the trials. Notice that when

the signal is occurring frequently, the observer says "yes" often. This gives him many hits, but also many false alarms. When he expects the signal only occasionally, he says "no" more often, thus reducing the number of false alarms but also reducing the number of hits. How, then, do we measure the observer's sensitivity? By our former definition of threshold (the point at which a signal is detected 50 percent of the time), the tone is clearly above threshold in the first instance, while in the second it is clearly below threshold. This does not make sense, since neither the tone's strength, nor the observer's sensitivity has changed. We need some way of separating the observer's sensitivity from his decision strategy.

We can look for such a method of analysis by exploring how the observer's responses change for a particular signal strength if we vary only his expectations. By holding constant the strength of the signal and varying only the relative frequency with which the signal occurs, we may plot a curve that indicates the relationship between the proportion of hits and false alarms as we vary the likelihood that the signal will occur. Figure 2-3 presents such a curve. This curve is called a **receiver operating characteristic curve** (frequently abbreviated **roc curve**). The terminology was inherited from the communications engineers who first developed signal detection theory. A more descriptive term is *isosensitivity curve*, since the curve represents the range of possible responses for one level of sensitivity. As in the previous example, the figure shows that when the signal is rare, the observer frequently says "no" even when the signal is presented. At the high end of the curve, where the signal occurs frequently, the observer says "yes" quite often even when the signal is not there.

An ROC curve reflects an observer's response pattern for one signal strength. If we increase the strength of the signal, we find that

Table 2-4. Stimulus present 90 percent of the time

Signal	Response	
	Yes	No
Present	0.95	0.05
Absent	0.63	0.37

Stimulus present 10 percent of the time

Signal	Response	
	Yes	No
Present	0.35	0.65
Absent	0.04	0.96

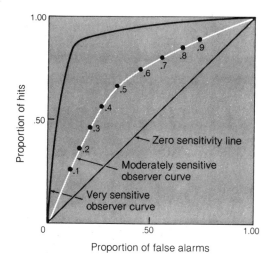

Figure 2-3 ROC curves. Notice how the shape of the curve changes for different levels of sensitivity. The black dots on the white curve represent results with the indicated probability of signal presentation.

the curve has a more pronounced bow, as shown by the curved black line in Figure 2-3. If we lower the signal strength, the curve becomes flatter and approaches the 45 degree line, which represents chance responding. Thus, the amount of bow in the curve can serve as a measure of the perceived signal strength. An alternative way of interpreting an ROC curve is in terms of variations in the sensitivity of the observer to a signal of a particular strength. Thus, the two curves in Figure 2-3 could also be interpreted as reflecting two different sensitivities of a single observer (the more bowed the curve, the more sensitive) or the curves of two different observers with different sensitivities to the same signal strength.

We may also vary the observer's response pattern, while holding the signal intensity constant, by varying the importance or the payoff for a given response. For instance, if we pay 10 cents for every correct detection of the stim-

ulus and do not penalize the observer for false alarms, the optimal strategy is to guess "yes" on every trial. This will maximize the amount of money that can be earned in the test situation. Contrast this to a situation in which we deduct 10 cents for each false alarm and do not reward for correct detections. Here, a reasonable observer would maximize the gains by saying "no" on every trial. Actually, most situations fall somewhere between these two extremes. For instance, we might pay our observer 10 cents for every correct response and deduct 5 cents for every wrong response. This situation is represented in a matrix of numbers as shown in Table 2-5. Such a set of rewards and penalties is called the **payoff matrix**. Changing the payoff matrix causes changes in an observer's response pattern in much the same way as varying an observer's expectations concerning stimulus frequency would. Thus an observer's *motives* as well as *expectations* affect responses during the detection experiment. Thus, by systematically varying the payoff matrix of an experiment, we can vary an observer's numbers of hits and false alarms and produce an ROC curve similar to that generated by varying the relative frequency of signals. Note that it is the observer's *response pattern* (the number of "yes" responses) that varies as the ROC curve is produced and not the *sensitivity to the stimulus*. Because the manipulation of motivation in this case is done by varying the payoff matrix, and thus the amount of money paid to an observer, this type

Table 2-5. A typical payoff matrix for a psychophysical experiment

Signal	Response	
	Yes	No
Present	10¢	−5¢
Absent	−5¢	10¢

of experiment has been given the snide term "sweatshop psychophysics."

Perhaps the theoretical and methodological bases for signal detection will become clearer if we look at the detection problem from a different conceptual angle. When no stimulus is present, an observer's sensory systems are still active, generating sensory noise. The amount of noise probably varies from moment to moment. This fluctuation in noise level is probably caused by physiological, attentional, and other variables operating on the sensory and perceptual systems of the observer. Signal detection theorists represent these fluctuations in the form of a **probability distribution**. This distribution is graphed in Figure 2-4 as the "signal absent" curve. The abscissa, or horizontal axis, is the amount of sensory activity (or sensation level), and the ordinate can be thought of as the likelihood of occurrence of any particular level of sensation over a great many trials. This means that even in the ab-

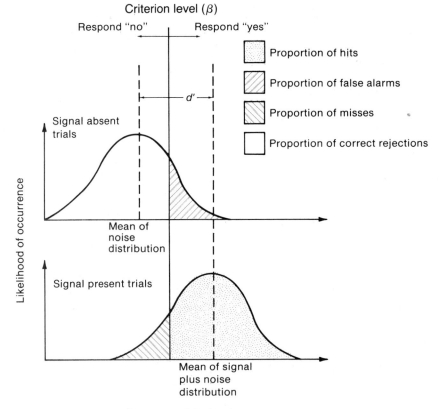

Figure 2-4 Illustration of how noise and signal plus noise distributions result in hits, misses, false alarms, and correct negatives for a particular criterion setting. Notice that the two curves are actually plotted on the same axes— they are separated for clarity. The curves would overlap if plotted together.

sence of any external signal, the observer experiences some level of sensation that is represented by a particular location along the abscissa. This level is experienced with a frequency represented by the height of the curve at that point.

When a signal is presented it occurs against this background of sensory noise. Of course, the signal produces some sensory response of its own, which then adds to whatever amount is already present. The effect of this would be the creation of a new distribution of sensory activity, the "signal present" curve. On average, the level of activity elicited by the signal added to the sensory noise is more intense than that of the noise alone. This is shown by the fact that its mean is shifted toward higher values of the sensory activity axis in Figure 2-4. When the signal is weak, however, it will not add enough sensory activity to make the two distributions (signal absent vs. signal present) completely distinct. The two distributions in Figure 2-4 would overlap if drawn on the same set of axes. You can see from Figure 2-4 that some levels of sensation could result either from presentations of the signal or simply from noise alone.

Imagine you are an observer sitting inside the head trying to decide if a signal has been presented. The only information you have is the intensity of the sensation. Remember, however, that sometimes the noise produces a sensation that is just as intense as that produced by the signal, as shown in Figure 2-4. As a rational observer, you would probably solve this problem by setting a **criterion** or cutoff point for sensation level. This is the value that you are willing to accept as probably indicating that a signal was present. If a sensation level is below the criterion (to the left in Figure 2-4), you respond "no"; if it is above the criterion, you respond "yes." This simplifies the problem greatly, since you must only decide, based on

your motives and expectations, where to put the criterion. From that point on, the experienced level of sensation more or less automatically determines the response. The criterion value is usually symbolized with the Greek letter β (pronounced "**beta**").

If this is what the observer is doing, then we can specify the proportions of hits and false alarms we might expect, depending on where he places his criterion. According to signal detection theory, the proportions of the various outcomes observed in an experiment (see Table 2-2) may be represented as that proportion of the *area* under the appropriate probability distribution curve to the right or left of the criterion location. Thus, if Figure 2-4 represents an actual situation, the proportion of signal present trials on which a "yes" response would be given (the proportion of hits) is represented by the area under the signal present curve to the right of the criterion, since the observer would say "yes" whenever the sensation level was above, or to the right of, the criterion. Similarly, the proportion of false alarms is represented by the area under the signal absent curve to the right of the criterion, since that is the proportion of trials on which the sensation level generated by the sensory system in the absence of a signal exceeded the criterion level set for the "yes" response. The other two possible outcomes are also represented in Figure 2-4.

The motivation and expectation effects on an observer's response pattern in a detection experiment now are interpretable. Essentially, these variables affect the placement of the criterion and, hence, the proportions of hits and false alarms. For instance, suppose that the observer is a radiologist looking for a light spot as evidence of cancer in a set of chest X rays (see for example, Swensson, 1980). If the radiologist thinks she has found such a spot, she calls the patient back for additional tests. The penalty for a false alarm (additional tests when no cancer is present) only involves some added time and money on the part of the patient, whereas the penalty for a miss (not catching an instance of real cancer) might be the patient's death. Thus, the radiologist may set a criterion value that is quite low (lax), not wanting to miss any danger signals. This means she will have many hits and few misses, but also many false alarms. This situation is shown in Figure 2-5A. On the other hand, if the observer is a radar operator looking for blips on a screen signifying enemy missiles, he might be much more conservative. Here the penalty for a false alarm could be war, while the penalty for a miss might be only a few seconds lost in sounding the alarm. He would therefore set a high (strict) criterion in order to avoid false alarms, but at the penalty of reducing the number of hits. This would be equivalent to the situation shown in Figure 2-5B. In this same manner, each point on any given ROC curve simply represents a different criterion setting.

Although we indicated that the location of the criterion alters the pattern of response, we never mentioned the effect of criterion location on the sensitivity of the observer. That is because there is no such effect. In signal detection theory, sensitivity refers to the average amount of sensory activity generated by a given signal compared with the average amount of noise-generated activity. This is similar to the everyday use of the word sensitivity. Thus, a radio receiver that produces a large electrical response that allows a weak signal to be heard above the background static is more sensitive than one that produces only a small electrical response to that signal, which may then be obscured by static and noise.

Within our present framework, the perceptual analog of sensitivity is the distance between the centers (means) of the signal absent and the signal present distributions. This is

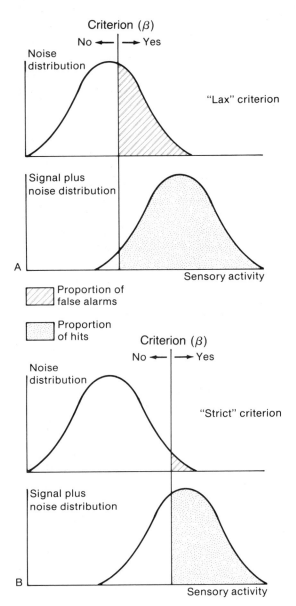

Figure 2-5 The effect of motives or expectations on criterion placement and proportion of hits and false alarms.

merely a measure of the difference in average sensation levels as a function of the presence or absence of a signal. We call this distance measure of sensitivity **d′**. When the distributions are far apart and overlap very little, as in Figure 2-6B, d' is large and the ROC curve is far from the diagonal and sharply curved. When the distributions are close together and overlap to a great extent, d' is relatively small as in Figure 2-6A. The corresponding ROC curve is close to the diagonal, which you may remember represents zero sensitivity. Signal detection theory attempts to measure an observer's sensitivity to a signal independently of his decision strategy, while acknowledging that both might affect the actual responses made in the experimental setting. Unfortunately, the actual computation of d' and β are somewhat complicated, involving a reasonable degree of knowledge of both algebra and statistics. In addition, some quite stringent statistical assumptions about the data must be met. Because of this, a number of alternative measures, which are easier to calculate and don't involve as many restrictions, have been devised. One that seems quite attractive involves a measure of sensitivity called **A′**, and a measure of criterion called **B″**. The equations we will present were derived by Grier (1971) although the measures were first suggested by Pollack and Norman (1964) and Hodos (1970), respectively. Remember, A′ and B″ are not exactly the same as d' and β, but can be used in the same way and have the same psychophysical rationale. Actual computation of these simpler measures of sensitivity (A′) and criterion (B″) from hit and false alarm proportions is demonstrated in Computation Box 2-1.

This must seem like an unusually elaborate procedure for investigating a seemingly simple problem, namely, the determination of the minimal amount of energy necessary for stimulus detection. However, an observer is a liv-

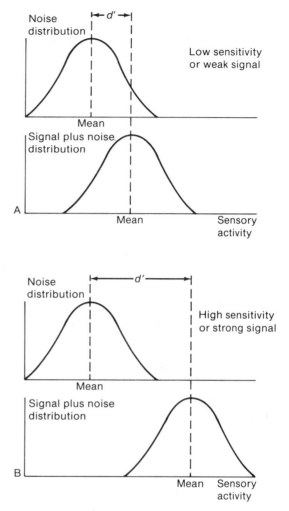

Figure 2-6 The effect of sensitivity and signal strength on d′.

ing organism whose expectations and motives affect his or her perceptual behaviors and judgments nearly as much as stimulus reception itself. These nonperceptual effects must be removed if we are to look at the pure sensory responses. Our original notion of an absolute threshold has proved to be too primitive. The detection threshold is simply a convenient

Computation Box 2-1. Computation of sensitivity and criterion

To calculate measures of sensitivity (A') and criterion (B''), you will need to know only the proportion of hits (PHIT) and the proportion of false alarms (PFA) obtained from a typical signal detection experiment. To calculate A' and B'' simply substitute values for PHIT and PFA into the equations below.

$$A' = \frac{1}{2} + \frac{(PHIT - PFA) \cdot (1 + PHIT - PFA)}{4 \cdot PHIT \cdot (1 - PFA)} \quad (1)$$

$$B'' = \frac{PHIT \cdot (1 - PHIT) - PFA \cdot (1 - PFA)}{PHIT \cdot (1 - PHIT) + PFA \cdot (1 - PFA)} \quad (2)$$

To interpret the numbers you obtain and to compare them with the more complex measures discussed in the text, you should know that d' ranges from a value of 0 (meaning zero sensitivity) on upward (although values above 3 are rare). For A', a completely insensitive observer would produce a value of 0.5, while perfect performance would produce an index of 1. Beta can assume any value greater than zero, although scores be-

low 1 mean a lax criterion (a bias toward saying "yes"), while scores above 1 indicate a more stringent criterion (a bias toward saying "no"). B'' varies between -1 and $+1$, with negative scores indicating lax criteria and positive scores indicating stringent criteria. To provide a few examples and comparisons, we have calculated the sensitivities and criteria for the data shown in Tables 2-3 and 2-4, and they appear in the table below.

		Sensitivity		Criterion	
Proportion of hits (PHIT)	Proportion of false alarms (PFA)	d'	A'	β	B''
0.75	0.25	1.3	0.8	1.0	0.0
0.95	0.63	1.3	0.8	0.3	−0.7
0.35	0.04	1.3	0.8	4.4	0.7

statistically defined point. As an alternative, we may use the d' measure, which provides an index of the observer's sensitivity to stimuli, instead of the traditional threshold measures.

RECOGNITION

The doctor listened very carefully, paused for a moment to adjust the stethoscope to a more comfortable position and listened again to the sounds emanating from the patient's chest. The sounds were quite clear and distinct. The problem was simply to decide whether they indi-

cated a normal or a pathological heartbeat. This doctor is wrestling with a problem that does not involve stimulus detection, for the sounds are clearly above the detection threshold. However, it does involve the *recognition* of the occurrence of one of a number of possible alternative stimuli. To recognize or identify a stimulus is one of the major tasks that the perceptual system is asked to perform.

The difficulty of any recognition task depends, in part, on the number of possible stimulus alternatives an observer is asked to distinguish. Consider an observer who claims she can discriminate her brand of cola from all others. Suppose we gave her two unmarked glasses of cola and asked her to sample them and try to recognize her own favorite brand. If she did select the correct brand we would not be very surprised, since she would be expected to select her favorite brand 50 percent of the time by chance alone, even if her taste buds were nonfunctional. If our expert selected her brand out of 25 brands presented to her, we would be much more likely to take her claim seriously, since the probability that she would by chance alone find her brand out of 25 alternatives is only 1/25. Measures of the difficulty of the recognition task must therefore take into account the number of stimulus alternatives.

Information theory

To solve the problem of specifying the difficulty of a recognition task, psychologists in the early 1950s turned to work arising from the efforts of engineers to assess the performance of radio and telephone communications systems. Books by Shannon and Weaver (1949) and by Wiener (1961) made it clear that the problems faced by the psychophysicist and by the communications engineer were quite similar. The engineer deals with a message that is transmitted through a communication channel and decoded by someone or something at the receiver end. The degree to which the final decoded message reflects the original message depends, in part, on the ability of the system to transmit information without distortion (this is what is meant by the fidelity of a system) and on the complexity of the input. The psychophysicist has an analogous problem. Stimulus information is transmitted to an observer through a sensory system, and it is then decoded in the central nervous system. The degree to which the observer's identification of the stimulus corresponds to the actual stimulus input will be affected by both the ability of the sensory system to handle the stimulus input without distortion and by the complexity of the input.

The quantitative system for specifying the characteristics of the input message is known as **information theory**. Information theory is *not* really a theory at all, but rather it is simply a system of measurement. The amount of information in a given stimulus display is defined so that the nature of the object being measured is irrelevant. What, then, do we mean by information? We mean what the everyday use of the word implies. If you tell us that this week will contain a Sunday morning, you have conveyed very little information, since we know that every week contains a Sunday morning. If you tell us that this Sunday morning there will be a parade in honor of Jiffy the Kangaroo, you have conveyed a great deal of information because you have specified which one out of a large number of possible alternative events is about to occur.

One way to quantify information is to define it in terms of the questions a person must ask to discover which member of a stimulus set has occurred. Suppose you had only two possible alternatives, A and B, and you were to search for the target among them. You need only ask, "Is it A?" to determine unambiguously which alternative had been selected as the target. If you receive the answer "no," you know immediately that B is correct. Similarly, if you had to determine which of four stimuli, A, B, C, or D, had been chosen as the target, you could determine it with two questions. The answer to the question, "Is it A or B?" reduces your number of possible alternatives to two, since a "no" answer reveals that it is either C or D, while a "yes" indicates that it is A or B. We already know that only one more question is necessary in order to identify the correct item. Each necessary question, structured to eliminate exactly *half* of the alter-

Table 2-6. Log₂n for selected numbers

Number of stimulus alternatives (n)	Number of bits (log₂n)
2	1
4	2
8	3
16	4
32	5
64	6
128	7
256	8

natives, defines a **bit** of information. Bit is a contraction of the words *binary digit* (which can be either a 0 or a 1, that is, there are *two* possible digits).

The number of bits of information needed to determine exactly one stimulus alternative is the logarithm to the base 2 of the total number of possible stimulus alternatives. The logarithm of a number n to the base 2, written $\log_2 n$, is merely the power to which the number 2 must be raised to equal n. Thus, if we have four alternatives we must raise 2 to the second power (that is, $2^2 = 2 \times 2 = 4$) and $\log_2 4 = 2$. Similarly, Table 2-6 gives the corresponding number of bits for n alternatives (a more detailed table can be found in Garner, 1962). Each time the number of stimulus alternatives is doubled, the amount of information rises by one bit. Of course, for intermediate values the number of bits will not be a whole number (for example, seven alternatives gives 2.81 bits).

Channel capacity. How many bits of stimulus information can an observer process and still have perfect recognition? Let us first look at a group of stimuli selected from a one-dimensional physical continuum, such as sound or light intensity. The number of stimuli from one continuum that a subject can differentiate has been found to be surprisingly small. For the judgment of the pitch of a tone, Pollack (1952) found it to be about 2.3 bits, which is equivalent to about 5 stimulus alternatives. Garner (1953) found much the same result for loudness, around 2.1 bits. Eriksen and Hake (1955) measured several visual continua and found information transmission to be limited to 2.34 bits for brightness, 2.84 bits for size, and 3.08 bits for hue. Overall, the number of stimuli that may be recognized perfectly on any single continuum turns out to be approximately seven, plus or minus two, depending on the particular stimulus continuum being tested (see Miller, 1956; Norwich, 1981).

It is important at this point to define the concept of **information transmission**. To do this, let us consider an observer as a channel, in the way that communications engineers do. Our observer may be represented as in Figure 2-7. A stimulus is presented to the observer, who is asked to try to recognize it. By "recognition" we mean giving a response that is the correct, agreed-upon label for the particular stimulus presented. We can say that information is transmitted by the observer to the extent that the responses given match the actual labels of the stimuli presented. That is, if the observer correctly recognizes a stimulus and gives the correct label as a response, information (the correct label) has been transmitted from one end to the other, through the channel represented by the observer. If the response matches the stimulus perfectly for all stimuli, then the observer is a perfect information transmitter.

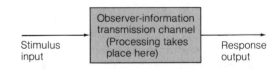

Figure 2-7 A human information channel.

Consider an example in which we are calling out alphabetic letters from a set containing eight items: *A B C D E F G H X*. If the observer correctly identifies the letter (response) that we have called out (stimulus), then she has reduced her uncertainty from three bits of information (eight alternatives) to zero; hence, she has transmitted three bits of information. Suppose that recognition is not perfect. This means that only some of the information is being transmitted. Thus, if the observer hears a faint "eee" sound, with the first part of the letter cut off, she does not know exactly which letter was called out. However, she can eliminate *A*, *F*, *H*, and *X*, which have no "eee" sound; hence, she has reduced the number of stimulus alternatives by half, and we would say that one bit of information has been transmitted. In general, the greater the probability that the observer will recognize the stimulus—that is, the more she "picks up" from the presentations—the more information she is capable of transmitting.

Consider a hypothetical experiment in which each of four stimuli are presented 12 times and observers are asked to identify which stimulus was presented. In Table 2-7 observer A shows perfect information transmission because every time stimulus 1 is presented, our observer correctly recognizes it, and every time 2 is presented, it is named correctly. In Table 2-7 observer B shows poorer information transmission. Notice here that when stimulus 2 is presented, the observer calls it stimulus 2 most of the time; but sometimes, he calls it stimulus 1 and sometimes he calls it stimulus 3. When he does say that it is stimulus 2, however, there is a fair likelihood that it is stimulus 2. He is much better than observer C, who seems to be responding without reference to the stimulus presented. Observer C is transmitting none of the available stimulus information. Formulas for computing the amount of infor-

Table 2-7. Stimulus-response matrices for three observers

Observer A: Perfect information transmission

Stimulus	Response			
	1	2	3	4
1	12			
2		12		
3			12	
4				12

Observer B: Some information transmission

Stimulus	Response			
	1	2	3	4
1	8	4		
2	2	8	2	
3		2	8	2
4			4	8

Observer C: No information transmission

Stimulus	Response			
	1	2	3	4
1	3	3	3	3
2	3	3	3	3
3	3	3	3	3
4	3	3	3	3

mation transmitted in such experiments may be found in Garner and Hake (1951).

If we now consider the information transmission measured in a number of experimental studies, we find that when the stimuli vary along only one sensory dimension (for example, pitch or loudness), and their number is small, observers are capable of perfect recognition. However, when the number of stimuli exceeds seven or so, that is, 2.5 to 3.0 bits of information, errors are made. We have reached the limit of the observer's ability to differentiate among the stimuli. This limit is called (again using communication theory terminology) our observer's **channel capacity**. A typical measurement of channel capacity is shown in Figure 2-8. Notice that even though we increase the amount of information available in the display, our subject has reached his limit of recognition (about 2.5 bits) and can transmit no more information.

Seven seems to be a very small number of stimuli to be able to recognize. We all know that singers, for example, seem able to recognize (indeed sing) hundreds of different songs. Every one of us can certainly recognize and differentiate dozens of faces and thousands of words. How can this be, in light of our inability to transmit more than about three bits of information per stimulus dimension?

You might think that if the stimuli were more widely spaced and discriminable, channel capacity would be higher. The discriminability of stimuli, however, has very little effect on recognition (Pollack, 1952). Another possible explanation is that our everyday performance is explained by practice or repetition. Except in extreme cases, where a person might have years of intensive practice on a single dimension, the practice effect is also not large enough to explain our everyday performance. For instance, you hear a new word today and now you can recognize that word with ease, even though you have only encountered it once. You can also recognize that this word is different from every other word in your vocabulary. We are not at all suprised at such a performance, yet this type of recognition may involve the reduction of uncertainty by some 16 bits (or more, depending on the total number of words in your vocabulary). Given that our channel capacity is so limited for any single stimulus dimension, how can this occur? The answer seems to depend on the *number of dimensions* along which the stimulus varies.

For example, Pollack (1953) found that if he varied only pitch, information transmission averaged about 1.8 bits, while if he varied only loudness, information transmission was about 1.7 bits. When both dimensions were varied simultaneously, however, information transmission was 3.1 bits, clearly more than was obtained for either dimension separately, although not the 3.5 bits expected if the information transmission on the separate dimensions were simply summed in such situations. As one adds new dimensions to the stimuli, recognition performance steadily increases. Certain ways of combining dimensions seem to produce better performances, by making stimuli "stand out" more clearly, or they capitalize on the small gains obtainable by familiarity (Monahan and Lockhead, 1977). Thus by proper selection of stimulus dimensions, Anderson and

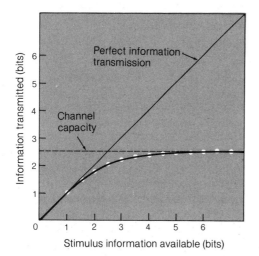

Figure 2-8 Channel capacity. The straight diagonal represents perfect information transmission. The curve represents typical performance. The dotted horizontal line is channel capacity.

Fitts (1958) were able to have information transmission levels of 17 bits on a single flashed stimulus. This means that their subjects could perfectly discriminate one stimulus out of more than 131,000 alternative stimuli!

The importance of stimulus dimensions and how they are combined has led modern investigators to place less emphasis on the *quantity* of information available and more emphasis on the *quality*, or kind, of information and the characteristics of the information processor (see Garner, 1974; Neisser, 1967). The basic ideas of information theory, especially those associated with the number of stimulus alternatives, have been important in calling attention to critical issues in recognition. They have taken their place as foundation concepts, almost assumptions, and modern researchers build on them rather than study them for their own sake. Chapter 12 considers some of these modern extensions of and alternatives to information theory in the study of pattern recognition.

DISCRIMINATION

The artist glances at his model's hair and then back down at the paint on his palette. He mutters to himself, "Still not the same." He daubs a bit more black, mixes the color through, and glances up again. "That is a perfect match," he grunts. This artist is engaging in a special form of recognition task. He is determining whether two colors are the same or different. He does not care what the color actually is, it can be "burnt sienna" or just plain "brown." He cares only whether or not it matches his model's hair color. The artist is engaged in an act of *discrimination*. Discrimination problems ask the question, "Is this stimulus different from that?"

The study of discrimination has focused on

the question, "By how much must two stimuli differ in order to be discriminated as not the same?" Suppose the melody "Oh Susanna" were to be played on a piano once in the key of C and once in the key of G. Are these two musical stimuli the same or different? The answer to this question depends on the stimulus dimension being judged. If we are judging whether the melodies are the same or different, we would answer differently than if we were judging the key in which the melodies are played.

To avoid such confusions, the standard discrimination experiment involves variation of stimuli along only one dimension. Thus, in a study of the discrimination of weights we might hold the size and shape of our stimuli constant and vary only the weight. In the earlier studies, observers were presented with pairs of stimuli and asked to make the appropriate response, "heavier," "lighter," or "same," or some similar set of judgments appropriate to the stimulus dimension being judged. One of these stimuli was designated the **standard**. This is a stimulus that appears on every trial. It is compared to a graded set of similar stimuli differing along the dimension being studied. The graded stimuli make up the set of **comparison stimuli**. This is simply a variant of the method of constant stimuli, which is used to determine the absolute threshold, with the addition of a standard. We are also measuring a threshold here, only this is a threshold for the perception of a difference between the standard and the other stimuli. It is called a **difference threshold**.

As psychophysicists worked with the measurement of difference thresholds for various stimulus dimensions, they found that observers used the "same" response category whenever they were unsure or unwilling to actually state a perceptible difference. Thus, experimenters soon resorted to only two response alternatives instead of three. For example, in a weight judgment experiment, the observer would only be permitted to respond that the comparison stimulus is either "heavier" or "lighter." If he feels that the comparison and the standard are the same, he is still forced to indicate (by guessing) in which direction they appear to differ. The advantage of this procedure was demonstrated by the painstaking work of Brown (1910), who was able to show that in a weight judgment experiment, stimulus differences as small as 0.2 g (which is about 0.008 ounce) produced more correct than incorrect judgments, even when the observer felt that the stimuli were the same and that he was merely guessing.

The results from such an experiment are easy to display. In the weight judgment experiment, for instance, the standard was presented with each comparison stimulus many times. We can plot the proportion of the presentations on which any given stimulus was judged heavier than the standard. Such a plot is illustrated in Figure 2-9. This plot is similar to results from a classic experiment on weight judgment by Brown (1910). He used a 100 g standard and a set of comparison weights ranging from 82 to 118 g in 1 g steps. Each comparison stimulus was judged 700 times against the standard stimulus. Notice that the shift from reports of "lighter" to reports of "heavier" is not very abrupt, as it would be if the threshold was always a single, unique value. Rather, we find a gradual change in the probability of a "heavier" response as the stimulus changes from much lighter than the standard to much heavier. Since the change is gradual, we again must make some decision regarding how we will define the difference threshold. The point where $p(\text{heavier}) = 0.5$, that is, the stimulus was called "lighter" 50 percent of the time and "heavier" 50 percent of the time, is not appropriate. This 50 percent point probably represents the stimulus that appeared most like the

standard, since the choices are evenly divided on either side of it. Therefore, it has been called the **point of subjective equality**. The stimulus for which $p(\text{heavier}) = 1.0$ represents perfect discrimination (because here a physically heavier stimulus is judged heavier 100 percent of the time). The stimulus where $p(\text{heavier}) = 0.5$ represents no perception of difference. Therefore, the point $p(\text{heavier}) = 0.75$ (halfway between these values) represents a value where the *difference* is noted 50 percent of the time. Following similar reasoning, $p(\text{heavier}) = 0.25$ is the point at which a stimulus difference in the lighter direction is noted 50 percent of the time. By convention, we take the interval from the 0.25 point to the 0.75 point, called the **interval of uncertainty**, and divide it by 2 to give us a value that we call the **just noticeable difference**, or *jnd*. The *jnd* computed for the data in Figure 2-9 is about 4 g. This means that when a pair of stimuli are separated in weight

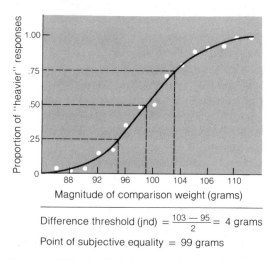

Difference threshold (jnd) $= \frac{103 - 95}{2} = 4$ grams

Point of subjective equality = 99 grams

Figure 2-9 Typical data from the method of constant stimuli in discrimination with calculations of difference threshold (jnd) and point of subjective equality.

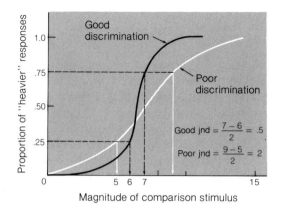

Figure 2-10 Difference thresholds (jnds) for observers of different sensitivity.

by 4 g, the subject will be able to detect the difference between them about half the time. You can probably see that the *jnd* is simply the average of the threshold for "greater than" and the threshold for "less than." In other words, it represents the threshold for "different," averaged across the direction of the differences.

If discrimination is good, we would expect very small differences between stimuli to be noticed. This corresponds to a small *jnd*. In Figure 2-10 the black line shows a good discriminator with a *jnd* of 0.5 units, while the white line shows a poor discriminator with a *jnd* of 2 units. As the *jnd* increases in size and discrimination ability decreases, the curve begins to flatten. The extreme of no discrimination at all would be represented by a horizontal line parallel to the abscissa at $p(\text{heavier}) = 0.5$.

You may have noticed an interesting aspect of the data pictured in Figure 2-9. The point of subjective equality is not equal to the standard in these data. The stimulus that *appears* to be equal to the standard of 100 g is actually 1 g lighter. This is a typical result in many psychophysical experiments involving the presentation of stimuli that are separated in time. The stimulus presented first (generally the standard) is judged to be less intense than the later stimulus. This effect has been named the **negative time error**. It is negative because the standard is judged less intense than it should be. Fechner (1966/1860) and Wolfgang Kohler (1923) thought this error was caused by the fading of the image or the memory trace of the sensation of the standard with the passage of time. Work done with auditory stimuli has shown, however, that with proper selection of a time interval, the error can be positive rather than negative (Kohler, 1923). Such errors are probably the result of particular cognitive or judgmental factors, which as we have seen before, tend to influence even the most apparently simple perceptual tasks (Hellstrom, 1979).

Weber's law

Is the *jnd* a fixed value for any given sense modality, or does it vary as a function of the nature of the stimulus input or the state of the observer? Following the lead of Ernst Heinrich Weber (1834), Fechner (1966/1860) conducted an experiment where he measured the *jnds* for lifted weights using standard weights of different magnitudes. We may plot the size of the *jnd*, that is, the amount by which we must increase the stimulus so that it is discriminable as different from the standard 50 percent of the time, against the magnitude of the standard. This has been done for some illustrative data in Figure 2-11. First, notice that the *jnd* is not a constant value. It appears to increase in a linear fashion with the size of the standard. In other words, as the stimulus magnitude increases, so does the size of the change needed for discrimination to occur. The intuitive force of this relationship is illustrated in an example proposed by Galanter (1962), "if in a room with ten candles you had to add one more in order to detect an increase in illumination, then if the room contained one hundred it

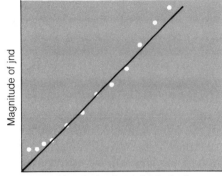

Figure 2-11 Effect of intensity of standard on difference threshold (jnd).

would be necessary to add ten candles in order to detect the same apparent increase in illumination . . ." (p. 133). This relation between the size of the *jnd* and the size of the standard intensity is called **Weber's law** after its discoverer.

Weber's law is simply written as

$$\Delta I = KI$$

where ΔI is the size of the *jnd*, I is the intensity of the standard stimulus, and K is a constant.

The constant K is always a fraction and is equal to $\Delta I/I$. It indicates the proportion by which the standard stimulus must be increased in order to detect a change. This fractional value is called the **Weber fraction**. Thus, if the Weber fraction is 0.02, it means that we must increase the intensity of one stimulus by 2 percent for a difference between it and another stimulus to be detected. This proportion (the Weber fraction) is the same, regardless of the strength of the standard stimulus. In a weight judgment experiment, for example, to discriminate a stimulus as different from a 2 g standard, the weight must be increased by only 0.04 g ($2 \times 0.02 = 0.04$). To discriminate a stimulus as different from a 200 g standard, it must be increased by 4 g ($200 \times 0.02 = 4$). A simple demonstration of Weber's law is given in Demonstration Box 2-2.

Conceptually, consider the Weber fraction to be a measure of the overall sensitivity of a sensory system to differences along a stimulus continuum. The larger the Weber fraction, the larger will be the *jnds* for any stimulus dimension, hence the bigger the change needed for discrimination. Note that K has no units (like grams), so that it does not depend on the physical units used to measure I and ΔI. Thus,

---

Demonstration Box 2-2. Weber's law

It is easy to demonstrate Weber's law for the perception of heaviness. You will need three quarters, two envelopes, and your shoes. Take one quarter and put it in an envelope and put the remaining two quarters in the other. If you now lift each envelope gently and put it down (use the same hand), it is quite easy to distinguish the heavier envelope. Now insert one envelope into one of your shoes and the other envelope into your second shoe, and lift them one at a time. The weight difference should be almost imperceptible. In the first instance the targets differed by the weight of the quarter and the difference was discriminated easily. In the second instance, although the weight differential was the same (one quarter), the overall stimulus intensity was greater because shoes weigh much more than the envelopes and the quarters alone.

Table 2-8. Typical Weber fractions $\Delta I/I$ (based on Teghtsoonian, 1971)

Continuum	Weber fraction
Brightness	0.079
Loudness	0.048
Finger span	0.022
Heaviness	0.020
Line length	0.029
Taste (salt)	0.083
Electric shock	0.013
Vibration (fingertip)	
60 Hz	0.036
125 Hz	0.046
250Hz	0.046

we can compare Weber fractions across different stimulus dimensions without having to worry about how the stimulus values were measured. The Weber fraction simply represents the average ratio of *jnd* size to the size of the standard level at which the *jnd* was measured, over an entire range of standard values. Table 2-8 presents typical Weber fractions for a variety of continua. As you can see, some of the *K*s are relatively large (for example, those for brightness and loudness), while some are quite small (for example, electric shock).

How well does Weber's law fit the data? For many years, there was considerable argument about this issue. Measurements were taken in many sense modalities to check the relation. The clearest picture of the results is obtained by plotting the value of the Weber fraction, $\Delta I/I$, against the standard stimulus intensity. If the Weber fraction is actually constant, we should see a horizontal line, parallel to the abscissa. Figure 2-12 shows a composite of data from loudness discrimination experiments by Miller (1947) and Riesz (1928). There is considerable deviation from the expected constancy at both extremes. Although these deviations at the extremes look very large, this is only be-

cause we have plotted the stimuli in logarithmic units. The flat middle part of the curve actually exceeds 99.9 percent of the total range of measured intensities. Thus, Weber's law is a useful summary in spite of the deviation of the data from a perfect fit.

Signal detection theory in discrimination

Although signal detection theory was presented (and first developed) in the context of the detection problem, it can be extended to the discrimination situation. Certainly there are decisional components that influence whether or not an observer discriminates a difference between two stimuli. To use the signal detection procedure to assess discrimination, we must redesign the Method of Constant Stimuli experiment so that the observer is asked to say which of two very similar stimuli was presented on a given trial. This is like a recognition experiment with only two stimuli.

The signal detection analysis of this experiment is quite similar to that used for detection. Instead of trying to ascertain whether the sensation experienced on a given trial came from

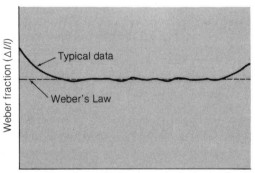

Figure 2-12 Typical data for test of Weber's law. The dotted line is predicted by Weber's law: $\Delta I/I = K$.

the signal or the noise distribution, the observer must decide whether it is from the Signal 1 or Signal 2 distribution. If the stimuli are very similar, the sensory response curves would overlap when plotted on the same set of axes, and an observer would be faced with a situation very similar to that faced by the observer in the absolute detection situation. Look back at Figure 2-4 and mentally relabel the two distributions "Signal 1" and "Signal 2." Two stimuli can give rise to a variety of different sensation levels, with different probabilities of occurrence. Since the curves cover the same general area of the sensation axis, there is no way to be certain which stimulus elicited a given sensation level on any one trial. The best the ideal observer can do is to place a criterion somewhere on the sensation axis and simply determine whether the sensation level experienced is above or below that criterion. If above, the appropriate response would be that the presented stimulus was a 2; if below, a 1. Just as in the absolute detection situation, where the observer places the criterion will greatly affect the proportions of different responses he gives. In turn, criterion placement will be affected by the observer's expectations as to the relative frequency of presentation of the two stimuli and the observer's present motivational biases.

As in the detection experiment, different criterion placements will define an isosensitivity curve when we plot the proportion of hits against the proportion of false alarms. The measure of sensitivity to the difference between the two stimuli is still called d' and is still unaffected by changes in the criterion. Actually, d' is determined by the physical difference between the two stimuli and the sensitivity of the observer's sensory system; both are factors that determine the difference between the levels of sensation evoked by the stimuli. Thus d' represents a measure of just how discriminable two very similar stimuli are. As such, it is closely related to the difference threshold and to the Weber fraction (Treisman, 1976; Treisman and Watts, 1966).

Reaction time

We have been looking at stimuli that are difficult to discriminate correctly. Even when we are working with stimuli well above the difference threshold, we may feel that some discriminations are easier to make than others. Red is more easily differentiated from green than from orange. When we are working with sets of stimuli that exceed the difference threshold, the frequency methods we have used to this point are too crude to measure interstimulus differences in detectability or discriminability. To provide a more sensitive measure we must turn to one of the oldest techniques in sensory psychology: **reaction time**. Reaction time is defined as the time between the onset of a stimulus and the beginning of an overt response. It was first introduced in 1850 by one of the early giants in perception and physiology, Hermann von Helmholtz, who used it as a crude measure of the speed of neural conduction in a limb.

There are two varieties of reaction time. **Simple reaction time** involves pressing or releasing a telegraph key (or making some other simple stereotyped response) immediately upon detecting a stimulus. **Choice reaction time** involves making one of several responses depending on the stimulus presented (for example, press the right-hand key for a red stimulus and the left for a green). Simple reaction times are generally used in detection paradigms. We have known for a long time that the stronger a stimulus the faster the reaction time. Figure 2-13 shows typical median reaction times to the onset of a tone plotted against the stimulus intensity (Chocolle, 1940). When

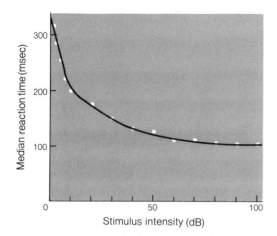

Figure 2-13 Effect of stimulus intensity on simple reaction time (based on Chocolle, 1940).

the stimulus intensity is low and near the detection threshold (although it is still quite detectable), the reaction times are longer. Thus, when the stimulus is more difficult to apprehend, reaction time is longer. Similar results have been obtained for visual stimuli (Cattell, 1886; Grice, Nullmeyer and Schnizlein, 1979). Simple reaction time has also been used to measure discrimination. Here, however, the subject had to detect a change in stimulus intensity. The larger the change in the stimulus (either an increase or a decrease), the shorter the reaction time (Welford, 1980).

Choice reaction time has been used in studies of discrimination and recognition. These reaction times tend to be somewhat longer than simple reaction times (Posner, 1978). The classic discrimination experiment utilizing reaction time was done by Henmon (1906). In this experiment the observer had two response keys—one for each hand. In one instance, the observer was presented with pairs of lines differing only in length and told to depress the key corresponding to the side on which the line was longer. Henmon found that the greater

the difference between the line lengths the shorter the reaction time. He reported similar results for colors and tones.

A striking example of the relationship between choice reaction time and the discriminability of stimuli used a slightly different technique. In an experiment by Shallice and Vickers (1964), observers were required to sort decks of cards into piles according to which of two lines on the cards appeared longer. The time it took them to sort the cards was the measure of their reaction time. This measure is, of course, the sum of a number of reaction times, where we consider the sorting of each card as a single response. The standard stimulus in this experiment was a 4.5 cm line. In the data shown in Table 2-9, we see that the more difficult the discrimination, the longer the sorting time. A simple demonstration of this effect is given in Demonstration Box 2-3.

Crossman (1953) has shown that these reaction time differences are related both to the discriminability of the stimuli and to the amount of information they contain. We are referring to information in the technical sense discussed in the section on recognition. If this is the case, choice reaction times should increase as we

Table 2-9. Differences in reaction time as a function of differences in line lengths measured via card sorts (based on Shallice and Vickers, 1964)

Difference in length (cm)	Sorting time (sec)
1.1	39.4
0.9	40.0
0.7	40.1
0.5	41.0
0.4	42.0
0.3	42.9
0.2	46.5
0.1	52.4

Demonstration Box 2-3. Reaction time and stimulus discriminability

Take a deck of common playing cards and select out of it 10 of the picture cards (Kings, Queens, and Jacks) and 10 numbered cards from the red suits (hearts and diamonds) to make up a new deck of 20 cards. Compose another deck of 20 by using the numbered cards (include the aces) of the black suits (clubs and spades). Shuffle each deck separately and place it in front of you, face down. Next you need a clock or a watch with a sweep second hand. Wait until the second hand reaches the 12, pick up one of the decks and be-

gin to sort it into two piles. The first deck gets sorted into number and picture cards, while the second gets sorted into spades and clubs. Note the time it takes to sort each deck. You may want to repeat the task a couple of times so that you are sorting smoothly. Notice that the sorting time for the spades and clubs (a more difficult task since it involves making small form discriminations on similarly colored cards) is longer than the easier discrimination task of sorting picture and number cards.

Table 2-10. Reaction time as a function of number of stimulus alternatives (based on Merkel, 1885)

Number of alternatives	Reaction time (msec)
1	187
2	316
3	364
4	434
5	487
6	534
7	570
8	603
9	619
10	632

increase the number of response alternatives, and indeed, this result has been known for many years. Merkel (1885) showed with number stimuli that the reaction time increased as the number of response alternatives increased. The data in Table 2-10 show this clearly.

Hick (1952) attempted to explain these results by postulating that the observer extracts information from the stimulus display at a constant rate. The more information that

must be obtained from the display, the longer the reaction time. In an experimental situation, where a display of lights served as stimuli and finger pressings of telegraph keys served as responses, he found a linear function between reaction time and the logarithm of the number of stimulus alternatives. This relation, called **Hick's law**, states that choice reaction time is a linear function of the amount of information in the stimulus. You may demonstrate effects of the number of stimulus alternatives on reaction time by consulting Demonstration Box 2-4.

SCALING

The dog trainer glanced at her new Saint Bernard pupil and estimated his shoulder height to be 75 cm and his weight to be 80 kg. In so doing she was actually engaged in the perceptual act called *scaling*. Scaling attempts to answer the question, "How much of X is there?" X can be a stimulus magnitude, a sensation magnitude, or the magnitude of such other complex psychological variables as similarity or even pleasantness.

A scale is a rule by which we assign numbers to objects or events. The scale attempts to represent numerically some property of objects or events. There are a variety of different types of representations that may be established, and each has its own characteristics (see Stevens, 1946). Perhaps the most primitive and unrestricted type of scale is a **nominal scale**. Its etymology specifies its nature, since "nomin" is derived from the Latin word for "name." When numbers are assigned in a nominal scale, they serve only as identity codes or surrogate names. The numbers imply nothing more about the quantity of some property than does the number on a football jersey.

Whenever we are dealing with something for which it is possible to say that an object or event contains more or less of the property than some other object or event, we can create an **ordinal scale** of that property. An ordinal scale simply ranks items on the basis of some quantity. An example might be the "Best Seller" or "Top Fifty" lists that order books or records on the basis of how many have been sold. It is clear that although this scale may prove to be more useful for measurement than a nominal scale, we are still quite restricted in what we can do with the numbers on such a scale.

The third type of scale is the **interval scale**. It not only answers the questions implied by the labels "more" and "less" but also tells "by how much?" The interval scale employs not only the sequential properties of numbers but also their spacing, or the *intervals* between them. A good example of an interval scale is the scale of temperature represented by the common household thermometer. Here the size of the difference between 10 and 20° C (50 and 68° F) is exactly the same as between 40 and 50° C (104 and 122° F). Such scales are very useful, as they allow for the application of most statistical techniques. Interval scales suffer from one major drawback, however. They do not have a *true* zero point; rather, convenience or convention usually dictates where the zero will be. Thus, in the Centigrade scale of temperature, the zero point is located at the freezing point of pure water.

The most numerically powerful scale is the *ratio scale*. The creation of this type of scale is possible only when equality, rank order, equality of intervals, and a true zero point can be determined experimentally. Unfortunately, ratio scales are most often found in the physical rather than in the behavioral sciences. Such things as weight, density, and length can be measured on ratio scales since the zero points are not arbitrary. For example, 0 g represents the complete absence of weight, and we can meaningfully say that 10 g is twice as heavy as 5 g. Negative values of weight exist only in the fantasies of dieters.

All sensory qualities cannot be scaled in the same way. Some perceptual experiences have an underlying aspect of intensity (for instance, brightness), while others do not (such as hue). When we are dealing with a stimulus or an experience in which it makes sense to ask "How much?" or "How intense?" we have a **prothetic continuum** (Stevens and Galanter, 1957). Changes from one level of sensation to another come about by adding or subtracting from what is present. Thus, when we increase the weight of a stimulus, the corresponding psychological sensation of "heaviness" increases. Such prothetic continua can be meaningfully measured on scales of any of the types we have discussed. In the other type of sensory continuum, changes in the physical stimulus result in a change in the apparent quality rather than the apparent quantity of a stimulus. When we have a stimulus or experience in which the only question that it makes sense to ask is "What kind?" we are dealing with a **metathetic continuum**. Thus, a change in the wavelength of a light may cause its appearance to change from red to green. Psychologically, there is no quantitative difference between these two hues; they just appear to be different. Occasionally both types of continua will be present in the same sense impressions. For instance, in touch, the amount of pressure applied is a prothetic continuum, while the location of the touch is a metathetic continuum. Metathetic continua can be dealt with using nominal scales, but scales that imply order have generally not been successfully applied to such sensory qualities (but see Schneider and Bissett, 1981).

Indirect scaling: Fechner's law

When the perceptual investigator attempts to establish a sensory scale in which numbers will be assigned to the intensity of sensations, two alternative approaches are possible. The first is a **direct scaling** procedure in which individuals are asked to assess directly some aspect of the strength of the sensation. Although this might be the easiest procedure, it is often difficult for the untrained observer. In addition, many early psychologists distrusted the accuracy of such direct reports because there seemed to be no easy way to convert them to numerical values. For this reason, **indirect scaling** methods, based on discrimination ability, formed the basis for the first psychological scales. Using an indirect procedure is not necessarily bad. After all, we measure temperature indirectly, using the height of a column of mercury as our indicator.

The first person to attempt to describe the relationship between stimulus intensity and sensation intensity was Gustav Theodor Fechner. To do this, he had to invent a way to measure the quantity of the sensory experience. As his starting point, he assumed that Weber's law was correct, which as we have seen, does hold over a wide range of stimuli. Fechner's next assumption engendered a good deal of controversy and experimental testing. He assumed that the subjective impression of the difference between two stimuli separated by one *just noticeable difference* was the same regardless of the absolute magnitude of the two stimuli. Thus, if we take two dim lights that are separated by one *jnd* and we take two lights that are 30 or 40 times brighter, but again separated from each other by one *jnd*, we should perceive the two pairs of stimuli as differing by equal sensory steps. Finally, Fechner assumed that sensation differences could be represented by adding or subtracting *jnds*.

If we accept Fechner's postulate that Weber's law is true and that the subjective sizes of all *jnd*s are equal, then only a small *physical* change is necessary to achieve a 1 *jnd* change for a weak stimulus, while a *large* change is needed for a 1 *jnd* change

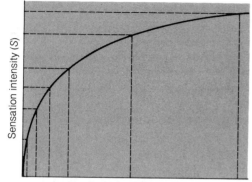

Axis labels: Sensation intensity (S) — vertical; Physical stimulus intensity (I) — horizontal.

Figure 2-14 Fechner's law. It takes larger and larger differences between stimuli (I's) as stimulus intensity increases to give rise to the same size differences between sensations (S's).

when the physical stimulus is intense. Perceptually, this means that the intensity of the sensation grows rapidly for weak physical stimuli and more slowly as the physical stimulus is made more intense. The relationship between the intensity of the sensation and the intensity of the physical stimulus is shown in Figure 2-14. This curve is described by the equation,

$$S = K \log I$$

where S is the magnitude of sensation a stimulus elicits, I is the physical magnitude of the stimulus (units above the absolute threshold stimulus magnitude), and K is a constant that depends on the value of the Weber fraction ($\Delta I/I$). This equation is called **Fechner's law**. The actual mathematical procedures by which Fechner derived this relationship are discussed by Falmagne (1974) and Baird and Noma (1978), among others. We are using the number of *jnd*s above the absolute threshold as a measure of the strength of the sensation generated by a given stimulus (S), and we are saying

that the equation above relates this number to the physical intensity of the stimulus (I). The constant K is different for different sensory and psychological continua. Remember that this is an indirect scale since the strength of the sensation is never measured directly. To create this scale we need measure only the size of the *jnd*. Once that has been determined, the rest is easy and requires only counting *jnd*s. Fechner's technique was to use some aspect of the discriminability of stimuli as an index of the intensity of an observer's sensory impression.

Direct scaling

Since Fechner's time, many psychophysicists have insisted that indirect scaling is neither necessary nor preferable. Because we are interested in the *apparent* intensity of a stimulus to an observer, why not simply require judgments based on how intense a stimulus seems to be? The observer's responses could then be used directly to establish a scale of measurement for the psychological attribute. The first attempt to do this was undertaken in 1872 by one of Fechner's contemporaries, a Belgian investigator named Plateau. To test Fechner's law he had eight artists mix a gray that was halfway between a particular black and a white. Notice that this requires direct relative judgments of three stimuli, the black, white, and gray. Fechner's law predicts that this psychological midpoint should correspond to the average of the logarithm of the intensity of the black stimulus and that of the white stimulus. Unfortunately, the results, although somewhat similar to the prediction, did not fully support Fechner's law. Rather, the grays mixed by Plateau's artists seemed to fall halfway between the cube roots (1/3 power) of the intensities of the black and the white stimuli. This numerical discrepancy suggests that Fechner's law may be only an approximation to the relationship between physical and sensory intensity. We care about such mathematical deviations because a major purpose of scaling is to make possible a precise description of the relationship between the strength of the physical stimulus and the strength of sensations.

Category judgment. Sanford was among the early investigators who attempted to measure sensation directly. As early as 1898, he had worked out a technique that involved having observers judge a number of envelopes, each of which contained different weights. The subjects were instructed to sort the weights into five categories. Category 1 was to be used for the lightest weights, and category 5 for the heaviest, with the remaining weights distributed in the other categories in such a way that the intervals between the category boundaries would be subjectively equal. Thus, the difference in sensation between the upper and the lower boundaries of category 1 should be the same as that of category 2. In other words, all categories should be the same size. This method has been called **category scaling** or **equal interval scaling**. A similarity exists between this method and a recognition task, except that in category scaling we usually have fewer categories than stimuli. Also, of course, there is no such thing as a correct or an incorrect answer, since the very nature of the experiment implies that we cannot know in advance what a correct category assignment might be.

If our observer has spaced the category boundaries equally in terms of the magnitude of the sensory differences among them, we can, without making any other assumptions, mark off equal category intervals (to represent the midpoints of the categories) along our ordinate and label them with the category names. We can plot the average category label assigned to each stimulus intensity over several trials. The curve we obtain for typical data

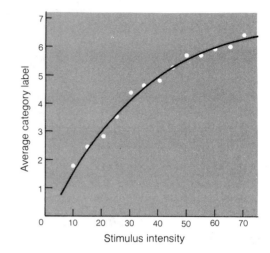

Figure 2-15 Some typical data from a category judgment experiment. The dots represent average category judgments of the various stimulus intensities.

(Figure 2-15) is concave downward and closely approximates the curve predicted by Fechner's law (Figure 2-14). The fact that we can predict the shape of the category scale from simple discrimination data is quite impressive. To Sanford it seemed support for the contention that a logarithmic relationship exists between physical stimulus intensity and perceived magnitude.

Since Sanford's work, category scaling has been studied in great detail. Category scales have been found to be relatively stable over several different manipulations, including the labels applied to the categories (numbers versus words) and the number of categories used (Stevens and Galanter, 1957). Other variations in procedure, however, dramatically affect the form of the scale. For example, how the stimuli presented are spaced along the physical intensity dimension (Carter and Hirsch, 1955) and how often the various stimuli are presented (Parducci, 1965) both affect the relation of the category scale to the stimulus values on physical scales. Also, the range of stimulus intensities presented is important (Parducci, 1965), and the category judgments themselves are affected by the memories of previous stimuli and responses (Ward, 1972). These biases indicate that we should use caution in interpreting scales of measurement formed from category judgments, although some authors argue that they are nonetheless the best type of scales to use (for example, Anderson, 1970b).

Magnitude estimation: Stevens' law. Although in category judgments, observers are directly responding to variations in stimulus magnitude, there is still some "indirectness" involved. Thus, stimuli that are similar but still discriminably different from one another may be grouped in the same category. Also, responses are limited to a few category labels. S. S. Stevens popularized a procedure called **magnitude estimation** that avoids these problems. The method is so simple and direct that one wonders why it had to be "invented" at all. In this procedure, observers are simply asked to assign numbers to stimuli on the basis of how intense they appear to be. Stimuli are usually judged one at a time, and the only restriction on responses is that numbers lower than zero cannot be used.

In a typical magnitude estimation experiment, in which we wish to scale the apparent length of lines, we would start by showing a *standard stimulus* that serves as the starting point for the observer's judgments. We might then say, "This stimulus has a value of 10. You will be presented with several stimuli that differ in length. Your task is to assign numbers to these other stimuli in relation to the one with a value of 10. Thus, if you see a line that appears to be twice as long as this one, you should assign to it the number 20. If you see a line one-fifth as long, you should assign to it the number 2. You may use any numbers you choose as long as they are larger than zero." In this task the number assigned to the standard stimulus is called the **modulus**. It serves to keep the numerical estimates of different subjects within the same general range of values. As you can see, this is a very direct way to attempt to measure sensation. The nature of the task (where a stimulus judged to be m times larger than the standard is given a number m times as large) implies that the resultant scale might be a ratio scale. There is, however, continuing debate on this point.

Stevens fully expected the results of such experiments to confirm Fechner's law. When he plotted the data from an experiment in the magnitude estimation of loudness (Stevens, 1956), however, he found that the graph differed from what a logarithmic relationship between stimulus and sensation intensity had led him to expect. The equation he ascertained that best described the relationship of the median magnitude estimates to the stimulus intensities was

$$L = aI^{0.6}$$

where L is the subjective loudness obtained through the observer's magnitude estimates, a is a constant, and I is the physical intensity of the sound, and 0.6 is a power to which I is raised. In succeeding years, Stevens and a host of others produced magnitude estimation scales for a multitude of sensory continua. All these scales seemed to be related to the physical stimulus intensities by the general relationship

$$S = aI^n$$

where S is the sensory intensity and n is a characteristic exponent that differs for different sensory continua. Since this relation states that the magnitude of the sensation is simply

Table 2-11. Representative exponents of the power functions relating psychological magnitude to stimulus magnitude (based on Stevens, 1961)

Continuum	Exponent	Stimulus conditions
Loudness	0.6	Both ears
Brightness	0.33	5° target—dark
Brightness	0.5	Point source—dark
Lightness	1.2	Gray papers
Smell	0.55	Coffee odor
Taste	0.8	Saccharine
Taste	1.3	Sucrose
Taste	1.3	Salt
Temperature	1.0	Cold—on arm
Temperature	1.6	Warmth—on arm
Vibration	0.95	60 Hz—on finger
Duration	1.1	White noise stimulus
Finger span	1.3	Thickness of wood blocks
Pressure on palm	1.1	Static force on skin
Heaviness	1.45	Lifted weights
Force of handgrip	1.7	Precision hand dynamometer
Electric shock	3.5	60 Hz—through fingers

the intensity of the physical stimulus raised to some power, this relationship is often called the **power law**, or after its popularizer, **Stevens' law**.

In the power law the magnitude of the sensation change, given a change in stimulus intensity, depends on the size of the exponent. In general, the exponent for any one continuum is quite stable. As long as the experimental situation is kept reasonably standard, the average exponents produced by different groups of observers for the same continuum are quite similar. Some of them are small fractions (like 0.3 for brightness), some are close to 1 (as for line length), while others are quite large (as 3.5 for electric shock). Some typical exponents for a number of continua are given in Table 2-11.

If we plot some of the relationships between judged sensory intensity and the physical stimulus intensity, we find that the curves for power functions with different exponents (n) have dramatically different shapes. This can be seen in Figure 2-16. With exponents of less than 1 (for example, brightness), the curves are concave downward, meaning that as the stimulus becomes more intense, greater stimulus changes are needed to produce the same degree of perceptual change. When exponents are greater than 1 (for example, shock), the curves are concave upward, meaning that as stimuli become more intense, the same physical stimulus change produces an even larger perceptual change than at lower stimulus intensities. Since each sensory continuum might give a different curve describing the relationship between sensory and physical intensity, it is fortunate that a simple procedure exists that allows us to estimate the power function from any set of data. If we plot the logarithm of the average magnitude estimates (the average numbers observers assign to their sensations)

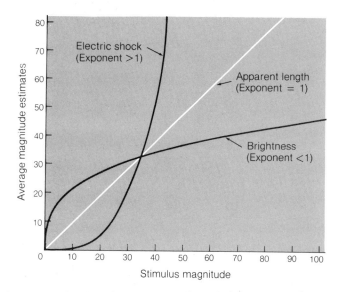

***Figure 2-16 Power functions for brightness,
length, and electric shock. Notice how the*** ***shape of the curve changes as the exponent
changes.***

against the logarithms of the stimulus intensities, any curve of the general form $S = aI^n$ will appear as a straight line. In Figure 2-17 the curves in Figure 2-16 have been replotted in this way. We can now estimate n from the curve by measuring the distances marked Δy and Δx in the figure and computing $\Delta y/\Delta x$. The constant a is the point at which the line crosses the vertical axis or ordinate. Demonstration Box 2-5 allows you to perform a magnitude estimation experiment for yourself.

We mentioned earlier that category judgments are subject to several sources of bias, and thus category scales should be constructed and used with caution. Unfortunately, although magnitude estimations have proved to be quite useful, and average magnitude estimations behave quite lawfully, they nonetheless are also subject to a variety of biases. The particular stimulus used as the standard, the modulus used, the range of stimuli presented, the clarity

of the stimuli, how people use numbers, and previous stimuli and responses can all affect observers' magnitude estimations (see for example, Baird, Lewis, and Romer, 1970; Poulton, 1979; Ward, 1973, 1979). Relatively bias-free scales may be produced by carefully choosing stimuli and procedures (Poulton, Edwards, and Fowler, 1980), but as we have noted many times before, it is impossible to eliminate completely the observers' judgmental inclinations, habits, or strategies from any such perceptual task.

You might wonder why category judgments seem to give a logarithmic relationship that supports Fechner's law, while magnitude estimates seem to give a power law to describe the growth of the sensation. Actually, Stevens and Galanter (1957) found that category judgments only approximate a logarithmic relationship. Since then several investigators (Marks, 1968, 1974; Gibson and Tomko, 1972; Ward,

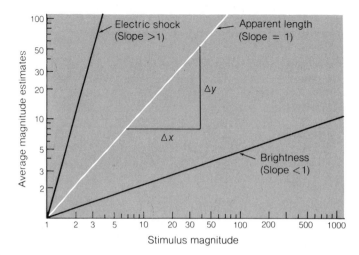

Figure 2-17 The same power functions as in Figure 2-16 plotted on logarithmic axes. In such "log-log" plots, all power functions become straight lines, with the slope of the straight line determined by the exponent (n) of the power function.

1971, 1972, 1974) have shown that category judgments also fit the power law, but with exponents (n) that are about half the size of those produced by magnitude estimation. Marks (1974) and Torgerson (1961) have suggested that these different results reflect different but equally valid ways of judging the same sensory experience. For example, if my 10 kg dog and my 100 kg brother both gain 1 kilogram in weight, we may ask, "Have they both gained the same amount?" If we are making an equal interval judgment (analogous to that required for category scaling), the answer is yes, since both have increased by 1 kg. If we are making an equal ratio judgment (magnitude estimate), my dog has increased his body weight by 10 percent and my brother has increased his body weight by only 1 percent. Thus, the weight gain is far from the same. Both judgments require estimates of the magnitude of a single event, and both are useful, but the scales (and resultant stimulus-sensation curves) are different.

Cross-modality matching. If the size of the exponent varies with the nature of the response, you might wonder whether these scales tell us more about how humans use numbers than they do about how sensation varies with stimulus intensity (see Zwislocki and Goodman, 1980). In order to counter such criticism, Stevens invented a scaling procedure that does not use numbers at all. In this technique, an observer adjusts the intensity of a stimulus until it appears to be as intense as another stimulus from a different sensory continuum. Thus, you might be asked to squeeze a handgrip until the pressure felt as strong as a particular light was bright. This procedure is called **cross-modality matching**, since the observer is asked to match sensory magnitudes *across* sensory modalities. Actually, magnitude estimation can also be viewed as a form of cross-modality matching in which the number continuum is matched to a stimulus continuum (Oyama, 1968; Stevens, 1975).

When we plot the data from cross-modality

Demonstration Box 2-5. Magnitude estimation of loudness

To produce a graded set of sound intensities for this demonstration you will need a long ruler, a coin (we've designed the demonstration for a quarter), an empty tin can or water glass, a soft towel, and a friend. Place the can on the folded towel and have your friend drop the coin from the designated height so that the coin hits the can on its edge only once and then falls onto the towel (silently, we hope). You should sit with your back to the apparatus.

At the start, your friend should drop the coin from a 70 cm height. Try to remember how loud that sounds, and assign it a value of 10. If you feel that a test sound is twice as loud as the first sound, call it 20, if it's half as loud call it 5, and so on. You may use any numbers you feel are appropriate as long as they are greater than zero. Your friend should then drop the coin from heights of 1, 10, 70, 100, and 200 cm, in some mixed order, while you call out the number corresponding to its apparent loudness and your friend records your judgment for each stimulus (height). Do this for two or three runs through the stimuli, and then average your magnitude estimates for each height.

To determine if these judgments follow a power law, plot them on the log-log coordinates provided in the accompanying graph. The vertical axis is the logarithm of the magnitude estimate while the horizontal axis is the logarithm of the sound intensity, based on the height of the coin drop. Draw the straight line that best fits the data points. Usually, the data points fall close to such a line and do not curve significantly. You can compute directly the exponent (n in the power law $S = aI^n$) by computing the slope of your straight line. Simply pick two points on the line and measure Δx and Δy for these points with a ruler, as pictured in Figure 2-17. Now divide Δy by Δx, and you should get a value somewhere around 0.3. This exponent means that the sensation of loudness increases less rapidly than does the actual sound intensity.

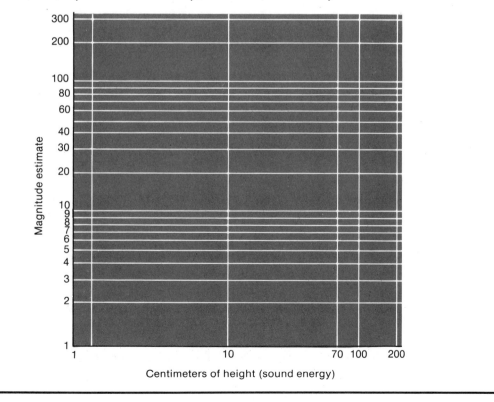

Centimeters of height (sound energy)

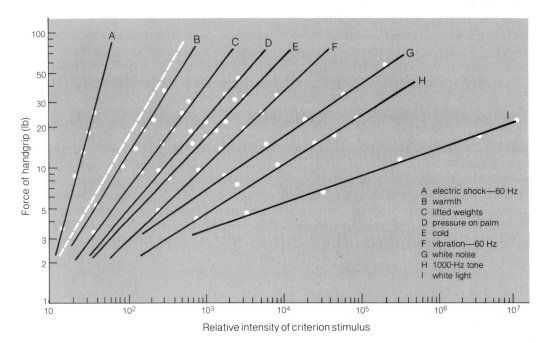

Figure 2-18 Cross-modality matching data for nine different psychological stimulus continua with force of handgrip as the response continuum. Because the values on both axes are logarithmically spaced, all the straight lines indicate power function relationships **between stimulus and response magnitude. The dotted line has an exponent of 1.0. (From S. S. Stevens, in W. A. Rosenblith, Ed., Sensory Communication. New York: Wiley, 1961, copyright 1961 by the MIT Press.)**

matching experiments on log-log axes (as we did for magnitude estimation experiments), we find that the average matches fall onto a straight line. Despite the fact that we no longer use numerical estimates from the observers, the data still obey the power law for sensory intensities. Figure 2-18 shows this for a number of modalities matched against handgrip pressure.

Cross-modality matching is often more difficult to use than direct magnitude estimation because the subject must adjust one of the sensory continua in order to give a response, rather than simply report a number or category label. Furthermore, in spite of Stevens's hopes, cross-modality matches are still affected

by a variety of biases (see for example, Baird, Green, and Luce, 1980; Ward, 1975, 1979). Because the psychophysicist wants to obtain as accurate an estimate of the exponent as possible, in order to describe precisely the relationship between the physical stimulus and its perceived magnitude, new refinements of the classical category and magnitude scaling procedures are always being introduced (Meyer, 1981). For instance, a recent modification of the cross-modality matching technique makes the task somewhat easier for the observer and seems to give somewhat more reliable results. This procedure is called **magnitude matching** (J. C. Stevens and Marks, 1980; Ward, 1982a). The observers do not actually match the sensory magnitudes in this task; rather they judge two different sets of sensory stimuli (for instance, lights and sounds), both of which are intermixed in the same experiment. The observer tries to use the same scale as the stimuli alternate between the modalities. The experimenter later uses mathematical techniques to determine the relationship between the two sets of judgments, and also to estimate the exponents of the power functions for the two sensory modalities. The theoretical importance of any such **mixed-modality psychophysical scaling** techniques rests in the exponents derived from them for the power law. These exponents indicate how the perceived intensities of stimuli change as the physical intensities change. Remarkably, the exponents usually agree, regardless of the technique used to estimate them. In addition, they generally agree with the values obtained from traditional magnitude estimation techniques (Stevens, 1975; Teghtsoonian, 1975). Although more precise scales may emerge, it seems likely that the power law is a reasonable description of how perceived intensity is related to stimulus intensity.

Adaptation level theory

Part of the circus strong man's job was to carry various members of the animal cast onto the circus train. One visitor watched in amazement as one after another the strong man lifted the dancing ponies and placed them in their railroad car. "Aren't they heavy?" asked the visitor. "Not if you've just carried three elephants," came the reply. The essence of this apocryphal tale is that no stimulus can be appreciated in isolation. Stimuli are seen in the context of the stimuli that precede them. Sportscasters of average height look like midgets when interviewing groups of professional basketball players

but like giants when interviewing professional jockeys. They have, of course, not changed height, but their apparent size has changed as a result of the frame of reference provided by the heights of those around them. Contextual effects have long been known to influence judgments of sensory magnitude in many psychophysical tasks, even when the context is in a modality other than the one being judged. You can experience this kind of context effect by using Demonstration Box 2-6.

Helson (1964) systematically attempted to explain how the magnitude of one stimulus can affect our judgments of the magnitude of other stimuli. His theory has both quantitative and qualitative aspects. In Helson's theory, the organism is thought to accommodate itself to the changing environment around it. This accommodation involves establishing a *reference level* against which all other stimuli are judged. Stimuli below this reference, or **adaptation level**, are judged in one way (to be weak) and stimuli above it in another way (to be intense). Stimuli at or near the adaptation level are judged to be medium or neutral. This implies that all judgments are relative. A stimulus is not simply weak or intense, it is weak or intense when judged against the subjective adaptation level.

For Helson, adaptation levels are established by pooling the effects of three classes of stimuli. The first class is called **focal stimuli**. These stimuli are the center of an observer's attention and are usually the stimuli she is asked to judge. Clearly, the magnitude of these stimuli will in some way determine the observer's judgments. This is the basic assumption of all scaling procedures. The second class of stimuli is called **background stimuli**. These are stimuli in which the focal stimulus is embedded. They provide the immediate background against which a focal stimulus is judged. The final set of stimuli is the *residual stimuli*. These are

---

Demonstration Box 2-6. The effect of visual context on judged weight

You will need two envelopes for this demonstration. One should be rather small (about 7 by 13 cm or so) and one should be large (approximately 20 by 28 cm). Put 15 nickels in each envelope. With the same hand, lift the large envelope and next lift the small. Which appears to be heavier? You will probably feel that the small envelope was considerably heavier although the weights were physically equal. This is an example of how a visual context (the envelope size) can alter our perception of heaviness. The same weight in the context of a smaller container seems heavier than when judged in the context of a larger container.

---

stimuli that are not current for the observer. They are the residue of stimuli the observer has experienced in the past. If you like, they are the sum of the observer's past experiences. To be more concrete, consider the example in which we judged the height of sportscasters surrounded by basketball players or jockeys. The physical height of a sportscaster is the focal stimulus. The contextual stimuli are provided by the heights of the surrounding athletes. The residual stimuli come from having seen athletes of different heights in the past. All these stimuli pool together to form the adaptation level.

Helson (1964) defines the adaptation level quantitatively as a weighted product of all three classes of stimuli: the focal, which we shall designate F, the background, B, and the residual, R. Thus, the formula for adaptation level becomes

$$\text{Adaptation level} = F^{w1}\ B^{w2}\ R^{w3}$$

where $W1$, $W2$, $W3$ are simply weighting coefficients that reflect the importance of any one class of stimuli in the determination of the overall adaptation level. Helson (1959) generally rewrites this formula as

$$\text{Log } AL = W1 \log F + W2 \log B + W3 \log R$$

which shows clearly that we are dealing with a type of weighted average. This formulation is not totally arbitrary. It is based on category judgment data similar to those used to test Fechner's law, and it provides a surprisingly good approximation to a large class of judgmental data. While there have been some interesting recent extensions of adaptation level theory (Restle, 1971, 1978), there are also a number of other quantitative formulations that make some slightly different assumptions about how stimulus magnitudes affect each other. These formulations result in some different mathematical expressions (Anderson, 1970b, 1975). All these alternatives, however, still acknowledge that surrounding stimuli, stimuli experienced in the past, and patterns of attention, as well as the actual stimulus judged, can affect our judgments of stimulus intensity.

Such shifts in our judgment of stimulus magnitude may be observed in many different tasks. For instance, consider a simple experiment by Engen and Tulunary (1956) in which subjects were required to find a weight that appeared to be exactly half the weight of a standard. They found that the mean weight judged to be one-half as heavy as the standard was consistently lighter for an ascending series of comparison weights (starting with the light weights and moving gradually to heavier) than

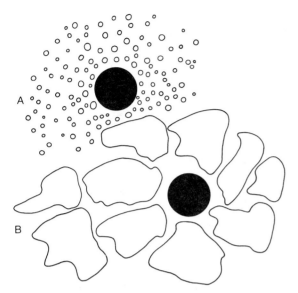

Figure 2-19 The circle surrounded by smaller elements appears larger than the circle surrounded by larger elements, although both are the same size (Based on Coren and Girgus, 1978).

for a descending series. Thus, the weight judged half as heavy as a 300 g weight was 179 g for a decending series (with the heavier weights of the series forming the context) but only 140 g for an ascending series (with judgments made in the context of lighter weights).

Similar shifts owing to context effects can also produce certain visual illusions (Coren and Girgus, 1978). For instance, consider Figure 2-19. The two black circles are physically the same size, although they appear to be different. It is easy to predict this illusory effect if you recognize that the adaptation level, when you are looking at circle *A*, is shifted toward the smaller size of the surrounding elements, while the adaptation level in the region of *B* is much larger. Because of this, circle *A* is above its adaptation level, hence appears larger, while

circle *B* is below its adaptation level and hence appears smaller.

There may be no simple relationship between stimulus magnitude and perceived magnitude. What we perceive is not simply a photographic reproduction of the stimuli in the environment, but it is affected by all the myriad forces that have impinged upon us in the past and that now provide the context for the perceptual situation in which we find ourselves. We will find that these conditions hold for all the sensory modalities that we shall study in the following chapters. Perception is an active process, and processes within the observer can sometimes be more important in determining the sensory experience than factors in the external environment.

The psychophysical measurement techniques introduced in this chapter will appear in many disguises throughout the rest of the book. We usually will not stop and identify these techniques or the rationale for using them. The methods by which perceptual data are collected, however, are important because the measurement technique will frequently interact with the phenomena to be measured. We find, for example, that when we look at raw recognition scores in one experiment, red and green are equally discriminable from orange because the differences are correctly recognized 100 percent of the time. On the other hand, when we measure reaction times, it takes longer to discriminate red from orange than green from orange, indicating a difference in discriminability. Is this a contradiction of fact? Not necessarily. Every method of measurement is tuned to a different task and often measures a different psychological function. In everyday language you can say that the answer you get depends on the question you ask.

GLOSSARY

The following definitions are specific to this book.

A' A measure of sensitivity, similar to *d'* in signal detection theory.

Absolute threshold The value of the minimal amount of energy required to detect a stimulus.

Adaptation level A subjective reference point against which stimuli are judged both quantitatively and qualitatively.

B″ A measure of bias or criterion, similar to β in signal detection theory.

Background stimuli Adaptation level theory term for stimuli that form a context for a focal stimulus but are not judged by an observer.

Beta β In signal detection theory, the criterion for sensation level that separates a "yes" response from a "no" response.

Bit The amount of information in a stimulus measured by the number of questions needed to halve the number of stimulus alternatives.

Category scaling A psychophysical scaling method where stimuli are grouped in a predetermined number of categories on the basis of their perceived intensity (equal interval scaling).

Catch trials Trials where no stimulus is presented. Used in threshold measuring experiments.

Channel capacity The limit to the number of bits of information that an observer can transmit on a single sensory dimension.

Choice reaction time Reaction time to make different responses to different stimuli.

Comparison stimuli A graded set of stimuli differing along a specific dimension, which are to be judged relative to a standard stimulus.

Correct negative Signal detection theory term for a trial when a stimulus signal is absent and the observer's response is "no."

Criterion In signal detection theory, a subjective value of sensation above which a stimulus is judged to be present (see Beta).

Cross-modality matching A scaling procedure where the observer adjusts the intensity of a stimulus until it appears to be as intense as another stimulus from a different sensory continuum.

d' In signal detection theory, the distance between the means of the signal absent and the signal present distributions.

Detection The perception that a stimulus is present.

Difference threshold The minimum amount of stimulus change needed for two stimuli to be perceived as different 50 percent of the time.

Direct scaling A procedure where individuals are asked to assess directly some aspect of the strength of a sensation.

Discrimination The act of discerning stimulus differences.

Equal interval scaling *See* Category scaling.

Error of anticipation A change in response before the perception actually changes.

Error of perseveration Continuing with the same response although the perception has changed.

False alarm In signal detection theory a trial in which a stimulus signal is absent but the observer responds "yes."

Fechner's law The logarithmic relationship proposed by Fechner between the intensity of sensation and the intensity of physical stimulus, $S = K \log I$.

Focal stimuli An adaptation level theory term for stimuli at the center of observers' attention, usually those being judged.

Hick's law A law stating that choice reaction time is a linear function of the amount of information in the stimuli to be differentiated.

Hit In signal detection theory a trial when a stimulus signal is present and the observer response is "yes."

Indirect scaling A method, based on discrimination ability, by which individuals' experiences of the strength of sensations are measured indirectly.

Information theory A quantitative system for specifying the difficulty of a recognition task.

Information transmission The degree to which the observer's response correctly represents the information in the stimulus.

Interval of uncertainty In a discrimination experiment, the difference between the stimulus intensity judged greater than the standard 25 percent of the time and the stimulus intensity judged greater 75 percent of the time.

Interval scale A scale where differences between scale values are meaningful but that has no absolute zero point.

Just noticeable difference (*jnd*) The stimulus difference noticed 50 percent of the time, computed as the interval of uncertainty divided by 2.

Magnitude estimation A psychophysical scaling procedure requiring the observer to assign numbers to a stimulus on the basis of apparent intensity.

Magnitude matching A technique where observers make magnitude estimates of stimuli from two different sensory continua intermixed in the same experiment.

Metathetic continuum A stimulus continuum involving quality of sensation, such as color or pitch.

Method of constant stimuli A method for determining thresholds in which each of a number of stimuli above and below the proposed sensory threshold are presented and judged repeatedly.

Method of limits A method for determining thresholds in which stimulus intensity is systematically increased or decreased until a change in response occurs.

Miss In signal detection theory the trial when a stimulus signal is present and the observer response is "no."

Mixed-modality scaling A psychophysical scaling procedure in which stimulus intensities are matched across sensory modalities; it includes magnitude matching and cross-modality matching.

Modulus In magnitude estimation, the standard numerical value assigned to one of the stimuli at the beginning of the judgment procedure; it determines the range of numbers to be used by the observer in the procedure.

Negative time error In discrimination experiments, when the point of subjective equality is lower than the value of the standard stimulus.

Nominal scale A scale in which scale values can only be used as names of events and thus reflect only whether they are identical or not.

Ordinal scale A scale involving the ranking of items on the basis of more or less of some quantity.

Payoff matrix In signal detection theory a set of rewards and penalties given an observer based on his or her performance in a psychophysical experiment.

Point of subjective equality The comparison stimulus intensity that appears most like the standard in a discrimination experiment.

Power law The relation that the magnitude of sensation varies as the intensity of the physical stimulus raised to some power. Also known as Stevens' law, $S = aI^n$.

Probability distribution A graphic representation of the likelihood that a given event will occur.

Prothetic continuum A psychological continuum that involves quantitative aspects (how much) of stimulation, such as loudness or brightness.

Ratio scale A measurement scale in which the rank order, spacing, and ratios of the numbers assigned to events have meaning; it also has an absolute zero point.

Reaction time The interval between the onset of a stimulus and the beginning of an overt response.

Receiver operating characteristic (ROC) curve In signal detection theory the plot representing how the probabilities of hits (ordinate) versus false alarms (abscissa) change as the criterion changes.

Recognition The act of identification of a stimulus.

Residual stimuli Stimuli that are no longer present but that affect the current adaptation level.

ROC curve *See* Receiver operating characteristic curve.

Scaling The measurement of how much of something is present.

Signal detection theory A mathematical, theoretical system that formally deals with both decisional and sensory components in detection and discrimination tasks.

Simple reaction time   Reaction time for simply detecting the onset of a stimulus.

Staircase method   A method for measuring absolute thresholds where the experimenter alters the direction of changes in stimulus strength each time the observer changes his or her response.

Standard   A stimulus against which the comparison stimuli are judged in a discrimination experiment.

Stevens' law   *See* Power law.

Weber fraction   The proportion by which the standard stimulus must be increased in order to detect change, $K = \Delta I/I$.

Weber's law   The relation that the size of the just noticeable difference (*jnd*) increases in a linear fashion with the size of the standard, $\Delta I = KI$.

The visual system

ALTHOUGH PERCEPTION OCCURS within the brain, the brain's only contact with the external environment is through our sense organs. Thus, we are reminded of the old saying, "The eyes are the windows to the world." The physical properties of this "window" should affect the nature of our perception in the same manner as the physical properties of a glass window affect the view. If the window is colored, the world we perceive will be tinted. If the window is dark or dirty, our ability to discern objects will be reduced. If the window is curved, and magnifies the images, our perception of the sizes of objects viewed through the glass may also be distorted. Thus, it is important for us to know the nature of the "window" through which we look at the world, or more simply, to understand the physiological makeup of the eye.

LIGHT

Each of the sensory systems is maximally responsive to a different form of physical stimulation. Thus, taste and smell respond to chemical stimuli, touch to mechanical pressure, and hearing to the vibration of air molecules. The physical stimulus for sight is electromagnetic radiation. The particular form of electromagnetic radiation that produces a visual response is called "light."

In 1704, Sir Isaac Newton advanced the theory that light, or for that matter any form of electromagnetic radiation, acts as if it were a stream of particles traveling in a straight line. Each particle is called a **quantum**. Particles of radiation that we register as light are called **photons**. The intensity of light is then given by the number of photons. Although this conception of light is extremely useful in physics, it is only important to the understanding of vision when we deal with stimuli that are relatively dim. At low levels of light, we often describe intensities as the number of photons reaching the visual receptors. Clearly, the smallest amount of light possible is a single photon.

While light often acts as if it were a stream of particles, at other times it acts as if it were made up of waves. James Clerk Maxwell (1873) showed that light does not travel in a straight line but rather as an oscillating wave. He suggested that if we consider the change in the electromagnetic field surrounding the train of photons, we can treat light as if it were purely a wave phenomenon, with the wavelength defined as the physical distance between the peaks of the photon waves.

The wavelengths of electromagnetic energy vary over a broad range, from trillionths of a centimeter to many kilometers in length. Very short wavelengths are not registered as light, nor are very long wavelengths. As Figure 3-1 shows, very short wavelengths include gamma rays, X rays, and ultraviolet rays. Longer wavelengths vary from those that we call electricity to the broadcasting wavelengths associated with television and radio (which may be more than 100 meters in length). The section of the electromagnetic spectrum that we see as visible light is really quite small, extending from 380 to about 760 nanometers. A **nanometer** (usually abbreviated nm) is a billionth of a meter. The older method of specifying wavelength was in **millimicrons** (abbreviated mμ). Perceptually, variations in wavelengths correspond roughly to the hue or color of light. In normal eyes, wavelengths of about 400 nm are seen as violet, 500 nm are seen as blue-green, 600 nm are seen as yellow-orange, and 700 nm are seen as red. Unfortunately, the perception of color depends on much more than simply wavelength, as you will discover in Chapter 7.

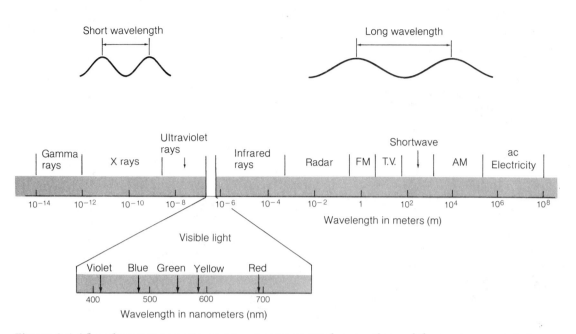

Figure 3-1. The electromagnetic energy spectrum. We have enlarged the region containing visible light.

THE STRUCTURE OF THE EYE

If we consider the vertebrate eye, we find that a single basic plan is common from the level of the fish all the way up through the higher mammals. A schematic diagram of the human eye is shown in Figure 3-2.

In most vertebrates, the eyes lie in protective bony sockets within the skull. They are spherical structures about 20-25 mm in diameter. The outer covering, which is seen as the "white" of the eye, is a strong elastic membrane called the **sclera**. The eye is not made of rigid materials, and it maintains its shape by internal fluid pressure.

The typical eye has something analogous to a lens at its opening. The function of the lens is to gather light hitting it and to concentrate it into a single point of focus. The front of the eye contains a region where the sclera bulges forward to form a clear, domelike window, about 13 mm in diameter, called the **cornea** (Martin and Holden, 1982). The cornea, the first optically active element in the eye, serves as a simple fixed lens that begins to gather light and concentrate it. Because the cornea is extended forward, it actually allows reception of light from a region slightly behind the observer, as is shown in Demonstration Box 3-1.

Behind the cornea is a small chamber filled with a watery fluid called the **aqueous humor.** This fluid is similar in nature to the cerebrospinal fluid, which bathes the inner cavities of the brain. This is not surprising since embryological evidence has shown that the

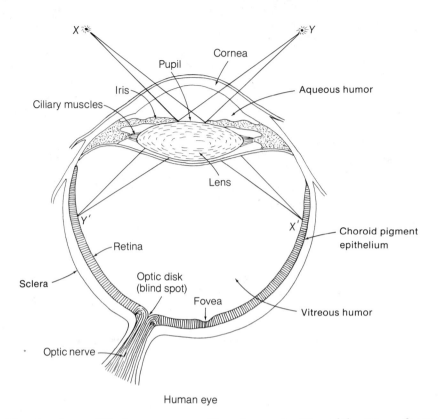

Figure 3-2. The structure of the human eye, with a demonstration of the image formation of two targets (X and Y).

neural components of the eye actually develop from the same structures that eventually form the brain.

When you look at a human eye, your attention is usually captured by a ring of color. This colored membrane, surrounding a central hole, is called the **iris**. When you say that a person has brown eyes, you really are saying that he has brown irises. The actual color, which may vary from blue through black, appears to be genetically determined. The iris controls the amount of light entering the eye. Although blue eyes may have been viewed as more appealing by poets, dark brown and black irises shield the eye from light more effectively. Light enters through the hole in the iris, called the **pupil**. The size of the pupil is controlled by a light reflex. When the light is bright, the pupil may contract to as little as 2 mm in diameter, while in dim light it may dilate to more than 8 mm. This is about a sixteenfold change in the area of the aperture. Demonstration Box 3-2 shows how you may observe the effect of light on pupil size.

The constriction of the pupil serves an important function. Despite the fact that the eye needs light to function, there are some advantages to viewing the world with a small pupil. Although the amount of light entering the eye is reduced, imperfections in the lens produce

Demonstration Box 3-1. Vision "behind" the eye

It is easy to demonstrate that the visual field actually extends to a region somewhat behind the eye. In order to do this, simply choose a point that is some distance in front of your head and stare at it. Now raise your hand to the side of your head as shown in the figure, with your index finger extended upward. Your hand should be out of view when you stare at the distant point. Now, wiggle your finger slightly, and bring your hand slowly forward until the wiggling finger is just barely visible in your peripheral vision. At this point stop and, with your head as still as possible, move your finger directly in toward your head. You will notice that your hand will touch a point on your temple somewhat behind the location of the eye, indicating that you were actually seeing somewhat "behind yourself."

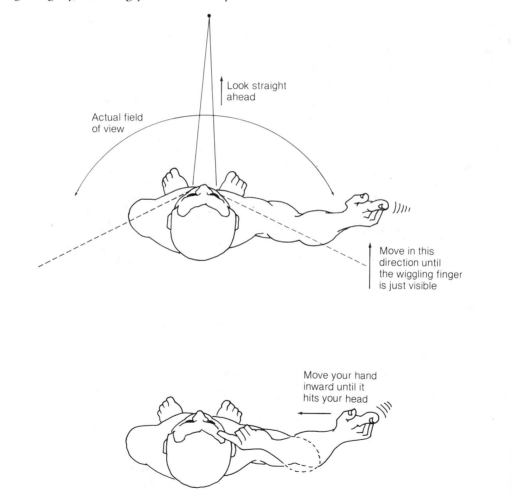

fewer distortions with a small pupil, and the depth of focus (which is the range of distances over which objects are simultaneously in focus) is vastly increased. We might say that the eye takes advantage of better light by improving its optical response. In dim light, the ability of the eye to resolve or discriminate details (called **acuity**) is less important than the increased sensitivity obtained by increasing the amount of light entering the eye; thus the pupil increases in size to let in more light. Pupil size also changes as a function of emotional and attentional variables. Under conditions of high interest, the pupil tends to be large, a cue often used by smart traders as an index of a customer's interest in an item. Clever customers often negate the usefulness of this cue in bargaining situations by wearing dark glasses. Similarly, the dimness of candlelight dilates the pupils and makes lovers appear to be more attentive and interested.

The lens: focusing the eye

Most vertebrate eyes contain a **lens**. The lens is located directly behind the pupillary aperture. Because the curvature of the lens determines the degree to which light is bent (refracted), it is critical in bringing an image into focus at the rear of the eye. The process by which the lens varies its focus is called **accommodation**. The lens changes focus by changing its shape (Dalziel and Egan, 1982). The natural shape of the human lens tends to be spherical, but when the ciliary muscles that control it relax, the pressure of the fluid in the eyeball and the tension of the zonal fibers connecting the lens to the inside wall of the eye cause it to flatten. Under these conditions, distant objects should be in focus. Contraction of the ciliary muscles, which hold the lens in suspension, removes tension from the lens and it regresses to a more spherical shape. When it is rounder, near objects are in focus. The effect of lens shape on point of focus is shown in Figure 3-3.

An individual's age is important in determining the focusing ability of the lens. The ability to accommodate is not present at birth. A newborn infant, until about the age of one month, can only focus on objects that are approximately 19 cm away (Dobson and Teller, 1978). Images of targets closer or farther away than 19 cm are proportionally blurred. During the second month of life, however, the accommodative system begins to respond more adaptively (see Chapter 16).

The ability of the lens to change focus decreases with increasing age after about 16 years. The inner layers of the lens die and lose some of their elasticity (Weale, 1963); thus, it becomes more difficult for the ciliary muscles to change the curvature of the lenses to accommodate to a near object. This results in a form of **refractive error** (light refracting or focusing error) called **presbyopia**, which simply translates to "old sighted." Functionally, this condition increases the **near point** distance. The term, near point, refers to how close an object may be brought to the eye before it can no longer be held in focus and becomes blurry. Older persons without corrective lenses in reading glasses often hold reading material abnormally far from their eyes in order to focus adequately.

Another feature of the lens that warrants mention is the fact that it is not perfectly transparent. The lens is tinted somewhat yellow, and the density of this yellow tint increases with age (Coren and Girgus, 1972*a*). The yellow pigment screens out some of the blue light and ultraviolet light entering the eye. It also alters our perception of color somewhat because it selectively absorbs some wavelengths of light and not others. Thus, a mother and daughter may argue vehemently about

whether the color of a particular garment is blue or green, totally oblivious to the fact that each views the world through a different yellow filter because of their age difference.

An eye having normal accommodative ability is called **emmetropic**. Sometimes there is too much or too little curvature in the cornea or, alternatively, the length of the eye is too short or too long, so that the accommodative capacity of the lens is not sufficient to bring targets into focus. If the eye is too short, or if the light rays are not bent sharply enough by the cornea, distant objects are seen quite clearly, but it is difficult to bring near objects into focus. The common term for this is farsightedness, while the technical term is **hypermetropia**. If the eye is too long, or if the light rays are bent too sharply by the cornea, near objects are sharply in focus, but distant objects are blurry. This condition is called nearsightedness, or **myopia**. The optical situations that result from these difficulties are shown in Figure 3-4.

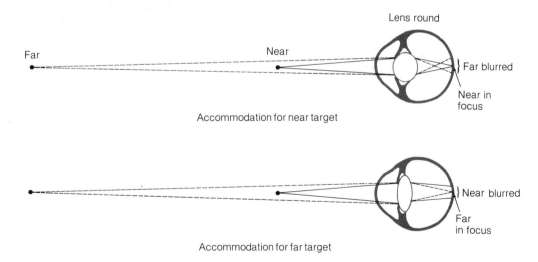

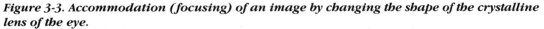

Figure 3-3. Accommodation (focusing) of an image by changing the shape of the crystalline lens of the eye.

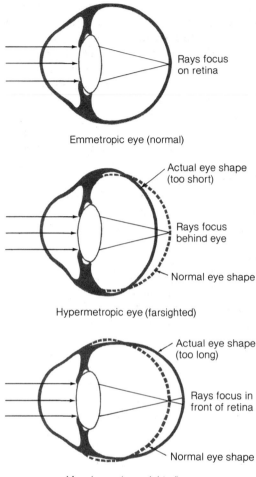

Emmetropic eye (normal)

Hypermetropic eye (farsighted)

Myopic eye (nearsighted)

Figure 3-4. Three common refractive states of the eye.

The retina

The large chamber of the eye is filled with a jellylike substance called the **vitreous humor**. This substance is generally clear, although shreds of debris often can be seen floating in it. Try staring steadily at a clear blue sky and you should note shadows moving across your

field of view; these shadows are from floating debris in the vitreous humor.

The image formed by the optical system of the eye is focused on a screen of neural elements at the back of the eye called the **retina**. The term retina derives from a Latin word meaning *net*, because when one surgically opens up an eye (or views its interior with an optical device such as an ophthalmoscope) the most salient feature is the network of blood vessels lining the inner cavity of the eye. Demonstration Box 3-3 shows you how you can observe these blood vessels in your own eyes.

The sheet of neural elements that makes up the retina extends over most of the interior of the eye. In diurnal, or daylight-active, animals, the retina is backed by a light-absorbing dark layer called the **pigment epithelium**. This dark pigment layer serves the same purpose as the black inner coating in a photographic camera. It reduces the amount of reflected and scattered light that could blur or fog the image. For nocturnal, or night-active, animals, the detection of light is more important than image clarity, so the light that penetrates the retina is reflected back through the retina by a shiny surface known as the **reflecting tapetum**. This reflecting surface permits the light to pass through the retina twice (once as it enters and once as it is reflected), effectively doubling its intensity. Although this results in a sizable increase in sensitivity, it is obtained at the expense of a considerable degrading of the image through fogging and blur, especially at higher illumination levels. The existence of this reflecting surface explains why cats and other animals have eyes that seem to glow in the dark when a flashlight is pointed toward them.

The retina of the eye is a predominantly neural layer of tissue, about the thickness of a sheet of paper. It is in the retina that the light is changed, or *transduced*, into a neural re-

Demonstration Box 3-3. Mapping the retinal blood vessels

For this demonstration you will need a pocket penlight, and a white paper or light-colored wall. Hold the penlight near the outside canthus (corner) of your eye. Now, shaking the bulb up and down you will see a netlike pattern on the light surface. This pattern is generated by the move- ments of the shadows of your retinal blood vessels across your retina. By steadily shaking the bulb with one hand and tracing the shadows with the other, you can produce a map of your own retinal blood vessels.

sponse. Structurally, the retina consists of three main neural layers diagrammed in Figure 3-5.

The outermost layer of the retina, closest to the scleral wall, contains the **photoreceptors**. Two types of photoreceptors are distinguishable on the basis of their shapes. The long, thin, cylindrical cells are called **rods**, and the shorter, thicker, somewhat more tapered cells are called **cones**. The outer segments of the photoreceptors contain pigments that actually absorb the light and begin the visual process.

The next layer consists of **bipolar cells**, which are neurons with two long extended processes. One end receives information from the photoreceptors, and the other end sends information to the third layer of retina, the large retinal **ganglion cells**. After the initial response to light, these three cell types carry the information toward the brain.

In addition to photoreceptors, bipolar cells, and ganglion cells, there are two types of cells that have lateral connections. Closest to the

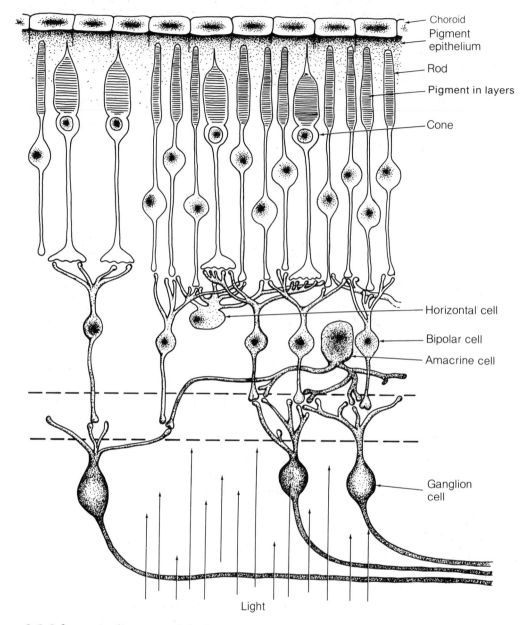

Figure 3-5. Schematic diagram of the human retina.

Demonstration Box 3-4. The macular spot

Under appropriate conditions it is possible to see the macular spot in your own eye. In order to do this you will need a dark blue or purple piece of cellophane. Brightly illuminate a piece of white paper with a desk lamp. Now, while looking at the paper with one eye, quickly bring the piece of cellophane between your eye and the paper. Now as you look at the paper you see what appears to be a faint circular shadow in the center of it. The sight of the shadow may only last for a couple of seconds. Sometimes its visibility can be improved by moving the cellophane in front of and away from your eye, so that you have a flickering colored field. Some individuals can see the spot when staring at a uniform blue field, such as a clear summer sky. This percept is caused by the fact that the yellow pigment in the macula absorbs the blue light and does not let it pass. This causes a circular shadow, which can be briefly seen. It is often called Maxwell's spot, after James Clerk Maxwell, who noticed its presence during some color-matching experiments.

---

receptor layer are the **horizontal cells**. These cells typically have short dendrites that are extensions of the cell body and a long horizontal process that extends some distance across the retina. The second set of cells that are lateral interconnecters are called **amacrine cells**. Amacrines are large cells found at the layer between the ganglion and bipolar cells, and they seem to interact with spatially adjacent units. The function of horizontal cells seems to be to allow interactions between adjacent photo-receptors or bipolar cells, while amacrine cells permit adjacent bipolar cells, or adjacent ganglion cells to communicate with each other (Frisby, 1980; Kolb, Nelson and Mariani, 1981; Naka, 1982).

The actual photoreception occurs within the rod and cone cells. Contrary to what one might expect, the orientation of rods and cones is inverted, with the pigment-bearing end pointing toward the rear of the eye rather than toward the lens. In other words, the retina is like a transparent carpet lying upside down on the floor of a room, with the pile of the carpet corresponding to the rods and cones. Incoming light must traverse through the carpet (the retina) before it reaches the photoreceptors.

While this arrangement might appear somewhat counterproductive, it actually makes good sense. The photoreceptors need a rich oxygen supply. To meet this need, many blood vessels lie in the epithelial layer at the rear of the eye. If the retina were "right-side up," so many blood vessels would be needed that the light input would be partially blocked. Therefore, the "upside-down" organization is more functional.

The fovea. Not all parts of the retina are of equal importance in the perceptual process. The most important section of the human retina is located in the region around the **optic axis**, an imaginary line that passes through the center of the pupil (see Figure 3-2). If one views a human retina through an ophthalmoscope one notes a patch of yellow pigment located in the region of the optic axis. This area is called the **macula lutea** (or just macula), simply translated to the "yellow spot." Demonstration Box 3-4 describes a procedure that allows you to see your own macula. In the center of the macula is a small depression that looks much like the imprint of a pinpoint about ⅓ mm in diameter. This small circular depression is called the **fovea centralis**, or

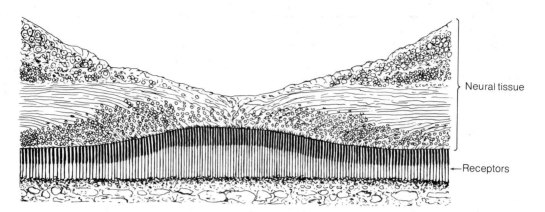

Neural tissue

Receptors

Figure 3-6. Sketch of a cross section through the fovea. Light comes from the direction of the top of the page.

translated, the "central pit." The fovea is critical in visual perception. Whenever you "look" directly at a target, your eyes are rotated so that the image of the target falls on the foveal region.

The fovea is unique in its structure and is schematically depicted in Figure 3-6. In the center of the foveal depression, the upper layers of cells are apparently pushed away so that the light passes through a much thinner cellular layer before reaching the photoreceptors. The photoreceptors themselves are quite densely packed in this region. This section of the retina contains only cones. There are no rods at all here. Foveal cones have a different shape than the cones of the periphery shown in Figure 3-5. They are much longer and thinner, so that they somewhat resemble rods. While cones normally range between 0.002 and 0.008 mm in diameter elsewhere on the retina, in the fovea they are as thin as 0.001 mm.

In a laborious study, Osterberg (1935) examined the retina of a human eye that had been removed as the result of an accident. By fixing the fresh retina in a suitable fluid, it may be preserved indefinitely. Thus, the topography, or distribution, of the rods and cones can be studied at leisure. Osterberg actually counted the number of rods and cones in this human retina and found that there were no rods in the center of the fovea, as we have already indicated. Outside the fovea the number of cones rapidly decreases. The number of rods, on the other hand, rapidly increases as one leaves the foveal region and reaches a peak concentration at about 20 degrees in the periphery; they then decrease in frequency again. This general distribution (which has been verified several times) is shown in Figure 3-7.

Rods and cones. The presence of two types of retinal photoreceptors suggests the existence of two types of visual function. In the early 1860s the famous retinal anatomist Max Schultze found that animals that are predominantly nocturnal, such as owls, have retinas that contain only rods. Animals that are only active during the day, such as the chipmunk and pigeon, have retinas that are all cones. Animals that are active in the twilight, or during both day and night, such as rats, monkeys, and humans, have retinas composed of both rods and cones. On the basis of these observations Schultze offered what has been called the **duplicity,** or **duplexity, theory** of vision. He maintained that there are two separate visual systems. The first, for vision in dim light, is dependent on the rods, and the other, for vision under daylight or bright conditions, is dependent on the cones. Vision under bright light is called **photopic** (meaning "light vision"), while vision under dim light is called **scotopic** ("dark vision").

Soon after Schultze's initial theoretical suggestions, more behavioral evidence was collected by other researchers to support the idea that the eye contains two different visual systems. Some fascinating data come from clinical studies of humans who were born with retinas lacking in rods or cones. In individuals whose retinas contain no rods, or only nonfunctioning rods, an interesting visual anomaly occurs. Although such individuals seem to have normal vision under daylight conditions, when the light dims beyond a certain point (to a twilight level of intensity), they lose all sense of sight and become functionally blind. These individuals are called **night-blind**. The implication is that in the absence of rods, scotopic vision is lost. A quite different pattern is found in individuals lacking in functioning cones. Normal levels of daylight are quite painful for these

persons. They totally lack the ability to discriminate colors and have quite poor visual acuity. Under dim levels of illumination, however, they function normally. The existence of such **day-blind** individuals indicates that a functioning cone system is necessary for normal photopic vision and also for the perception of color. The specifics of the perception of brightness and color will be discussed in Chapters 6 and 7.

Before a rod or a cone can signal the presence of light, it must first interact with the light in some way. Chemically, such interaction involves absorbing, or capturing, one or more photons. Any substance that absorbs light is called a pigment. A substance that absorbs a great deal of light would appear darkly pigmented, absorbing most of the incoming photons and leaving very few to bounce back to the eye of the viewer. As noted earlier, the outer segments of both the rods and the cones contain visual pigments. If you return to Figure 3-5, you will see the pigments arranged in layers in the outer segments of the photoreceptors.

Rods and cones do not contain the same pigment. The visual pigment in the rods of

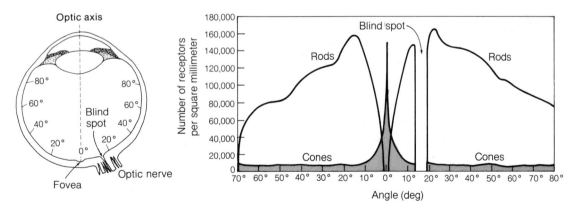

Figure 3-7. The distribution of rods and cones in the human retina. The left-hand figure gives the locations on the retina of the "angle" *relative to the optic axis on the right figure (modified from Lindsay and Norman, 1977).*

vertebrates was first successfully isolated in 1876, when Franz Boll extracted a brilliant red pigment from the frog retina (which contains predominantly rods). He noted that this pigment bleached, or lost its apparent coloration, when exposed to light. Such a reaction indicated that the substance was photosensitive. Boll further noted that the pigment regenerated itself in the dark. Thus, it fulfilled the elementary requirements of the visual pigment in that it responded by changing chemically in the presence of light, yet it still remained capable of resynthesizing itself. Kuhne took up the study of this pigment in 1877, and in one extraordinary year, laid the groundwork for our understanding of its action. This pigment has been named rhodopsin (which means "visual red" rather than "visual purple" as it is sometimes called). In the century since the work by Boll and Kuhne, we have been able to detail much of the photochemical reaction in rhodopsin.

Basically, rhodopsin is a compound made up of two parts, a **retinene** part and an **opsin** part. The retinene part is structurally similar to Vitamin A, which is in fact necessary for its synthesis. The retinene portion of the rhodopsin molecule is quite complex. As is the case for many organic compounds, the molecule can exist in several different shapes, called *isomers*. When a molecule of rhodopsin absorbs light it isomerizes, or changes shape, which is the only effect light has on rhodopsin. The resultant substance is unstable and rapidly goes through several chemical changes (all resulting in unstable intermediate substances) until the molecule splits into retinene and opsin. The energy for this chain reaction is provided by light. The isomerization triggers a neural response through some mechanism not yet fully understood. Some theories suggest that the process opens pores in the rod membrane, which allows certain ions to flow inward, while others maintain that the action blocks

the flow of another class of ions. In any event, the result is a change in the electrical state of the rod, resulting in a hyperpolarization, or positive voltage shift, across the rod membrane, which then triggers the horizontal and bipolar cell responses (Hubbell and Bownds, 1979).

Rhodopsin regenerates in the dark from the retinene and opsin with the help of vitamin A and other enzymes. Some evidence indicates that light actually provides the energy to resynthesize rhodopsin, although this process is too complex to discuss here. The chain of chemical events involved in the bleaching and resynthesis of rhodopsin is shown in Figure 3-8 (Blazynski and Ostroy, 1981; Rodieck,

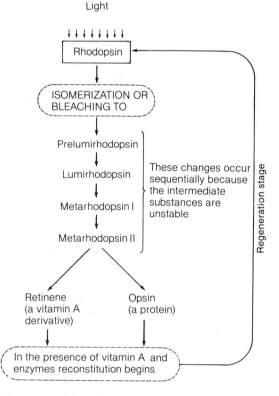

Figure 3-8. The rhodopsin cycle.

1973). Notice that Vitamin A is vital to the re-synthesis, and in the absence of Vitamin A, rhodopsin cannot be formed. In isolated communities where fish products or appropriate vegetables are not available, the absence of Vitamin A in the diet shows up in "epidemics" of night blindness, as the rods become nonfunctional (Wald, 1968).

The identification and analysis of cone pigments has proved to be more difficult and elusive than that of rhodopsin. We have learned, however, that a purple-colored pigment called **iodopsin** ("visual purple") is present in the cone cells of some birds. Iodopsin breaks down upon exposure to light into retinene and another form of opsin. Opsins are large, complex protein molecules. The opsin found in cones is often called **photopsin** to distinguish it from that in rods, which is called **scotopsin**. It is a slightly different protein from the opsin found in the rods. The retinene, however, appears to be the same in rods and cones. Research indicates that all photopigments, regardless of the animal species studied, are composed of the same retinene and a specific protein or opsin that is characteristic of each pigment (Dartnall, 1957; Metzler and Harris, 1978). In some manner, these photochemical reactions result in electrochemical neural responses that pass on to the bipolar cells. From the bipolar cells, the neural information is passed to the retinal ganglion cells, and from the retinal ganglion cells, the information passes out of the eye.

NEURAL RESPONSES TO LIGHT

In order to get information out of the eye and into the brain, the axons of the retinal ganglion cells extend in a transverse fashion across the retina and gather together to exit from the eye. This is done through a hole in the retina and the scleral wall. The resulting bundle of axons (the long fibers of nerve cells) forms the **optic nerve**. The center of the optic nerve contains the blood vessels that sustain the metabolic needs of the eye. Since the bundle of axons must push its way through the retina, there are no photoreceptors in this region. Because of this, there can be no visual response to light striking this portion of the retina, and it is appropriately called the **blind spot**. The circular pattern of neural axons as they form the nerve to exit the eye has led anatomists to refer to this as the **optic disk**. You may easily demonstrate the absence of vision in this region of the retina by referring to Demonstration Box 3-5.

The output of the retina is transmitted to the brain via the optic nerves. The nerve impulses transmitted via the ganglion cell axons that make up the optic nerve are not "raw" sense data but are the result of a large amount of neural processing that has already taken place in the retina itself. In order to understand how much processing has occurred, consider that there are some 120,000,000 rods and another 5,000,000 cones in each human eye. There are only about 1,000,000 axons in each optic nerve. Each receptor cell does not have its own private channel to the brain; rather the responses of a large number of photoreceptors are represented in one optic nerve fiber. This occurs when the combined activity of the 125,000,000 rods and cones, plus the output of several million more intervening bipolar, horizontal, and amacrine cells, converge on the much smaller number of ganglion cells. We shall soon see that the information is modified and distilled as it is collected.

Because the information carried to the brain by a single ganglion cell can represent the combined activity of a large number of rods and cones, a single ganglion cell may respond

---

Demonstration Box 3-5. The blind spot

The region of the retina where the optic nerve leaves the eye contains no photoreceptors and thus is blind. You may demonstrate this for yourself by using the figure here. Close your left eye and with your right eye look at the X in the figure. Keeping your eye on the X, move the page toward you. At some point the little open square will seem to disappear. At this point its image is falling on your blind spot. Notice that when you have the page at the correct distance, not only does the square seem to disappear, but also the line appears to run continuously through the area where the square should be. This indicates that we automatically "fill in" missing information. We fill it in with material that is similar to nearby visible material. This accounts for why you are not normally aware of the blind spot. You are simply supplying the missing information to fill in this "hole" in the visual field.

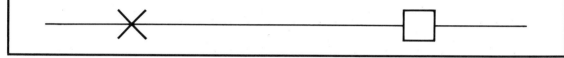

---

to light from a sizable region of the retina. Such a region, or area of the retina, in which light alters the firing rate of a cell, is called that cell's **receptive field**. A single ganglion cell serves as a clearinghouse for information coming from a substantial zone of receptor cells in the retina. In order to understand how visual information is processed, we must know how specific ganglion cells respond to various forms of light stimuli. It may be useful, however, to digress a bit to discuss the nature of neural responses in general.

The nature of neural activity

The human nervous system contains approximately 10–14 billion neurons. Each neuron is a separate unit composed of three parts. These three parts are a **cell body**, an **axon**, and **dendrites**. The axon and dendrites are extensions of the cell body. Although each neuron or cell is discrete, it communicates with other cells by means of its **axon terminals** (the ends of the axon). The place where the axons of one cell come into proximity with the cell body, dendrites, or axon of another cell is called a **synapse**. All these structures are diagrammed in Figure 3-9.

All neural activity is electrochemical. The inside of a cell is negatively charged relative to the outside. This electrical difference, or **potential** across the cell membrane, is about −70 millivolts (mV). Under these unstimulated conditions the cell is in the resting state. Because of the electrical potential difference, we say that the cell is **polarized**. When an externally applied stimulus causes a reaction in a cell, the potential of the cell either becomes less negative by moving toward 0 mV, or it increases its degree of negativity by moving away from 0 mV. The word **depolarization** describes the movement of the potential toward zero, while the movement toward increasing negativity is called **hyperpolarization**. When a stimulus evokes a response in a neuron, this response is electrochemical, and it involves either depolarization or hyperpolarization.

The neural responses in the parts of the ret-

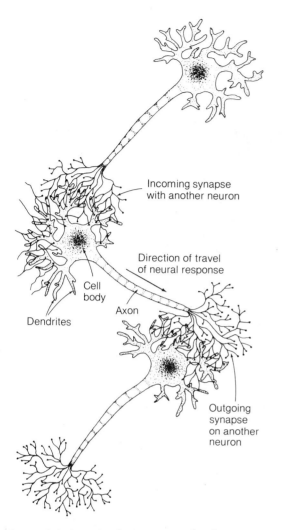

Figure 3-9. A typical neuron and a few connections to other neurons.

Incoming synapse
with another neuron

Direction of travel
of neural response

Cell
body

Axon

Dendrites

Outgoing
synapse
on another
neuron

is a small depolarization (a movement from −70 mV toward 0 mV), which is suddenly followed by a large and rapid shift from a negative to a positive potential. This shift, diagrammed in Figure 3-10, occurs within about 1 msec. This rapid depolarization is quickly reversed and followed by a period of hyperpolarization, after which the potential returns to the resting level of −70 mV. These changes in electrical potentials in the axon constitute the **action potential**, or **spike potential**, that can be recorded by various cellular recording devices. Increased stimulation does not change the size of the spike potential, but rather it increases the number of responses per unit time. You might imagine that each neural response is a gunshot and the excitement of the gunman is measured by the speed of weapon firing. Thus, the number or frequency of responses reflects the level of stimulation.

Neural responses are measured using microelectrodes (whose tip might be 0.01 mm in size or smaller). The electrical activity of the cell is detected by the electrode, amplified,

ina that respond first (namely, photoreceptors, bipolars, and horizontal cells) involve a continuous graded change in electrical potential; however, this is not the case for the amacrines and retinal ganglion cells and for virtually all successive neurons in the system. Instead there is a complex and rapid change in the electrical state of these cells. First, there

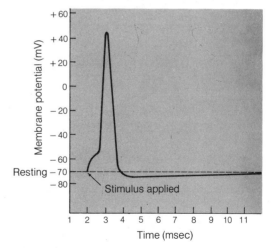

Figure 3-10. The electrical response of a neuron ("spike potential") to a stimulus.

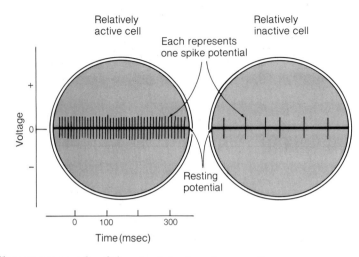

Figure 3-11. Oscilloscope records of the electrical response of a neuron.

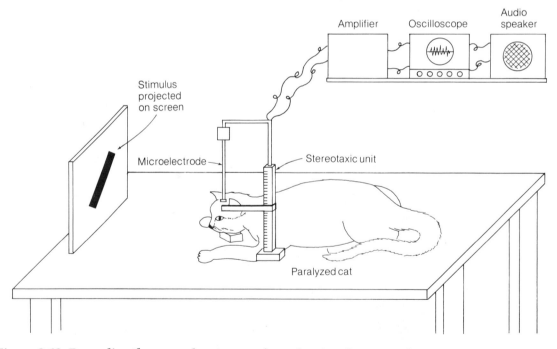

Figure 3-12. Recording the neural responses from the visual system of a cat.

and usually displayed on an **oscilloscope**, which is a sensitive voltmeter that displays voltage changes over a period of time. Figure 3-11 shows both an excited cell and a relatively unexcited neural cell.

The use of microelectrode techniques to record the activity of single neurons has produced some of the most exciting data in the field of sensory physiology. Generally, the procedure involves the application of a muscle relaxant combined with local anesthetics to reduce the discomfort of the restraining device used to hold the animal. Such restraining devices are called **stereotaxic instruments**, and they permit a researcher to place electrodes in the brain accurately. Figure 3-12 shows a cat in a stereotaxic instrument. The cat is viewing a screen upon which stimuli are presented, and the electrode in the brain is attached through a set of amplifiers to an oscilloscope and also to a speaker. The responses of a neuron are displayed, as shown in Figure 3-11, as a series of rapid, brief, electrical changes, which produce the characteristic neural "spike" on an oscilloscope screen. When a loudspeaker is included in the recording system, the neural response is transformed into a series of pops or clicks, where each click is caused by a single neural impulse. A researcher can then listen to the neural response, and the eyes are free to tend to other matters. An increase in the rate of clicking means an increase in the frequency of cell firing, and a decrease means a reduction. The ear can easily recognize whether there is an increase or a decrease in the rate of response.

Neural activity in the retina

Most contemporary studies of the response to light of retinal ganglion cells have followed the lead of Hartline (1940) and Kuffler (1953),

who inserted an electrode through the eye of an anesthetized cat and recorded from single ganglion cells in the retina. Generally researchers have found that when a single small spot of light is displayed on the screen, thereby stimulating the retina of the animal observing it, three different types of responses from a cell may be elicited, depending on the location of the spot in the field. The first type of response, the one typically expected when a neuron is excited, is a burst of neural impulses immediately following the onset of the stimulus. This response is called an **on response**. Alternatively, the cell can give a burst of impulses immediately following the termination of the stimulus. Such a response is termed an **off response**. Some responses appear to be hybrids because both the presentation of *and* the removal of the stimulus cause a burst of neural impulses. Such responses are designated **on-off responses**. Typical examples of these responses are shown in Figure 3-13.

When investigators use very small stimulus

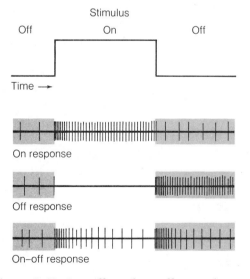

Figure 3-13. On, off, and on-off neural responses in the optic nerve.

lights (about 0.2 mm in diameter), the nature of the retinal ganglion cell response tends to vary from on, through on-off, to off, depending on the location of the stimulus. A map of the shape of the overall receptive field of the retinal ganglion cell (the region of retinal stimulation to which the cell responds) shows that the response types are distributed circularly, with two distinct zones in each receptive field. Typically, the receptive field has a relatively circular center that produces on responses when stimulated. That is, the ganglion cell gives an on response to the onset of a light stimulus in that region. The outer portion of the receptive field gives the opposite result. That is, the onset of a light does not produce a response, but its cessation does. Between these two regions, roughly at the boundary between the on and off regions, is the narrow region where on-off responses occur. A typical receptive field is shown in Figure 3-14, where

on response regions are marked by plus signs and off by minus signs (remember on-off responses occur at the border between these regions).

As Figure 3-14 indicates, some receptive fields have the opposite organization, with the central region producing off responses when stimulated and the surrounding region showing on responses. The retina contains approximately equal numbers of off-center cells and on-center cells. Recent evidence indicates that the ganglion cells that show the on- and off-center responses are visibly different. Apparently, the off-center cells make contact with their respective bipolar cells at a more peripheral level in the retina (closer to the photoreceptors) than do the on-center cells (Kaneko, Nishimura, Tachibana, Tauchi, and Shimai, 1981; Nelson, Kolb, Robinson, and Mariani, 1981).

Recently, attention has turned to an analysis of the conduction speed of neural information

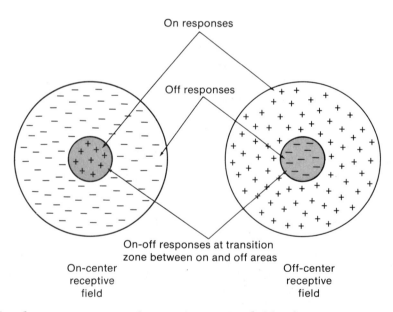

Figure 3-14. Circular center-surround retinal receptive fields of two types.

from the retina to the brain, as well as the form of the response. These observations have revealed three types of cells in the retina, each with different characteristics. They have been given the completely atheoretical names of W, X, and Y cells. We know most about the X and Y cells (Lennie, 1980; Rodieck, 1973). Overall, the Y cells have the fastest neural conduction speeds of about 40 meters per second, while the X cells respond with conduction speeds of one-half that of the Y cells. The most sluggish are the W cells, which are physically very tiny and conduct very slowly (10 meters per second). Also, they do not seem to have a center-surround organization in their receptive fields (Rodieck, 1973; Stone and Hoffman, 1972).

X and Y cells differ along a number of important dimensions. Both cells have the center-surround, on-off arrangement that we have described. X cells, however, are physically smaller than Y cells and have smaller center-surround receptive fields. Proportionally, there are many more X than Y cells, and they differ in terms of their distribution across the retina. Most X cells are found in and around the fovea. Virtually no Y cells are found in the foveal region, and the number of Y cells increases as we move outward into the peripheral retina. The characteristic neural response pattern of X and Y cells also differs. X cells, when stimulated, respond in a rather sustained manner, continuing their neural activity as long as the stimulus remains. Y cells, however, have a much more transient response. They tend to give a burst of activity when the stimulus comes on or goes off.

Another difference between X and Y cells is illustrated in Figure 3-15. Part *A* shows a schematic drawing of the receptive field of a retinal ganglion cell, where half the field is evenly illuminated with light while the other half is dark. Suppose that we now switch the illumination to the pattern shown as part *B* or *C*. If

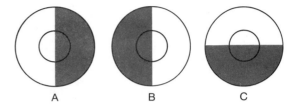

Figure 3-15. If the illumination pattern on a center-surround receptive field was half light and half dark as shown in A, and then was shifted to a new orientation (either B or C), an X cell would not respond to a change, while a Y cell would.

we were stimulating an X cell, it would continue to respond exactly as it had been responding. In other words, as long as the same amount of illumination is present in the center and surround, the X cell does not distinguish between the different locations of illumination. On the other hand, any switch in the pattern of illumination will provoke a vigorous response in a Y cell, since changes in the distribution of illumination across a region of the field are usually caused by movement. This suggests that Y cells may be specialized for movement detection, while X cells are specialized for the analysis of stationary patterns (Kruger, 1981; Sherman, 1979).

THE VISUAL PATHWAYS

The axons of the retinal ganglion cells gather together and push their way out of the eye at the blind spot. This bundle of axons, which forms the optic nerve, is the beginning of the pipeline of information that eventually ends in the brain. Two distinct anatomical routes lead to the common end point, however, and each carries somewhat different information.

The primary visual pathway is the

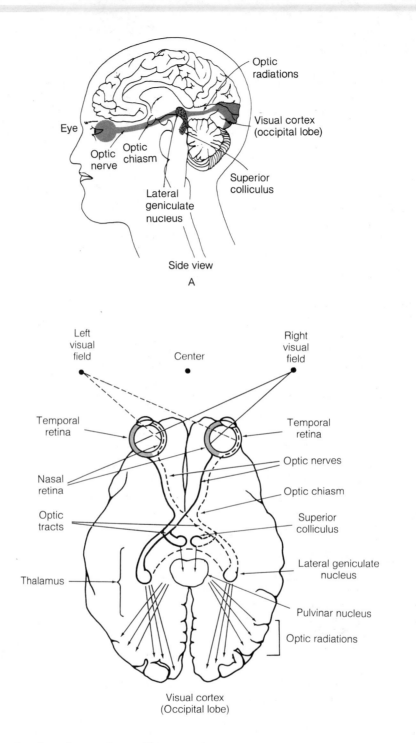

Figure 3-16. The visual pathways from the eye to the visual cortex.

geniculostriate system, and the secondary pathway is the **tectopulvinar system**. Both begin in the same fashion, with the information traveling out of the eyes along the optic nerves. As shown in Figure 3-16, the first significant event occurs when the two optic nerves come together at a point that looks like an X. This point is called the **optic chiasm** (from the Greek letter χ or "chi"). In lower animals, the optic nerve from the right eye crosses completely to the left side of the head and vice versa. In many mammalian species, particularly those that seem to use combined input from the two eyes to obtain better depth perception (this will be discussed more fully in Chapter 10), some of the fibers do not cross. In primates, such as humans, approximately one-half the optic nerve fibers cross to the opposite side of the head. These fibers represent the two inside, or nasal, *retinas*. Those from the outside, or *temporal*, halves of each retina do not cross but continue on the same side. Such an arrangement implies that each half of the visual field will be projected to the opposite side of the brain. One must also remember what is happening optically to keep the situation straight. Because the crystalline lens in the eye imposes an up-down, right-left reversal of the retinal image, the right visual field projects onto the nasal half of the retina of the right eye and the temporal half of the retina of the left eye. The axons from both these half-retinas (or hemiretinas) terminate in the left side of the brain. Thus, information from the right side of your field of view ends in the left side of your brain, and vice versa as shown in Figure 3-16*B*.

As we begin to trace the visual pathways, we will need a few maps to help us. A general map is given in Figure 3-16. We shall provide you with a few additional ones as we progress.

The geniculostriate system

Beyond the optic chiasm, the pathway is no longer called the optic nerve but rather the **optic tract**. For most primates, the major termination for the optic tracts is reached after the fibers pass around the hypothalamus and synapse in the **lateral geniculate nucleus** of the thalamus. The lateral geniculate is arranged in six layers, each of which seems to receive input from only one eye, with little binocular interaction.

Electrophysiological studies of the lateral geniculate have shown that these neurons are spontaneously active, which means that they are always producing some number of neural impulses, even in the dark. Although surprising, spontaneity is a characteristic of brain cells. We do not fully understand why this activity maintains itself. Perhaps because the neurons are alive and announce this by occasional random responses. This continuing train of responses augments the information coding capacity of the cells as we shall see.

As is the case with the retinal ganglion cells, lateral geniculate cells do not respond to visual stimuli unless the stimulation occurs within their receptive fields. Thus, a particular lateral geniculate neuron provides information about the location of an object in space because it responds only to those objects projected onto the patch of retinal receptors that defines its receptive field. These receptors, in turn, respond only to objects in a particular region of the visual field. Generally, the receptive fields of the lateral geniculate cells are similar to those of the retina. If we map a lateral geniculate cell by projecting points of light onto a screen in the visual field in front of an animal, we find that the cell response appears somewhat similar to that of a retinal ganglion cell. For instance, most such cells have an on-center and an off-surround, or the reverse. In addition, lateral geniculate cells, which are fed by X and Y cells in the retina, show X-like and Y-like responses to moving and stationary stimuli (Lehmkuhle, Kratz, Mangel, and Sherman, 1980; Lennie, 1980; So and Shaply, 1981).

There is, however, one quirk that makes these lateral geniculate responses somewhat more interesting. Recent evidence suggests that some cells respond differentially not only to the location of a light but also to its color (Boynton, 1979; Hurvich, 1981). For instance, DeValois and DeValois (1975) report that there are cells in the lateral geniculate of monkeys that respond with an increase in their firing rate when the center of their receptive field is stimulated by a red spot of light, whereas they show a decrease in their activity levels from the spontaneous firing rate when the center is stimulated by a green light. This finding suggests the possibility of encoding both color and location information in the same cells.

When the axons of the lateral geniculate neurons leave the geniculate, they form a large fan of fibers called the **optic radiations**. These fibers eventually synapse with cells in the cortex in the rear (or *posterior*) portion of the brain.

This portion of the brain is known as the **occipital lobe**. Several labels have been used to refer to this region of the brain. The most popular system for locating parts of the cortex is the numbering system devised by Brodmann (1914) based on the appearance of cells. In Brodmann's numbering system, this primary area of visual function (that is, the place where the fibers from the lateral geniculate terminate) is designated **area 17**. Since, when sliced vertically the cortex has a banded appearance, this region is also called the **striate** (striped) **cortex**. Probably the most informative label used for the area is the **primary visual cortex**. Some of the geniculate fibers also project to an area adjacent to area 17, which is area 18. It is one of the regions known as the **extrastriate cortex** (*extra* has the meaning here of beyond), which is usually regarded as part of the **secondary visual cortex**. Figure 3-17 maps these areas, and others that we shall discuss shortly.

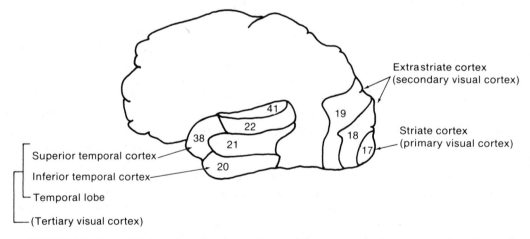

Figure 3-17. The principal visual response regions of the cortex and associated regions showing Brodmann's numbering of the areas.

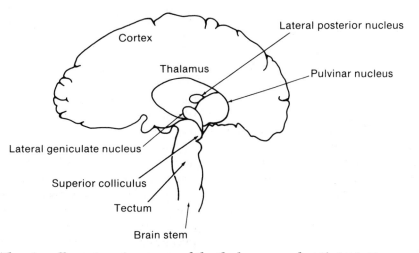

Figure 3-18. The visually responsive areas of the thalamus and optic tectum.

The tectopulvinar system

A second pathway to the visual cortex is also indicated in Figure 3-16. This pathway begins when a number of fibers from the optic tract branch off to go toward the brain stem. Most pictures of the brain do not show the brain stem or midbrain structures because they are hidden by the cortex. Figure 3-18 shows schematically where these structures are located, and we have marked off some of the areas that are of concern to us.

The region of the brain stem of interest is, in an evolutionary sense, a much older, more primitive visual center known as the **tectum**. Most of the visual processing of some lower animals occurs here. The part of the tectum that receives most of the incoming fibers is the upper pair of what appear to be four bumps on the back (or *dorsal*) surface of the brain stem; these bumps are known as the **superior colliculi**. Not all of the retinal ganglion cell types project to the superior colliculi, however. Only Y and W type inputs come here. X inputs seem only to be part of the geniculostriate

system, while Y and W cells seem to be part of both.

From the superior colliculi, the pathway continues on to the thalamus. Rather than projecting to the lateral geniculate nuclei, however, the pathways go to the **pulvinar** and the **lateral posterior nuclei**, which are located nearby, as you can see from Figure 3-18. From here, the fibers project to the cortex. None is destined for the primary visual cortex (area 17), but rather they are destined for the secondary visual areas (areas 18 and 19).

Do the two different visual pathways serve different perceptual functions? Basically, it seems that the geniculostriate system is involved in the detailed perception of patterns and, perhaps, colors (Van Essen, 1979), while the tectopulvinar system coordinates the localization of objects in space and the guidance of eye movements (Flandrin and Jeannerod, 1981; Guitton, Crommelink, and Roucoux, 1980; Wurtz, 1976). Perhaps the most dramatic demonstrations of these separate functions come from studies of lower vertebrates. In one classic study, G. E. Schneider (1969)

showed that removal of the lateral geniculate nuclei of the golden hamster left the animal with an inability to recognize patterns,
while removal of the superior colliculi left it
with the ability to recognize patterns, but with
an inability to localize them well enough to
approach them. This type of result seems consistent with the speculation that the two anatomically different visual pathways serve the
different functions of localization and recognition, although some overlap in function seems
likely.

THE VISUAL CORTEX

There are more than 100 million neurons in
the visual cortex. Only the smallest fraction of
them has been thoroughly studied in attempts
to discover their response characteristics.
What we do know of these cells is based
largely on research done with microelectrodes. Such studies have employed techniques similar to those used in the mapping of
the receptive fields for the retinal ganglion and
lateral geniculate cells. Much of the pioneer
work was done by David Hubel and Torstein
Wiesel, who received the Nobel prize in 1981
for their research effort.

In the early 1930s, Lashley (1931) established the importance of area 17 of the cortex
for the perception of patterns and forms. He
removed the visual cortex of rats, while Kluver
and Bucy (1937) did the same for monkeys.
With this section of the cortex missing, the animals were unable to discriminate patterns, although brightness perception was still intact,
probably maintained by the tectopulvinar system. Thus, decorticate animals could be trained
to discriminate light from dark, but could not
respond to the shape of the targets.

Within the striate cortex a rather direct to-
pological (point for point) mapping of the external visual world exists, with specific points
in the environment corresponding to specific
points in the cortex. Most information about
this mapping has been obtained clinically from
cases of accident or war injury, where penetrating missile wounds have injured specific
parts of the cortex. When a piece of the occipital cortex is damaged in this way, the patient is blind in part of the visual field. Such a
damaged area is called a *lesion*. The blind
patch in the visual field is called a **scotoma**
(meaning dark spot). By studying such lesions,
researchers can map the correspondence between sections of cortex and parts of the visual field. The cortical map does not correspond exactly with the external scene in all its
dimensions. For instance, the fovea is represented by an inordinately large quantity of cortex relative to its actual size on the retina. This
is in accord with its disproportionate importance relative to other retinal regions. When
we note that points on the cortex correspond
to points in the visual field, we do not mean to
imply that if one looks at a house there is a
house-shaped pattern of electrical excitation in
the cortex. Rather, much of the analysis of features of a particular visual input occurs within
individual cortical neurons located close together in the cortex.

Neural activity in the cortex

Following the methodological procedures of
Hubel and Wiesel (1962, 1979), many investigators have mapped receptive fields of cortical cells in animals. For instance, recording
electrodes have been placed (or *implanted*)
in cortical cells in area 17 to measure cells'
electrical responses to stimuli projected onto a
screen in front of the animal. (DeValois, Yund,
and Hepler, 1982; Heggelund, 1981*a*, *b*).

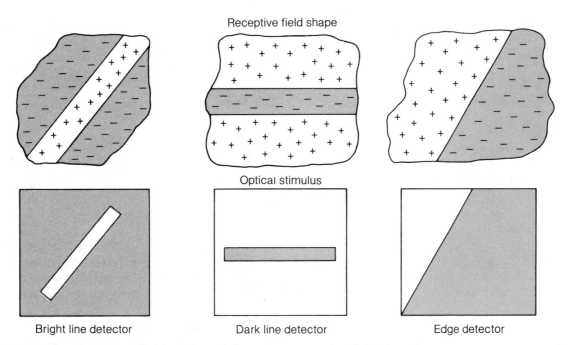

Receptive field shape

Optical stimulus

Bright line detector · Dark line detector · Edge detector

Figure 3-19. Receptive fields of "simple" corti-cal cells: a plus sign means a region in the receptive field that gives an on response, and a minus sign indicates an off response.

When cortical cells are mapped in this way, one still finds the familiar circular on and off regions found for ganglion and lateral genicu-late cells. The majority of the measured recep-tive fields, however, have elongated central regions. A map of some such cells is shown in Figure 3-19. This type of cell, which Hubel and Wiesel labeled a **simple cell**, generally has no spontaneous activity at all and never seems to respond to diffuse illumination covering the whole screen. Sometimes such cells respond to small spots of light. Because of the elonga-tion of the central region of the receptive field, however, the best stimulus for such a cell is a dark or light bar or line flashed in the appro-priate location in the receptive field. Fig-ure 3-19 shows the receptive fields that might be mapped from several simple cells. Beneath each of them you will see the stimulus that produces the maximal response for each re-ceptive field. Notice that in every case the edge between the light and the dark must be at a particular orientation in a particular loca-tion. If the edge of the line is flashed on the receptive field at a different angle, a greatly re-duced response may be obtained, or perhaps no response at all. For this reason such cortical cells are said to have an *orientation specific-ity*, which the simple circular center-surround cells do not. An older terminology referred to such cells as **orientation detectors**, or **line detectors**.

Other kinds of neurons in the visual cortex seem to be tuned to even more complicated pattern properties of the stimulus. These more elaborate feature-analyzing neurons have been labeled **complex cells**. They have larger re-ceptive fields than do simple cells, although their size may vary tremendously. Like simple cells, complex cells respond maximally to stimuli when they are in a particular orientation. They rarely respond to any flashing patterns, however. What they prefer is a bar or edge moving somewhere within the receptive field. The location within the receptive field does not appear to be particularly important. In other words, the complex cells seem to generalize their response over a wider area of the visual field. Figure 3-20 shows the response of a complex cell to two different moving light slits, one in the optimal, and the other in a nonoptimal orientation. Notice that both direction of movement and orientation are important factors in determining the response.

Unfortunately, the complex cells do not ex-

Preferred orientation and direction

Preferred orientation and nonpreferred direction

For nonpreferred orientations, direction does not make a difference

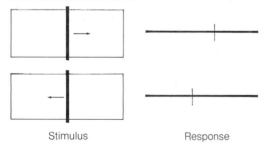

Stimulus   Response

Figure 3-20. Some typical "complex" cortical cell responses.

haust the types of cells recorded in the cortex. At a slightly more sophisticated level are certain special complex cells, which are often called **hypercomplex cells**. These cells respond not only to the orientation and to the direction of movement of the stimulus, but also to the length, to the width, and even to certain features of shape, such as the presence of corners. Figure 3-21 shows an example of some hypercomplex cell responses.

Organization of cortical cells

The different cell types are not randomly intermixed in the visual cortex. Actually, a detailed structure spatially separates particular cell types. The cortex in area 17 is arranged in six layers, numbered 1 to 6, beginning with the outermost (surface) layer. The only layer receiving direct inputs from the lateral geniculate body is layer 4. This layer contains the largest number of simple cortical cells in addition to cells with the simple circular center-surround receptive field found at the lower levels of the visual system. Above this level, in layers 2 and 3, nearly 90 percent of the cells have strong orientation sensitivity. Layers 5 and 6 contain certain special complex cells, with those in layer 5 being quite large and particularly sensitive to the direction of stimulus movement, while layer 6 contains rather long, narrow, directionally sensitive cells. This arrangement is depicted in Figure 3-22.

The directional sensitivity of cells is not distributed randomly either. Instead, cells with a particular orientation sensitivity tend to be aligned in a column, as diagrammed in Figure 3-23. As we move across the cortex, the orientation specificity shifts by about 10 degrees per column. Moving in the other direction, we encounter columns of cells that have the same orientation sensitivity; however, each column looks at a slightly different section of

Length detector

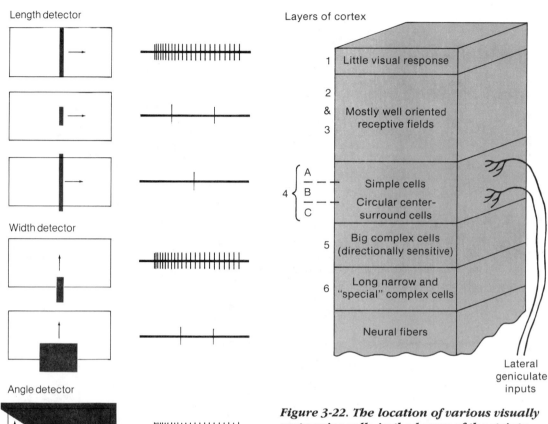

Width detector

Angle detector

Stimulus Response

Figure 3-21. Some typical "hypercomplex" cortical cell responses.

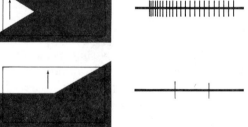

Layers of cortex

Figure 3-22. The location of various visually responsive cells in the layers of the striate cortex (area 17).

the visual field, thus forming a "slab" of cells with a specific orientational tuning.

One final aspect of the organization of the cortex must be mentioned. Each cortical cell tends to be more responsive to one eye than to the other. These right eye and left eye inputs are also spatially separated, with a slab of cells responding to one eye located next to one driven by the other eye. They are systematically arranged in alternating stripes across the cortex. A region of cortex containing all 360 degrees of orientational specificity, and including a region responsive to both the left eye and the right eye, forms a larger unit, which is sometimes called a **hypercolumn**. Such a piece of cortex might be between 0.5 and 1 mm square, and 2 mm deep. We have diagrammed a hypercolumn in Figure 3-23. Our catalog of cell types and arrangements does not exhaust all the forms of special

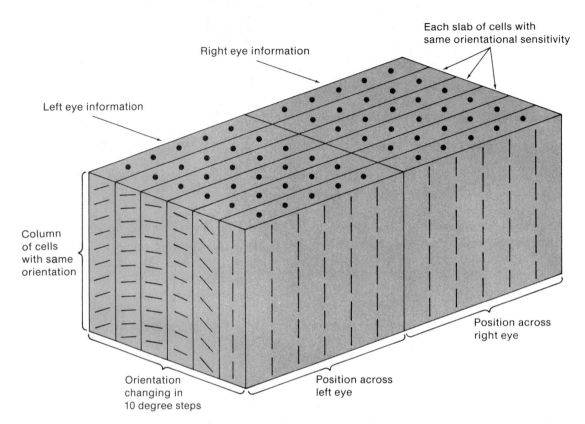

Right eye information

Left eye information

Each slab of cells with
same orientational sensitivity

Column
of cells
with same
orientation

Position across
right eye

Orientation
changing in
10 degree steps

Position across
left eye

*Figure 3-23. A diagram of a hypercolumn,
which is a small region of the visual cortex
that contains inputs from both eyes and all*
*visual orientations separated spatially, as
shown.*

receptive field properties that may be perceptually important. We shall mention others when we talk about brightness, spatial frequencies, color, and depth perception in later chapters. For the moment, however, this discussion of cell types gives a general idea of the types of visual analysis that may be monitored at the single cell level in the primary and secondary visual cortex. Such a detailed architecture, spatial arrangement, and specificity at the cellular level is bound to elicit certain forms of theoretical speculation. Thus, the existence of orientation-specific or feature-specific cells in the cortex suggests that pattern perception

may take place by decomposing visual stimuli into component features or contours. These contours are then resynthesized at a later point according to some plan or template (Frisby, 1980). Certainly, many pattern recognition machines have been built using this principle. For instance, the machine that reads the numbers on your bank check is tuned to respond to certain, highly stylized, numerical stimuli by matching the patterns on paper to internally represented codes. Unfortunately, in mammalian species the significance of such feature extraction cells for the perceptual process has not yet been determined. We know that if we alter an animal's visual experience from birth, we can alter the distribution of orientations to which cortical cells are responsive. The significance of such changes will be discussed later when we deal with the effects of experience in Chapter 17.

The temporal lobes

Both the geniculostriate system and the tectopulvinar system have inputs to the secondary visual areas 18 and 19. From here the information seems to travel to the temporal lobes of the brain, which roughly correspond to the region of the brain directly behind the temples of your skull (Rockland and Pandya, 1981). Here, recent evidence suggests, there are additional "maps" of the visual field, and some quite complex visual processing takes place. In order to localize these *tertiary visual areas*, you might look back at Figure 3-17.

The first part of this region to be studied was the lower portion, called the **inferotemporal cortex**. The visual significance of this section of cortex was accidentally discovered by Kluver and Bucy in 1937 while observing monkeys that had undergone surgery that removed most of both temporal lobes. The researchers called the syndrome that they observed **psychic blindness**. The animals could reach for and accurately pick up small objects; hence, they were clearly not blind. However, they seemed to have lost the ability to identify objects by sight. An example of this is shown in what was named the **concentration test**. Here, a piece of food or a metal object is presented to the monkey approximately every 30 seconds. Generally, a normal monkey will eat the food, and discard the nail or steel nut after examination by mouth. Within a few trials, a normal monkey will let the metal objects pass by and select only the food. For the ani-

mals with inferotemporal lobe loss, however, both the food and the inedible object were picked up on virtually every trial. The animal showed no evidence of learning to discriminate between the targets. Wilson (1957) found that such monkeys could discriminate between an inverted and an upright L by touch, yet with inferotemporal lesions, they could not make the same discrimination visually. This syndrome is similar to a human defect called **visual agnosia** (Kolb and Whishaw, 1980). Such patients can see all parts of the visual field, but the objects they see mean nothing to them. Patients with lesions of the right temporal lobe also show deficits on a variety of visual tests. For instance, they have difficulty in placing pictures in a sequence that relates a meaningful story or pattern. They also have difficulty in learning to recognize new faces. Furthermore, such patients make poor visual estimates of the number of dots in an array, have difficulty recognizing overlapping figures, have poor memory for nonsense forms, and generally have poor picture memory. We'll have more to say about such agnosias when we consider some clinical conditions in Chapter 17.

Needless to say, some investigators have begun to map single neurons in the inferotemporal cortex. Some microelectrode measurements in the monkey brain have produced startling results, suggesting that neurons found in this part of the brain have amazing response specificities. Although this research area is quite new, neurons sensitive to size, shape, color, orientation, and direction of movement have already been discovered in this region of the brain (Desimone, Albright, Gross, and Bruce, 1980). There is even a report that one neuron produced its best response when the stimulus was the outline of a monkey's paw. Gross, Rocha-Miranda, and Bender (1972) report that one day they discovered a cell that seemed unresponsive to any light stimulus. When they waved their hand in front of the stimulus screen, however, they elicited a vigorous response from the previously unresponsive neuron. They then spent the next twelve hours testing various paper cutouts in an attempt to find out what feature triggered this specific unit. When the entire set of stimuli were ranked according to the strength of the response they produced, the researchers could not find any simple *physical* dimension that correlated with this rank order. The rank order of stimuli in terms of their ability to drive the cell, however, did correlate with their apparent similarity (at least for the experimenters) to the silhouette of a monkey's hand. The relative adequacy of a few of these stimuli in producing a neural response is shown in Figure 3-24. Interestingly enough, fingers pointing downward elicited very little response compared with fingers pointing upward or to

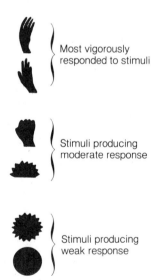

Figure 3-24. The stimuli shown were used to excite a neuron in the inferotemporal cortex of a monkey. Notice that the more handlike a stimulus is, the more vigorous is the response.

the side. An animal looking at its own hand would most likely see a hand with fingers pointing upward. Such complex response specificity has been observed a number of times in this region of the cortex (Desimone and Gross, 1979).

Even more startling degrees of stimulus analysis seem to be emerging from a region of the temporal lobe called the **superior temporal cortex**. Here, Bruce, Desimone, and Gross (1981) found cells in monkeys that responded selectively to drawings of faces. The more realistic and monkeylike the face, the stronger the response. Distorting the stimulus by removing the eyes, scrambling the features, or presenting a cartoon caricature resulted in weaker responses. Thus, it seems possible that in your temporal cortex there might be a template for the perception of your grandmother, your car, and many other familiar stimulus shapes.

Figure 3-25 is a summary of the flow of visual information from the retina of the eye, through the various visual centers, as we have discussed it in this chapter.

GLOSSARY

The following definitions are specific to this book.

Accommodation   The process by which the lens of the eye varies its focus.

Action potential   A large rapid change in electrical potential of an axon.

Acuity   The ability of the eye to resolve or discriminate details.

Amacrines   Large, laterally interconnecting neurons found in the retina.

Aqueous humor   The fluid occupying the small chamber between the cornea and the lens of the eye.

Area 17   According to Brodmann's numbering sys-

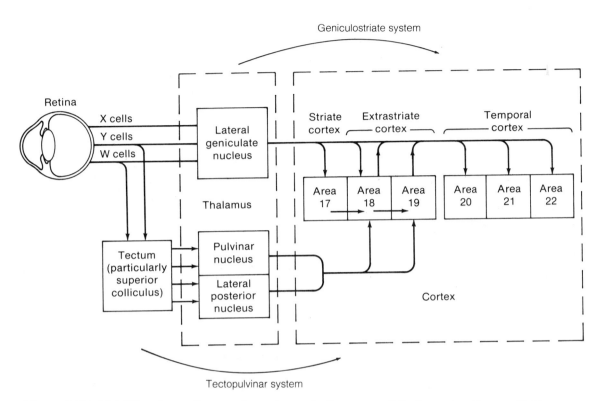

Figure 3-25. A highly schematic overview of the visual system; indicating the two visual pathways and their connections with the major subcortical and cortical centers.

tem, another name for the primary visual cortex, which is part of the occipital lobe of the brain.

Axon The extended portion of a neuron that conducts the action potential to other cells.

Axon terminal The end of the axon through which action potentials trigger reactions in other cells.

Bipolar cell A neural cell in the retina between the photoreceptor and ganglion cells.

Blind spot A portion of the retina through which the optic nerve passes and therefore an area without photoreceptors. This region shows no response to light.

Cell body The main part of a cell (for example, a neuron) containing the nucleus.

Complex cells Cells in the visual cortex that respond to features such as orientation and direction of movement. These cells usually have large receptive fields.

Concentration test A method for determining the ability to discriminate objects following inferotemporal lobe loss.

Cone A short, thick, tapering cell in the photoreceptive layer of the retina, used in bright-light and color vision.

Cornea The transparent, domelike part of the eye formed by the bulged sclera. It serves as a fixed lens.

Day blind The condition of absence or nonfunctioning of cones resulting in visual difficulty under bright-light conditions.

Dendrite   The parts of neurons that receive stimulation from axons of other neurons.

Depolarization   A change in the electrical potential of a neuron toward zero volts.

Duplexity theory of vision   *See* Duplicity theory of vision.

Duplicity theory of vision   The concept of two separate visual systems, rod-dependent (low-light) vision, and cone-dependent (bright-light) vision.

Emmetropic   An eye with normal accommodative ability.

Extrastriate cortex   In the visual system, Brodmann's areas 18 and 19, the secondary visual cortex.

Fovea centralis   A small depression in the retina that contains mostly cones and where acuity is best.

Ganglion cells   The third layer of the retina through which impulses travel after the photoreceptor and bipolar cells.

Geniculostriate system   The primary visual pathway passing through the lateral geniculate nuclei to the cortex.

Horizontal cells   Retinal cells with short dendrites and a long axonal process that extends horizontally.

Hypercomplex cells   Cortical cells that respond to complex stimulus features regardless of where they occur in the receptive field.

Hypercolumn   A larger unit of the cortex, sensitive to input from both eyes and to a full range of orientation specificity.

Hypermetropia   Farsightedness.

Hyperpolarization   The change of the electrical potential of a cell toward increasing negativity.

Inferotemporal cortex   The cortical region located in the temporal lobes of the brain, which may be associated with recognition abilities and pathologically with agnosia.

Iodopsin   The cone pigment present in some birds. *See* Opsin.

Iris   The opaque, colored membrane that controls the amount of light entering the eye by changing the size of the pupil.

Lateral geniculate nucleus   The first major relay center for optic nerve fibers leaving the retina. It is in the thalamus in primates and is part of the geniculostriate pathway.

Lateral posterior nucleus   A visual center in the thalamus. It is part of the tectopulvinar pathway.

Lens   A transparent body in the eye of primates. Its shape can be changed, thus altering the focus of the retinal image.

Line detectors   *See* Orientation detectors.

Macula lutea   A yellow pigmented area centered at the fovea.

Millimicron   The thousandth part of a micron, or the millionth part of a millimeter. Now usually called a nanometer.

Myopia   Nearsightedness.

Nanometer (nm)   A billionth of a meter (a millionth of a millimeter).

Near point distance   The nearest point to which an object may be brought to the eye and still remain in focus.

Night blindness   A condition resulting from an absence of functioning rods, in which individuals cannot see under low-light (twilight) conditions.

nm   *See* Nanometer.

Occipital lobe   The rear portion of the brain, which serves as the primary visual processing center.

Off response   A neural response commencing with the termination of a stimulus.

On response   A neural response commencing with the onset of a stimulus.

On-off responses   Responses of neurons caused by both the onset and termination of a stimulus.

Opsin   The protein part of the rhodopsin pigment.

Optic axis   An imaginary line though the center of the pupil and terminating in the center of the fovea.

Optic chiasm   The point at which the two optic nerves meet and the nasal fibers cross to the contralateral side.

Optic disk   The region of the retina where the optic nerve leaves the eye. *See* Blind spot.

Optic nerve   A bundle of axons leading from the retinal ganglion cells.

Optic radiations The large fans of fibers spreading out from the lateral geniculate nucleus to the occipital cortex.

Optic tract The path of the optic nerve after the optic chiasm.

Orientation detectors Cortical cells that respond best to visually presented lines at a particular orientation.

Oscilloscope A sensitive voltage-measuring device used to display the electrical activity of a cell.

Photon The smallest unit of light energy.

Photopic Vision under bright-light conditions.

Photopsin The protein segment of the photochemical in cones.

Photoreceptors Photosensitive cells in the retina (rods and cones).

Pigment epithelium The light-absorbing dark layer backing the retina in diurnal animals.

Polarization The electrical resting state of a cell, where the inside of the cell is charged negatively relative to the outside.

Potential The difference between the electrical charge inside a cell and the electrical charge outside.

Presbyopia Farsightedness found in older individuals.

Primary visual cortex The first layer of the occipital lobe that receives input from the lateral geniculate, Brodmann's area 17; also known as Striate cortex.

Pulvinar nucleus A visual center in the thalamus and part of the tectopulvinar pathway.

Psychic blindness The ability of animals to locate objects without being able to identify them.

Pupil The opening in the iris of the eye through which light enters.

Quantum A particle of any form of electromagnetic radiation. See Photon.

Receptive fields For any particular cell, the region of the visual field in which a stimulus can produce a response.

Reflecting tapetum The shiny surface backing the retina in some nocturnal animals.

Refractive error A light-bending or focusing error.

Retina The rear portion of the eye containing photoreceptors and neural elements.

Retinene Part of the rhodopsin pigment, similar to vitamin A.

Rod A long, thin cyclindrical photoreceptor used in low-light vision.

Sclera The strong, elastic outer covering, seen as the "white," of the eye.

Scotopic Vision under low-light conditions.

Scotoma A localized blind spot.

Scotopsin The protein portion of rhodopsin.

Secondary visual cortex Includes Brodmann's areas 18 and 19; receives fibers from both visual pathways.

Simple cell A cortical cell that responds to lines of particular orientation and location.

Special complex cells *See* Hypercomplex cells.

Spike potential *See* Action potential.

Stereotaxic instrument A device that permits accurate placement of electrodes.

Striate cortex *See* Primary visual cortex.

Superior colliculus The first way station in the tectopulvinar pathway; located in the tectum of the brain stem.

Superior temporal cortex An area of the temporal lobe implicated in visual stimulus analysis.

Synapse The point at which the axons of one cell come into proximity with the cell body or dendrites of another cell.

Tectopulvinar system A secondary pathway to the visual cortex branching off from the optic tract toward the brain stem.

Tectum A primitive visual center in the brain stem.

Visual agnosia A syndrome in which all parts of a visual field are seen, but the objects are without meaning.

Vitreous humor The jellylike substance filling the large chamber of the eye.

4

The auditory system

IN ONE OF THOSE STRANGE HISTORICAL occurrences, Alexander Graham Bell developed the telephone while studying the physiology of the ear to help the deaf learn to deal with a world of sound. Perhaps the leap was not too great, however, for if the eye is our window to the world, then the ear must be our microphone. Just as an understanding of the physical nature of light and of the anatomy and physiology of the eye is important to understanding the psychology of vision, an understanding of the physical nature of sound and of the anatomy and physiology of the auditory system is crucial to our understanding of hearing. The ear is a remarkable physical instrument. An engineer trying to duplicate the function of the ear would have to compress a sound system of immense complexity into a space of approximately 2 cubic centimeters. Such a system would have to contain many sophisticated components, including an impedance matcher, a wide-range mechanical analyzer, a mobile relay-and-amplification unit, a multichannel transducer to convert mechanical energy to electrical energy, a system to maintain a delicate hydraulic balance, and an internal two-way communications system (Stevens and Warshovsky, 1965). So much complicated apparatus suggests that the analysis of sound waves, from their origin in the external environment to the final stage where we "hear" a sound, involves several different mechanisms and stages of information processing.

SOUND

Sound is similar to mechanical pressure. If you have ever attended a rock concert, you probably have felt the actual mechanical pulsations, especially those from the bass instruments, that may cause the floor, seat, and the air about you to seem to vibrate. You are feeling the results of the movements of air molecules being pushed forward in waves by the cone of the speaker. Perhaps it is easier to understand this process if we consider what happens when we pluck a guitar string, causing a sound. We can see the string vibrate. This vibration causes the sound as the strand of steel or nylon collides with the air molecules around it. These molecules, in turn, collide with others, causing air compression as the string moves forward and rarefaction as it moves back. This movement results in a **wave** of mechanical energy, as is shown in Figure 4-1. Such collisions are, of course, not perfectly efficient in transferring the original collision energy, so the wave tends to become less intense as it moves farther away from the original source. Consequently, its ability to move or vibrate other objects decreases. Sound waves are alternations of rarefaction and compression of an elastic medium (for example, water, air, and walls) in which they travel. In air, for instance, the original vibrating surface first compresses the nearby air molecules into a smaller space by colliding with them and moving them closer together. Then, when the surface moves away from the air molecules during the second part of its vibration, it causes a rarefied region where there are relatively few air molecules. This cycle is repeated in the vibration, and the alternations of compression and rarefaction are transmitted for great distances, although in actuality the individual air molecules simply move back and forth over very small distances. Since sound involves vibration of parts of the medium through which it travels, it cannot pass through a vacuum. The necessity of a medium for the existence of sound waves was demonstrated by Robert Boyle in 1660, when he pumped the air out of a jar and then failed to hear the sounds made by a watch suspended by a thread in the jar.

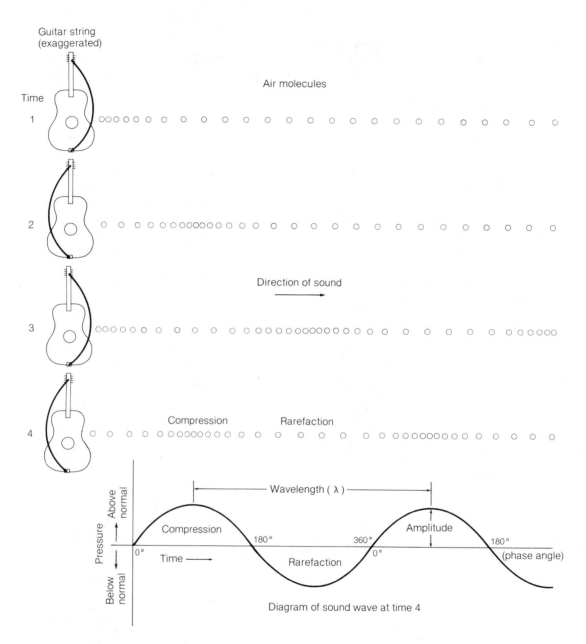

Figure 4-1. The nature and description of a simple sound wave in air.

The speed of sound varies according to the medium in which it travels. The elasticity and density of the medium are important, with sound traveling faster in a denser or more elastic medium. The speed of sound is rather slow compared with that of electromagnetic waves. Sound travels at approximately 340 m/sec in air, while in water it travels at about 1360 m/sec.

A simple sound wave

Any sound wave may be described by specifying certain values. The simplest wave is sinusoidal (so called because the trigonometric sine function describes it mathematically). Figure 4-1 shows the alternate compressions and rarefactions of air molecules over time from the vibrating string of a guitar. When we plot the air pressure as it varies over time, we get the wave shown in the figure. Its **wavelength** (represented by the Greek letter λ) is the distance from one peak to the next peak. The wavelength represents a single **cycle** of the wave. The **frequency** (f) of the wave is, by convention, the number of cycles the wave is able to complete in one second. The unit used to measure frequency is **Hertz** (Hz), named after the German physicist Heinrich R. Hertz. One Hertz is equivalent to one **cycle per second**. The frequency of a sound wave is important to our later discussion, since it is related to (although not the same as) the perceived pitch of the sound. The range of tone frequencies that seem to have pitch for most people is from about 20 to 20,000 Hz. Sounds below 20 Hz are sensed as vibration while sounds above 20,000 Hz are not heard at all except by young children. Other animals, such as bats and dolphins, can hear frequencies several times as high as the upper limit for humans.

The intensity of a sound wave is related to its **pressure amplitude**. This is a measure of compression or rarefaction in the air or other medium at the peaks or valleys of the sound wave. For a sine wave in air, the pressure amplitude is the maximum amount by which the wave causes the pressure (force per unit area) to differ from the normal atmospheric pressure (which is about 1,000,000 dynes/cm^2). The maximum pressure *variation* the ear can tolerate is about 280 dynes/cm^2 above atmospheric pressure, whereas the minimum pressure detectable (average for adults of all ages) is of the order of 0.0002 dynes/cm^2 (above atmospheric). For these threshold-level sound waves, the air molecules are displaced (on average) about 0.0000000001 cm, which is about one-tenth the diameter of an average air molecule. Obviously, the ear is an extremely sensitive organ with a broad response range.

In order to express conveniently this wide range of sound sensitivity, we use some special measures. When dealing with sound as energy units, we can speak of the difference between two levels by asking by how many powers of 10 (the logarithm) one energy level exceeds another. If one energy level is one million times greater than another (10^6 times greater), we say that it is 6 **bels** greater (a measurement unit named after Alexander Graham Bell). It is more convenient, however, to speak in terms of **sound pressure levels**, which represent the actual force against the ear, rather than in terms of sound energy. Because of the mathematical differences in units, this doubles the number of bels when we speak of ratios of sound pressure levels. Since a bel is a rather large unit relative to normal hearing levels, the most common unit used is the **decibel**, which is one-tenth of a bel. The formula for decibels (dB) is

$$\text{Number of dB} = 20 \log (P/P_0)$$

where P is the sound pressure level we wish to express in decibels, and P_0 is the standard reference level. The standard reference level is psychologically meaningful because it is actually the average value of the threshold for sound, measured in adults at 1000 Hz (0.0002 dynes/cm^2). Decibels are particularly suited to express the relationships between sound pressure levels since they compress the large range of possible pressures into more manageable units. Table 4-1 gives typical values of sound pressure levels expressed in decibels for some representative sounds. The table shows that as the measured intensity of a sound increases, subjective loudness also increases. Intensity is related to (but not identical to) loudness.

A final important parameter of sound waves is **phase**, which is important when two or more simple waves are compared. Phase refers to the particular part of the compression-rarefaction cycle a wave has reached at one instant of time. If two waves are at exactly the

same part of their respective cycles at the same instant (so that their peaks and valleys coincide), they are said to be **in phase**. If their peaks and valleys do not coincide, the two waves are **out of phase**. How much they are out of phase is expressed in terms of **phase angle**. A single cycle is assigned 360 degrees (as in circular motion); thus, a portion of a cycle can be specified by number of degrees from 0 to 360 (see Figure 4-1). If one wave is at its 90 degree point (its peak) when another wave is at its 180 degree point (crossing the zero pressure-difference line), then the two waves are 90 degrees out of phase. If we remember that these waves simply describe increases and decreases in mechanical pressure at various moments in time, it should be clear that different sound waves (patterns of pressure) that occur at the same time can interact with each other. If two waves are perfectly in phase (0 degrees out of phase), their peak and minimum pressures coincide; hence, they add strongly to each other's intensities. When two waves of the same frequency are 180 degrees out of phase, one reaches its minimum as the other is reaching its maximum, and they cancel each other's effects; therefore, we would not be able to hear the interacting sound waves.

Typical everyday sounds are more complex than the simple sine waves we have discussed. Only a few sound sources, such as tuning forks or electronic instruments, produce "pure" sounds, which are composed of a simple sine wave variation of compression and rarefaction. Sounds produced by musical instruments, the human voice, automobiles, waterfalls, and so on, have enormously complex cycles of compression and rarefaction. These complexities result from the interaction of many different waves of different frequencies and phases. Such complex wave forms produce **timbre** of the sounds (see Chapter 8 for a detailed dis-

Table 4-1. Sound pressure levels (intensity levels) of various sound sources

Source	Sound level (dB)
	200
Manned spacecraft launch (from 45 m)	180
Loudest rock band on record	160
Pain threshold (approximate)	140
Large jet motor (at 22 m)	120
Loudest human shout on record	111
Heavy auto traffic	100
Conversation (at about 1 m)	60
Quiet office	40
Soft whisper	20
Threshold of hearing	0

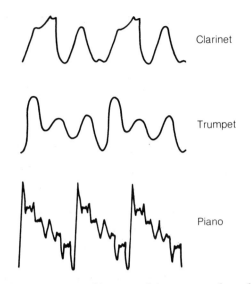

Figure 4-2. Complex sound waves produced by three musical instruments.

cussion of how this occurs). We can differentiate among the sounds of a trumpet, a clarinet, a piano, and a violin quite easily, because the wave forms they produce, even when they are playing the same musical "note," are quite different. You can see in Figure 4-2 that instruments produce very complicated wave forms. They are described by breaking each one into a set of simpler sine waves, which then add together to produce the more complicated wave forms. This method was invented by the French scientist Jean B. J. Fourier in the course of his studies of heat conduction. Fourier proved a mathematical theorem that states, in essence, that *any* wave form that is continuous and periodic can be represented as the sum of a series of simple sine waves with appropriate wavelengths, phases, and amplitudes. As it turns out, these simple waves have frequencies related to each other by simple mathematical ratios. Figure 4-3 shows an example of the decomposition of a complex wave form into its **Fourier components**.

Speech sounds may also be broken into their Fourier components, with results that are quite useful for the understanding of speech perception (see Chapter 13). The ear itself acts in some ways as a sound analyzer, decomposing complex sounds into their individual components. This fact is known as **Ohm's acoustical law** after the physicist George Ohm. Demonstrate this effect for yourself using Demonstration Box 4-1.

THE STRUCTURE OF THE EAR

Evolution and anatomy of the ear

The human ear is a complex piece of biological engineering. Yet biologists have traced its origins to simple organs in quite primitive animals (Stebbins, 1980; van Bergeijk, 1967). All vertebrate ears seem to have evolved from the sense of touch. Whether primitive or advanced, they seem to be specializations of

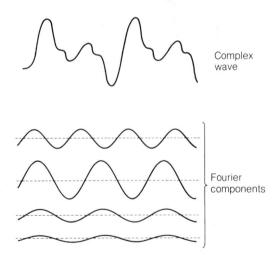

Figure 4-3. Fourier components (sine waves) of a complex sound wave.

Demonstration Box 4-1. Ohm's acoustical law

This demonstration is best done with a piano or a guitar. If neither is available, take two glasses and fill one with water so that it makes a fairly high note when struck with a butter knife. The other should be relatively empty, so that it produces a low note. Using piano, guitar, or glasses, sound a high note and then a low note. Now sound both simultaneously. Although the resultant chord is a complex sound, you can still pick out both the high and the low notes. They do not lose their individual identities. A few moments of practice will help you to resolve the sound. With enough practice a person can learn to separate as many as six or seven different components of a complex "clang." This separation of sound components by the auditory system is known as Ohm's acoustical law.

---

groups of cells with protruding hairs, much like those found on the skin of your arm. In fact, we can use the skin to demonstrate a number of phenomena associated with human hearing. One of the first steps in the evolution of the modern mammalian ear was the "lateral line." The lateral line is a linear array of nerve endings in the skin of fish and some amphibians from which protrude jellylike masses in which are embedded sensory hairs. Often these hairs are pigmented and form a horizontal line that runs the length of the animal's body. As the water moves or vibrates because of sound or other stimuli, these sensory hairs bend. In a sense, the fish does not so much "hear" sound as "feel" it.

In addition to the lateral line system, some types of fish have primitive internal ears that work on much the same principles as do human ears. It is believed that these internal ears evolved from a specialized, deeply sunken part of the lateral line system. In such fish, vibrations in the water cause similar vibrations in an air bladder in the fish's body cavity. From there the vibrations are passed on to a series of small bones, derived from some of the vertebrae and ribs, and then to a complex organ called the labyrinth, whose looping passages are filled with fluid. This fluid contains hairs that are sensitive to the movements of the liquid in the labyrinth caused by the vibrations picked up by the air bladder. These hairs send the auditory information to the fish's brain by way of sensory nerves. In many of its elements, this system is quite similar to that found in humans, even to the composition of the fluid in the labyrinth. A variety of other animals have ears that are considered to be outgrowths of these primitive versions. An interesting transition form is that of the frog. A tadpole has a hearing apparatus similar to those of fishes. Sound waves are picked up by the lung and transmitted to the inner ear (the labyrinth) and from there to the brain. During metamorphosis into a frog, however, the ear changes. It develops an external membrane (the eardrum) that takes the place of the lung in the tadpole hearing system.

Another major component, which is common to all mammals and birds, is the **cochlea**. The cochlea also appears in the "crocodilian" reptiles. It is a specialized extension of the labyrinth that contains a long membrane covered with sensory cells from which (of course) hairs protrude. Its name (which means "shell") is derived from its coiled seashell appearance in mammals.

All mammalian ears have the same basic

parts, although they differ somewhat in proportions (with the elephant, of course, having one of the largest). There are also differences in sensitivity. Bats, dolphins, and dogs have extraordinarily keen hearing over a wide range of frequencies. The ears of mammals differ from those of birds, reptiles, and fish in that mammalian ears typically have three small bones to transmit vibrations to the labyrinth, rather than the single bone found in these other species. Békésy (1960), in a series of detailed studies, established that all these various types of ears function in a similar manner. He was able to link many of the performance differences with differences in the physical properties of the ears (such as in the length of the cochlea). Thus, the human ear, with which we will be concerned in the remainder of this chapter, is part of a large family of roughly equivalent organs. This fact makes it possible to extend the results of studies of other mammalian ears to the human auditory system.

Physiology of the human ear

Let us follow a sound wave through the structure of the human ear and trace the information pathways to the brain. The ear can be divided into three major parts, the **outer**, **middle**, and **inner** ears. Figure 4-4 is a schematic representation of the human ear. The

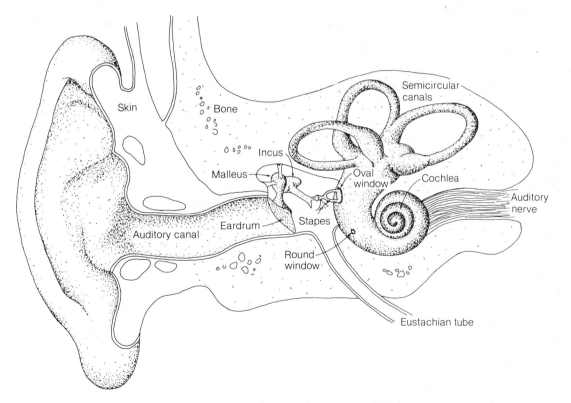

Figure 4-4. The human ear (based on Lindsay and Norman, 1977).

outer ear consists of the **pinna**, which is the fleshy part of the ear visible from the outside. Only mammals have pinnae, and they are thought to function primarily to channel the sound waves into the **auditory canal**. The pinna may also be involved in the localization of sound. Some mammals, such as bats and dogs, have highly mobile pinnae that allow them partially to select the direction from which sounds are received. The sound waves that enter the auditory canal are channeled along it until they encounter the **eardrum** (or **tympanum**). The eardrum vibrates in resonance with incoming sound waves, moving back and forth at a high rate for high-frequency sounds, and more slowly for low-frequency sounds. As we mentioned when discussing sound, these vibratory movements are quite small. For frequencies in the middle of the audible range (1000–6000 Hz), the shape of the auditory canal actually helps to concentrate the sound and to increase its force against the eardrum.

The middle ear consists of a set of three tiny bones (ossicles): the **malleus** (hammer), the **incus** (anvil), and the **stapes** (stirrup). These bones transmit the vibrations of the eardrum to the transducer mechanism located in the inner ear. Some interesting and important subtleties of operation of this part of the ear may help explain why the complex system of ossicles evolved. The middle ear amplifies sound waves in two ways as it transmits them to the cochlea. First, the energy of a sound wave may be approximately doubled by its transmission through the ossicles since they operate mechanically as a system of levers. Second, the area of the oval window is only about one-fifteenth that of the vibrating area of the eardrum. Elementary physics tells us that a given force applied to two surfaces of different areas yields a greater force per unit area on the smaller surface; thus, the forces applied to the

oval window by the stapes are an additional 15 times greater than those at the eardrum. In total, the middle ear amplifies sounds by a factor of about 30. This amplification is needed because the tiny motions of the air molecules caused by the sound wave must ultimately cause the entire body of cochlear fluid to vibrate. Without this amplification, only very intense sounds would be heard.

A second important aspect of the operation of the middle ear is the ability of the ossicle system to selectively decrease the amplification it provides by means of a change in its relative orientation against the oval window. Sounds in the normal range of intensity cause the stapes to push directly on the fluid in the vestibular canal. For very intense sounds, however, the axis of rotation changes and the effect of the stapes on the fluid of the vestibular canal is greatly reduced. In addition, a muscle attached to the stapes contracts via a neuromuscular reflex when intense low-frequency sounds strike the ear, while another muscle attached to the eardrum contracts to stiffen the eardrum. These mechanisms make the eardrum less able to vibrate in sympathy with sounds in the canal, and together, all these mechanisms protect the ear from long-lasting excessive stimulation by loud sounds.

The bones of the middle ear are surrounded by air. The air pressure is kept approximately equal to that of the atmosphere surrounding the observer by means of the **eustachian tubes**, which open into the back of the throat. The equalization of pressure on either side of the eardrum is important since a pressure differential would cause the membrane to bulge and stiffen, resulting in less responsiveness of the eardrum to the sound striking it. If the eustachian tubes were not present, the pressure on the inner side would gradually drop due to absorption of the air by the surrounding tissue. However, the eustachian tubes open briefly

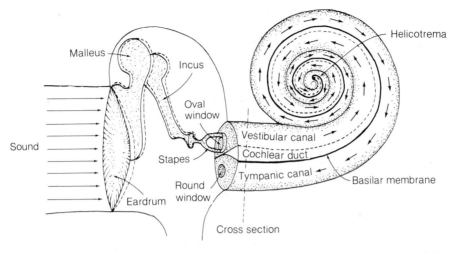

Labels: Malleus, Incus, Oval window, Stapes, Round window, Eardrum, Sound, Helicotrema, Vestibular canal, Cochlear duct, Tympanic canal, Basilar membrane, Cross section

Figure 4-5. Movements of the eardrum in response to sound are transmitted by the ossi- *cles to the fluid in the canals of the coiled cochlea.*

every time we swallow, allowing air to flow into the middle ear cavity from the mouth and lungs. This process equalizes the air pressure on both sides of the eardrum. Sometimes, for example, when we have a head cold, the eustachian tubes become blocked, and the pressure in the middle ear cannot adjust to that of the outside air. Also, when we climb to cruising altitude in a commercial jetliner, the cabin pressure may become considerably lower than the pressure within our middle ear at the time of takeoff. Instances of inequalities in internal versus external air pressure, such as the two described here, can cause you to experience temporary hearing loss and even some pain.

We have already noted that the footplate of the stapes rests on a membrane called the **oval window**. This is the only part of the inner ear directly receiving sound vibrations. The oval window is at one end of one of the three canals that make up the **cochlea**. As can be seen from Figure 4-5, the cochlea consists of three canals that run down its length. Two of these, the **vestibular** and the **tympanic canals**, are

connected at the apex of the cochlea by an opening called the **helicotrema**. They are filled with a fluid resembling saltwater. Since this fluid is relatively noncompressible, a point is needed where the pressure from the vibration of the stapes at the oval window is released. This release point is provided by the **round window**, which is a membrane at the base of the cochlea that opens onto the middle ear. When a movement of the stapes causes the fluid to move away from the oval window, the round window bulges. This indicates that fluid has been displaced, and the resulting pressure change has been transmitted through the helicotrema into the tympanic canal and to the round window at its base. This system allows any vibration of the stapes to set up similar vibrations in the internal fluid in the cochlea. The way in which this system works makes it clear why we need so much amplification of the sound energy in the middle ear. The amplification is necessary to allow small and relatively weak displacements of the eardrum to cause the entire body of cochlear fluid to

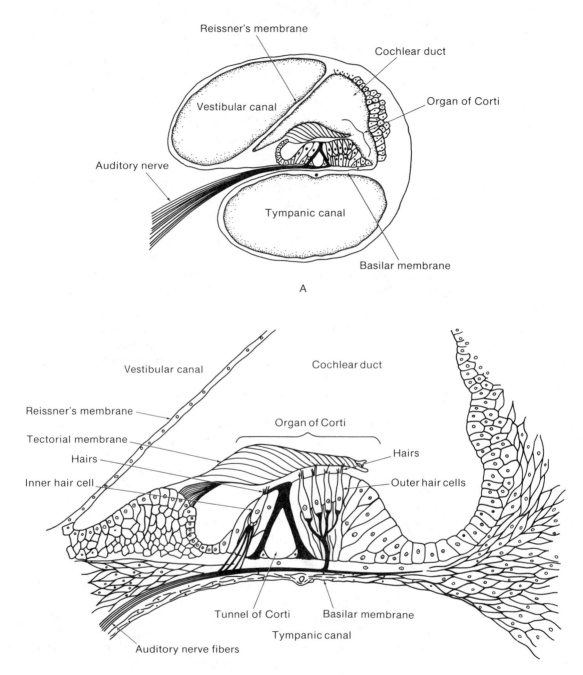

Reissner's membrane

Cochlear duct

Vestibular canal

Organ of Corti

Auditory nerve

Tympanic canal

Basilar membrane

A

Vestibular canal

Cochlear duct

Reissner's membrane

Tectorial membrane

Organ of Corti

Hairs

Hairs

Inner hair cell

Outer hair cells

Tunnel of Corti

Basilar membrane

Auditory nerve fibers

Tympanic canal

B

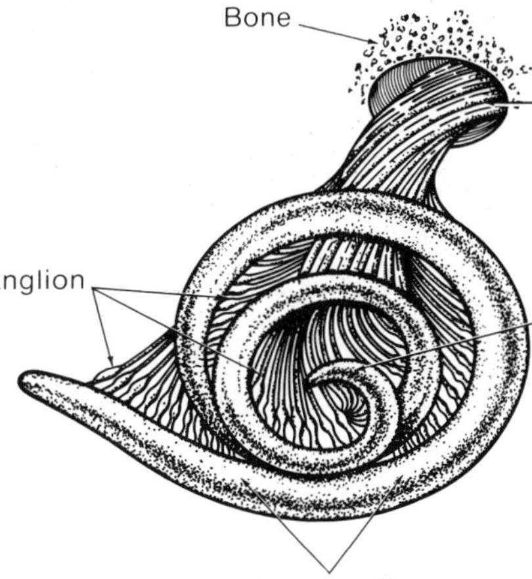

Bone

Auditory nerve

Spiral ganglion

Apex

Scala media
(all boney parts of cochlea removed)

C

Figure 4-6. (A) A cross-section of the cochlea reveals its three canals and the organ of Corti, the auditory receptor. (B) The detailed structure of the organ of Corti (based on Gulick, 1971). (C) A view of the cochlea with the bone and scula tympani removed, leaving only the soft membrane and neural tissue.

vibrate in the same fashion as the eardrum (Schubert, 1978).

The third canal of the cochlea, the **cochlear duct**, is relatively self-contained. It neither opens to the middle ear nor joins the vestibular or tympanic canals. It is formed by two membranes that run the length of the cochlea: **Reissner's membrane** and the **basilar membrane**. Together they form a rough triangle with the wall of the cochlea (Figure 4-6A). The cochlear duct is also filled with a different kind of fluid. Reissner's membrane is very thin (only two cells thick) and has no function other than to form one wall of the cochlear duct. The basilar membrane is the functionally important one. In humans it is about 3 cm long and varies in width from about 0.08 mm near the base (where the windows are) to about 0.5 mm at the apex (where the helicotrema is). It is also about 100 times stiffer at the base than at the apex. A third membrane, located within the cochlear duct, is also important. The **tectorial membrane** extends into the cochlear duct from Reissner's membrane, and touching it are some of the hairs of the **organ of Corti** (Figure 4-6B). This is the part of the cochlear duct that accomplishes the final transduction of the mechanical energy of a sound wave into electrochemical energy interpretable by the nervous system. The organ of Corti rests along the entire length of the basilar membrane. It is composed of about 23,500 cells, which resemble the cells of the skin in that hairs protrude from them. A single row of about 3000 **inner hair cells** is found on the inner side (left side in Figure 4-6B) of the **tunnel of corti**, while three or four rows of **outer hair cells** are located on the outer side. Inner hair cells have about 40-60 hairs each, which extend into the viscous fluid that fills the cochlear duct under the tectorial membrane but which apparently do not touch the membrane (Lim, 1980). Each outer hair cell may have as many as 100-120 hairs protruding from it. The tallest hairs are firmly embedded in the tectorial membrane; the shorter hairs apparently do not touch the membrane but move with the taller hairs as a unit. About 30,000 nerve fibers, whose cell bodies are located in the **spiral ganglion**, form synaptic connections on the bases of the hair cells. About 95 percent of them, called **radial fibers**, make one-to-one connections with the inner hair cells (about 10 per inner hair cell). The other 5 percent of fibers from the spiral ganglion, called **outer spiral fibers**, each make synaptic contact with about 10 outer hair cells. No outer hair cell receives more than about four such contacts (Spoendlin, 1978). Figure 4-6C shows a general picture of how the fibers of the spiral ganglion cells innervate the cochlea. The radial fibers have a large diameter and are probably myelinated, while the outer spiral fibers are smaller in diameter and probably unmyelinated, hence they will have slower neural conduction times. In addition, the two types of fibers come from ganglion cells that have a noticeably different shape (Kiang, Rho, Northrop, Liberman, and Ryugo, 1982). Given so many structural differences, it is likely that these two different sets of fibers carry different types of auditory information. The axons of these spiral ganglion cells make up the auditory nerve, which is the neural pathway to the brain.

Wave motion on the basilar membrane

Sound waves cause the bones of the middle ear to vibrate, and the vibration of the last of these bones (the stapes) causes the oval window, and thus the cochlear fluid, to move back and forth at the same frequency. This movement causes pressure differences across the cochlear duct and movements in the basilar membrane, stimulating the sensory cells of the organ of Corti. Two important aspects of the transduction of mechanical energy into electrochemical energy are accomplished here. The first is the movements of the basilar membrane that result in the stimulation of the sensory cells, and the second is the actual transduction mechanism itself. We will discuss each of these in turn.

The movements of the cochlear fluid cause mechanical waves to travel down the basilar membrane from the base (near the oval window) to the apex. Such a wave is really a traveling bend, or kink, that moves down the length of the basilar membrane, much like the motion when you crack a whip. Figure 4-7 is a schematic drawing of such a wave. The existence of these traveling waves was demonstrated by Georg von Békésy, who received the Nobel Prize for his work on the mechanics of the ear. The waves themselves travel very quickly, going from the base to the apex in about 3 msec (Kitzes, Gibson, Rose, and Hind, 1978). The wave is initiated in the stiffer, narrower part of the basilar membrane and travels toward the looser, broader part. The stiffer parts react first, and the reaction is progressively slower as the membrane becomes broader and looser.

The variations in elasticity and width of the basilar membrane are responsible for the direction and the speed of the traveling wave. They are also responsible for differences in the size or amplitude of the wave. Békésy was able to demonstrate that the basilar membrane reacts differently to sound stimuli of different frequencies. Although the entire basilar membrane vibrates for any given stimulus, each

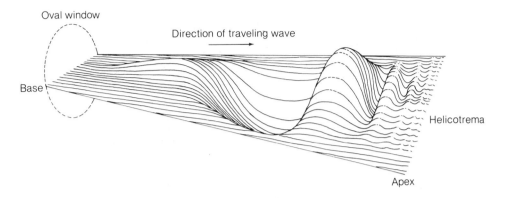

Figure 4-7. A traveling wave on the basilar membrane.

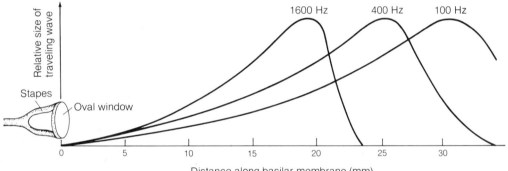

Figure 4-8. A graph of the relative sizes of traveling waves along the basilar membrane for three different frequencies of tone. Notice *that as the frequency increases, the waves reach their maxima nearer the oval window and stapes (base).*

different frequency of a sound wave has a different place along the basilar membrane where the traveling wave reaches its maximum. Traveling waves caused by low-frequency sounds grow steadily in size as they travel toward the apex of the membrane and do not reach a maximum until they reach a place near the apex. High-frequency sounds, on the other hand, create traveling waves that reach their maximum near the base of the basilar membrane and then quickly dissipate, causing little

deformation of the membrane near the apex. This is shown in Figure 4-8, which displays the amplitude of the traveling wave at different places along the basilar membrane for pure tones of several different frequencies. This characteristic action of the basilar membrane in response to sound provides a basis for the frequency analysis of complex tones, as well as for the more basic ability of distinguishing between pure tone stimuli of different frequencies. Demonstration Box 4-2 shows you how

---

Demonstration Box 4-2. The skin as a model for the basilar membrane

The basilar membrane is set into vibration by incoming sound stimuli. How the membrane vibrates, however, depends on the frequency of the sound input. Low frequencies tend to cause vibrations of significant magnitude along the entire length of the membrane, while high frequencies cause vibrations that are significant only near the base. You can easily demonstrate the frequency-specific nature of membrane vibration by using your forearm as a model of the basilar membrane; forearm skin has about the same resiliancy and elasticity as the basilar membrane. First, lightly rest your forearm against a surface that is vibrating at a high frequency (such as an electric shaver

with nonrotating heads). Notice that the vibratory feeling (transmitted from the place where the skin touches the vibrator) covers only a small, localized region. Next, rest your forearm lightly against a similar area of a surface vibrating at a lower frequency (a washing machine is an excellent source of such vibrations). Notice that the lower frequency pulsations seem to travel the entire length of the arm, up to the elbow. In a similar fashion, lower sound frequencies induce waves that extend over the length of the basilar membrane, while higher frequency waves are restricted spatially in their effects.

---

to demonstrate the differences in the ability of low and high frequencies to travel down a membrane.

Mechanisms of transduction

Thus far we have been discussing the ear as if it were a purely mechanical device. The organ of Corti, which rests on the basilar membrane, is the site of the transduction of sound energy from its mechanical form to the electrochemical energy that is the language of the nervous system (see Chapter 3). The movements of the basilar membrane described above cause the basilar membrane and the tectorial membrane to move laterally with respect to one another. Since the outer hair cells are attached at their base to structures connected to the basilar membrane, and the longest hairs are embedded in the tectorial membrane, a shearing force is applied to these hairs, causing them to bend. This bending of the hairs is thought to be the final mechanical step in the transduc-

tion process. The bending somehow produces electrical or chemical changes, or both, in hair cells that in turn trigger electrical activity (spike potentials) in the neurons of the spiral ganglion. The actual process involved in converting a bending force in a hair cell to a neural response is still not fully understood (Brown, 1975; Dallos, 1981).

Current notions suggest that the inner hair cells may be bent in a somewhat different way. Since they appear not to make contact with the tectorial membrane, they are not subject to the shearing force applied to the longest hairs of the outer hair cells. It is possible that they do make contact with the tectorial membrane as a result of the movements of the basilar membrane and are bent when they rub against it (Crane, 1982). It is also possible, however, that they are bent by the flow of the viscous fluid in the cochlear duct caused by these same movements (Dallos, 1978). Although it may seem to be a less efficient means of producing a bending force, the most recent evidence indicates that there are no systematic differences between the sensitivities of inner and outer hair cells to pure tones (Dallos, Santos-Sacchi, and Flock, 1982).

ELECTRICAL ACTIVITY OF THE AUDITORY NERVE

We have followed sound energy to the point at which it is converted into patterns of electrical activity (spike potentials) in the auditory nerve. From this point on, we can use the same techniques of electrophysiological recording that we used to investigate the visual system to study the neural processing of auditory information. When electrodes are inserted into single axons in the auditory nerve, we can record the electrical activity of individual neurons in response to a variety of sounds.

As a first guess, one might suppose that the auditory system would be responsive only to simple physical aspects of the sound, namely frequency and intensity. Actually, some cells seem to mimic visual processing in that they are quite selective and respond to complex aspects of the stimulus. Thus, when we record the responses of single axons in the auditory nerve, we find that some respond only to complex noises and are completely unresponsive to pure tones. Others respond only to such brief transient sounds as clicks. Still others respond to a wide variety of different frequencies of pure tones. Apparently, auditory encoding is quite complex even at this peripheral level. Thus, in much the same way that we found selective analysis taking place early in the visual system, similar selectivity seems to be characteristic of audition.

Although neurons possessing a great many different types of response characteristics seem to be present in the auditory nerve, one type of neuron is extremely common. Such

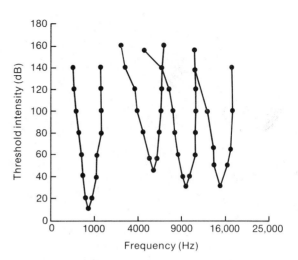

Figure 4-9. Threshold response curves for auditory nerve fibers in the cat (based on Whitfield, 1968).

neurons are often called **tuned neurons**, in analogy to the way we "tune in" a radio station to its broadcast frequency. Figure 4-9 shows the absolute thresholds (minimum intensity of sound that stimulates a neuron to fire above its resting rate) of some typical neurons of this type. The results are called **threshold response curves**, and as can be seen from the figure, each neuron has a best, or *characteristic*, frequency where its absolute threshold is lowest. The sensitivity of neurons decreases (the threshold is higher) as one moves away from the best frequency in either direction. Another way of looking at the tuning of such an auditory neuron is to present a tone, varying in frequency but fixed in intensity. A graph of the response rate of a tuned neuron measured in this way is often called a **tuning curve**. Such a tuning curve is shown in Figure 4-10. In the auditory nerve there are neurons tuned to frequencies over the entire range of hearing.

The tuned nature of these cells probably

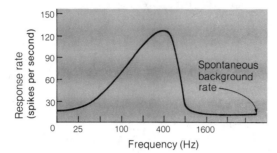

Figure 4-10. Tuning curve of a typical auditory nerve fiber (based on Lindsay and Norman, 1977).

comes about because of the mechanical properties of the basilar membrane (Khanna and Leonard, 1982). Most of the tuned auditory nerve fibers that have been studied are connected to inner hair cells (Kiang et al., 1982; Liberman, 1982). Remember that different parts of the basilar membrane vibrate maximally to different frequencies of sound, and it is this vibration that causes the hair cells to bend and in turn initiates the neural response. A hair cell will respond most vigorously when a tone of a certain frequency creates a traveling wave on the basilar membrane that has its maximum amplitude near the location of that hair cell. The frequency of this tone will be the frequency to which the neuron that synapses with that hair cell is "tuned." Other frequencies of sound of this same intensity will cause less vigorous movement of the basilar membrane at that location, less vigorous bending of the hair of the hair cell, and thus less vigorous responding of the neuron.

Mechanical action may not be the entire answer to the question of how neural tuning occurs. Most measurements of the mechanical tuning curves of the basilar membrane (similar to those of Figure 4-8) give curves that are less sharp (change less steeply with frequency)

than the tuning curves measured in auditory nerve fibers (Dallos, 1981). One suggestion is that the outer hair cells help to sharpen the auditory nerve tuning curves, because destruction of such cells tends to result in broader tuning curves (Lynn and Sayers, 1970; Schmiedt, Zwislocki, and Hamernik, 1980). Further evidence for interaction between inner and outer hair cells comes from a finding called **two-tone inhibition** (Rose, Galambos, and Hughes, 1959; Sachs and Kiang, 1968). This phenomenon occurs when recording from an auditory fiber that is stimulated by its characteristic, or tuned, frequency and is responding vigorously. If a second tone of a different frequency, which is moderately close to the tuned frequency, is now briefly presented, the response rate in the tuned neuron drops. Such an inhibitory response may result from the action of outer hair cells (Javel, 1981). This is supported by the fact that two-tone inhibition disappears when outer hair cells have been selectively damaged by a drug (Schmiedt et al., 1980). Such inhibition may be a mechanism that sharpens the neural tuning curves, since it involves the suppression of response frequencies other than the tuned one.

What is the nature of the information about intensity and frequency carried from the ear to the brain? One suggestion, at least for low frequencies, states that frequency may be directly encoded in the neural response (Johnson, 1980; Rose, Brugge, Anderson, and Hind, 1967). Thus, if the frequency of the stimulus is 100 Hz, the firing in the auditory nerve will tend to be at approximately 100 Hz. This does not mean that any given individual neuron fires at this frequency. Rather, individual neurons seem to fire at fixed points in the cycle of the sound wave. For example, one neuron may fire at every second peak of the wave (and thus at 50 Hz), while another may fire at every fifth peak (and thus at 20 Hz). This is called **phase-locking**. For a great many neurons firing out of phase with one another there will tend to be a spike (or several) occurring at every peak of the wave (and thus at 100 Hz). This ability of the auditory nerve to follow the frequency of the stimulating sound wave (up to about 4000 Hz) has been a central component of several theories of pitch perception (for example, Wever, 1970) that will be discussed in Chapter 8. The pattern of response of the whole auditory nerve rather than the responses of individual neurons may be involved in conveying information to the brain.

The importance of pattern of response in the auditory nerve cannot be overestimated. Even though many cells in the auditory nerve may be tuned to the same characteristic frequency, they may still vary in terms of their threshold intensities over a range of about 20 dB (Evans, 1975). Once the intensity of a sound has exceeded a cell's threshold, further increases in intensity up to 30-50 dB above the threshold value will increase its rate of response. At this point the neuron is firing as fast as it can and is said to be **saturated**. These facts imply that for a sound of a given intensity and frequency, there will be a population of neurons all firing at different response rates. This situation is represented hypothetically in Figure 4-11. Stimuli of different frequencies tend to cause different populations of neurons to fire above their background rates. As the intensity of the stimulus increases, other neurons, tuned to nearby frequencies, may also be recruited, resulting in an increase in the number of neurons responding, as well as an increase in their response rate. Thus, the whole pattern of auditory activity changes with changes in the stimulus. Frequency seems to be indicated by *which* neurons are firing, while intensity seems to be roughly indicated

by *how many* are firing, and to a minor extent *how fast* they are firing (Whitfield, 1978).

THE AUDITORY PATHWAYS

Figure 4-12 diagrams the principle pathways taken by auditory information in the brain. The auditory pathways are somewhat more complex than the visual pathways. First, the bipolar cells of the spiral ganglion receive information from the organ of Corti. The axons of these bipolar cells make up the auditory nerve, which then goes to the **cochlear nucleus**, located in the lower back part of the brain. The auditory nerve fibers enter the **ventral** (front) **cochlear nucleus**, where each divides into at least two branches. One branch synapses with cells in the ventral cochlear nucleus, while the other proceeds to the **dorsal** (back) **cochlear nucleus**. The cells of the ventral cochlear nucleus send about half their axons to the **superior olive** on the opposite side of the brain and half to the one on the same side. The cells of the dorsal cochlear nucleus send their axons up a pathway known as the **lateral lemniscus** on the opposite side of the brain, eventually to terminate in the **inferior colliculus**. Thus, most of the information from the right ear is processed first by the left side of the brain, and vice-versa. The cells of the two superior olives also send most of their fibers to the inferior colliculi (which are located just below the superior colliculi, discussed in Chapter 3). At the level of the inferior colliculus considerable fiber crossing takes place from one side of the brain to the other, so that both inferior colliculi have full information about what is going on in the other inferior colliculus.

Most cells in the inferior colliculi send

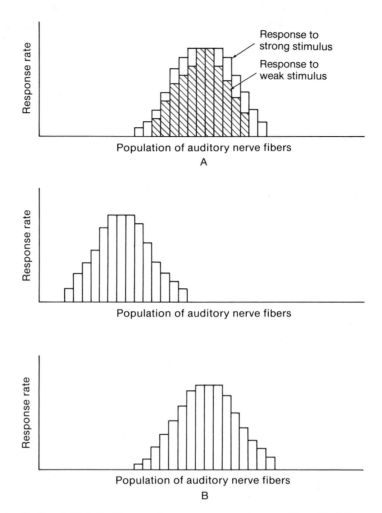

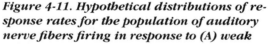

Figure 4-11. Hypothetical distributions of response rates for the population of auditory nerve fibers firing in response to (A) weak versus strong stimuli of the same frequency and (B) stimuli of the same strength but of different frequencies.

axons to the **medial geniculate**, although a few go to the superior colliculi as well. Since the superior collicular pathway has been implicated in visual localization, perhaps the auditory fibers that go there also carry information about location. This sound localization information could then be related to visual data to yield a more complete "picture" of space (see

Chapter 8). From the medial geniculate, fibers project to a part of the temporal cortex that is often called the **primary auditory projection area**, or Brodmann's area 41. The adjacent Brodmann's area 22 also receives axons directly from the medial geniculate, although fewer of them (these regions of the brain were pictured in Figure 3-17).

Electrical activity of the lower auditory centers

We have already discussed the response patterns found in the fibers of the auditory nerve. Although some of them respond only to clicks or other non-pure-tone stimuli, the majority of the fibers are axons from "tuned" neurons. Tuned neurons respond to a range of frequencies of pure-tone sounds, but each has a "preferred" band of frequencies where it is most sensitive and produces its maximum response. Similar "tuned" neurons are found in the cochlear nucleus, superior olive, inferior col-

liculus, and medial geniculate. Also, as described for the auditory nerve, there is a region of nearby frequencies that produces an inhibition of response (as in two-tone inhibition) in these same cells.

In addition to the frequency tuning of cells in the more central nuclei of the auditory pathway, a number of more complex neural response patterns appear. When Pfeiffer (1966) recorded from single neurons at the cochlear nucleus of adult cats, he found a variety of different types of neural responses to a simple tone. **On neurons** gave a burst of responses immediately after the onset of the tone burst

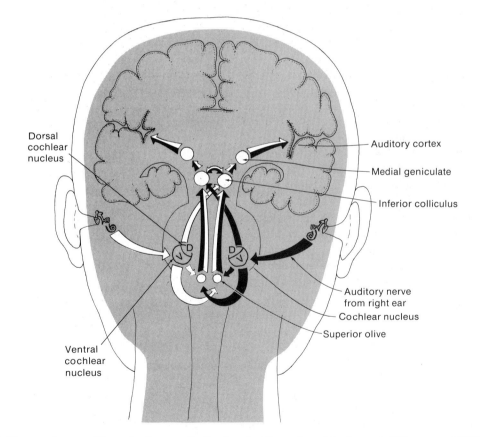

Figure 4-12. The major auditory pathways in the brain (based on Lindsay and Norman, 1977).

and then ceased responding to the tone, no matter how long it persisted. **Pauser neurons** exhibited a similar burst of firing at the onset of a tone, but this was followed by a pause and then a weaker sustained response until the tone was turned off. **Choppers** gave repeated bursts of firing followed by short pauses, with the vigor of successive bursts decreasing. **Primarylike neurons** gave an initial vigorous burst of firing when the tone was turned on, then the firing rate decayed to a lower level that was sustained for the duration of the tone.

In addition to these response patterns, a response analogous to the **off responses** observed in the visual system seems to exist. These cells actually reduce their response rate below their spontaneous activity level at the onset of the tone and then give a burst of activity at its offset. An interesting variation of this is the presence of "tuned" cells that *reduce* their activity level when a stimulus different from the "best" one is present. Of particular interest is a set of cells that are reminiscent of the on-center/off-surround cells observed in the visual system (Chapter 3). Rather than having a receptive field that consists of a region in space, these cells have a "receptive field" consisting of a band of frequencies. For instance, there are cells in the medial geniculate with "W-shaped" receptive patterns. W-shaped neurons respond above their background rate of firing to a particular "best" frequency and below the background rate for frequencies directly below and directly above the "best" frequency. The firing rate gradually returns to background level for frequencies progressively more removed from the "best" frequency and its surrounding "worst" frequencies (see Webster and Atkin, 1975). This type of correspondence between properties of neurons in different sensory systems is quite common, although each sensory system also displays coding principles idiosyncratic to its own stimulus modality. It appears that we are dealing with basically the same kinds of neural units at the electrophysiological level, regardless of the sensory system considered. It is as though some master technician found a useful biological coding scheme for stimuli and simply modified it to fit the various requirements of different sensory systems.

Because different points along the basilar membrane vibrate most strongly for various different frequencies of sounds, we refer to the response of the basilar membrane as **tonotopic** (from the Greek *tono*, for tone, and *topus*, for place). This means that we are actually representing sound frequencies with a sort of spatial code. This spatial encoding also seems to be preserved at other points in the auditory system. In the cochlear nucleus of the cat, Rose, Galambos, and Hughes (1960) recorded the responses of single cells to pure tones as a microelectrode was moved through the tissue. As the electrode was pushed along, the frequency of stimulus that gave the best response (highest rate of firing) changed systematically, going from high near one edge of the nucleus to low near the other. This indicated that the cells were arranged in an orderly spatial layout, with cells tuned to similar frequencies lying closer together in the nucleus than those tuned to different frequencies. Similar tonotopic arrangements of cells have been reported for the auditory nerve and other noncortical nuclei (Gulick, 1971; Webster and Atkin, 1975). In general, the tonotopic organization of the basilar membrane is preserved even in the cortex, where we find cells that respond to high frequencies clustered in some areas, and cells that respond to low frequencies clustered in other areas. Figure 4-13 shows this clustering for the cat auditory cortex (where Ⓗ marks high-frequency areas and Ⓛ marks low-frequency areas). This result has been extended to humans by some ingenious

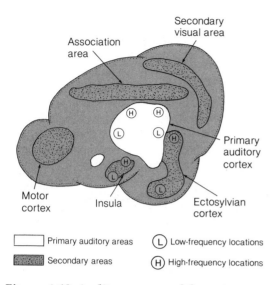

Association area
Secondary visual area
(H) (H)
(L) (L) (H)
Primary auditory cortex
(H)
(L)
Motor cortex
Insula
(L)
Ectosylvian cortex

▢ Primary auditory areas (L) Low-frequency locations
▨ Secondary areas (H) High-frequency locations

Figure 4-13. Auditory areas of the cat cortex.

measurements of the magnetic field created in the brain by its electrical response to sounds (Romani, Williamson, and Kaufman, 1982). The researchers found that the maximum brain activity observed in the auditory centers of humans varies in depth as the frequency varies. High frequencies are deep, while low frequencies lie near the surface of the brain. These results are consistent with the idea that the frequency of sound waves is coded primarily by *place* (*which* neurons are firing), both on the basilar membrane and in the central auditory system.

THE AUDITORY CORTEX

Studies of nonhuman animals have provided us with most of the information we now possess about the physiology of sensory systems. For the lower levels of analysis, we can be fairly confident that we can generalize the concepts to humans. When we begin to discuss the cor-

tex, however, we are on shakier ground. The human cortex is more complex than that of most of the common experimental animals (such as the cat, the preferred subject of such studies), so that generalization of findings to humans is more tenuous. Nonetheless, animal studies have yielded a significant amount of useful information on the activity of the auditory cortex. Figure 4-13 shows the wide variety of areas on the cat cortex that have been shown to be responsive to sound stimuli. In this chapter, we shall be concerned mainly with the primary auditory areas, but a large number of nonauditory areas respond to sound stimuli, especially association and visual areas. Presumably, similar responses occur in the human cortex, especially in the speech and general association areas.

Cells in the auditory cortex exhibit a variety of complex responses to sound stimuli. In the approximately 60 percent of the cells that respond to pure tones, there occur *on* responses, *off* responses, *on-off* responses, and more general *excitatory* and *inhibitory* responses (see Figure 4-14). These responses, of course, resemble the response patterns of cells in the visual system. The other 40 percent of the cells seem to respond selectively to more complex sounds, including noise bursts, clangs, or clicks.

Another complex type of neuron found in the auditory cortex of the cat is the **frequency sweep detector** (Whitfield and Evans, 1965). These cells respond only to sounds that change frequency in a specific direction and range. Some cells respond only to increases but not to decreases in frequency in the same range. Others respond to decreases in frequency but not to increases. A third type responds only to increases in frequency for low-frequency tones. Because these types of stimuli are often encountered in everyday speech and music, such detectors, if present

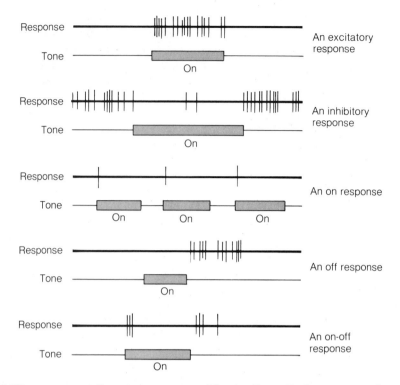

Figure 4-14. Different types of response to pure tones recorded from neurons in the auditory cortex of the cat (from I. C. Whitfield, **The Auditory Pathways.** *London: Arnold, 1967).*

in humans, could have an important role in speech and music perception. Certainly they have obvious utility for the cat, whose "war cries" and "love calls" consist of just such types of sounds. These cortical neurons respond to sound patterns in much the same way that visual cortical neurons respond selectively to light patterns. There are even auditory analogs to the highly specifc visual cells (face and paw detectors) observed in the temporal cortex, which we described in Chapter 3. Swarbrick and Whitfield (1972) found cells in the auditory cortex of the squirrel monkey that are sensitive to the vocalizations of other squirrel monkeys, while Funkenstein, Nelson, Winter, Wolberg, and Newman (1971) dem-

onstrated that some of these cells are unresponsive to the presentation of simple tones, although they respond vigorously to the presentation of extremely complex vocalizations. Watanabe and Katsuki (1974) found cells in cat auditory cortex that, in addition to being tuned to a specific band of frequencies, responded with a unique pattern of activity to recordings of cat vocalizations. Interestingly, these cortical cells did not respond with the same pattern of activity to any of the individual components of the cat vocalization. This indicated that the cells were integrating the outputs of cells from lower levels of the auditory pathway that do respond to simpler components of the sound pattern. We could say that the lower level cells were detecting the various features of the vocalization, and the cortical cell was responding only to the combination of all the features (Whitfield, 1980).

Although these physiological findings are quite intriguing and suggestive, the ultimate test of any hypotheses about the significance of neural encoding or analysis of auditory patterns rests on data about an individual's actual auditory percepts. In Chapter 8 we shall consider *what* is heard and try to integrate it with our present knowledge of *how* it is heard.

GLOSSARY

The following definitions are specific to this book.

Auditory canal   The channel conducting sound waves to the eardrum.

Basilar membrane   The membrane within the cochlea of the ear upon which the organ of Corti lies.

Bel   The basic unit used to measure the relative intensity of a sound wave.

Chopper   A neuron that gives repeated bursts of impulses followed by short pauses, with the vigor of successive bursts decreasing, in response to the presentation of a pure tone.

Cochlea   A snail-shaped part of the labyrinth of the ear that contains the auditory receptors.

Cochlear duct   One of the three canals in the cochlea.

Cochlear nucleus   A structure in the lower back part of the brain receiving input from the auditory nerve.

Cycle   In sound, the completion of a full sequence from air rarefaction to compression.

Cycles per second   The unit used to measure frequency of sound waves, now usually referred to as Hertz.

Decibel   The unit used to measure relative sound intensity; one-tenth of a bel.

Dorsal cochlear nucleus   The back half of the nucleus in the lower back part of the brain where the auditory nerve fibers end.

Eardrum   The membrane at the end of the auditory canal that vibrates in resonance with incoming sound waves.

Eustachian tubes   Channels from the back of the throat to the middle ear; when we swallow they open and allow the air pressure in the middle ear to equalize with the outside.

Fourier components   Simple sine waves that add together to form a complex waveform.

Frequency   The number of cycles a sound wave completes in one second.

Frequency sweep detector   A neuron that responds only to sounds that change frequency in a specific direction and range.

Helicotrema   An opening, between the vestibular and tympanic canals, at the apex of the cochlea.

Hertz   The unit (cycles per second) used to measure the frequency of sound waves.

Incus   One of the three middle ear bones involved in sound conduction to the cochlea. Also known as the *anvil.*

Inferior colliculi   Auditory processing centers in the midbrain that are the termini for cells of the superior olives.

In phase   The peaks and valleys of sound waves coincide over time.

Inner ear   The part of the ear containing the cochlea.

Inner hair cells   Cells found on the inner side of the tunnel of Corti.

Lateral lemniscus   The neural pathway in the brain that contains axons from cells in the dorsal cochlear nucleus that synapse with cells in the inferior colliculus on the opposite side of the brain.

Malleus   The first of the inner ear bones. Also called the hammer.

Medial geniculate   The brain structure through which the output of inferior colliculi cells are channeled to the cortex.

Middle ear   The part of the ear consisting of the ossicles, malleus, incus and stapes that transmit the eardrum vibrations to the inner ear.

Off responses   Neural responses that commence with the termination of stimuli.

Ohm's acoustical law   The auditory system separates complex sounds into simple (Fourier) components.

On neurons   Neurons that fire immediately and exclusively after the onset of a tone.

Organ of Corti   The part of the cochlear duct that transduces mechanical sound wave energy into electrochemical energy interpretable by the nervous system.

Out of phase   The peaks and valleys of sound waves do not coincide over time.

Outer ear   The pinna, the auditory canal, and the eardrum.

Outer hair cells   Cells found on the outer side of the tunnel of Corti.

Outer spiral fibers   Fibers extending from the spiral ganglion to the outer hair cells.

Oval window   A membrane in the cochlea that receives sound vibrations from the stapes.

Pauser neurons   Those neurons, similar to on-response neurons, that exhibit an initial response to stimuli, followed by a pause, and then a weaker, sustained response until the stimulus stops.

Phase   The particular point in the compression-rarefaction cycle of a sound wave at one instant of time.

Phase angle   The degree to which one sound wave is out of phase with another, considering a complete cycle as 360 degrees.

Phase-locking   The tendency of individual neurons to fire at fixed points in the cycle of a sound wave.

Pinna   The fleshy visible parts of the outer ear.

Pressure amplitude   A measure of the degree of compression or rarefaction at the peaks or valleys of a sound wave.

Primary auditory projection area   The area of the temporal cortex that receives most of the fibers from the medial geniculate; Brodmann's area 41.

Primarylike neuron   A neuron that gives an initial burst when fired in response to a stimulus and then continues firing at a lower level until the stimulus is stopped.

Radial fibers   Fibers extending from the spiral ganglion to the inner hair cells.

Reissner's membrane   One of two membranes making up the cochlear duct.

Round window   The membrane at the base of the cochlea opening onto the middle ear.

Saturated   The point at which a neuron cannot fire any faster, even if stimulus intensity is increased.

Sound pressure level   The log-relative pressure amplitude; measured in decibels.

Spiral ganglion   The cells whose axons form the auditory nerve, which is the neural pathway to the brain.

SPL   Sound pressure level.

Stapes   The final bone in the chain of middle ear ossicles. Sometimes called the stirrup.

Superior olive   The brain termini for axons leading from the ventral cochlear nuclei.

Tectorial membrane   Within the cochlear duct, the membrane extending from Reissner's membrane in which some hairs of the organ of Corti are embedded.

Temporal cortex   The cortex of the brain on the sides near the temples.

Threshold response curve   A graph of neural absolute threshold as a function of sound frequency.

Timbre   A sound attribute associated with the components of a complex sound wave.

Tonotopic   Whenever the place of response to a sound depends on the frequency of the sound.

Tuning curve   A plot showing the rate of firing of an auditory neuron for different frequencies of sound wave; it usually has a single peak.

Tuned neuron   A neuron that responds optimally to tones of a characteristic frequency.

Tunnel of Corti   A structure in the cochlea.

Two-tone inhibition Inhibition of neural response to a characteristic or "best" frequency that occurs when a second tone of a different frequency is presented; inhibition occurs during and for a brief period after the presentation of the second tone.

Tympanic canal One of three canals running through the cochlea.

Tympanum *See* Eardrum.

Ventral cochlear nucleus The front half of the nucleus in the lower back part of the brain where the auditory nerve fibers end.

Vestibular canal One of three canals running though the cochlea.

Wave The pattern of air molecule motion that characterizes sound.

Wavelength The distance in a sound wave from one peak to the next.

The chemical and
mechanical senses

116

I guessed vaguely from my mother's signs and from the hurrying to and fro in the house that something unusual was about to happen, so I went to the door and waited on the steps. The afternoon sun penetrated the mass of honeysuckle that covered the porch, and fell on my upturned face. My fingers lingered almost unconsciously on the familiar leaves and blossoms which had just come forth to greet the sweet southern spring. I did not know what the future held of marvel or surprise for me . . . We walked down the path to the well-house, attracted by the fragrance of the honeysuckle with which it was covered. Someone was drawing water and my teacher placed my hand under the spout. As the cold stream gushed over one hand . . . (Keller, 1931, pp. 21-22).

What can you say about the person who wrote the above passage? Did it occur to you that all those vivid sensory impressions came from someone who was completely blind and deaf? It takes someone like Helen Keller to point out that the so-called "minor senses" (touch, taste, and smell) can provide us with a rich and accurate picture of the world. Humans, primates, and birds are unique in their reliance on the visual and auditory sensory systems. Many other animals are equipped with less effective visual and auditory organs, or none at all. However, they perform amazing feats through the use of a variety of other sensory systems, which are often much more sensitive and discriminating than ours. In this chapter, we shall explore the physiology of some of these "other" sensory systems, including *smell*, *taste*, the *skin senses*, the *kinesthetic* senses, the *vestibular* senses, and the sensation of *pain*.

THE GUSTATORY (TASTE) SENSE

Presumably, life began in a bowl of chemical soup that we call the sea. Various substances suspended or dissolved in water were important to the survival of primitive living things. Some substances provided food, some gave warning, some caused destruction. The most primitive, one-celled organisms clearly could not use anything like visual or auditory sensory systems, which require large numbers of specialized cells. They relied on chemical or mechanical interactions with their environment mediated by the cell's outer membrane. This was the first, primitive "sensory system" used by living things. As life evolved, multi-celled animals could afford a "division of labor" among the many cells composing their bodies. Specialized cells were grouped together to pick up chemical information from the surroundings. For example, on the surfaces of their bodies, fish have pits that are lined with cells responsive to a variety of chemical and mechanical stimuli. Insects and other invertebrates have such cells located on their antennae.

Although two anatomically separate systems developed, in the sea, there was little differentiation between taste and smell. All important chemical stimuli were dissolved or suspended in the same substance—water. When life moved on to land, the two existing chemical receptor systems came to serve different functions. The taste system became a "close-up" sense, which provided the last check on the acceptability of food. Smell turned out to be useful as a distance sense, and as we shall see later, may be based on an entirely different principle of animal-environment interaction.

Taste stimuli and receptors

The physical stimuli for the taste system are substances that can be dissolved in water, although the extent to which they can be dissolved in lipids (fats) may be more important to what they taste like (Gardner, 1979). As is usual for physical stimuli, the amount of a substance present is related to the intensity of the taste we experience. However, what property (or collection of properties) gives rise to the various different taste qualities is still unknown in detail. A variety of possibilities exists, such as the size of the individual molecules of the substance, how a molecule breaks apart when it is dissolved in water, or how the molecule interacts with cell membranes. Unfortunately, just what aspects of a stimulating substance cause its characteristic taste will be known only when we agree on the basic dimensions of taste.

There is general agreement that there are at least four primary taste qualities: *sweet, salty, sour,* and *bitter*. These taste qualities are associated with some general types of molecules. A sweet taste is generally associated with so-called "organic" molecules, which are made up mostly of carbon, hydrogen, and oxygen in different combinations. These organic molecules are commonly called sugars, alcohols, and so forth. Other sweet substances, like saccharine, are also organic chemicals, but they are quite different from "natural" sweeteners, such as sugars, in their molecular structure. Many sweet-tasting substances have a particular structure in common, termed the AB,H system, that consists of two negatively charged atoms (represented by the letters A and B) and a positively charged hydrogen atom (H) arranged in a special way. It is thought that this molecular structure selectively interacts with special parts of some taste receptors to cause them to respond (see Bartoshuk, 1979). Bitter taste is closely related to sweet taste. Many substances that taste sweet in small amounts taste bitter in large amounts (for example, saccharine). Also, a number of chemicals containing nitrogen (such as strychnine, caffeine, quinine, and nicotine) taste bitter. The relationship between sweet and bitter is further strengthened by the fact that bitter tasting

molecules also often contain an AB,H system. In bitter substances, however, the components have a different spatial arrangement than they do in sugars.

A salty taste is elicited by molecules that, when dissolved in water, break into two electrically charged parts called *ions*. For example, common table salt has two atoms, one sodium and one chlorine. When dissolved in water, the atoms break apart. The sodium atom is now a positively charged ion, and the chlorine atom is a negatively charged ion. The ratio of the weights of these positively and negatively charged ions may be related to how salty a substance tastes. When the ratio is relatively low, substances taste salty. A high ratio is associated with substances that taste bitter (see Wyburn, Pickford, and Hirst, 1964). In very low concentrations, salts tend to taste sweet. Finally, we have the sour taste. Sour substances also break into two parts when in solution, but they are usually acids (such as hydrochloric, sulphuric, acetic, and nitric acid) rather than salts. In all these substances, hydrogen is the positively charged ion. The behavior of the hydrogen seems to be directly related to the sourness of such acids, but other properties must also be important because most acids taste sweet or bitter instead of sour. Thus, while we can relate some aspects of chemical stimuli to the tastes they produce, this relationship is not simple. A taste is probably the result of several different properties of the physical stimulus interacting with the properties of the receptor cells (see for example, Faurion, Saito, and MacLeod, 1980).

The major receptors for taste are groups of cells called **taste buds**. The taste buds are located in little bumps on the tongue called **papillae**. Although three different types of papillae contain taste buds, there is no simple relationship between their locations and their sensitivity to different taste sensations. There are also some taste receptors scattered over

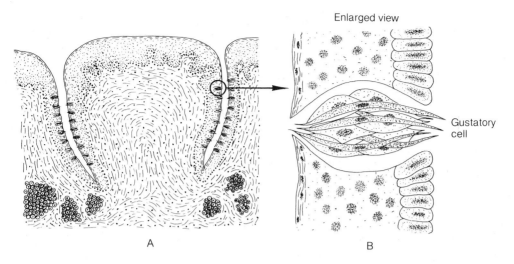

Figure 5-1. (A) A typical papilla with taste buds (one is circled). (B) Enlarged picture of a single taste bud (from Wyburn et al., 1964).

parts of the mouth other than the tongue, but they do not seem to play a major role (except perhaps in wine tasting and other gourmet activities). Figure 5-1A shows the distribution of the taste buds within one kind of papilla. Each taste bud consists of several receptor cells (perhaps as many as 30) arranged like the closed petals of a flower (Figure 5-1B). There are about ten thousand taste buds in your mouth when you are young, although their number decreases with age.

Within each taste bud, the individual cells are continually developing. Each cell has a life span of only a few days, so the composition of the taste bud changes continuously, with some immature cells (around the outside), some mature cells (near the inside), and some dying cells always present (Beidler and Smallman, 1965). No one knows why these cells have such a short life span; perhaps they are somehow damaged when they respond to substances in the mouth. Each taste cell in the taste bud is a leaflike cell that resembles a skin cell (from which it probably evolved). A slender projection from the top end of each

cell lies near an opening onto the surface of the tongue called a **taste pore**. It is thought that the actual reception mechanism for taste is located in these slender processes. Presumably, some aspect of the stimulating substance causes a change in the cell wall of the taste cell, which in turn causes the cell to generate an electrical current and stimulate the nerve cell(s) connected to it. Because there are several different taste qualities, there may be several specialized receptor processes that encode taste information. A number of theories for the action of such receptor processes have been proposed recentiy (Bartoshuk, 1978; Kennedy and Halpern, 1980; Tancredi, Lelj, and Temussi, 1979); however, the issue is still controversial.

Neural responses in taste

Three large nerves carry fibers from the taste buds. They run from the tongue to the *solitary nucleus*, which is located in the brain stem (the lower back part of the brain). From the solitary nucleus in the brain stem, taste information is carried to the thalamus, and from there to the area of the sensory cortex that receives information from the region of the face.

As in vision and audition, most of our knowledge of the electrical activity of the taste system has come from studies of nonhuman animals. A variety of studies has shown that taste fibers respond to an increasing intensity (concentration) of the stimulus by increasing their overall rate of firing. One of the few studies that actually used human subjects for direct recording (Diamant, Funakoshi, Strom, and Zotterman, 1963) capitalized on the fact that taste pathways from the front of the tongue must be cut during one type of ear surgery. Electrical activity in response to taste stimuli was recorded from this nerve during the operation. The data from these patients show that the amount of neural response grows as the logarithm of the intensity of the stimulus (in this case, table salt), much like the responses in vision and audition to increasing stimulus intensity (see Chapters 3 and 4). As in most modalities, the neural code for intensity seems to be the overall amount of firing of all the sensory fibers.

How is taste *quality* encoded? At first it was thought that there would be "sweet receptors," "salt receptors," and so on, one for each taste quality. Most receptor cells, however, seem to respond to all four basic kinds of taste stimuli although at different rates (Arvidson and Friberg, 1980; Kimura and Beidler, 1961). The same sort of responsiveness to most stimulus types has been found in the solitary nucleus and in the thalamus as well (Doetsch, Ganchrow, Nelson, and Erikson, 1969; Scott and Erickson, 1971).

Actually, there is no theoretical need for specialized taste receptors as long as the various neural units have different stimulus-specific response rates. If this condition is met, then the code for taste quality could be an **across-fiber pattern** of neural activity (Erickson and Schiffman, 1975; Pfaffman, 1955). Figure 5-2 shows how this might work. Notice that although all the fibers respond to all taste inputs to some extent, the pattern of firing across the four diagramed fibers is different for each quality. Thus, for a sugar stimulus (S) we find fiber *A* responding vigorously, *B* moderately, and *C* and *D* only weakly. For salt (NaCl), *A* and *D* respond weakly, while *B* responds strongly and *C* nearly as vigorously. Erickson (1963) was actually able to show such distinct across-fiber pattern differences. These patterns become somewhat less distinct in the thalamus (Doetsch et al., 1969; Scott and Erickson, 1971).

Although there do not seem to be taste receptors that respond only to one of the four basic taste qualities, different gustatory nerve fibers seem to be "tuned" to certain taste stimuli, much as auditory nerve fibers are tuned to certain frequencies of sound (see Chapter 4). Such fibers respond most vigorously to their "best" substances and less vigorously to others. Eventually, it may be possible to classify such fibers into a few classes, corresponding to the basic taste qualities (Frank, 1975; Pfaffman, Frank, and Norgren, 1979). The response patterns shown in Figure 5-2 could thus also be interpreted as those characteristic of such tuned fiber types. On the basis of such data, Pfaffman (1974) proposed the **labeled-line theory** of taste quality encoding. The basic idea is that each taste fiber encodes the intensity of a single basic taste quality, that associated with its "best" stimulus. To the extent that a stimulus activates the "sweet" fibers, it tastes sweet; to the extent it activates the "bitter" fibers, it tastes bitter. This means that such a "simple" stimulus as NaCl could have a complex taste if it activated several types of fibers and this seems to happen. For example, salts tend to taste both salty and sour (Bartoshuk,

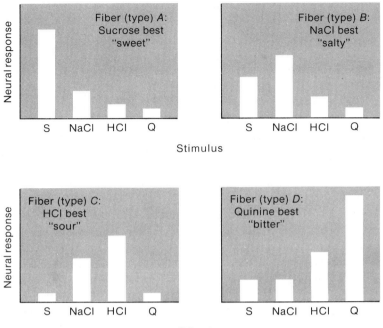

Figure 5-2. *Using the across-fiber pattern theory, consider each graph to represent the response of a unique taste fiber to the various stimuli. Using the labeled-line theory, consider each graph to represent the average response of a group of more-or-less equivalent taste fibers.*

1978). This theory is compatible with the across-fiber pattern approach, except that here the code for taste quality is a profile across a few fiber types rather than a pattern across many thousands of unique fibers.

Although it is unknown whether labeled-lines exist along the entire taste pathway, cortical neurons most responsive to the four basic tastes seem to be localized in different parts of the taste cortex (Yamamoto, Yayama, and Kawamura, 1981). Furthermore, it is likely that some recoding of the taste information takes place in the cortex. There may be specific cortical cells that give an "on" response to some taste stimuli and an "off" response to others, similar to the feature-specific cells in the visual cortex discussed in Chapter 3 (Funakoshi, Kasahara, Yamamoto, and Kawamura, 1972).

THE OLFACTORY (SMELL) SENSE

When we have a bad head cold, food seems flavorless, and yet it is our nasal passages that are most affected by the cold, not our mouths, where the taste receptors are located. A major part of the experienced flavor of food and drink is caused by the odor of the substance (Brillat-Savarin, 1971/1825; Hyman, Mentyer, and Calderone, 1979; Murphy and Cain, 1980). When our nasal passages are clogged with mucus, our olfactory (smell) receptors cannot function properly. This affects both our ability to smell and to experience flavor; much of the richness and subtlety of our experiences with food and drink come from their odors.

Some organisms that live in water have two anatomically different types of organs that respond to dissolved chemicals. Life on land has exploited the fact that one of these systems also responds to the molecules of various types that are continually floating about in the air. These molecules carry information about the organisms or objects from which they have been detached. For instance, we leave molecules of ourselves on the ground and in the air near the ground wherever we walk. Insects and some higher animals secrete volatile chemicals (pheromones) whose molecules waft through the air to other members of the species. The specific molecules secreted can carry messages about fear and sexual availability, among other things (see Chapter 9). Species that possess sensory systems that respond to such low concentrations of molecules in the air can take advantage of this information, hence improving their ability to survive.

Smell stimuli and receptors

What aspects of a molecule give it the quality of evoking the sensation of smell? First, it must come from a volatile substance (one that has a gaseous state at ordinary temperatures—in other words something that can evaporate) because air currents carry the molecules to the smell receptors in the nose. The most volatile substances, however, do not necessarily smell the strongest. Water, which has a high volatility, has no smell at all. In fact, the extent to which a smell stimulus separates itself chemically from water (hydrophobicity) is highly correlated with the perceived intensity of that

stimulus (Greenberg, 1981). On the other hand, musk, which has a low volatility, is quite a powerful odorant. Musk is used to make some of our most expensive perfumes.

In general, any molecules may be described as having a specific size, weight, shape, or *vibration frequency*. Vibration frequency has to do with the fact that atoms in a given molecule are not held firmly in place but move around in a characteristic pattern at predictable speeds that are different for different substances. Wright (1977, 1982) has suggested that the vibration frequency may be the critical property that determines the quality of a smell. We can measure the vibration frequency of a molecule by determining how infrared light (light with a wavelength longer than 700 nm) is absorbed by the substance. Such measurements are quite useful in predicting smell responses to various substances. Substances that have similar infrared absorption characteristics (that is, vibrate at the same frequencies) seem to have similar smells (Wright and Burgess, 1975).

Another possible critical property of smell molecules is the shape of the molecule (Amoore, Johnston, and Rubin, 1964). Although an old suggestion, in its modern form it is proposed that there are submicroscopic indentations of different shapes on the receptor surface, and only molecules of a certain "shape" can fit into these indentations (as a key fits into a lock). When the molecule fits into the corresponding indentation it changes the state of the cell membrane and produces a neural response. Given the complexity of smells, it seems likely that all these different properties we have been discussing play a part in our sensory response to odorous molecules.

The receptor cells that interact with the smell stimuli are located in a relatively small area in the upper nasal passages (see Figure 5-3). This area is called the **olfactory epithelium**, which actually translates to "smell skin." The

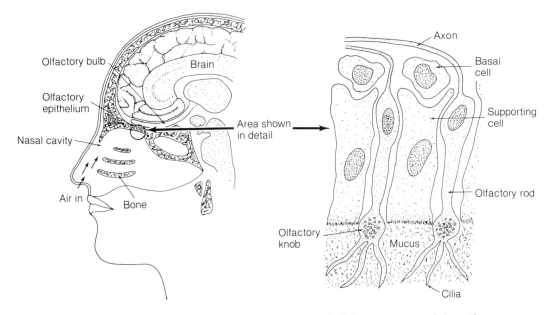

Figure 5-3. Anatomy of the olfactory system and a detail of the structure of the olfactory epithelium.

actual receptor cells are oval in shape. Each sends a long extension (called the **olfactory rod**) toward the surface of the olfactory epithelium. In addition, the receptors send their axons toward the brain. The olfactory rod of the receptor cells reaches up toward the surface of the epithelium, where it expands to form a knob. From this knob protrude a number of **olfactory cilia**, which are hairlike structures embedded in mucus secreted by a set of special glands found nowhere else in the nasal passages. These cilia are probably the receptor elements that make contact with the smell stimulus (Cagan and Rein, 1980). Both the number of cilia per receptor and the total number of receptors seem to be correlated with olfactory sensitivity. Animals that have more receptors and more cilia per receptor have much keener senses of smell than do humans. Humans are at the lower end of the scale of smell sensitivity. For example, a dog

has about 100 million olfactory receptors as opposed to only about 5 million in humans. Also, a dog has 100−150 cilia per receptor as opposed to a paltry 6−8 cilia in humans (Brown, 1975).

The mechanism by which the stimulus molecules cause an electrical response in the receptors of the olfactory epithelium is still a mystery. There are two major theories, based on two of the physical properties of odorous molecules that we have mentioned already. The **lock-and-key theory** maintains that molecules of various shapes fit into special sites on the receptor membrane (probably on the cilia or the knobs from which they protrude) like a key fits into a lock. When a molecule fits into a receptor site, a change in the structure of the cell membrane results, perhaps allowing electrically charged substances into or out of the cell and generating an electrical current (Amoore, 1970). The **vibration**

theory maintains that the stimulus molecule ruptures certain chemical bonds in the cell membrane, causing the release of stored-up energy, which in turn generates an electrical current. Which bonds are ruptured in which cells depends on the unique vibration frequency of each stimulus molecule. Again, the interaction should take place in the cilia (Wright, 1977, 1982).

In the lock-and-key theory, once a stimulus molecule has served as a key for a particular lock, it would be stuck there. In the vibration theory, a single stimulus molecule could bounce along over the olfactory epithelium like a rubber ball, having broken chemical bonds in cell after cell (causing them to give a neural response) without being detained by any of them. This latter mechanism is consistent with the high sensitivity of the olfactory sense, which can respond to the presence of only a few molecules of a volatile substance. For example, a dog can detect butyric acid (contained in sweat) at a concentration of 1 g spread throughout the entire volume of air above a city the size of Boston, up to a height of 100 m (Droscher, 1971). One difficulty of the vibration theory, however, is that the stimulus molecule may have to penetrate the mucous covering in order to contact the receptor cell. This would make it unlikely that a single molecule could move very far over the receptor surface. This is no problem at all, however, for the lock-and-key theory.

Neural responses in smell

The olfactory receptor cells send their axons through tiny holes in a bone at the top of the nasal cavity to form the **olfactory nerve**. The nerve goes straight to the **olfactory bulb**, which is located in front of and below the main mass of the brain (see Figure 5-3). The axons of the receptors and the dendrites of cells from the olfactory bulb form complex clusters of connections in the bulb. These clusters may be grouped according to the type of receptor involved (Kauer, 1980). One type of olfactory bulb cell seems to send axons directly to the primary sensory cortex for smell, which is located on the temporal lobe of the cortex. Another type of cell sends axons to a variety of lower brain centers, as well as to the smell cortex. The number of fibers leaving the olfactory bulb is *much* smaller (about a thousand times smaller) than the number entering it, so presumably many receptor cells contribute to the activity of each of the cells in the olfactory bulb and later centers (Allison, 1953). The major route of information from the olfactory bulb to the smell cortex is called the **lateral olfactory tract**. After the primary smell cortex, the neural pathways become extremely complex and are not well understood.

The electrophysiology of the olfactory system has not been studied thoroughly; as we mentioned earlier, however, a number of studies have found that the intensity of the neural response varies directly with the intensity of the stimulus. Most contemporary investigators have focused on the more subtle problem of how different smell qualities are signaled to the brain. They have tried to find evidence of specific types of receptors for different types of stimuli. One major study was that of Ottoson (1956), who measured the electrical response of the entire olfactory epithelium to various stimuli. He discovered that passing a puff of odor-laden air across the epithelium resulted in a unique type of electrical response, a slow change in the electrical charge of the receptor cells. This change is thought to generate spike potentials in the axons of these cells.

With improved experimental techniques, Gesteland, Lettvin, Pitts, and Rojas (1963) were able to record the responses of single receptors in the olfactory epithelium. They recorded both the slow potential response to

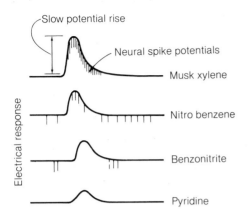

Figure 5-4. Slow potential and spike potential responses of olfactory receptor cells to four different smell stimuli (based on Gesteland et al., 1963).

stimuli and the spike potentials generated in the axons of the receptors by the same stimuli. These two types of electrical responses are shown one on top of the other in Figure 5-4. As you can see in the figure, this particular receptor responded vigorously to a musky odor, less to nitrobenzene, hardly at all to benzonitrite, and not at all to pyridine. The researchers (Gesteland et al., 1963) thought these responses indicated the existence of the sought after receptor types, although they were cautious in making this interpretation. Such caution seems to have been well founded, since later recordings from single cells in the epithelium, olfactory bulb, and in cortical and lower brain centers that receive olfactory information have tended to indicate that each neural unit responds to a broad range of stimuli (Giachetti and MacLeod, 1975; Cain and Bindra, 1972; MacLeod, 1971; O'Connell and Mozell, 1969). The same sort of across-fiber patterns that are found in taste seem to be present in the olfactory system, and it seems likely that the "code" for smell qualities will be found in these patterns (Erickson and Schiffman, 1975). At present there

is no evidence that olfactory fibers fall into groups like the taste fibers. Furthermore, a labeled-line theory for olfaction based on such a grouping would be somewhat cumbersome, requiring many more types of labeled lines than for taste, since a small list of primary smells does not exist for olfaction (see Chapter 9).

THE CUTANEOUS (SKIN) SENSES

All living things have a "skin" of some kind. Probably the most important function of the skin is to *define* the organism, that is, to set boundaries in space, inside of which exists the organism and outside of which exists the environment. The skin is an *interface* (a place where two systems meet) between the organism and the environment, and it is in intimate contact with it. In the most primitive one-celled organisms, the skin is the cell membrane, and it is responsible for all the organism's contacts with its environment. These contacts include such functions as taking in food, excreting waste, isolating the inside of the cell from damaging outside substances, and responding to all sorts of external stimuli. Although more advanced organisms, such as mammals (including humans), have more specialized organs to handle these tasks, their skins are also complex and important organs. The skin plays a role in respiration, temperature regulation, and protection. It also has a wide variety of sensory functions, and produces the sensations we call touch, heat or cold, and pain.

Skin stimuli and receptors

The skin responds to a variety of physical stimuli. When we press an object against the skin,

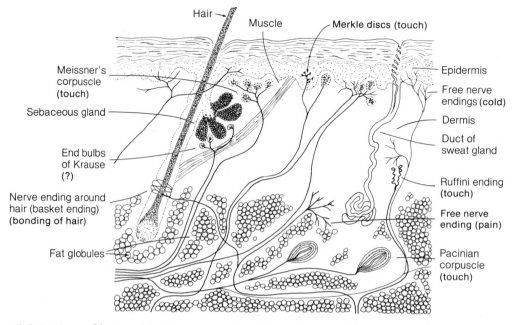

Figure 5-5. A piece of hairy skin in cross section (based on Woolard, Weddell, and Harpman, 1940).

it deforms the surface and we experience the sensation of touch, or pressure. When an object makes contact with a hair, causing it to bend, we also experience touch. The temperature of the object with which we touch the skin also elicits a sensation. Whether it is warmth or cold depends both upon the temperature of the stimulus and upon the temperature of the skin (see Chapter 9). Finally, the skin responds to electrical stimulation. For mild stimulation, a type of touch sensation is usually felt, although temperature can also be experienced. When the stimulation becomes intense, the sensation usually becomes painful.

In humans the skin has a very complex structure. Figure 5-5 is a diagram of the most important structures in **hairy skin** that covers most of the human body. A different kind of skin, found on the palms of the hands, soles of the feet, fingers and toes, and other places, has no hairs protruding from it. This is called

glabrous skin. Although there is a thick outer layer of dead cells in glabrous skin, there are also many free nerve endings embedded in this layer. This makes such skin effective protection but also extremely sensitive to stimulation. All skin consists of two basic layers. The outer layer, called the **epidermis**, consists of several layers of tough dead cells that lie on top of a single inner layer of living cells. The inner layer divides constantly to generate the protective layers above. The inner layer, called the **dermis**, contains most of the nerve endings in the skin. Under these two layers is usually a layer of fat cells. In addition to these layers, the skin contains a variety of hairs, muscles, glands, arteries, veins, and capillaries. Some of these elements are shown in Figure 5-5.

Figure 5-5 also shows some of the most common nerve endings in the skin. Although it is certain that at least some of these nerve endings are the receptors for the skin sensations, it

has been difficult to specify exactly which ending is responsible for which sensation. In fact,
all the nerve endings seem to respond somewhat to all the different types of stimulation.
Although some researchers argue that these
different types of nerve endings are merely histological or neurological artifacts (see Geldard,
1972), some progress has been made in asso-
ciating various receptor types with nerve fibers that have different response characteristics and that respond selectively to mechanical,
thermal, or painful stimuli. In particular, most
"corpuscular" endings (nerve endings with
small bodies or swellings on the dendrites),
including the Pacinian corpuscles, Meissner
corpuscles, Merkle discs, and Ruffini endings,
seem to be associated with various types of fibers selectively responsive to touch stimuli.
Noncorpuscular, or so called "**free**," **nerve
endings** in subcutaneous fat are associated
with pain fibers (see Vierck, 1978). Free nerve
endings projecting into the epidermis seem to
be associated with cold fibers (Hensel, 1981).
Modern electrophysiological and histological
techniques should succeed eventually in identifying the nerve endings associated with the
several types of nerve fibers that exist farther
along in the touch pathways. Much progress
has already been made with regard to Merkle
discs and Pacinian corpuscles (Gottschaldt and
Vahle-Hinz, 1981).

As an example of how a skin receptor responds to stimulation, let us consider the **Pacinian corpuscle** (see Figures 5-5 and 5-6).
The Pacinian corpuscle has been studied extensively because it is large, easily accessible,
and occurs in nearly all animals that have complex nervous systems. The elegant work of
Loewenstein and his colleagues (see Loewenstein, 1960) involved peeling away the surrounding layers of the cell (much as we would
peel an onion) to allow a mechanical stimulus
to touch the axon itself. They were able to
show that such a stimulus operates directly

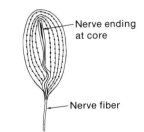

Figure 5-6. A Pacinian corpuscle.

on the axon of the nerve by deforming its
membrane. This mechanical action causes numerous tiny holes in the membrane to open,
allowing electrically charged particles to flow
from one side of the membrane to the other.
This process in turn causes an electrical current to flow between the point of stimulation
and another point on the axon. Finally, this
electrical current generates a spike potential
that jumps along the axon and carries the message of stimulation to the brain. The surrounding layers of material in the Pacinian corpuscle
seem to be present simply to make the effect
of the stimulus less intense. Temperature could
act in a similar way, perhaps by controlling
chemical reactions that would affect the ability
of electrically charged particles to cross the
cell's membrane. Electrical stimuli probably
trigger spike potentials directly. We do not
know whether this is the case for all the cutaneous nerve endings, but it is reasonable to
suppose that they all operate in a similar way.

Neural responses in the skin senses

Because there are so many different types of
nerve endings in the skin, you might think that
the nerve pathways to the brain would be
hopelessly complex. They are complex, and
yet there is a simple organizational plan at
work. The plan depends on two major

principles associated with the type of nerve fiber and the place of termination.

The type of nerve fiber is important because different types of nerve fibers carry different types of information to the brain. Fibers can be classified in at least three ways: (a) according to the type of stimulus that excites them (mechanical, temperature, or noxious), (b) according to the way they respond to those stimuli (slow or fast adapting), and (c) according to whether they have large, ill-defined receptive fields or small, well-defined ones. For example, in humans, at least four different types of fibers respond to mechanical deformation of glabrous skin: rapidly adapting fibers with small, well-defined receptive fields; similar, but slowly adapting fibers; slowly adapting fibers with large, ill-defined receptive fields; and rapidly adapting fibers with large, ill-defined receptive fields (Vallbo, 1981). Such fibers are reminiscent of the sustained versus transient activities of the X and Y fibers that leave the retina of the eye (see Chapter 3).

The second major principle is that *where* on the skin a particular nerve ends determines where its information goes in the brain, regardless of the type of fiber it represents. All the sensory information from the skin is passed to the spinal cord through 30 pairs of nerves (one member of each pair for each side of the body). There are also four cranial nerves that collect cutaneous information from the head region. These inputs are gathered into two main pathways to the brain, which carry different types of information.

The first system is called the **lemniscal system**. The nerve fibers that make up this path are large and conduct information quickly. The inputs are passed through the **medulla**, then the **thalamus**, and finally arrive at the sensory cortex, located in the **parietal region** of the brain (the upper central region). An interesting aspect of the lemniscal system is that the inputs from the right side of the body termi-

nate on the left side of the brain, and vice versa. This system has fibers that respond mostly to touch and movement, although temperature fibers have also been found (Hensel, 1981).

The second major pathway is called the **spinothalamic system**. This pathway is rather slow and is made up of many short fibers instead of a few long axons. It also passes through the thalamus (but through a different area), and then moves through the **reticular formation** to the sensory cortex. It seems to have relatively equal inputs to both sides of the brain. This pathway carries information about temperature as well as touch. Some recent evidence suggests that one of its prime functions is to convey the sensation of pain (discussed in the last section of this chapter).

An important property of the skin is the fact that sensory activity in one region can interfere with sensory activity in nearby regions. If the distance between two stimuli is appropriate, a reduction may even occur in the perceived magnitude of the sensation. It seems that the receptive fields in the skin have the same sort of excitatory-center, inhibitory-surround organization observed in the visual system (Békésy, 1967). Demonstration Box 5-1 shows how you can experience this phenomenon yourself with touch stimuli.

The relationship between regions of the body that are stimulated and cortical regions of the brain that respond to the stimulation is quite regular. One classic "map" of these relationships was created by Penfield and Rasmussen (1950). These investigators electrically stimulated the sensory cortex of patients during brain operations. As various points on the cortex were stimulated, the patients reported the sensations that they felt, for example, the tingling of one leg. The resulting sensory map of the body is shown in Figure 5-7. Notice that the spatial location of stimulation on the skin is preserved in the

Demonstration Box 5-1. Inhibitory interactions on the skin

In this demonstration you will see how skin sensations interact. You will need two fairly sharply pointed objects such as two toothpicks or two bristles from a hairbrush. The demonstration will work better if you ask a friend to control the stimuli. Do not use anything like a knife, for you will be pushing the point quite strongly against your skin. First, try pressing one point against the skin of your palm. Notice the spread of sensation around the stimulated point. Now put the two points as close together as you possibly can. Push them together on the same place on your palm. Notice that you feel only one point, although two are present. Now move the two stimulating points slightly apart. You should *still* feel only one point. Repeat this procedure several times, moving the points apart by a little more each time and paying careful attention to whether the sensation feels like two points or one on your skin. If you are pushing hard enough and paying close attention to your sensations, at just about the separation where the two points begin to feel like two distinct points on the skin, you should have a surprising experience. The magnitude of the sensation from the two points should diminish greatly, perhaps vanish altogether for a short time. The sensation should be very faint, even though two toothpicks (or brush bristles) are pushing with some force

against the skin. As you then move the points even farther apart, you will perceive two distinct, full strength sensations, appropriately separate on the skin. This phenomenon is explained by the overlapping of regions of excitation and inhibition in adjacent receptive fields of the skin, as shown in the accompanying figure.

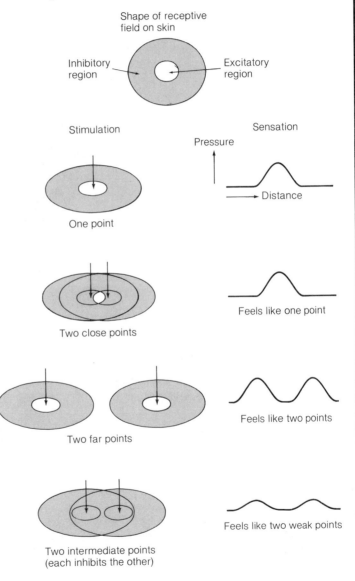

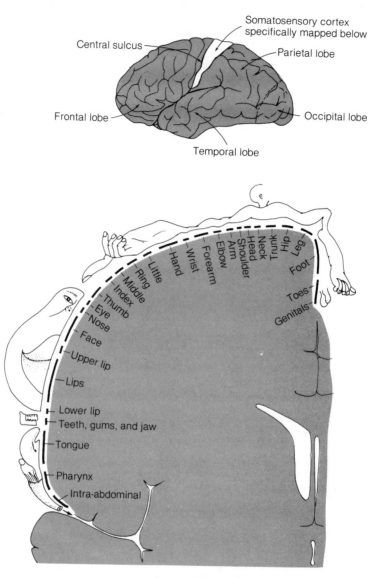

Sensory homunculus

Figure 5-7. Penfield and Rasmussen's (1950) topographic map of projections of "touch" nerve fibers on the sensory cortex. The length of the line next to the drawing of each body part is proportional to the area of sensory cortex subserving that body part (from W. Penfield and T. Rasmussen, The Cerebral Cortex of Man. Copyright 1950 by Macmillan Publishing Co., Inc., renewed 1978 by Theodore Rasmussen).

spatial location of activity in the cortex. More recently, details of how the cells in the touch cortex encode information about touch stimuli are being revealed. For example, these cells respond to movement of ridges across the skin in much the same way cells in the visual cortex respond to moving edges in the visual field (Darian-Smith, Dreyer, Hollins, and Young, 1982; Whitsel, Sugitani, Heywood, Karita, and Goodwin, 1979). You can experience one of the consequences of a cortical map that encodes the stimulation of adjacent regions of the skin into adjacent cortical locations of activity by trying Demonstration Box 5-2.

The skin responds not only to touch, but also to temperature. Two types of nerve fibers seem to respond when the skin is cooled or warmed. **Cold fibers** respond to cooling of the skin with an increase in firing relative to their resting rate, and to warming with a firing decrease. **Warm fibers** respond to warming with an increase in firing rate and to cooling with decreased firing (see Hensel, 1981). Also, after an initial change in firing rate in the direction appropriate to the type of stimulus and the type of receptor, both types of fibers gradually adopt a steady rate of firing. This "resting" rate is related to the *absolute* temperature of the skin (and thus of the receptor).

Cold and warm fibers have different patterns of response over a broad range of skin temperatures. This is shown in Figure 5-8, which is from the work of Zotterman (1959). As you can see in the figure, the cold fibers respond in the range from about 13 to 35°C (55 to 95°F) and again from about 45 to 50°C (113 to 122°F). Above this limit the receptors become damaged and the response falls off. Warm receptors respond from about 23°C to about 47°C (73 to 117°F) with a peak at about 38° C (just above body temperature at 100°F). The cold fibers have peaks at about 25°C (77°F) and again at about 50°C (122°F). These *steady-state* responses provide information about the absolute temperature of the skin. This information is quite important since internal body temperature must be maintained within a narrow range of values (around 37°C or 98.6°F) (see Hensel, 1981). Demonstration Box 5-3 allows you to experience the consequences of

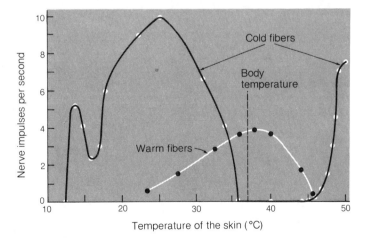

Figure 5-8. Steady discharge of cold and warm fibers in the cat as it varies with skin temperature (based on Zotterman, 1959).

Demonstration Box 5-2. Aristotle's illusion

The famous Greek philosopher-scientist Aristotle noticed an interesting illusion of touch that is quite easy to demonstrate. Hold your fingers as shown in Figure A and touch the point between them with a pencil as shown. Notice that you feel one item touching you and the sensation of one single touch. Now cross your fingers as shown in Figure B, touching yourself again with a pencil in the place indicated between the fingers. Notice that you feel two distinct touches. The effect may be stronger if you close your eyes during the touches. The simplest and most plausible explanation of the illusion is that when the pencil is stimulating the insides of the two fingers (Figure A), the touch information is being sent to overlapping or adjacent areas of the touch cortex, resulting in the sensation of one touch. When the pencil is stimulating the outsides of the two fingers because of your finger contortions, the information is being sent to two separate areas of the touch cortex, allowing you to experience two distinct touches. Such a cortical mapping is quite reasonable, since commonly a single object between two fingers would be expected to stimulate adjacent skin surfaces, hence should be encoded as a single touch source. It is normally not possible, however, for a single object to stimulate the outsides of two different fingers, and so two different touches should be experienced in these circumstances. The cortical mapping reflects these common situations.

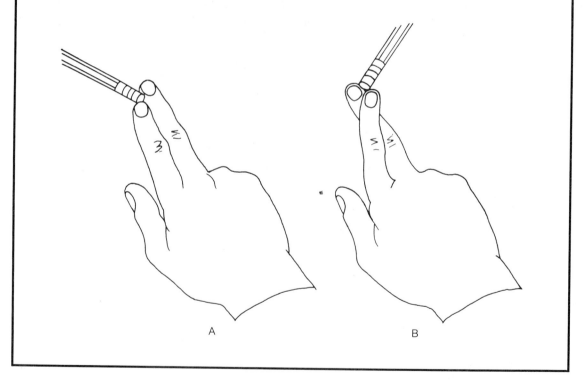

A   B

Demonstration Box 5-3. The heat grill

For this demonstration you will need two pipe cleaners bent as shown in Figure *A*. Be careful to bend the pipe cleaners so that they fit together closely when both are laid on a table, as shown in Figure *B*. Place one pipe cleaner in a glass of cool water and the other in a glass of very warm (not unpleasantly hot) water. Take the pipe cleaner out of the glass of cool water, and place it on a flat surface. Working quickly, take the pipe cleaner out of the glass of warm water and arrange it to form the configuration shown as Figure *B*. As soon as this is done, place your forearm over the set of pipe cleaners and press down as shown in Figure *C*. The temperature sensation you receive will probably be quite surprising. Although the stimulus consists of alternately cool and warm surfaces,

you will feel no coolness. Observers usually get a sensation of an intense stinging heat. Some people may find the heat sensation sufficiently intense to cause them to withdraw their arm. The temperatures of the pipe cleaners are such (if you followed directions faithfully) that receptors of both cold and warm fibers in the same general area of the skin are being stimulated near their optimum. Usually this does not happen. When it does, you mislead your brain by making both the cold and the warm fibers fire near their maxima. The brain processes this information as emanating from a single, very hot stimulus. (Note in Figure 5-8 that for very hot stimuli, the cold fibers would be firing vigorously as well as the warm fibers.)

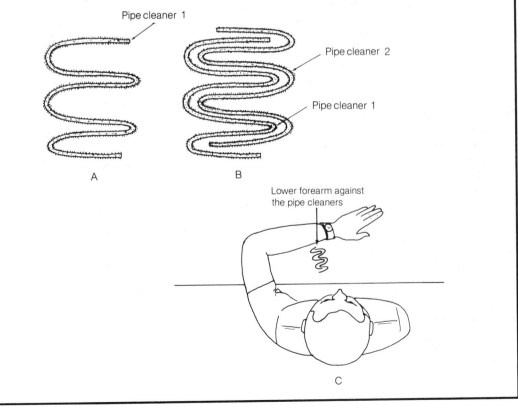

Pipe cleaner 1

Pipe cleaner 2

Pipe cleaner 1

A

B

Lower forearm against
the pipe cleaners

C

having both cold and warm fibers stimulated optimally, something that usually only happens when the skin reaches temperatures dangerous to its integrity.

THE KINESTHETIC SENSES

Thus far we have been talking about receptors that respond to information generated by the world around us. Now we shall consider some of the sensory information generated within our own bodies. In this section we will discuss some of the more general systems that signal whether we are moving or stationary, inform us of the position of body parts, and also tell us something of the body's chemical state.

One of the things that distinguishes animal from plant life is the ability to move about in the world. In higher organisms, specialized receptor systems inform the brain about the position of the limbs or the orientation of the body. The bodies of such organisms (including humans) are literally enmeshed in a web of sensory receptors, which accurately monitor the positions of various parts so that appropriate action can be initiated. In many cases the signals of these sensory systems are not perceived consciously, but rather they are used in controlling reflex actions that maintain an upright posture.

Kinesthetic stimuli and receptors

The overt physical stimulus to which the kinesthetic system responds is movement (the root *kine* is from the Greek word for movement). Some information about position is available, however, even when no movement is taking place. This information is generated by our continuous battle against gravity. Both

movement and postural responses involve tension, compression, or twisting forces on the muscles, tendons, or joints of limbs. These physical forces should be considered the stimuli for kinesthesis. Any position of the body, even supine and fully relaxed, results in a complex pattern of muscular tensions and compressions and the consequent mechanical forces acting on tendons and joints. The relative intensities of the various forces, or changes in those intensities over time, signal body movement and posture.

Just as in the surface layers of the skin, a great many sensory receptors are scattered throughout the body. First, at least two types of nerve endings exist in the deeper layers of tissue beneath the skin: **free nerve endings** and **Pacinian corpuscles** (both of which we encountered in the last section). The free nerve endings are thought to be responsible for pain sensations. The Pacinian corpuscles provide our sense of deep pressure (which can be felt even when the overlying skin has been anesthetized). A variety of other specialized receptors (such as a carbon dioxide sensor) are located on or in many of our vital organs. Although the visceral organs themselves are rather insensitive to touch, temperature, or pain stimuli (with the obvious exception of the stretching or twisting forces that cause, for example, gas pains), these organs are surrounded by muscle. This muscle is supplied with a variety of nerve endings that are responsive to the movements of the viscera. Finally, a number of types of nerve endings are located in and around our joints in the muscles that move our limbs.

Matthews (1933) divided the receptors in the muscles into three major types, two of which are shown in Figure 5-9. His first type is called the A endings, which have two subtypes. The A_1 endings are often called "flower-spray" endings because they look like a bou-

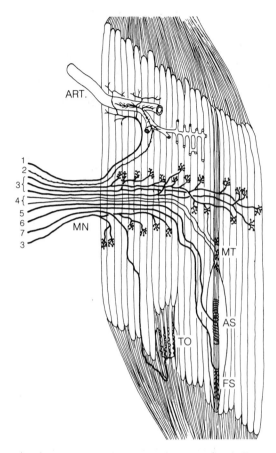

Figure 5-9. Nerve endings in muscle. 1, Free nerve endings around an artery; 2, efferent nerves that regulate the size of the artery; 3, motor nerves that cause the muscle to contract; 4, more motor nerves; 5, Matthews type A₂, or annulospiral, nerve endings on a muscle spindle; 6, Matthews type A₁, or flower-spray, nerve endings on the same muscle spindle; 7, Matthews type B, or Golgi tendon organs, nerve endings on a muscle tendon. Matthews type C endings, or Pacinian corpuscles, are not shown (from Creed, Denny-Brown, Eccles, Liddell, and Sherrington, 1932).

quet of flowers against the muscles where they synapse. The A₂ type are wound around strands of muscle fibers called muscle spindles. Both types respond to stretching of the muscle and therefore have been called **stretch receptors**, or **spindle organs**, since they both attach to muscle spindles. This type of nerve ending is found also in great numbers in the joints between limbs. Matthews's second type, the B endings, look much like the flower-spray endings but are attached to the tendons that connect the muscles to the bones. B endings are also called **Golgi tendon organs**. They respond to both stretching and contraction of the muscle, while the spindle organs respond only to stretching. Matthews's third type of receptor, which he labeled C, is thought to be the Pacinian corpuscle (Geldard, 1972). Although important in the cutaneous senses, the C receptor probably plays little role in kinesthesis. There seem to be few such Pacinian corpuscles in muscles or near joints. In addition to all the above receptors, muscles and joints are well supplied with the free nerve ending that may be responsible for pain sensations in these areas.

Neural responses in kinethesis

The variety of receptors we have described send their messages to the brain by way of the two major neural pathways described previously for touch: the lemniscal system and the spinothalamic system. Most of the fibers follow the lemniscal pathway, except for the free nerve endings, many of which follow the spinothalamic pathway. There are also a great many branchings and interactions of these two pathways with others of less importance. The nerves that terminate on muscles or tendons and in joints project to the same region of the cortex we described for the skin senses. Thus, information about stimuli touching the skin of the arm and about the position and movement of the arm are both projected to the same area of the cortex. The cutaneous information, however, is kept separate from the position and movement information even at the cortical level (see Vierck, 1978).

Let us look at the signals generated by these kinesthetic receptors. Figure 5-10 shows an electrophysiological recording from a nerve fiber that terminates in the knee joint of a cat. The limb is being bent and returned to its original position. The movement of the limb is signaled by a sudden change in neural re-

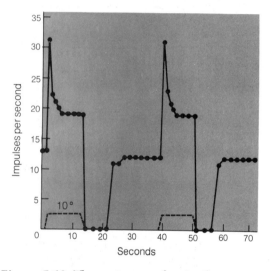

Figure 5-10. The response of a single nerve fiber that terminates in the knee joint of a cat. The dotted lines represent bending of the knee joint by 10 degrees. This "slow-adapting" fiber gives a large initial burst of impulses to the bending, which then gradually declines to a stable rate of firing above background (no bending). When the limb is "unbent," there is an inhibition of responses, so that nerve firing is below background rate, and then firing rate climbs back to the background rate (from Boyd and Roberts, 1953).

sponse rate. The size of the change indicates the speed of movement. The resting level of neural response signals the static position of the limb. Fibers that act in this manner are often called **slow-adapting fibers**, because it takes several seconds for them to find a new resting rate of firing corresponding to a new limb position. Cells with similar response characteristics are also found higher in the kinesthetic system at sites in the thalamus and cortex (Mountcastle, Poggio, and Werner, 1963; Mountcastle and Powell, 1959). In addition, more rapidly adapting fibers and "postural neurons" (which respond only when a joint is in a particular position) have been found in the cortexes of monkeys, along with neurons that act much like "feature-detectors" for the different limb components of particular postures (Costanzo and Gardner, 1981; Gardner and Costanzo, 1981). Virtually all positional and movement information comes from the receptors located in the joints (Adams, 1977). The other kinesthetic receptors may serve to give us the sensation of strain when lifting something, or of pain. Their major role seems to be to provide information to control our postural reflexes, automatically adjusting our muscle tension to the requirements of whatever load we are carrying.

THE VESTIBULAR SENSE

In the last section, we mentioned that much sensory input does not give rise to conscious sensations. In such cases, sensory information regulates various physiological states such as muscular tension. This is also true of the vestibular system. The vestibular system's major functions are to assist in the maintenance of an upright posture and to control eye position as we move our heads while viewing various

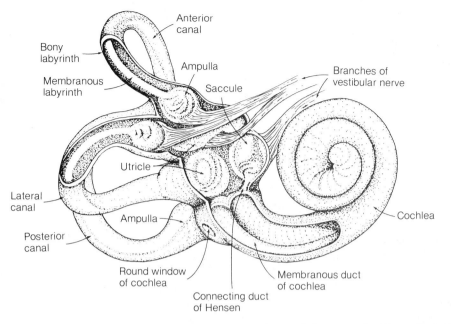

Figure 5-11. A diagram of the right inner ear showing the cochlea (which houses the auditory receptor), the semicircular canals, the *utricle, and the saccule (from F. A. Geldard,* **The Human Senses,** *2nd ed. New York: Wiley, 1972).*

stimuli. Neither one is a conscious operation.

Some of the most primitive organisms have organs that are sensitive to changes in motion of the body. In primitive invertebrates, such as the crayfish, these organs are called **statocysts**. Each consists of a fluid-filled cavity lined with hair cells. A tiny stone in the cavity called a **statolith**, or "still stone," rests on the hairs. When the animal accelerates, the stone lags behind because of its inertia, thus bending the hairs on which it rests. This action generates an electrical response to the movement. If the animal is tilted, the stone rolls along over a number of different hairs, bending them and generating a different response that indicates tilt. The function of such organs is to signal the animal's orientation with respect to gravity. More advanced invertebrates, such as squid and octopus, have statocysts that approach

vertebrate vestibular organs in complexity. Their statocysts are multichambered and have the ability to detect acceleration in several planes (Stephens and Young, 1982).

Primitive vertebrates have organs that have a similar function; they are called **otocysts**, and the bones they contain are called **otoliths**. Notice that these terms each contain the root *oto*, meaning ear. These organs are usually closely associated with the ears, since both the auditory receptors and the vestibular organs probably evolved from pits on the surface of hairy skin. In mammals, these organs are protected from damage by the skull. In humans, the **bony labyrinth** in the head contains the cochlea (which is the auditory organ) and the **semicircular canals**, the **utricle**, and the **saccule**, which make up the vestibular organs (see Figures 5-11 and 4-4).

Vestibular stimuli and receptors

The effective physical stimulus for the vestibular organ is a change in the rate of motion, or **acceleration**, like that which occurs when we jump up and down, spin in a barber chair, take off in a jet plane, or simply stand up and walk. The semicircular canals and their associated receptor organs seem particularly well suited for monitoring rotary acceleration (such as turning around or falling down). The other two organs, the utricle and the saccule, seem to respond primarily to linear acceleration (for example, when we take off in an airplane).

The movement-receptive portion of the semicircular canals is called the **crista** and is found in swellings (called **ampullae**) at the bases of the semicircular canals (Figure 5-11). The crista consists of an array of sensory cells from which tiny hairs protrude. This is shown in Figure 5-12A. The hairs are embedded in a jellylike material called the **cupola**. When the head accelerates, the fluid in the canals causes

the cupola to move. This in turn causes the hairs to bend, generating neural responses. As the head continues to move at a particular rate of speed, the cupola gradually comes back to its resting position, no longer bending the hairs, and no longer causing a response in the sensory cells. This is why the effective stimulus is acceleration rather than steady movement.

The receptor organ found in the utricle and the saccule is called the **macula**, shown in Figure 5-12B. It functions much like the statocyst we discussed before. As in the crista, tiny hairs protrude from the sensory cells in the macula. Embedded in a jellylike substance, these hairs lag behind when the head is accelerated, bending the hair cells and generating an electrical response to the acceleration. When the otoliths catch up to the rest of the head, which would happen if the acceleration ceased and motion became steady, the hairs are no longer bent. When this happens, no response is generated, even though the head may be traveling at

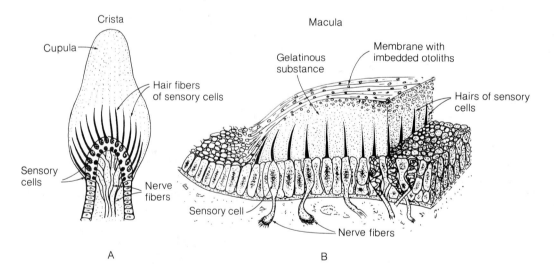

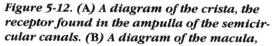

A   B

Figure 5-12. (A) A diagram of the crista, the receptor found in the ampulla of the semicircular canals. (B) A diagram of the macula, *the receptor found in the utricle and the saccule (from F. A. Geldard,* **The Human Senses,** *2nd ed. New York: Wiley, 1972).*

Demonstration Box 5-4. *Vestibular stimulation and eye movements*

For this demonstration you will need a friend and a little space. Have your friend hold her arms out and spin around (like a whirling ice skater) until she becomes dizzy. This continuous rotation sets up currents in the semicircular canals that trigger the compensatory eye movement system. Now stop your friend from turning and look into her eyes. You will notice that the eyes drift steadily in one direction, and then snap back and start to drift again. This type of repetitive eye movement is called **nystagmus**. It is a reflex movement that is evoked automatically by the vestibular stimulation caused by fluid currents in the semicircular canals.

---

thousands of kilometers per hour relative to the earth.

Neural responses in the vestibular sense

The hair cells from both the crista and the macula send their information to the brain stem via the eighth cranial nerve. From there most of the nerve fibers go to the **vestibular nuclei** (still in the brain stem). After this, the sensory pathways become complicated and somewhat obscure. Projections to the cerebellum and to the cortex exist, but they are different in different animals (see Correia and Guedry, 1978). Most of the fibers leaving the vestibular nuclei are motor, or **efferent, fibers**. One major group of such fibers forms a pathway to the muscles that move the eyes. Szentagothai (1950) discovered that each pair of eye muscles receives fibers from a different semicircular canal. The arrangement indicates that muscles that move the eye in a particular plane are controlled by nerve fibers originating in the semicircular canal that respond to acceleration in that plane. Acceleration in a particular direction causes compensatory eye movements in the opposite direction. This allows the eyes to remain fixed on an object even though the head is turning in various directions. The relationship between eye movements and vestibular stimulation is shown in Demonstration Box 5-4.

Lowenstein and Sand (1940) performed a classic study that illustrates the electrophysiology of the vestibular system. They recorded the electrical activity of single nerve fibers from the crista of a ray (a kind of fish) while the entire labyrinth was rotated on a turntable. They found that as long as the head was accelerating, the fibers responded. The fibers increased their response rate for acceleration in one direction and, when the acceleration was in the *opposite* direction, they responded by giving *fewer* impulses per second than at the resting rate. Thus, as in other sensory systems, both excitatory and inhibitory responses to physical stimuli occur. Lowenstein and Sand (1940) also showed that the magnitude of the response (impulses per second in single fibers) varies directly with the magnitude of the stimulating acceleration. Stimulus intensity seems to be encoded in a manner similar to that in other sensory systems. There are at least two other types of nerve fibers, one of which always responds to acceleration (regardless of direction) with an increase in firing rate. The other only responds with decreases in firing rate.

The fibers connected to the hair cells of the macula respond to their stimuli somewhat more simply. Two types of responses have been described. The first is an increase in the rate of neural firing when the head is tilted; the second is a rate increase when the head is returned to its original position (Wyburn et al., 1964). Although there have been some studies of cortical responses to acceleration of the head, little detail is known about these responses. One fact that has emerged is that inputs from vestibular, kinesthetic, and visual systems converge in the cortex, so that our sensations of "turning," for example, depend in a complex way on all these inputs (Mergner, Anastosopolous, Becker, and Deecke, 1981; Parker, 1980). One striking example of this complex interaction is the phenomenon of motion sickness, which is often caused by a mismatch between visual and vestibular or kinesthetic inputs. A great deal of effort is being put into studying this aspect of human reaction, especially because of its importance in space travel under zero-gravity conditions.

PAIN

The shrill squeal of the siren seemed to pierce his head like a knife. The pain was exquisite. Then came a brilliant flash of light; he blinked, trying to somehow relieve the savage pain flooding in through his eyes. He stumbled, barking his shin on a log, and another bright, fierce pain penetrated his consciousness. On top of all this, the old World War II shrapnel wound in his hip began to throb with a dull, sickening ache. Finally, he found the water, diving into a dark, cool world that promised to soothe his battered body. But something was wrong with the water; instead of cooling it was burning. His head seemed to explode as the caustic liquid burned its way along his nasal passages and forced its way between his lips. Finally, and almost gratefully, he lost conscious-

ness, his body succumbing to an assault it was never meant to experience.

Pain is a complex experience. It is usually associated with damage to the body of an animal, and in humans, it is usually accompanied by myriad emotions and thoughts. Some sensory psychologists consider pain to be a sensation in its own right. Other psychologists argue that pain is not a sensation at all, but rather an emotion, or even a bodily state akin to hunger or thirst (see for example, Wall, 1979). Perhaps the best view is a compromise. The experience of pain seems to have identifiable sensory characteristics; therefore, we shall treat it as a separate sensory modality. We must be aware, however, that interactions with other sensations and with more complex cognitive processes are important for a complete understanding of pain phenomena.

Pain stimuli and receptors

The evolutionary significance of pain may be twofold. First, it is essential that an animal be able to respond appropriately to environmental situations that could destroy it. It must respond by avoiding such situations in the future or terminating the ongoing dangerous stimulus. Light, sound, touch, and temperature, when they occur at high intensities or for prolonged durations, can destroy the receptors that are specialized to receive them. If such potentially damaging intensities are not signaled quickly to the brain, the organism will be damaged beyond repair. This is often the unfortunate fate of those humans who are born without a well-functioning pain sense (see Sternbach, 1963). Second, pain seems to have the effect of requiring a person to cope appropriately with an injury if it does happen. In fact, many people who receive serious injuries do not feel pain until quite a while, sometimes several hours, after they occur (see Melzack, Wall, and Ty, 1982). Their pain seems to have the function of inducing them to be still in order that healing may occur, or to seek treatment for the injury. When an injury first occurs, more important responses than pain may be appropriate, for example escape or fighting for life. In this view, the biological significance of pain lies in its ability to promote healing (see Wall, 1979). During the recovery phase, the stimulus for pain is the injury itself, and the function of pain is not to warn but to promote recovery.

All pain does not arise from overstimulation or serious injury. Certain kinds of painful experiences arise from only moderately intense stimulation, such as a pin prick or salt touching an open wound. On the other hand, overstimulation can sometimes occur without eliciting pain. For instance, pain is not experienced as the concentration of sugar stimulating the tongue increases. At present it is difficult to say exactly what stimulus properties are responsible for the experience of pain. The best statement would probably be that several different stimulus qualities can arouse pain. Stimuli that cause warning pain perhaps share the potential for causing damage to the integrity of the organism, while the stimulus for pain that promotes healing is the actual damage itself.

The best candidates for pain receptors are the free nerve endings with which the skin and the rest of the body are particularly well supplied. As we mentioned earlier in this chapter in the discussion of the skin senses, free nerve endings in the subcutaneous fat under the dermis of the skin have been found to be connected to nerve fibers associated with pain (see Vierck, 1978). It has been suggested that we could isolate the pain receptors if we could find some area of the body that only experiences pain. For a while it was thought that the cornea of the eye was such a place. The cornea is exquisitely sensitive, and almost any stimulus will cause pain, even a tiny speck of dust. Also, it is known to contain only free nerve endings (Tower, 1943). Careful work by several investigators (for example, Giraldez, Geijo, and Belmonte, 1979; Nafe and Wagoner, 1937), however, has established that the cornea is capable of a variety of sensory experiences, including touch and perhaps temperature. Free nerve endings, therefore, must be capable of responding with signals that are experienced as sensations other than pain.

Another view puts less emphasis on the receptors than on the nerve fibers that carry information away from the site of stimulation on the body. As we mentioned earlier in discussing touch pathways to the brain, some of the fibers are fast conductors and some conduct nerve impulses more slowly. Many authors, stimulated by the early work of Henry Head (1920), have proposed that the fast system (lemniscal) is specialized for highly discriminative, complicated processing of information. The slower system (spinothalamic), which is also the more primitive one, is said to carry less complicated information, such as pain, temperature, and rudimentary touch. Because all types of nerve endings can send information through both types of systems, it is uncertain just how such a division of labor comes about. This view is appealing on some physiological grounds, however, and is consistent with some interesting psychological phenomena. Consider for example the occurrence of **double pain**. This is the experience of two distinct peaks of pain, differing in quality and separated in time, arising from a single pain stimulus. In one explanation, the first pain arises from the fast fibers, while the second arises from the slow ones. You may be able to experience this for yourself if you try Demonstration Box 5-5.

Demonstration Box 5-5. The production of double pain

This demonstration uses the method of Sinclair and Stokes (1964) to generate two pains for the price of one. Double pain is experienced only under certain conditions. When these conditions are met, people report a first, sharp stinging sensation, followed about one second later by a more intense burning pain that may spread to a wider area and fades more gradually. Although most people, under the appropriate conditions, experience this sequence without being told what to expect, we are telling you now so that you will have a good chance to experience it. For this demonstration you will need to find a source of hot water, something to measure its temperature, and two medium-sized bowls to hold it in. You want to produce two water baths: one at 35°C (95°F) and one at 57°C (135°F). If you have access to a thermometer (a meat thermometer is fine for this demonstration), this would obviously be the best way to measure the temperatures of the baths. If you don't have a thermometer, simply mix 3½ cups of very hot tap water with 3½ cups of cold tap water for the 35°C bath. To keep it at about this temperature, add a little hot water every minute or so. To create the 57°C bath, combine 6⅔ cups of hot tap water with ⅓ cup of cold tap water. Immerse your entire hand in the 35°C bath for about 10 minutes. When this time has elapsed, mix the 57°C bath, and carefully insert your finger into it until the water comes up past the second joint of the finger. Count "one-thousand-one" to yourself, and then withdraw your finger. Pay careful attention to the sensations you experience. Notice that first you feel a sharp stinging and then about a second later a burning feeling. You may try the experiment again and again without fear of any damage if you immerse your hand in the 35°C bath between trials, and always limit your immersion in the 57°C bath to one second. If you wish, you can try varying the temperatures of the two baths to find the limits of the conditions under which the phenomenon will occur. Also, in calculating the formulas for the two baths, we assumed that the cold tap water in your area has a temperature of about 10°C (50°F), and the hot tap water a temperature of about 60°C (140°F). If your water temperatures vary significantly from these, you will have to adjust the proportions of each to make up the baths.

Neural responses to pain stimuli

The electrophysiology of the pain system(s) has been studied by applying noxious stimuli (such as electric shock, pinching, or pricking) to animals and recording the responses of neurons at various levels of the nervous system. It is assumed that these stimuli cause pain for the animals, as they usually do for humans, but this may not always be the case. Unfortunately, simply knowing that a particular stimulus was present cannot guarantee that a particular sensation was present. Thus, injured humans, particularly those engaged in some demanding activity such as battles or athletics, often do not feel pain although horribly wounded, presumably because of conflicting and more urgent responses. We know, however, that certain nerve fibers appear to fire only when their receptive fields are stimulated by noxious stimuli. For example, Poggio and Mountcastle (1960) found such neurons in the cat's thalamus, and Casey and Morrow (1983) found similar neurons in the thalamus of awake monkeys. Another group of investigators stimulated various areas of animals' brains while looking for responses indicating discomfort. Although several candidates for a pain center in the brain have been found, probably no one region of the brain can claim to be exclusively responsible for the pain experience (see Casey, 1978).

Perhaps the most interesting electrophysiological fact about pain is that the two types of fibers that are involved in pain, and in the other cutaneous and kinesthetic sensations, seem to act in opposition to each other. Mel-zack and Wall (1965; see also Melzack, 1973a) devised an ingenious conceptual model of pain, called the **gate-control theory**, based on the interaction of these two systems. This theory provides the foundation for most modern accounts of a variety of pain phenomena and so it is important to understand it thoroughly at this point. Figure 5-13 presents the theory diagrammatically. Let us go through it

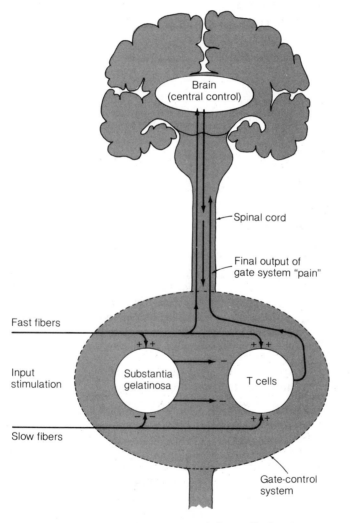

Figure 5-13. An illustration of the "gate-control theory" of pain.

step by step, since there are several aspects to keep in mind.

First, notice in Figure 5-13 that both fast and slow fibers have connections with the **substantia gelatinosa** (a part of the spinal cord) and with the first **transmission cells** (T cells). The T cells are part of the set of slow fibers that make up the spinothalamic pathway and send pain information up the spinal cord to the brain. The fast (lemniscal) fibers also have a direct connection to the brain (or "central control," to use Melzack's terminology), which can in turn send information back down the spinal cord to the **gate-control system**. Notice in the figure that the connections of both the fast and the slow fibers to the T cells are marked with a plus sign, meaning that they increase neural activity in, or excite, those cells. The reactions of these fibers on the substantia gelatinosa are different, however. The fast fibers excite the substantia gelatinosa (+), while the slow fibers inhibit its action (−). When the T cells are stimulated beyond some value, we experience pain. A normal stimulus, say a touch, would mostly stimulate the fast fibers, which have lower thresholds. This would excite the substantia gelatinosa, thus causing it to inhibit the T cells, keeping them below the value that is sensed as pain. A noxious stimulus, however, would stimulate slow as well as fast fibers. Because the slow fibers inhibit the substantia gelatinosa, this allows the T cells to fire more vigorously, and pain is experienced. The substantia gelatinosa then is the "gate" for the T cells. The fast fibers close this gate, while the slow fibers open it. Melzack and Casey (1968) suggested that the central pathway to the gate can also be responsible for closing it, so that other perceptions, cognitions, and emotions could be responsible for changing the nature of a potentially painful experience.

A fascinating extension of gate-control theory deals with the traditional Chinese tech-

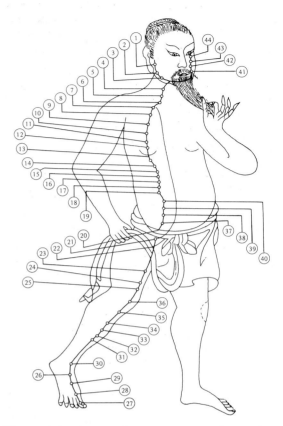

Figure 5-14. A typical acupuncture chart. The numbers indicate sites at which needles can be inserted, and then either twisted, electrified, or heated. An impressive analgesia results in many cases.

nique for alleviating pain called *acupuncture* (from the Latin *acus*, meaning needle, and *pungere*, meaning to sting). In this technique, long thin needles are inserted at various sites on the body (see Figure 5-14). The needles may occasionally be twirled, heated, or have electrical current passed through them. Although Western doctors have been cautious about accepting acupuncture as a valid means of reducing pain, most (though not all) studies support its effectiveness (see P. E. Brown,

1972; Chapman, 1978; Cheng, 1973; Clark and Yang, 1974). Generally speaking, chemical anesthetics act to inhibit the slow fibers, but do not affect the fast fibers. This allows the substantia gelatinosa to inhibit the T cells and close the pain gate. Acupuncture may work by increasing the activity in the fast fibers (Melzack, 1973b). This would have the effect of stimulating the substantia gelatinosa more strongly and, thus, again reducing the pain-producing activity of the T cells. In order to explain how a needle in the arm can ease a toothache, or a needle in the foot can ease sinus pain, we would have to postulate higher level gates, perhaps in the thalamus, that work in a similar fashion. Perhaps the anesthetic of the future will not be a needle filled with novacaine, but merely a needle.

GLOSSARY

The following definitions are specific to this book.

Acceleration   A change in the rate of motion.

Across-fiber pattern   A pattern of neural activity in which various neural units have different stimulus-specific response rates.

Ampullae   Swellings at the base of the semicircular canals containing the crista.

Bony labyrinth   The structure inside the head that contains the cochlea and the vestibular organs. It is made of very hard bone.

Cold fibers   Neurons that respond to cooling of the skin by firing at a more rapid rate and to warming of the skin by decreasing their firing rate.

Crista   The movement-perceptive portion of a semicircular canal.

Cupola   A jellylike material in which the hairs of the crista are embedded.

Dermis   The inner layer of skin, containing most of the nerve endings.

Double pain   The phenomenon of two distinct peaks of pain, differing in quality and separated in time, from one single pain stimulus.

Efferent fibers   Neural fibers that carry outgoing information from the brain to muscles or other action systems.

Epidermis   The outer layer of skin.

Free nerve endings   Noncorpuscular, branching nerve endings in skin, joints, etc., that may be receptors for pain and temperature stimuli.

Gate-control theory   A conceptual model of pain based on the interaction of slow fibers in the spino-thalamic system and fast fibers in the lemniscal system.

Gate-control system   In the gate-control theory of pain, the substantia gelatinosa and its connections to fast and slow fibers and T-cells.

Glabrous skin   A type of skin that has no hairs (for example, on lips, fingers, and toes); it is highly sensitive to stimulation.

Golgi tendon organs   Nerve endings attached to tendons that respond to both stretching and contraction of muscle.

Hairy skin   A type of skin covering the human body from which numerous hairs protrude; it is both a protective and stimulus-sensitive covering. *See also* Glabrous skin.

Labeled-line theory   A theory of taste in which each taste fiber encodes the intensity of a single basic taste quality, that to which it is most sensitive.

Lateral olfactory tract   The main route, composed of axons, from the olfactory bulb to the smell cortex.

Lemniscal system   Composed of large, rapidly conducting nerve fibers; one route of information conduction from the skin, muscles, and joints to the brain.

Lock-and-key theory   A theory that suggests that variously shaped molecules fit into holes in the walls of cells in the olfactory epithelium, much as a key fits into a lock, and that when this occurs, a chemical change takes place causing a neural response.

Macula   The receptor organ of the utricle and saccule; it is responsive to linear acceleration.

Medulla   The part of brain attached to the top of the spinal cord.

Nystagmus   Reflexive, short oscillations of the eyes often evoked by vestibular stimulation.

Olfactory bulb   The olfactory center in front of and below the main mass of the brain that receives input from the olfactory nerve.

Olfactory cilia   Hairlike projections extending from the knoblike end of the olfactory rod, protruding through the surface of the olfactory epithelium.

Olfactory epithelium   The small area of oval-shaped cells in the upper nasal passages that respond to smell stimuli.

Olfactory nerve   The bundle of axons of smell receptor cells that passes through the top of the nasal cavity.

Olfactory rod   A long extension from smell receptor cells to the surface of the olfactory epithelium.

Otocysts   In primitive vertebrates, fluid-filled cavities that function to maintain balance and attitude to gravity. *See* Statocysts.

Otoliths   Bony bodies in otocysts.

Pacinian corpuscle   A corpuscular nerve ending found in skin and joints, sensitive to mechanical deformation.

Papillae   Small bumps on the tongue where taste buds are located.

Parietal region   The upper central region of the brain housing the part of the sensory cortex responsible for touch.

Reticular formation   Part of the brain stem, associated with attentional processes.

Saccule   A vestibular organ contained in the bony labyrinth. It responds to linear acceleration.

Semicircular canals   Vestibular organs contained in the bony labyrinth.

Slow-adapting fibers   Nerves that mediate neural responses in kinesthesis.

Spindle organs   *See* Stretch receptors.

Spinothalamic system   A slow pathway of short fibers conducting information to the brain from the skin, muscles, and joints.

Statocysts   In primitive invertebrates, motion-sensitive cavities lined with hair cells.

Statolith   A tiny stonelike body resting on the hairs of statocysts and responding to motion or position of the animal.

Stretch receptors   Nerve endings attached to muscle spindles that respond to stretching of the muscle.

Substantia gelatinosa   Part of the spinal cord implicated in pain transmission through the gate-control theory.

Taste buds   The group of cells in which the major receptors for taste are located.

Taste pore   An opening in the surface of the tongue leading to the taste cells extending from the taste bud.

Thalamus   A region of the lower brain that relays sensory impulses to the cortex.

Transmission cells   In the gate-control theory of pain, cells that transmit pain impulses to the brain.

Utricle   A vestibular organ contained in the bony labyrinth. It responds to linear acceleration.

Vestibular nuclei   Way stations in the brain stem on the route of nerve fibers from the crista and macula to the cerebellum and cortex.

Vibration theory   The suggestion that a stimulus molecule ruptures chemical bonds in the cell membrane of olfactory epithelium receptor cells, causing the release of stored energy, in turn generating an electrical current.

Warm fibers   Neurons that respond to warming by firing more rapidly and by reducing the firing rate with cooling.

Brightness and spatial frequency

THE FOLLOWING SCENE MUST HAVE been played countless times on cinema screens in Grade B horror movies.

It is night, and in the darkness, two old ragged beachcombers are moving along the water's edge. Suddenly, one stops.

"Hey, Charlie, I think there's something out there."

"W-What is it?"

"I can't make it out. It's some sort of glow. It's too dim to make out what it is."

This scene illustrates the most basic property of vision, namely, that it depends on the presence of light, and the most primitive visual percepts are simply reactions to the intensity of the incoming energy. These responses are represented in consciousness as a brightness or glow. We often sense the presence of light before sufficient energy exists for us to apprehend shape or form. Thus, the next line in the above scenario usually goes, "It's getting brighter," and then as the energy becomes sufficient to apprehend the object itself, "Oh my God! It's some sort of creature!" As we shall see, the perception of brightness is much more complex and surprising than the script of this particular film.

PHOTOMETRIC UNITS

Electromagnetic energy, or light, can vary along three dimensions: intensity, wavelength, and duration. All dimensions are important in the perception of brightness, although brightness varies most directly with intensity. Of course, to make sense of the perceptual effects, we must first be able to specify the physical intensity of the stimulus. This is not as simple as it seems.

Based on the visual effects produced by visible radiation, the process of light measurement is known as **photometry**. Photometric units are used to describe the stimulus, and these units are, by convention, expressed in terms of energy. Unfortunately, over the years a confusing array of photometric units have been developed. Most of them were designed for some specific purpose or by some technical or academic subdiscipline that needed to specify an amount of light present. The result is chaos. Even among the most scholarly, few can tell you how many *nits* there are in an *apostilb* or a *blondel*, or how these units are related to a *candle* or a *lambert*. In 1960, an International Conference on Weights and Measures established the *Système International d'Unités*, which is a uniform system of measurement (known commonly as **SI**). Throughout this book we use these **standard units**. Should your reading bring you into contact with some of the older forms of photometric measurement, we can only refer you to some more advanced texts such as Wyszecki and Stiles (1967) to try to make sense of the quantities involved.

Basically, there are two ways in which light can reach the eye: (a) Directly from a radiating source such as a light bulb, fluorescent tube, a firefly, or the sun, or (b) by reflection from surfaces that have radiant energy falling on them, such as walls and paper. Different types of measures are used for these different types of light input. All photometric units, however, are ultimately based on the amount of light emitted from a single candle. The nature of this *standard candle*, its photic energy, and the specific measures derived from it have been fixed (albeit somewhat arbitrarily) by an international body called the *Commission Internationale de l'Eclairage*, usually known as the **CIE**.

Each different aspect of light is designated by its own name and requires a different measurement unit. Thus, the amount of energy

Table 6-1. Photometric units

Photometric term	What is measured?	Unit	How measured?	Comments
Radiance or luminous flux	Radiant energy from a light source	Lumen	A candela is the light of a 1 lumen source at a distance of 1 m shone on a square meter	Defined in terms of a standard candle
Illuminance	Light falling on a surface	Lux	Actually 1 lumen/m^2	As the source moves farther away illuminance decreases
Luminance	Light reflected from a surface	Candelas per square meter	Lumens reflected from a surface	Independent of distance of eye from surface
Reflectance (albedo)	Proportion of light reflected from surface	% reflectance	$\dfrac{\text{Luminance}}{\text{Illuminance}} \times 100$	Really ratio of reflected to incident light
Retinal illuminance	Amount of light incident on the retina	Trolands	1 candela/m^2 seen through pupil of 1 mm^2 area	Roughly 0.0036 lumens/m^2 through a 1-mm^2 pupil
Brightness	Phenomenal impression of light intensity	Not yet agreed upon but bril is best contender	Relative matching and scaling techniques	Psychological rather than physical quantity

coming from a light source is called **radiance**. The unit of radiance is defined in terms of the standard candle, which produces an energy of slightly more than one one-thousandth of a watt at a wavelength of 555 nm. This quantity of luminous energy is called a **lumen**. The amount of light falling upon a surface is another photometric quantity called **illuminance**. The amount of light reflected from a surface is called its **luminance**, while the proportion of light falling on a surface that is reflected is called its **reflectance**. The amount of light reaching the retina is called the **retinal illuminance**. Finally, the phenomenal impression of the light intensity of a stimulus is called its **brightness**. Thus, if we have a slide projector shining on a screen, the amount of energy leaving the bulb determines its *radiance*, the amount of light falling on the screen is its *illuminance*, the amount of light reflected from the screen is its *luminance*, and our perceptual or phenomenal impression is the *brightness* of the screen. Table 6-1 summarizes the most common photometric quantities, how they are measured, the units used, and some of their specific properties.

Before becoming too involved with measurement, however, it is important to remember that, perceptually, brightness is not explained simply by the amount of light reaching the eye. As we noted in Chapter 2, when we plot the brightness sensation against the physical stimulus intensity, we get a nonlinear relationship. The apparent brightness measured by a direct scaling technique (such as magnitude estimation) grows approximately as the cube root of the physical intensity (to be precise, the phenomenal sensation grows at a rate equivalent to the light intensity raised to the 0.33 power). This means that if you had a theater stage illuminated by eight lights and you wished to increase the perceived brightness of the area, doubling the number of lights so that you now have 16 would not double the perceived brightness but would only increase it by one-third. If you wanted to double the phenomenal brightness, you would have to increase the number of lights to 64! Figure 6-1 shows the general shape of this relationship graphically. Notice that the curve in Figure 6-1 resembles the logarithmic curve of Fechner's law (remember Chapter 2 and Figure 2-14). Although this would not be the case for power functions with larger exponents (as, for example, for electric shock), the resemblance of the power and log laws for brightness means that the old custom of measuring brightness in terms of logarithms of photometric values still provides a relatively accurate representation of the relationship between the physical stimulus and the sensation. For this reason, various photometric values, such as the brightness scales used in television studios, are frequently presented in logarithmic units, especially when designed for visual purposes. This serves to equalize the sizes of the sensory changes as a function of changes in physical intensity. The unit of brightness in the graph in Figure 6-1 is the **bril,** which was suggested by S. S. Stevens. Each bril represents about one-tenth of a log unit above threshold, in much the same way that a decibel (see Chapter 4) represents one-tenth of a log unit above threshold in audition.

FACTORS IN BRIGHTNESS PERCEPTION

Adaptation

The perception of brightness depends on the current state of sensitivity of the eye in much the same way that the brightness of the final photographic image depends on the sensitivity of the film. An amount of light that will produce a faint image on insensitive film will produce an overly bright image on very sensitive film. You are probably aware of the effects of changing sensitivity when you walk from a darkened room into the bright sunlight, only to find that everything appears to be so bright and "washed out" that a few moments must pass before objects are visible clearly. The opposite occurs when you walk from a bright exterior into a darkened room. Now everything appears to be very dark, and objects are difficult to resolve in the gloom. After a while you can discern objects, although the accommodation to the darkness takes somewhat longer

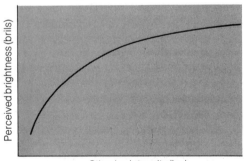

Figure 6-1. *The nonlinear relationship between stimulus intensity and brightness.*

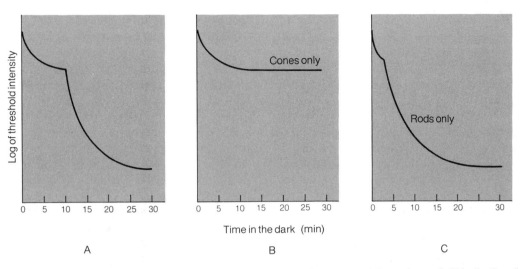

Time in the dark (min)

A B C

Figure 6-2. (A) *The normal time course of* *dark adaptation,* (B) *dark adaptation in the* **cones (or central fovea), and (C) *dark adap-* *tation in the rods (or periphery).***

than the adaptation to the brighter environment. We call the process of adaptation to a darker environment **dark adaptation** and that to a brighter environment **light adaptation**. Although we cannot remove our daylight retina and put on the twilight one in the way that we change film in a camera to accommodate changes in lighting conditions, the sensitivity of our eyes changes through these two adaptation processes.

We can monitor directly the changes in sensitivity associated with dark adaptation. First, we adapt an observer to bright light by putting him in a brightly lit room for a few minutes; then we turn off the lights. Now we test to find the observer's *absolute threshold* for the detection of light. This is done at fixed time intervals after the onset of darkness, using one of the standard psychophysical methods outlined in Chapter 2. Such an experiment usually reveals that the observer first needs relatively strong stimuli to reach threshold; however, the eye rapidly becomes more sensitive over the first minute or two, at which point it begins to

stabilize at a level that is about 100 times more sensitive (2 log units) than when we initially turned off the light. After about 10 minutes of darkness, the sensitivity begins to rapidly increase again. During this second period, the threshold drops quickly for 5 or 10 minutes, then begins to stabilize, reaching a relatively constant level after about one-half hour. When we graph the change in threshold for a typical observer, as we have done in Figure 6-2A, we can see a break, or *kink*, in the sensitivity curve. The kink indicates a change in the rate of dark adaptation.

Whenever a sudden transition or break is found in a curve, it often suggests that a second mechanism or process has come into operation. This is confirmed in the present case by the fact that phenomenal changes are occuring at about the same time. For instance, if we used a greenish light (or nearly any color, for that matter) to measure the threshold, the observer would be able to identify the color throughout the first 10 minutes or so of the test session. At about the point at which the sensitivity suddenly begins to increase again, the test stimulus would seem to lose its color and become grayish. An old proverb is based on this loss of color vision under dim levels of illumination: "At night, all cats are gray."

In Chapter 3 we talked about the differences between rods and cones. At that time, we reviewed some evidence indicating that rods were found predominantly in animals active during the twilight hours (or in conditions of dim illumination), while cones are found predominantly in the retinas of animals that are active during daylight. It was suggested that cones function to provide **photopic**, or daylight, vision (including the perception of color), while rods provide **scotopic**, or twilight, vision. Humans have both rods and cones; hence, the two segments of the dark adaptation curve may represent separate rod and cone contributions. The cones seem rapidly to reach their level of maximal sensitivity. The rods take longer to adapt. When they do, the threshold begins to drop, but at the expense of a loss in color vision. The point at which the adaptation of the rods catches up to that of the cones is the break in the dark-adaptation curve shown in Figure 6-2A.

We can verify this experimentally. Suppose we return to the experimental situation that we used to track the course of dark adaptation. Now we change the stimulus so that we are focusing a tiny pencil of light only on the fovea when we take threshold measurements. Since the fovea contains only cones (Chapter 3), we can track dark adaptation in cones. Such an experiment gives us the data shown in Figure 6-2B. Notice that this curve looks just like the first segment of the curve in Figure 6-2A. No second increase in sensitivity occurs, no matter how long we continue in darkness. To demonstrate the lower, or rod, portion of the curve we repeat the experiment, only now we

focus our pencil of light about 20 degrees from the center of the fovea, where the retina contains predominantly rods. When we do this, we get the curve shown in Figure 6-2C, in which the first rapid change (attributable to cone action) is almost completely absent. An even more spectacular way to show the separate rod and cone origin for the two portions of the dark adaptation curve was provided by Hecht and Mandelbaum (1938). They placed a normal observer on a vitamin A–deficient diet for 57 days. Since this vitamin is critical for the synthesis of rhodopsin, the pigment in rods, the diet effectively eliminated the action of these receptors. After 57 days, the observer had a dark adaptation curve similar to that in Figure 6-2B. Not only was the rod portion of the curve almost totally absent, but the individual was almost completely "night-blind" and unable to see dimly illuminated targets. By the way, the observer completely recovered when he went back to his normal diet. Perhaps such naturally occurring instances as this have given carrots, a vegetable high in vitamin A, their reputation for being "good for the eyes." Overall, these experiments indicate that two separate physiological mechanisms are involved in the perception of brightness: the cone system for brighter illumination and the rod system for dimmer illumination. Some evidence even suggests that when bright light is present and the cones are active, they actually inhibit or "turn off" the action of the rods (Drum, 1981).

There is still much to be learned about the nature of the adaptation process. Clearly, any incoming light will bleach the available photopigments in the rods and cones, and time will be needed for them to regenerate (remember the rhodopsin cycle shown in Figure 3-8). As more pigment becomes available, the sensitivity of the eye should increase. While such a process does seem to play a role (MacLeod, 1978), dark adaptation actually involves changes in the sensitivity and responses of neural processes as well (Green and Powers, 1982). Later in this chapter we shall see that even higher cognitive responses may influence our perception of brightness.

Retinal locus

As we saw in Figure 3-7, rods and cones are unequally distributed across the retina. The fovea contains only cones, which are less sensitive to weak stimuli, while the more sensitive rods are more plentiful in the periphery. Suppose the apparent brightness of a light depended directly on the sensitivity of the stimulated receptors, as well as on the intensity of the light. If that were the case, then moving a constant light stimulus across the retina, stimulating less sensitive cones near the fovea and more sensitive rods in the periphery, should change the apparent brightness of the light. This has been verified experimentally (Drum, 1980; Osaka, 1981). Peripheral targets appear brighter. It is also embodied in a bit of folk wisdom. At some time in antiquity scientists noted that looking directly at a dim object, such as a star, could cause it to disappear from view. Early astronomers looked at a point off to the side of a star in order to let its image fall upon the more sensitive peripheral retina (containing mostly rods). This technique allows such a dim target to be perceived more clearly, under conditions of dim illumination. If you ever try this yourself, look at a point about 20 degrees of visual angle from the star you wish to see. This would allow the star's image to fall on the part of the retina where the density of rods is greatest, giving both maximum sensitivity and maximum acuity.

Wavelength

The wavelength of the light stimulating the eye will also affect our perception of its brightness. For instance, yellows (medium wavelengths) almost always appear to be brighter than blues (short wavelengths). The usual procedure for assessing the relative brightness of lights of different colors is to use a *bipartite target*. This is simply a circular target that has been divided in half. One half contains the *standard color* that is to be matched in brightness, and the other half is the *comparison color* that is adjustable. Systematically pairing various colors and then matching their apparent brightness provides a set of measures of the relative amounts of energy needed to produce equal sensations of brightness for various wavelengths of light. For convenience, the wavelength requiring the least energy to equal the brightness of the standard is set at a value of 1.0. All other wavelengths, being less effective, are assigned values less than 1, depending on their relative brightnesses. Once this conversion has been made, a curve can be plotted as in Figure 6-3. Such a curve is called a **luminosity curve**. Notice that we actually have two curves in this figure. The first is labeled *photopic* and represents the results we would obtain from the matching experiment if we were working at daylight levels of light intensity. It has a peak sensitivity for wavelengths around 555 nm, and the apparent brightness falls off rapidly for shorter (toward the blue) or longer (toward the red) wavelengths. If we repeat this matching experiment under conditions of dim illumination, in which we are operating only on rod vision, the observer will not actually be aware of the color of the stimuli, and both halves of the field will appear gray regardless of their wavelength. Nonetheless, some wavelengths still look brighter than

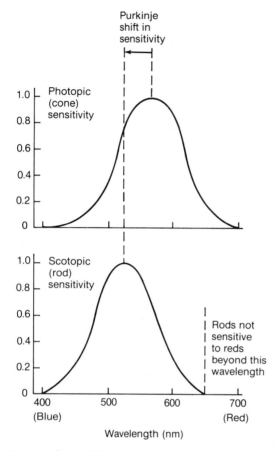

Figure 6-3. Differences in relative sensitivity to various wavelengths under photopic and scotopic illumination conditions.

his honor this phenomenon is referred to as the **Purkinje shift**. He first noticed the change while looking at his garden as twilight was falling. As the light dimmed, certain colors began to change their apparent brightness. Thus, reds that had been bright relative to blues and greens began to look darker, while the bluer tones appeared to brighten. Because scotopic vision lacks the sensation of color, daylight greens or blues change to moonlight grays, while daylight reds change to moonlight blacks. Demonstration Box 6-1 allows you to experience this shift in sensitivity for yourself.

There is an interesting application of the Purkinje shift. You may remember from watching war movies that the briefing rooms next to airstrips or the control rooms of ships and submarines are often depicted as illuminated by red light. This red is not used solely for dramatic effect in the film but is actually used in such settings. At the red end of the spectrum, rods are relatively insensitive, but cones still function at these longer wavelengths if there is sufficient stimulus intensity. Thus, the cones may be used while the rods are beginning to dark adapt. The dotted line in Figure 6-3 shows a wavelength where this is true. Thus, pilots about to fly night missions, or sailors about to stand the night watch, can be briefed or can check their instruments, then go directly into the dark without waiting the many minutes necessary to completely dark adapt.

others. Thus, we can map out the *scotopic* luminosity curve in Figure 6-3. Under these conditions the curve is somewhat different, with a peak around 505 nm. Thus, the curve is shifted toward the short wavelengths, suggesting that we may be more sensitive to blue light under dim light viewing conditions.

The change in the apparent brightness of different wavelengths as we alter the intensity of the light was first noted by the Czechoslovak phenomenologist Johannes E. Purkinje, and in

Time and area

In addition to intensity, wavelength, and retinal location of the stimulus, our ability to detect a spot of light depends on other stimulus properties. For instance, a photographer knows that when she is taking a picture under dim illumination she may have to lengthen the exposure time in order to collect enough light to

Demonstration Box 6-1. The Purkinje shift

For this demonstration you will need a dark room and some way of providing a light whose intensity you can vary without altering its color. A good method is to use a television set as a light source. This may be done by tuning the set to an unused channel and turning the contrast control to a minimum. This reduces the visibility of the random dots that normally appear on the screen. Now, if you darken the room so that the television is the only source of illumination, the brightness control on the set will be a means of controlling the room light. An alternate procedure in the absence of a television is to turn on a light in a room and enter a closet, shutting the door after you. The amount of light entering the closet can be controlled by opening the door by differing amounts. Turning your back to the door allows for a diffusion of the light to any target that you wish to be illuminated. Unfortunately, if the outside room is well lit, opening the door by a few centimeters will provide a good deal of light;

hence, control of illumination may be improved by dimming the light in the outside room.

Now, look at Color Plate 1 in Chapter 8. Here we have two colored spots, one blue and one red. When viewed in moderate or bright light (the brightness control on the television is set to high, or the closet door is more widely ajar), the blue and the red spot appear to be approximately equal in brightness. Now, make the light very dim (close the door almost completely, or turn down the brightness control on the television). In the bright light, you were viewing the spots with cone vision. Now, if you dim the lights sufficiently, only rod vision will be activated. After 5–10 min, as your eye dark adapts, the blue spot will appear to be significantly brighter than the red spot. In fact, the red spot may actually disappear. The effect may be accentuated by staring at the white spot. This shifts the images away from the fovea to an area of the retina containing a greater number of rods.

---

adequately register the image on the film. In bright sunlight, a short exposure will usually do. Actually, the same amount of physical energy is necessary to expose the film properly in each case; it just takes longer to collect the requisite amount under dim illumination. In physics this relationship is known as the **Bunsen-Roscoe law**. This law describes the photochemical reaction of any light-sensitive substance, whether film or visual pigment. We find that there is a similar trade-off between stimulus duration and stimulus intensity in vision when we are dealing with the problem of the absolute threshold for the detection of brightness. We can express this relationship using simple algebra. If we define C as the critical value necessary to reach threshold (that is, the minimum perceptible brightness),

I as the stimulus intensity, and T as the stimulus duration, the relationship is $T \times I = C$. When applied to vision, this is known as **Bloch's law**. Thus, for a given stimulus, we may increase the likelihood of detection by either increasing the intensity of the stimulus or increasing its duration of presentation, with the limitation that the time versus intensity trade-off does not work over durations greater than one-tenth of a second. This value may vary a bit, being somewhat longer if you are completely dark adapted and somewhat shorter if you are very light adapted (Montellese, Sharpe, and Brown, 1979). If the duration is greater than about 1/10 sec, the probability that you will detect a stimulus is no longer affected by stimulus duration, but depends only on stimulus intensity.

The size of the stimulus is also important in determining its detectability. In Chapter 3, we noted that there is a good deal of neural convergence in the visual system. A number of rods or cones may converge on the same bipolar cell. Similarly, several bipolar cells may converge on the same retinal ganglion cell. Consider a hypothetical example. Suppose four neural responses per second activate a bipolar cell, and that bipolar cell has four receptors converging upon it. If we provide a tiny spot light, which is only strong enough to elicit one response per second from the retinal receptor, and the light is only wide enough to stimulate two receptors, the bipolar cell will not respond. If we double the size of the stimulus so that all four receptors are illuminated, however, the bipolar cell will be receiving a total of four responses per second and it will become activated. Thus, as the area of a stimulus increases, even if its intensity does not change, the likelihood increases that we will recruit enough photoreceptors to begin a chain of neural activity. An alternative conceptualization is in terms of retinal receptive fields, such as those illustrated in Figure 3-14. Increasing the stimulus size might be thought of as simply "filling in" the center of the receptive field with light, thus adding more *on* responses to the overall activity.

For relatively small areas, covering visual angles of 10 minutes (') of arc or less (about 1 mm viewed at arm's length), there is a direct relationship between area and intensity. If A signifies the area stimulated, and I and C are again stimulus intensity and critical threshold value, respectively, we can describe the relationship as $A \times I = C$. This is known as **Ricco's law**. Thus, we can increase the likelihood of stimulus detection by either increasing its intensity or increasing its area of stimulation.

For stimulus sizes greater than 10', increasing the area has a reduced effect. The effect of area on detection for larger stimuli is described by $\sqrt{A} \times I = C$. In other words, for larger stimuli, a greater increase in area is needed to achieve the same reduction in threshold. This second area-intensity relationship is known as **Piper's law**. Beyond 24 degrees of visual angle, no further benefit is gained by increasing the size of the stimulus, and the likelihood of detection depends solely on the intensity.

Because these effects are supposedly a result of the summation of neural responses converging on a single retinal ganglion cell, a few additional relationships might be expected. For instance, the degree of summation (or convergence) varies as we move across the retina, with more convergence upon a single ganglion cell found in the periphery. Receptive fields are smaller in the foveal region (Randsom-Hogg and Spillman, 1980). This suggests that increasing simulus area might have a different effect at different positions across the retina, with the area increases facilitating detection more for stimuli in the periphery, and this seems to be the case (Lie, 1980).

Maximum sensitivity

After this discussion, you may be wondering just what the ultimate limit of sensitivity might be if the stimulus were adjusted to the optimal wavelength, size, and retinal position, and the observer were fully dark adapted. The classic experiment to answer this question was conducted by Hecht, Schlaer, and Pirenne (1942). They found that the threshold for the perception of a brightness sensation occurred when only 10 quanta of light (photons) were stimulating the retina. Further computations showed that at this ultimate threshold it was probable that each of 10 rods was responding to a dif-

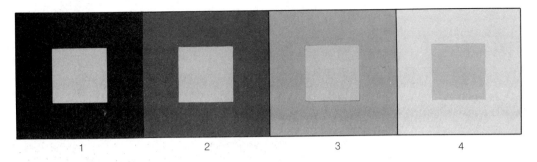

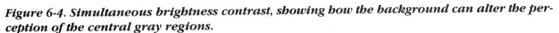

Figure 6-4. Simultaneous brightness contrast, showing how the background can alter the perception of the central gray regions.

ferent one of the 10 quanta. This is, of course, the maximum sensitivity that is possible theoretically. Even at higher levels of illumination, however, it is possible to show that fluctuations of only a few photons may affect our perception of brightness, thus showing the exquisite sensitivity of the eye as a light detector (Krauskopf and Reeves, 1980; Zuidema, Gresnigt, Bouman, and Koenderink, 1978).

BRIGHTNESS CONTRAST

Strange as it may seem, our perception of the brightness of targets often depends more on the luminance of adjacent objects than on the luminance of the target itself. Figure 6-4 shows four small squares, each of which is surrounded by a larger square. The central squares are printed in the same gray; thus, the amount of light that reaches your eye from each is the same. Notice, however, that the apparent brightnesses of these small squares are not equal. Their brightnesses vary depending on their background, with the grays printed on dark backgrounds appearing lighter than the grays printed on light backgrounds. This perceptual effect is called **simultaneous brightness contrast**.

Everyday experience tells us that our perception of brightness will increase as the amount of light reaching our eye increases. Unfortunately, our perceptual experiences often defy such common sense. Despite increases in the amount of light reaching the eye, a target may actually *decrease* its apparent brightness, depending upon the brightness of the background upon which it rests. This explains why the color black on a television screen appears darker than the apparent blackness of the screen when the set is turned off and no light is emitted from it at all! This surprising paradox is shown in Demonstration Box 6-2.

The fact that the targets vary in brightness as a function of the intensity of their background suggests that there is some form of spatial interaction present, perhaps between adjacent retinal regions that are illuminated by the target. Notice that targets on a light background, such as target 4 in Figure 6-4, appear to be darkened. The brightness response from the part of the retina exposed to target 4 has been reduced. This suggests some sort of inhibition of the brightness response as a function of activity in surrounding retinal areas.

Actually, physiological evidence indicates that such inhibitory spatial interaction does take place in the eye. Most of this evidence has

Demonstration Box 6-2. The interaction of luminance and background

For this experiment you will need your variable light source again (either the closet or the television). Hold up Figure 6-4 and look at the central squares, with your light source providing a low (but not dim) level of illumination. As you increase the level of illumination from its lowest value, the center target in square 1 should grow brighter. Now repeat the procedure while looking at the center target in square 4. Notice that as the luminance level increases, this target square actually gets darker. Since all the center squares are identical in reflectance, the differences in their apparent brightnesses depend solely upon their backgrounds. This may seem strange because we tend to associate black with the absence of light. Since you are already in a room or a place that potentially can be darkened, turn off all the light sources and close your eyes (to eliminate any stray illumination). Notice that what you are seeing is not black, but rather a misty gray (often called "cortical gray"). Thus, the absence of light is gray, not black. Only in fields that contain some areas of bright illumination can real black be seen.

been collected from *Limulus* (the horseshoe crab), an animal commonly found on the eastern shores of the United States. *Limulus* has several sets of eyes, but the ones that are most important for research purposes are the lateral eyes, which are faceted (as in the eye of a fly). In such a compound eye, a separate optical system exists for each facet, and each has its own primitive retina. Since each eyelet has its own optical nerve, this arrangement spreads out the neural fibers somewhat.

With skill (and a dissecting microscope) a researcher can isolate a single nerve fiber, drape it over an electrode, and record its electrical activity. Much of the work on the visual system of *Limulus* has been carried out in the laboratories of the Nobel-prize–winner, H. K. Hartline and his frequent collaborator Floyd Ratliff. They were able to demonstrate the inhibitory neural interactions between nearby receptors using a very simple but elegant experiment (Hartline and Ratliff, 1957). First, they monitored the responses from the cell in *Limulus* that is functionally equivalent to a ganglion cell, called the *eccentric cell*, while the receptor attached to it was stimulated. The fact that the onset of the light increased the activity of the cell, of course, indicated that its activity was controlled by stimulation of the particular receptor they had illuminated. Let us call this ganglionlike cell and its receptor A. Next Hartline and Ratliff illuminated a receptor located a short distance away (call this one B). There was no change in the activity of A, indicating that there were no excitatory connections between A and B. Next the researchers went back and again stimulated A, and while the light remained on at A, they turned on the light at B. Now they observed that the stimulation of B actually *decreased* the response of cell A. This experiment is shown diagrammatically in Figure 6-5. The importance of these results is that they demonstrate that visual cells may be inhibited by the activity of adjacent visual units. This process is called **lateral inhibition** because the inhibition acts laterally (sideways) on adjacent cells. The amount of inhibition any given cell applies to its neighbors depends on how strongly it is responding and how close the cells are to each other. The more a cell is stimulated, and the closer it is to another cell, the more intensely it will inhibit the other.

It is now easy to understand why the target

in square 1 seems to be lighter than the target in square 4 in Figure 6-4. In the part of the retina exposed to the bright surround (square 4), many cells are active, and as a consequence of this activity, they are inhibiting their neighbors. This inhibition from the bright surround should reduce the neural response rate to the central square, making it appear dimmer. The part of the retina exposed to the target on the dark background (square 1) does not receive as much inhibition from its less strongly stimulated neighbors. Because the amount of stimulation from the target is the same but the amount of inhibition from the surround is less, square 1 appears to be brighter. Thus, lateral inhibition is a basis for explaining brightness contrast effects.

Lateral inhibition can also explain more complex effects observed in other stimulus configurations. Ever since the 1860s, when

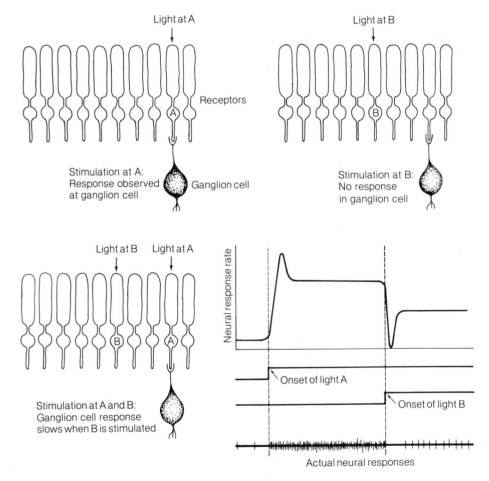

Figure 6-5. Lateral inhibition: Stimulation at A produces a response in the ganglion cell, while stimulation at B does not. Stimulating B *while* A *is active depresses its response due to lateral inhibition (from Lindsay and Norman, 1977).*

Ernst Mach studied patterns with an intensity distribution like that shown in Figure 6-6B, investigators have been intrigued by a particular brightness phenomenon it generates (Weale, 1979). Figure 6-6A shows a uniform dark and a uniform light area, with an intermediate zone that gradually changes from dark to light. When we look closely at the stimulus in Figure 6-6A, however, we do not see a uniform change in brightness flanked by two uniform areas. Instead, two bands or blurry lines are visible at the points marked by the arrows in the figure. One is darker than any other part of the figure and the other is brighter. These lines are called **Mach bands**, in honor of their discoverer, and their presence is explained by the process of lateral inhibition.

We have indicated the location of some retinal cells illuminated by the Mach-band-producing pattern in Figure 6-6C. Cell *b* is stimulated by bright incoming light, but it is also strongly inhibited by the activity of the adjacent cells *a* and *c*. Cell *d* is stimulated to the same extent as cell *b*. But on one side it is strongly inhibited by *c*, while on the other side it is somewhat more weakly inhibited by *e*, which is not receiving as much light. The important thing to derive from this discussion is the fact that cells *b* and *d* have the same degree of stimulation, but *d* is less strongly inhibited. In this case, we might expect that its corresponding response will be more vigorous than that in cells like *b*. This should cause the region around *d* to appear relatively brighter. Next, consider cell *i*. It is not stimulated very much, but neither are the nearby cells *h* and *j*. Thus, *i* is not being strongly inhibited by surrounding units. On the other hand, *g* is receiving the same small amount of stimulation as *i*. While *g* is weakly inhibited on one side by *h*, however, it is more strongly inhibited on the other side by *f* which is responding more vigorously because of the higher intensity of light

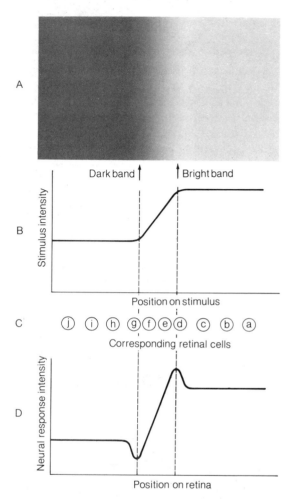

Figure 6-6. (A) a Mach band pattern, (B) the actual distribution of stimulus intensity, (C) corresponding retinal cells (see the text), and (D) neural response intensity distribution. (A and B based on Cornsweet, 1970).

falling on it. Thus, although *g* and *i* receive the same amount of stimulation, *g* is more strongly inhibited than *i*. This inequality will decrease its response, causing the appearance of an apparently darker region. The relationship between the input and the neural (and perceptual) response is diagrammed in Figure 6-6D.

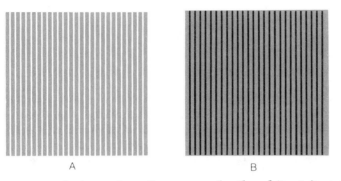

A B

Figure 6-7. Brightness assimilation, where the gray under the white stripes appears lighter than the gray under the black.

It is actually quite easy to produce a Mach band pattern for yourself. Demonstration Box 6-3 shows how to do this.

COGNITIVE FACTORS IN BRIGHTNESS PERCEPTION

The relatively simple manner in which changes in brightness can be explained by spatial interactions between retinal cells is quite exciting, especially given the apparent precision suggested by some relatively sophisticated mathematical descriptions of these interactions (Ratliff, 1965). Unfortunately, brightness perception is much more complex, and there are many instances in which predictions made from lateral inhibitory considerations may be wrong. As an example, consider Figure 6-7. The gray under the white stripes is identical to that under the black stripes. Notice, however, that the gray under the white stripes appears to be lighter than the gray under the black stripes. This is the opposite of the prediction one would make based on the action of lateral inhibition. The white stripes should darken the gray rather than lighten it. The phenomenal impression, then, is the reverse of brightness contrast, and it is called

brightness assimilation. The appearance of this effect seems to depend on a *cognitive* factor. The term *cognition* is used to cover all mental processes by which we come to know the world. Thus, processes such as learning, reasoning, intuition, and attention are all cognitive factors, as we noted in Chapter 1.

Attention seems to be a relevant variable for the appearance of brightness assimilation. Coren (1969a) demonstrated that the part of the visual field that captures your attention seems to show greater brightness contrast. Festinger, Coren, and Rivers (1970) extended this observation to explain brightness assimilation. They showed that regions of a field to which you attend show the expected brightness contrast against their surround, while unattended regions of the field show brightness assimilation. Observers usually describe the pattern shown in Figure 6-7A as a gray field with white lines *on* it and Figure 6-7B *as a set of black lines on* a gray background. Festinger et al. (1970) reasoned that the lines have a "figure-like" quality that captures the attention (this aspect of perception will be discussed more fully in Chapter 12). Since the gray is then a nonfigural background to which we pay little attention, it shows assimilation. If this is the case, then voluntary shifts in attention, so that concentration is focused on the gray regions,

Demonstration Box 6-3. Mach band patterns

Mach band patterns do not reproduce well in print. This is probably because the range of luminances possible from ink on paper is not very large. It is actually quite easy to produce your own Mach band pattern using a distribution of light. All you need is a card or a book that is opaque and has a straight edge, and a large light source. If you are in a room that has fluorescent or large frosted light fixtures in the ceiling, these produce a fine uniform source of illumination. When you hold the card near a surface, you cast a shadow. As shown in the accompanying diagram, there is a full shadow under the surface and full light on the other side. In between there is a graded shadow, the *penumbra*, which gradually moves from light to dark. Hold the card still and look at the brightness pattern, and you will easily see the dark and light Mach bands. You may increase the visibility of the bands by moving the card closer to the surface. This reduces the size of the penumbra and makes the area of gradual change in intensity steeper, as shown in the diagram. Since this puts the bright and dim areas nearer one another, it enhances the effect of the inhibitory process.

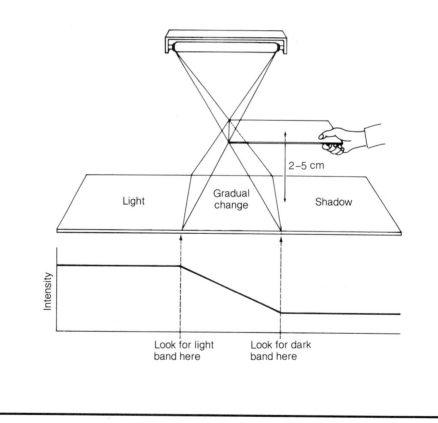

should alter the brightness effect from one of assimilation to one of contrast. The gray under the white stripes should now appear to be the darker member of the pair, and this is exactly what happens (Festinger, Coren, and Rivers, 1970). You can demonstrate this for yourself by focusing your concentration on the gray for a few moments, and soon the grays will appear to differ in a contrast direction, rather than showing brightness assimilation.

A similar attentional mechanism may account for the fact that we fail to notice recurrent periods of total "blackout" in the visual system. These periods occur when we blink, which we do about 10 to 15 times a minute. Each blink causes a total blackout for 100 to 150 msec, yet it goes unnoticed. When an observer consciously attends to the presence of blinks, some darkening is detected, yet direct measurements show that observers underestimate the duration of the blackout by 90 percent and also underestimate the amount of actual darkening by about 75 percent (Riggs, Volkmann, and Moore, 1981). This suppression is probably a cognitive adjustment to maintain continuity in the conscious flow of perception.

Some brightness effects depend on other cognitive factors, namely, the assumptions that the observer makes about the nature of the world, or even the way in which regions of the visual field *appear* to be arranged, as well as on simple lateral inhibitory interactions (Gilchrist, 1980). We shall have more to say about this in Chapter 14, where we discuss the issue of *brightness constancy*.

VISUAL ACUITY

Visual acuity refers to the ability of the eye to resolve details. There are different types of visual acuity, each dependent on the specific task or specific detail to be resolved. These details almost always involve brightness differences between a target, or part of a target, and its background. The type of visual acuity most commonly measured is **recognition acuity**, introduced by Herman Snellen (1862). This task uses the familiar *eye chart* found in most ophthalmologists' or optometrists' offices. An eye chart contains rows of letters of progressively smaller size. The observer is simply asked to recognize the letters on the chart. The size of the smallest recognizable letters determines acuity. Acuity is usually measured relative to the performance of a normal observer. Thus, an acuity of 6/6 indicates that an observer is able to identify letters at a distance of 6 meters that a normal observer can also read at that distance (you may be more familiar with the designation 20/20; 6 m is equivalent to 20 ft). In other words, the measured acuity is normal. An acuity of 6/9 means that an observer is able to read letters at 6 m that are large enough for a normal observer to read at a distance of 9 m. Here, the visual acuity is lower than normal. A more general means of specifying the limits of acuity is to use the minimum **visual angle** of a detail that can be resolved. The visual angle is simply a measure of the size of the retinal image. Figure 6-8 shows what is meant by visual angle and demonstrates a simple computation based on the size and the distance of the object. Generally speaking, a normal observer can resolve details of one minute of arc (about the size of a quarter seen at a distance of 81 m), although different tasks often produce different limits of acuity (Beck and Schwartz, 1979).

The recognition of letters on a Snellen chart is not the best way to measure acuity, because letters differ in their degree of recognizability. For instance, O and Q or P and F are letter pairs that are easily confused, whereas L and W or O and I are quite easy to discriminate. Because these differences might affect acuity measurements, Landolt (1889) introduced a

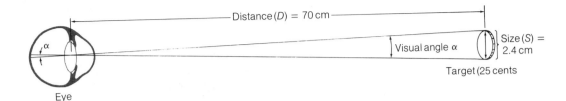

Figure 6-8. Computation of the size of the visual angle of the image of a quarter viewed at a distance of 70 cm (approximately arm's length), where the observer's line of sight is perpendicular to the lower edge of the coin. Tangent of visual angle = size/distance, therefore tan α = S/D = 2.4/70 = 0.034. Thus α is approximately 2°.

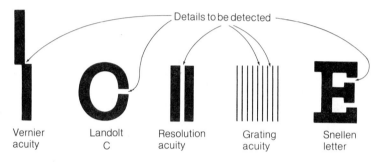

Figure 6-9. Some typical acuity targets and the details to be discriminated.

different recognition task that used circles with a gap in them as targets (see Figure 6-9). The gap can be oriented either up, down, to the right, or to the left, and the observer's task is to indicate the position of the gap. The circles differ in size, and the smallest detectable gap is the measure of acuity.

A variety of other tasks are used to measure visual acuity. The most primitive measure of acuity is simply the specification of the smallest target of any type that can be detected. The relationship between brightness perception and the acuity task is most apparent for this task, where the target is a light line or spot against a dark background, or a dark line or spot against a light background. **Vernier**, or **directional, acuity** requires an observer to distinguish a broken line from an unbroken line. **Resolution**, or **grating, acuity** is mea-

sured by an observer's ability to detect a gap between two bars, or the orientation of a grid of lines. This particular form of acuity task has certain theoretical implications, which we will discuss in the next section. Figure 6-9 shows examples of the various acuity targets with arrows pointing to the critical recognition detail. Notice that each detail is merely a region of the field where there is a change in luminance.

Because acuity tasks are closely related to brightness discrimination, it is not surprising to find that acuity varies as a function of the many factors that were shown to be important in the perception of brightness. For instance, the adaptive state of the eye determines the minimum details that can be discriminated under particular viewing conditions (Lie, 1980). Thus, if you step out of the bright sunlight into a dim room, you may find it impossible to read

---

Demonstration Box 6-4. Visual acuity as a function of retinal location

Visual acuity is best in the fovea. The range of clear vision extends less than 10 degrees away from the foveal center. Lay this book flat on the table and view the accompanying diagram from a distance of approximately 12 cm. Cover your left eye with your left hand and look directly at the point marked 0°. Without moving your right eye, you will note that the letter over the 0° mark is relatively clear, and that the letter at 5° is also legible. However, the letters at 10° and beyond begin to appear fuzzy, and the letters at 40° or 50° are virtually unreadable.

K	B	X	M	P	A	S
+	**+**	**+**	**+**	**+**	**+**	**+**
50°	40°	30°	20°	10°	5°	0°

---

even the large type of the headlines of a newspaper for a few moments. As your eyes adapt to the dim surroundings, however, you can soon easily read even fine print. Miller (1965) demonstrated that even a brief flash of light, bright enough to alter an observer's state of adaptation, could markedly reduce the observer's ability to detect and recognize acuity targets.

The detection of details in acuity targets also shows an interaction between time and stimulus intensity, very much like that described by Bloch's law for brightness detection. This means that you can increase the likelihood that the detail will be detected either by increasing the difference in the stimulus intensity of the target compared with its background, or by increasing the amount of time that the observer views the stimulus. While this relationship only holds for times less than 100 msec for brightness detection, the trade-off between time and intensity holds for up to 300 msec in acuity tasks in which observers are trying to detect details of the pattern (Kahneman, 1966; Kahneman, Norman, and Kubovy, 1967).

Retinal position is also as important for acuity as it is for brightness perception (Jennings

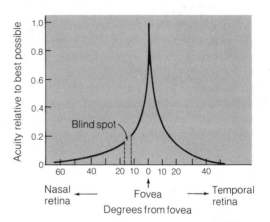

Figure 6-10. The distribution of visual acuity across the retina.

and Charman, 1981). The figure in Demonstration Box 6-4 allows you to experience the drastic reductions in visual acuity for targets that are imaged some distance from the fovea. When we measure relative acuity for various locations on the retina, we find that it varies as shown in Figure 6-10. Notice that acuity is best in the central fovea and drops off rapidly as we move out into the periphery. This curve looks remarkably like the distribution of cones across the retina diagrammed in Figure 3-7. It also looks much like the distribution of X cells in the retina (Peichl and Wassle, 1979). Direct physiological measurements of the responsiveness of X and Y cells shows that X cells have smaller receptive fields and seem to respond better to small stimuli. This has led a number of researchers to suggest that the limits of visual acuity are set by the prevalence of X cells, which are best designed for the detection and analysis of small details in stationary visual arrays (Andrews and Pollen, 1979; Robson, 1980).

To the extent that the part of the retina that is highest in visual acuity contains mostly cones, which then send their signals to X-type ganglion cells, we can predict some further interactions between brightness and acuity. Since cones operate only at higher levels of illumination, we would expect better acuity at higher illumination levels. When we measure the relationship between acuity and illumination directly, we obtain the curve shown in Figure 6-11. Notice that when the illumination

is low, in the scotopic (rod) range, acuity is poor, and it improves only slightly as the light intensity is increased. As we begin to shift into the photopic (cone) range, however, acuity improves rapidly. Of course, at too high a light level acuity is reduced again because of the effects of glare. Demonstration Box 6-5 provides a stimulus figure and instructions for demonstrating the relationship between acuity and illumination.

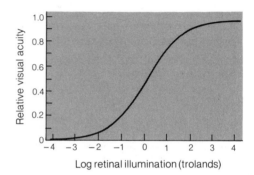

Figure 6-11. *The effect of illumination on visual acuity.*

Demonstration Box 6-5. Acuity and intensity

You will need your variable intensity light source again (either television or closet). Under very dim illumination, view the bundle of converging lines shown in the diagram. Notice that at some point, where the lines are relatively close together, you can no longer resolve individual lines and the bundle appears to be gray. This is the limit of your grating acuity under these conditions. Place your finger or the point of a pencil at the point where the individual lines are no longer resolvable. Now

gradually increase the intensity of the light source and notice that you can now begin to resolve lines at a higher point in the bundle. In fact, under normal room illumination, the lines in the area where acuity began to fail under lower illumination may now be discriminable. Notice also that the apparent blackness of the lines and whiteness of the paper (in other words the psychological contrast) also improves under higher light conditions.

One aspect of the relationship between acuity and illumination has important implications for some common situations. In 1789, Lord Maskelyne, Director of the Royal Greenwich Observatory, noticed that he became noticeably near-sighted at night. This tendency to accommodate the eye inappropriately near, even when the object of interest is far away, is referred to as *night myopia* (Leibowitz, Post, Brandt, and Dichgans, 1982). Practically, this degrades the sharpness of the retinal image, interfering with one's ability to see details under twilight and nighttime conditions. This reduction of acuity may be an important component in nightime driving accidents (Leibowitz and Owens, 1977).

SPATIAL FREQUENCY ANALYSIS

Spatial Fourier analysis

A complete description of the relationship between brightness perception and acuity must take into account a great deal of information. Imagine any test pattern of light. Next, realize that when this pattern stimulates the eye there are 20,000,000 or more retinal receptors, each receiving an amount of light ranging from 0 to many millions of units. Pity the poor perceptual researcher who must now find a method of describing all this activity (not to mention the poor brain that must interpret it). Must we catalog every point of light and its intensity before we can begin to speak analytically about the problems associated with the perception of brightness and how they reflect on our visual acuity? If such were the case, we would never make any progress. Many researchers realized this and began to look for a small set of relationships among the variables that affect brightness perception that could be used to

describe visual arrays, and that might shed some light on some of the brightness and acuity data that we have considered so far. The most successful attempt to date has been to use a mathematical technique based on **Fourier's theorem**, which implies that it is possible to take any light pattern and analyze it as a set of sine waves in much the same way sound can be analyzed as combinations of simple tonal sine waves (see Chapter 4). Here, however, instead of dealing with sound waves that vary in intensity over time, we will deal with light patterns that vary in intensity across a surface, that is, in space. According to Fourier's theorem, we should be able to generate any pattern of light by summing the appropriate sine waves. Looking at this in reverse, any visual pattern that we might wish to analyze can be described mathematically by decomposing it into the set of sine waves that added together to produce it.

You might recall from trigonometry (and from Chapter 4) that a sine wave is simply a regular, smooth, periodically repeating function that has some precisely specified mathematical properties. Figure 6-12*A* shows a graph of a sine wave and beside it a distribution of light that follows this mathematical description, growing more intense where the function rises and less intense where it falls. Such a pattern is properly called a **sine wave grating**, because its intensity varies sinusoidally as we move across the figure. Remember, Fourier's theorem says that by adding together (synthesizing) a number of such waves we can produce *any* specified brightness distribution. Thus, although individual sine wave patterns appear to have only blurry variations in brightness, by adding many of them together we can even produce light distributions that contain sharp corners, such as that shown as Figure 6-12*B*. This pattern is commonly called a **square wave grating**.

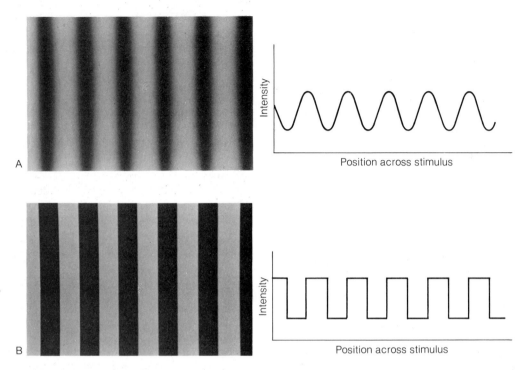

Figure 6-12. (A) A sine wave spatial distribu-
tion of light, and (B) a square wave spatial

distribution of light (based on Cornsweet,
1970).

Successive additions of the appropriate frequencies of sine waves (or more accurately the light distributions they represent) gradually gives a better and better approximation to the sharp corners of the square wave grating. Figure 6-13 shows this graphically. If we take this approach to describing the patterns of light that act as stimuli to our visual systems, we no longer have to catalog the intensity of every point in the pattern. Now we can fully describe a light pattern with a relatively compact mathematical expression indicating the particular sine wave frequencies to be added to reproduce it. Even if the mathematics sometimes becomes complex, it is still far simpler than the detailed description of the light hitting 20,000,000 or more individual retinal recep-

tors. (See Levine and Shefner, 1981, or Weisstein, 1980, for a more complete introduction to Fourier analysis.)

Modulation transfer function

Fourier analysis and synthesis provide more than a simple shorthand for the description of light patterns. They serve as powerful tools that may be used to analyze how the visual system responds to stimuli. Consider for a moment how you might test the fidelity of a photographic system. The simplest way of doing this is to use a series of gratings, such as those shown in Figure 6-12. Some of the gratings will have very broad bars and spaces. In such gratings, the light intensity rises and falls slowly as we move across the spatial extent of a surface, hence they are said to have *low spatial frequencies*. In other words, the frequency of changes in light intensity across space is low. Some other gratings will have narrow bars and spaces. In these gratings the light intensity changes rapidly (at a high rate) as we move across space, hence they are said to have *high spatial frequencies*. Now we will photograph each grating to see how well it is reproduced. At some point, when the bars and spaces become quite narrow, the system will reach its limit. The lens will no longer be able to resolve the individual bars, and all the bars and spaces will merge into a gray blur. This is exactly the same type of task we would use to measure the resolution acuity of human observers, except that here we are looking at the resolution acuity of an optical system. When photographic engineers do this type of analysis for an optical system, they measure its resolution in terms of the maximum number of lines per inch that can be resolved. Because very finely packed arrays of lines, corresponding to high spatial frequencies, cannot be resolved and are blurred, we say that optical systems *attenuate* the high frequency components of the pattern. A graphic or mathematical description of how certain spatial frequencies are lost because the system cannot resolve them, while others are retained because they are within the system's resolution capacity, is called the **spatial modulation transfer function**. It measures the system's ability to "transfer" to the final image a spatial modulation (or intensity change over space) present in the target stimulus.

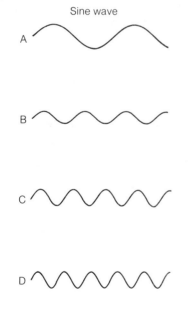

Figure 6-13. Gradually adding higher frequency sine waves to the distribution leads to better approximations of a square wave through the process of Fourier synthesis.

 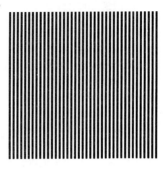

Figure 6-14. The effect of spatial frequency on the apparent brightness and contrast of pat- *terns. Notice that the higher frequency pattern has less apparent contrast.*

To assess the visual system's limitations in resolving changes in light intensity over space, *contrast matching* is used to measure the modulation transfer function in humans. Consider the two targets shown in Figure 6-14. Although both are square wave gratings, the one on the left is of a lower spatial frequency than the one on the right. Despite the fact that the physical contrast is the same in the two figures, the psychological contrast (the apparent difference between light and dark regions) is much less for the higher frequency (you can increase this difference by propping the book up and stepping back a foot or two). In a contrast matching task, observers would be asked to match the apparent contrast of such targets (or more usually sine wave gratings) by adjusting the intensities of the light and the dark regions until the two patterns matched. In this way, we could map the differences in visibility of various spatial frequencies. An alternative method involves measuring the threshold for detecting sine wave gratings as different from uniform stimuli. Subjects are presented with a sine wave grating at a particular spatial frequency. Using one of the psychophysical procedures we discussed in Chapter 2, the size of the intensity variation between the bright and the dark regions of the grating

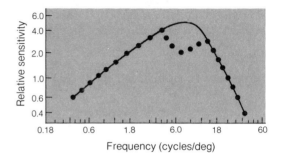

Figure 6-15. The modulation transfer function that shows the relative visibility of targets of various spatial frequencies. The solid line represents the normal transfer function, while the dotted line represents the transfer function after selective adaptation to a 6 cycle/degree stimulus.

is adjusted until the observer can just barely distinguish the stripes that define the grating pattern as different from a uniform gray.

When we measure a typical modulation transfer function for a human observer, it looks like the solid line shown in Figure 6-15. As the graph shows, human observers are quite sensitive to spatial frequencies around 6 cycles per degree (6 cycles of the sine wave over a degree of visual angle). As spatial frequency becomes higher, we gradually lose our ability to resolve spatial intensity differences. This loss at higher frequencies is probably a result of the fact that the eye is an optical system, containing a lens, and any such system has a high-frequency cutoff. Notice also that there is some loss of resolution in the lower spatial frequencies (less than six cycles per degree). This loss results from the fact that as the bars and spaces become wider, the lateral inhibitory interactions that sharpen the contours and increase apparent brightness differences between adjacent regions become less effective. In much the same way, Demonstration Box 6-3 showed that Mach bands were accentuated when the intensity changes were near one another. Thus, intensity changes are most effective in producing the phenomenal impression of a brightness difference when these changes occur at intermediate spatial frequencies (as determined by the Fourier analysis). When intensity changes occur too frequently within the visual image, they are difficult to resolve. Similarly, when the physical changes are too infrequent, there is no perception of brightness differences. Thus, the modulation transfer function provides a convenient basis for predicting the apparent brightness of many types of stimulus configurations.

Neural spatial frequency channels

Imagine an extremely self-assured scientist sitting at his home computer, complete with all the programs necessary to do Fourier analyses of any light patterns that might happen to be of importance or interest, muttering to himself, "If *I* find Fourier analysis so useful in analyzing patterns of light, maybe the visual system does too. Perhaps the visual system is designed to conduct some sort of spatial frequency analysis for any given pattern of light. Certainly, if it did, it would benefit from the same sort of concise description of the incoming light pattern that I obtain, and could thus also avoid the separate analysis of millions of responses of millions of individual photoreceptors."

Actually, this suggestion is not as strange as it might seem. At a general level, the first stage of spatial frequency analysis can be accomplished by mechanisms that we know exist and have already discussed. These mechanisms are the circularly organized retinal receptive fields described in Chapter 3. Recall that each of these has an excitatory, or *on*, region that, when stimulated by light, gives an increase in neural response rate, and an inhibitory, or *off*, region, that gives a decrease in the neural response rate when stimulated by light (and a burst of responses upon the light's termination). Before we discuss how such an arrangement can do a spatial frequency analysis, we must first introduce a bit of terminology. Every cycle of a sine wave grating has both a dark and a light phase, as we saw in Figure 6-12. This means that the dark stripe (or the light stripe) would be one-half the sine wave cycle. Now we can tell you that every circular receptive field is "tuned" to a sine wave frequency the half cycle of which is equal to the size of its central excitatory or inhibitory region. To visualize this type of structure, consider Figure 6-16.

Suppose we have an *on-center* receptive field of the size illustrated in the figure. If the spatial frequency is too low, that is to say the stripes are too wide, the fields of illumination will fall on both the center and the surround. Even though the central *on* region of the field is stimulated, there is an equal degree of stimulation of the inhibitory surrounding *off* regions of the receptive field. Because of lateral inhibitory interactions, the two types of responses tend to cancel each other. Thus, the total response of the ganglion cell with this

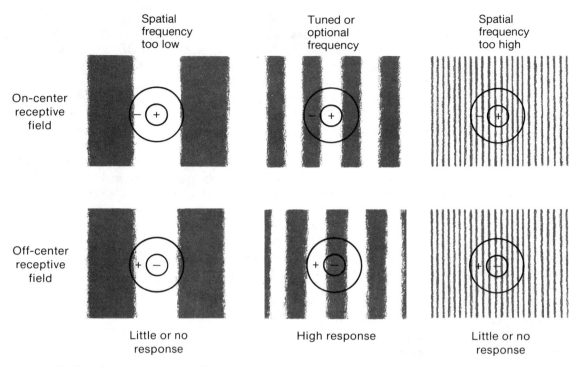

Spatial frequency too low

Tuned or optional frequency

Spatial frequency too high

On-center receptive field

Off-center receptive field

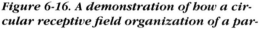

Little or no response

High response

Little or no response

Figure 6-16. A demonstration of how a circular receptive field organization of a par- *ticular size can perform a crude spatial frequency analysis.*

receptive field is low. Now consider the other extreme, where the spatial frequency is very high, and there are many stripes falling across the field. The *on* and *off* regions of the field would each be stimulated by about equal proportions of light and dark, again producing little or no net response. Finally, consider a spatial frequency in which the half cycle width is approximately the same as the central region of the receptive field. If the bright stripe now covers the central region of the *on* center cell, there will be a vigorous *on* response. There will be little inhibition from the surrounding *off* region, which lies mostly in darkness from the dark half of the cycle. Thus, the net response to this grating would be quite strong. Notice that the same sort of analysis of

spatial frequency can occur in the *off-center* cell, only here the optimal response is obtained when the dark half of the cycle is over the central region of the receptive field. Each receptive field is maximally responsive to a specific spatial frequency of light intensity changes.

This crude analysis of spatial frequencies could serve as the first step of a Fourier decomposition of the incoming stimulus pattern if a few additional requirements were met. First, there must be a broad range of receptive field sizes so that "tuning" would be fine enough to determine many of the spatial frequencies that make up the pattern. This requirement is fulfilled easily since, as noted in Chapter 3, X and Y cells differ in their ranges of receptive field size, with X cells tuned for higher frequencies than Y cells (see Lennie, 1980). Thus, there may be a number of different *channels* in the visual system, each tuned to a different range of spatial frequencies. The second major requirement would be higher level cells, perhaps in the visual cortex, that preserve the spatial frequency information extracted by the tuned receptive fields of the retinal ganglion cells. There is evidence that such cells exist in the cortex. These cells have not only preferred orientations of response, but also preferred ranges of spatial frequency (Derrington and Fuchs, 1981; DeValois, Albrecht, and Thorell, 1982). The fulfillment of these requirements does not *prove* that Fourier analysis occurs in the visual system; however, it suggests that the equipment to perform such an analysis exists.

Selective adaptation

A number of perceptual results suggest that there are separate channels in the visual system signalling the presence of specific spatial frequencies. Most of these findings emanate from an experimental technique involving **neural satiation**, or fatigue, also often called **selective adaptation**. (Note that this is quite a different use of the word adaptation than that associated with dark or light adaptation discussed earlier in the chapter.) In this procedure, an observer is exposed to a specific spatial frequency for a moderately long time (perhaps several minutes). If there is a specific group of neurons tuned to that particular frequency, they will, of course, immediately start responding when their optimal stimulus appears. If the stimulus remains in view for a long period of time, these neurons will continue to respond, until they are eventually too fatigued to respond vigorously any longer.

Since this fatigue might last for a minute or two after exposure to the *adapting stimulus*, we have then effectively eliminated, or temporarily disabled, a particular group of spatial frequency channels.

As an example of how this technique works, suppose we begin by measuring the *modulation transfer function* of an observer, just as we did to produce the solid line in Figure 6-15. Now we have an observer stare for a while at a grating of about 6 cycles per degree, in order to fatigue the spatial frequency channels associated with this middle range of frequencies. When we next measure the observer's transfer function, we get the results shown as the dotted line in Figure 6-15. Notice that there is a depression in sensitivity around the adapted spatial frequency, indicating that these tuned frequency channels have been fatigued and hence no longer respond as effectively. Of course, the region of reduced sensitivity will vary depending on the specific spatial frequency channels that were satiated or fatigued (Harris, 1980; Graham, 1980).

There is one particularly interesting perceptual effect that can be produced using this technique. Remember that spatial frequency roughly corresponds to the size of elements in a pattern. Thus, low spatial frequencies correspond to large elements, or in our gratings, to wide stripes, while high frequencies correspond to smaller elements. Suppose we had somehow disabled all the low spatial frequency channels. With only the high frequency channels operating, they would dominate the percept. In addition, their response to larger pattern elements would be weaker than the response of the channels optimally tuned to those elements but now not responding due to fatigue. Since the action of these higher frequency channels usually signals the presence of high spatial frequencies, we might expect that the pattern would appear to be dominated

Demonstration Box 6-6. Selective adaptation of spatial frequency channels

If you look at the pattern, you will see that one of the squares on the left has broad bars (low spatial frequency) and the other has narrow bars (high spatial frequency). The pattern on the right contains two gratings, both of which have the same spatial frequencies, but they are neither as high nor as low as the ones on the left. Hold the illustration about 80 cm away from you. Now look at the horizontal bar between the upper and lower patterns on the left for about 20 or 30 sec. Move your gaze from one portion of the bar to another, but keep your eyes on the bar. As you look steadily at the bar, the channels tuned to low spatial frequencies from the upper part of your visual field

and these tuned to the high spatial frequencies from the lower part of your visual field are fatiguing, or adapting. Now if you transfer your gaze quickly to the dot between the identical gratings on the right, you will notice that they no longer seem to be the same. The top part of the grating now appears to be spaced more finely, with thinner stripes, than those on the bottom. The low frequency channels have been disabled in the upper region of the visual field. With more high spatial frequency channels active, the percept is shifted toward higher frequencies; hence, the stripes are seen as smaller and more dense. The opposite effect is occurring in the lower region of the field.

 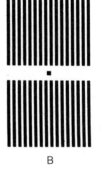

A   B

by high frequency (smaller) elements compared with a situation where all channels were operating normally. Demonstration Box 6-6 allows you to demonstrate this effect for yourself.

While spatial frequency analyses provide an interesting new approach to the problems of brightness and acuity, they do not provide us with the complete answer, any more than does lateral inhibition. The final perceptual response that emerges as a particular brightness, size, or detail, involves the operation of all

levels of the perceptual system. In later chapters we shall see how some of the higher cognitive factors interact with the mechanisms we have discussed so far.

GLOSSARY

The following definitions are specific to this book.

Adaptation   A reversible change in sensitivity as a result of prolonged or ongoing stimulation.

Bloch's law The trade-off relationship between stimulus duration and stimulus intensity in their effect on absolute threshold; $T \times I = C$.

Brightness The phenomenological impression of the intensity of a light stimulus.

Brightness assimilation The perceptual effect that is the reverse of brightness contrast. Here, added white lines lighten a stimulus and black lines darken it.

Bril A unit for measuring the apparent brightness of stimuli.

Bunsen-Roscoe law The physical law defining the photochemical reaction of any light-sensitive substance as a function of the intensity and duration of light exposure.

CIE The *Commission Internationale de l'Eclairage*, an international committee responsible for light measurement.

Dark adaptation An increase in the eyes' sensitivity after a change from a high to a low level of illumination.

Directional acuity *See* Vernier acuity.

Fourier's theorem A theorem that implies that a complex pattern of light can be mathematically analyzed as a set of simple sine waves.

Grating acuity *See* Resolution acuity.

Illuminance The amount of light falling on a surface.

Lateral inhibition The process of adjacent visual units inhibiting one another, for example, the more a cell is stimulated, the more it responds and inhibits its neighbor cells.

Light adaptation The change in visual sensitivity when an individual moves from a darker environment into a lighter one.

Lumen The unit of luminous energy equal to the light emanating from a standard candle, which is slightly more than 0.001 watt at a wavelength of 555 nm.

Luminance The amount of light reflected from a surface.

Luminosity curve A plot of the relative brightness of light of different wavelengths.

Mach bands The perception of dark or light lines at regions near abrupt changes in an intensity gradient.

Neural satiation A process in which specific groups of neurons fatigue in response to optimal and continuous stimulation. Also called selective adaptation.

Photometry The process of light measurement in reference to its visual effects.

Photopic A term for high light (daylight) visibility conditions and vision under these conditions.

Piper's law The trade-off relationship between area and intensity in the detection of stimuli between $10'$ and $24°$ of visual angle in size; $\sqrt{A} \times I = C$.

Purkinje shift The change in the apparent brightness of different wavelengths in a light- as opposed to a dark-adapted state.

Radiance The amount of energy coming from a light source.

Recognition acuity A type of visual acuity commonly measured by means of letter recognition and scaled relative to a norm of visibility at 6 m distance from the observer.

Reflectance The proportion of incident light that a surface reflects.

Resolution acuity An observer's ability to detect a gap between two lines, or the orientation of a grid of lines.

Retinal illuminance The amount of light reaching the retina.

Ricco's law The trade-off relationship between area and intensity in the detection of stimuli smaller than $10'$ of visual angle in size; $A \times I = C$.

Selective adaptation *See* Neural satiation.

Scotopic A term for low light (night) visibility conditions and vision under these conditions.

Simultaneous brightness contrast A target area of a given luminance appears brighter when surrounded by a dark background than when surrounded by a light background.

Sine-wave grating A pattern of light intensity that varies from light to dark following sinusoidal gradations.

SI   The *Système International d'Unités*; a uniform system of light measurement.

Spatial modulation transfer function   A graphical description of the way in which an optical system's ability to resolve spatial modulations (intensity changes over space) varies with spatial frequency.

Square-wave grating   Sharply alternating light and dark stripes.

Standard units   Uniform measures of photic energy established by international convention.

Vernier acuity   The measure of an individual's ability to distinguish a broken line from an unbroken line.

Visual acuity   The ability of the eye to resolve visual details.

Visual angle   A measure of the size of the retinal image.

Color

A COUPLE SAT WATCHING THEIR NEW color television set. When a commercial appeared on the screen, the woman commented, "I often wonder why humans developed color vision. After all, if we never saw anything but shades of gray, history would have run its course, science would have emerged, and except for the effect it would have had on art, we would have survived well enough as a species."

"I'm not so sure," replied the man. "My dad was color-blind, but didn't find out until he was nearly fifty. He was always doing strange things. He couldn't be trusted to pick tomatoes from the garden because he was always mixing up the ripe and the green ones. We finally suspected that something was wrong when he commented that he admired cherry pickers for their ability to recognize shapes. 'After all,' he said, 'the only thing that tells 'em it's a cherry is the fact that it's round and the leaves aren't. I just don't see how they find 'em in those trees!'"

It is surprising to many of us to find out how important color is in determining our ability to discern aspects of our world. For instance, consider Figure 7-1. Although the figure appears to be a random collection of gray shapes, there is a word hidden in it. Each letter is composed of a series of similar shapes. If you study the figure for a moment, you will see how difficult it is to detect the word (if you can do it at all), despite the fact that the shape and brightness information are there. Now turn to Color Plate 2, where we have added color to the figure. Notice that, now, the word actually leaps out. Color provides an important stimulus dimension that aids in the localization and identification of targets. For some species, color vision is a matter of life and death. For instance, if bees lacked color vision, their task of locating the nectar-bearing flowers hidden among shrubs, grasses, or leaves would be almost impossible. The survival of this species may well depend on its ability to spot a glint of color that indicates the presence of blossoms.

COLOR STIMULUS

The human eye registers as light wavelengths between 360 and 760 nm. Sir Isaac Newton was able to show that stimuli of different

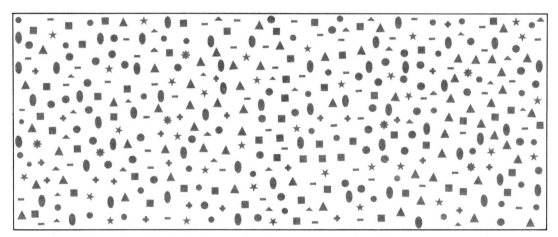

Figure 7-1. Can you find the hidden word? If not turn to Color Plate 2.

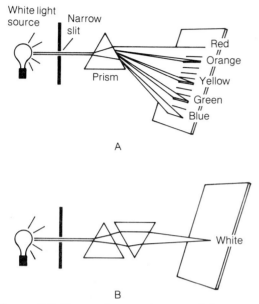

Figure 7-2. Newton's experiments: (A) separation of white light into its various wavelengths gives the color spectrum; (B) recombination of the colors gives white light.

wavelengths within this range produce different color sensations. Newton's experiment was quite simple. He took a glass prism and allowed some sunlight to pass through it from a slit in a window shade. When he held a sheet of white paper on the other side of the prism, the light no longer appeared to be white; rather, it took the form of a colored spectrum, looking much like the arrangement of lights in a rainbow (see Figure 7–2A). Newton knew that light bends when it passes through a prism, and that the amount of bending (technically called refraction) depends on wavelength. There is less refraction of the longer wavelengths (600–700 nm) and greater bending of the shorter wavelengths (400–500 nm). Thus, a prism takes various wavelengths of light, which make up sunlight, and separates them according to wavelength. The fact that we see this spread of light as varying in hue

seems to show that color perception depends on the wavelength of the light. Table 7-1 shows some typical color names associated with some selected wavelengths of light. Newton inserted another prism (in opposite orientation) so that the light was now refracted in the direction opposite to the effect of the original prism. This, of course, recombined all the wavelengths into a single beam. Now when he placed a piece of paper into this beam, it again appeared to be white, with no hint of the original colors that went into the combination. This indicates that the sensation of white results from a mixture of many different wavelengths (see Figure 7-2B).

An important technical distinction should be made here: Figure 7-2 does not describe how white light is broken up into "colored light." Colored light does not exist; rather, what exists is visible radiation of different wavelengths. If there were no observer, there would be no color. Newton pointed this out when he said, "For the rays, to speak properly, are not colored. In them is nothing else than a certain Power and Disposition to stir up a sensation of this or that Color." Thus, when we talk about the color stimulus, we should actually speak of radiation of different wavelengths, since the

Table 7-1. Wavelengths of light and associated color sensations

Color name	Wavelength (nm)
Violet	450
Blue	470
Cyan	495
Green	510
Yellow-Green	560
Yellow	575
Orange	600
Red	660
Purple	Not a spectral color but a mixture of "red" and "blue"

sensations of red, green, blue, and any other color reside in the observer. Having made this technical distinction, we must admit that it is extremely convenient to talk about red light or green light, and for the sake of brevity, we will not hesitate to do so in some of our later descriptions. However, when we refer to a "blue light," we are referring to those wavelengths of light that *elicit the sensation of blue*, namely, the shorter wavelengths in the visible spectrum.

Objects appear to be colored because they reflect to our eyes only selected wavelengths of light. Consider a common object, such as an apple, with white light falling on it. It appears red. We have seen already that white light, such as sunlight, is a combination of all wavelengths. Because the light stimulus that reaches our eyes produces the sensation of red, all the wavelengths except the longer (red-appearing) ones must have been absorbed by the surface of the apple. Colored objects or surfaces contain pigments that selectively absorb some wavelengths of light, while the rest are reflected and thus reach our eye. It is this selective "subtraction" of some wavelengths from the incoming light that gives an object its color. If a surface does not absorb any of the wavelengths reaching it but reflects them all uniformly, it appears to be white rather than colored. Color filters work in much the same way, that is, by absorbing some wavelengths of light. For instance, if a white light is projected through a green filter, the resulting beam is green. This means that the filter has absorbed most of the long and short wavelengths, allowing only the medium-range, or green-appearing wavelengths, to reach the eye.

You should be alerted to the fact that simply specifying the wavelength, or wavelengths, in a stimulus does not fully describe the way the color appears to an observer. For instance, a stimulus with a dominant wavelength of

570 nm may appear yellow, while another with the same wavelength composition may appear brown. For this reason, factors other than wavelength are used to classify colors.

Color appearance systems

Suppose that you were marooned on a desert island that had a beach covered with pebbles of many colors. Lacking anything else to do, you set about the task of classifying the colors of all the pebbles in some meaningful way. The first classification scheme that might come to mind would involve grouping stones together on the basis of their hues. Thus, you would build a pile of red stones and another of green stones, and so forth. Once you have your piles of stones, you would have to look for some meaningful arrangement for the piles. For instance, you might notice that orange seems to fall, in terms of appearance, somewhere between red and yellow. The yellow-greens, of course, seem to fall between yellow and green. Once you reach the blue end of your line of stones, however, you might run into a bit of a problem. The purple stones seem to fall somewhere between the blues and the reds. This means that a straight line arrangement is not adequate. Instead, you might arrange the pebbles as shown in Figure 7-3.

This crude color arrangement scheme is circular. You have probably seen it before in books on art, decorating, or design. It is usually called the **color circle** or **color wheel** in such sources. In this arrangement, you have separated the colors according to **hue**, which is the psychological dimension that most clearly corresponds to variations in wavelength. Let us consider the effect of wavelength on sensation by looking at the effects produced by pure, or **monochromatic, stimuli**. A monochromatic stimulus contains only one wavelength (from

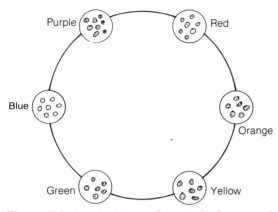

Figure 7-3. A primitive color circle for encoding the colors of pebbles.

the Greek *mono*, meaning one, and *chroma*, meaning color). These stimuli are similar to those found in the spectrum generated by Newton's prismatic separation of light and, therefore, are often called **spectral colors**. Such monochromatic stimuli do not produce all the hues found in the color wheel. For instance, we find that no single wavelength produces the sensation of purple. This sensation requires a mixture of blue and red wavelengths. Similarly, there is no place in the spectrum where we can find a red that does not have a tinge of yellow. In order to achieve such a hue, we must add a bit of blue (short wavelength) light.

Meanwhile, back on the beach, it has become clear that your color wheel classification scheme based only on the psychological attribute of hue seems incomplete. A close look at the piles of pebbles reveals marked color differences. For instance, among the red pebbles, you might find some that are a deep red color, while others are pink. Another group may be almost pure white with only a hint of red coloration. Physically, this observation corresponds to the dimension of **purity**. Clearly, the purest color one could get would corre-

spond to a monochromatic or spectral hue. As we add other wavelengths, or white light, the color appears to become "washed out." This psychological attribute of color appearance is called **saturation**. It is actually quite easy to integrate saturation into the color circle by simply placing white in the center. Now imagine that the various degrees of saturation correspond to positions along the spokes, or radii, emanating from the center of the wheel. The center represents white (or gray) and the perimeter represents the purest or most saturated color possible. Figure 7-4 shows the color wheel modified to include saturation. Notice that the point corresponding to pink (a moderately desaturated red) would be plotted near the center along the line connecting red and white, while a crimson would be plotted farther away from the center along the same line.

To the average observer, hue and saturation do not completely describe all the visible nuances of color. It is quite possible to have

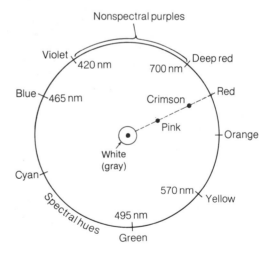

Figure 7-4. The color circle, modified to allow the encoding of both hue and saturation. Spectral colors are on the outer rim, white is in the center.

two colors match in both these attributes but still appear to be different. For instance, a blue spot of light projected onto a screen would not appear to be the same as another spot identical in all regards except that it has been dimmed by a light-reducing filter put in front of it. Thus, the sensory quality of **brightness** (which we discussed in Chapter 6) must be worked into our system of describing colors. Because we have already used the two dimensions capable of being reproduced on a flat piece of paper, it is clear that the addition of a third color dimension (brightness) forces us to use a solid instead of a flat representation.

The shape of the three-dimensional color space can be derived from common observation if we recognize that at high brightness levels or at very low brightness levels colors seem "weak" or "washed out," meaning that they are of low saturation. Thus, the hue circle must shrink, since saturation seems to vary over a more confined range, and very high degrees of saturation are never observed at very high or very low levels of brightness.

If we combine the three attributes of hue, saturation, and brightness, we derive something that looks like Figure 7-5, which seems to be a pair of cones placed base to base. This figure is usually called the **color spindle**, or the **color solid**. The central core as we move up or down represents brightness and consists of all the grays running from white (at the top) to black (at the bottom). We can imagine that at each brightness level, if we sliced through the color solid in the direction shown in the diagram, we would get a color circle in which the hue would be represented along the perimeter. Totally desaturated colors (the grays) are at the central core, as we've already noted; hence, saturation is represented by moving from the center outward. This is the basic representation used in many color appearance systems. Probably the most popular among

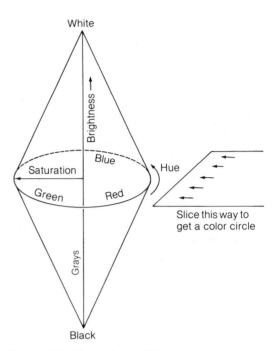

Figure 7-5. The color solid.

psychologists is the one developed by Munsell (1915) in use and modified by Newhall, Nickerson, and Judd (1943) to agree with the way in which typical observers arrange color stimuli. To classify colors, you can use a **color atlas** in which each page represents a horizontal or a vertical slice through the color solid. Color samples that illustrate colors found in varying locations in the color solid are given in such atlases, allowing the observer to identify and to label any given test color.

Color mixture

Pure colors of a single wavelength are usually produced under precise laboratory conditions. Most of the light reaching your eye is composed of a mixture of many different wavelengths. Generally, the **dominant wavelength**

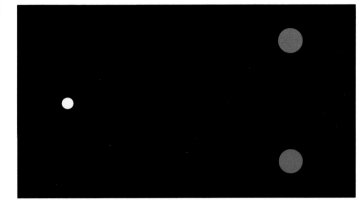

Color Plate 1

Color Plate 2

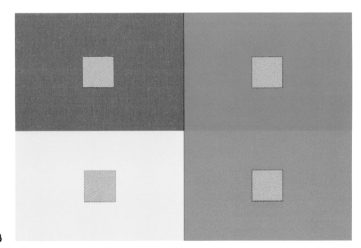

Color Plate 3

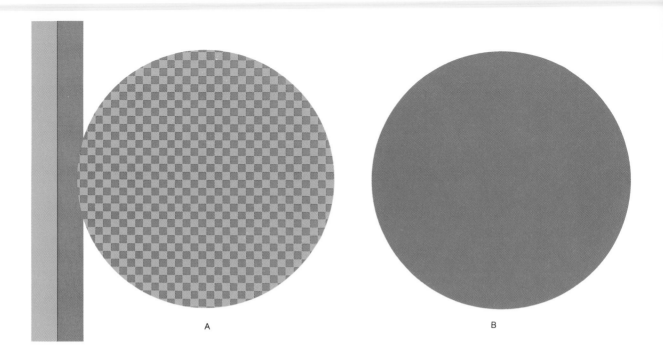

A   B

Color Plate 4

Color Plate 5

Color Plate 6

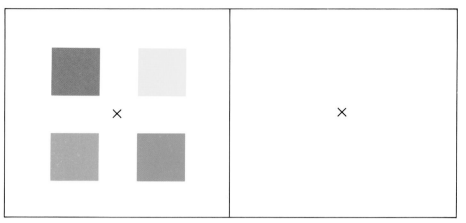

Color Plate 7

A Read through this list of color names as quickly as possible.
Read from right to left across each line.

RED	**YELLOW**	**BLUE**	**GREEN**
RED	**GREEN**	**YELLOW**	**BLUE**
YELLOW	**GREEN**	**BLUE**	**RED**
BLUE	**RED**	**GREEN**	**YELLOW**
RED	**GREEN**	**BLUE**	**YELLOW**

B Name each of these color patches as quickly as possible.
Name from left to right across each line.

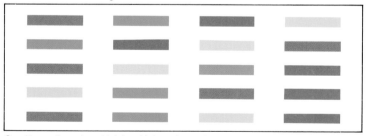

C Name the color of ink in which each word is printed as quickly as possible.
Name from left to right across each line.

RED	**BLUE**	**GREEN**	**YELLOW**
YELLOW	**BLUE**	**RED**	**GREEN**
BLUE	**YELLOW**	**GREEN**	**RED**
GREEN	**BLUE**	**YELLOW**	**RED**
BLUE	**YELLOW**	**RED**	**GREEN**

Color Plate 8

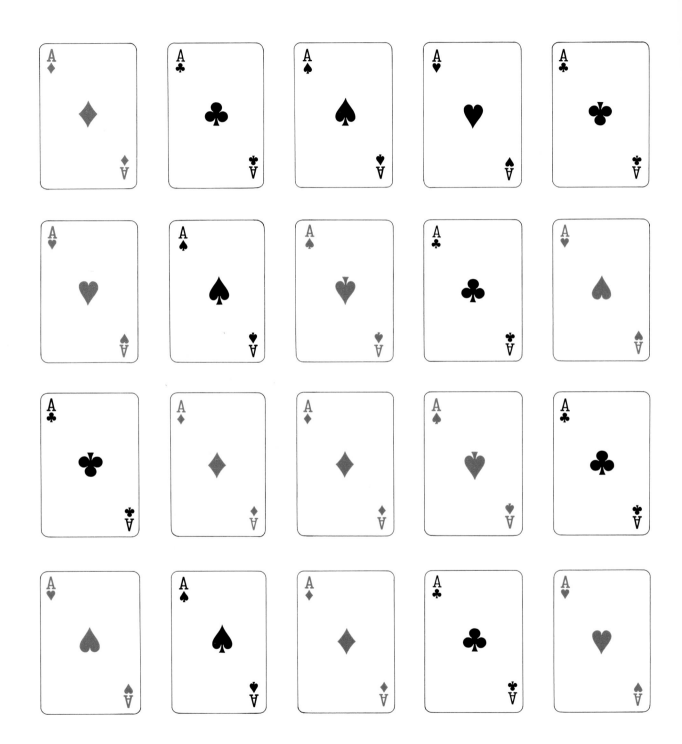

Color Plate 9

will determine what hue you see, although this is not always the case. When we combine two or more wavelengths of light, we see a new color, with a different psychological hue and saturation. Once the colors are mixed, the eye can no longer determine the individual wavelengths that make up the mixture. One can have a pure yellow light of 570 nm and another that matches it, composed of a mixture of a 500 nm green and a 650 nm red. Colors that appear to be the same but are made up of different wavelengths of light are called **metameric colors**. You will not be able to distinguish between these hues, nor will you be able to isolate the red and the green that went into the mixture.

There are two types of color mixtures. The first and the simplest to describe is called **additive color mixture**. Additive mixtures occur when we mix light. For instance, if we project a red circle on a screen, the light reaching the eye from the projected point is red. If we project a blue circle on the screen so that it partially overlaps with the red circle, the light reaching the eye from the region where the circles overlap contains both blue and red light. Each new wavelength projected onto the screen adds to the mixture of wavelengths reaching the eye. Figure 7-6A shows a situation that might occur if we used three projectors with the first projecting a red beam, the second a green beam, and the third a deep blue beam. If the circles of light were arranged so that they partially overlapped with one another, we would get a series of additive mixtures. For instance, where the red and deep blue overlap, we get a reddish purple generally called magenta. Where the deep blue and the green overlap, we get a lighter hue tending toward a green, usually called cyan. Something that some people find quite surprising happens where the red and green overlap. In this region we perceive yellow. Where all three

beams overlap we see white. Demonstration Box 7-1 shows another way to get additive color mixtures.

You cannot duplicate these results using paints. If you tried mixing all your paints together to get white, you would get a shade of

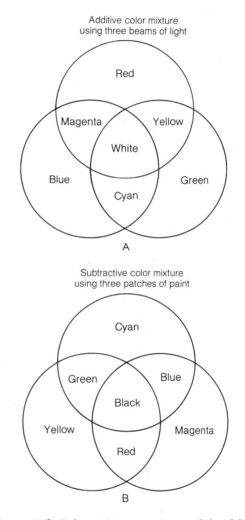

Figure 7-6. Color-mixture systems: (A) additive color mixture using three beams of light; (B) subtractive color mixture using three patches of paint.

Demonstration Box 7-1. Color mixture

There is a simple way to obtain additive color mixtures without using projected beams of light. Consider Color Plate 4A, in which you see a checkerboard of tiny red and green squares. In Color Plate 4B you see a yellow disk. Prop up the book so that you can see the Color Plates when you move across the room. Now, standing at a distance, look back at the figures. What formerly appeared to be red and green now appears to be yellow and should match the yellow disk. At a distance, the optics of the eye can no longer resolve the individual squares. The light from each of them smears, or blurs, across the retina giving rise to the color mixture effect.

This technique is similar to the technique used in your color television set. If you take a magnifying glass and hold it up to the screen, you will see that each region is made up of a series of tiny dots. When you sit at normal viewing distance, you can no longer resolve the individual dots. They have combined within the eye to give you an additive color mixture. A similar technique was used by the French painter Seurat, who replaced the traditional irregular brush stroke used in painting with meticulously placed dots of color. Thus, instead of mixing paints on his palette, he allowed the mixture to be accomplished optically within the eye of the onlooker viewing the painting from an appropriate distance.

gray instead. This is because pigments do not work in the same way as lights. Something that appears red, such as a tomato, will have a surface pigment that absorbs most of the short and medium wavelengths, reflecting to your eyes only the longer (red) wavelengths. On the other hand, a pigment that gives you a color similar to grass green might absorb most of the long wavelengths and the short wavelengths, reflecting to your eye mainly the middle wavelengths. When you mix the red and the green paints together, the mixture contains the middle wavelengths that are reflected by the green, but these same wavelengths are absorbed by the red pigment; hence you are subtracting *all* the wavelengths from the mixture, leaving only a muddy gray.

Because pigments work by subtracting or absorbing wavelengths of light, mixtures of pigments are called **subtractive color mixtures**. Such pigment mixtures produce colors that are considerably less predictable than mixtures of lights because the wavelength-absorbing property of pigments is complex and variable. For example, Figure 7-7 shows the wavelengths reflected by some typical pigments. Notice how irregularly they reflect the light, so imagine the problems in predicting what the resultant mixes might reflect and absorb.

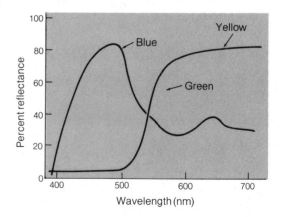

Figure 7-7. The relative wavelength composition of a blue, a yellow, and a green pigment.

Suppose, however, that we were dealing with relatively simple pigments, where the yellow reflected only the middle and long wavelengths, the cyan only the long and middle wavelengths, and the magenta reflected only the long and short wavelengths. If we now painted circles of these pigments so that they overlapped, we would get a crude representation of the expected results in subtractive color mixtures. Because yellow pigments absorb all the short wavelengths, and the cyan pigment absorbs all the long wavelengths, their mixture absorbs both the short and the long wavelengths, leaving only the middle, or green-appearing portion of the spectrum. When we combine yellow with magenta, we find that the yellow subtracts the short wavelengths and the magenta subtracts the middle wavelengths; hence, only the long, or red-appearing, wavelengths remain. In a similar fashion, overlapping cyan and magenta leaves us with only the blue wavelengths, because all others are subtracted; hence, the mixture produces blue. Clearly, when all three pigments overlap, everything is absorbed and we get black, as shown in Figure 7-6*B*. In general, it is more convenient to deal with additive color mixtures since they are easier to conceptualize.

Although the color wheel provides a convenient way of predicting the appearance of additive color mixtures, it *describes*, rather than *explains*, how colors interact. To use the color wheel to predict a color mixture is actually quite simple. Suppose we mix a spectral red (about 650 nm) with a spectral yellow (about 570 nm). Figure 7-8 depicts this process where the two colors in the mixture are represented by the line connecting them. For instance, if we combine the yellow and the red in equal proportions, we will get a color that corresponds to the dot in the center of the line. We can determine what this color will look like simply by drawing a line from the

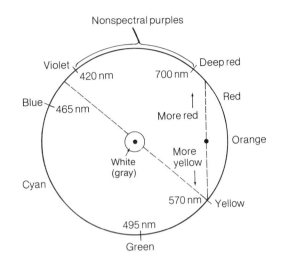

Figure 7-8. Using the color circle to predict color mixtures.

center of the color circle through the dot to the perimeter. When this is done, we find that we would get an orange corresponding to about a 600 nm spectral stimulus. Increasing the amount of yellow would shift the point along the line in the direction indicated, making it closer to the yellow hue. Adding more red would shift the point in the other direction along the line. You will notice that we started out with two spectral, or pure, hues (marked on the perimeter). The resultant mixed color, however, is a hue that is no longer on the perimeter. It is closer to the center of the color wheel. The purest colors possible are placed on the perimeter of the color wheel; colors that are more desaturated are found closer to the center of the circle (nearer white or gray). A color mixture is less saturated than either of the two component colors that went into it. *No mixture of colors can ever be quite as saturated as a monochromatic or spectral color.*

Mixing more than two hues (or hues containing more than a single wavelength) is a little more complex. If we were mixing three colors, the resultant color sensation would be given by the center of a triangle produced by connecting the three colors. If the amount of each hue differed, the center point of the triangle would shift toward the dominant hue.

CIE color space

An interesting effect occurs when we mix two colors that are exactly opposite to each other on the color circle. For instance, mixing a violet with a yellow along the lines shown in Figure 7-8 results in a colorless gray. When the proportions are correct, this mixture lies in the center of the circle. Colors whose mixture produces such an achromatic gray are known as **complementary colors**.

An important fact about color mixtures emerged in the 1850s. The German physicist and physiologist Hermann von Helmholtz (1821–1894) and the Scottish physicist James Clerk Maxwell (1831–1879) carried out a set of color matching experiments. They reported that by combining an appropriate set of three monochromatic light sources in appropriate amounts, they could match any other hue. These three wavelengths were to be known as **primaries**. In fact, the choice of primaries is rather arbitrary. One must select colors that are reasonably far apart, with the requirement that the mixture of any two of them alone will not match the third one. In 1929, Wright made a set of measurements where observers matched the hue of the various spectral sensations. He selected as his primary colors a red of 650 nm, a green of 530 nm, and a blue of 460 nm. The observers matched the color of two patches of light, where the first was the test color and the second could contain any combination of the three primaries. His results, shown in Figure 7-9, indicate the relative amounts of

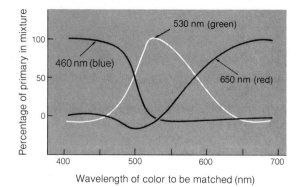

Figure 7-9. The proportion of each primary (a 460 nm blue, a 530 nm green, and a 650 nm red) needed to match any spectral color.

each of the three primaries needed to match any given wavelength. Notice that some of the values are negative, indicating that some of the particular primary had to be added to the test sample in order to reduce its saturation to the point where it could be matched by a mixture of the two remaining primaries. In other words, some matches could be made only if one of the three primaries was not included in the mixture *and* additional color was added to the test sample. The fact that any given color can be matched by an appropriate combination of the three others has important theoretical implications, which we will discuss later. In addition, it has led to another means of specifying colors that has been agreed upon by the Commission Internationale de l'Eclairage (CIE). This international commission adopted a set of standard primary wavelengths, and by adopting a certain shape of color diagram, they created the **CIE color space** that describes color mixtures with more accuracy.

The fact that any selected color can be matched by a mixture of three appropriately selected primary colors suggests an alternate way to specify the hue of a stimulus. We can specify the stimulus in terms of the proportion of the three primaries needed to reach this match. Geometrically, this suggests a triangular space with a primary color at each corner. Color mixtures may then be represented in the same way as they are on the color circle. Thus, yellow, which is a mixture of red and green, is represented by a point on the line between red and green. If we add more red, the point moves toward the red primary, and if we add more green it moves toward the green. As in the color circle, white is represented by a point in the middle, and is composed of an equal proportion of the three primaries. Also, as in the color circle, a red of lower saturation (the whitish red, or pink) would be represented by a point moved in toward the center. Such a diagram is shown in Figure 7-10.

In 1931 a special commission of the CIE standardized the procedure for specifying the color of a stimulus. The commission decided to use a color space created by the mixing of three primaries as we did above. Unfortunately,

if we select any three actual spectral primary colors, a number of perceptual and mathematical problems result. The major one is that some colors cannot be represented accurately within the triangle. Thus, a pure spectral yellow cannot be represented, since any color mixture can never be as saturated as the pure spectral color itself. To solve this perceptual problem, the CIE selected three *imaginary* primary colors and arranged the primaries at the corners of the triangle shown in Figure 7-11. These imaginary primary colors are more saturated than it is possible to get with any real colors. (Remember, this is simply done so that all colors can be represented within the space.) Notice that we have labeled the horizontal and vertical axes of the triangle *X* and *Y*.

We can now represent any color as a point in the color space. We can plot a mixture of three colors by using a point that has only two spatial coordinates because the **CIE color**

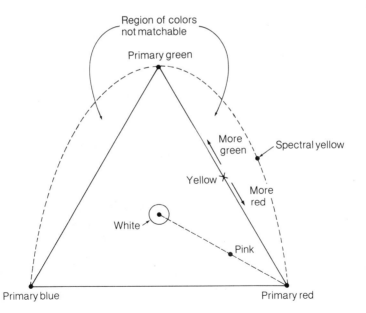

Figure 7-10. Specifying colors using a color triangle.

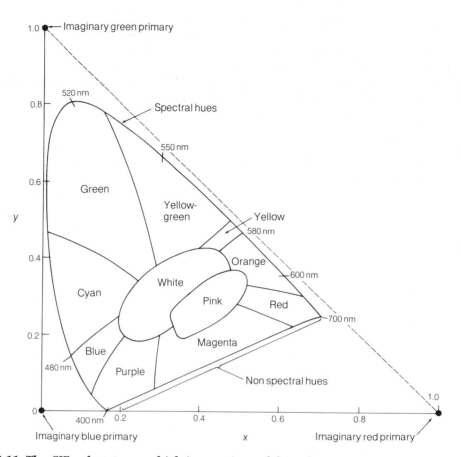

Figure 7-11. The CIE color space, which is a variant of the color triangle system using three imaginary "super" primaries.

space has been arranged so that Y represents the proportion of green in the mixture, and X represents the proportion of red in the mixture. The proportions of red and green and blue in any mixture must sum to a proportion of 1.0 (think of these as representing percentages, where all the items must sum to 100 percent of the light). If we know the total proportion of green and red in the mixture, we need only subtract this value from 1.0 to find the proportion of blue. Arranging the color space as shown automatically gives us these totals when we plot the X and Y coordinates of any

color. The actual colors that can be perceived do not fill the full triangle (remember, the primaries we are using are imaginary supercolors). Instead, they fill a horseshoe-shaped area, with the spectral colors forming the outside boundary. We have labeled this area on the figure so that you can see the regions filled by various colors. Thus, if we had a color 0.2X and 0.6Y, we would know that it was composed of 20 percent red and 60 percent green, and subtracting from a total of 100 percent, we would know that it contained 20 percent blue. Looking at the figure, you can trace out the X and Y

coordinates and see that this color would look green.

Brightness is not represented in any space on this diagram. As in the color space we discussed earlier, brightness requires a third dimension. Thus, the color space in the figure can be pictured as a single slice through a three-dimensional color space just as we demonstrated in Figure 7-5. This third dimension would be called Z. Using the CIE color system, we can specify any color stimulus by using its **tristimulus values**, which are simply the X and Y coordinates for the hue of the stimulus and a Z coordinate for the brightness of the stimulus.

THE PHYSIOLOGY OF COLOR VISION

To this point, we have dealt with the physical stimulus, some methods of specifying the appearance of a color, and some aspects of combining various wavelengths of light. None of the foregoing descriptions specifies *how* a particular color sensation arises. To understand this process, we must deal with both physiological and psychological factors. Let us consider these factors in light of the two major theoretical positions that have emerged during the last 150 years.

Trichromatic color theory

Much research has gone into the search for the physiological basis of color vision. One of the earliest findings was discussed in Chapter 6, where it was reported that no color vision is found under scotopic levels of illumination, when only the rods are active. These observations indicated that cones are the retinal receptors that provide the first stage of the color response. Therefore, the first question to be

answered is how the cones provide information about the wavelength of the incoming light.

Most normally sighted people can discriminate among thousands of colors. Holding brightness and saturation constant, however, the average human observer can discriminate at least 200 different hues. Suppose that we wished to create an artificial eye with this same ability. The simplest procedure would require a separate cone that responds to each of the discriminable hues. Unfortunately, such a scheme is not practical. For any given colored stimulus, we would only have 1/200 of the cones active. This means that our visual acuity would be much poorer than research has shown it to be. In addition, such a system would mean that our acuity measured under white illumination would be many times better than our acuity measured under monochromatic stimulation. This is also experimentally false.

An alternative scheme would be to have only one type of retinal cone with 200 different signal codes by which it could indicate the discriminable hues. This could be done with a sort of neural Morse code. Although such a neural Morse code may play a part in some aspects of color vision (as we shall see later), the evidence for such a mechanism is still controversial. Research evidence suggests that each cone contains only one pigment. If so, how would the cone itself "recognize" the wavelength of the light? The only thing that the cone "knows" is the amount of pigment that has been bleached. Although different wavelengths of light may bleach more or less pigment, simply increasing or decreasing the intensity of the stimulus could also cause such a state of affairs. It therefore seems unlikely that a single cone would be able to discriminate 200 hues.

An answer to the dilemma was suggested almost 200 years ago by Thomas Young

(1773–1829). Young suggested that only a few different retinal receptors, operating with different wavelength sensitivities, are necessary to allow humans to perceive the number of colors they do. He further suggested that perhaps as few as three receptors would do. His theoretical notion was revived in the 1850s by Helmholtz. As we have already noted, Helmholtz and Maxwell were able to show that normally sighted observers need only three primaries to match any color stimulus. These data were taken as evidence for the presence of three different receptors in the retina. Since the usual color matching primaries consisted of a red, a green, and a blue, it was presumed that there were three types of receptors, one responsive to red, one to green, and one to blue. Since these receptors are cones, and cones operate by the bleaching of pigment, we may suggest three hypothetical pigments. The first we would call **erythrolabe** (translated from the Greek, this means red-catching), another called **chlorolabe** (meaning green-catching), and the third pigment would be called **cyanolabe** (meaning blue-catching). This **trichromatic theory** (from the Greek *tri*, meaning three, and *chroma*, meaning color) finds some convincing support in the realm of defective color vision.

Color vision defects. Virtually all individuals differ in some way from what is usually called "normal" color vision. Some individuals, however, show drastic deficiencies in their ability to discriminate colored stimuli. In popular speech, such individuals are called **color blind**. This term is much too strong, since only a very small percentage of individuals are totally incapable of discriminating colors. According to a trichromatic theory of color vision, we should be able to predict five different varieties of color abnormality. The first, and most drastic, would be found in individuals who have no functioning cones. Because

such individuals could use only the rod system for seeing, they would be expected to have no color discrimination ability. In addition, they should find photopic, or daylight, levels of illumination to be quite uncomfortable. A slightly less drastic malady is one in which only one variety of cone is functioning in addition to the rods. With this problem, a person should be able to see under both photopic and scotopic conditions but would still lack any color discrimination ability. Any wavelength of light hitting one of the functioning rods (or the single cone system) would produce some bleaching of the pigment. Even though different wavelengths might bleach different amounts, this is not enough to allow color discrimination, since the response produced by any one wavelength of light can be matched merely by adjusting the intensity of any other. In other words, the individual with no functioning cones, or the one with only one functioning cone type, responds to light in much the way that a sheet of black and white film does. All colors are recorded simply as gradations in intensity of the response. Such individuals are called **monochromats**.

One might also suppose that some individuals, rather than lacking two or three sets of cones as does the monochromat, might only have one malfunctioning cone system. Given two functioning cone systems, individuals should have some color perception. Of course their color perception would differ from that of a normally sighted observer. They should be able to match all other colors with a mixture of two primaries. Such individuals are usually called **dichromats** (from the Greek *di*, meaning two, and *chroma*, meaning color). The existence of such individuals has been known since the 1700s. The famous English chemist Dalton was such a dichromat, a fact he learned rather late in his life. Supposedly, it first came to his attention when he wore a scarlet robe to receive his Ph.D. degree. Since he was a Quaker, a sect that shuns bright colors, this caused quite a scandal until it became clear that woolen yarn dyed crimson and yarn dyed dark blue-green appeared the same to him.

There are three predictable forms of dichromacy, depending on whether it is the red-, green-, or blue-responding cones that are inoperative. The specific confusions one would get are predictable from the color matching curves of normal observers shown in Figure 7-9. Dalton's type of color defect is usually referred to as **protanopia** (the Greek prefix *protos* means first, and red light is generally designated as the first primary). A protanope would be insensitive to long wavelengths normally perceived as red light. If a red light were made very much brighter than a green light, a protanope could easily confuse them. A color-normal observer would perceive that the light was brighter than the green and also that they differed in hue. Dalton described his subjective experiences when viewing a spectrum such as that produced by Newton's prism. Most individuals perceive six different colors, blending one into another. Dalton reported, "To me it is quite otherwise. I see only two, or at most three distinctions. These I should call yellow and blue, or yellow, blue, and purple. My yellow comprehends the red, orange, yellow, and green of others and my blue and purple coincide with theirs."

The most common form of dichromacy is called **deuteranopia** (the Greek prefix *deuteros* means second, and green light is by convention the second primary). Individuals with deuteranopia presumably have a malfunction in the green cone system. If you have deuteranopia, you are still able to respond to green light; however, you cannot distinguish green from certain combinations of red and blue.

Trichromatic theory also predicts a third form of dichromacy based on the absence or malfunction of the blue cone system. Although a name existed for this phenomenon, **tritanopia** (from the Greek *tritan*, for the third primary), there was no report of this difficulty for many years. Some years ago, however, a magazine article appeared as part of an intensive search throughout England that managed to find 17 such individuals. These individuals, instead of seeing the spectrum as composed of blue and of yellow as do other dichromats, see the longer wavelengths as red and the shorter ones as bluish-green. The discovery of this last class of individuals seems to provide strong support for a trichromatic theory of color vision.

Color defects are a fairly common problem. Some instances of it are relatively mild and result in what we call **anomalous trichromatism**. Although individuals with anomalous trichromatism do not act exactly as a dichromat would, their matches require more red (**protoanomaly**) or more green (**deuteranomaly**) than the color matches of non-defective individuals. They seem more like dichromats than like color-normal individuals. If we count all individuals with any form of color deficiency, we find that just over 8 percent of all males show such color weaknesses, while slightly less than 0.05 percent of all females show similar defects.

What colors does a dichromat actually see? While it is not possible to know how the colors of a dichromat compare with those seen by a color-normal observer, a glimpse into the visual world of the color defective has been provided by a rare person who was deuteranope in her left eye, but color-normal in her right eye. Graham and Hsia (1958) had this observer adjust the color seen by her normal eye so that it appeared to be the same hue as the color seen by her defective eye. The results of her matches are shown in Figure 7-12. As shown, the colors over the entire range of red

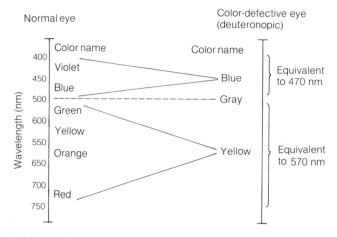

Figure 7-12. Color matches of a normal eye to a "color-blind" eye (deuteranopic) in the same observer (based on Graham and Hsia, 1958).

to green (from about 700 to 502 nm) all appear to have the same yellow hue (about 570 nm), while all the colors from green to violet appear to be blue (matching a 470 nm stimulus). The region that appears to be blue-green to the normal observer (around 502 nm) was perceived as a neutral gray in the defective eye.

Physiological basis of trichromatic theory. Although the data from color mixing and color defects seem to support a trichromatic theory of color vision, direct physiological evidence for the three cone pigments did not appear until the 1960s. The measurement procedure involved is conceptually simple but technically quite difficult (Brown and Wald, 1964; Marks, Dobelle, and MacNichol, 1964; Bowmaker and Dartnall, 1980). It involves a device called a **microspectrophotometer**. With this device, a narrow beam of monochromatic light is focused on the pigment-bearing outer segment of a cone. As tiny amounts of light of various wavelengths are passed through the cone, the amount of light absorbed at each wavelength is measured. The more light of a given wavelength that is ab-

sorbed by the cone pigment, the more sensitive is the cone to light of that particular wavelength. Such measurements were taken using cones from the retina of goldfish, monkeys, and finally, on cones from the retinas of humans. The results are unambiguous: There are three major groups of cones. The most recent measurements, taken from a human eye that had to be removed surgically (Bowmaker and Dartnall, 1980) show maximum absorptions in the ranges of 420, 534, and 564 nm, respectively (rods have a maximum absorption of 498 nm measured on this same eye, using the same technique). Figure 7-13 shows the relative absorption of these three pigments (where 1.0 is the maximum amount absorbed by the pigment). Clearly, on the basis of their sensitivity peaks, we should call the short-wavelength-absorbing pigment "violet," the middle "yellow-green," and the long wavelength "orange" if we wished to be more precise than the red, green, and blue labels we have been using.

Rushton (1962, 1965) introduced a technique called *reflection densitometry*, based on the same general principle but not requiring a microspectrophotometer, that is capable of measuring the absorption of cone pigments in living human observers. He sent a beam of light into the eye and then took measurements on the amount of light reflected back out of the eye. By taking the difference between the amount of light sent into the eye and the amount reflected (corrections are also applied for various interfering factors, such as absorption by blood vessels and light scattering in the eye), an estimate is obtained of the amount of light at each wavelength absorbed by the photopigments in the living human eye. The eye is next flooded with a light of a particular distribution. For example, red light might be expected to activate the long-wavelength-catching pigment most strongly; hence, with continued exposure, this pigment would be "bleached out." After the continuous exposure, the amount of light absorbed at each wavelength is measured again, and the exact pattern of absorption of the red pigment shows in the difference between light reflected from the "bleached" and "unbleached" retinas. Rushton

concentrated his beam on the fovea, since cones alone populate this region. He was able to obtain absorption curves similar to those shown in Figure 7-13 for pigments marked "red" and "green." He reasoned further that protanopes and deuteranopes, according to trichromatic theory, should be missing one or the other of the two longer-wavelength pigments. When he used his procedure with color-defective observers, he found that they were missing the appropriate pigments. Rushton could not find evidence for cones containing blue-matching pigment in the fovea. This fact suggests that all observers are dichromats, specifically tritanopes, for targets seen in central vision. This conclusion has also been verified using psychophysical techniques (Bornstein and Monroe, 1978; Williams, MacLeod, and Hayhoe, 1981).

Actually, we have known for a long time that the color response varies over regions of the retina. The central foveal region is relatively blue-blind. The distribution of sensitivity to red and green is limited to an area of about

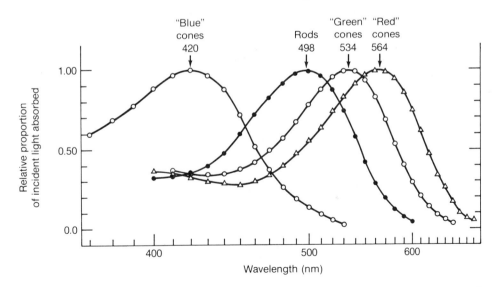

Figure 7-13. The relative absorption of various wavelengths of light by the three different cone types and the rods of a human (based on Bowmaker and Dartnall, 1980).

20–30 degrees around the central fixation point. Yellow and blue can be discriminated at up to 40–60 degrees. If we go into the far periphery of the retina, we find that individuals are totally color-blind in this region. Figure 7-14 shows a map of the color sensitivity of the retina. You may trace this sensitivity for yourself to see how your own color discrimination varies across the retina, by using Demonstration Box 7-2. Although the evidence for trichromatic theory is quite strong at the retinal level, a number of perceptual phenomena cannot be explained by the existence of three pigments alone. Such data suggest that the neural coding of color information is not simply the addition of responses from three separate color channels.

Opponent-process theory

The German physiologist Ewald Hering (1964/1878) was not completely satisfied with a trichromatic theory of color vision. It seemed to

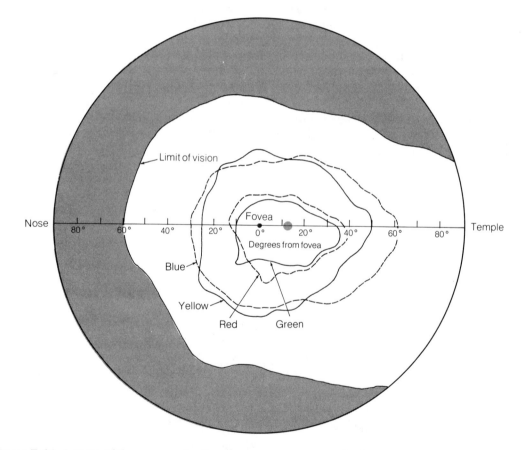

Figure 7-14. A map of the zones of color sensitivity of one observer's right eye. Each line represents the limit of the area (from the center) where the marked colors can be seen.

Demonstration Box 7-2. Color sensitive zones on the retina

Color perception is best in the central region of the retina. You can observe the changes in color discrimination for different parts of the retina by using Color Plate 5. Lay this book flat on a table and view the color plate from a distance of approximately 12 cm. Cover your left eye with your left hand and look directly at the point marked 0 degrees. Without moving your right eye, notice that the four colored dots (red, green, blue, and yellow) have clearly discriminable hues at the point marked 0 degrees. At 10 degrees, you may find some difficlty discriminating between the red and the green. At 20 degrees, only the blue and the yellow should have clearly discriminable

hues, while at 50 or 60 degrees, the four dots should be virtually indistinguishable as far as hue is concerned, with each taking on a shade of gray.

Another way to demonstrate this is to take a small orange piece of paper and put it on a sheet of gray. Now, keeping your head fixed, look off to the side of the orange target. If you keep moving your eyes outward, eventually you will reach a point where the orange will look yellowish, meaning that you have now imaged it beyond the red sensitive zone. If you continue to move your eyes outward, you may even reach a point where the orange no longer looks colored at all, but merely appears gray.

---

him that human observers acted as if there were four, rather than three, primary colors. For instance, when observers are presented with a large number of color samples and asked to choose those that appear to be *pure* (defined as not showing any trace of being a mixture of colors) they tend to select four, rather than three, colors. These unique colors almost always include a red, a green, and a blue, as trichromatic theory would predict; however, they also include a yellow (Bornstein, 1973). Boynton and Gordon (1965) showed that with the color names red, yellow, green, and blue, English-speaking observers can categorize the entire range of visible hues (some stimuli seem to require a combination term containing two primaries, such as yellow-green). Figure 7-15 shows the way in which adult observers distribute their hue names. Clearly, there are four overlapping hue name categories, corresponding to red, green, blue, and yellow. We cannot simply attribute the results to learning or language use. For example, Bornstein, Kessen, and Weiskopf (1976) showed that four-

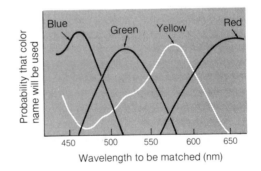

Figure 7-15. The relationship between color names and wavelengths.

month-old infants tend to see the spectrum as if it were divided into four hue categories. They did this by repeatedly presenting a given wavelength of a light until the infants became visually bored and stopped looking at the light (a process called **habituation**). They next monitored how much time an infant spent looking at a second wavelength of light. They found that when the second wavelength was selected from another hue name category (based on the adult data), the infants spent more time looking at it than they did at a wavelength selected from the same hue category. This suggests that, to infants, stimuli within a given hue category are somehow similar; hence, it seems they categorize hues into the same four groups that the adults do.

Hering looked at another aspect of the subjective experience of hue. He noted that certain color combinations are never reported by observers. For instance, one cannot have a yellowish-blue, nor can one have a greenish-red. This led Hering to suggest that the four primaries were arranged in opposing pairs. One pair would signal the presence of red or green, while a separate pair would signal blue or yellow. This might be accomplished by having a single neuron whose activity rate increased with the presence of one color (red) and decreased in the presence of its opponent color (green). Since the cell's activity cannot increase and decrease simultaneously, one could never have a reddish-green. A different opponent process cell might respond to blue and yellow. A third unit was suggested to account for brightness perception. This unit might be called a black-white opponent-process cell. We need not limit our discussion to speculation, however, since physiological evidence exists that bears directly on the issue of opponent-process coding of color information.

Physiological basis of opponent process theory.

At the time when Hering first suggested an opponent-process mechanism for the neural encoding of hue information, there was no physiological evidence to support such a speculation. Perhaps the single most important finding of twentieth century sensory physiology was that neural responses are subject to both excitatory and inhibitory influences caused by interaction between neighboring units. We introduced you to several such systems in Chapters 3 and 6. In fact, Chapter 6 discussed how many brightness phenomena can be explained by the presence of a *spatially* opponent mechanism on the retina, where excitation in one region causes inhibition in another. If we could also find *spectrally* opponent organization, where stimulation by one wavelength of light causes excitation in a cell, and stimulation by a wavelength in another region of the spectrum causes inhibition of that cell's neural response, then we would have a physiological unit that corresponds to the mechanism postulated by Hering.

The first evidence that different wavelengths of light could cause opponent effects in neural response was offered by Svaetichin (1956), who inserted an electrode into the cell layers of the retina of the goldfish. When he recorded the responses to light transmitted by the horizontal cells (units at the first cellular layer beyond the cones, as noted in Chapter 3), he found that responses vary depending on the wavelength of the light reaching the cones. These neural responses were not in the form of the typical action potential found in most neurons, but rather were graded shifts in the electrical polarization of the cells. Svaetichin found that not only did the strength of response vary as the wavelength was changed, but more importantly, the electrical sign of the response was different for long and short wavelengths. Figure 7-16 shows the pattern of responses recorded by Svaetichin and MacNicol (1958). Notice that the spectral sensitivity of the units marked green-red and blue-yellow are exactly what we would need for these cells. For instance, the cell marked green-red would respond with a large positive signal if the unit were stimulated with a long-wavelength light (around 650 nm). This positive response could signal red. If the unit were stimulated with a greenish hue (around 500 nm), it would give its peak negative response, thus signaling

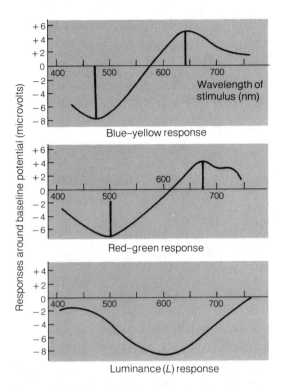

Figure 7-16. *Graded electrical response of retinal cells to various wavelengths of light (based on Svaetichin and MacNichol, 1958).*

the presence of green. If we simultaneously stimulated this unit with both a red and a green stimulus, the positive and negative responses would cancel each other and no signal would result. Red and green oppose each other, and we can never have the same unit simultaneously signaling both red and green. Such graded potentials are usually called **S potentials** after their discoverer, Svaetichin, and the cells that give these responses are called *C-type* horizontal cells, where *C* stands for color. Also notice that another form of cellular response is shown in the figure; it is marked *L*. This type of cell responds to the intensity of the light regardless of the wavelength. These *L-type* horizontal cells could be the basis of

the black-white response hypothesized by Hering.

At the level of the retinal ganglion cells, there is clearly an opponent process coding; however, now it takes on a spatial distribution (Boynton, 1979; De Monasterio, 1978). The general form of this encoding involves the center-surround organization of receptive fields that we discussed in Chapter 3. Suppose that we shine a tiny red spot on the eye, while recording from a retinal ganglion cell. In some cases, as the size of the spot increases, the vigorousness of the neural response increases up to some point. After that point, further increases in the size of the red spot have no influence on the cell's response. Notice that this is quite different from the type of response seen when white light is used (as in Chapters 3 and 6), where increasing the size of the spot starts to produce a reduction of response rate as it begins to enter the inhibitory region of the receptive field. If we repeat the experiment with a green spot, we find that the cell appears unresponsive when the green spot is in the center of the receptive field; as the spot becomes larger, however, or as it is moved into the surround field, the resting level of activity is reduced. Thus, we have a cell that has the property of being excited by red and inhibited by green, if the stimulus is the appropriate size and in the appropriate location on the retina. Of course, an equal number of cells is found with the opposite organization (green excitatory center, red inhibitory surround) in addition to cells in which the centers are inhibitory and the surrounds are excitatory. The visual system, once having come upon a particular organizational scheme, seems to like to exhaust all possible combinations.

Farther along in the visual system at the lateral geniculate nucleus, this particular arrangement can easily produce cells that generate a spectrally-opponent-signal with appropriate stimulus arrangements. In Chapter 3, we discussed some of the work of DeValois and his co-workers (DeValois and DeValois, 1975, 1980). They found that cells in the lateral geniculate of monkeys were also color coded, similar to the color coding of the retinal ganglion cells. These units showed a resting level of activity (in terms of neural responses per unit time) even in the absence of any light stimulation. When the eye was stimulated by large spots of light, the response pattern changed. Some cells responded more vigorously when the eye was stimulated with short wavelengths of light and decreased their response rate below their spontaneous (dark) activity level for long wavelengths of light. Other cells acted in exactly an opposite manner. As with the S potentials, two different classes of cells were reported. Each had different patterns of response as a function of wavelength, similar to what is needed for a red-green cell and a blue-yellow cell. Since the lateral geniculate receives its input directly from the retinal ganglion cells, this is exactly the pattern of results that we would expect. Thus, returning to our earlier example, if we have a red excitatory center in a receptive field, we should get increased response for a large area red light while the green inhibitory surround would completely ignore its presence. On the other hand, a large green spot would cause an inhibitory response and be ignored by the red excitatory center, and so forth. Typical responses from lateral geniculate cells can be seen in Figure 7-17. As Figure 7-17 shows, there are three cell types. One responds differentially to short and moderately long wavelengths (blue-yellow), one responds differentially to moderately short and long wavelengths (red-green), and one does not show different opponent processing but rather responds simply to the amount of luminance reaching the eye. The spectrally tuned cells code both chromatic and spatial information

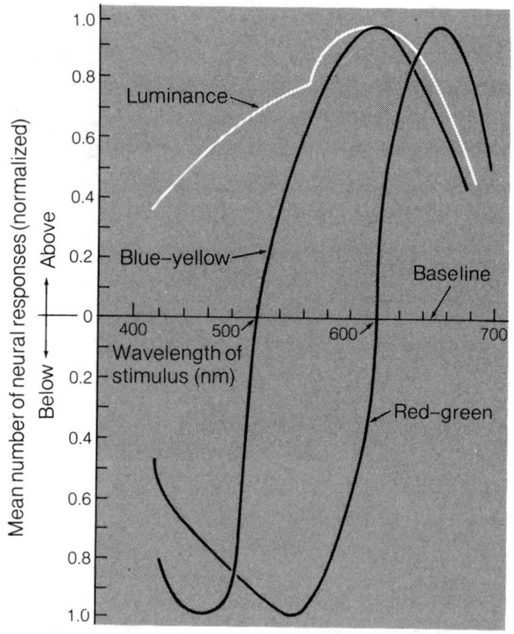

Figure 7-17. *The neural response rate for cells in the lateral geniculate relative to their resting response rate, for stimulation by lights of different wavelengths (based on De-Valois and DeValois, 1975).*

in the responses. This means that whether a given wavelength will produce an increase or a decrease in neural response may also vary as the spatial position of the stimulus spot is varied within the receptive field of the cell.

The processing of color information in the visual cortex has now become somewhat clearer, although much remains to be learned. Hubel and Wiesel's pioneering study in 1968, which recorded electrical responses from single cortical cells, showed that some cells in the monkey cortex respond differently as a function of the color of the test stimulus. Since then, evidence suggests that perhaps 50 percent or more of cortical cells are color sensitive (Jacobs, 1976). This responsiveness to color appears in addition to the responsiveness to orientation, motion, and so forth, found in both simple and complex cortical cells (Gouras and Kruger, 1979; Kruger and Gouras, 1980; Michael, 1981). In one complex cell, one might find that the largest response is for a red line of a particular orientation moving in a specific direction, whereas another cell might show its maximum response for a green line. The Mc-Collough after-effect is an interesting demonstration of how orientational and color responsiveness are connected (Harris, 1980; Mc-Collough, 1965, Stromeyer, 1978). Demonstration Box 7-3 allows you to see this effect for yourself.

As we saw in Chapter 3, visual coding in the cortex is highly organized, both across and down into the cortical surface. Similar organization is found for color coding. Penetrating into the cortex are vertical columns, or slabs, where all the cells will be color responsive, while in others, no color responsiveness appears (Michael, 1981). Within a color column, all cells show color sensitivity; however, each might be tuned to different colors, orientation, or eye of input.

As we penetrate the cortex vertically, we find types of cells that show an increase in response when the eye is stimulated with some colors and a decrease in response when stimulated with others. Once again, there is a spatial factor in this response. For example, a cell might respond by increasing its activity to red in the center of its receptive field while it would also respond by decreasing its activity for green stimuli in the surround. In layer 4 of the cortex, however, there are cells that have a double opponent process. If there is a red excitatory center, a cell will increase its response to red in the center, but instead of ignoring red in the surround, the cell actually decreases its firing. The opposite organization in the same cell holds for green, with a green spot on the inside producing a decrease in re-

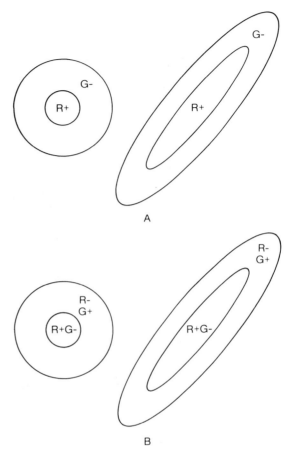

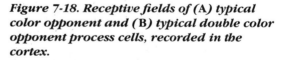

Figure 7-18. Receptive fields of (A) typical color opponent and (B) typical double color opponent process cells, recorded in the cortex.

sponse, while the green spot on the outside produces an increase in firing (Michael, 1978a, b). Figure 7-18 shows typical receptive fields of these types. Such double opponent process cells would respond most vigorously to contrasting colors placed next to one another, such as a red surrounded by a green. A schematic outline of the arrangement of color processing in a section of striate cortex, as we currently know it, is shown in Figure 7-19.

Demonstration Box 7-3. McCollough's demonstration of the interaction between color and form

Through repeated exposure to colored stimuli at a particular orientation, the cortical cells that are tuned to that combination of stimuli will become fatigued. When we next show a set of noncolored stimuli at the same orientation, these cells respond more weakly. This gives us colored aftereffects. The particular color that is seen is usually the complement to the fatigued color. Thus, for instance, if you fatigue the green response you will get red, the blue response you will get yellow, and so forth. Of particular interest here is the fact that these aftereffects are orientation specific and seem to be a result of the selective fatigue of cortical cells tuned to color and orientation (Harris, 1980, Stromeyer, 1978).

To perform this demonstration, first notice that the figure in this box is completely achromatic. Now, turn to Color Plate 6, and notice the two colored grids, one containing vertical green lines

and the other horizontal red lines. To fatigue the cortical cells, simply look at the green grid for about 5 seconds, then shift your gaze to the red grid for another 5 seconds, then back again to the green grid for 5 seconds, continuing this alternation for about 2 or 3 minutes. When that inspection period has passed, look back at the figure in this box and you will find that it appears to be colored. Now the vertical white bars appear reddish (the green response to vertical lines has been fatigued), and the horizontal bars appear greenish (the red response to horizontal lines is diminished). Notice also that turning the book sideways or tilting your head so that the orientation of the lines changes on your retina will change the colors of the lines. This demonstration illustrates the intimate relationship between color and form that was predictable from our knowledge of the cortical coding of color and orientation.

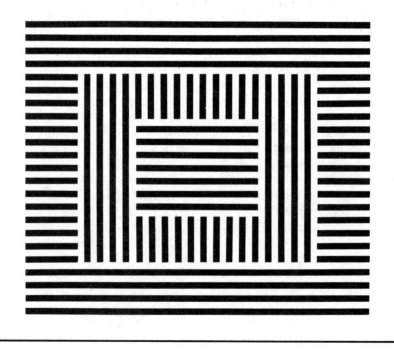

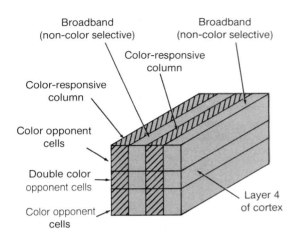

Figure 7-19. The arrangement of color-responsive cells in the cortex.

Models of color coding

How can a four-primary, opponent-process (or "push-pull") system exist when the retina seems to operate with a three-color pigment system? Actually, Hurvich and Jameson (1974) have suggested a **neural wiring diagram** that indicates the way in which cones, each containing only one of three pigments, could produce opponent responses at the postretinal level. An example of how such a wiring diagram might work is shown in Figure 7-20. It requires only that certain cones *excite* cells farther along in the system, while other cones *inhibit* the response rates of other cells. Engineers hit upon a similar system when they designed color television. The color in the original scene is first analyzed into its red, green, and blue components by the camera and then transformed into two color-difference (or opponent-process) signals (plus an intensity signal). After reception at its distant location, the signals are reconverted into red, green, and blue signals by the television set. This technique was selected because it required considerably less information to be transmit-

ted through each channel, thus providing good fidelity and increased economy. Perhaps similar considerations of economy and fidelity underly the organization of our visual systems.

An alternative neural coding theory for color was first suggested by Troland (1921) and recently has been revived. It claims that separate neural channels may not be needed for the various primary hues. Instead, information may be sent through common channels, with the color information carried by way of a sort of neural Morse code. Here, specific patterns of neural responses with specified time intervals could signal various colors. If this is the case, then it should be possible to create the subjective impression of color by flickering white light on and off in a pattern that mimics the usual neural code. Several investigators

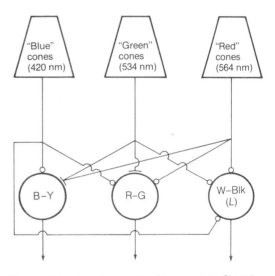

Figure 7-20. A schematic diagram indicating how a three-pigment system might be connected to produce an opponent process neural response. The lines represent the connections. The round and the flat connections differ in that one is excitatory and the other is inhibitory (which is arbitrary). Numbers indicate the wavelength of maximum sensitivity.

Demonstration Box 7-4. Subjective colors

You have already encountered subjective colors in Demonstration Box 1-2, where colors appeared in a stationary stimulus. A more powerful set of subjective colors, produced by flickering black and white patterns, began as a toy invented by C. E. Benham in 1894. It was painted on a top and meant to be spun; hence the pattern is often referred to as **Benhams's top**. The pattern is shown in the figure below. Cut out this pattern (or carefully reproduce it), and mount it on a piece of thin cardboard. Punch a hole in the marked center region and insert a nail or a round pencil. Now spin the pattern as shown. Colors should appear when the pattern is spun at a moderate speed. If you

are spinning clockwise, the inner bands should be slightly red, the next yellow, then green, and the last blue or violet. The order of the colors should reverse if you spin the pattern counterclockwise. The color effects arise because of the specific patterns of flickering white and black set up by each band. These patterns mimic the flashing on-and-off light patterns used to study subjective colors in a laboratory setting.

If you alter the adaptive state of your eye by staring at a white surface for a minute, you will notice that the perceived colors on each line will be different (Karvellas, Pokorny, Smith, and Tanczos, 1979).

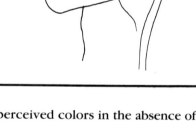

have been able to do exactly this, namely, generate the appearance of colors by pulsing white lights on and off (Festinger, Allyn, and White, 1971; Jarvis, 1977; Piggins, Kingham, and Holmes, 1972). Young (1977) has even managed to do this by pulsing tiny electric currents into the eye to simulate the supposed neural code. There is one phenomenon that this theory explains very well. It is the appearance of **subjective colors**. Subjective colors are perceived colors in the absence of the appropriate wavelengths of light, which can be made to appear in certain flickering black and white displays. A procedure for creating subjective colors for yourself is shown in Demonstration Box 7-4. Interestingly, people who show color defects for real colors also show the same pattern of color defect for subjective colors (White, Lockhead, and Evans, 1977).

Most contemporary researchers accept the

fact that several mechanisms may be involved in color perception. It seems that there is an initial trichromatic coding at the level of the cones, followed by opponent processing at the higher neural levels, with perhaps, some additional information provided by the time relationships in the overall patterns of neural response.

COLOR PERCEPTION

The wavelengths of light that are present are not the only factors that determine our perception of hue, as is demonstrated by the existence of subjective colors. A number of factors, such as stimulus intensity and duration, as well as the characteristics of surrounding stimuli, can also alter perceived color.

Intensity and duration

Increasing evidence suggests that information for color and brightness involve different visual channels (Boynton, 1978; Favreau and Cavanagh, 1981). Perhaps the best evidence for this is the fact that their time courses are quite different. Responses to color changes are much slower than responses to brightness changes (Bowen, 1981). It is also clear, however, that the perception of hue may interact with the intensity of the stimulus. If intensity levels are low, only rods will be active and no color will be seen. Even beyond the cone threshold, however, the perceived hue of a stimulus will change depending on the stimulus intensity. Specifically, if we increase the intensity of red or yellow-green stimuli, they not only appear brighter but also begin to take on a more yellow hue. Similarly, blue-greens and violets begin to appear bluer when the intensity is increased. This phenomenon is called

the **Bezold-Brucke effect**, in honor of its two discoverers. It is quite easy to demonstrate, as is shown in Demonstration Box 7-5. Although the basis of the Bezold-Brucke effect is not yet fully understood, it is clear that it is neural in its origin (Coren and Keith, 1970; Nagy, 1980). This effect may come about because the red-green cells are slightly more sensitive than the blue-yellow cells. Thus, we can discriminate between red and green at lower intensity levels. Because the blue-yellow units become more active at higher intensity levels, hues tend to be dominated by these colors when stimuli are bright (Hurvich, 1981).

Prolonged exposure to colored stimuli also produces a shift in the perception of hue. For instance, should you view the world through a deep red filter for a sufficient period of time, you would find that when the filter was removed the world would take on a blue-green tint. The fatiguing of a specific color response is called **chromatic adaptation**. It is believed that such adaptation effects are caused by either selective bleaching of one particular photopigment or fatigue of one aspect of an opponent-process color response system. Suppose you looked through the red filter for a long period of time. The red-catching pigment becomes bleached, or the red response in the red-green unit becomes fatigued. Now, when you view a white surface, the absence of red pigment (or the weakness of the red response) causes the blue and green systems to account for a greater proportion of the total activity. This gives the white a cyan (blue-green) tint. When such fatigue effects, due to prolonged stimulation, are localized (that is, confined to one region of the retina), they are called **afterimages**. Demonstration Box 7-6 provides a stimulus for the production of color afterimages. You will notice when performing this demonstration that the hue of the afterimage tends to be a *complementary* hue of the stimulus producing the afterimage.

Demonstration Box 7-5. The Bezold-Brucke effect

For this demonstration you will need three pieces of colored cellophane, glass, or celluloid to serve as color filters. One should be a red, the other a green, and the last a yellow. Take a white sheet of paper that is brightly illuminated with room lighting, and cast a shadow over one-half of the paper. Looking through the red filter, you will notice that the hue of the red seen on the bright half of the paper is noticeably yellower than the hue seen on the shadowed portion. When you peer through the green filter, you should experience the same effect. On the other hand, looking through a yellow filter should not cause an apparent change in hue. Thus, the brighter one makes a red or a green, the more yellow it will appear. This is a demonstration of the hue shift, associated with increasing stimulus intensity, called the Bezold-Brucke effect.

Another way to see this effect is to simply look at an incandescent light bulb (60 – 100 W) through the red or the green filter. You will notice that the light bulb appears to be yellow, despite the presence of the filter. Since the red filter only allows the long (red) wavelengths of light to pass, and the green only allows the middle (green) wavelengths through, no yellow is reaching your eye. Thus the yellow appearance of the bulb is caused by the Bezold-Brucke hue shift that occurs when the intensity of the stimulus is high.

Demonstration Box 7-6. Color afterimages

You can easily demonstrate negative or complementary color afterimages using Color Plate 7. Here you will see four square patches of color: red, green, blue, and yellow. Notice that there is a black x in the middle of this pattern. Stare at the black x for about two minutes while keeping the plate under reasonably bright illumination. At the end of this period, transfer your gaze to the black x to the right of the figure. You should see a pattern of colored squares that is the exact complement of the pattern originally viewed. Where the red patch was, you will see green; where the green patch was, you will see red; where the blue patch was, you will see yellow; and where the yellow patch was, you will see blue. These are the complementary color afterimages caused by the fatiguing of the color response during the time you were staring at the color patches.

Spatial interactions

As you may recall from Chapter 6, the brightness of a stimulus can be affected by the intensity of adjacent stimuli. The general nature of the interaction is inhibitory, so a bright surround makes a target appear dim. Inhibitory interactions between adjacent color systems can also occur. This results in hue shifts. Such a phenomenon is called **simultaneous color contrast**. Consider Color Plate 3. Notice that this figure has four brightly colored patches, each of which surrounds a small central target. The target on the red patch appears to be slightly green, while that on the green appears to be slightly red. The target on the blue patch appears to be slightly yellow, while that on the yellow patch appears to be slightly blue. In fact, each target is exactly the same gray. The apparent tinge of hue that appears in the target results from spatial interactions. You might be able to increase the strength of this effect by viewing Color Plate 3 through a sheet of tracing paper or thin tissue.

Jameson and Hurvich (1964) have suggested that color contrast arises from mechanisms similar to those that cause brightness contrast, namely, an active retinal neuron tends to inhibit the responding of adjacent units. If we consider the target on the red background, we have a situation where the red response system is highly activated. In turn, these active neurons will inhibit the red response in the gray patch. Inhibition of the red response results in the emergence of the complementary, or opponent, green response in this region. We then see a tinge of green hue in the gray. The results are similar to those observed in chromatic adaptation, except that there is an instantaneous neural response rather than a prolonged fatigue effect. The response does not seem to depend on an alteration of sensitivity to colored light, but rather only affects the perceived hue in the surrounded areas (Kinnear, 1979).

Contrast-induced colors act very much like real colors in their ability to produce other perceptual effects. For instance, Anstis, Rogers, and Henry (1978) induced quite strong contrast colors on surrounded gray patches (as in Color Plate 3) and found that observers developed negative afterimages to the contrast colors, just as though they had been viewing real colors!

Age and physical condition

Although an individual may have normal color vision when tested at one stage in life, color discrimination ability may change over a lifetime. Aging seems to alter color vision. Perhaps this is because the crystalline lens of the eye grows more yellow as an individual ages;

hence, we look through a gradually darkening yellow filter (Coren and Girgus, 1972a). Other effects may also account for age changes in color vision. For instance, aging seems to bring about a gradual deterioration of blue-yellow vision (Lakowski, 1962; Verriest, 1974). Most individuals are unaware of such changes because the onset is quite slow; the effect gradually accumulates, however. Since the perception of hue is subjective, we seldom have opportunities to assess whether our perception agrees with that of others. Does your red appear to be the same as that of your friends? Clearly, this is an unanswerable question.

Physical conditions can also result in losses in the ability to discriminate colors. Such acquired color vision losses are called **dyschromatopsias**. Several diseases or physical conditions lead to such dyschromatopsias. For instance, diabetics tend to suffer losses of color discrimination in the blue-yellow system, although the red-green system appears to be appears to be relatively unaffected (Lakowski, Aspinall, and Kinnear, 1972). Such color losses can be aggravated by a number of factors. For instance, diabetic women who take oral contraceptives show significantly greater discrimination losses in the blue-yellow range (Lakowski and Morton, 1977), and alcoholics also show similar losses in their sensitivity to blue (Reynolds, 1979). Thus, changes in the perception of color are possible throughout an individual's lifetime.

Cognitive factors in color perception

Although color is a basic sensory experience, nonsensory factors also affect the perceived color of an object. In addition, color may interact with other nonperceptual behaviors.

Memory color. The remembered color of familiar objects often differs from the object's actual color. When observers are shown color samples and later asked to match them from an array of colored chips, systematic errors are made. Observers tend to pick chips of greater brightness when asked to remember bright colors and greater darkness when asked to remember dark colors. (Bartleson, 1960; Newhall, Burnham, and Clark, 1957). When asked to remember and match colors of familiar objects with characteristic hues, we remember apples or tomatoes as being more red than the actual objects, bananas are more yellow in memory than in the bunch, and grass is greener than it is on the lawn. Because of this memory effect, many photographic film manufacturers have chosen to modify the spectral reproduction ability of color film so that the reproduced colors are richer than they are in nature. Because television engineers have not made a similar correction, color memory distortions may account for part of our feeling that the picture reproduced on a color television set is an unfaithful reproduction of real color.

Memory color effects tend to creep into certain other matching tasks. For instance, if you are asked to match the color of a Valentine's Day heart or an apple, both of which have been cut out of orange paper, you will match them with a truer red than you would match an oval or a triangle cut out of the same material. A banana-shaped figure, or one labeled "lemon," is matched with a truer yellow. It seems as if the remembered color blends with the observed stimulus, altering the percept toward the ideal, or prototypical, color of an object (Bruner, Postman, and Rodrigues, 1951; Delk and Fillenbaum, 1965; Harper, 1953; White and Montgomery, 1976). The color you remember is probably "better" than the color that is present; on the other hand, the color you see now may be tinged by your memory's hue.

Culture and color. As we noted earlier, a speaker of the English language is content to describe hue differences using four basic categories: red, yellow, green, and blue. This is not the case for native speakers of many other languages. Many languages have no separate names for green and blue, while others use the same name for yellow and green, or red and yellow. There are some languages that only distinguish red as a separate color and have no names for the other hues. It is often argued that an interaction exists between language and perception, and that when one has separate names for separate sensory experiences, these labels make discriminations easier. In other words, members of the Lakuti tribe, who have only a single term for blue and green, may see the two colors as more similar to each other than do English speakers, who have separate words for these stimuli (Whorf, 1956). The suggestion that different language terms for colors indicate different perceptual abilities has been presented in many different forms. For instance, Robertson (1967) suggested that an evolutionary development has taken place in both the color-perceiving ability of humans and in the color terms encoded in the language. He suggested that the first discriminations were between red and green, then the discrimination ability for yellow evolved, and finally, that for blue. He analyzed a number of ancient languages and found such evolutionary trends. One could conclude from such evidence that the ancient Greeks were relatively weak in their ability to perceive colors because their language has only a limited set of color names.

Actually, when one directly measures the ability of individuals to match, discriminate, or reproduce colors (rather than just to name colors), the picture changes. It seems as if the number of color names in a language does not affect one's ability to make such discriminations (Berlin and Kay, 1969; Bornstein, 1973; Bornstein, 1975). Such findings indicate the danger in assuming that cognitive effects are occurring in the absence of direct perceptual measurements.

Color impressions. Color does more than provide us with additional information about stimuli. It has emotional consequences. It delights and depresses. It makes humans feel warm or cold, tense or relaxed. For instance, a manufacturer of detergent found that the color of the detergent box made a difference in how the user evaluated the strength of the detergent. Women were given the same detergent in three boxes, which differed only in color. When the detergents were rated after use, the women felt that the detergent in a yellow-orange box was too strong with ruinous effects on some of the clothes. The detergent in a blue box was too weak, while the one with both blue and yellow-orange flashes seemed to be most effective (Kupchella, 1976).

Color can even produce sensory impressions that are characteristic of other senses. It is almost universal to call the short-wavelength (blue) colors "cool," while the longer wavelengths (yellow) tend to be called "warm." Perhaps these labels arise because the cool of the night is first broken by the red of the dawn, with midday characterized by the yellow of sunlight and warmth. As the yellow begins to disappear and the blue of twilight begins to predominate, temperatures again grow cool. Many years and many generations of such an association might stamp in this warm-cool relationship. In an era when the conservation of energy is important, it is interesting to note that people will turn a heat control to a higher setting in a blue room than they will in a yellow room. It is as if they are trying to compensate thermally for the coolness that has been visually induced (Boynton, 1971). In a similar vein, Alexander and Shansky (1976) have shown that dark saturated colors are perceived as being associated with a greater sensation of "weight" or "heaviness."

Color adds an aesthetic quality to our lives.

We refer to an interesting person as a "colorful" character. We refer to the announcer who adds extra detail and insight to a sports broadcast as the "color man." We refer to exciting events as "colorful." Certainly, in the absence of our ability to distinguish chromatic stimulation, our life would be "colorless" in all senses of that word. Remember, however, that color is a psychological achievement, not a direct effect of the physical variation of wavelengths of light. If you still doubt this statement, it will probably be instructive to turn back to Demonstration Box 1-2 to see colors develop in your mind where no physical variations in wavelength exist.

GLOSSARY

The following definitions are specific to this book.

Additive color mixture   Color mixture resulting from the mixture of lights of different wavelengths.

Afterimage   A visual sensation that continues after an intense or prolonged exposure of a part of the retina to a stimulus.

Anomalous trichromatism   A defect in color vision in which color matches made by an individual are systematically different from normal, although the three primary color systems are still functioning.

Benham's top   A black and white pattern that when rotated produces subjective colors.

Bezold-Brucke effect   The shift in the apparent hue of a color as the intensity is changed.

Brightness   The psychological impression of light intensity.

Chlorolabe   Green-sensitive cone pigment.

Chromatic adaptation   Lowered response to color stimulus resulting from previous exposure to other chromatic stimuli.

CIE color space   A standard system used to describe colors, based on the mixture of three imaginary "super" primary wavelengths.

Color atlas   A book in which each page represents a horizontal or a vertical slice through the color spindle.

Color blindness   A condition in which individuals lack the ability to make discriminations on the basis of wavelength of light.

Color circle   *See* Color wheel.

Color solid   *See* Color spindle.

Color spindle   A three-dimensional model in which the relationships between hue, brightness, and saturation are depicted.

Color wheel   A circular scheme in which colors are separated according to hue, with complementary colors placed directly across from each other.

Complementary colors   Colors whose mixture produces an achromatic gray or white.

Cyanolabe   The blue-sensitive cone pigment.

Deuteranomaly   A condition in which individuals' color matches require more green than those of color-normal individuals.

Deuteranopia   A form of color blindness associated with the confusion of reds and greens owing to insensitivity in the green system.

Dichromats   Individuals whose color vision is defective, allowing all hues to be matched with two rather than three primaries.

Dominant wavelength   The wavelength of a monochromatic stimulus that best approximates the hue of a color mixture.

Dyschromatopsias   Acquired color vision losses.

Erythrolabe   The red-sensitive cone pigment.

Habituation   The process by which an observer ceases to respond, or reduces the magnitude of a response, to a repetitious stimulus presentation.

Hue   The term denoting the psychological dimension most clearly corresponding to wavelength of light and most often termed "color" in common language.

Metameric colors   Colors that appear to be the same but are composed of different wavelengths.

Microspectrophotometer   A device for measuring the amount and wavelengths of light emanating from microscopic target areas.

Monochromatic stimulus   A stimulus that contains only one wavelength of light.

Monochromats   Individuals who see color as simply gradations of intensity, due to malfunctioning of two or three cone systems.

Neural wiring diagram   A schematic that illustrates how pigment-specific cones could produce opponent responses at the postretinal level.

Primaries   Three monochromatic light sources in appropriate amounts that, when combined, can match any other hue.

Protoanomaly   A condition in which individuals' color matches require more red than those of color-normal individuals.

Protanopia   A form of color blindness resulting in the confusion of reds and greens owing to insensitivity in the red system.

Purity   A spectrally "pure" stimulus is composed of only one wavelength.

S potentials   Graded electrical retinal cell responses that vary in direction and strength depending on the wavelength of the stimulus.

Saturation   The psychological attribute of a color associated with "how much" of a hue is present.

Simultaneous color contrast   A process in which inhibitory interactions between adjacent color systems cause hue shifts.

Spectral Colors   Pure monochromatic stimuli such as those produced in a prismatic spectrum.

Subjective color   Colors that are consciously experienced but not associated with any wavelength change in the physical stimulus.

Subtractive color mixture   Color mixture resulting from the selective absorption of wavelengths, usually by pigments.

Trichromatic theory   The theory that color vision is based on three primary responses.

Tristimulus values   The combination of the stimulus hue and brightness coordinates used in the CIE color system for describing any color stimulus.

Tritanopia   The color vision defect in which yellows and blues are confused owing to reduced blue sensitivity.

Hearing

THE YOUNG DANCERS MOVED IN UNI-
son. Two lines of lithe bodies in black
leotards swayed, seemingly pulled about like
marionettes by the throbbing beat of the loud
music. The choreographer watched a moment,
then turned to her visitor and said, "It's really
hard to believe that they are all deaf, isn't it? I
never understand how they keep in time to
the music. They claim that they just 'feel' the
rhythm and the sound."

In fact, many striking similarities exist between the sense of touch and the sense of
hearing. The sense of touch is generally
evoked by mechanical pressure against some
part of the body, and the sense of hearing is
similarly evoked by mechanical pressure. For
auditory sensation, the pressure is caused by
the collision of vibrating air molecules with
the eardrum, as we discussed in Chapter 4. We
can often actually "feel" some sounds. For instance, at a rock concert, we might feel the
pulsating throb of the amplified music physically assailing the whole surface of our body.
This aspect of sound recently led some movie
theaters to install large speakers that emit intense low-frequency sounds, giving audiences
an opportunity not only to hear but also to feel
an earthquake or an explosion. The close relationship between touch and hearing is also apparent in the evolutionary history of hearing
organs. Modern ears seem to have evolved
from a vibration-sensitive line that extends the
length of the body of certain species of fish.
Scientists have not yet agreed whether this
primitive "lateral line" is actually an organ of
touch or one of hearing (see Chapter 4).

At the subjective level, however, the senses
of hearing and touch have many qualitative differences. Although we may feel the air vibration associated with the sound stimulus, we
also "hear" it, which is quite a different sensory experience. Psychologically, a sound has
many attributes of its own. While the sensation

of touch shares with sound the psychological
attributes of location and duration, sound also
has the qualities of *loudness, pitch, timbre,
volume, and density*. While some of these sensory qualities seem to be associated with particular aspects of the physical stimulus, the
sensation is often not directly predictable
merely from knowing the physical stimulus.

DETECTION OF SOUNDS

Clearly, the minimum auditory experience is
the detection of the presence of a sound. What
determines the minimum sound intensity we
can hear? You may recall that in Figure 4-1 we
showed a simple auditory stimulus (pure tone)
as a sine wave. In that representation, the amplitude of the sine wave represented the intensity of the stimulus, or the pressure exerted by
the vibrating air molecules as we described in
Chapter 4.

In determining an observer's absolute threshold for sound presented through earphones,
we measure the sound pressure level associated with the threshold stimulus very close to
the eardrum. At threshold, this value is called
the **minimum audible pressure**. One might
argue that this is a rather artificial situation
since the sound wave at the eardrum has already been amplified somewhat and distorted
during its travels through the ear canal. Another, perhaps more natural, procedure would
be to determine the absolute auditory threshold for an observer sitting in an open space
that is free of echoes and other distortions.
In this situation, sounds are presented by a
speaker placed at various angles to the observer's ear, and the intensity of the threshold
stimulus is measured at the location of the observer's head. This measurement of threshold
is called the **minimum audible field** (indica-

210

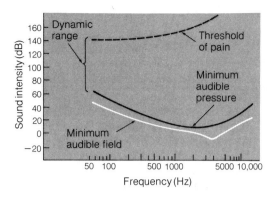

Figure 8-1. The dynamic range of hearing from minimum audible intensities to the threshold of pain (based on Sivian and White, 1933).

ting that the intensity of the threshold stimulus was measured in a free field, rather than directly at the eardrum).

In a classic study at Bell Telephone Laboratories, Sivian and White (1933) systematically varied the frequency of the pure tone stimulus as they took a series of threshold measures under carefully controlled conditions. Sivian and White's results are shown in Figure 8-1. Notice that the absolute threshold varies as the frequency of the stimulus varies. The ear appears to be most sensitive to sounds with frequencies between 1000 and 5000 Hz. We are about 100 times less sensitive to a sound at 100 Hz than we are to a sound at 3000 Hz. Notice that the minimum audible field measurements are considerably lower than the minimum audible pressures. The reasons for this are rather complex, the most important of which is probably that the free field situation allows resonances and amplifications from the shape of the pinna (the outer cup of the ear) and the ear canal to come into play. This is supported by the fact that we are most sensitive to sounds of 3000–4000 Hz in free field presentation. This is in the range of the natural resonance frequency

of the external ear canal. From an adaptive point of view, the benefit that humans derive from increased sensitivity in this particular range of frequencies may at first seem obscure, since most of the important frequencies used in speech are lower than 1000 Hz. A somewhat macabre possibility, as Milne and Milne (1967) speculate, is that we leave a "channel open—as though reserved for emergencies—for any high pitched scream." In fact, screams of agony or terror, especially those of females, do sometimes reach the 3000 Hz range. You can demonstrate for yourself the effect of frequency on your ability to detect sounds using Demonstration Box 8-1.

The lower limit of sensitivity for the ear seems to be determined by the sound of blood rushing through the tiny vessels in the middle and inner ear, while the upper limit is determined by the stimulus intensity that produces pain. The difference between the absolute threshold and the pain threshold for a particular frequency of sound waves defines the **dynamic range** of the ear for that frequency (see Figure 8-1). For stimuli with frequencies between about 1000 and 5000 Hz, the ear has a dynamic range of up to 150 dB, which is equivalent to a 7.5-millionfold increase in sound pressure from the weakest sound detectable to the most intense sound tolerable. Few stereo systems can approach the dynamic range with which you were born.

The dynamic range of the ear is distinct from the frequency range over which our ears respond to sound. Young adults can hear sounds between about 20 and 20,000 Hz. Some young children can hear sounds with frequencies up to about 27,000 Hz. Unfortunately, with age, a progressive loss in hearing capacity occurs, particularly for higher frequencies, so that this range gradually decreases as we grow older. Demonstration Box 8-2 provides a simple test for the upper limits of your own hearing.

Demonstration Box 8-1. Sound frequency and threshold

Many people are aware of the problems associated with replaying recorded music so that it sounds as it did when it was recorded. Recording techniques reproduce the frequency produced by musical instruments, but the replay is usually at a lower intensity. Most of the sounds of musical instruments lie in frequency ranges where the absolute threshold is most affected by changes in frequency. Thus, unless you listen to recordings of an orchestra at reasonable intensity levels, you will not hear many of the frequencies produced by the instruments. Many high-quality audio amplifiers have been modified to include circuits that compensate for such psychological mechanisms. These circuits are set to emphasize very low and very high frequency sounds.

For this demonstration you will need a radio or another sound source that produces orchestral music. A cheaper unit, such as a portable radio or your car radio, both of which lack loudness compensation circuits, would be perfect. Find a station (or a record) where a full orchestra is playing. Turn down the sound and listen to the instruments you can hear. Now, gradually turn up the sound. As you do this, you will find that you become more aware of the bass violin and cello, the larger brass pieces, such as the tuba, and some of the lower notes of the harp or bassoon, as well as some of the higher tones from the violins, flutes, and piccolos. When the volume has been considerably increased so that you can hear the entire orchestra and many of the pieces (placing you ear close to the speaker helps), gradually turn down the volume again. Now, many of the lower and higher frequency instruments seem to disappear as certain frequencies they produce drop below threshold. The middle frequencies of the orchestra, however, are still quite audible.

Demonstration Box 8-2. High-frequency hearing limits

You can make a simple test of your own high-frequency hearing using your television set. Turn it on and then lower the sound completely. Now lean over the back of your set and listen for a soft, high-pitched whine. If you can hear it, this means that you can detect frequencies on the order of 16,000 Hz. Now, try this test on someone who is considerably older than you are and then with someone who is much younger. You should find that the older individual cannot hear this sound, while the younger one can. You might also try moving away from the set (if possible) until you can just hear the sound. This is your "threshold distance." Now have your other observers do the same and determine their threshold distances. The greater your threshold distance, the more sensitive is your ear to these high-frequency sounds.

Temporal, frequency, and binaural interactions

A number of factors other than frequency and intensity determine our ability to detect sounds. One of these factors is the duration of the stimulus. The auditory system seems to act as if a fixed amount of sound energy is necessary to stimulate the ear sufficiently so that we hear a sound. It doesn't seem to matter if this energy comes at a high intensity over a short time interval or at a lower intensity over a longer time interval. We can describe this relationship algebraically as:

$$T = I \times D$$

where I is the intensity of the sound, D is its duration, and T is a constant value necessary to reach threshold. Thus, brief sounds must be more intense than longer sounds in order to be detected with the same likelihood. This relationship holds approximately for threshold sounds up to a duration of about 200 msec. Beyond 200 msec, increasing stimulus duration does not seem to improve our ability to detect sound. You may recall that in Chapter 6 we discussed a similar relationship between time and intensity in the visual system.

We have been talking about increasing the likelihood that a sound will be heard by increasing its duration. We may also increase the likelihood that a sound will be heard by increasing the number of different tones, or frequencies, that are presented together. Thus, if we simultaneously present two tones, neither of which would reach threshold by itself, we may achieve an audible stimulus. Each tone could actually be about half the intensity needed for threshold. It seems the nervous system adds the neural responses of different tones, producing a composite response based on the sum of the intensities of the various single stimuli. The tones should not differ in frequency by too much, however, or their energies will not sum, and the threshold intensities will be the same as if we presented each tone alone. Just as there was a critical duration beyond which temporal summation did not occur, there is a critical band of frequencies beyond which adding tones does not facilitate detection (Scharf, 1975). This critical band is not the same width for all frequencies. It is much narrower for low frequencies than it is for high frequencies. Thus, if we start with a 400 Hz tone, adding a tone between 350 and

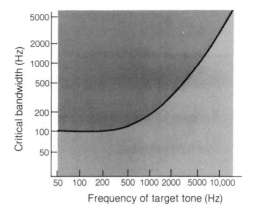

Figure 8-2. Relation between critical bandwidth, in which added tones will facilitate detection, and frequency of target tone.

450 Hz will improve our ability to detect the sound, while adding a tone beyond these limits will not. If we started with a 5000 Hz tone, however, any added tone between about 4500 and 5500 Hz would improve our ability to detect the sound. Figure 8-2 demonstrates how the critical bandwidth varies with frequency.

An additional factor affects our ability to detect the presence of sound stimuli. When sounds are presented to both ears as opposed to only one, absolute thresholds are lowered. Presentations to one ear are called **monaural** (from the roots *mon*, for one, and *aural*, for ear); presentations to two ears are called **binaural** (from the root *bi*, for two). At first it was believed that this was only because one of the ears was more sensitive than the other, and the most sensitive ear determined the absolute threshold (Sivian and White, 1933). However, more recent work (Chocolle, 1962) has shown that the threshold for two-ear stimulation is about one-half that for one-ear stimulation. An interesting aspect of the interaction between the ears is that the two stimuli do not have to occur simultaneously in the two ears. If the tones are presented to the ears one at a time, and the total stimulus duration of the combined input is less than 200 msec, the pair of tones will be detected even if each individual tone is only about one-half the intensity needed to reach threshold when presented monaurally (Schenkel, 1967).

In addition to lowering the absolute threshold, presentation of the same stimulus to the two ears causes the subjective impressions of loudness from each ear to add together (see, for example, Marks, 1979b). Thus, a binaural presentation will sound about twice as loud as a monaural presentation of the same tone. If you have a sound source nearby, such as a radio or a television, you can demonstrate this for yourself by assessing the loudness when you hear the source with two ears, then covering one ear, and noting how the apparent loudness diminishes.

Auditory masking

We have all been in a noisy meeting, convention, or theater and found that we could not hear or understand a speaker very well. When the crowd quiets down, however, we find that the speaker's voice is audible immediately. This observation illustrates that whether a particular sound can be heard or not depends not only on its own intensity but also on the presence of other sounds in the environment. The last section discussed one way in which sounds can interact with one another to facilitate hearing. In the present situation the effects are reversed. Now, we present an observer with a sound, which is audible by itself, and then add another sound, only to find that the target tone can no longer be heard. We usually say that the second tone (the **masker**) has **masked** the first (the **target**). When target and masker are presented at the same time, we have **simultaneous masking**. A masking sound does not simply make all other tones more difficult to

hear. Masking sounds act rather selectively. A set of experiments demonstrating this phenomenon was done by Zwicker (1958), who masked target tones using a narrow band of noise with a middle frequency of 1200 Hz. He measured the threshold intensity for a listener to detect a target tone with and without the masking stimulus. When he measured the amount of masking for several different frequencies of target tone, he obtained the results shown in Figure 8-3. As you can see from the figure, as we increase the intensity of the masking stimulus, we must increase the intensity of the test tone for it to be audible. The most striking aspect of these data, however, is the asymmetry of the masking effect. The greatest masking is found for tones that have frequencies that are very similar to the masker itself. The effect of the masker seems to spread upward, affecting a set of tones higher in frequency than the masking sound. Tones of a lower frequency, however, are relatively unaffected.

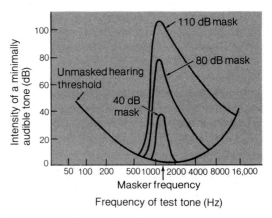

Figure 8-3. Thresholds for a pure tone target in the presence of a narrow band of masking noise centered at 1200 Hz. The higher the curve, the higher the threshold, hence the more effective the masking (based on Zwicker, 1958).

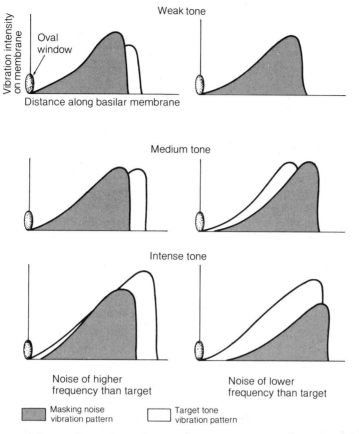

Weak tone

Medium tone

Intense tone

Noise of higher
frequency than target

Noise of lower
frequency than target

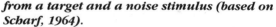

Masking noise
vibration pattern

Target tone
vibration pattern

*Figure 8-4. The interactions of patterns of
vibration of the basilar membrane resulting
from a target and a noise stimulus (based on
Scharf, 1964).*

Why does the added noise most effectively
mask tones higher in frequency than itself?
The answer may lie in the physiology of the
ear. Turn to Figure 4-8 (page 103), which
shows how the vibration pattern of the basilar
membrane varies with the frequency of a pure
tone. Notice that tones of low frequencies produce a very broad vibration pattern, extending
over much of the membrane, while tones of
higher frequencies produce vibration patterns
nearer to the oval window and not extending
as far along the membrane. Now look at Fig-

ure 8-4. Notice that when we have a weak test
tone and the noise is of a higher frequency
than the target, the pattern of vibrations set up
in the basilar membrane by the masking noise
only extends across part of the membrane. Because the lower frequency target tone vibrates
more of the membrane, the target's pattern extends beyond the flank of the vibration pattern
produced by the masker. Thus, the target is detectable. However, the vibration pattern produced by the target tone when the noise is of a
lower frequency than the target is completely

Demonstration Box 8-3. Auditory masking

To experience several different masking phenomena, you need two major sources of sound, one for a masking sound, and one for the target sound that will be masked. Good sources are the noise of a car engine for a masking sound and the car radio for a source of target sounds. If you have a car with a radio, get into it and turn on the radio without starting the engine. Find some music with a good range of frequencies. Classical music is best, but any music will do. Modern music with a lot of steel guitar (country) or electrically amplified guitar (rock) is also good. Take particular note of the high and the low frequencies. Turn the volume knob on the radio to an intensity where you can just barely hear these frequencies. Now start the car motor. Press on the accelerator (with the car out of gear!) to make the engine turn over at high revolutions per minute. This creates a source of intense broad-band masking noise. Now listen for the high and the low frequencies that were clearly audible in the music before you started the car engine. Turn up the volume until the high and

low frequencies (which should now be masked) are just barely audible again and take notice of the difference between the volume settings before and after the noise was introduced. You could map out a masking curve for particular frequencies in a piece of music by varying the revolutions per minute of the motor to vary the intensity of the noise and by varying the frequency of the sounds whose audibility you are using as a criterion for radio volume adjustment. Note that even with intense masking noise, you can still hear the middle frequencies, where most of the singing is, while the higher and lower frequencies are masked. This is a reflection of the superior sensitivity of the ear to these frequencies. You also experience *speech masking* in your car. When the masking noise is of sufficient intensity (be careful not to damage your engine), even the middle frequencies (where most speech sounds occur) are masked, and you cannot understand the singer or the radio announcer.

---

covered by the masker's vibration pattern, and it is not detectable as a separate tone. The intensity of the higher frequency test tone in the presence of low-frequency noise must be increased before its own vibration pattern extends beyond that of the masker and can be detected as a separate tone. You can experience some aspects of the frequency-specific effect of a masker by performing Demonstration Box 8-3.

Although sound masking effects seem to be largely explained by the interaction of the patterns of vibration on the basilar membrane, this explanation is clearly not adequate for all masking phenomena. For example, consider what happens if target and masker are not

presented at the same time. If the masker is presented first, followed after some **interstimulus interval** by a brief target, the lowered ability to hear the target is called **forward masking**. Many studies (see Zwislocki, 1978) have found, as you might expect, that the forward masking effect increases as the intensity of the masking sound increases, and decreases as the interstimulus interval increases. For interstimulus intervals longer than 300 msec, there is no measurable forward masking. Also, in general, the lower the frequencies of both the target and mask pair, the more masking takes place (Jesteadt, Bacon, and Lehman, 1982). In addition, the same asymmetry we discussed above for simultaneous masking shows up in forward masking: There is little masking of target tones with frequencies lower than the masker, but a great deal for target tones of frequencies higher than the masker. It is unlikely, however, that we can explain these effects by interaction of excitation patterns on the basilar membrane, since the excitation of the masker is not present when the target is presented at a later time. Some sort of interaction of more central neural processes must be involved. For the situation discussed above, it is likely that the masker is lowering the sensitivity of the hair cells, or their synapses with auditory nerve fibers, to stimulation by the target tone, thus raising the threshold for that tone.

What happens when the target tone preceeds the masker? Nothing, you might think; how could the masker's effect appear before the masker does? Yet **backward masking** does occur, albeit somewhat differently from forward masking. For instance, your ability to hear a click may be reduced if another click follows it by as much as 25 msec (for loud masking clicks). Backward masking is more difficult to measure for tones than for clicks, because tones must extend over a longer period of time. Some backward masking does occur, however. When a tone is masked with noise, the masker may have some effect on the threshold of a tone that is turned on up to 400 msec before the masker is turned on (Wright, 1964). The explanation of these backward masking effects is still not clear. One possibility is that inhibition caused by the masker could build up faster than excitation caused by the target tone, thus overlapping with it in time and canceling it to some extent, even when the target occurs appreciably earlier than the masker.

In addition to separating target and masker in time, we can separate them by presenting a target sound to one ear and a masking sound to the other. This is called **central masking**, since again there can be no interaction of the sounds on the basilar membrane, and the masking is therefore assumed to take place in more central brain areas. In this situation, the masker must be much more intense (about 50 dB) than when a masking sound is presented to the same ear as the target tone. Under these conditions, it can be shown that the effect of the mask is usually much more symmetrical and does not spread so widely as we vary the frequency of the test tone (Zwislocki, Damianopoulos, Buining, and Glantz, 1967). Only when the frequency of the masking sound is quite low (less than 200 Hz) does the usual asymmetric spread of masking to higher frequencies appear (Billings and Stokinger, 1977).

When one looks at the interaction between the two ears, one occasionally encounters some strange and interesting phenomena. For example, Hirsh (1948) presented a pure tone plus a broad band noise (that is, one containing many frequencies) to the same ear. He adjusted the target so that it could just be heard above the background of noise. Next, he presented some additional noise to the other ear, so that the two noises were in phase (meaning that the peaks and valleys of sound pressure coincide, as we discussed in Chapter 4). Under these circumstances, the target tone, instead of being more difficult or perhaps impossible to hear, became more clearly audible. To reach the threshold value again, it was necessary to *lower* the target's intensity. What seemed to be happening was that the two masking tones were masking each other. Again, since the two noise masks were coming into different ears and did not share the same basilar membrane, the interactions must have been occurring more centrally, that is, in the brain. Such central interactions become very important when we consider the processing of meaningful sounds, such as occur when we are listening to speech (see Chapter 13).

Sound discrimination

In some respects, the problem of masking is really a discrimination problem, of much the same sort as that discussed in Chapter 2. The observer's task is to discriminate the target tone from the masking tone or noise. We may simplify this problem somewhat by asking the basic discrimination question for the perception of sound: "How different must two sounds be in order for the difference to be detected reliably?" To answer this question precisely, we must separate the two physical dimensions upon which a sound stimulus may differ, namely, intensity and frequency.

Let us begin by considering our sensitivity to intensity changes. A good deal of care must be taken when studying such abilities, since turning a tone on or off, or changing its frequency or intensity abruptly, can create the perception of a "click." In a threshold situation, an observer might respond to this click rather than to the actual intensity or frequency change in which we are interested. Because of this, Riesz (1928), at the Bell Telephone Laboratories, resorted to a rather elaborate technique based on a phenomenon known as **beats**. When we listen to two simultaneous tones that are similar in intensity but slightly different in frequency, we may perceive the occurrence of beats. These beats are perceived as a single tone that seems to throb, much like the vibrato of a singer. In short, the perception is of an alternate rising and falling in loudness. The frequency with which the loudness fluctuates is precisely the frequency difference between the two sounds that are combined. The air compressions in the sound waves will add

to each other when the maximum of one wave is occurring at the same time as the maximum of the other, and subtract from each other when a maximum of one wave coincides with the minimum of another. For example, when two tones differ by 3 Hz, the maxima of the two sound waves will coincide (add) three times each second. The sound will thus seem to wax and wane at 3 Hz (three times per second). As we increase the size of the frequency difference, soon the beats will be no longer discriminable. At a large enough difference between the two tones, the sound begins to take on a harsh or rough and grating quality. Figure 8-5 shows how two sound signals can combine to form a separate beat frequency.

Riesz (1928) used the perception of beats to determine the limits of intensity discrimination in an observer. He presented a tone that was clearly audible by itself (say, at a frequency of 1000 Hz). He next presented another tone that was close enough in frequency (say, 1003 Hz) so that it would cause the perception of beats if it were intense enough. He gradually increased the intensity of the added sound until the listener first detected the fluctuation in loudness caused by the beating. On the basis of this, he could compute the difference threshold, without contaminating the sound with the harsh clicking of sudden changes in intensity at onset or offset of the stimulus.

You will probably recall from Chapter 2 that one measure of our ability to discriminate between two stimuli is given by Weber's fraction. We defined the Weber fraction as $\Delta I/I$ where ΔI is the intensity change necessary to be just noticed, and I is is the standard stimulus from which the change is taken. This fraction represents the proportion by which a stimulus must be changed in order for us to detect that change. Thus, a Weber fraction of 0.5 means we must increase (or decrease) the intensity

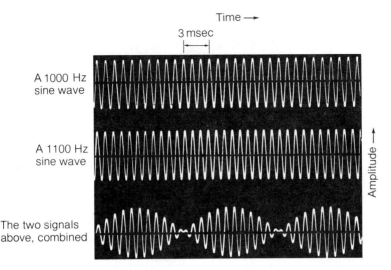

Figure 8-5. A 1000 Hz sine wave is added to a 1100 Hz sine wave to give a beat frequency of 100 Hz. This means that the beat pattern re- *peats every 10 msec as the overall envelope of sound pressures varies (from Lindsay and Norman, 1977).*

of a stimulus by 50 percent in order for a subject to discriminate the change.

We can use the Weber fraction as a measure of our ability to discriminate sounds from one another. In general, studies of the difference threshold for intensity have shown that a Weber fraction of about 0.33 describes auditory performance. Figure 8-6 shows Riesz's (1928) results for how the Weber fraction varies as we vary the intensity of the standard (*I*) stimulus. Notice that we have plotted four different curves for four different frequencies. As you can see, the size of the Weber fraction is smallest (discrimination is best) for stimuli in the middle range of frequencies. Increasing or decreasing the frequency results in a decrease in our ability to discriminate intensity changes, although such variations in discrimination with changes in frequency are not always found to be as large as those shown here (see, for example, Jesteadt, Wier, and Green, 1977). For moderate stimulus intensities, the Weber fraction is

rather constant. It would, of course, be perfectly constant if Weber's law were completely true, as we discussed in Chapter 2. More modern measurements (using pure tone stimuli that were turned on and off gradually in order to avoid the spurious click we mentioned earlier) seem to indicate even less of a violation of Weber's law, with much less of a rise in the Weber fraction at lower intensities (Green, Nachmias, Kearny, and Jeffress, 1979). Figure 8-6 shows that the auditory system is capable of detecting an approximately 20 percent change in stimulus intensity across a broad range of frequencies and intensities, covering the stimulus range where most of our everyday hearing takes place.

We have discussed only studies of sound discrimination where the stimuli were presented to a single ear (monaural presentation). You might expect that, just as is the case with detection, it would be easier to discriminate intensities of sounds presented to both ears

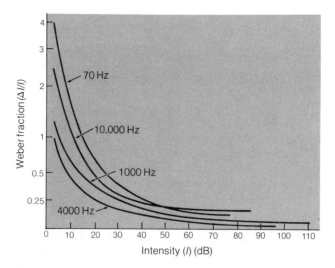

Figure 8-6. Intensity discrimination measured in terms of the Weber fraction for various intensities and frequencies of standard stimuli (based on Riesz, 1928).

(binaural presentation) than those presented only to a single ear. This is in fact the case. Jesteadt and Wier (1977) found that intensity difference thresholds were about 33 percent smaller when the stimuli were presented simultaneously to both ears than when they were presented to one or the other ear alone. This probably occurs because the binaural presentation gives the observer two chances to hear the difference (one in each ear) rather than just the single chance available when monaural presentation is used.

Thus far, we have dealt with the question of discrimination of differences in intensity of sound stimuli. We may also ask, "By how much must two tones differ in frequency for this difference to be noticed?" Again, the classic study was done at the Bell Telephone Laboratories by Shower and Biddulph (1931) (you might guess that the telephone company would have an interest in discovering the limits of our ability to discriminate sounds). The basic experiment involves presenting an observer with a tone of a given frequency and intensity and

then varying (modulating) the frequency of the tone by larger and larger amounts until the observer is just able to detect a change in pitch. Again, we may measure the limits of discrimination using the Weber fraction. In this case, however, the fraction consists of $\Delta f/f$, where f represents the frequency of the standard tone and Δf represents the change in frequency necessary to be just noticed as different from the standard. Figure 8-7 shows Shower and Biddulph's measurements of the Weber fraction for frequency discrimination for a number of different intensity levels and a broad range of frequencies. Notice that above 1000 Hz the Weber fraction is constant and quite small (around 0.005). This means that if we presented a listener with a tone with a frequency of 1000 Hz and another tone of 1005 Hz, this small difference in frequency (one-half of 1 percent) would be detectable. At lower intensity levels our discrimination of frequency differences is not quite this good.

As was the case for intensity discrimination, more recent studies of the effect of intensity and frequency on the frequency difference threshold have used as stimuli tones that are turned on and off gradually for brief durations (500 msec or so). The method of constant stimuli (see Chapter 2) applied to these stimuli then yields a measurement of the difference threshold. The most comprehensive of the modern studies was done by Wier, Jesteadt, and Green (1977). Their results were similar to those of Shower and Biddulph (1931) in form; that is, the Weber fraction for frequency depended on both frequency and intensity in a way similar to that shown in Figure 8-7. Finally, as was the case for intensity discrimination, binaural frequency difference thresholds are about 33 percent smaller than are monaural ones (Jesteadt and Wier, 1977).

Sound localization

Sounds are usually perceived as having a location in space, as emanating from sources to the right or left, in front of or behind, above or below our bodies. Some sounds appear to come from close by, others from a distance. Our auditory systems use a variety of aspects of sound to construct a sort of *auditory space*, with our bodies at the center. Within this space sounds can be localized and their sources approached ("Hey, Jill, nice to see you!") or avoided ("Grrrroooowwwlll").

Direction cues: simple tones. When a sound comes from some distance away and from a particular angle to the listener, a number of cues indicate the direction to the right or left, or **azimuth**, of the sound source. Figure 8-8 shows a typical situation when a sound is coming from a source positioned at about 45 degrees azimuth. Notice that one ear receives the sound directly from the source, while the other ear is in what could be called a **sound shadow**. The shadowed ear receives only those sounds from the source that are *bent* around the head, or *diffracted* by the edge of the head. The presence of a sound

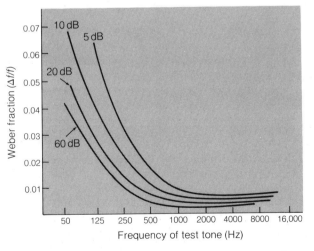

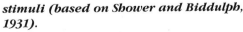

Figure 8-7. Frequency discrimination measured in terms of the Weber fraction for various intensities and frequencies of standard stimuli (based on Shower and Biddulph, 1931).

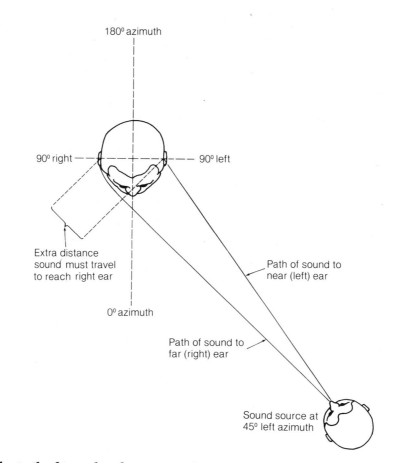

Figure 8-8. The path of sound to the two ears for a sound source at 45 degrees left azimuth (based on Lindsay and Norman, 1977).

shadow means that the sound intensity at one ear is less than the intensity at the other ear.

Careful measurements have been made of **intensity differences** between the ears as both the azimuth of the sound source and the frequency of the emitted sound are varied. These measurements have shown that the intensity difference between the ears increases as a sound source is moved toward the side. In addition, while low-frequency sound waves (those less than 3000 Hz) bend around the head quite readily, high-frequency tones tend to rush past the hidden ear unless deflected

into it. This exaggerates the intensity differences caused by the presence of a sound shadow for higher frequency sounds. The changes in intensity difference as the angle of the sound source changes can be a cue to direction. A large intensity difference between the two ears indicates that the source of the sound is positioned to one side. The greatest intensity difference occurs when the sound source is located at 90 degrees azimuth. The ear receiving the loudest input is perceived as closest to the source of the sound.

When a sound source is at an angle, sound

must travel different distances to reach the two ears. This is always the case unless the sound source is positioned at either 0 or 180 degrees, when the ears are at equal distances from the source of the sound. Because sound takes time to travel through space, there is a **time difference** in the arrival of the sound at the two ears. For example, for a sound at 0 degrees azimuth, there is no time difference between the stimulation of the right and the left ears since they are at equal distances from the sound source. For a sound at 90 degrees azimuth in either direction, however, the ear closer to the sound is stimulated approximately 0.8 msec earlier than the hidden ear.

Intermediate azimuths result in intermediate values for this time difference. Such a time difference may be a cue to the location of the sound source and may result in the experience of an apparent direction for it. You can demonstrate the effects of this time difference on direction perception for yourself using Demonstration Box 8-4.

Under certain circumstances, the time difference between the stimulation of the two ears results in a **phase difference**. If a sound is arriving earlier at one ear, it will be in a different portion of its cycle of compression and rarefaction of the air molecules than the sound arriving at the other ear (this aspect of sound

---

Demonstration Box 8-4. Time differences and auditory direction

For this demonstration you will need a length of rubber hose, or flexible plastic tube. Hold one end up to each ear as shown in the figure. Now, have a friend tap the tube using a pencil. At the point where you tap, you start a sound wave moving in both directions down the tube. If you tap so that there is a longer section of tube on one side, the sound must travel farther before reaching one of your ears. This delay is perceived as a shift in direction of the sound. Notice how the sound seems to change direction as you tap on different parts of the tube causing different patterns of sound delays.

is discussed fully in Chapter 4). This is especially true for low-frequency sounds, where the time taken to complete one cycle is more than the maximum time difference in the arrival of sound at the two ears. For example, it takes a 1000 Hz tone exactly 1 msec to complete one cycle. If such a tone arrived 0.5 msec earlier at one ear (as it would if the sound source were positioned at about 62 degrees azimuth), it would always be 0.5/1, or 1/2 cycle ahead of the sound arriving at the opposite ear. Although phase difference could be considered a cue to sound direction, it provides ambiguous information when we consider the full range of sound frequencies. For instance, with a tone of 10,000 Hz at 62 degrees azimuth, the time difference between the arrival of the sound at the two ears would once again be 0.5 msec. However, a 10,000 Hz tone takes only 0.1 msec to complete one cycle. This implies a phase difference of 0.5/0.1, or 5 cycles. Thus, the sound at the ear closest to the source is 5 cycles ahead of the sound arriving at the more distant ear. However, every cycle is identical. Therefore, how can the observer tell just what the phase difference may be? It could be 5, 4, 3, 2, or 1 cycles, since they are all alike. Some ambiguity is attached to the use of phase difference information as a cue to sound localization. Even at the lower frequencies, where potentially it could be more useful, the same pattern of phase delay is characteristic of sounds positioned opposite to one another (in reference to a line drawn through the head in any direction).

In 1907, Lord Raleigh proposed a dual, or two-process, theory of sound localization. He suggested that we localize low frequency sounds by using time or phase differences, or both, at the two ears, and we localize high-frequency sounds by using the intensity differences at the two ears caused by the sound shadow and differences in their distance from the sound source. This notion has been con-

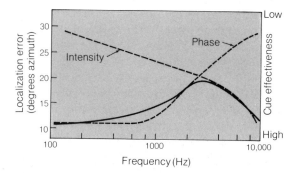

Figure 8-9. Relative cue effectiveness in arbitrary units for interaural intensity and phase differences (dashed lines) as a function of frequency. The solid line shows mean localization errors as a function of frequency (from Hearing: Physiology and Psychophysics, by Lawrence W. Gulick. Copyright 1971 by Oxford University Press, Inc. Reprinted by permission; data from Stevens and Newman, 1934).

firmed by later research. For example, Stevens and Newman (1934) had observers with their eyes closed make judgments as to the direction of a sound source. They played sounds of different frequencies from a variety of azimuths and recorded the listeners' errors of localization for each sound. Their data are shown in Figure 8-9. The solid line in this graph represents a summary of the data they collected, with errors averaged over all the locations at a particular frequency. As you can see, most errors occur in the region of 1500–3000 Hz. Fewer errors occur both above and below this frequency range. One can interpret this as indicating the efficient use of at least one cue in the low- and high-frequency ranges. Performance is worst in the midrange, however, where neither cue to localization is particularly useful. This interpretation has been confirmed by Mills's (1958) work on the **minimum audible angle**, which is the smallest amount of movement of a sound source that can just be detected. Minimum audible angle also varies as a function of frequency and location of a sound source; the variations are consistent with those observed in experiments like those of Stevens and Newman (Mills, 1960).

Direction and distance cues: complex tones. When we are in an ordinary room, the sound from any source may go bouncing around the room, reflecting from the walls, ceiling, and floor many times before it reaches our ears. Figure 8-10 illustrates this phenomenon. Why do we not experience an overwhelming auditory confusion as these sounds ricochet around us? Typically, we respond only to the first of the many replicas of a particular complex sound in echo-producing surroundings. We do not respond to the echos that arrive several milliseconds later. In fact, we do not even experience echos until the reflecting surface, which hurls the sound back at us, is far enough away so that the echos take a substantial time to reach us (more than 34 msec or so). Groups of sounds that arrive at interstimulus intervals of less than 35 msec are fused together into one sound. The first arrival appears to to be the major determinant of where in space we perceive the sound source to be. This phenomenon is called the **precedence effect** and has been studied extensively by Wallach, Newman, and Rosenzweig (1949; see also Zurek, 1980). Their experiments indicated that the earliest of a pair of fused sounds (separated by 2 msec) was 6-10 times more important than the later of the pair in determining the perceived direction of the sound source. Wallach et al. (1949) also pointed out that the precedence effect is an important part of our ability to listen selectively to one source of sound out of a larger group of competing sounds (see the discussion of the cocktail party problem in Chapter 15). You can experience the effects of precedence on the localization of sound by using Demonstration Box 8-5.

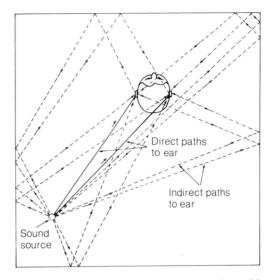

Figure 8-10. Some of the echoes produced by sound reflecting from the walls of a room. Unless the walls are quite far away, the echoes are not perceived (from Lindsay and Norman, 1977).

Under appropriate conditions, echoes can be important to the judgment of the location of sounds. For example, blind individuals apparently use echoes to help them locate obstacles and thus avoid them (Supra, Cotzin, and Dallenbach, 1944; Worchel and Dallenbach, 1947). Such animals as bats and whales have highly developed **echolocation systems**, similar to sonar, which they can use to locate objects with the same facility with which we use our eyes (see Neuweiler, Bruns, and Schuller, 1980 for a review).

There are a number of other cues to the spatial location of complex sounds. Head movement has been shown to be important both in resolving ambiguities of location, such as whether the sound is in front of or in back of the observer, and in providing a feeling that the sound is *out there* as opposed to inside the head (Wallach, 1939). It has also been argued that the *pinnae* (the fleshy parts of the ears

---

Demonstration Box 8-5. Precedence and the one-speaker stereo illusion

For this demonstration you will need a radio, phonograph, or tape recorder that has stereo speakers located about 2 m apart. Turn on some music and stand about midway between the two speakers, facing a point between them. You will notice that the sound seems to envelop you. It comes from both sides, and you can clearly identify sounds coming from one speaker or the other. Take a few steps (you need not go very far) toward the side where one speaker is located. After only a step or two you will suddenly find that all the sound seems to be coming from the speaker nearest you.

You no longer get any sensation of sound coming from the more distant speaker (although it still affects sound quality as you can demonstrate by turning it off). A few steps to the other side will reverse this effect, making it appear as though all the sound is coming from the other speaker. As you move toward a speaker, you alter the time that it takes for the sound to reach your ears. The precedence effect then takes the sound arriving first and emphasizes it, giving you the impression that all the sound emanates from that source.

---

outside of the head) delay (Batteau, 1967) or amplify (Flannery and Butler, 1981) sounds of different frequencies by different amounts. Such differential delays and amplifications apparently provide cues as to the location of complex sound sources since a positive relation exists between the apparent location of sounds and the amount of delay or amplification provided by the pinnae.

Distance information is also carried by complex sounds. One major source of this information is the relative intensity of a sound, with nearer sources being louder. Changes in sound distance are coded reliably by changes in sound intensity (Mershon and King, 1975). Of course, any intensity could be produced by a sound source that is farther away. Thus, this cue is unreliable for absolute distance unless the sound is a familiar one. We know through experience what a bell on an ice cream truck or a car engine sounds like when the sound is made relatively close to us. At some other time, we can use this knowledge to judge how far away a similar sound source may be by the loudness of the sound.

Another important source of distance information is the relative amount of **reverbera-**

tion in the impinging sound. As we stated above, sound reaches our ears both directly from a source and after being reflected from (*reverberating* from) various surfaces such as walls (see Figure 8-10). In general, as a sound source gets farther away from an observer, the amount of sound that directly reaches the ears decreases more rapidly than the amount reaching the ears after reverberation. Thus, the relative amount of "reverberation sound" (which has a distinct quality, like an echo) is a cue to the distance of a sound source from an observer. Békésy was one of the first to investigate this cue systematically. In 1938 (Békésy, 1960), he showed that altering the proportion of reverberant sound alters judgments of perceived distances of sounds. More recent work (Butler, Levy, and Neff, 1980; Mershon and Bowers, 1979; Mershon and King, 1975) has confirmed and extended this earlier work.

Another cue to distance that seems to be as compelling as the amount of reverberation is the frequency makeup, or *spectrum*, of a complex sound. Sounds that are composed mostly of high frequencies seem to come from quite nearby, and the more the sound is dominated by low frequency components, the farther away its source seems to be. Butler et al. (1980) suggested that this is because more distant sounds typically are more dominated by low frequency components and that we have learned this through a lifetime of experiencing such sounds and locating their sources.

A final important cue to the distance of a sound source is the presence of a compelling visual object that *could* be the source. The ventriloquist's dummy seems to talk because its mouth moves while the ventriloquist's does not (if the ventriloquist is a good one). Of course, echoes and reverberation do not play a role in this effect (Mershon, Desaulniers, and Amerson, 1980). In addition, the illusion that a sound is coming from a likely visual object can be so compelling that it can affect the perceived loudness of the sound. If the sound seems to emanate from far away, it sounds louder than if it seems to emanate from close by (Mershon, Desaulniers, Kiefer, and Amerson, 1981). Observers seem to correct for the fact that actual sound intensity diminishes rapidly as the distance from the sound source increases, a phenomenon termed *loudness constancy* (see Chapter 14 for a discussion of constancies).

Physiological mechanisms. There are neurons in the auditory system that respond best to binaural stimuli that reach the two ears at slightly different times or intensities (see Erulkar, 1972, for a review). Different neurons have different "best" interaural time differences, or different "best" interaural intensity differences. In other words, different neurons are "tuned" to different time or intensity differences between the two ears. Because these differences are cues to the location of sounds, we could say that these tuned neurons encode sound location much as neurons tuned to sounds of different frequencies encode frequency. It is possible that such neurons constitute a kind of map of auditory space, with each

neuron having a region of auditory space to which it responds best, a sort of "auditory receptive field" much like the visual receptive fields discussed in Chapter 3. There are problems with this idea, however. The major one is that the tuning of the neurons is too gross to account for the accuracy with which animals, including humans, can localize sounds. In other words, the auditory "receptive fields" of these neurons are too large to account for the degree of accuracy shown in actual behavioral data. In some species, such as the barn owl, much smaller, more intricately organized auditory receptive fields have been found using electrophysiological recording techniques (Knudsen and Konishi, 1978a). An interesting nuance in the barn owl is that the receptive fields of the neurons have a center-surround organization (Knudsen and Konishi, 1978b). That is, not only do they fire above their background rate to stimuli in their "best" areas of space, but also they are inhibited in their response by sounds in areas outside their "best" areas, thus resembling, in many ways, the center-surround organization of neurons at various levels of the visual system (see Chapter 3) and the auditory system (see Chapter 4). So far there has been no direct evidence that such neurons exist in the auditory systems of mammals, but it is certainly possible that the time and intensity difference detectors are preliminary stages leading to such neurons. Interaction of time and intensity difference detectors that have a center-surround organization could give rise to higher level neurons that have relatively restricted receptive fields and might allow a fairly accurate mapping of auditory space.

SUBJECTIVE DIMENSIONS OF SOUND

So far, we have concentrated on an observer's ability to detect the presence of a sound, or to discriminate one sound from another. Such analyses, however, do not deal directly with the subjective quality of a sound as experienced by an observer. Early in the history of the psychological investigation of audition, experimenters were inclined to believe that there would be a direct correspondence between the experienced qualities of the sensation and the physical stimulus. For a long period of time it was taken for granted that every *qualitatively different psychological variable* would reflect almost perfectly some corresponding *quantifiable physical variable*. For example, it was believed that the subjective dimension of loudness was a direct reflection of the physical dimension of *amplitude* of the sound wave stimulus. In similar fashion, it was believed that the subjective dimension of *pitch* (whether a sound appears to be high or low) was simply the psychological experience of the *frequency* of the sound wave. Even today we occasionally find references to frequency and intensity when we really should be speaking of pitch and loudness. This sort of mechanistic viewpoint has been opposed by many investigators, who have pointed out that we should separate concepts and expressions that describe our conscious or phenomenal experience from those that describe the physical stimulus. The subjective qualities of loudness and pitch are complex perceptions that depend on the interaction of several physical characteristics of the stimulus, as well as the physical and psychological state of the observer. Thus, we must distinguish between the physical dimensions that refer to the characteristics of the vibrations we call sound stimuli and the phenomenal qualities or subjective experiences, which should probably be called *sound attributes*.

The deeply rooted older view maintained that at best the observer could be expected to distinguish only two phenomenal dimensions (loudness and pitch), because there are two predominant physical dimensions (intensity and frequency). Actually, we can differentiate many qualitative differences in sound stimuli. Such differences include not only *pitch* and *loudness*, but also the **perceived location** of a sound (where it seems to come from), its **perceived duration** (how extended in time it appears), its **timbre** (that complex quality that allows us to distinguish a note played on a clarinet from the same note played on a violin), its **volume** (the sense in which it fills space and seems large or small), its **density** (a complex feeling of the compactness or hardness of the sound), as well as **consonance** or **dissonance** (how two tones seem to "go together" or "clash"). Our auditory experience is composed of these and other qualitative feelings, and it is not simply the registration of the frequency and the intensity of the stimulus. We have already discussed sound localization, and we will discuss others of these subjective qualities in more detail in the sections that follow.

Loudness

We cannot predict a subjective experience totally from one physical dimension. However, the experienced loudness of a sound is affected greatly by stimulus intensity. As we increase the amplitude of the sound stimulus, we increase its apparent loudness. The experience of loudness, however, is *not* identical to stimulus intensity, and decibels are *not* measures of phenomenal loudness.

In order to study loudness, we must use psychophysical scaling procedures such as the magnitude estimation techniques we discussed in Chapter 2, or the matching of one stimulus to another on a different sensory continuum (cross-modality matching). Stevens (1956) did a classic study of this type using magnitude estimation. He gave an observer a standard stimulus tone and a set of tones that varied in intensity but had the same frequency (1000 Hz) as the standard. The standard tone was assigned a value of 100 units of loudness. The observer simply assigned numbers to the variable tone on the basis of its perceived loudness. Thus, a tone that sounded twice as loud as the standard would be called 200 units, and a tone that sounded half as loud would be called 50 units. Stevens found that the perception of loudness varied according to a simple equation: $L = aI^{0.6}$, where L is the apparent loudness, I is the physical intensity of the sound (in units of pressure amplitude), and a is a constant. The loudness of the stimulus was increasing as approximately the 0.6 power of the physical sound pressure. Other exponents have also been found, depending on the specific stimuli used and the test conditions employed (Marks, 1974). For example, the exponent of the power function varies with stimulus frequency, being somewhat larger for frequencies lower than 1000 Hz (Scharf, 1978).

On the basis of his own work and that of others, Stevens suggested a new unit by which to measure loudness. He called this unit the **sone**. One sone is defined as the loudness of a 1000 Hz stimulus at an intensity level of 40 dB. For most of the stimulus range, a linear relationship exists between the loudness measured by the logarithm of the number of sones and the intensity measured in decibels. To double the loudness (for instance, from 1 to 2 sones), we have to increase the intensity of the sound by about 10 dB. For very weak sounds (below 20 dB), however, the change in apparent loudness is much more rapid with increases in intensity. This relationship is shown in Figure 8-11, which also indicates the loudness in sones of some typical sounds. Table 8-1 summarizes the definition of sones and shows how sones relate to sound intensity.

Sound intensity does not provide a full description of how loud a sound will be. For ex-

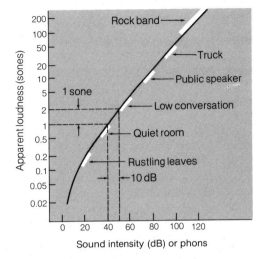

Figure 8-11. The relationship between loudness (measured in sones) and stimulus intensity (measured in decibels) or phons.

ample, our perception of the loudness of a tone is also affected by its frequency. A typical procedure to measure the relationship between frequency and loudness involves presenting an observer with a standard tone of a given frequency and intensity. She is then asked to adjust the intensity of another tone (differing only in frequency) until it matches the loudness of the first. When this is done for a number of comparison tones, we can plot a curve that describes the intensity at which tones of varying frequencies appear to be equally loud as the standard tone. Such a curve is called an **equal loudness contour**.

A series of such equal loudness contours is shown in Figure 8-12. Each curve represents a different sound intensity in decibels for the standard tone. Notice that the lines are not flat. If sounds of various frequencies sounded equally loud when they were the same intensity, all the curves would be straight lines. The fact that the contours rise and fall with frequency (much as the graph of absolute threshold varied with frequency) means that tones of

Table 8-1. Audiometric units

Audiometric term	Unit	What is measured?	How measured?
Pressure amplitude	Dyne/cm²	Variation of sound pressure from atmospheric	Measure peak compressive force per 1 cm² area
Sound pressure level	Decibel (dB)	Ratio of pressure amplitudes of two sounds	$20 \log(P/P_o)$
Frequency	Hertz (Hz)	Number of cycles of compression/rarefaction	Count cycles per second
Loudness	Sone	Subjective impression of sound intensity	1 sone = loudness of 1000 Hz tone at 40 dB
Loudness	Phon	Association of loudness with decibel value of 1000 Hz tone	1 phon = loudness equivalent to that of 1000 Hz tone at 1 dB
Pitch	Mel	Subjective impression of sound frequency	Pitch of 1000 Hz tone at 60 dB is 1000 Mels

equal intensity but of different frequencies appear to differ in loudness. Tones of less than 1000 Hz, or greater than around 6000 Hz, must be considerably more intense to match the loudness of tones between 1000 and 6000 Hz. Thus, tones in the middle range of frequencies sound considerably louder than equally intense tones outside this range.

What if we wished to compare the loudness of tones of frequencies other than 1000 Hz, say an 8000 Hz, 40 dB tone and a 400 Hz, 30 dB tone? Figure 8-12 shows that both tones fall close to the 30 dB contour. This means they are both approximately equal in loudness to a 1000 Hz, 30 dB tone, and thus they also match each other in loudness. We could be more precise and specify their loudness in sones by finding the loudness in sones of the 1000 Hz, 30 dB tone. By graphic (see Figure 8-11) or computational methods we find this to be about 0.46 sone. Thus, both the 8000 Hz, 40 dB tone and the 400 Hz, 30 dB tone have a loudness of 0.46 sone. Although we could compare the loudness of tones of any frequencies and amplitudes using this method, it is somewhat cumbersome. A simpler procedure would be to specify the decibel level of the 1000 Hz tone that matches each test tone in loudness and to compare the respective 1000 Hz tone decibel levels. In fact this procedure is often used, and a special unit of loudness has been defined to make it easy to talk about. The loudness of a test tone of any amplitude and frequency expressed in **phons** is just the sound pressure level, in decibels, of the 1000 Hz tone that is equal to the test tone in loudness. Thus, the loudness of the two tones we have been discussing is just 30 phons, since they are both equal in loudness to a 1000 Hz, 30 dB tone. Phons are simply decibel values of a 1000 Hz tone. However, phons and sones are not simply two different measures of the same thing. Sones are a measure of subjective loudness and can be used to compare differences between any pair of tones. Phons simply associate any pure tone with a 1000 Hz tone of equal subjective loudness. Because phons are simply decibel values of a 1000 Hz tone, they are not measures of subjective loudness any more than are any other decibel values.

Table 8-1 summarizes essential aspects of these audiometric units.

There are other factors that also influence the apparent loudness of a tone. One is the length of time the tone is sounded. For tones briefer than about 200 msec in duration, we must increase intensity to match the loudness of a longer tone. We could create an equal loudness contour, of a type similar to that for variations with frequency, by having a standard of fixed duration and requiring an observer to match its loudness with a comparison tone of different durations. When we do this we get a curve similar to that shown in Figure 8-13. Thus, a 2 msec burst of sound must be 15 dB in order to sound as loud as a 90 msec burst at 5 dB. This sort of finding suggests that the auditory system may sum all the inputs coming

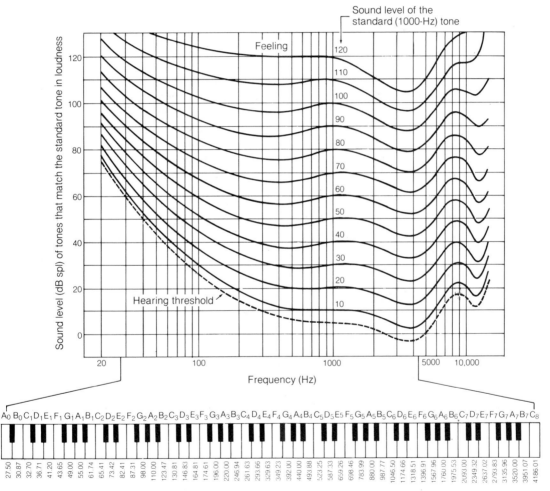

Figure 8-12. Equal loudness contours. The numbers on the curves represent the number of phons. (from Lindsay and Norman, 1977; data from Robinson and Dadson, 1956).

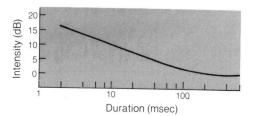

Figure 8-13. Equal loudness contour showing the changes in intensity needed to maintain a constant loudness as the duration of the standard is varied (from **Hearing: Physiology and Psychophysics,** *by Lawrence W. Gulick. Copyright 1971 by Oxford University Press, Inc. Reprinted by permission).*

in over a 200 msec window of time (Gulick, 1971).

The duration of the stimulus can have another effect on our response to loudness. If a tone is presented for a very long time, the stimulus gradually seems to decrease in loudness. We can measure this effect by having an observer match the loudness of the persistent or adapting tone to that of a comparison stimulus (usually of a different frequency). As the adapting stimulus remains on for longer and

longer periods of time, the intensity of the matching stimulus must be decreased. This indicates that the loudness of the adapting stimulus has itself decreased. This process is called **auditory adaptation**. A related phenomenon, called **auditory fatigue**, is caused by exposing the ear to very intense sounds. The resultant *reduction* of loudness of other stimuli presented after the intense sound ceases may persist for a considerable period of time, depending on the intensity and duration of the stimulus. For instance, Postman and Egan (1949) exposed observers to an intense sound (115 dB) for 20 minutes. They then measured the sensitivity of their observers over a period of several days. The results are shown in Figure 8-14. The horizontal line represents pre-exposure sensitivity, while the other curves represent the hearing loss, which could be interpreted as a reduction in loudness, for varying periods of time after the exposure to the stimulus. As can be seen, the largest hearing loss immediately follows the exposure to the intense noise; however, it does persist to a measurable extent over a period of 24 hours. You can experience an interesting analog to this experiment using Demonstration Box 8-6.

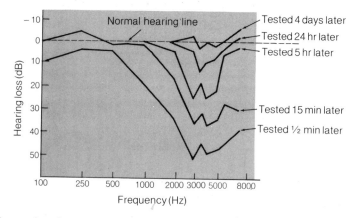

Figure 8-14. Prolonged reduction of loudness following exposure to an intense (115 dB) *stimulus for 20 min (based on Postman and Egan, 1949).*

Demonstration Box 8-6. Auditory adaptation

During an average day you are exposed to many noises and sounds, from individuals who talk with you, from stereos, televisions, radios, and numerous other sources. Set a radio or a stereo to an intensity level where the sound seems comfortable for listening in the evening before you go to bed. At the day's end, your auditory system has adapted to the ongoing, persistent noise of the day. When you awaken in the morning, however, you may find that the radio, set to the same sound level, will appear to be too loud. During the night your ears have recovered from the auditory adaptation caused by exposure to the sounds you heard during the previous day. The quiet of the night has given you a chance to recover your sensitivity, hence all sounds now seem louder. This may explain why an alarm clock, whose bell seems low and pleasant when bought one evening in a department store, will seem so jarring and loud the following morning.

Another factor that influences our perception of loudness is the complexity of the stimulus. Most laboratory experiments in audition have used tones of a single frequency, while most of the sounds we hear in our everyday environment are made up of mixtures of a large number of frequencies. We can match the intensity of a pure tone to that of a complex sound in much the same way as we matched tones of different frequencies to a 1000 Hz tone when we constructed the phon scale. We simply ask listeners to adjust the intensity of a pure tone of 1000 Hz until it matches the loudness of the complex tone, giving a new kind of equal loudness contour.

Suppose we take a complex sound composed of a group of frequencies centered around that of a standard tone. We can systematically increase or decrease the range of frequencies included. We usually refer to the range of frequencies as the **bandwidth**. Figure 8-15 displays an equal loudness contour for a complex sound with a center frequency of 1000 Hz. Note that as the bandwidth of the sound is increased, the intensity at each of the component frequencies must be decreased in order to keep the overall intensity of the sound the same. Notice also that when only a small

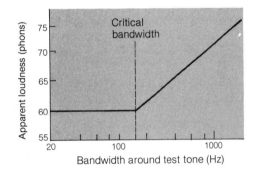

Figure 8-15. The effect on loudness of increasing the bandwidth of frequencies in a complex tone (based on Gulick, 1971).

band of frequencies makes up the complex sound, increasing the bandwidth does not affect our perception of the loudness of the stimulus. This is reasonable, since the overall intensity of the sound is not changing but only the number of different frequencies included in it. Notice, however, what happens when the frequencies reach a critical bandwidth of about 160 Hz. From this bandwidth onward, loudness begins to increase as we include a greater number of frequencies, although the overall intensity of the sound is unchanged (Gulick, 1971; Scharf, 1978).

Researchers have acknowledged that loudness depends on all the factors we have been discussing, including the frequency, duration, and complexity of the tone. However, they have persisted in a search for one simple underlying physiological variable that might serve as the basis for our phenomenal experience of the loudness of a sound. The most frequent suggestion is that our sensation of loudness simply depends on the total amount of neural activity per unit time taking place in some region of the brain. In Chapter 4 we discussed how the overall level of neural activity in the auditory nerve is primarily a function of the intensity of the sound reaching the ear. Since the primary physical determinant of loudness is sound intensity, it seems reasonable to suppose that the amount of neural activity in some higher brain center corresponds, at least generally, to our sensation of loudness. This is supported by evidence that the relationship between the amount of neural activity and the sound intensity follows the same sort of power function that we observe when we look at the relationship between sound intensity and the loudness sensation (Stevens, 1975). In the auditory nerve, the exponent of this power function is similar to that derived from magnitude estimation experiments for loudness (about 0.6), although exponents obtained at higher levels are somewhat smaller and often do not correspond closely to those measured from magnitude estimations of the same subjects (Wilson and Stelmack, 1982). Stevens suggested that the power function obtained for loudness is determined by the operating characteristic of the ear [the way in which it transduces (transforms) sound energy to neural activity], and that the remaining levels in the auditory system only relay the total intensity of the firing onto the next center, with the message ultimately "becoming" loudness at some more central site in the brain.

Recent studies of neural responses in the auditory system of the cat indicate that the situation might not be so simple. Atkinson (1976, 1978) found evidence for a power function between stimulus intensity and the amplitude of the neural response in the medial geniculate body (an auditory area in the lower brain) and in the superior colliculus (a brain area that receives both auditory and visual inputs). This seems to suggest that there is a direct relationship between the magnitude of neural activity and the percieved loudness of a stimulus. This position, however, must be modified somewhat since Atkinson also reported that when he used very intense sounds (stimuli that sound like clicks to humans), these same neurons responded with less overall activity than they did for less intense sounds. Some kind of inhibitory response seems to set limits on the range of loudnesses that can be signaled. This finding also suggests that our phenomenal impression of loudness is not simply a reflection of the amount of neural activity, although the two are related in some ways (Atkinson, 1982).

Pitch

Every time you sing or play a musical scale, you are varying the subjective experience of **pitch**. Your *do*, *re*, and *mi* differ in this tonal quality. The most important physical determinant of our perception of pitch is the frequency of the sound stimulus. The high notes on the piano have higher frequencies than the low notes. For instance, the dominant frequency of A-4 (the forty-ninth key on the piano counting from the left to the right) is 440 Hz. The dominant frequency of the A note one octave higher (A-5, or the sixty-first key from the left) is 880 Hz (turning back to Figure 8-12 might help you to visualize this).

Perhaps the first demonstration of the relationship between frequency and pitch was performed by Robert Hooke in 1681. Hooke placed a card against a wheel that had teeth notched in it. He then spun the wheel. The spinning teeth hit the card and the resultant vibrations sent out a sound wave—a sort of rough buzzing musical note. When the speed of rotation was increased, the frequency of vibration of the card increased, and so did the pitch of the note. The relationship between frequency and pitch had been established. For centuries thereafter, the terms pitch and frequency were used interchangeably on the assumption that pitch rises and falls in exact step with frequency.

Perhaps the most commonly used measure of the pitch of a sound is the musical scale, which is basically logarithmic in nature. Any note one octave higher than another note of the same name has exactly twice the frequency of the lower note. Thus, the note A-3 (the thirty-seventh key from the left) has a frequency of 220 Hz, while A-4 (the forty-ninth key from the left) is one octave higher and has a frequency of 440 Hz (again see Figure 8-12). The musical scale has undergone very little change over the years, although some attempts have been made to adjust the spacing between the notes in an attempt to represent more accurately the pitches of different musical notes. For example, there is a version of the musical scale called the **equal temperament scale** (W. D. Ward, 1970). Here, each octave is divided into 12 equal parts representing standard intervals between the musical notes. These intervals are called semitones, and each semitone can be further divided into 100 cents. Thus, an octave consists of 1200 cents, and the pitch of any tone can be precisely described in terms of in what octave it is located in and how many cents it lies above the lowest tone in that octave. This scale has proved to be

quite useful for musicians, although there are still arguments about the spacing of the standard intervals within an octave. The reason for such arguments seems to lie in the fact that the musical scale is not a direct representation of the psychological scale for pitch.

The most useful psychological scale for pitch to date is the **mel** scale proposed by Stevens, Volkman, and Newman (1937). Like the sone scale of loudness, the mel scale can be created by various psychophysical scaling techniques. For instance, in one experiment, the researchers created a sort of electronic piano with 20 keys and 20 corresponding knobs set above the keyboard. Turning a knob varied the tone produced by the corresponding key through a wide range of frequencies. Subjects were asked to sit before the keyboard and to tune the "piano" to produce pitch intervals that appeared to be equally wide. The results were somewhat surprising. Subjects did not tune the piano to equal steps on the frequency scale, nor did they tune them to equal steps on a scale of musical intervals.

As in other psychophysical scaling techniques, one must designate a standard against which all other items will be scaled. By definition, a sound with a frequency of 1000 Hz and an intensity of 60 dB has been assigned a pitch of 1000 mels (see Table 8-1 for a summary of measures of frequency and pitch). This frequency lies between the notes B-5 and C-6 on the piano (the sixty-third and the sixty-fourth keys from the left). When we compare the mel scale with the musical scale, we find several large discrepancies. For instance, the one octave difference between C-3 (Key 28) and C-4 (Key 46) is 167 mels, while the one octave difference between C-6 (Key 64) and C-7 (Key 76) is 508 mels. Such measurements confirm the feelings, often expressed by musicians, that the higher musical octaves sound "larger" than the lower ones. It is as if there is more

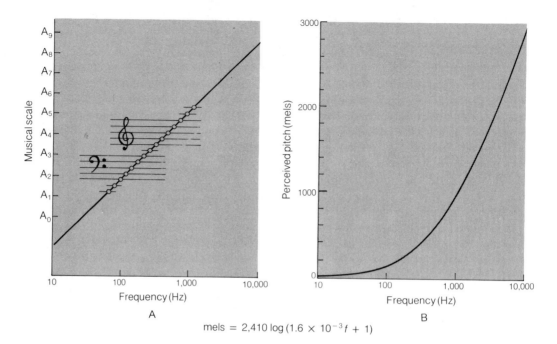

$$mels = 2,410 \log (1.6 \times 10^{-3} f + 1)$$

Figure 8-16. (A) The relationship between frequency and the musical scale and (B) the relationship between mels and frequency (from Lindsay and Norman, 1977).

"psychological distance" between the keys on the high end of the piano than on the low end. The relationships between mels, frequency, and the musical scale are shown in Figure 8-16.

Just as a variety of factors other than sound intensity affect the perceived loudness of a sound, factors other than frequency affect its perceived pitch. The very existence of the mel scale demonstrates that pitch is not identical to frequency, since when asked to find a sound that is half the pitch of a standard sound, an observer does not produce a sound that is half the frequency of the standard. Perhaps the major physical factor, other than frequency, that affects the perceived pitch of a pure tone is its intensity. In a classic demonstration, first performed over a quarter of a century ago, an investigator struck a tuning fork tuned to middle

C (C-4, or 262 Hz) a few feet from the ear of a trained singer. The singer was asked to sing the note she heard, and she reproduced the sound with reasonable accuracy. Next, the investigator held the same tuning fork a few inches from her ear. This increased the intensity of the sound reaching her ear, but it left the frequency unchanged since a tuning fork (when properly struck) produces sounds of only a single frequency. Nonetheless, the pitch that the singer heard did change. She now sang a note that was considerably lower in pitch than middle C, clearly demonstrating that sound intensity affected perceived pitch.

Using an experimental technique similar to that used in producing equal loudness contours, we can produce **equal pitch contours**. The observer can be asked either to adjust the intensity of one of two tones that differ in frequency until the two tones match in pitch (Stevens, 1935) or to adjust the frequency of one of two tones that differ in intensity until it matches the other in pitch (Gulick, 1971). Figure 8-17 shows the results from one observer measured by Stevens (1935). The graph shows the percentage change in the frequency necessary to keep the pitch constant as intensity is changed. The ordinate was chosen so that lines curving upward mean that the pitch is increasing (sounds higher), while lines curving downward mean that the pitch is decreasing (sounds lower). As the figure shows, varying the intensity of the tone greatly alters its perceived pitch. For higher-frequency tones, the pitch tends to rise as intensity increases, whereas for lower-frequency tones, an increase in intensity tends to lower the pitch.

Another factor that affects our perception of pitch is the duration of the stimulus. A pure tone that lasts for only a few milliseconds is always heard as a click, regardless of the frequency. Before a tone is perceived to have the quality of pitch, one of two conditions must be met. For high-frequency tones (greater than

1000 Hz), the minimum length of time the stimulus must be sounded is around 10 msec. For low-frequency tones (less than 1000 Hz), at least 6-9 cycles of the sound wave must reach the ear before it is perceived to have pitch. This means that most lower frequency tones must last for considerably longer than 10 msec before they have pitch (Gulick, 1971). Even for tones that exceed the minimum duration for number of cycles, the tonal quality continues to improve as the duration is increased up to about 250 msec. Listeners are better able to discriminate between tones of different frequencies when their duration is longer. You may recall that the loudness of a tone also increases as we increase stimulus duration up to around 200-250 msec. Perhaps 1/4 of a second represents some sort of fundamental time period for sensory systems such as the ear. Our phenomenal impressions of the world seem to be based on averages or sums of energy changes taken over this small window of time, similar to the psychological moment we discuss in Chapter 11.

Theories of pitch perception. The realm

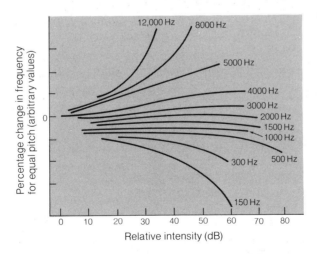

Figure 8-17. The relationship between apparent pitch and stimulus intensity for one observer (based on Stevens, 1935).

of pitch perception has proved to be a testing ground for the major theories of auditory perception. Several tests have been based on some interesting characteristics of our subjective impressions of sound. Suppose we created a complex sound by adding together several different sinusoidal sound waves. The auditory system conducts its own waveform analysis of the complex sound, and we are able to perceive the pitch of the various components separately. For instance, if two tones are played at the same time, you perceive a musical chord containing two distinct pitches. You do not hear a single, unitary sound (as you discovered in Demonstration Box 4-1). The visual system lacks this property of analyzing light stimuli into their component frequencies (wavelengths). In vision, two stimulus frequencies are combined into a single experience, and the individual components cannot be resolved in consciousness (this was discussed in Chapter 7 when we dealt with color perception).

When we are considering a complex stimulus composed of several sound wave frequencies, the lowest (usually most intense) frequency sound wave is called the **fundamental**. Musical instruments tend to produce complex sounds in which **harmonics** (frequencies higher than the fundamental) occur at whole number multiples of the fundamental frequency. For example, we have already noted that a sound wave of 220 Hz corresponds to a musical note that we call A (it would be A-3, or the thirty-seventh key from the left on the piano). When a musical instrument sounds this note, the complex waveform produced will also contain some sound energy at frequencies of 440 Hz, 880 Hz, 1320 Hz, and so on. These are called *high even harmonics* (because they represent frequencies of 2, 4, and 6 times the fundamental frequency). Actually, the characteristic sound of an instrument depends on the specific harmonics it produces. This quality, which gives the characteristic sound to a par-

ticular instrument, is called its **timbre**. Different instruments emphasize different higher harmonics (sometimes called *overtones*). The number of higher harmonics, or overtones, and their strength determines the complex phenomenal perception that allows us to distinguish between a note played on a piano and the same note played by plucking a violin or a guitar string. Thus, the pitch of a sound is greatly determined by the frequency of the fundamental, while the timbre is determined by the harmonics. Helmholtz (1863) summarized the various subjective feelings pertaining to the composition of a complex tone. This summary is shown in Table 8-2.

Because the fundamental frequency is the greatest common denominator of all the harmonics present in a complex sound, we could correctly determine the fundamental from our knowledge of the way in which harmonics work. For example, if we had harmonics of 600, 900, and 1200 Hz, the fundamental frequency would be 300 Hz. As we noted earlier, a waveform normally contains both a funda-

Table 8-2. Sound composition and timbre (based on Helmholtz, 1863)

Makeup of complex tone	Subjective impression
Fundamental alone	Soft
Fundamental plus first harmonic	Mellow
Fundamental plus several harmonics	Broad or full
Fundamental plus high harmonics	Sharp
Fundamental intense, harmonics less intense	Full
Harmonics intense, fundamental less intense	Hollow
Odd harmonics (for example, 1, 3, 5) dominating	Nasal
Frequency ratios of 16:15, 9:8, 15:8, 7:5, or 7:6	Rough or screeching

mental frequency and several higher harmonics. It is possible (through the use of special electronic filters) to remove the fundamental frequency without changing the higher harmonic structure. Alternatively, we could present together a set of pure tones that had a particular fundamental without presenting the fundamental (for example, 600, 900, and 1200 Hz tones without the 300 Hz fundamental). Such an artificial sound complex, from which the fundamental frequency is missing, is called a stimulus with a **missing fundamental**.

An interesting and puzzling problem comes from a particular illusion associated with the missing fundamental. Suppose you are presented with two complex sounds. One contains the fundamental and higher harmonics, and the other does not contain the fundamental frequency but contains only the higher harmonics. The illusion lies in the fact that both sounds appear to be the same. In both cases, the pitch will sound like that associated with the fundamental frequency, even though the fundamental frequency is not physically present in the waveform of the second sound. This unusual phenomenon of hearing plays an important role in a test of the two major theories of pitch. The first is based on the **place principle** and the second is based on the **frequency principle**.

More than a hundred years ago, Helmholtz became intrigued by the fact that the ear could separate a complex sound stimulus into its component simple frequencies. He observed that since the basilar membrane consists of many fibers stretched across its triangular shape, we could think of it as a harp with strings. He suggested that the longer strings resonate to (that is, vibrate in sympathy with) lower frequency tones, while the shorter strings resonate to tones of higher frequency. Thus, if we sounded a complex tone it would be automatically decomposed into its component frequencies on the basilar membrane.

Each different tone would cause a different *place* on the membrane to vibrate. This is the place principle.

This basic idea was later supported and modified by Békésy in a series of precise experiments that ultimately won him the Nobel Prize (see Békésy, 1960). His basic procedure was to cut tiny holes in the cochleas of guinea pigs and to observe the basilar membrane with a microscope as the ear was being stimulated by tones of different frequencies. He discovered that high-frequency tones maximally displace the narrow end of the basilar membrane near the oval window, while tones of intermediate frequency cause displacement farther toward the other (wider) end of the basilar membrane. Unfortunately, the action of the basilar membrane was not quite as simple as Helmholtz's resonance notion, since low-frequency tones activated the entire membrane (see Chapter 4). This fact, together with the result that tones of intermediate frequency also displace a fairly broad area of the membrane, made it unlikely that differential displacement or vibration of the basilar membrane is sufficient to fully explain our ability to discriminate pitch (at least for lower to intermediate frequencies).

The place theory also has difficulty in explaining the phenomenon of the missing fundamental. Helmholtz attempted to deal with this experience by suggesting that the transduction process in the middle ear introduces distortion before the waves enter the cochlea. This distortion could then create a new fundamental frequency, so that the fundamental is present inside the cochlea even though it is missing in the stimulus that contacts the outer ear. Békésy (1960) modified this notion somewhat so that the distortion became part of the response of the basilar membrane, which was said to respond "as if" the fundamental were also physically present.

Unfortunately, several experimental results

throw doubt on this distortion hypothesis for the missing fundamental. The basic form of such experiments (Patterson, 1969) involves the presentation of pairs of tones, such as 2000 Hz and 2400 Hz, which would produce a missing fundamental of 400 Hz. If we now add a low-frequency band of noise to the complex wave, centered around 400 Hz, we would expect that when the noise is sufficiently intense it would be very effective in masking the fundamental tone, since it is stimulating the approximate place on the basilar membrane that place theory assumes to be vibrating. Nevertheless, despite the presence of this noise, the pitch of the complex wave is still perceived to be that of the fundamental frequency. Since the missing fundamental phenomenon cannot be explained by distortions in the ear, or the local response of the basilar membrane, it presents a problem for a place theory.

The second major class of theory is based on the frequency principle. It also has a long history. It was first championed by August Seeback in the 1840s (Green, 1976) and has been carried forward to the present by Wever (1970). This theory argues that the vibrations of the basilar membrane reproduce at least partially the vibrations of the incoming sounds. The frequency of the sound is transmitted by the pattern of neural excitation resulting from this vibration. This situation is analogous to the microphone end of a telephone transducing the pattern of vibrations into variations of electrical signals as it vibrates in unison with your voice. According to this theory, pitch is determined by the frequency of impulses traveling up the auditory nerve. The greater the frequency, the higher the pitch. Some studies have shown that for tones of up to about 4000 Hz, the electrical response of the auditory nerve tracks the frequency of the tone (see Chapter 4). A tone of 500 Hz produces a pattern of response that contains some 500 bursts of electrical responses per second in the nerve,

while a tone of 1000 Hz produces twice as many responses.

Such a theoretical position could explain the missing fundamental. Since there are many harmonics but only one fundamental frequency, masking the region of the fundamental should not appreciably change the overall pattern of sound excitation. The low frequency of the fundamental may actually be signaled by the neurons that respond to the higher harmonics, since it is these neurons that convey most of the information about the pattern of excitation. This may seem somewhat topsy-turvey in that we are saying that the fundamental is *not* fundamental, yet consider the example we used earlier in our discussion. Given a sound wave with harmonics of 600, 900, and 1200 Hz, the fundamental is inferred to be 300 Hz. In much the same way that we *infer* the fundamental from knowledge of the harmonic structure, a higher auditory center could infer the fundamental from the pattern of excitation reported by neurons that respond to higher frequencies (see Javel, 1981). This can be verified to a certain extent by the following experiment. We again present an individual with a pair of tones, such as 2000 and 2400 Hz tones to produce a missing fundamental of 400 Hz. If we now introduce a high-frequency band of noise, centered at about 2200 Hz and extending for several hundred Hertz on either side of it (which should mask the higher harmonics), the missing fundamental is no longer heard (Patterson, 1969).

Additional experiments give a similar picture. If we present one component of a complex sound, say 600 Hz, to one ear, and another, say 800 Hz, to the other ear, a missing fundamental corresponding to 200 Hz is perceived (Houtsma and Goldstein, 1972). Here there could be no activity on either basilar membrane corresponding to that created when a 200 Hz pure tone stimulates it, since each membrane was stimulated only by a single tone far from 200 Hz. Missing fundamental pitches seem to be perceived using a different mechanism than that used for the pitch of pure tones.

A number of problems still exist with a frequency theory for pitch perception. One difficulty is that an individual neuron cannot fire at high enough rates to account for the perception of high-frequency signals. Actually, an individual neuron can conduct only about 1000 impulses per second. Thus, the ability of the auditory nerve to track frequencies above this point (up to about 4000 Hz—see the discussion of phase locking in Chapter 4) has to be explained in terms of a **volley prinicple** (Wever, 1970). This argues that there is cooperation between neural fibers so that they fire in groups or squads. While one neuron is "reloading," its neighbor can discharge. The overall effect is that the neural pattern of firing is in direct correspondence to the frequency of the stimulus, since if one counts the total number of discharges, or volleys, per unit of time, they correspond to the frequency of the stimulus. An example of how this can work is shown in Figure 8-18.

A major problem with a volley or frequency principle of pitch perception is that we require

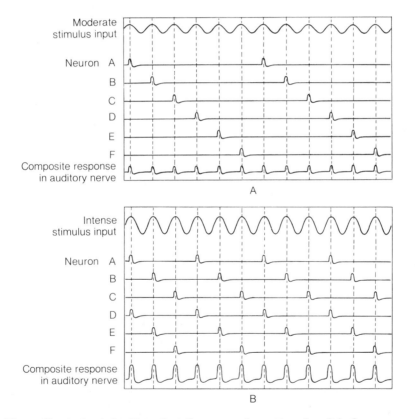

Figure 8-18. The volley principle. Note that the composite neural response follows the frequency of the stimulus. However, for the weaker stimulus (A), fewer neurons are firing in each volley than fire for the stronger stimulus (B).

the frequency of neural firing to encode both the intensity and the frequency of the sound. Although at first this seems impossible, one way to resolve the problem is to differentiate a concept of overall *density* of neural activity from one of a *number* of volleys (or bursts of firing) per unit time. The density of neural firing could be defined as the total number of neurons responding in each volley, or if you will, the number of "shots" being fired in each volley down the auditory nerve. An increase in the intensity of the sound, while not changing the volley frequency, could increase the number of neurons joining in the firing, or cause the rate of each individual neuron to increase somewhat. If all the neurons were connected to some higher center that ascertained pitch by the frequency of volleys and loudness by the number of responses per volley, the problem would be solved. An example of how this could work is also shown in Figure 8-18.

Since both the place principle and the frequency principle seem to be supported by some data, it seems likely, as Wever (1970) has suggested, that the ultimate explanation of pitch will include some aspects of both theories. Wever has proposed that in humans pitch is coded by the frequency principle for frequencies lower than about 4000 Hz (the theoretical upper limit for volleying). The use of this volley mechanism for the perception of lower pitches may be supported by an individual's learning and experience (Terhardt, 1974; Hall and Peters, 1982). For frequencies from 500 to 20,000 Hz, the place principle seems capable of explaining pitch perception. Below 500 Hz, however, the vibration pattern on the basilar membrane seems too broad to explain our excellent pitch perception. Notice that for frequencies between 500 and 4000 Hz, both principles are operating. This could explain the superior performance of the ear for sounds in this range compared with sounds of higher

or lower frequencies. Frequencies outside this range must rely on only one mechanism, hence performance is poorer.

The place-frequency compromise is supported by a good deal of research. In one of the most intriguing studies, Simmons, Epley, Lummis, Guttman, Frishkopf, Harmon, and Zwicker (1965) placed electrodes in the auditory nerve corresponding to different parts of the basilar membrane of a subject's deaf ear. They found that electrical stimulation at different locations produced perception of different pitches. This of course supports the place principle. Varying the frequency of the electrical stimulus from about 20 to 300 Hz, however, produced the appropriate changes in pitch perception, regardless of the place where the stimulating electrode was located. This supports the frequency principle. Clearly, both mechanisms are needed to explain such data.

MUSIC PERCEPTION

Valerie had just spent the entire afternoon sitting in a soundproof room, listening to a series of pure tones through a pair of earphones. As each tone was presented, she had had to make a judgment of its pitch on a scale from 1 to 100. The tones had varied in frequency, intensity, and duration, and in some cases several had been presented together so that they sounded like a chord or like some kind of musical instrument. Valerie was tired. The afternoon had been indescribably boring, and being a highly motivated observer she had worked very hard to give consistent, useful responses. As she left the audition lab she was thinking to herself, "I'm sure glad I'm going to the symphony tonight. Let's see, they're playing one of Bach's Brandenburg Concerti. That should be relaxing. I can't wait till I get there. It will help scrub all this afternoon's silly *sounds* out of my mind."

What distinguishes mere collections of sounds from music? Isn't music the same kind of stimuli—just sounds that vary in frequency, intensity, duration, and timbre? The answer seems to be that music is created by the context, or relationship of a sound to those preceeding and following it. In contrast, the sounds Valerie judged in the afternoon's experiment were presented one at a time and separated from one another in an attempt to make them relatively independent of one another. In the experiment, Valerie had never felt that the sequence of sounds was music. Earlier in this chapter we discussed some of the results from experiments such as the one in which Valerie was an observer. When a musical context is provided for such judgments, however, and the listeners have had some experience with music, an entirely new set of phenomena emerges (Krumhansl and Shepard, 1979).

One of the most striking examples of this new set of phenomena is the difference between musical pitch and acoustic pitch. We have indicated that the mel scale (acoustic pitch) is somewhat inconsistent with the musical scales that have been proposed. In both, sounds vary along the dimension musicians call **tone height**, or whether a sound appears to be of higher or lower pitch. But in music, there are other relations between the pitches of sounds than those of tone height. For example, in a musical context, sounds that are exactly one octave apart (say C4 and C5) seem more similar than do sounds separated by less than one octave but with different names (say C4 and G4). In other words, as we ascend the musical scale (do, re, mi, and so on), the dos sound similar to each other, as do the res, and so forth. The tendency for tones exactly one octave apart to sound similar musically means

that a simple one-dimensional scale will not suffice for *musical pitch*. Rather, each note seems to be cycling through again with a different quality. This is reminiscent of the situation we discussed in Chapter 7 for color. There, when dealing with the dimension of hue, we found that we seemed to be moving around a circle, recycling from red through yellow, green, blue and purple, then back to red. In color we could vary independently the brightness dimension linearly, without changing the identity of the hue. We found that to represent the range of colors we had to use a three-dimensional scheme. A similar problem seems to exist with musical sounds. Thus, as early as 1846, Drobisch proposed that musical pitch might be represented as a helix, an idea that has persisted until the present (see Shepard, 1982). Figure 8-19 shows a representation of this type.

The new aspect of musical pitch represented in the figure is called **tone chroma**, a name that shows its psychological similarity to what we mean by hue in the realm of color perception. As with hue, tone chroma is represented by a circle. Tone chroma can be seen in the figure as the circular component of the helix, while tone height is represented by the vertical component of the helix. One complete turn of the helix (a 360 degree rotation in the horizontal plane) represents a single octave, and all notes with the same name project on a line drawn down the helix onto the same point on the chroma circle at the bottom. For convenience we have labeled the spiral with some names of musical scale notes corresponding to the piano keyboard represented in Figure 8-12.

While the usual laboratory experiment in pitch perception is able to isolate tones that seem to vary only in tone height, it is also possible to produce a series of sounds that vary only in tone chroma (moving around the

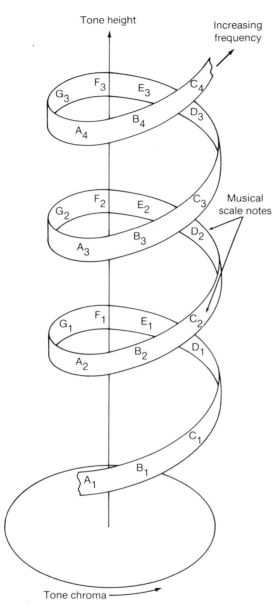

Figure 8-19. A regular helix represents the two aspects of musical pitch, height and chroma.

chroma circle in Figure 8-19) yet that seem to ascend in height (Burns, 1981; Pollack, 1978; Shepard, 1964). You can try this for yourself in Demonstration Box 8-7.

Recent work has confirmed the importance of the chroma circle in musical pitch but also has indicated that other relations between musical tones are also quite important (see Krumhansl and Kessler, 1982; Shepard, 1982). For example, when one tone is exactly 1.5 times the frequency of the other (a 3-to-2 ratio, or a *perfect fifth*), the two tones seem to "go together" or sound better together than when the tones are separated by other frequency steps (except for the octave step). These other relations, both between tones and between keys (a particular group of tones that compose the set from which a melody is chosen), require a much more complicated representation, and agreement on it has not yet been reached (see Krumhansl and Kessler, 1982; Shepard, 1982). What is certain is that such relations, which play an important role in music theory, do have a perceptual reality, at least for musicians, and must be taken into consideration in any description of music perception.

How well can people identify musical notes? In music, one frequently hears of individuals who have "perfect pitch." Such musicians are able to identify a musical note (for example, C4 on a piano) even when it is presented in complete isolation from other tones (although they do occasionally misidentify the octave in which it is located). However, when these musicians are presented with pure, sine-wave tones, they can identify the notes correctly only about half the time (Lockhead and Byrd, 1981). Although this is better than the performance of those without perfect pitch, who tend to be correct on only about 8 percent of the trials, it is not "perfect." Clearly, musicians who have perfect pitch are using more than

---

Demonstration Box 8-7. The tonal staircase

Shepard (1964) invented a series of complex tones generated by a computer that when listened to in sequence seemed to continually increase in pitch. That is, each step between tones was perceived as being a step upward in pitch. Shepard, however, used a trick in generating this series of sounds, and in fact the series ended where it had begun, completing a journey around the chroma circle (see Figure 8-19), and the continuing rise in pitch was an illusion. It is rather difficult to produce Shepard's series of sounds without complex equipment, but it may be possible for you to hear the illusion anyway. First, fill a glass partially full of water; a crystal glass would be best, perhaps a wine glass, but any glass with a "ring" should do. Now tap the glass gently with a knife or other im-

plement to make it ring. Continue tapping gently to produce a series of complex sounds. Each sound will be slightly different from the others in its frequency components because of variation in the way the knife strikes the glass. The series of sounds produced this way can often be heard to ascend or descend in pitch continuously, much in the way Shepard's sounds did, even though the sounds are highly similar and the fundamental frequency probably does not change. This illusion is quite similar to the visual staircase illusion shown here. The stairs seem to climb endlessly but never get anywhere. This is probably the most striking demonstration of the reality of the quality of tone chroma in musical sounds.

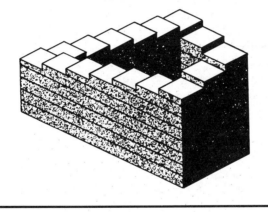

---

the fundamental frequency of the musical notes to identify them; they are probably using the higher harmonics of the musical note (for example, piano note) to aid in identification. From their own reports, such musicians claim to judge chroma by comparing the test note with an internal (remembered) standard for each note, while the people without perfect pitch simply seem to guess at chroma.

The spacing between musical notes is called a **musical interval**. In the music of the Western world, scales have been arranged with logarithmic musical intervals, because frequency intervals that are equal on a logarithmic scale are perceived as being approximately equal intervals of musical pitch. For example, if you heard an interval generated by a pair of notes with frequencies of 200 and 400 Hz and another generated by a pair with frequencies of 2000 and 4000 Hz, they would seem to be equally large. When three or more musical notes are played at the same time, we have a **chord**. Chords provide much of the characteristic sound that we call music (see for example, Krumhansl, Bharucha, and Kessler, 1982). Formal music theory provides a somewhat complicated system for naming chords, too complicated to discuss here. Briefly, chords too are defined in terms of the ratios of the frequencies of the tones that compose them. Chords that have components that stand in the same frequency relationship are given the same name, irrespective of the octave. For example, an E major chord is composed of the notes E, G#, and B, no matter whether that means E4, G#4, and B4 or E6, G#6, and B6. This aspect of musical pitch too is consistent with the logarithmic helix shown in Figure 8-19, since the logarithmic spacings between the notes remains the same regardless of tonal height or absolute frequency.

So far we have described a few of the most important individual components or aspects of musical sequences. Any sequence of tones, however, also has properties that give an overall pattern to the sound sequence and are quite important to its musical character. These properties include the sequence of pitch changes and the proportion and sizes of the various ascending and descending intervals. They are global overall properties since they are perceived in relationship to one another, rather than as individual features (Cuddy, Cohen, and Mewhort, 1981; Deutsch, 1978). In fact, melodies can even be recognized on the basis of such global properties alone. These global cues are often described collectively as the **contour** of a piece of music. Contour means much the same thing here that it does in visual pattern perception (see Chapter 12). It is the general *shape* of the sequence of musical sounds, defined in terms of rises and drops in frequency. Figure 8-20 shows some examples of musical passages that share a contour even though they are in different positions on the musical scale.

A typical piece of music consists of a rather long sequence of different notes and chords, rather similar to a long string of sounds uttered by a person making a speech. And just as we perceive a complicated hierarchy of words, phrases, sentences, and so on, as we listen to someone speaking (see Chapter 13), we also organize music in a hierarchical fashion. Combinations of notes form *motives* (pronounced "mo-teefs"), combinations of motives form *phrases*, and so on (Deutsch, 1978).

How are these combinations formed perceptually? Notes are grouped together according to principles that strongly resemble those that govern visual pattern perception, suggesting that the perception of music and melody is a form of auditory pattern perception. Of particular interest in this regard are the *Gestalt laws of grouping* that we will discuss in greater detail in Chapter 12 when we deal with the perception of visual form. There are several major principles that tend to organize which notes or chords are grouped together (see Deutsch, 1978). The first of these is *pitch range*. Notes that are close together in pitch will tend to be perceived as part of the same perceptual unit, while notes that are far apart in pitch are perceived to be in separate groups. This principle is related to the Gestalt law of *proximity*. The visual equivalent of this principle can be seen in Chapter 12, Figure 12-6. Whenever the same instrument plays both a melody and an accompaniment, they are played in different pitch or frequency ranges so that the melody will be the *figure* (the part that stands out perceptually) and the accompaniment will be the

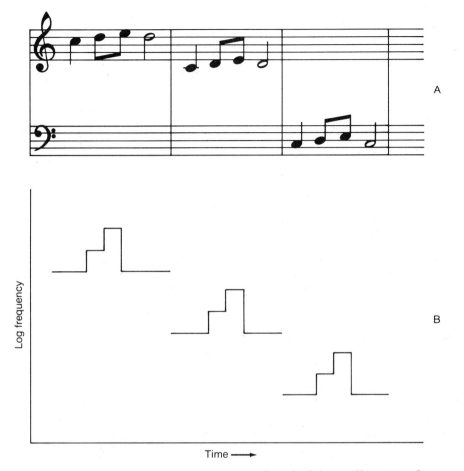

Figure 8-20. When a melodic sequence is transposed to different positions on the mu- **sical scale (A) it still retains the same contour (B).**

ground (or background against which the melody is imaged). For example, a folk guitarist often plays an ongoing accompaniment on the bass strings of the guitar while playing a melody on the treble strings.

Another principle that maintains perceptual grouping in music is based on *timbre*. Different musical instruments play the same notes with different timbres that give them their characteristic sounds and allow us to identify which instrument is playing any given note. When several instruments are playing simultaneously, the observer tends to group those of similar timbre into units, following a principle analogous to the Gestalt law of *similarity* (see Chapter 12, Figure 12-6). Much symphonic music uses this principle to separate phrases that have a similar fundamental frequency range but a different musical message. Also, timbre provides an additional principle of

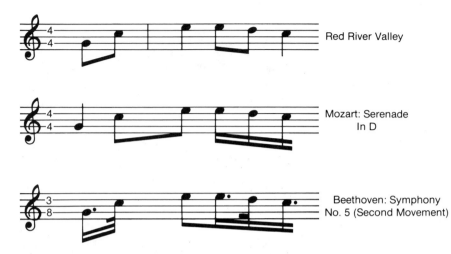

Figure 8-21. Three musical excerpts that have the same tonal contour and note sequence. Duration differences of the individual notes, however, give rise to three distinct musical experiences when the sequences are played.

grouping to that of pitch range when different instruments play different parts of a piece (as in the lead and rhythm guitar parts of a piece of modern rock music).

The final principle is called *good continuation* in a direct analogy to the Gestalt principle of the same name (again, Chapter 12, Figure 12-6 provides a visual analog of this principle). Sequences of frequency changes in the same direction (for example, ascending the scale) tend to be perceived as part of the same sequence, while changes in direction between sequences of notes tend to act as boundaries between segments (Deutsch and Feroe, 1981)

So far, we have concentrated on variations in frequency of musical notes or combinations of notes, neglecting the other major dimension of musical sounds—their duration. You probably learned in grade school that written sequences of musical notes indicate, not only the height (frequency) of the note to be played, but also its duration. Thus, a quarter note is held for half the duration of a half note, and so forth.

The duration of notes, as well as their tone height is vital in determining our perception of melody. You can see this in the three musical excerpts in Figure 8-21. All have the same tonal contour, and the sequence of musical notes is the same. They differ only in the durations of the notes, but this difference causes a tremendous diversity in the perceived melody. The first is the beginning of the familiar American folk song "Red River Valley," the second is the opening of Mozart's "Serenade in D," while the third is the beginning of the second movement of Beethoven's "Symphony No. 5." If you know how to play a musical instrument, you might want to try these phrases for yourself, just to hear how different they sound.

A sequence of sounds of various durations possesses **rhythm** and **tempo**. Tempo is the perceived speed associated with the presentation of a sequence of sounds. Rhythm is the perceived organization in time of the sequence of sounds. When listeners are presented with a sequence of sounds, they spontaneously organize it into subsequences consisting of an accented sound followed by at least one and sometimes several unaccented sounds (Bolton, 1894). This is why the ticking of a clock seems to go "tick, tock, tick, tock," despite the fact that every ticking sound emitted by the clock is identical. This spontaneous organization occurs when the sounds are presented at rates between 10 per second and 1 every two seconds and seems to be optimal at rates of 2 to 3 sounds per second. Under some circumstances, the percept may vary the degree of accenting of sounds so that a fairly complex rhythmic structure is perceived, despite a physical stimulus that is nothing more than a regular sequence. In the perception of music, these perceptual rhythms are superimposed on a deliberately manipulated rhythmic structure. This rhythmic organization is achieved by making use of principles of grouping similar to the Gestaltlike principles we already mentioned above. It interacts with the organization induced by the variations in pitch of the musical notes, making it easier to perceive the structure of the music (Deutsch, 1978; Handel and Oshinsky, 1981). Demonstration Box 8-8 shows how sounds may be grouped together by varying the rhythm or timing between them.

Demonstration Box 8-8. Rythmic grouping

In this demonstration you will produce a series of tapping sounds as stimuli. In order to indicate how your taps should be distributed in time, let us establish a sort of rythmic notation. Whenever we present a *V* it indicates a tap, while a hyphen indicates a brief pause. First, tap this simple sequence *VV-V*. Listen carefully, and notice that the first two taps seem to "go together" or form a unit, while the last seems to stand alone. Now, repeat this sequence of taps several times and try to mentally change this organization so that you have two groups with the first tap (*V*) forming one and the last two taps (*V-V*), forming the other. Notice that no effort of will allows you to do this. The two taps that are close together in time seem to go together and the other does not. This is analogous to the Gestalt principle of grouping by proximity that we shall discuss in Chapter 12.

Next, try the sequence *VVV-V-V-VVV-V-V-VVV* and so on. Notice that this is a repetition of three quick taps, followed by two slow taps. Notice that now the three taps form one group, while the two slow taps form another perceptually. It is virtually impossible to hear this in any other way. This is analogous to the Gestalt principle of similarity (the visual analog is shown in Figure 12-6).

While you are tapping, you can see that perceptual groups or clusters can be formed by frequency or timbre differences despite the absence of rhythmic differences. Begin by steadily tapping a surface with your pencil. Make sure that the tapping rhythm is steady and unchanging. Now take a piece of paper and slip it between the surface and your pencil and notice that the sound quality changes. Without changing your rhythm, slip the paper in and out so that you are tapping *table, table, paper, paper, table, table*, and so on. Notice that the sounds seem to take on a grouping, with the table taps together and the paper taps together, and it seems, despite the fact that you are tapping quite steadily and monotonously, that the sounds have a rhythm that goes table, table, pause, paper, paper, pause, table, table, and so forth. Here, grouping by perceived similarity has imposed an apparent rhythm on the sound sequence.

Music has many more aspects than those few we have discussed here. In addition, we are now beginning to find that certain neural mechanisms may be critical to music perception. Perhaps, comparisons between the music of different cultures may yield some insights into which aspects of music depend on learning the musical vocabulary of a particular culture and which depend on mechanisms that characterize all human beings (Deutsch, 1982). Until such data are available we will continue to listen to a symphony of theories and speculations.

GLOSSARY

The following definitions are specific to this book.

Auditory adaptation   Decrease in loudness of a sound with prolonged exposure to it.

Auditory fatigue   A prolonged reduction in auditory sensitivity following exposure to very intense sounds.

Azimuth   The direction of a sound source indicated as degrees around a circle.

Bandwidth   The range of frequencies of a complex sound.

Beat   When two tones similar in intensity but slightly different in frequency are presented, they are perceived as a single tone that varies in intensity, much like the vibrato of a singer.

Binaural   Sound presentations to both ears, from the roots *bi* and *aural*, for "two" and "ear," respectively.

Chord   A simultaneous presentation of three or more musical tones.

Consonance   The quality of two tones "going together."

Contour   The general "shape" of a sequence of musical notes in terms of changes in tone height.

Density   The feeling of the compactness or hardness of a sound.

Dissonance   The quality of two tones being discordant, or "clashing."

Dynamic range   For a particular frequency, the difference between the absolute threshold and the pain threshold, measured in decibels.

Echolocation system   A system used by some animals, such as bats and whales, to locate objects by analyzing sound waves reflected from them.

Equal loudness contour   A curve describing the intensities at which tones of varying frequencies appear to be equally loud.

Equal pitch contour   A curve describing the frequencies at which tones of varying intensities appear to have the same pitch.

Equal temperament scale   A version of the musical scale where each octave is divided into 12 equal parts, called semitones, that are further divided into 100 cents.

Frequency principle   The principle of pitch theory that asserts that sound frequency is encoded in the frequency of neural impulses traveling up the auditory nerve.

Fundamental   The lowest, usually the most intense, frequency sound wave in a complex stimulus.

Harmonics   Frequencies that are whole number multiples of the fundamental frequency in complex sounds.

Intensity difference   A difference in sound intensity caused by the presence of a sound shadow; a cue to the direction of high frequency sounds.

Interstimulus interval   The time span between the end of one stimulus and the beginning of the next.

Masking   The phenomenon whereby an audible tone can no longer be heard because of the added presentation of another tone.

Mel   A scale used for apparent pitch.

Minimum audible angle   The smallest amount of movement of a sound source that can be detected.

Minimum audible field   The absolute threshold for a sound presented and measured in a free field.

Minimum audible pressure   The threshold stimulus intensity for hearing for stimuli presented through earphones and measured at the eardrum.

Missing fundamental The absent lowest (and usually most intense) frequency in a complex sound.

Monaural Sound presentations to one ear, from the roots *mon* and *aural*, for one and ear, respectively.

Musical interval The perception of the separation in musical pitch between two musical sounds.

Perceived duration The apparent extension in time of a sound.

Perceived location The place where a sound seems to come from.

Phase difference The difference in the phase of a sound wave reaching each ear caused by the different distances the sound wave has to travel to reach each ear from a source located other than at 0 degrees or 180 degrees azimuth.

Phon The intensity (in decibels) of a 1000 Hz tone that matches a given tone in subjective loudness; used to compare the subjective loudnesses of tones of different frequencies and intensities.

Pitch The psychological attribute of sound associated with different sound frequencies (that is, high or low tones).

Place principle The theory of hearing suggesting that each different tone causes a different place on the basilar membrane to vibrate.

Precedence effect The use of the first sound stimulus to arrive at the ear as a major determinant of the spatial location of the sound source.

Reverberation A cue in determining the distance of a sound source; reverberant sound is sound that reaches the ears after having bounced off some surface.

Rhythm The perceived organization in time of the sequence of sounds.

Sound shadow An area in space where sound is diffracted by the edge of the head.

Sone A unit used to measure the apparent loudness of a sound.

Tempo The perceived speed with which a sequence of sounds is proceeding.

Timbre A sound attribute associated with the complexity of the sound wave.

Time difference Sound takes different amounts of time to travel to the two ears when its source is at azimuths other than 0 degrees or 180 degrees; this is a possible cue to the direction of the sound source.

Tone chroma A "circular" dimension of musical pitch that connects similar notes of different octaves.

Tone height The simple "vertical" dimension of musical scales.

Volley principle The theory that neural fibers fire in groups, one group of neurons firing while another group "recharges."

Volume The sense in which a sound fills space and seems large or small.

Taste, smell, touch, and pain

THE JUNGLE MAN STOPPED AND LOOKED at the fresh gash in the tree. He touched his tongue to it. The lingering taste of metal verified that humans were near. He turned and sniffed the wind. There it was—the faint scent of two men. He could tell by the scent that they were city people, not from the jungle. He could also tell by the message in the wind that she was with them.

Do you know anyone who tastes or smells this keenly? Probably not. Such accounts are common only in fiction. We humans are quite inferior to many other animals in our abilities to taste and smell. We rely more heavily on our sense of sight and hearing. Nonetheless, chemical and mechanical sense experiences are important to all of us: the flavor of food, the smell of fire, the touch of a loved one, the pain of an injury. Some humans even approach the performance of our Tarzanlike example, at least for certain dimensions. For instance, consider the abilities of a wine or tea taster or a perfumier. We also seem to excel at experiencing pain. We fear the dentist's chair almost as much as our ancestors might have feared the inquisitor.

TASTE

Taste thresholds and adaptation

What are the limits of a human's sensitivity to taste? It is difficult to study the thresholds for taste stimuli, since there are so many different stimuli to consider. Thus, we find that thresholds vary with the varying viscosity of the mixture to be tasted (Paulus and Haas, 1980) or with its temperature (Paulus and Reisch, 1980). The study is further complicated by the fact that the various parts of the tongue and mouth are not equally sensitive to different stimuli.

Let us begin by seeing how we can measure physically the amount of a taste stimulus present at any moment. Although there is some debate on the appropriate measurement procedures for taste stimuli, one useful measure is the **molar concentration** of a substance (Pfaffman, Bartoshuk, and McBurney, 1971). Molar concentration is based on the weight of a substance dissolved in a given amount of a solvent (usually water, when we deal with taste). A solution is said to have a concentration of one *mole* if the molecular weight of the substance (in grams) is added to enough water to make one liter of solution. Different solutions with the same molar concentrations have the same number of stimulus molecules in a given volume of liquid.

Once we have decided how to specify the stimulus concentrations, we can begin to measure thresholds. We must be careful to note, however, that the region of the mouth or tongue stimulated also affects our sensitivity. For many years it was thought that the back of the tongue was especially sensitive to bitter taste, while the front of the tongue was more sensitive to sweet and salty stimuli, and the sides of the rear part of the tongue were most sensitive to sour stimuli. Work by Collings (1974), however, altered this picture. She used as a stimulus a tiny piece of filter paper that had been soaked in a stimulus solution. This gave precise control over the location of the stimulus on the tongue. Figure 9-1 shows a summary of her results for four different parts of the tongue and the soft palate. For the bitter substance, the lowest threshold on the tongue is at the front. For this substance, however, an even lower threshold occurs on the palate. The tip and back of the tongue are most sensitive to sweet, while the front and sides are most sensitive to salt.

Individuals often differ in marked ways in their sensitivity to certain tastes. This was shown

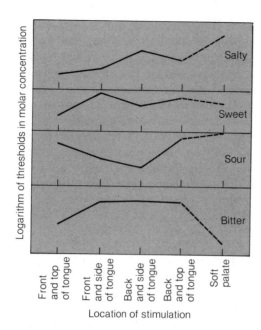

Figure 9-1. Average absolute thresholds for four different taste stimuli at four locations on the tongue, and at a location on the soft palate (based on Collings, 1974).

in a study by Blakeslee and Salmon (1935), who tested the taste thresholds of 47 people using 17 different substances. Figure 9-2 summarizes some of their results. Most substances, such as table salt or saccharine, have a narrow range of thresholds for different people. For others, however, such as vanillin or phenylthiocarbamide, large individual differences in sensitivity exist. These latter two substances are interesting because some people are apparently "taste-blind" to them. That is, at ordinary concentrations, some people cannot taste these substances at all. Phenylthiocarbamide (PTC) produces a bitter taste for those who are sensitive to it, but a large group of people seem to be taste-blind for PTC. If the stimulus is intense enough, however, even the taste-blind can taste PTC, as Figure 9-2 shows. One

similarity between taste blindness for PTC and color vision deficiencies (discussed in Chapter 7) is that both appear to have a genetic component and tend to run in families.

You might be surprised to learn that another substance associated with taste blindness is caffeine, the stimulant found in coffee (Hall, Bartoshuk, Cain, and Stevens, 1975). For caffeine, the taster and nontaster groups are not as distinct as they are with PTC, but the range of thresholds is still quite large and two groups clearly appear. Furthermore, tasters of PTC

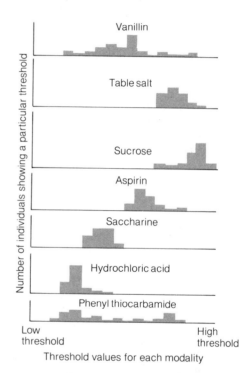

Figure 9-2. Frequency distributions of absolute thresholds of 47 observers to various taste stimuli. Phenylthiocarbamide (PTC) and vanillin have particularly wide ranges of thresholds, and PTC clearly shows two modes—tasters with low thresholds and nontasters with high thresholds (based on Blakeslee and Salmon, 1935).

tend to be tasters of caffeine and vice versa, indicating that a common mechanism may be responsible for this threshold variation. This is not due simply to a general "bitter" taste mechanism, for in the same study Hall et al. (1975) found that thresholds to two other bitter-tasting substances were unrelated to thresholds for PTC and caffeine. Similar results have been found for the bitter and sweet tastes of saccharine (Bartoshuk, 1979). In general, the attempt to explain such cases of taste blindness by postulating deficiencies in a particular taste system (as is often possible for color deficiencies) has not succeeded very well.

Taste thresholds can also be affected by stimuli that have reached the tongue before the threshold test. The taste system adapts readily to continued stimulation of the same type, and this adaptation temporarily raises the absolute threshold for the particular substance to which it has been adapted. Figure 9-3 shows an example of the effects of previous stimulation on absolute threshold. Here, both the adapting stimulus and the test stimulus were table salt (NaCl). As you can see from the figure, the absolute threshold varied both with how long the tongue had been exposed to the adapting stimulus and the strength of the stimulus (Hahn, 1934, O'Mahoney, 1979). Similar effects can be demonstrated for the effects of adaptation on sensory intensity (Gent, 1979). This sort of adaptation explains why some people salt their food again and again at dinner. As they eat, they adapt to the salty taste and come to need more salt to experience the taste at the same level. You can avoid resalting your food if you eat something that is not salty between bites of salty food (see Halpern and Meiselman, 1980). As Figure 9-3 shows, recovery from adaptation is virtually complete in about 10 sec, no matter how much salt was eaten previously.

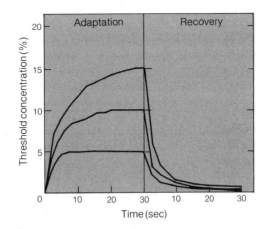

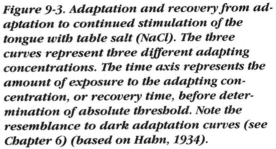

Figure 9-3. Adaptation and recovery from adaptation to continued stimulation of the tongue with table salt (NaCl). The three curves represent three different adapting concentrations. The time axis represents the amount of exposure to the adapting concentration, or recovery time, before determination of absolute threshold. Note the resemblance to dark adaptation curves (see Chapter 6) (based on Hahn, 1934).

Adaptation to one substance can also have an effect on the threshold for (and the subsequent taste of) different substances. This is called **cross-adaptation**. For example, adaptation to one salt will raise the threshold to other salts. Similarly, exposure to a sour substance will raise the threshold to other sour stimuli. In some cases, exposure of the tongue to one stimulus may actually *lower* the threshold to another taste stimulus (or make its taste more intense). This special case of cross-adaptation is called **potentiation**. Thus, adaptation to an acid, while reducing the sourness of another acid, may increase the sweetness of a sugar. Adaptation to urea (the bitter substance contained in human urine) will increase the intensity of salty sensations (McBurney, 1969). Perhaps the most striking phenomenon associated with cross-adaptation is

Demonstration Box 9-1. The taste of water

Water has a distinctive taste, especially when you have been eating or drinking some other substance before you taste the water. In this demonstration, you will be able to make water taste sweet, bitter, sour, or salty. Although you may not be able to (or want to) try all of the demonstrations, be assured that all of them work under the carefully controlled conditions of the laboratory (Bartoshuk, 1974). The most pleasant of the demonstrations requires that you eat a few cooked artichokes of any variety (canned, fresh, or frozen) and then taste a sip of water. Be sure to thoroughly mash the artichoke onto your tongue and palate while eating it. Water tasted after eating the artichoke usually tastes sweet. Another way to ob-

tain the sweet taste is to swish a mouthful of strong (caffeinated) coffee on the tongue for 30 sec before tasting tap water. A foolproof way to make anything taste sweet is to eat miracle fruit first. This fruit is not readily available, however, so it is more difficult to demonstrate. To make water taste bitter or sour, take some very salty water and swish it around in your mouth for 30 sec and then spit it out. Afterwards, taste some tap water. Something that has been tried in the laboratory but that you may not want to try is to swish some urea (a major component of urine) on the tongue for 30 sec. Tap water tasted after this treatment tastes salty.

the variability of the taste of ordinary tap water with adaptation to various substances. In fact, all four basic tastes can be induced in water by previous adaptation to a suitable taste stimulus (McBurney and Bartoshuk, 1972). You can experience this for yourself by trying Demonstration Box 9-1.

Taste intensity and qualities

Our ability to discriminate intensity differences in taste, regardless of the stimulus tested, is really quite poor. The Weber fraction (which measures the fractional amount by which two stimuli must differ for them to be discriminated as different, as we discussed in Chapter 2), ranges from a relatively poor 1/10 to an awful 1/1, making taste the least sensitive of the senses by this criterion (Pfaffman, et al., 1971).

To see how the sensation of taste grows as we increase the stimulus intensity, a number

of investigators have used the magnitude estimation technique discussed in Chapter 2. In general, they have found that the sensation increase is described by a typical power function of the form $S = aI^n$, where S is the sensation, I is the intensity of the stimulus, a is a constant, and n indicates the rate at which the sensation increases. The exponent n is usually greater than 1 (that is, for table salt it is 1.4, and for refined cane sugar it is 1.3). This means that at greater concentrations a small addition to the stimulus produces a larger change in the sensation than if the same amount were added to a weaker solution (Moskowitz, 1970; Stevens, 1969). This is exactly the opposite of the situation in vision and hearing, where the corresponding exponents are less than one and changes in weaker stimuli are perceived as greater. An important caution here is that we must be careful to specify exactly the conditions under which such exponents are measured, for they are greatly affected by adaptation. For example, O'Mahoney and Heintz

(1981) found an exponent for NaCl of only about 0.7 under conditions somewhat different from those used by other investigators.

Several studies have compared the changes in the rate of neural response with changes in stimulus intensity to the psychophysical data. They have shown that the two types of response vary with stimulus intensity in a similar fashion (Borg, Diamant, Oakley, Strom, and Zotterman, 1967; Diamant and Zotterman, 1969). It seems likely that our sensation of the intensity of a taste is directly related to the overall amount of neural activity evoked by the stimulus, which in turn depends on the intensity (molar concentration) of the stimulus.

Modern psychophysical scaling techniques have also been used to look at the relationships among taste *qualities*. In 1916, Henning proposed that we could specify the qualities of all tastes using a specially shaped three-dimensional geometrical space, in much the same way we specified colors in Chapter 7. He proposed that this space would be in the form

of a pyramid, with the primary tastes at the corners. Intermediate tastes would be represented by points on the surface of this space, which is shown in Figure 9-4A. Schiffman and Erickson (1971) used a sophisticated mathematical technique to test this notion. The technique is based on the judged similarity between stimuli. Using a procedure called multidimensional scaling, observers' similarity judgments can be converted into a set of distances between points in a geometric space with the smallest possible number of dimensions. Figure 9-4B shows their results. Notice that Henning's taste pyramid fits reasonably well into this space. This has been verified in another study, using a larger set of stimuli (Schiffman and Dackis, 1975). Such techniques have also been used to explore the relationships between the tastes of more similar substances, such as sodium salts (Schiffman, McElroy, and Erickson, 1980) and sweeteners (Schiffman, Reilly, and Clark, 1979) and to try to discover the physical and psychological

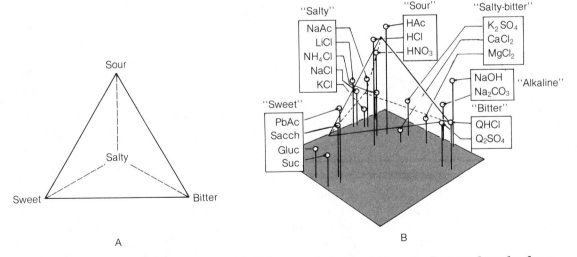

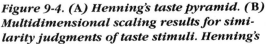

Figure 9-4. (A) Henning's taste pyramid. (B) Multidimensional scaling results for similarity judgments of taste stimuli. Henning's taste pyramid is superimposed on the three-dimensional space to show the correspondence (from Schiffman and Erickson, 1971).

properties that underlie the similarity judgments. In general, multidimensional scaling
does provide results that are consistent with
the existence of the four primaries: sweet,
salty, sour, and bitter, as shown in Figure 9-4,
although there is some controversy about
other relevant facts (see Erickson and Covey,
1980; McBurney and Gent, 1979). It seems
likely that investigators will continue to refer
to four basic taste qualities because they provide a useful summary of most of our research
findings in taste. However, their interpretation
may change. For example, it has been suggested that each of the basic tastes should be
considered a separate sensory modality, much
as the skin senses can be separated into touch,
warmth, cold, and pain (McBurney and Gent,
1979).

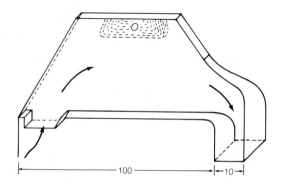

*Figure 9-5. A model of the nasal passage used
by Stuiver to calculate the proportion of molecules in a smell stimulus that reaches the
olfactory epithelium (O). Air follows the path
indicated by the arrows. Stimulus molecules
reach O via eddy currents (like the eddies in
a stream). (From H. De Vries and M. Stuiver.
In W. A. Rosenblith (ed.),* Sensory Communication. *New York: Wiley, 1961, copyright 1961 by
the MIT Press.)*

SMELL

Smell thresholds and adaptation

A dog's sense of smell can be amazingly acute.
Droscher (1971) tells the story of a dog trainer
who had worked with dogs for years. He
brought his dog to a university professor for
testing. He felt that the dog's ability was "su-
pernatural" since it could track people by
scent, even if they were wearing rubber boots!
Actually, the dog was simply using its acute
sense of smell to detect the millions of sweat
molecules that leaked through the rubber
boots. Why can't we smell such things? Actually, the sensitivity of each smell receptor is
about the same for humans and dogs. However,
the dog has many more smell receptors than
humans, with more hairlike cilia projecting
from each (see Chapter 5).

In the early 1960s Stuiver studied the absolute sensitivity of human smell receptors by
making a model of the nasal passages around
the olfactory epithelium. He used this model
to calculate just how much of an olfactory
stimulus actually arrived at the surface of the
epithelium (see Figure 9-5). When threshold
stimuli were considered, he found that it takes
eight molecules at most to stimulate a single
receptor in the human. Considering all aspects
of the manner in which molecules of odor
stimuli are distributed in the nose, it can be
argued that a single receptor cell needs to be
contacted by one stimulus molecule in order
to respond (De Vries and Stuiver, 1961). Quite
clearly, this is the greatest sensitivity that any
single olfactory receptor cell could have,
hence a dog's (or any other animal's) receptors
cannot be more sensitive than a human's. Because the dog has more receptor sites, however, the likelihood that a very weak stimulus
will actually stimulate the olfactory receptors
and produce a noticeable sensation is greater
for the dog (see Marshall and Moulton, 1981).

More traditional attempts to determine the

absolute threshold for various odors encounter problems similar to those found when measuring taste sensitivity. Thresholds vary across methods. They seem to depend on the purity of the odorant, the way in which it is delivered to the olfactory epithelium, and how the stimulus intensity is measured. Different substances also have different thresholds. Some of these factors seem to affect the ability of various molecules to stick to the receptive surfaces, rather than the actual sensitivity of individual smell receptors.

In much the same way that we found individual differences in taste sensitivity, there are also individual differences in smell sensitivity. Some individuals are relatively "odor-blind" to certain substances (see Engen, 1982, for a good discussion). Amoore (1969, 1975, Amoore, Pelosi, and Forrester, 1977) has reported the results of an extensive search for instances of odor blindnesses as a part of his plan to identify the primary odors. By 1975 he was able to report 76 different **anosmias** (odor blindnesses), ranging from the smell of skunk to the smell of vanilla. Some of these are quite common; for example, about one out of three individuals cannot smell a strong stimulus of 1,8 cineole, which produces a camphorous odor (Pelosi and Pisanelli, 1981). On the other hand, some anosmias are quite rare, as when only four people out of 4030 couldn't smell a strong stimulus of n-butyl mercaptan, which has a foul, putrid odor. Amoore was able to classify these 76 anosmias into about 31 classes, each of which might represent a primary odor quality. Wright (1978a) suggested that such specific anosmias may indicate that humans have two classes of olfactory receptors. Members of the first class are called *specialists*, because they respond to only one or two specific odorants. The second class contains *generalists*, which respond to many different odorants, which may be chemically quite dissimilar. Such a two class olfactory sys-

tem has been found for some insects already (see Schneider, 1969).

As in most sensory systems, adaptation affects smell thresholds and the perceived intensity of an odor. It even affects the pleasantness of odors (Cain and Johnson, 1978). One of the great disappointments of wine tasting is that the aroma and the bouquet of the wine seem to last only for a few sniffs. The rich complexity of a great wine soon fades into a bland, featureless odor, even for the most experienced "smeller," unless one takes frequent breaks of about 15 sec. Luckily, the odors of sweaty bodies, rotten eggs, or the sulfurous smell of air pollution also soon fade away, if you continue to sniff.

An important early study of adaptation of the smell sense was that of Moncrieff (1956). He studied the effects of previous exposure to an odorant on the threshold for that odorant (**self-adaptation**). He also looked at the way in which exposure to one odorant affected the threshold for different odorants (**cross-adaptation**). As you might expect, the largest loss of sensitivity was found for conditions of self-adaptation. Cross-adaptation effects varied with the similarity of the smells of the two stimuli. Stimuli with similar smells gave large cross-adaptation effects, while those that differed in smell gave smaller effects. Surprisingly, all the adapting odors had some effect on observers' sensitivity for the others. This means that it was not possible to classify the various stimuli into a small number of primary classes. This is similar to Amoore's conclusions based on anosmias.

Cain and Engen (1969) looked at the effects of adapting stimuli on the perceived intensity of odorants. They used a magnitude estimation procedure (such as those described in Chapter 2), and found that the higher the concentration of the adapting stimulus the greater the reduction in the apparent intensity of the test stimuli presented afterward. This relationship does not hold for extreme test stimulus values, however, since *very* intense test stimuli all appeared to arouse about the same sensory response, regardless of the state of adaptation.

Smell intensity and qualities

When we consider how the intensity of an odor varies as stimulus intensity is varied, we again find it useful to refer to the exponent of the psychophysical power function to describe this relationship. As is the case with the various taste substances, the exponents of power functions fitted to magnitude estimations of odor intensity differ across the various odors scaled. Cain (1969) found that exponents ranged from about 0.7 to a low of about 0.15. Remember that the higher the exponent the faster the sensation increases as we increase stimulus intensity. Cain reported that the size of the exponent is directly related to the degree of water solubility of the odorant, with exponents for completely water-soluble odorants always about 2.5 times as large as those for non-water-soluble odorants. More recent work by Wright (1978b, 1978c) showed that the exponents for various odorants can be predicted from the specific ways in which the odorant molecules interact with receptor cell membranes.

In absolute terms, the sense of smell is remarkably acute. Although for a long period of time it was thought that humans could not discriminate between different odor intensities very well, most recent measurements indicate that the olfactory system is more sensitive than the taste system in this regard. In fact, the olfactory system may be as sensitive as the visual or auditory system in discriminating changes in intensity, with Weber fractions as low as 0.05 (Cain, 1977).

As in all the other sensory modalities, at-

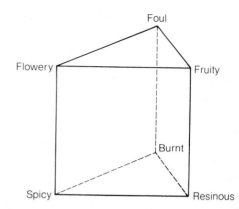

Figure 9-6. Henning's smell prism. Six "primary" odors are at the corners; the surfaces represent stimuli that resemble more than one primary.

tempts have been made to isolate a small set of "primary" smell qualities. If such could be found, then all olfactory sensations could be predicted as the result of a combination of these primary responses. As we have already seen, the data from adaptation and anosmias do not suggest such a small cluster of primaries for smell. The classical attempt to describe smell primaries was that of Henning (1915). Figure 9-6 shows his "smell prism," which had six primary qualities arranged at its corners.

Although it was a standard representation of the "smell primaries" for quite some time, Henning's prism apparently does a poor job of describing the perceived relationships among odorants. When multidimensional scaling techniques are used to provide a geometrical representation of odor similarity judgments, in much the same way as for taste judgments, neither Henning's smell prism nor any other readily identifiable classification scheme emerges. Figure 9-7 displays some representative results from this kind of study. The result has led some investigators (for example, Erickson and

Schiffman, 1975; Southwick and Schiffman, 1980) to speculate that only a complex set of physicochemical considerations could account for the interrelationships shown in the qualities of smell stimuli. Such results seem consistent with Amoore's (1975) suggestion that there may be as many as 31 primary odors. Some of these particular primaries seem to be associated with receptor systems that respond to odors produced by the human body. These are the same types of odors emitted by most animals in situations relevant to the survival of the species, such as danger and sexual contact, and humans seem to respond to this class of stimuli as well.

Some smells seem to have a special biologi-

cal significance for humans. Around the turn of the century, Ellis (1905) noticed that both men and women often emit strong odors during sexual excitement. Some researchers contend that some human behavior may be under the control of these olfactory stimuli (see, for example, Comfort, 1971). Chemicals secreted by animals that transmit information to other animals (usually of the same species) are called **pheromones**. While it has long been recognized that such olfactory signals are important for many animal species, the possibility that scents affect human behavior directly has been entertained only recently. As one might expect, manufacturers of colognes and perfumes, ever searching for ways to enhance the

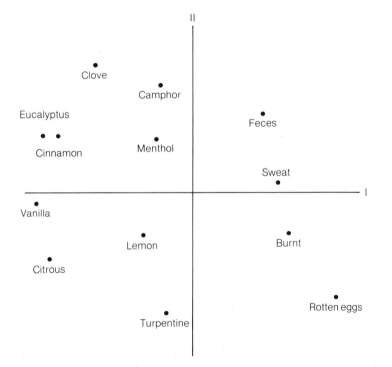

Figure 9-7. A composite replotting of selected odors from multidimensional scaling of similarity judgments of odor pairs (Schiffman, 1974). Dimension I is thought to be "pleasantness." This mapping bears little resemblence to Henning's smell prism (Figure 9-6).

sales of their products, have immediately responded to this suggestion. In fact, a number of products are now on the market that contain *alpha androstenol*, which is known to be an effective sexual pheromone for pigs and also occurs in some human secretions.

Before we discuss the data available on humans, we will provide a context by describing some of the work done on other animals. Pheromones were first studied, indeed discovered and named, in insects (see Wilson, 1971). There are two major types: **releasers**, which upon reception by an animal "release," or automatically trigger, a specific behavioral response, and **primers**, which trigger glandular and other physiological activities in the recipient. Most of the aspects of the lives of insects, particularly such social insects as ants, bees, and termites, are regulated via communication by pheromones. Insects attract their mates, recruit fellows for food gathering or fighting, and recognize each other and their own species via releasers. Queen ants, bees, and termites control swarming, new queen production, proportion of types of workers, and so on, using primers. The important thing to remember about insect pheromones is that usually a *specific chemical*, produced by a *specific gland*, and detected and recognized by a *specific (or specialist) receptor* is involved in such communication. Insect behavior is directly under the control of these pheromones.

Mammals, of course, are much more complex animals than insects, and the effects of such olfactory stimuli are a bit more subtle. A variety of pheromone-related effects have been found, however, in several species, including rodents, dogs, and monkeys (see Brown, 1979; Keverne, 1976). Mammalian releaserlike effects include the mutual recognition of mother and young offspring. Male and female sexual attraction is also affected by such scents, as is easily demonstrated by observing the effect on the

male of the odor of a female dog in heat. Other pheromones elicit aggression in males, inhibit agression in females, and are used for such signaling purposes as trail marking or defining territorial boundaries. Primerlike effects include effects of scents on the estrus cycle of females, the age at which puberty is attained, and even the likelihood of becoming pregnant.

Some effects of pheromones have been observed in monkeys, a species that is close to humans on the evolutionary scale. Here, however, the story is even more complex. Some early research looked at the effect of vaginal secretions from female monkeys in estrus (that is, those that are sexually receptive) on the copulating behavior of males. Early work seemed to indicate that a powerful pheromone was involved. Normally, male monkeys seldom attempt to engage nonestrus females sexually. Such behavior could be elicited, however, if the females' sexual skins had been rubbed with the secretions of the sexual skins of females who were in estrus. These secretions, presumably containing pheromones, were dubbed *copulins* (Michael and Keverne, 1968; Michael, Keverne, and Bonsall, 1971). Later work indicated that the suspected releaser pheromone was not as powerful as had been thought, and that monkey sexual behavior was under the control of many interacting factors, only one of which was the smell of the partner's sexual skin (Goldfoot, Kravetz, Goy, and Freeman, 1976; Keverne, 1976). In fact, in all the pheromonelike effects studied with mammals, the communications delivered by chemical means have not been found to be as imperative as they are with insects. Mammals have more complex brains, and their behavior is controlled in much more complex ways by environmental factors, only one of which is odorants.

When we consider humans, the behavioral effects of pheromones seem to be most subtle, since social and learning factors influence our behavior even more than they do that of other mammals. Some very interesting results, however, indicate that smells may play an important, although probably subordinate, role in many aspects of human social behavior. First, two separate studies (McBurney, Levine, and Cavanaugh, 1977; Russell, 1976) have demonstrated that people can reliably detect their own body odor from among a set of similar stimuli contributed by other people. The actual stimuli were collected by having people wear T-shirts for several days. When asked to rate the pleasantness of the body odors and to describe the individual whose odor they were smelling, there was a remarkable degree of consistency across people. In general, the individuals having unpleasant odors were usually described as if they also would be likely to have socially undesirable traits. They were supposedly dumb, ugly, fat, and unhealthy. The more pleasant odors were described as coming from people with the more desirable traits (McBurney et al., 1977). Subjects seemed able to discriminate reliably the sex of an odor donor; the odors of males were characterized as "musky" while female odors were described as "sweet" (Russell, 1976), although not all studies produced the same result (Doty, Orndorff, Leyden, and Kligman, 1978).

Human sensitivity to human odors seems to be present from an early age. For instance, Russell (1976) found that a small sample of 2-week-old babies reliably responded to the odor of their own mother's breast and not to that of a strange mother; this ability may exist as early as 6 days after birth. One of the necessary conditions for most odor identification, at least in adults, seems to be a lot of experience with the odor and its label (Cain, 1979). Certainly, the relationship between parents and children contains much such experience. We might thus expect that parents could recognize the odors of their own offspring, and that perhaps siblings could recognize each others' odors as distinct from those of other children. This seems to be the case, raising the possibility that smell plays an important role in interactions among humans from the same family (Porter and Moore, 1981).

A second line of research with humans has been aimed at finding a sex attractant based on releaser pheromone action. The most promising candidate for such a substance is the substance *alpha androstenol* mentioned earlier, which causes a sow to become immobile, and thus receptive to a boar's sexual advances, when the boar secretes it in his saliva. Because alpha androstenol is also present in human apocrine (a gland in the underarm region) sweat, it may play a role in human sexual attraction, especially since humans have been shown to reliably discriminate among axillary (underarm) odors. A few published studies have found positive effects. For example, Cowley, Johnson, and Brooksbank (1977) found that androstenol affected ratings of various social characteristics of hypothetical applicants for a job and affected male and female ratings differently. Kirk-Smith, Booth, Carroll, and Davies (1978) similarly found that women in photographs were rated as more sexually attractive by both men and women wearing surgical masks impregnated with androstenol than by those wearing control masks. Such results are exciting to perfume manufacturers (and, perhaps, to the sexually deprived), but they may not be easy to interpret. Rogel (1978) critically reviewed a number of such studies along with those of monkeys and concluded that although it is possible that olfaction does influence many aspects of social behavior, it would be wrong to believe that human behavior could be controlled, to the extent seen in lower mammals, by such pheromones. This means that human sexual choice, contrary to the claims of some perfume manufacturers, is apt to be more a matter of higher mental processes than of primitive responses to sexual odors.

TOUCH

Given the fact that any point on our body's surface can evoke the sensation of touch, it is surprising how often this modality is ignored. For instance, we seldom consider that major components of most sexual experiences are touch sensations. The very act of touching another person, in Western society, is considered an act of considerable intimacy, whether it is the gentle touch of a friend or lover or the violent punch of an aggressor.

Touch thresholds and adaptation

One of the most striking aspects of our sense of touch is the variability of sensitivity from one region of the body to another. Figure 9-8 shows the absolute touch thresholds for several different regions of the body (excluding most of the erogenous zones, which probably contain some of the lowest thresholds). Such thresholds are obtained by applying a small rod or hair (pig bristles were used in some of the earliest work) to the surface of the skin with differing amounts of force. When an investigator continues to use the same hair, these thresholds can be expressed in terms of the amount of force applied to the hair, as they are in Figure 9-8. Thus, the higher the bar, the greater the force needed, and the lower the sensitivity. It is probably best, however, to ex-

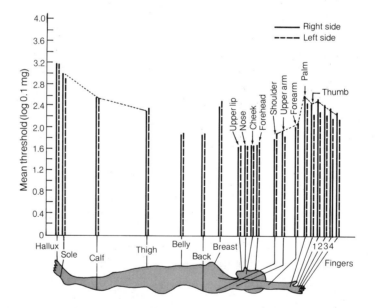

Figure 9-8. Absolute pressure thresholds for different regions of the female skin. Relative values for males are similar but average thresholds are somewhat higher. (From S.

*Weinstein, in **D. R. Kenshalo, ed., The Skin Senses,** 1968, Courtesy of **Charles C Thomas, Publisher, Springfield, Illinois.**)*

press absolute thresholds in units of force per unit area, since the actual stimulus is the change in the amount of tension in the skin and not the force itself (Frey and Kiesow, 1899). At any rate, it is apparent in Figure 9-8 that absolute thresholds vary considerably over the body surface.

Even more dramatic variations of threshold exist within a relatively small area of skin, say, the surface of the arm. If you explore a 2 × 2 cm area on your forearm with a toothpick or hairbrush bristle, pressing with the same light pressure every time you touch the skin (just enough to make the bristle bend slightly), you will discover a number of spots that respond to this stimulus with a distinct sensation of touch. You will also find a large number of places that will give only a faint sensation, or none at all.

The sensitivity of the skin is often tested using a *vibrating* stimulus, which alternately applies and releases a force to the same small surface region at frequencies ranging from 20 to 20,000 Hz. Generally, vibrating the touch stimulus results in a lower absolute threshold. That is, when the stimulation is intermittent (on again—off again) the skin seems to be more sensitive. This is reasonable since it is the change in the tension in the skin that is the stimulus for touch sensation, and the vibrations cause these changes continually. The frequency of vibration of a vibrotactile stimulator on the skin affects its threshold in much the same way that the frequency of a sound wave affects the threshold of hearing. Also, similar to responses of the ear, the skin is sensitive only to a limited range of frequencies of vibration. The range most investigators agree upon is from about 40 to about 2500 Hz. Some researchers, however, have claimed that under special conditions sensations can result from stimuli of frequencies up to 20,000 Hz (Verrillo, 1975).

One aspect of all tactual stimuli is that each touch sensation seems to be located at a particular place on the skin. Our ability to localize the sensation accurately varies across different regions of the skin. Localization accuracy seems to be related directly to the amount of neural representation each area has in the touch cortex. In general, the greater the representation of a particular area, the smaller are the errors of localization for that area (the relative cortical representation of areas of the body was shown in Figure 5-7). One way to measure our sensitivity for localization is to introduce a second stimulus and to measure the **two-point threshold**. This refers to a fact discovered by Frey, who found that two-touch stimuli (such as the points of a drawing compass) will be felt as a single touch if they are close enough together. The two-point threshold is a measure of the distance between stimuli before they are felt as two separately localizable touches. It was during investigations of this kind that Békésy (1967) discovered inhibitory interaction in the skin (see Demonstration Box 5-1). A comprehensive determination of two-point threshold was provided by Weinstein (1968). A summary of his results is shown in Figure 9-9. Notice the remarkable differential sensitivity of the lower face and the hands, and even the feet. Presumably this reflects the use of these areas in manipulation of objects. The high sensitivity of the feet may be left over from our primate ancestors, who could manipulate objects with their feet! Another interesting aspect of touch localization is studied in Demonstration Box 9-2.

Touch sensations adapt, as do all other sensations. This can be shown by simply applying a stimulus to the skin and observing the gradual disappearance of the sensation. Zigler (1932) demonstrated this adaptation using several different areas of the body. He reported

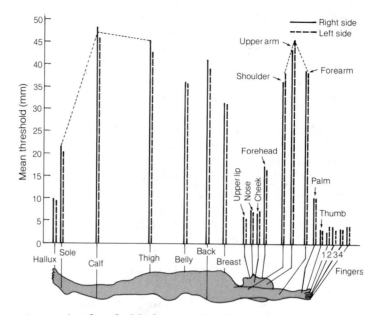

Figure 9-9. Average two-point thresholds for different regions of the male skin. Relative values for females are similar but lower in value overall. (From S. Weinstein, in D. R. **Kenshalo ed., The Skin Senses, 1968, Courtesy of Charles C Thomas, Publisher, Springfield, Illinois.)**

that the heavier the stimulus, the longer it took for the sensation to disappear. On the other hand, the larger the area covered by the stimulus, the less time it took for the sensation to disappear. You can demonstrate this result using Demonstration Box 9-3.

Another technique for measuring adaptation is to present a stimulus for some period of time and then to introduce a second stimulus. The observer is asked to adjust the intensity of the second stimulus until it matches the sensation caused by the first. Since adaptation has reduced the apparent intensity of the first stimulus, the difference between the magnitudes of the two stimuli is a measure of the amount of adaptation that has taken place. This technique assumes that the two stimuli would be matched in magnitude of sensation if they were equal in intensity. Using this technique, von Frey and

Goldman (1915) determined that adaptation to touch stimuli is similar to that for other modalities. The adaptation is very rapid for the first second or so and then gradually slows down. After 3 sec, the sensation level has decreased to about 1/4 of the beginning value.

Békésy (1959) used this same technique to measure the time course of adaptation for vibratory stimuli, which generally takes longer than adaptation for static stimuli. Again, different parts of the body respond differently. Thus, on the lip the adaptation is complete after about 20 sec. For the forearm, however, loss of sensation is more gradual, and adaptation is not complete even after 60 sec. These longer adaptation times are consistent with the greater effectiveness of the vibratory stimulus.

Demonstration Box 9-2. Touch localization

Békésy has studied localization in all the major sensory modalities and has discovered similar phenomena in all of them. One of the most striking is the discovery that a touch can be localized as being outside of the body under the appropriate circumstances (Békésy, 1967). We will demonstrate a somewhat simpler phenomenon that apparently depends on the difference in arrival times of neural impulses from different parts of the skin surface to the primary sensory areas of the brain.

Touch your two index fingers together. Try to concentrate on experiencing *where* the sensations of touch are felt, that is, on which of the two fingers. Most people report sensations of about equal intensity from both fingertips. Now touch your fingertip (either one) repeatedly to your lower lip with light, quick touches. When asked to say where the sensation is, most people report that they feel it mostly on the lip and little or not at all on the fingertip, even though both are of about equal sensitivity and are being stimulated

approximately equally. Now use the same finger to touch, with the same light, quick touches, your little toe or your ankle. Most people now report that the sensation seems to be located mostly in the finger, rather than in the toe or the ankle, even though both are being equally stimulated. As it turns out, it takes somewhat more than 1 msec longer for the nerve impulses to travel from the fingertip to the brain than for them to travel from the lip to the brain. Similarly, it takes more than 1 msec longer for impulses to travel from the foot to the brain than from the finger to the brain. The impulses that arrive at the brain first (providing the difference is more than 1 msec) seem to dictate where the sensation will be experienced, even though the two places on the skin are being stimulated equally. The various other parts of the body fall in between these extremes, but in all cases the localization depends on the relative lengths of the pathways from the touching parts to the brain.

Demonstration Box 9-3. Touch adaptation

For this demonstration, you will need a watch with a sweep second hand, two pieces of cardboard (cut into small circles with diameters of about 1 cm and about 4 cm), and a friend. Lay one piece of cardboard on the skin of your friend's back and record the amount of time before the sensation of touch disappears. Repeat this with

the other piece of cardboard. Try the experiment again, only this time press gently on the cardboard. Notice that the lighter touches and the larger surface area stimulations disappear faster from consciousness. Thus they show faster adaptation.

Touch intensity and qualities

When measuring the subjective intensity of touch stimuli, vibrating stimuli are often used because they do not adapt as quickly. A study

by Stevens (1959) demonstrated that magnitude estimations of the intensity of a 60 Hz vibratory stimulus on the fingertip followed the standard psychophysical power function, with the apparent intensity of the touch stimulus increasing with increasing physical intensity with an exponent of about 0.95. More recent measurements using single mechanical pulses applied to the skin of the hand found that magnitude estimates of sensation intensity produce similar results for both hairy and glabrous skin (see Chapter 5), but that exponents were somewhat lower for glabrous (0.55–0.86) than for hairy (0.70–1.41) skin (Hamalainen and Jarvilehto, 1981).

It was mentioned earlier that the action of a vibratory stimulus on the skin is quite similar to that of sound on the ear in that sensitivity is greatest for certain stimulus frequencies (see also, for example, Gescheider and Verrillo, 1982; Marks, 1979a). This means that for a given physical pressure, some vibration frequencies give a more intense touch sensation than others. This can be seen in Figure 9-10, which shows a set of equal-sensation curves, for a vibrating stimulus on the skin, that are

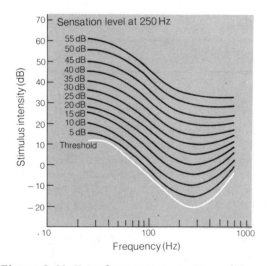

Figure 9-10. Equal-sensation contours for a vibrating stimulus. These contours are quite similar to equal-loudness contours over the same range of frequencies (see Figure 8-9) (from Verrillo, Fraioli, and Smith, 1969).

highly similar to the equal-loudness contours we presented in Figure 8-12. Here, maximum sensitivity seems to be in the region of about 200–400 Hz, with sensitivity decreasing dramatically as frequency declines. Notice that stimulus intensity in Figure 9-10 is measured in decibels (compared with a displacement of the vibrator surface by one-millionth of a meter, which then represents 0 db). This makes the vertical scale a logarithmic scale similar to the logarithmic decibel scale used in hearing (see Chapter 5).

The sense of touch has the ability to discriminate complex stimuli, which in turn represent ideas. Most of you have probably heard about Louis Braille's tactile pattern alphabet, used by blind people to "read" any suitably translated book or paper. In this alphabet, patterns of raised dots on paper play the role of the patterns of ink on paper that sighted people use for letters. The speed with which an experienced blind person can read with this alphabet is a testimoney to long hours of practice (as is any form of reading) but also to the remarkable sensitivity of the touch system. Of course, the final interpretation of these patterns of touch stimuli involves a number of complicated cognitive processes (Krueger, 1982).

Braille is not the only method that conveys pattern information by way of the touch modality. An alternate method was invented by a group of individuals who wanted to find a more direct substitution of touch patterns for those of vision. White, Saunders, Scadden, Bach-y-Rita, and Collins (1970) developed a **vision substitution system** in which a television camera is used to scan a visual pattern. The information gathered by the television camera is then converted into a pattern of vibrating points on the skin of the back of an observer (see Figure 9-11). The subjects can move the camera to view different parts of the

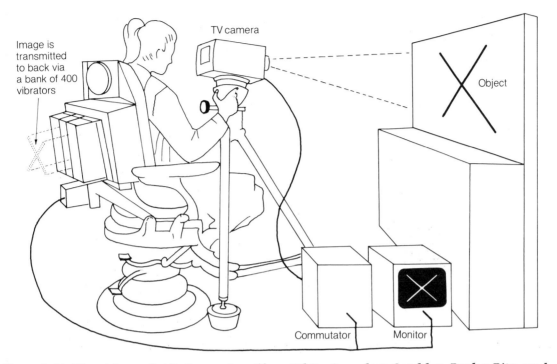

Figure 9-11. The vision substitution system (from White, Saunders, Scadden, Bach-y-Rita, and Collins, 1970)

visual scene. When visual stimuli are presented tactually in this way, observers can recognize a wide variety of different stimulus patterns (up to 25). Remarkably, the relative distance of several visual objects in a scene can be perceived from the tactile pattern. Even visual illusions can be experienced in a tactile pattern on the back. These types of findings raise questions similar to those raised by visual and auditory pattern perception. Thus, one might ask if there are also such feature detectors for touch. The findings also point to the importance of higher level cognitive processes in even the simplest types of perceptual experiences.

Reading in Braille requires that the paper or book be translated into Braille. This is especially difficult to do with newspapers and magazines, which are numerous in their pub-

lication. The **Optacon** (Bliss, Katcher, Rogers, and Shepard, 1970) works similarly to the vision substitution system except that the size of the visual field scanned is about one printed letter, and the pattern of vibrations corresponding to each letter is formed on the fingertip instead of the back. After approximately 50 hours of training, blind users can read untreated material at about 20 words per minute. Experienced users attain rates as high as 60 words per minute. In 1977, nearly two thousand blind people were using the Optacon for reading (Craig, 1977). This device is now being used for research into the mechanisms of tactile pattern perception (see for example, Craig, 1981; Loomis, 1981). Such research promises to reveal more about both the capacities and limitations of tactile perception and perhaps about processes of pattern recognition common to all sensory modalities.

WARMTH AND COLD

Are you cold right now? Are you warm? Probably you are feeling rather neutral, that is, comfortably unaware of any temperature sensations. Our bodies contain a remarkable system of thermal sensors that trigger reflexes that in turn regulate the flow of blood in the blood vessels in our skin, the activity of the sweat glands, and the tiny muscles located around the roots of hairs in the skin. When our internal body temperature is too high (above 37°C), the blood vessels of the skin dilate, allowing more blood to flow and thus radiating more heat into the air. We also begin to sweat, losing heat both by the conduction of the overheated sweat to the surface of the skin where it can radiate more efficiently and also by the cooling of the skin surface through the process of evaporation. When we are too cold, the blood vessels in the skin contract, thereby slowing heat loss, and we begin to shiver, which generates more heat from our muscles. The thermal sensitivity of the skin plays a major part in this complex, mostly reflex-operated temperature-regulating system that keeps our internal body temperature around 37°C (98.6°F) (see Hensel, 1981). Usually the system functions so well that we do not notice any temperature sensations, at least in temperate environments. The ability of this system to regulate body temperature is limited, however, and when the limits are exceeded, the body needs to take more dramatic steps, such as changing clothing or starting a fire. These actions bring the temperature of the skin's environment within its safe limits again. Such necessities are signaled by the conscious sensations of warmth and cold.

Thermal thresholds and adaptation

Because the skin works to maintain a constant internal body temperature, sensations of warmth and cold are generally caused by departures from a particular reference skin temperature level called **physiological zero**. Thus, to talk about "cold" means a stimulus that has caused the *skin temperature* to drop below physiological zero. This reference temperature is a floating neutral point, based on the temperature to which the thermal receptors in the skin have adapted. There is a **neutral zone** around physiological zero, within which no sensation will be felt if a stimulus within that temperature range is applied to the skin. This zone is seldom more than a couple of degrees on either side of the zero, but it varies in width depending on what the zero point is, where on the body the change occurs, and what kind of stimulus is applied. A good average value for physiological zero in a temperate environment (room temperature) would be around 33°C (91°F). At room temperature, such a skin temperature maintains the internal body temperature at about 37°C (98.6°F).

The measurement of absolute thresholds for warm and cold sensations is complicated by the fact that relatively complete adaptation to thermal stimuli takes place over some range of temperatures, and that thermal sensations are relative to the temperature to which the skin has become adapted. Several techniques have been used to measure adaptation. Typically, an area of the skin is exposed to very high or low temperatures for some period of time (usually by dipping it in water at the required temperature), and then a threshold for warmth or cold is determined. In a different technique, observers are exposed to a particular thermal stimulus and asked to report when they no longer feel any thermal sensation at that temperature. For instance, Kenshalo and Scott (1966) had observers change the temperature of a sophis-

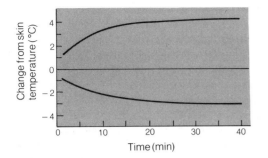

Figure 9-12. Adaptation to thermal stimuli. Each curve represents the average amount of adjustment by four observers to maintain a just noticeable warm or cool sensation with a thermal stimulator. Thermal changes closer to the 0 line than the curves are felt as having neutral temperature (based on Kenshalo and Scott, 1966).

ticated thermal stimulator just enough to maintain a detectable sensation, while they adapted the skin to a given thermal level. The stimulator started at the previously measured temperature of the observer's skin. Adjustments were made whenever the experimenter asked for them, every minute at first, and then every 5 min for up to 40 min. Figure 9-12 shows the results obtained for four observers. Using this technique, Kenshalo and Scott (1966) found that complete adaptation occurred over a range of about 4–8°C centered around the average skin temperature. This then serves as an experimental measurement of the neutral zone around the physiological zero set by adaptation. Notice that when adaptation has not fully occurred (early in the period), the neutral zone is actually quite narrow (perhaps about 1 degree), but it widens as the adaptation becomes more complete.

Overall, the sensation of warmth or coldness of any given stimulus is determined largely by the adaptation temperature of the skin before the stimulus is applied. (You can experience this in Demonstration Box 9-4). Absolute

thresholds for these sensations can be defined as the amount of temperature change (from the adapting temperature) necessary to cause an experience or a report of warmth or cold. A determination of absolute thresholds by Kenshalo, Nafe, and Brooks (1961) found that sensitivities differ for upward and downward changes in temperature, depending on the adapting temperature, with sensitivity to lowering of temperature greater when skin temperature is cold, but better for rises in temperature when skin temperature is warmer, as can be seen in Figure 9-13. Thus, at relatively high or low temperatures, we are more sensitive to fluctuations in temperature, especially those changes that indicate greater deviation from our normal body temperature. This makes sense, since very low or very high thermal values can be dangerous for the body, hence the detection of thermal changes is more important when the stimuli are more extreme. The minimum threshold values obtained seem to be about 0.1°C of temperature change from the adapting temperature.

As with other aspects of touch, the exact place on the body surface to which the stimulus is applied also determines our sensitivity to warmth and cold. The head region is the most sensitive to warm stimuli, with the limbs least, and the trunk intermediate. On the other hand, the trunk, particularly the back, is the most sensitive to cold stimuli, with the limbs intermediate and the head least (J. C. Stevens, 1979). This is easy to demonstrate for yourself using pieces of metal that have been dipped in water of different temperatures (pay attention to the intensity of the sensations aroused by the stimuli on the various parts of your body).

Actually, there are significant differences in sensitivity to warmth and cold, even over a small patch of skin. If the thermal stimulus has a small area (perhaps the size of a pin head), it is possible to find some spots that yield only sensations of warmth and others that produce

---

Demonstration Box 9-4. The dependence of thermal sensation on physiological zero

For this demonstration, you will need to create three water baths of different temperatures. You can use a meat thermometer to measure the temperatures or try the following formulas.

Assuming that your tap water has temperatures of 10°C (cold) and 60°C (hot), you can make a 30°C bath by adding 3⅔ cups of cold tap water and 2⅓ cups of hot tap water to a bowl. A 35°C bath requires 3 cups each of hot and cold tap water. For a 40°C bath, use 2⅓ cups of cold water and 3⅔ cups of hot water. It is best to have a friend help with preparing the water baths and with keeping them at a nearly constant temperature (by adding a little hot water every minute or so). Your friend can then try the demonstration while you make the baths.

First prepare the 30 and the 40°C baths. Place one hand in the 30°C and one in the 40°C bath. Keep the hands in the baths for about 5 min. Under these conditions most people report that after 5 min there is no longer any sensation of warmth or cold, although the cooler bath initially felt cold

(as it should have relative to your average skin temperature of about 33°C) and the warmer one felt warm. Now prepare the 35°C bath (quickly, if you are doing it by yourself), and plunge both hands into it at once. The hand that was in the 30°C bath should now feel as if it is in warm water, while the other hand (40°C) will feel as if it is in cool water. Since the water is actually the same for both hands, but their physiological zero has been changed by the previous 5 min adaptation period, the sensations of warmth and cold must be caused by the relationship of the stimulus temperature to the current temperature of the skin (physiological zero). You can experiment with this phenomenon further by trying out more extreme adapting temperatures and adapting to them for longer times. See if you can find points beyond which all stimuli feel either warm or cold. Changes in temperature near these points only result in changes in the intensity of that sensation, rather than resulting in a change in sensation quality (Kenshalo and Scott, 1966).

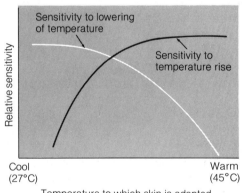

Figure 9-13. Sensitivity to increases and decreases in temperature varies as a function of the adaptation temperature of the skin.

only sensations of cold. There are also regions that produce no temperature sensations at all (although they may respond to touch). Figure 9-14 shows a set of maps of such warm and cold spots from an area of 1 cm² on the skin of the upper arm (Dallenbach, 1927). The spots were mapped on four successive days so that the permanence of the spots could be determined. As you can see from the figure, the spots tend to be in the same places from day to day. Since all these spots are innervated only by free nerve endings, the difference between the cold and warm spots probably has to do with the type of nerve fiber generating these nerve endings. It seems that cold fibers are typically larger in diameter and myelinated,

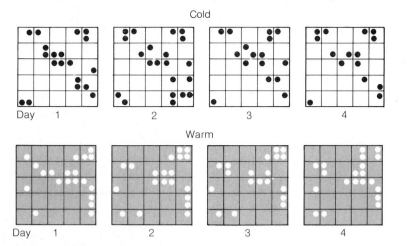

Figure 9-14. Maps of cold and warm spots on a 2 cm square area of the skin of the upper arm of a single observer on four successive days. Notice how the spots tend to be in the same places from day to day. (From K. M. Dallenbach, American Journal of Psychology, 1927, 39, Copyright the University of Illinois Press.)

while warm fibers are smaller and unmyelinated (Hensel, 1981).

Thermal intensity and qualities

Because of the complexity of the situations under which warm and cold sensations occur, perhaps you think that it would be difficult to measure the apparent intensity of thermal stimuli. We can, however, measure these sensations using direct scaling techniques such as those discussed in Chapter 2. For instance, Stevens and Stevens (1960) had observers make magnitude estimations of the thermal sensations caused by the application of warm or cool pieces of aluminum to the skin of the forearm. They used stimuli above the average skin temperature [about 33°C (91°F)] for warm sensations and stimuli below this temperature for cold ones. They found that warm and cold sensations also follow the psychophysical power law when measured in this way, with

exponents of the power functions for warmth around 1.6 and for cold about 1.0. The sensation of warmth grows somewhat more rapidly with stimulus intensity than does that of cold.

Because of the close relationship between the sensations of warmth and cold, it should not surprise you to learn of some very interesting and somewhat paradoxical phenomena associated with thermal stimuli. One of these, called **paradoxical cold**, was discovered by Max von Frey in 1895. He found that if cold spots (such as those illustrated in Figure 9-14) are touched with a very warm stimulus above 45°C (113°F), a sensation of cold will result. The opposite phenomenon, paradoxical warmth, has been much sought after, but never demonstrated convincingly. This asymmetry is consistent with the tendency of nerve fibers that respond to cooling (cold fibers) to respond both in the range of temperatures between about 12 and 35°C (54−95°F) and between 45 and 50°C (113−122°F). Warm fibers respond only in the range between about

25 and 47°C (77–117°F) (Zotterman, 1959; see also Chapter 5). When the skin temperature rises above 47°C (117°F), only the cold fibers respond. Therefore, very high temperatures actually result in sensations equivalent to very cold temperatures, both of which are felt subjectively as cold.

PAIN

Throughout human history, pain has been recognized as an important experience, capable of motivating the basest and the most beautiful of human actions. Although everybody acknowledges its importance in human experience, nobody is quite sure just what it is. Most individuals would agree that most pain is unpleasant, and indeed many authors simply classify pain as an emotional or affective experience that is the opposite of pleasure. This is consistent with the fact that pain seems to have no specialized sense organs. Furthermore, it does not convey information about any single class of stimulus energy in our environment. It comes from anywhere and everywhere and can be experienced in virtually every part of the body. It may even function to promote healing, once an injury has occurred, rather than to indicate the presence of dangerous stimuli (see Chapter 5).

On the other hand, when we experience pain it has a distinct sensory quality. Also, much of the physiological evidence implies that the neural response identified with pain travels along specific pathways, and analgesics that lessen pain can leave the other senses unaffected (see Chapter 5). Pain apparently has absolute and differential thresholds, it adapts, and it can be measured in a variety of ways. Thus, pain acts much like a separate sensory system. Although the sensory versus the emotional (and now the healing promotion) view-

points of pain have resulted in intense controversies in the history of psychology, there is no consensus as to exactly how we should define and deal with the concept of pain. In this section, we take the stand that pain as a warning or as an immobilizing experience has both affective and sensory aspects. We will review first the available information on the sensory aspects and then proceed to consider some of the more interesting recent work on analgesia, particularly on the substances known as endogenous opiates.

Pain thresholds, intensity, and adaptation

To treat pain as a sensation, we must first define a pain threshold. Usually this is taken to be the intensity of a stimulus that will just barely produce a sensation of pain. Obviously, thresholds vary across the different conditions under which they are measured, since pain can be aroused in so many different ways. As in the case of touch and thermal sensitivity, specific tiny points on the skin respond selectively to pain. These points give the sensation of pain for stimuli that do not produce painful sensations when applied to places other than "pain points." The distribution of such pain points over the body also seems quite variable, as can be seen from Table 9-1.

One major advance in the standardization of conditions for measuring the pain thresholds was made by Hardy, Wolff, and Goodell (1943). They used a device that focused an intense beam of light on the ink-blackened forehead in order to produce a painful heat stimulus. Since the device used radiant heat as a stimulus, it could be controlled and measured precisely. They called the device a **dolorimeter**, from the Latin *dolor* or pain, and *meter*, to measure. This development permitted the investigation of the various conditions that affect the level of the pain threshold. The exact thresholds

Table 9-1. Distribution of Pain Sensitivity (Based on Geldard, 1972)

Skin region	Pain "points"/cm²
Back of knee	232
Neck region	228
Bend of elbow	224
Shoulder blade	212
Inside of forearm	203
Back of hand	188
Forehead	184
Buttocks	180
Eyelid	172
Scalp	144
Ball of thumb	60
Sole of foot	48
Tip of nose	44

measured in this way are of little importance to us here, since the units of any pain threshold stimulus vary with the pain-producing device or stimulus modality. However, Hardy et al. (1943) were able to show that pain thresholds acted very much like the thresholds for other sensations. Pain thresholds were shown to be relatively stable as long as the conditions were stable, but they varied systematically with changes in the neurological, pharmacological (drugs), or psychological state of the individual. Since then, these results have been replicated many times. More recently, even social situations have been shown to affect pain thresholds (Craig, 1978).

One can discriminate whether two pains are the same or different in intensity, indicating that pain has a differential threshold too. The first good measurement of the differential threshold was done by Hardy, Wolff, and Goodell (1947) using a modification of the dolorimeter. Because the authors felt the knowledge was important, they served as their own subjects and as a result experienced both a great amount of pain and considerable tissue damage. They even moved the site of the painful stimulation from the forehead to the forearm because the latter was more easily cared for when blistered by the pain stimuli. These rather extreme measures resulted in some important results. They found that the differential threshold could be measured for pain and that it is reproducible under constant conditions. Moreover, Hardy et al. (1947) also found that the Weber fraction remains remarkably constant (as Weber's law would assert) at about 0.04 over quite a large range of stimulus intensities. This indicates that we are quite sensitive to variations in pain intensity. Weber fractions begin to increase dramatically at only the highest stimulus intensities. At the extremes, however, the data were not very reliable, because the skin damage sustained made it difficult for the observers (the authors themselves) to concentrate on the pain intensities.

Hardy et al. (1947) also created the first scale of pain intensity. Since they had established the validity of Weber's law for pain, they merely added up *jnd*s, as Fechner had done, to create a scale of pain intensity based on the discriminability of painful stimuli. They appropriately called this scale the **dol scale** (again based on the Latin *dolor*). Later scales of pain intensity were created by more direct methods. Stevens (1961) obtained magnitude estimations of the intensity of pain produced by electric shocks. He found that the magnitude estimations were a power function of the stimulus intensity with an exponent of about 3.5, making pain produced by electric shock the sensory modality with the highest power function exponent. This implies that the sensation of pain grows faster with increasing stimulus intensity than does any other sensory experience. The actual size of the exponent varies as a function of a variety of stimulus and even social factors (Craig, Best, and Ward, 1975; Sternbach and Tursky, 1964), and more recent studies have typically obtained somewhat lower exponents, usually under 2.

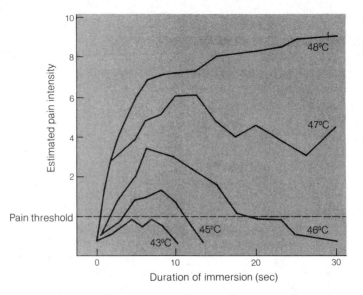

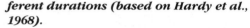

Figure 9-15. Average estimations of pain in-
tensity from hot water immersions of dif-
ferent durations (based on Hardy et al.,
1968).

If we want to argue for a sensory basis for the experience of pain, we must ask if pain sensations adapt as do all other sensations. Dallenbach (1939) demonstrated that pain caused by needles, heat, and cold does adapt. Heat-induced pain was studied by Hardy, Stolwijk, and Hoffman (1968) by having observers judge the degree of experienced pain as they sat with their hands in hot water over a period of time. As can be seen from Figure 9-15, adaptation is complete for the lower temperature pain stimuli, which were only mildly painful, and less complete for the more painful stimuli. Adaptation may not take place at all for the extremely painful stimuli.

Analgesia and endogenous opiates

Because pain is unpleasant, it is only natural to seek to minimize it. After it has served its function of warning us that our body is about to be

or already has been damaged, the pain signal is no longer necessary or desired. Yet strong pain signals often persist, or indeed may occur for the first time, well after the damaging stimulus is gone. This may be because the pain induces us to remain relatively immobile, so that healing may proceed optimally (Wall, 1979). Humans, however, are not content simply to accept this immobilizing pain, nor do they desire to experience the pain from surgery or illness. Thus, they have assembled an impressive array of analgesics and anesthetics to rid themselves of pain. The major focus of much pain research seems to be the discovery of new ways to induce analgesia. The most potent and reliable method of pain alleviation involves chemicals that are ingested (such as aspirin) or are injected into nerves or muscles (such as the Novocaine used by dentists). We can even buy sprays or tubes of salve that contain substances that cause a temporary analgesia on cut or burned skin. For more severe pain, we resort to narcotic drugs (such as morphine, an opium derivative) or opt for unconsciousness (as with ether or chloroform).

While studying how some of the more powerful opium-based drugs produce analgesia, researchers made a discovery that helped advance our understanding of how our bodies control pain naturally. Opiates interact with specific receptors in the brain to produce their analgesic and intoxicating effects. Since the brain has receptors for this family of chemicals, it seemed likely that there must be a class of chemicals present naturally in the body that also interact with these receptors. Presumably, such **endogenous opiates** (meaning opiates generated from within) should exhibit analgesic properties similar to those of opium derivatives. Several such substances were discovered by biochemists in the early 1970s (see Kosterlitz and McKnight, 1981; Snyder, 1977). Two major classes of internally generated chemicals, the **enkephalins** and the **endorphins**, have significant analgesic effects and seem to react with the same sites that opiates do. When bodily levels are raised artificially (by administration of extra amounts of these substances), the endorphins seem to be the more potent and longer lasting. The opiumlike action of these endogenous substances is further demonstrated by the fact that their analgesic action can be blocked by the administration of *naloxone*, a potent antagonist of opiates such as morphine, which is often administered to those who have taken overdoses. Administration of naloxone by itself makes people who are under stress more sensitive to pain, presumably because it blocks the effectiveness of endogenous opiates released naturally under these circumstances (Schull, Kaplan, and O'Brien, 1981).

Specific sites in the brain seem to be responsible both for the generation of endogneous opiates and for the analgesic effect caused by them. For example, electrical stimulation of certain parts of the thalamus can produce strong analgesic effects. This analgesia is reversible by naloxone and is less strong for individuals who have developed a tolerance, or relative insensitivity, to morphine. This finding suggests that this part of the brain may be one site where endogenous opiates are produced (see Akil and Watson, 1980). Individuals who suffer from chronic pain have lower than normal levels of some endogenous opiates in their spinal fluid, and electrical stimulation of the brains of such people produces both analgesia and dramatic increases in the levels of endorphins in their spinal fluid (Akil and Watson, 1980; Terenius and Wahlstrom, 1975).

Our conscious experience of the intensity of pain seems to be affected, not only by the magnitude of the pain stimulus, but also by chemical regulators, generated internally, and acting directly on specific areas of the central nervous system. It may also provide clues as to the mechanisms involved in the nonchemical methods for the reduction of pain. For example, in many instances, purely psychological factors seem to induce reduced sensitivity to pain. For example Willer, Dehen, and Cambier (1981) found that the psychological stress caused by the anticipation of a painful shock actually resulted in analgesic effects. Presumably, the stress triggered the endogenous opiate system. Similar factors seem to be involved in some of the more "mysterious" reports of reduced pain sensitivity. Several studies have established that pain reduction achieved through acupuncture (see Chapter 5) is reversible by naloxone and thus seems to be mediated at least in part by release of endogenous opiates (Akil and Watson, 1980; Kosterlitz and McKnight, 1981). Similarly, placebo effects are sometimes reversible by naloxone, again suggesting that some opioid system is involved.

The brain/chemical interaction we have been discussing provides only an incomplete picture of the factors influencing our perception of pain. For instance, many forms of pain reduction, such as that achieved through hypnosis, do *not* appear to be mediated by endogenous opiates (Akil and Watson, 1980; Kosterlitz and McKnight, 1981). Not all forms of "mysterious" analgesia can be explained by asserting that a pain reduction procedure causes release of endogenous opiates into the nervous system. The most recent evidence suggests that humans have two pain control systems, and that only one of them involves endogenous opiates (Akil and Watson, 1980; Watkins and Mayer, 1982).

Some of the most interesting analgesic procedures involve cognitive processes. These include such techniques as suggestion, attitude, concentration of attention, and social modeling (see Craig, 1978; Wolff and Goodell, 1943). The efficacy and the interpretation of these techniques vary, but there is no doubt that they are real. Pain thresholds can be reduced dramatically by several of the techniques. For instance, social modeling, where observers see another person's reactions to painful stimuli before judging the painfulness of the same stimuli for themselves, has been reported to affect both d' and physiological reactivity to painful electric shocks (Craig and Prkachin, 1978). Demonstration Box 9-5

Demonstration Box 9-5. Cognitive effects on pain: the Lamaze technique

A cognitive technique to alleviate the pain of childbirth is now being taught in many places in North America and Europe (see Beck and Siegel, 1980). The basic idea was that of a French medical doctor named Lamaze. One demonstration of how this technique works requires a friend to assist you.

Have your friend grasp your leg just above the knee with a hand. Have your friend squeeze gently at first, then with steadily increasing force until you can feel a fairly severe pain. This should convince you that the stimulus is actually painful. Now you have three things to practice simultaneously. First, you have to breathe in a particular way. To do this you must take five short panting breaths in a row, followed by a strong blow outward (pant-pant-pant-pant-pant-blow). Repeat this pattern during the entire period during which the painful stimulus might occur. Do not breathe too quickly for you might hyperventilate and get dizzy. If you do get dizzy, stop for a moment and then start up again at a slower pace. Second, you

must count the breaths (1-2-3-4-5-blow) or say a short poem or nonsense sentence over and over again to the rhythm of your breathing ("Am I a bird or a *plant?*"). Third, you must concentrate your visual attention on (look intently at) some clearly visible object during this entire period. Practice these behaviors for a few minutes until you feel fairly confident of your ability to maintain them for a couple of minutes. Then have your friend give you the gradually increasing pressure on the leg, while you do your breathing. Under these conditions, if your concentration is really intense, you might not feel the pain (or the pressure) at all, or at least it will be of much lesser intensity. According to the Melzack-Wall-Casey (Melzack and Casey, 1968; Melzack and Wall, 1965) approach to pain, what is happening here is that your central control system is closing the pain gate. Thousands of mothers claim that this basic technique of concentrating on something removed from the source of the pain effectively alleviates the pain and distress of childbirth.

allows you to assess the effectiveness of one form of cognitive control of the perceived intensity of pain.

Quite clearly, these results suggest that the perception of pain is complex, involving a number of different levels of control. One can see how these many levels may be integrated into one system by considering the *gate control theory* of pain. In Chapter 5, we discussed Melzack and Wall's (1965) proposal of a neural gate in the spinal cord composed of the substantia gelatinosa (a part of the spinal cord) and some T cells that transmit pain information through the spinal cord to the brain (see Figure 5-13). Activity in fast-conducting nerve fibers from the surface of the body tends to close this gate, while activity in slow-conducting fibers tends to open it. According to this theory, pain is experienced when the T cells are transmitting at a high rate. The theory describes not only spinal control, however, but also allows inputs from higher levels of the nervous system to open or close the gate. Thus cognitive factors, motivational states, attentional factors, or other stimulation such as high-intensity hissing noises, electricity, or music could all be responsible for controlling the gate via the pathway *descending* from the brain to the spinal cord gate. These descending pathways seem to be most strongly implicated in analgesia caused by release of endogenous opiates. Perhaps activation of the descending pathways causes release of endogenous opiates into the spinal cord, thus closing the pain gate (Watkins and Mayer, 1982). On the other hand, the mechanism involving the substantia gelatinosa does not seem to use endogenous opiates to produce its effects.

We do not understand fully the story about the perception of pain. However, we now have a hint about why the second-century physician Galen prescribed the shock from an electric fish for a headache, while a twelfth-century English doctor prescribed wearing a copper bracelet on the left hand to relieve a pain in the right hand, both claiming successful analgesic results. Perhaps they were stimulating the endogenous opiate pain control system, rather than simply engaging in "empty superstition."

GLOSSARY

The following definitions are specific to this book.

Anosmia Relative insensitivity to an odor.

Cross-adaptation Exposure to one taste affecting the threshold stimulus taste of other substances; also experienced in odor perception.

Dolorimeter A device used to measure pain threshold.

Dol scale A scale of pain intensity based on the discriminability of painful stimuli.

Endogenous opiates Analgesia-inducing opiates produced naturally by the brain.

Endorphins One of the major groups of endogenous opiates.

Enkephalins One of the major groups of endogenous opiates.

Molar concentration The amount of a substance dissolved in a given amount of solution, 1 mole equaling the molecular weight of a substance in grams added to enough water to make 1 liter of solution.

Multidimensional scaling A procedure by which similarity judgments can be represented geometrically.

Neutral zone A temperature range surrounding physiological zero. Stimuli within this range feel neither warm nor cold.

Optacon A system, similar to the vision substitution system, that converts printed letters into vibration patterns on the fingertip.

Paradoxical cold The phenomenon of cold spots

in the skin responding to warm stimuli with a sensation of cold.

Pheromones   Chemicals secreted by animals that transmit information to other animals.

Physiological zero   A neutral point in the perception of heat and cold, usually taken to be the skin temperature.

Potentiation   A case of cross-adaptation in which exposure to one taste stimulus lowers the threshold to another taste stimulus.

Primers   Pheromones that trigger glandular and other physiological responses.

Releasers   Pheromones that trigger specific behavioral responses.

Self-adaptation   The effects of previous exposure to an odorant on threshold sensitivity for that same odorant on subsequent exposures.

Two-point threshold   The minimum distance necessary between two pointed touch stimuli (such as two toothpicks) so that they will be felt as two distinct sensations.

Vision substitution system   An instrument that converts a visual pattern from a television camera into a pattern of vibrating points on the skin of the back; used for the visually impaired.

10

Space

ONE DAY A TOURIST STOPPED HIS CAR on a road to ask a young boy the distance to Douglasville.

The boy looked up and said, "It's 24,999 miles the way you're going, but if you turn around it isn't more than four."

We live in a three-dimensional space composed of distances and directions. It is a commonplace task for us to estimate the distance between our hand and the pencil we wish to grasp and to calculate unconsciously the direction of arm movement needed. We can even estimate whether our coffee cup is a few inches nearer or farther away than the pencil. These extractions of spatial information are made automatically and with remarkable accuracy.

The perception of depth, distance, and direction are vital to our survival. We must know how far we are from the edge of a cliff or we may stray too close and fall. We must further know the direction of the edge from our bodies, otherwise we might step toward it rather than away from it. We cannot get cut by a knife edge pictured in a flat photograph, but the real blade extending toward us in space can produce painful contact. Thus, our lives and safety may depend on the accuracy of our spatial perception.

Space perception involves a number of different aspects. The first is called **egocentric localization**. Most of us are familiar with the word *egocentric* in everyday use, where it pertains to a person who is concerned only about his own activities and their effect on himself. In the context of space perception, the word egocentric means that we have a good sense of where our bodies are positioned relative to other objects in the external environment. The concept of space perception also includes the ability to make **object-relative localizations**. Just as we can correctly estimate our own position relative to other objects, we can also perceive the distance between objects in the environment.

Another aspect of space perception involves the comprehension of whether an object is flat (as in a two-dimensional picture) or solid (three dimensional). The accomplishment involved in seeing objects in depth is quite amazing, given that the basic information available to the nervous system is just a flat image projected on our retinas. How do we accomplish these spatial organizations? The current consensus states that we organize our world by using a combination of different sources that give us information about spatial arrangements. Some of these sources are structures within the sensory systems themselves, others appear to arise from properties of the physical world and the way in which our sensory systems interact with it, and still others have to do with cognitive interpretive processes that are called into play.

DEPTH AND DISTANCE

Our discussion will start with **cues** that allow us to have the impression of depth or distance in pictures, drawings, or photographs, as well as in the physical world. Notice that we use the word *cue* rather than clue. In the theater, a *cue* is a signal that prompts an action from an actor who then automatically goes to the next line in the script. A *clue* suggests deliberate consideration that leads to the deduction of the correct answer. Since we derive depth from stimuli using mostly unconscious, automatic processing, the "triggers" that "prompt" the perception of depth will be called *cues*. The cues used by an artist, or those we interpret from photographs, are usually called **pictorial** or **monocular cues**, since they appear in pictures and only require one eye to regis-

ter (remember a camera has only one eye).
Occasionally, they are also called *static cues*
because the registration of depth information
requires neither the object nor the observer
to move. These cues serve as the basis for our
perception of monocular depth.

Pictorial depth cues: light

Our visual experience depends on the transfer
of light from an object in the external world to
the eye of the observer. A number of depth
cues depend on characteristic ways in which
light travels to the eye, or ways in which it interacts with the medium (usually, air) through
which it passes.

Interposition or overlay. Most objects in
the world are not transparent. Thus, if one object is in front of another, relative to the observer's point of view, it will block parts of the
more distant one behind it from view. In other
words, light from distant objects cannot pass
through opaque objects that stand between
them and the observer. This results in portions
of more distant objects being hidden from
view by the closer objects that impede the
complete transmission of the light stimulus
to the eye. This depth cue is called **interposition**, or **overlay**. In Figure 10-1 the square is
seen as the most distant object because it appears partially covered by another object. The
triangle appears to be at an intermediate distance because it blocks a portion of the square,
in addition to being covered partially by the
circle. The circle, however, seems to be closest
to you because it is seen in full view; light reflected from a full circular surface has an un-
impeded path to your eye.

Shadowing. There are several depth cues
that depend on the way in which light interacts with objects. The first, and most obvious,
of these is **shadowing**. Light travels in straight

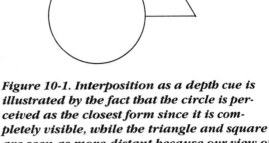

*Figure 10-1. Interposition as a depth cue is
illustrated by the fact that the circle is perceived as the closest form since it is completely visible, while the triangle and square
are seen as more distant because our view of
them is partially blocked.*

lines, thus parts of an object that form outgoing "bumps" intercept the light and are usually
bright, while dents have surfaces shielded from
the light and are in shadow. Thus, an object
that has some protruding or indented portions
will show a distribution of shadowing. Figure 10-2A shows a flat gray disk with no shadowing and no apparent depth. When we add
shadows, it is seen immediately as a three-
dimensional sphere (Figure 10-2B). The use
of the shadowing cue seems to involve the assumption that light generally comes from overhead. Notice that Figure 10-2C looks like a
"bump" protruding from the surface while
10-2D looks like a "dent." This is because the
upper portion of 10-2C is brighter (as would
be expected if a bump were illuminated from
above), while 10-2D is shadowed in its upper
portion (as a dent illuminated from above
would be). Turning the figure upside down reverses this shadowing effect and also reverses
the apparent depth, turning C into the dent
and D into the bump.

Aerial Perspective. The air is filled with
light-absorbing and light-scattering molecules

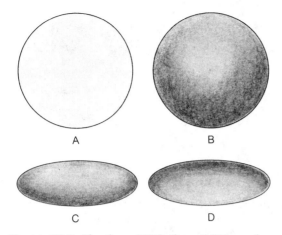

Figure 10-2. Shadows. With the addition of shadowing, a flat surface (A) can be made to appear as a solid object (B). Also, because we assume overhead lighting, shadowing can cause differences in the direction of perceived depth. (C) is seen as a "bump," while (D) is seen as a "dent." If you turn the book upside down, the direction of depth (bump vs. dent) will change.

even on the clearest of days. Therefore, as light passes through the air, it tends to be absorbed and somewhat scattered by these minute particles of dust and moisture in the atmosphere. One type of scattering is caused by large particles and results in the production of a uniform distribution of light or a blurring of the image. The second type of scatter is related to the effect of particles that are small in comparison with the various wavelengths of light. Here, the degree of scatter depends on the specific wavelength of light, with short wavelengths (blue) undergoing more scatter than the longer wavelengths (Uttal, 1981). The combined effect of these processes means that the image of a very distant object, such as a distant mountain, will be slightly bluer in hue and hazier in appearance. Such changes in appearance provide information about distance. This cue is

called **aerial perspective**. In some geographic regions (such as the prairies of the United States and Canada), considerable errors in distance judgments can result since the clear dry air reduces aerial perspective. Thus a plateau that on a clear day appears to be only 1 or 2 miles away across a dry sector of Wyoming may actually be 20 or 30 miles distant.

Relative Brightness. The last depth cue in this group is called **relative brightness**. Ittelson (1960) has shown that the brighter of two identical objects (viewed in a dark room that allows no other cues to be used) will be seen as closer. The luminance of a lighted surface or object does not decrease with distance, but the light from more distant objects must travel through the atmosphere for a greater distance. Therefore, increased absorption of the light by the particles in the air could account for the perception of a diminished brightness with increasing object distance, even though the distances are not as great as those described in the context of the aerial perspective cue. For this reason, Uttal (1981) has proposed that the use of brightness differences as a cue to depth be considered to be a special case of aerial perspective, and be related to the interaction between light and the air through which it passes.

Pictorial depth cues: size and object relations

As objects vary in their distance from the observer, the size of the retinal image changes. Consider Figure 10-3A; notice that the more distant person casts a smaller retinal image. These regular changes in the retinal image as a function of changes in distance can be used as sources of spatial information.

Size. We utilize changes in **retinal image size** in making judgments of depth or distance.

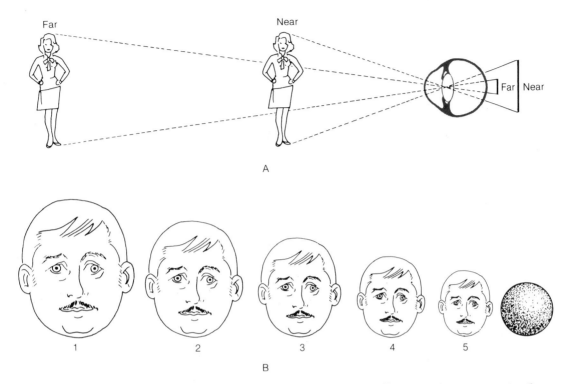

A

B

Figure 10-3. The size cue to distance. (A) Objects of the same physical size produce smaller retinal angle sizes with increasing distance from the observer. Thus, relatively speaking, smaller images are perceived as more distant. (B) The interaction between familiar and relative size (See Demonstration Box 10-1).

For example, Figure 10-3B shows a row of faces that seems to recede in space because of the decreasing image size. Thus, the comparison of the sizes of objects in the visual field, relative to each other, is an important part of the process of distance and depth estimation.

Our familiarity with the actual size of the targets plays a role in these judgments. We presume that all the faces in Figure 10-3B are the same physical size, and hence that their retinal size differences are caused by differences in distance. Ittelson (1951) demonstrated the importance of more cognitive factors, such as familiarity with the size of the targets judged. He presented observers with

a series of playing cards. One of the playing cards was normal in size, a second was twice normal size, and a third was one-half normal size. He found that observers judged the double-sized playing cards as much closer to them than the normal-sized ones. As you might expect, the half-sized cards were judged to be much more distant. Ittelson conducted his experiment under conditions that have come to be called *reduction conditions*. This means that the observers were making their distance judgments under conditions that did not allow them to use any of the other distance cues.

Epstein and Baratz (1964) showed that **familiar size** is a potent cue for the perception

---

Demonstration Box 10-1. Familiar size and distance

Look at Figure 10-3B. Notice the row of faces that seems to recede into the distance. Off to the right is a ball. Imagine that it is a ping-pong ball or a golf ball. Study the figure for a moment and decide which face is at the same distance as the golf ball. Then return to this box. Now imagine that the ball is a volleyball or a basketball. Which face is at the same distance as the ball? Notice that the ball "moved backward" in depth when you assumed it was a larger object. This shows how retinal size and familiar size work together to give you an impression of depth or distance.

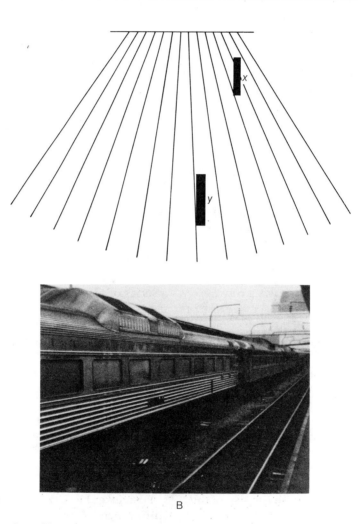

B

Figure 10-4. Examples of linear perspective.

of distance. They found that differences in image size led to differences in distance estimates when the objects used in an experiment were ones that had a familiar size. If we see a very tiny elephant, we can use our knowledge that elephants are relatively large creatures to deduce that the elephant has not shrunk in size but rather has moved away from us and is now more distant. You may demonstrate the effect of familiar size for yourself by following the instructions in Demonstration Box 10-1.

Perspective. **Perspective** is simply an extension of the size cue to distance. Look at Figure 10-4A. Here you see lines that seem to converge. If the lines represented physically parallel structures, the changing size of the spacing between the lines would result from increases in their distance from the observer. Thus, pole X appears to be farther away than pole Y, since it is asssociated with lines that are closer together due to the perspective cue. Figure 10-4B is a photograph that shows how linear (line) perspective really operates. We know that the sides of the train are parallel, thus the roof is parallel to the underside. However, as these parallel lines recede into the distance (in this case, as they recede toward the

entrance of the railway station), they appear to converge, or form an angle. In the physical world, parallel lines converge toward a *vanishing point* as their distance from the eye increases. Thus, there is a continuous variation in visual angle size, from large to small, as continuous surfaces recede in depth. Probably the best example of this is to stand in the middle of a railroad track and take note of how the tracks appear to converge as they become more and more distant from you, until they appear to disappear into a point.

Texture gradient. J. J. Gibson made an important contribution to our knowledge of depth perception when he studied **texture gradient**, a cue that combines both linear perspective and relative size information. A *texture* is any collection of objects (Caelli, 1982), and the *gradient* (continuous change) is the change in the relative size and compactness of these object elements. The more distant points of the texture have smaller elements and are more densely packed together (Gibson, 1950). This cue is sometimes called detail perspective. Figure 10-5A shows a texture of dots. It is usually seen as a plain receding in depth. On the other hand, Figure 10-5B typically is seen

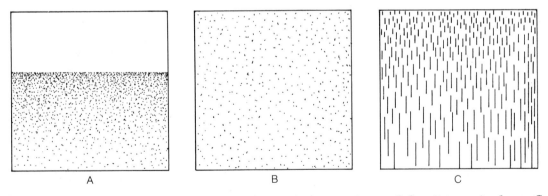

A   B   C

Figure 10-5. Examples of texture gradients in (A) and (C), which appear as surfaces receding in depth. (B) has no decreases in element size or spacing and thus is perceived as a flat surface.

as a flat surface, since the texture is uniform and unchanging. Figure 10-5C shows a texture of lines that again seems like a plain receding toward the horizon. Sudden changes in texture usually signal a change in the direction or distance of a surface. Thus, Figure 10-6A shows how the gradient changes when we shift from floor to wall; Figure 10-6B shows how the gradient changes at a cliff or step down.

Height in the plane. Another cue to distance, which rests in the relationships between objects in external space, is **height in the plane**, or relative height. This cue refers to where an object is relative to the horizon line. In Figure 10-7, post B seems farther away than post A because its base is closer to the horizon line. Therefore, it is higher in the plane, or higher in the picture plane if we consider this a two-dimensional representation. The reverse holds for targets above the horizon. Bird C

seems farther away than bird D because it is *lower* in the picture plane. In other words, proximity to the horizon line signals the greater distance.

Motion

We have been discussing depth cues that are derived from properties of the external world, cues that are often mimicked by artists to obtain three-dimensional interpretations of two-dimensional surfaces. Some cues to depth and distance, however, are not available to the artist or still photographer, although perhaps a cinematographer can make use of them. These cues involve the changes that come about in the pattern of retinal stimulation as we move, or are moved, through the world.

Motion parallax. One such movement

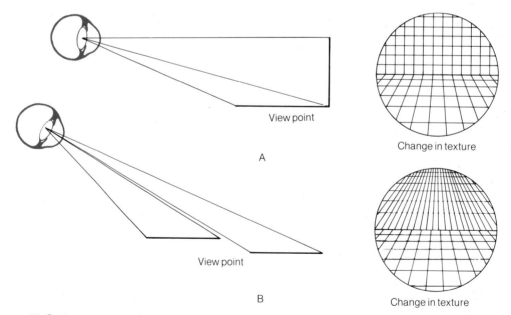

Figure 10-6. How texture changes at (A) a corner, and (B) an edge next to a sharp drop in depth.

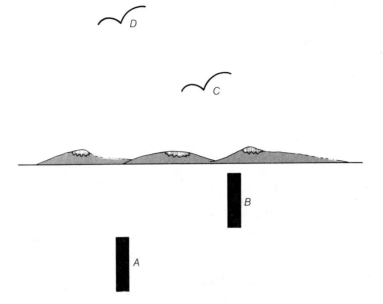

Figure 10-7. Height in the plane. Proximity to the horizon will determine which elements in the diagram are perceived as more distant.

In this case, B and C are seen as being farther away because they are closer to the horizon line.

cue concerns the pattern of object motion as you travel past it. Suppose you were traveling in a car or bus and looking at the scene in Figure 10-8. Let us also suppose that your direction of movement is from right to left and that you are gazing at the spot marked "fixation point." Under these conditions, all the objects closer to you than the fixation point would appear to move in a direction opposite to your movement. On the other hand objects that are farther away will appear to move in the same direction you are moving. Not only the direction, but also the speed of movement varies with the objects' proximity to you and to your point of fixation. This cue to distance is called **motion parallax**.

Motion perspective. An interesting variation of the linear perspective cue involves motion. In linear perspective, all objects and

points in space seem to converge as they recede into the distance. When we directly approach a surface, objects and points in space seem to diverge outward from a point directly in front of our eyes and straight ahead of our movement. Walking down a corridor while looking at a distant point gives the flow pattern shown in Figure 10-9. The cue is often called **motion perspective**, or optical expansion (Gibson, Kaplan, Reynolds, and Wheeler, 1969). These flow patterns are thought to be one of the depth cues that airline pilots use when landing an aircraft (Regan, Beverley, and Cynader, 1979). The specific patterns and how they blur and streak across the retina convey information about the surfaces and objects in the environment and their relationship to the observer (Harrington, Harrington, Wilkins, and Koh, 1980; Prazdny, 1982).

Fixation point

Your movement

*Figure 10-8. Motion parallax. When an ob-
server moves, objects at varying distances
from the observer will appear to move in dif-*
*ferent directions at differing speeds. These
differences can serve as cues for the relative
distance of objects.*

Physiological cues to depth and distance

We have considered cues for depth and distance
that depend on the geometry of the world and
the way light interacts with objects. Certain
other cues for distance arise simply because
of the way the visual system is structured.
These **structural**, or **physiological, cues**
may also play a role in our perception of depth.

Accommodation. In Chapter 3 we discussed the action of the crystalline lens when
the eye changes its distance of regard. As you
may remember, when we shift our gaze from
one object in the visual field to another that
lies at a different distance from us, the lens
changes shape (actually, it changes its amount

of curvature) so that the new object of regard
is focused on the retinal surface (Dalziel and
Egan, 1982). This process is called *accommodation.* Only a lens of one particular curvature will clearly focus the retinal image of any
given object viewed at a specified distance
from the eye. For instance, relaxed accommodation (or a relatively thin lens) is necessary if distant objects are to be focused clearly
on the retina, while a curved lens is needed to
image closer objects on the retinal surface. Because we are continually changing the tension
on the ciliary muscles, which control the lens
shape, it seems reasonable that the particular
pattern of muscular tension needed to bring an
object into focus could provide important

information about the relative distance of objects from the eye. Another source of information from the accommodative system that may provide a distance cue is the blur in the retinal image when an object is not in focus (when the degree of accommodation is incorrect for a particular viewing distance). It has been shown that in the absence of all other depth information, observers can judge that two spots of light presented in complete dark-ness are at two different distances in external visual space. Since accommodation cannot be correct for both stimuli simultaneously, the observer could be making these accurate distance judgments based on the information that, at any point in time, one of the lights will be slightly out of focus or blurred on the retina (Kaufman, 1974).

Unfortunately, accommodation by itself can only give information about distance and

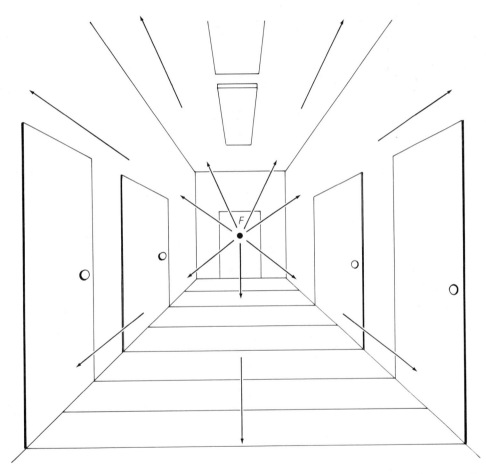

Figure 10-9. Optical expansion. Movement toward and away from objects causes typical expansion and contraction patterns that can provide information about distance. F marks the point of fixation toward which the observer is moving.

depth over a limited range of observer-to-object distances (Graham, 1965). The lens reaches its fullest point of relaxation when an object is about 3 meters away from us. If the object moves beyond that distance, the lens will no longer change its degree of curvature. A similar restriction exists for close objects. Once a target has come within 20 cm of the face, the lens has reached its point of maximum curvature. Thus, there is only a limited range over which accommodation of the lens alone can provide adequate information about distance and depth (Kaufman, 1974). Hochberg (1971a) has surveyed a body of literature spanning 70 years of research into the distance information available from accommodation in

the absence of other cues. He concludes that accommodation is not a very good cue to distance even within the range where it could potentially work (20-300 cm from the observer).

Convergence and divergence. Other physiological cues for distance arise from the fact that we have two eyes—we are *binocular* observers. Since the best visual acuity is obtained when the image of a target is on the foveal region of the eye, eye movements are executed to bring the image to the fovea. When an object is close to the observer, the two eyes must rotate inward (toward the nose), as shown in Figure 10-10A. Such a movement is called *convergence*. When a target is farther away, the eyes must engage in an

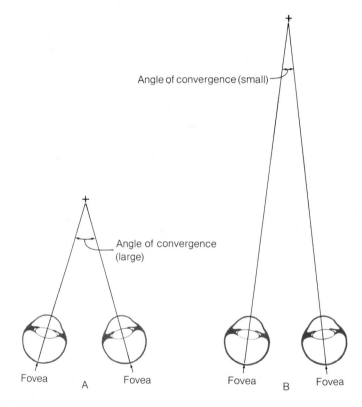

Figure 10-10. Convergence. Convergence angle changes as a function of fixation dis- *tance. This may provide some information about target distance.*

outward rotation (toward the temples) in order to **bifoveally fixate** (the technical term for the situation in which an image stimulates both foveas) the target (see Figure 10-10*B*). This movement is called **divergence**. Each target distance (up to about 6 meters) is associated with a unique angle between the eyes (usually called the *convergence angle* as indicated in Figure 10-10*A* and *B*) and, hence, a unique pattern of muscular contractions. Thus, information about the amount of ocular rotation needed to image the targets on both foveas could serve as a cue to target distance. Unfortunately, much dispute still exists about the usefulness and reliability of convergence as a distance cue (Gogel, Gregg, and Wainwright, 1961; Hochberg, 1971a).

Binocular disparity and stereopsis.
The last of the physiological cues for depth is probably the most important. In humans the two eyes are horizontally separated by the nose. This separation results in a distance of up to 6.5 cm between the pupils. While such a separation may not seem important, it results in the two eyes having different directions of view and, hence, different images. You can see this for yourself in Demonstration Box 10-2. The two images are said to be disparate, and the process by which the disparate views come to be merged into one common percept is called **fusion**.

Because the process of fusion is not perfect, many parts of the total visual image remain disparate. This failure of the two eyes' views to merge completely gives rise to double vision, or **diplopia**. Although consciously we are not aware of diplopia under normal conditions, we can learn to see the double images. Demonstration Box 10-3 shows how this is done. Notice that in this demonstration the pattern of double images is different, depending on whether the unfused image is in front of or in back of the target you have fixated. These **crossed** and **uncrossed images** (see Demon-

stration Box 10-3 for the definition of these terms) can serve as a cue to the relative distance of objects. Objects more distant than the point of fixation are seen in uncrossed disparity, while closer objects are seen with crossed disparity. Only objects at about the same distance as that of convergence will be fused and seen singly. If we map out all the points where targets are at about the same convergence or fixation distance in external visual space, we have traced out an imaginary curved line called the **horopter**. The region immediately surrounding this hypothetical curved line, which includes all points in external space that are fused or seen as single images, is called **Panum's area** (named for Panum, one of the early researchers in the area of binocular vision). A diagram of the horopter and the surrounding area of fused images is shown in Figure 10-11. The shape of the horopter will change with varying fixation distances; however, it is a convenient way to talk about the zone of fused images surrounded by areas of unfused or disparate images.

Fusion also occurs because each eye contains **corresponding retinal points**. When stimulated by light input from the same visual stimulus, the two monocular images merge into one because corresponding retinal areas represent a common visual direction in the visual areas of the brain. It does not matter that the two eyes view the world from different directions, since the corresponding retinal areas are matched in direction in the brain. The foveas of each eye are corresponding retinal points. The horopter represents the zone in external visual space that stimulates corresponding retinal points for one fixation distance.

The physicist Wheatstone (1838) is credited with the discovery of **stereopsis**. This term is used to describe the ability to see depth based solely on the disparity of the two retinal images. He maintained that when two objects are

Demonstration Box 10-2. Binocular disparity

You can see the difference between the views of your eyes by holding a pencil up near your nose as shown below. The tip of the pencil should be toward you and angled slightly downward. Now alternately close each eye. The pencil seems to swing back and forth. With your right eye open, it appears angled toward the left, while with the left eye open, it appears angled toward the right. With both eyes open, the fused view is of a pencil straight ahead of your nose.

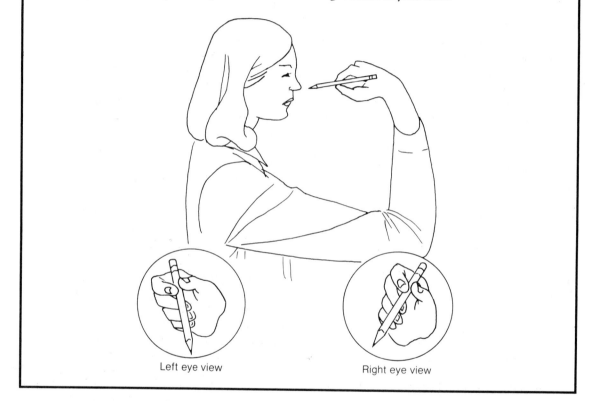

Left eye view   Right eye view

located physically at different depth planes, the two eyes cannot possibly get the same view of these two objects. We saw this in Demonstration Box 10-2 and can also see it in Figure 10-12. In the figure, the two rods are spatially separated in depth. The image of the two rods differs for the right and for the left eyes. The rods are more widely separated in the right eye's image than in the image in the left eye. Thus, the images in the two eyes are disparate; in other words, they are not exactly alike.

Wheatstone drew a flat picture of the right eye's view of the two rods and another flat picture of the left eye's view of the two rods. He then positioned them so that the right eye could only see the right eye view and the left eye could only see the left eye view. Curious

Demonstration Box 10-3. Double images and disparity

Find a piece of transparent colored material like cellophane (any hue will work). Place it before your right eye. If you wear glasses you can affix it to the frame over the lens in front of your right eye; if not, use a piece of tape to hold it to your forehead. Now align two index fingers directly in front of your nose with the closer finger about 10-20 cm from your nose and the farther finger about 8 cm behind the closer one.

Now that you have arranged the appropriate situation, fixate your nearer finger. However, simultaneously try to pay attention to what the far finger looks like. This is a pretty difficult feat to accomplish at first, but with practice you should be able to fixate one target while simultaneously paying attention to what is going on beyond the fixated area. When you fixate the near target, you will notice that two images of the far target will be seen. The fact that one eye is viewing the image through a colored filter should help make the presence of double images beyond the fixation point more apparent. If you switch your fixation to the farther object, the closer of the two targets will appear as a double image. Targets that lie away from the area surrounding the point of fixation are not fused into a single image. They produce *disparate* retinal images. Disparate, unfused images are always present in the visual field; however, we are usually not aware of them unless forced to attend to them as in this demonstration.

Once you have become comfortable with this procedure, fixate the near target and then close

the right eye. You should notice that the image of the far target (the uncolored image) appears to lie to the left of the nearer, fixated object. Now close the left eye and open the right and you will notice the opposite. The image of the far target (the colored image) now appears to lie to the right of the closer, fixated target. The fact that the right eye is seeing the right disparate image and the left eye is seeing the left disparate image means that when both eyes are opened the far target is seen in **uncrossed disparity**. On the other hand, the opposite will happen if you

change your fixation to the far target. Now the closer object appears as diplopic (double). If you once again alternately close each eye, you will notice that the right eye is now seeing the image that lies to the left of the fixated target (the colored image), while the left eye is viewing the image that lies to the right. In the case of double images that lie closer to us than the point of fixation, we have a situation of **crossed disparity**. As the text explains, these differences in disparity may be a cue to distance.

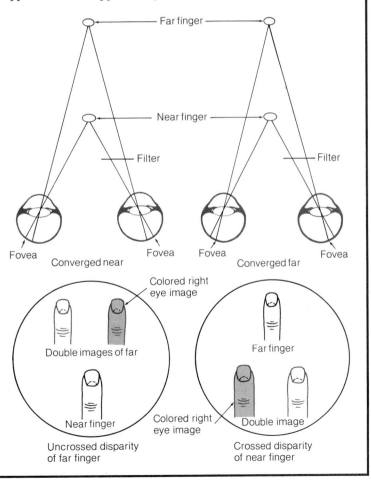

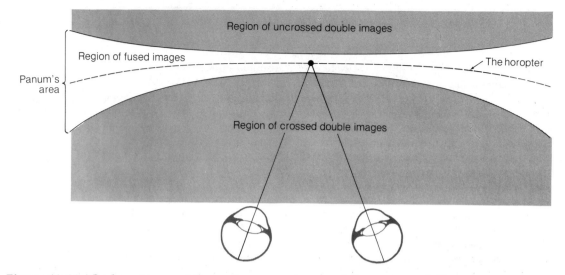

Figure 10-11. The horopter and Panum's area for one fixation distance. The regions of fusion and disparate images are shown. Crossed disparity is present at distances closer to the observer than the fixation dis-

tance, while uncrossed disparity is present beyond the fixation distance. The presence of disparate images may provide a cue to distance.

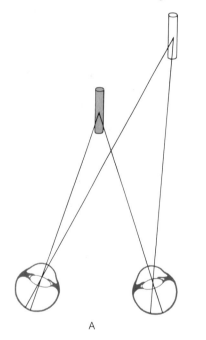

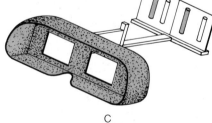

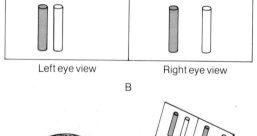

Figure 10-12. Disparate retinal images. (A) The two retinal images of a scene can be different because the two eyes view the world from slightly different directions. (B) A stereogram is a flat representation that mimics the

differences within the two retinal images. (C) A stereogram is viewed in a stereoscope that allows for the separate but simultaneous stimulation of the two eyes. The phenomenon is called stereopsis.

to see if he could simulate a real world depth situation by creating artificial disparity, he devised an optical instrument known as a **stereoscope** (a stereoscope allows you to place different stimuli into the two eyes simultaneously). He found that even though the pictures were actually flat, one of the rods appeared to be behind the other. For a period of time every Victorian living room had a stereoscope and a set of travel pictures that had been taken using a two-lensed camera, producing the "visual magic" of depth from flat images. While the trend toward more prurient photographic subjects ended this craze, it did not end the interest in stereoscopic depth.

Stereopsis has been one of the most widely studied of all the depth-producing processes, especially in the last 20 years. In the early l960s, investigators found disparity-tuned detectors in the visual cortex of the cat (see Pettigrew, 1978). Disparity-tuned detector cells act much like those described for other visual and auditory features in Chapters 3 and 4. For example, with a disparity value of 0, the targets are stimulating corresponding retinal points. If a cell gives a maximum response to this value, then that neuron represents a spatial locale that lies on the horopter, or the zone of fused images in external space. Neurons tuned to disparities greater than or less than 0, however, represent locations in space that lie in front of or behind the horopter. The existence of such disparity detectors indicates that cells in the visual cortex are providing information about the relative depth of targets located in external three-dimensional space. Each of the disparity detectors seems to be tuned to only one particular disparity value. Thus, populations of them are needed to represent all the possible disparity values in the visual scene. Some seem to be responsive only to stimuli that lie close to the horopter, while others are tuned to broad disparity values or to stimuli that lie far from the horopter (Aslin

and Dumais, 1980; DeValois and DeValois, 1980).

The specific properties of disparity-tuned detectors have been measured in cats, monkeys, and sheep, and their existence has been verified in a number of different laboratories (DeValois and DeValois, 1980; Pettigrew, 1978). These studies have demonstrated the possibility of a physiological basis to human stereopsis. However, the existence of disparity detectors in other species (and their proposed existence in humans), coupled with the existence of certain perceptual stereoscopic effects in humans, has started one of the most vigorous controversies in spatial vision. Consider Demonstration Box 10-4, which shows a random dot stereoscopic display. These displays were introduced by Julesz (1971) who used them to demonstrate the notion of **global stereopsis**. If you follow the instructions in Demonstration Box 10-4, you will see a dotted square floating in front of the background of random dots. In other words, the binocular view is an organized three-dimensional form despite the fact that the right and left eyes see only random dots. Figure 10-13 shows how the random dot stereograms are constructed. Notice that the central region of each side of the stereogram is disparate. In the combined view, this disparity operates to provide the appearance of a three-dimensional square.

How do we achieve this depth effect in random dot stereograms? If stereopsis is based on the action of disparity-tuned detectors, each of which responds to one disparity value in the array, any dot potentially could be combined with any other dot, with each of the many possible combinations producing a different depth. How is the one organized combination possible, given the multitude of possible depth combinations in this type of array? This question has been asked by many investigators interested in stereopsis. Many claim that the

Demonstration Box 10-4. Random dot stereograms and global stereopsis

You may demonstrate how depth cues can bring about the perception of a binocular form by using the accompanying figure. You will need a pocket mirror, which should be placed on the dotted center line of Figure *B* while you hold your head as shown in Figure *A*. Adjust the images until the two views seem to overlap and the frames around the outside seem to be at the same distance. Viewing it in this way, you will see a square form emerge, floating above the background, created completely by the depth cue of binocular disparity. Notice that this square simply can't be seen in either monocular view alone.

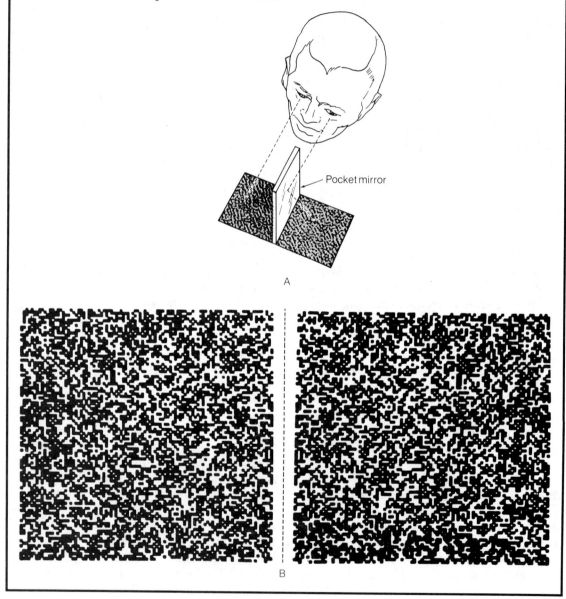

Left eye view   A   Right eye view

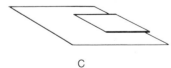

Displaced center square

B

C

Figure 10-13. (A) is a random dot stereo-gram. (B) shows how (A) is constructed, while (C) illustrates that a central square is seen floating above the background when the upper views are combined in a stereoscope (from B. Julesz, Foundations of Cyclopean Perception, *copyright 1971 by the University of Chicago Press).*

presence of disparity detectors, each of which is tuned to a specific disparity (or local disparity cue), is not enough to account for the global stereoscopic phenomena found in random dot stereograms. Consequently, a number of models or hypotheses have been developed to try and show how global stereopsis can be achieved by the action of disparity detectors in the human cortex. (see DeValois and DeValois, 1980; Julesz and Schumer, 1981). Most of the models assume that detectors tuned to the same disparity cooperate, while those tuned to different disparities inhibit each other. With a population of neurons working together in this fashion, only one depth solution would be common to this facilitatory-inhibitory process, and only one global stereoscopic view would be seen. Most of the current models of stereopsis tend to follow lines of reasoning that incorporate this notion (Julesz and Schumer, 1981).

Depth and distance: the interaction of cues

In natural viewing situations, we are exposed simultaneously to a number of sources of distance and depth information. Normally, they agree. For example, if interposition tells you that object *A* is closer to you than object *B*, other cues, such as relative size, will be in agreement with this type of visual organization. One way that we can demonstrate our dependence on the consistency of information from various depth cues is to look at pictorial representations and the effects that artists often achieve by manipulating this dependence. For example, look at Figures 10-14 and 10-15. Figure 10-14 shows two people walking down a long staircase that seems to recede away from the plane of the picture into depth. Notice that we have imposed the downward

Figure 10-14. Consistency of depth cue information. Notice how the cues of linear perspective, texture gradient, retinal size, and *height in the plane combine to convey the impression of two people descending a staircase that recedes in depth.*

Figure 10-15. Ambiguity of depth cues gives a confusing, difficult interpretation to a scene, as shown in Hogarth's 1754 engraving "False Perspective." The more you study this figure, the more contradictory depth cues you find.

direction, despite the fact that "down" has been drawn in the upper portion of the picture. A number of pictorial depth cues (familiar and retinal size, linear perspective, height in the plane) act together to support this interpretation. On the other hand, you can see the puzzling effects that occur when pictorial depth cues conflict with each other, as they do in Figure 10-15. In this case the depth relationships in the picture are ambiguous and confusing. This generates a high degree of artistic interest, but it is a situation that we could not tolerate or survive in if it existed in our everyday perceptual experience.

Perceptual investigators have been interested in the relative efficiency of each cue alone as well as in how various cues interact with each other. In this context, Jameson and Hurvich (1959) have reported that an observer's sensitivity to a difference in distance when all cues are available is close to the arithmetic sum of the sensitivities obtained with each cue alone. In other words, your sensitivity to a depth difference between two objects when texture gradient and interposition are present in the field is equal to the sum of your sensitivity to this depth difference when interposition is the only available cue, and when texture gradient is the only available cue. This additivity of depth cue effects has been confirmed in a more recent study by van der Meer (1979), who found that information from binocular disparity and linear perspective add together in the final judgment of perceived depth.

Much earlier work done by Schriever (1925), however, indicates that the interaction may not be that simple. He placed drawings and photographs of solid objects in a stereoscope. As you might expect, with only binocular disparity present, Schriever found good perception of depth. He then added additional cues to this stereoscopic array. He wanted to know whether the appearance of depth could be changed or reversed if such additional cues were placed in conflict with the binocular disparity cue to depth. For example, the disparity information might indicate that object A is closer than object B, while the linear perspective informaton might indicate the reverse effect. In general, Schriever found that the cue of binocular disparity tended to dominate the organization of the percept for all cues except interposition, which seemed to be the single most powerful depth cue he investigated.

Brunswick (1952, 1956) has argued that each separate distance and depth cue is ambiguous. Sometimes it may lead us to an incorrect interpretation of depth or distance within a scene. Thus, the power of a particular cue will be determined by its reliability and our past experience with its accuracy. This approach implies that our use of depth cues, and our ability to decipher how they interact with each other to organize a visual space, is a learned ability that becomes more efficient with experience. Brunswick's approach is shared by some investigators, but historically, the issue of the learned versus the innate nature of our spatial percepts has been a controversial one. It is often referred to as the *nativist* versus *empiricist* question (Hochberg, 1972). The nativists argue that these perceptual abilities and our capacity to use them are inborn, while the empiricists maintain that interaction with the world, through which we learn about its properties and organization, is crucial to our spatial awareness and abilities. One of the ways to explore this issue is to observe the behavior of young animals when they are placed in situations that call upon their abilities to perceive distance and depth. Since very young animals have limited experience with the world, their abilities to deal with such situations should shed some light on the role of inborn versus learned components in the perception of visual space.

The development of depth and distance perception

The study of newborn and very young animals is the principal technique used to study the origins of distance and depth perception. Investigators frequently use *controlled rearing* procedures that enable them to make a more exact statement about the experiential factors contributing to these perceptual abilities (as you may remember, we discussed some controlled rearing experiments in Chapter 3). A common form of controlled rearing is *dark rearing* (which is discussed more fully in Chapter 16). In this procedure, young animals are raised from birth (or very close to birth) to adulthood in total darkness, eliminating all externally generated visual experience. If experience with various visual depth cues is necessary for the development of depth perception, these dark-reared animals should have measurable impairments. If depth perception simply matures as the animal ages, then this restriction of visual experience should not affect its behavior. The only important variable should then be its chronological age.

One of the most popular methods of measuring depth perception in young animals has been the **visual cliff**, an apparatus devised by Walk and Gibson (1961). A diagram of the typical visual cliff is shown in Figure 10-16. In the visual cliff a central starting platform divides the floor of the apparatus into two sections. Each section provides a different kind of visual stimulation. The "shallow" section is a piece of glass that lies directly over a patterned surface. The "deep" section has the same patterned surface but is placed at some distance below the glass. Usually a young animal is placed on the central starting platform that separates the shallow and the deep sections. From this position, the animal can see that the shallow side is safe; however, the deep side, since it simulates a clifflike drop-off, is

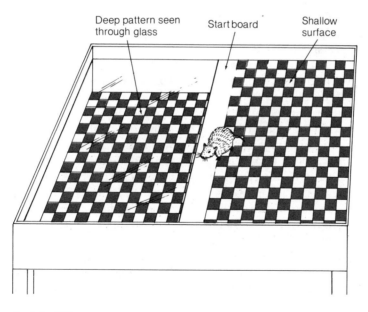

Deep pattern seen through glass   Start board   Shallow surface

Figure 10-16. The visual cliff.

perceived as dangerous. The experimenters assume that the animal wants to avoid a fall. Thus, the ability to perceive the drop-off in the visual cliff leads the animal to prefer walking on the shallow side to avoid any contact with the deep side.

Researchers have exposed a wide variety of animal species to the visual cliff. Walk and Gibson (1961) experimented with visual cliff behavior in infant and adult rats, chickens, and sheep, as well as turtles, goats, pigs, kittens, puppies, infant monkeys, and infant humans. In all cases, the animals preferred the shallow side over the deep side. Aquatic turtles did not show the marked preference for the shallow side that the other, more landbound species displayed. In like fashion, Walk (1962, 1964) showed that rabbits chose the shallow side consistently, but ducklings walked on either side with equal ease. Once again, ducklings are aquatic animals. The survival value of cliff avoidance may not be as pronounced in animals that spend much of their lives swimming, since changes in the depth of water are not as perilous as sudden sharp drops on land.

Although these cross-species studies are of interest, the visual cliff apparatus has been used primarily to generate data concerning the development of depth perception. The combination of controlled rearing followed by observations of behavior on the visual cliff has been a widely used experimental technique. Several interesting interactions between experience and innate factors have emerged from these studies. For example, Walk and Gibson (1961) reared kittens in the dark for four weeks. Initially, the kittens showed no depth discrimination on the visual cliff. As they received more experience in a lighted world, however, their depth discrimination rapidly improved. Thus, their lack of early visual experience caused initial deficits that were remedied by later visual experience. Tees and

Midgley (1978) have shown similar results in rats; the effects of early rearing in the dark on the rats' perception of depth are rectified by increasing their exposure to a normal lighted environment.

There seems to be a crucial age at which restricted or controlled rearing has an effect on an animal's depth discrimination. If the animal does not have visual experience during this sensitive period, then there is a measurable perceptual deficit; otherwise, dark rearing seems to have no effect (Aslin, 1981; Mitchell, 1981). A demonstration of how physical maturation, experience and sensitive periods interact was provided by Tees (1974). Dark-reared rats were compared with light-reared rats on their preference for the deep side versus the shallow side of the visual cliff. The animals were tested at 20, 40, 60, and 80 days after birth. In addition, the depth of the drop in the visual cliff was varied from 10 to 25 cm. Tees reported that the age of the animal and the size of the drop interacted. Both the light-reared and dark-reared rats, regardless of the age at which they were tested, preferred the shallow side when the depth difference between the two sides was 20 or 25 cm. At the two shallowest depths (10 and 15 cm) the young animals (20 days old) showed no effect of either light or dark rearing. Neither group showed a significant preference for the shallow side at that age. Thus, there was no significant effect of light rearing versus dark rearing at the two deepest depths (20 and 25 cms), nor was there an effect of rearing conditions for the young animals at the shallowest depths. It was only among the older animals (60 and 80 days old) that the effects of rearing conditions revealed themselves. At 60 and 80 days old, at least 75 percent of the light-reared rats, regardless of the depth difference, showed a preference for the shallow side of the visual cliff. The dark-reared rats, however, seemed to be insensitive to depth differences less than 15 cm. These data indicate that there may be inborn components in the ability of rats to discriminate depth on the visual cliff. These inborn components are probably sharpened through experience with depth cues in the environment.

The development of depth perception in humans. Similar data have emerged from studies with humans. The use of the visual cliff requires an animal that is old enough to be independently mobile. Therefore, to test human newborns who are still too young to crawl, other response measures have been employed. One such response involves a component of the *orienting reflex* (this will be discussed more fully in Chapter 15). When there is a change in stimulation in the external field, we find a series of physiological changes that coincides with the turning of attention toward novel or changed stimulation. One physiological change is the *deceleration* or slowing of the heartbeat when we orient toward a novel stimulus. There is evidence that this heart rate deceleration is part of a human observer's response of interest and attention to a novel and interesting stimulus (Graham and Clifton, 1966; Graham and Jackson, 1970). On the other hand, our heartbeat *accelerates*, or speeds up, as a component of our reaction to intense, alarming stimuli. This may be a defensive reaction against potentially dangerous stimulation. Therefore, changes in heart rate can be used by experimenters to differentiate between situations an observer finds alarming and those that are interesting or novel (Sokolov, 1960).

A number of investigators have used this technique to look at young infants' response patterns when they are placed on both sides of the visual cliff. For example, Campos, Langer, and Krowitz (1970) placed 2-month-old infants face down on the shallow side and then on the deep side of the visual cliff. Greater heart rate deceleration occurred when the infants were placed on the deep side. This was interpreted as indicating that the infant could discriminate between the two sides but was not sensitive to the danger of the drop-off. On the other hand, Schwartz, Campos, and Baisel (1972) found that nine-month-old infants showed a heart rate acceleration when placed on the deep side of the visual cliff. These results imply that for infants between two and nine months of age, the lack of visual stimulation indicating bodily support becomes a danger signal.

Most contemporary psychologists agree that capabilities to orient oneself in visual space are present at an early age. They also agree, however, that experience in the world plays some role in the full development of distance and depth perception. In this context, recent work with human infants on the visual cliff has emphasized the developmental components that contribute to an avoidance or lack of avoidance of the deep side of the cliff. Although early studies with infants of crawling age indicated that very few crossed the deep side of the visual cliff (Gibson and Walk, 1960), more recent studies have found that more than 50 percent of the crawling infants tested cross the deep side (Campos, Hiatt, Ramsay, Henderson, and Svejda, 1978). In an attempt to explain this lack of avoidance behavior (which on the surface appears to be disfunctional), investigators have argued that the age at which an infant begins to crawl is an important factor in determining whether or not she will avoid the deep side of the visual cliff. For example, Rader, Bausano, and Richards (1980) have proposed that there is a perceptual-motor "program" that matures as an infant grows older and directs crawling behavior. If an infant begins to crawl before this perceptual-motor program (which is assumed to be biological) comes under visual control, crawling will be controlled more by touch than by visual information. In other words, they argue that visual control needs a particular time period to develop, although an infant may begin to crawl before the development of this control. This argument predicts that infants who crawl at an early age (for example, before 7 months of age) will be more likely to cross the deep side of the visual cliff than infants who start to crawl at a later age during the first year of life. The infants who crawl at an early age are, theoretically, less responsive to the visual depth cues present in the cliff arrangement than the infants who crawl at a later age. Data support this prediction (Rader, Bausano, and Richards, 1980; Richards and Rader, 1981) and demonstrate the interaction between the maturation of a perceptual-motor ability and the degree of crawling experience in the development of cliff avoidance in human infants.

Unfortunately, the visual cliff testing situation is one in which many depth cues can be operating simultaneously to guide the infants' responses. Therefore, a number of investigators have studied the development of individual sources of depth information. One area that has received much recent attention is sensitivity to binocular disparity in human infants. Fox, Aslin, Shea, and Dumais (1980) have provided a demonstration of stereopsis in human infants. They presented moving random dot stereograms to infants between 2 and 5 months old. The infants wore special goggles allowing them to see a moving square floating in front of a background only if they could combine the disparate information from both eyes' views. As you remember from Demonstration Box 10-4, random dot stereograms are meaningless unless you can make use of the disparity cues hidden in each monocular view. Observers, unaware of the direction of stimulus movement, monitored and recorded the directions of the infants' gaze patterns. They

found that by the age of 3 months, infants showed reliable responsiveness to the stereoscopic display. It seems that sensitivity to disparity information develops at an early age. Other studies, using different measurement techniques, have confirmed this result; stereoscopic discrimination appears to be present in infants by the age of 3 to 4 months (Braddick, Atkinson, Julesz, Kropfl, Bodis-Wollner, and Raab, 1980; Hutz and Bechtoldt, 1980; Petrig, Julesz, Kropfl, Baumgartner, and Anliker, 1981).

Other studies have shown that infants and young children are also sensitive to pictorial depth cues. For example, several studies have shown that 6- to 7-month-old infants respond to linear perspective information (Kaufman, Maland, and Yonas, 1981; Yonas, Cleaves, and Pettersen, 1978). In addition, Yonas, Goldsmith, and Hallstrom (1978) have shown that by the age of 3 years, children can perceive depth in pictures that is appropriate to the direction of the shadows cast in the pictorial representation. One biologically important aspect of depth perception is motion perspective (a sensitivity to object motion toward the body) which protects the infant from impending collisions. It has been measured at ages as young as two to three weeks old (Ball and Vurpillot, 1976; Yonas, 1981).

These studies demonstrate that contemporary emphasis is on understanding the interaction between maturational and experiential factors in the development of depth perception. The earlier, very strict, dichotomy between the nativist and the empiricist has been replaced by an acknowledgment that there are both innate and learned components in depth perception. The innate components must mature, and certain types of experience can help or hinder the maturation of the ability to extract useful spatial information.

DIRECTION

At the beginning of this chapter, we stated that space perception includes not only the ability to judge distances, but also the ability to assess direction. In Chapter 8, we discussed factors that contribute to our directionalizing ability in the auditory modality, so here we will concentrate on describing judgments of visual direction.

Most judgments involve the direction of objects relative to the body. Howard (1982) has specified two types of visual directional judgments, which are coordinated in a complex way to give us a stable sense of up, down, right and left. The first type Howard calls *body-centric* direction, which uses, as a reference point, the midline of the body (an imaginary vertical line, parallel to the spine, passing

through the naval). The second type is called *headcentric* direction, which uses the midline of the head (an imaginary line passing through the middle of the nose) as another reference point for right and left. You can see that bodycentric and headcentric directions are different since the head can independently change its direction relative to the body. For example, an object may lie straight ahead of the midline of the body, but may lie to the left of the midline of a head that is turned to the right. The difference between bodycentric and headcentric direction is shown in Figure 10-17.

The visual straight ahead

If we think of the head or body as the center point of a circle, we can refer to **radial**

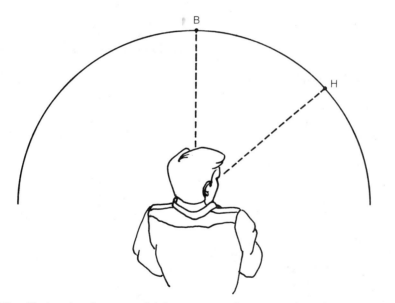

*Figure 10-17. The distinction between body-centric and headcentric directions. B is straight ahead of the body midline, while H is straight ahead of the midline of the head. No-*tice, *however, that these two straight ahead directions are two different points in visual space.*

direction as in the points of a compass (Rock, 1975). The point on this compass of radial direction that has received the most research attention is the visual *straight ahead* direction. First, we must know if the straight ahead direction is relative to the body or the head. Most researchers have concentrated on headcentric judgments of the straight ahead direction. When we talk about an object lying straight ahead of us, what do we mean? A first guess might be that objects directly in front of our eyes, whose images are stimulating the foveas of both eyes, would be seen as straight ahead. Instead, we localize the straight ahead direction as around the midline of the head, regard-

less of eye position. This implies that we are "taking account" of our eye position in our judgments of direction. The visual directions of both eyes, although slightly different because of their spatial separation in the head, are referred to a common **egocenter**. The visual egocenter is the position in the head that serves as our reference point for the determination of headcentric straight ahead. Because straight ahead seems to be in front of the center of the head, researchers often refer to direction in terms of a **Cyclopean eye**, a name derived from the mythical Greek giant *Cyclops*, who had a single eye in the middle of his forehead. Demonstration Box 10-5 shows

---

Demonstration Box 10-5. The common visual direction of the two eyes

You can experience how the visual directions of the two eyes are referred to one common direction in the center of the head. First, take a sheet of stiff cardboard (20 × 27 cm will do) and place it in front of the eyes as shown in the figure. Put a dot in the middle of the far end of the cardboard and stare at it while a friend marks the exact center position of each of your pupils on the end of the cardboard closest to your face. Next, draw lines from these marked points until they form an angle, or "V" (as pictured below). Finally, reposition the cardboard in front of your face at a point slightly below the eyes. Now, stare at the far point where the two drawn lines intersect, and you should see, in addition to the two lines you have drawn, an additional, somewhat more shadowy line running between them. This "new" line is the fusion of the views of the two eyes and should appear to point directly at a spot close to the midline of the head. This demonstrates that, although the direction of each eye's view is different (as shown by the spatial separation between the two drawn lines converging on the far point on which

you are fixating), the visual direction of the combined binocular view is referred to a common point between the eyes. This point is called the **egocenter**, or the **Cyclopean eye**.

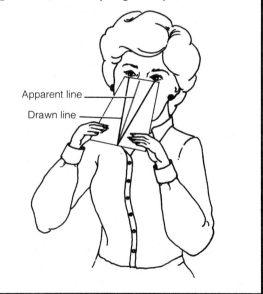

Apparent line
Drawn line

Demonstration Box 10-6. Sighting dominance and the straight ahead direction

The visual straight ahead may depend upon a single eye (Porac and Coren, 1976, 1981; Walls, 1951). Try the following demonstration to see how this works. Stand in front of a wall at a distance of about 3 m. Pick a point on the wall that is directly in front of you (a small crack or bump will do). Now, with both eyes opened, *quickly* stretch out your arm and align your fingertip with the point on the distant wall. When the alignment has been completed, alternately close each eye. You will find that the point on the distant wall will shift out of alignment for one of the eyes. However, the other eye will seem to be aligned with

the point on the wall whether one or both eyes are opened. The eye that maintains the alignment is called the **sighting dominant eye**. You will notice that regardless of which hand you use to perform the alignment, you will tend to line up a near (your fingertip) and a distant (the point on the wall) target in terms of the same eye. The presence of a sighting dominant eye, and our tendency to make a straight ahead alignment in terms of this eye, indicates that the locus of the egocentric straight ahead direction may be shifted toward the side of the sighting dominant eye.

---

how you can experience for yourself the referring of the visual direction of the two eyes to this common egocenter.

Unfortunately, this explanation of the determination of the visual straight ahead direction may be an oversimplification, since the two eyes are not used equivalently. When only one eye can be used, such as in peering through a telescope, 65 percent of all observers consistently use their right eye, while the remainder consistently use their left. This pattern is measurable even in young children (Coren, Porac, and Duncan, 1981). The preferred eye is usually called the **sighting dominant eye** (Porac and Coren, 1981a; Ruggieri, Cei, Ceridono, and Bergerone, 1980). Demonstration Box 10-6 shows how you can determine which eye is your sighting dominant eye.

In terms of the perception of direction, sighting dominance may be important because the visual direction associated with straight ahead may be positioned in front of the dominant eye or at least biased toward this eye (Porac and Coren, 1976, 1981). Thus, while information from both eyes is used in judg-

ments of the visual straight ahead (Ono and Weber, 1981), the location of the egocenter or Cyclopean eye may be influenced by the sighting dominant eye. Barbeito (1981) measured eye dominance in a group of observers using a method similar to that described in Demonstration Box 10-6. He then measured the position of the egocenter by asking observers to position two targets until they formed a straight line pointing directly at their heads. He found that his observers positioned the targets so that they pointed at a location between the eyes. For 90 percent of the observers, however, the visual egocenter did not lie directly between the eyes but was shifted toward the side of the sighting dominant eye. Howard (1982) has pointed out that the position of the sighting eye in the head plays a role in aligning objects in external space (as you saw in Demonstration Box 10-6). Information from both eyes is probably quite important in determining visual direction; eye dominance simply affects the placement of the egocenter, so that the Cyclopean eye may be viewed as slightly off center, shifted in its direction.

Our sense of straight ahead also varies with the visual information available. For instance, our ability to judge direction is much less stable in the dark. Also, specific visual configurations influence our judgments. If the observer is viewing a target, such as a square or rectangle, that is not centered in the visual field, there is a tendency to judge the straight ahead direction in terms of the center of the displaced square or rectangle. It is as if the perceptual system confuses what is straight ahead with what is centered with respect to the other contents of the visual field (Roelofs, 1935). This is demonstrated in Figure 10-18.

Development of direction perception

What about the innate versus the learned origins of direction perception? Here, the evidence is clearer than that encountered in our discussion of depth and distance. Animals lower on the evolutionary scale seem to have an inborn sense of direction. Hess (1950) has shown that immediately after birth, chicks peck at small objects with reasonable accuracy. If the images of targets are optically displaced to one side (using special lenses attached to hoods), the chicks systematically peck to that side, and this pattern of inaccuracy shows little improvement over time. In salamanders, it is possible to rotate the eye 180 degrees, inverting the retina. When this is done, the salamanders consistently swim and snap in the opposite direction when presented with a food lure (Sperry, 1943). Because the same results occur in similar operations during the animals' embryonic stage, visual direction clearly is innately related to the location of retinal stimulation in this species (Stone, 1960). In humans, however, there are learned components to the assessment of visual direction since we learn to compensate for optical distortions in spatial direction, as we shall see in Chapter 17.

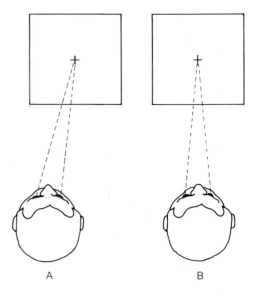

Figure 10-18. Shifts in the position of objects in the field of view can produce shifts in the perceived straight ahead direction. (A) Actual situation (+ to right side). (B) Perceived situation (+ straight ahead).

GLOSSARY

The following definitions are specific to this book.

Aerial perspective A distance cue in which distant objects appear hazy or less distinct because of the interaction of light with dust and moisture particles in the air.

Bifoveally fixate The situation in which an image stimulates both foveas.

Binocular disparity The difference in two monocular images resulting from the difference in direction of gaze of the two eyes.

Convergence The rotation of both eyes toward the nose as fixated objects become closer.

Corresponding retinal points Areas in the two retinas that share a common visual direction when the two monocular inputs are processed in the brain.

Crossed disparity (images) A cue for relative distance, where the unfused part of the image in the right eye appears on the left and that in the left eye on the right.

Cues Features of visual stimuli that prompt the perception of depth or distance.

Cyclopean eye An imaginary point midway between the eyes, thought to be used as a reference point for the straight ahead direction.

Diplopia Double vision.

Divergence The outward rotation of both eyes away from the nose as fixated objects become more distant.

Egocenter The position in the head that serves as the reference point for the determination of head-centric "straight ahead."

Egocentric localization The awareness of where our bodies are positioned relative to other objects in the external environment.

Familiar size The known or remembered size of objects.

Fusion The process by which disparate views are synthesized into one percept.

Global stereopsis Stereopsis not dependent on local contour elements (for example, as in random dot stereograms).

Height in the (picture) plane A cue for distance, referring to where an object is relative to the horizon.

Horopter An imaginary curved line in external space used to describe the region of fused images.

Interposition The depth cue based on the visual blocking of an object from view by another, closer object.

Monocular cues Depth information that requires only one eye to be used.

Motion parallax The relative apparent motion of objects in the visual field as the observer moves his head or body.

Motion perspective A depth cue based on the flow of elements in the retinal image as the observer moves.

Object-relative localizations The estimation of the relative positions of objects wihin the environment that are external to the observer.

Overlay *See* Interposition.

Panum's area The region around the horopter, where all images in space are fused.

Perspective The convergence of parallel lines as they recede into the distance.

Physiological cues *See* Structural cues.

Pictorial cues Cues for distance that can be found in photographs and pictures.

Radial direction In judging visual direction, using the body as the center point of a circle, we can refer to locations around the circle as points on a compass.

Relative brightness A depth cue in which the brighter of two otherwise identical objects will be seen as closer.

Retinal image size A potential depth cue based on the fact that the size of the retinal image of an object decreases with increasing distance from the eye.

Shadowing A depth cue based on differences in object or surface brightness that result from light interactions with textured surfaces.

Sighting dominant eye The eye the use of which is preferred in such monocular tasks as looking through a telescope.

Stereopsis The ability to see depth based solely on the disparity of the two retinal images.

Stereoscope An optical instrument enabling two different images to stimulate the two eyes simultaneously.

Structural cues Depth and distance cues based on the physiology of the visual system.

Texture gradient Distance cue based on variations in apparent surface texture as a function of distance from the observer.

Uncrossed disparity (images) A cue to distance in which the unfused part of the image in the right eye appears in the right field of view and that in the left eye appears on the left.

Visual cliff A device used for measuring depth perception in young animals.

11

Time and motion

THE EXASPERATED MOTHER GLARED AT her teenaged son. "Have you no sense of time?" she growled. "This afternoon you said you just wanted to talk on the phone to Judy for a few minutes and you were at it for two hours!"

"Mom, it only seemed like five minutes!"

"And tonight you said you were going to put in a full evening studying for your exams and you're back downstairs in ten minutes!"

"But Mom," came the puzzled reply, "It felt like I had been studying for three hours!"

The passage of time is a psychological experience. In some ways, however, time can be treated as a stimulus continuum, just as any other perceptual event has its physical stimulus. Fraisse (1963) has pointed out that our notion of time is tied to our experience of successive change. Changes occur continually, sometimes with the regularity of night following day, and sometimes with irregularity, such as moving to a new house. The swift or slow passage of time appears to be linked to our experience of a continual flux of events. Change is also responsible for the perception of motion. Here the change refers to spatial position. If an object is perceived to have changed its position from one moment to the next, then under appropriate circumstances, we perceive it as moving. Time and motion thus represent dynamic qualities of perceptual experience.

TIME

The study of time perception has posed many complex problems for investigators, since "time is not a thing that, like an apple, may be perceived" (Woodrow, 1951). Poppel (1978), who has summarized the research history of time perception, also has identified five types of psychological experience associated with the passage of time. Each form of time perception may be different from the others and may be maintained by different physiological or information processing mechanisms. The first is *duration estimation*, which is a report of how much time has elapsed between two events (for example, between the time that the alarm goes off and the time that you get out of bed). Such estimates use conventional time units, such as seconds and minutes. The second experience is *simultaneity versus successiveness*. Here one determines the minimum time interval separating two events before they are perceived to be occurring one after the other rather than at the same moment. The third experience is *order, or sequencing*, in which we assign time tags to events as they occur so that we can identify which came first, then next, and so on (for example, the correct order of digits in a telephone number that a friend gives you verbally). The fourth experience is the *subjective present*, which has been described by William James (1890) as the "saddle-back of time with a certain length of its own, on which we sit perched, and from which we look in two directions into time." In other words, the subjective present is the few seconds we experience as here and now, and all else is either past or future. Fifth, and last, is the action of *anticipation or planning*, or the ordered sequencing of events before they occur. This last aspect of time perception is especially important in such actions as talking in which we automatically plan and execute an ordered sequence of sounds that has meaning.

Two general theoretical approaches have guided research into all five areas of time perception. The first is called the **internal timer hypothesis**. This theory assumes that there is a biological or physiological basis to our perception of time. Just as we have a sense organ that is sensitive to light (the eye), we also must have a sense organ that keeps track of

313

time. The phrase "a sense of time" stems from this general orientation. The internal timer hypothesis has been particularly important in researching simultaneity and successiveness, because it suggests that the experience is determined by an internal clock that ticks at a particular rate. Events are perceived as simultaneous if they occur between the same two ticks of the clock and as successive if the clock ticks between their occurrence. Thus, it is not surprising to find that an issue for the internal timer hypothesis is the search for the basic unit of internal time.

In agreement with the idea of an internal clock are several lines of evidence suggesting that time is an integral aspect of naturally occurring processes. Many physical phenomena have their own rhythm or timing, for example, the day-night cycles, the cycles of the moon, and the cycles of the seasons. Living organisms often display rhythmic activities. Many flowers open at particular periods of the day, and the cycle of opening and closing may follow a temporal sequence. Certain physiological processes in animals have a cycle of periodic change. One of the most obvious of these is the waking-sleeping cycle. For humans, periods of wakefulness and sleep follow regular rhythms during a 24-hour period.

Other, more subtle physiological processes have their own periodic changes. For example, the pulse, blood pressure, and temperature of the body demonstrate day-night variations in humans and many animals. There is a difference of more than 1°C in body temperature between the coolest point, which occurs during the night, and the warmest point, which occurs during the afternoon. Other body functions also demonstrate rhythmic aspects. Heartbeats, electrical activity in the brain, breathing, walking, and finger tapping seem to occur at regular intervals. All these physiological processes, at one time or another, have

been suggested as candidates for an internal biological timing mechanism (Ornstein, 1969; Poppel, 1978; Treisman, 1963).

The second general approach to the investigation of the experience of time is the **event processing hypothesis**. This approach dismisses the notion that our perception of time depends on a continuous internal timer. Here, time is viewed as a purely cognitive process that is not tied to any objective or "clock" time. Our experience of time is based on the amount of sensory information processed during a particular interval. According to this view, time is not a real entity that we can perceive by means of a sensory system; rather, we experience time by the psychological events occurring over a physically defined period. The experience of time is not tied to any physiological process; it is a mental construct that comes about through our processing of differing amounts and types of incoming information. In effect, this approach involves a measure of time based on counting the number of events occurring to the observer rather than ticks of an internal clock. This approach has dominated research concerning duration estimation.

Before we go any further, let us be clear as to what we mean by time. These distinctions are important if you are to understand the research findings on time perception. Imagine that there are three clocks that control our lives. The first is a *physical clock*. Each tick of this clock represents a regularly occurring physical event, such as the vibrations of the nitrogen atom in ammonia (the international time standard) or the revolution of the earth around the sun (solar time). Physical time is marked off by the number of these regularly occurring events (conveniently grouped into such units as centuries or seconds). The second clock is a *physiological clock*. Each tick of this clock is represented by internally generated physiological events. Thus, we have regular sleeping and wakefulness patterns based on a **circadian rhythm** (from the Latin *circa dia*, meaning "approximately a day"), which ticks off approximately 24-hour units. Females have an approximately 28-day cycle marked off by the hormonal shifts of the menstrual cycle, while males manifest an approximately 9-week physiological cycle that is also based on hormonal fluctuations. Finally, our third clock is a *psychological clock*. This clock, which determines our conscious experience of time, is the clock we are concerned with here.

Duration estimation

The area of time perception most widely studied is that in which observers are asked to estimate the duration of some event. Both the internal timer and the event processing approaches have been used to explain duration estimation. According to our psychological clock, how long does an event endure? How does psychologically clocked time compare with physically clocked time? Our experience of brief (under 1 second) and relatively long (minutes, hours, and days) durations has been investigated.

First, let us consider the perception of time intervals less than one minute. Much of the research in the estimation of brief time periods has been psychophysical. For example, researchers have tried to pinpoint the form of the relationship between real or clock time and perceptual time in the manner that was discussed in the scaling section of Chapter 2. Considerable data support a linear relationship between perceived time and stimulus time (at least for intervals up to 10 seconds). There are some deviations from a simple relationship, however. Unfortunately, attempts to apply

more traditional psychophysical concepts to duration perception, such as Weber's law, have not proved to be always successful (Allan, 1979).

In general, when asked to estimate the duration of time intervals, observers tend to overestimate brief intervals and underestimate longer intervals (Ward, 1975; Woodrow, 1951). There also seems to be a particular duration that does not give rise to either an overestimation or an underestimation of its length. This duration, which seems to be around 0.7 seconds (700 msec), has been termed the **indifference interval** (Ornstein, 1969; Treisman, 1963). Because this duration is measured as equally long by both the physical (real passage of clock time) and psychological (estimated passage of clock time) clocks, some investigators have hypothesized that it represents the basic time unit of the internal timer.

Some data from duration perception support the contention that our experience of duration is tied to the amount and type of stimulus information we process during a given time interval, rather than to an internal clock (Ornstein, 1969). For example, let us look at a phenomenon called the **filled duration illusion**. A duration filled with stimulus events is perceived as longer than an identical duration empty of any external events. In other words, if we fill a 1-second interval with brief tones, this interval will be perceived as longer than an identical 1-second period defined only by a beginning and an ending tone (Ornstein, 1969; Thomas and Brown, 1974). The existence of this illusion supports an event processing approach to time perception. Because there are more stimuli to process within a filled duration, this period is perceived as longer than one identical in physical time but devoid of information processing requirements. A number of interesting variations to the filled duration illusion also imply a relationship between duration estimation and information processing. For example, observers judge the brief presentation of a word to be longer than a blank interval of the same length (Thomas and Weaver, 1975). However, an important aspect of time perception is the amount of actual information processed, rather than simply the number of stimulus events that occur. Thus, the presentation interval of familiar words is judged to be shorter than the presentation interval of meaningless verbal stimuli (Avant and Lyman, 1975; Avant, Lyman, and Antes, 1975). In both instances, an increase in the amount of information processing required during the interval (a word versus a blank and a meaningless group of letters versus a word) leads to increases in the estimated duration of the interval.

Research on longer time intervals (those extending over minutes, hours, or days) also suggests that both the internal timer and the event processing theories of time perception may be useful. For example, Hoagland (1933) suggested that if there were an internal timer, it would speed up or slow down with other physiological processes in the body. When Hoagland's wife was ill with a fever, he took the opportunity to engage in some experimental observations. He asked her to estimate 1 minute by counting to 60 at a rate of one number per second. When her body temperature was approximately 39°C (103°F), her perceived minute was only 37.5 seconds by objective clock time. Hoagland reasoned that at higher body temperatures, when physiological activities increase their speed, the internal timer ticks more rapidly than usual. This means that when asked to reproduce a given physical time interval, a person with a high body temperature produces an interval that is too short. An alternate way of looking at this is to note how our perception of physical (clock) time will change when psychological time is running quickly. A given physical duration will appear too long if a psychological clock is ticking faster than the physical clock, hence giving more ticks per unit time than normally occurs (see Figure 11-1).

Hoagland's observations lead us to expect

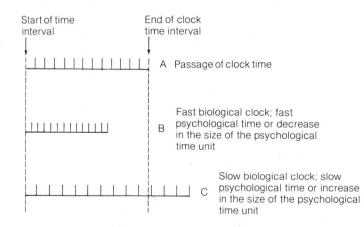

Figure 11-1. Each unit on lines A, B, C represents a unit of time. Those in B are one-half the size of those in A, while those in C are one and one-half the size of those in A. When the biological clock speeds up, leading to a de- *crease in the size of the psychological time unit, we tend to overestimate the passage of time, and clock time seems to "drag" by. The opposite occurs when the biological clock slows down.*

Demonstration Box 11-1. Body temperature and time perception

This demonstration is based on an experiment performed by Pfaff (1968). We know that our body temperature can fluctuate as much as 1°C during the course of a day. It is at its lowest point early in the day and tends to rise throughout the afternoon. Given this, try the following observations. Upon rising in the morning, try counting to 60 at the rate of what you perceive to be one number per second. You will probably need a friend to keep track of clock time for you so that you can relate your perceived minute to a clock

minute. Then take your temperature. (Do not take your temperature before you count, otherwise it may bias your counting rate.) Do this several times throughout the day, and keep a record of your results. If the theory is supported, you should find that your counting time will shorten (relative to a clock minute) as your body temperature increases. Thus, as the body clock speeds up, the passage of time tends to be overestimated and "clock" time seems to pass more slowly.

---

that lowering body temperature will have the opposite effect. Baddeley (1966) tested this effect with scuba divers diving in cold water off the coast of Wales. He asked the divers to count to 60 at a rate of one number per second. After the dive, when their body temperature was approximately 1°C lower than it had been before entering the water, they required approximately 70 seconds to count to 60. This result indicated that their internal timer was ticking at a slower rate than the external clock. The divers were counting time using the slower ticking rate of their internal timer. This led them to underestimate the passage of time. In other words, when your internal clock is too slow, physical time seems to whiz by (see Figure 11-1). You may demonstrate the effects of temperature on your own time sense by using Demonstration Box 11-1.

The notion of a physiologically controlled internal timer is also supported by data on the effect of drugs on the experience of time. As a general rule, people overestimate the passage of clock time when under the influence of stimulants and underestimate it when under the influence of sedatives (Fraisse, 1963). Conversely, a number of investigators have found

that such drugs as amphetamines and caffeine (both of which are stimulants) lead to a lengthening of time experience (Frankenhauser, 1959; Goldstone, Boardman, and Lhamon, 1958). General anesthetics, on the other hand, lead to a shortening of time experience (Adam, Rosner, Hosick, and Clark, 1971; Steinberg, 1955). Such drugs as marijuana, mescaline, psilocybin, and LSD seem to produce a lengthening of perceived time relative to a nondrug state (Fisher, 1967; Weil, Zinberg, and Nelson, 1968). It has been argued that all these changes in time perception are caused by physiological acceleration or deceleration of the internal timer.

A rather wide body of evidence supports the notion that our experience of longer periods of time involves the information processing requirements of stimulus events. Ornstein (1969) has provided evidence that durations filled with more elements are judged to be longer than durations filled with fewer elements (this is the filled-duration illusion discussed earlier). He presented his observers with tape recordings marking off the same physical time (approximately 10 minutes). The tapes differed from one another only in that sounds were recorded on the tapes at different rates. These rates varied from 40 to 120 tones per minute. In confirmation of the event processing hypothesis, in which time estimation is based on the amount of information processed during the interval, Ornstein found that the tape that had 40 tones per minute was judged shorter than the tape that had 120 tones per minute. Similar results have been reported in the visual and tactual modalities (Buffardi, 1971; Mescavage, Heimer, Tatz, and Runyon, 1971). Thus, durations filled with more events are judged to be longer than durations filled with fewer events.

Other experimental evidence supports the hypothesis that variations in time perception are caused by variations in information processing rates. For example, this hypothesis predicts that situations that increase our awareness or heighten our motivation to attend should lead to a lengthening of time perception, because when aroused, we attend to more stimuli and process information more rapidly. In a study by Filer and Meals (1949) subjects were given different motivational sets for performing simple tasks. Subjects who were told that a desirable goal would be obtained on completion of their tasks tended to overestimate the passage of time relative to conditions in which subjects were not given these expectancy sets. These findings are consistent with the folk saying that "a watched pot never boils," or the common experience of time dragging by as we await the fun of opening gifts on Christmas morning. More recent research, where in some instances observers actually were asked to watch a pot of water until it boiled, has confirmed the finding that expectancies concerning an event (for example, the boiling of water) lead to an overestimation of the passage of clock time (Block, George, and Reed, 1980; Cahoon and Edmonds, 1980). Ornstein (1969) would in-

terpret this as the result of the expectancy leading to a greater awareness of the input of information and thus a lengthening of subjective duration. A study by Falk and Bindra (1954) is consistent with this idea. They placed observers in a stress situation (receiving electrical shocks) and found that these observers also overestimated the passage of physical time.

Other factors, such as the complexity of stimuli being processed, also affect time estimates. Complex stimuli, which would be expected to cause an increase in attention and awareness, cause increases in subjective time estimates over situations in which less complex stimuli are being processed (Burnside, 1971; Ornstein, 1969). Given such data, it is possible to reinterpret the effects of various drugs on the perception of time from the event processing viewpoint. One could argue that any drug that increases alertness or results in a heightened state of awareness does not affect the speed of an internal timer but rather increases the amount of sensory input processed per unit of time. This, in turn, is what leads to the increase in perceived time.

Clearly, support exists for both the internal timer and the event processing hypotheses in the data on duration estimation. Neither of these viewpoints, however, provides a complete picture. Time is really an intangible aspect of our experience. We are aware of its effects but we do not experience it in ways that are similar to our experience of light or sound. The elusive nature of our experience of time makes it susceptible to variations resulting from individual styles, motivations, attitudes, and expectations. For example, estimates of a given duration may change as we vary an observer's perceptual task. If an observer is asked to reproduce a time interval, as opposed to giving a verbal estimate of its length, different types of data may result (Allan, 1979; Ornstein and Rotter, 1969). Similarly, duration judgments may also be affected by whether or not observers know in advance that they will be asked to make a time estimate (Hicks, Miller, and Kinsbourne, 1976) or by how often they are asked to repeat the time estimation (Hicks and Allen, 1979). There seem to be age differences in the ability to make accurate time estimates. For instance, when elementary school-aged children are asked to make estimates of the duration of a 1 second interval, their estimates are extremely variable. This variability in time estimation decreases with age. When 6- to 7-year-olds are given feedback as to the accuracy of the estimates, they do not seem to benefit. It is not until around the age of 8 years that children are able to improve their performance as a result of information about the accuracy of their time estimates (Smythe and Goldstone, 1957).

Such data indicate that the strategy an observer uses when estimating time can affect measurements of subjective duration. Although such data do not directly address themselves to the event processing hypothesis of time perception, they do seem more compatible with it than with the internal timer hypothesis. The data support the notion that the judgmental strategy and the distribution of attention in particular tasks can affect subjective estimates of duration, yet it is unlikely that these factors would directly affect the speed of a biological clock.

There may be a way to resolve the differences between the internal timer and the event processing hypotheses of time perception. Polzella, Dapolito, and Hinsman (1977) had observers estimate the duration of various dot patterns, which differed in terms of the number of stimulus elements they contained. They also varied the appearance of the dots on the left or the right sides of the visual field. You will recall from Chapter 3 that a target in

the left half of the visual field is imaged on the right side of the retina and vice versa. Furthermore, all stimuli imaged on the left side of the retina of either eye are first processed in the left cerebral hemisphere, while all those imaged on the right side of the retina are first processed by the right hemisphere. Polzella et al. (1977) found that when patterns were presented to the right visual field (the left hemisphere), duration estimates were more consistent with the internal timer hypothesis, while duration estimates of patterns presented to the left visual field (right hemisphere) were more consistent with the event processing hypothesis. They concluded that the left hemisphere of the brain relies on an internal timer to estimate duration, while the right hemisphere relies on event processing (Thomas and Weaver, 1975). Because both hemispheres are available for most tasks, both methods of estimating time may be used by observers in the majority of tasks involving time perception.

Simultaneity and successiveness

Although more evidence appears to support the event processing notion of time perception in research on duration estimation, the search for the basic timing unit or the basic timing rate has dominated research surrounding the perception of simultaneity and succession.

Stroud (1955) maintained that time is not a continuous dimension; rather, it is broken into discrete bits called *moments*. These **perceptual moments** are the psychological unit of time. We have already mentioned that the *indifference interval* (the time interval where there is no discrepancy between perceived time and clock time, which is about 700 msec in duration) has been proposed as one value that represents the time interval between the ticks of the internal clock, or the perceptual moment. This appears to be too long an interval, however, given the accuracy of simultaneity and succession judgments. Drawing on various research findings (including patterns of electrical activity in the brain), Stroud estimated that each moment is about 100 msec in duration. According to this point of view, the shortest perceived duration a stimulus can have is one moment, or 100 msec. In addition, stimuli presented within the same moment would either be perceived as occurring simultaneously, or depending on the nature of the stimulus, would be indistinguishable. Stimuli presented in different moments would be perceived as sequentially presented, separated by a variable number of perceptual moments. White (1963) tested this notion by having observers estimate the number of clicks they heard. He presented the clicks at different rates up to 25 per second. Observers were fairly accurate at rates up to five per second. At the highest click rates, however, observers still estimated a presentation rate of six to seven clicks per second. This corresponds to a perceived rate of one stimulus every 150 msec. Thus, information could not be processed in "chunks" smaller than 150 msec, which would be the resolution limit of the internal timer.

Efron (1967) also tried to measure the perceptual moment. In one study he presented two brief pulses of light and asked observers to say which one was longer. One of the flashes was always 1 msec in duration. The other was of a variable duration. Both flashes were always perceived as the same length until the exposure time of the variable flash exceeded a value of 60 or 70 msec. At this duration, it was perceived as longer than the 1 msec flash. Efron concluded that the minimum duration of a stimulus in consciousness (which should be one perceptual moment) was around 60 or 70 msec.

Other types of research support a perceptual moment that is even shorter in duration, perhaps around 30 msec (Poppel, 1978). For example, reaction time studies (where observers are asked to react as quickly as possible to a stimulus input) have indicated that information is being processed at about the rate of 30 msec per item (Sternberg, 1975). The timing of well-trained motor tasks, such as typing or piano playing, also seems to support a 30 msec internal timing organization (Augenstine, 1962). Finally, Eriksen and Collins (1968) used a set of patterns, which if seen by themselves seemed random. If, however, two patterns were superimposed, either physically or psychologically, they contained a word. They found that when observers are shown patterns sequentially, recognition for the word was highest when the interval between the presentations is about 25 msec. This implies that the perception of simultaneity is maintained over only a 25 msec interval rather than one that approaches 100 msec. These data, taken together, indicate that the perception of simultaneity and succession may differ from the temporal relationships that exist in the physical stimulus. There is still controversy, however, over the unit of perceptual time, or how long it may be between ticks of the internal clock that monitors the time relationships between stimulus events.

Time and space

Perhaps the most intriguing aspect of time is the way it interacts with other sensory experiences. For instance, time and space affect each other. Suppose we flash two spatially separated lights in a dark room, one after the other. Now we ask an observer to estimate the distance between the two lights. As we increase the time between the offset of one light and the onset of the other, the observer's estimates of the distance between the two lights will also increase. This is called the **tau effect**. Exactly the opposite manipulation distorts time. If we decrease the distance between the two lights, keeping the time interval between the flashes constant, the observer reports that the time beween the offset of the first light and the onset of the second has shrunk. This is called the **kappa effect**. Both the tau and kappa effects illustrate that time and space exist in the consciousness of the observer and that they are not dictated by physical events alone. You can experience the tau effect for yourself by following the instructions in Demonstration Box 11-2.

Jones and Huang (1982) have argued that the tau and kappa effects arise because observers unconsciously apply certain hypotheses or assumptions about the nature of the perceptual situation. Here, observers treat the situation as if the first light were moving to the position of the second, despite the fact that there are actually two stationary but spatially separated stimuli. Once they assume that the lights are in motion, they next expect that a fixed distance is traversed in a given time. In other words, the longer the time, the greater the distance that can be covered, or conversely, the greater the distance, the longer the time it takes to traverse it. The tau and kappa illusions then occur through the application of these rules. Thus, when the time between flashes increases, we not only recognize that fact, but presume that the distance between the two stimuli (treating them as if they were end points from a path of movement) has also increased. This kind of explanation is quite consistent with many common behaviors that fuse judgments of time and distance. Thus, you might find yourself replying, when asked the distance between your residence and the campus of your university, "Well, it's about a 10 minute drive." This answer shows the interdependence of spatial extent and time judgments (and also the movement between two locations given a fixed speed) that have been hypothesized to give rise to the tau and kappa effects.

This explanation of the tau and kappa effects is reminiscent of the revolution created in physics when Albert Einstein proposed that time and motion do not have absolute values but can only be measured relative to one another. In his *theory of relativity* he maintained that physical time actually slows down as we move more quickly. We have already seen an example of *psychological relativity* in the kappa effect, where the distance an object is thought to move affects our judgment of time. In fact, time and motion are psychologically inseparable phenomena. Max Wertheimer demonstrated this interdependence in 1912 in another way. He began with two lights, separated in space, that could be flashed on and off sequentially. Next, he varied the time interval between the offset of the first light and the onset of the second light (we call this variable period the **interstimulus interval**). When the interstimulus interval was quite brief (less than 30 msec), observers reported that a light came on and *moved* from the first position in space to the second. If the interstimulus interval was longer than 200 msec, there was no perception of movement. Here, observers reported that they saw a light come on and then go off, followed by a second light that came on in a different position. This apparent movement is dependent on certain interstimulus intervals and also on the distance between the successive presentations of the stimuli. When the stimuli are separated by larger distances, longer time intervals between the stimuli are needed for apparent motion to be present (Farrell, 1983). Wertheimer called such apparent movement the **phi phenomenon**, although today the more usual term is

Demonstration Box 11-2. The tau effect

The **tau effect** is an interaction between time and space. Suppose that we have two pairs of stimuli, pair *A* and pair *B*. The members of each of the pairs are separated by the same physical distance, and we can alter the time interval between the offset of one member of the pair and the onset of the other. Under these conditions, we find that as we increase the offset–onset interval between the members of one pair, we will increase the perceived distance between them relative to the other pair of stimuli. Thus, increases in the time interval between successively stimulated points will lead to increases in the perceived distance between the two points.

Try the following demonstration. Cut an index card so that it has two points about 5 cm apart. Diagram *A* will help you visualize the stimulus. Make sure that the ends are rather narrow and come to a relatively sharp point. Simultaneously touch the ends of the notch to the underside of your forearm. Take note of the apparent distance between the two points of stimulation as they touch your skin. Next place one point on your skin. With a gentle twist of your wrist you can lift the point touching your skin and make contact with the other point. In other words, instead of stimulating your skin with both points simultaneously, you are applying the stimulation in a sequential order with one end of the notch following the other (see Diagram *B*). Under these circumstances, you should experience the distance between the two points of stimulation as longer than it was when the two stimuli were applied simultaneously. A sequential presentation means that the time interval between the offset of one stimulus and the onset of the second stimulus has increased. Thus the tau effect should operate to increase the perceived distance between the two points of stimulation on the skin during the sequential presentation. Try this experiment several times not only on yourself but on someone else. See how varying the time between touches varies the apparent distances.

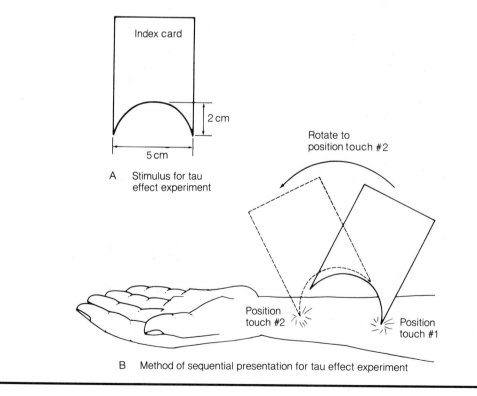

Index card

2 cm

5 cm

A   Stimulus for tau effect experiment

Rotate to position touch #2

Position touch #2

Position touch #1

B   Method of sequential presentation for tau effect experiment

---

Demonstration Box 11-3. Stroboscopic movement—the phi phenomenon

You can experience stroboscopic movement for yourself by following this simple demonstration. Take a small piece of paper and draw a short line (about 1 cm in length) in the center of it. Hold it directly in front of you at a distance of about 15–20 cm from your nose. Alternately close each eye while looking at the line. You will notice that the line seems displaced in the two separate views (this is due to the separation of the two eyes in space—see Chapter 11). Now alternately wink each eye in turn (you may have to do this with moderately rapid alternations between the eyes). At an appropriate rate of alternate winking, you will see the line apparently *move* between the two positions. This is phi, or stroboscopic, movement.

---

stroboscopic movement. Stroboscopic movement is interesting because it demonstrates that time relationships between stimuli can determine whether or not movement is perceived. It is also the basis of the apparent movement seen in motion pictures. Movies are, of course, made up of sets of projected still views of objects varying in spatial position, which are flashed in specific temporal sequences. The movement we see is illusory, just as in the phi phenomenon. You can demonstrate stroboscopic movement for yourself using Demonstration Box 11-3.

MOTION

Under normal viewing conditions, how do we perceive movement? At first, you might be tempted to say that we perceive motion when an image of an external object moves across the retinal receptors. We have just seen, however, that this condition is not necessary since stroboscopic movement exists. Actually, motion perception involves some fairly complex interactions among a number of different systems (see Sekuler, Ball, Tynan, and Machmer, 1982). For instance, it is possible for us to perceive movement when our eyes are in motion with the image of an object remaining fixed on only one portion of the retinal surface, such as when we follow a moving car with our eyes. There are also times when we should see movement but do not. Consider the fact that our eyes are in continual motion. This means that the images of stationary objects in the environment are sliding across our retinal receptors in stops and starts almost all the time. Despite all these image movements, we still perceive the world as stationary. Thus, movement of the retinal image does not fully account for the perception of motion. In general, there are two major movement perception systems that act together; they are the **image-retina system** and the **eye-head system** (Gregory, 1966). Both combine to determine whether a given movement on the retina has been caused by an observer or an eye movement, or whether it has been caused by the real movement of an external object.

The image-retina movement system

The image-retina system signals movement when there is motion in the retinal image but the eyes are stationary. This situation is diagrammed in Figure 11-2A. The image-retina system seems to operate by means of physiological *movement detectors*. These detectors may occur at several levels of the visual

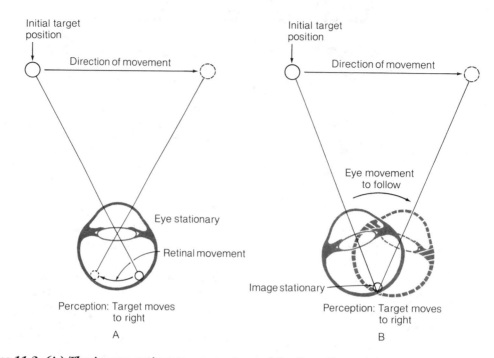

Figure 11-2. (A) The image-retina movement system. The image of the moving object stimulates the retina when the eyes are held stationary. This gives information about object motion, possibly as a result of the involvement of movement detecting cells. (B) One

of the functions of the eye-head movement system. When the eye pursues a moving target, the image remains stationary on the fovea of the eye, but we still perceive the movement of the object.

system. Thus, as we discussed in Chapter 3, the Y-type retinal ganglion cells are particularly well suited for the detection of movement, as opposed to the X-type cells, which are best suited for detail perception in stationary targets. At the cortical level, specialization for the detection of moving stimuli seems even clearer. Thus, we found numerous complex cells in the cortex of mammals responding only to moving targets. Furthermore, these cells seem to be directionally sensitive, strongly discharging when a properly oriented stimulus drifts in one direction across the visual field, and responding less strongly (or not at all) when the same stimulus moves through the vi-

sual field in the opposite direction (see Hubel and Wiesel, 1979). The actual degree of response specificity to moving stimuli may be quite strong. Thus, there are cells that respond not only to particular directions of movement but also to particular velocities or speeds of the moving targets (Orban, Kennedy, and Maes, 1981a,b). In fact there are some suggestions that the entire tecto-pulvinar pathway in vision may be specialized for the perception of movement and the direction of responses such as eye movements toward moving stimuli (Flandrin and Jeannerod, 1981; Guitton, Crommelink, and Roucoux, 1980; Van Essen, 1979).

A psychophysical technique called **selective**

adaptation can tell us about the nature of such movement-sensitive cells in humans (Sekuler, 1975). Its rationale is the same as the adaptation procedures we discussed in the spatial frequency section of Chapter 6. First, the eye is continually exposed to a moving pattern such as a field full of stripes. After prolonged exposure, the motion-specific cells that have been responding to the direction of the pattern's movement begin to fatigue and become less sensitive. In other words, we have adapted the visual system to movement in one direction by fatiguing the cells that are sensitive to that type of movement. When this is done, we find that an observer's sensitivity to movement of other patterns, which are moving in the same direction and at the same speed as the previously exposed *adapting pattern*, has been reduced. This drop in sensitivity, however, does not carry over to faster or slower movements, nor does it generalize to movements in the opposite direction (Sekuler, 1975; Sekuler and Ganz, 1963). Thus, the selective adaptation procedure gives results consistent with the idea that our brains contain movement-sensitive cells that have particular tuning for direction and velocity. To experience an interesting illusion thought to be caused by the fatigue of motion sensitive cells, try the demonstration in Demonstration Box 11-4.

The eye-head movement system

The second system, the eye-head movement system, operates in a very different fashion. It seems to have two tasks to perform. First, this system enables us to detect the movement of external objects when their images remain in stationary positions on the retina. This happens when we move our eyes to follow the path of a physically moving object as shown in Figure 11-2*B*, as when we track a swinging

pendulum from side to side. These types of eye movements, called **smooth pursuit movements**, function to keep the image of the target on the fovea (the most acute part of the retina). Since the image of the target remains on the fovea, if there is no patterned background across which the object is moving, the only way the observer can know the path or the speed of an object is to monitor the path and speed of the eyes' movements. Given this fact, it is remarkable that we can accurately report the shape and the length of the path of a moving target (Epstein and Hanson, 1977; Rock and Halper, 1969).

Unfortunately, since much of our information about the course of a moving target comes from the record of the path our eyes have traveled, discrepancies between the path of the stimulus and the path the eyes have followed can lead to perceptual errors. Actually, the eye does not pursue moving targets with perfect accuracy. There is a tendency for the eye to follow some distance behind, with the degree of the lag depending on the speed of the target (Puckett and Steinman, 1969; Fender, 1971). Under some circumstances, the eye never really catches up to the stimulus (Young, 1971). Festinger and Easton (1974) had observers track a spot of light moving over a square path. The eye lagged behind (as usual) and did not change direction as quickly as the spot; the spot had turned a corner of the square while the eye was still pursuing along a side. Because of this, when asked to describe the path of the target, most observers did not describe squares but paths such as those in Figure 11-3. These are the kinds of shape distortions one would predict, given that the eye was tracking behind the target. The importance of eye movements in this illusion is confirmed by the disappearance of distortion, and the square appearance of the path, when the eye views the moving light without trying to

Demonstration Box 11-4. The spiral aftereffect

To experience the **spiral aftereffect**, cut out (or trace) the accompanying stimulus and place it on the turntable of your stereo or record player as if it were a record. Let the stimulus rotate for about one minute while you stand over it and watch it closely. Stop the turntable and hold it so that it is completely stationary. You should notice that you now see a spiralling movement in a direction opposite to that in which the stimulus physically rotated. This is an illusory movement since the stimulus itself is no longer in motion. The spiral aftereffect is not well understood, but it may be due to the satiation or fatiguing of a particular group of movement detectors, which is caused by excessive stimulation in one direction of movement. It is one of several such movement aftereffects.

follow it. Similarly, Coren, Bradley, Hoenig, and Girgus (1975) have shown that the size of the circular path of a rotating spot of light can be distorted when the eye movements used to pursue the rotating light are erroneous.

The eye-head movement system also enables us to compensate for the effects of image motion on the retinal surface when it is generated by the observer and not by an external movement. Although we do not know exactly how this second movement system works, it must be based in part on a system that monitors the changing position of the eye in relation to the head, either when we are tracking a moving target or when we are scanning a stationary scene (Howard, 1982).

Figure 11-3. Festinger and Easton (1974) asked observers to follow the path of a moving spot of light. Although the physical path of the light was square, observers most often reported shapes like those shown (based on Festinger and Easton, 1974).

Two major theories have been proposed to explain the eye-head movement system. Sir Charles Sherrington (1906) suggested that motion is detected through feedback information from the six extraocular muscles that control eye movement. This feedback information, called proprioceptive or position information (see Chapter 5), allows the observer to monitor eye position. When proprioceptive information tells the brain that the eyes have moved, this allows the brain to interpret movement across the retina as observer generated rather than object generated. There is evidence that cells in the superior colliculus and in the cortex of the cat brain monitor eye position (Berkley, 1982; Krutz and Butter, 1980). These cells fire at different rates depending on the extent and direction to which the eye is turned (Donaldson and Long, 1980; Kasamatsu, 1976; Noda, Freeman, and Creutzfeldt, 1972). These cells could provide the information required to monitor eye position. Sherrington's theory is often called an **inflow theory** because the information "flowing in" from the eye muscles to the brain relays the crucial message for the interpretation of movement.

Hermann von Helmholtz (1962/1909) had a different view about how the eye-head movement system worked. He felt that it worked on an **outflow principle**. When the brain initiates an eye movement, signals are sent out commanding the eyes to move. In outflow theories, this signal (emanating from central regions in the visual system) cancels the movement information coming from the retina as the eyes move. Thus, the interpretation of the origin of movement does not come from information from the extraocular muscles, but from the message sent out by the brain initiating an eye movement. As in the case of inflow information, there seem to be cells in the cerebellum and the cortex of monkeys that contain information about eye position. Since these cells respond before the actual movement takes place, they could represent the source of outflow information (Miles and Fuller, 1975; Wurtz and Goldberg, 1971).

There is also experimental and observational evidence that the initiation of **voluntary eye movements** contains the outflow information that is an important aspect of the eye-head movement system. For example, try this experiment suggested by Helmholtz. Place your hand over one eye and tap or push the side of your other (uncovered) eye gently with your fingertips. This rotates the eye in a movement similar to one initiated by the brain. However, this movement is not typical of voluntary eye movements since the brain has not sent a signal to move the eye. When the eye is passively rotated in this fashion, the visual field will swing in the direction opposite to the movement of the eye. Thus, the visual field is stable only for eye movements initiated by signals from the brain.

To stabilize the visual field during eye movements, the eye-head movement system operates in a complex fashion. Signals to or from

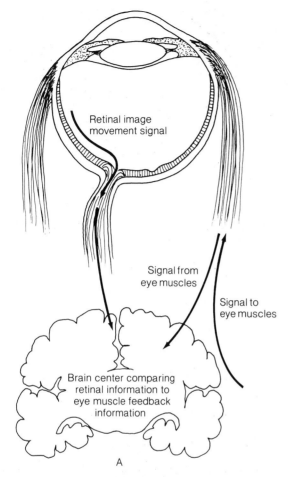

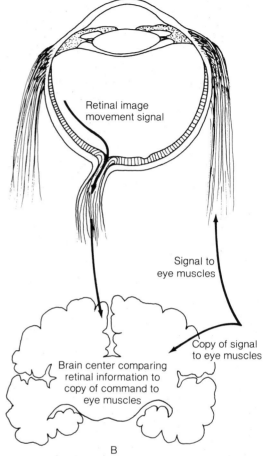

Figure 11-4. *The second function of the eye-head movement system is to maintain the stability of the visual world during eye movements. The inflow theory (A) states that this is accomplished by comparing movement signals from the retina with proprioceptive feed-* *back from the eye muscles, which indicates that the eye has moved. The outflow theory (B) maintains that commands from the brain to initiate voluntary eye movements cancel the movement information coming from the retina as the eyes move.*

the eye muscles (or both) are compared with signals from the retina indicating changes in retinal image position (Matin, 1982). Figure 11-4 illustrates the difference between the inflow and outflow theories of the eye-head movement system. As is the case with many

phenomena we discuss, both inflow and outflow information may be needed to provide a full explanation of this movement system. Table 11-1 presents a summary of the actions of the image-retina and eye-head movement systems. Demonstration Boxes 11-5 and 11-6 give

Table 11-1. The effect of retinal image change and voluntary eye movements on the perception of motion

Physical Target	Action of Eye	Retinal Image	Commands to Eye (Head)	Perception
Image-retina				
Moving	Stationary	Moves	None	Movement
Eye-head				
Moving	Tracks target	Stationary on fovea	Yes	Movement
Stationary	Moves	Moves	Yes	No movement
Stationary	Passively pushed	Moves	None	Movement in direction opposite eye motion
Image stabilized on retina	Moves	Stationary on retina	Yes	Movement in same direction as eye motion

---

Demonstration Box 11-5. Afterimages and apparent movement

One can readily experience one of the ways in which the eye-head movement system differentiates external from observer movement. The first thing that is needed is to generate a **stabilized retinal image**. Ordinarily, the retinal image is in constant motion and stimulates varying groups of receptors at a rapid rate. However, by quickly satiating or fatiguing a single group of retinal receptors, we can generate an image that maintains its position regardless of eye movements. Many of you are probably familiar with the technique used to give rise to such an image if you have ever had your picture taken with a flashbulb attached to the camera. If you looked at the light while it flashed, you may have noticed a purple dot that tended to linger in your field of view for some time after the picture was taken. This purple dot is called an **afterimage**. It is one example of a stabilized retinal image. The afterimage does not shift position on the retina. It stays in a constant position regardless of how we move our eyes. We can use the afterimage to demonstrate the operation of the eye-head movement system.

Perhaps the easiest way to generate an afterimage is to look at a rather bright but small source of light for a brief period of time. Make a 1-cm hole in an index card and hold it up in front of a light bulb. Look at the hole for a few moments and this should provide a clearly visible afterimage when you look away from the light. Now notice that each time you move your eyes the afterimage seems to jump in the same direction. This apparent movement is due to the action of the eye-head system.

Commands have been issued to the eye to move, yet the image remains on the same place on the retina. This could only occur if the image had moved as much as the eye (see Table 11-1). You may also notice that the image sometimes seems to drift smoothly from place to place. Again, the image never moves; the movement is signaled from the movements of your eyes. This is one example of how the action of the eye-head movement system can lead to illusions of motion.

Demonstration Box 11-6. The autokinetic effect

There is an interesting phenomenon in which movement is seen in the absence of any physical motion of the target. The word used to describe the occurrence is *autokinesis*, which means self moving. For this experiment, you will need a *very* dark room. No stray light of any sort should be visible. In addition, you will need a small dim point of light (a lighted cigarette works fine). Place the point of light about 2 m away from you and look at it steadily. After a few minutes it should appear to move, perhaps slowly drifting in one direction or another. Of course the light is still stationary; hence the movement is an illusion, which is called the **autokinetic effect**.

The autokinetic effect demonstrates the outflow principle that operates in the eye-head movement system. The visual system only monitors commands to initiate voluntary eye movements. However, these are not the only types of eye movements possible. Our eyes also exhibit invol-

untary eye movements. As you may have guessed, these are not monitored by the visual system. One type of involuntary eye movement is **eye drift**, and this is the mechanism that has been implicated in the autokinetic effect (Matin and MacKinnon, 1964). When we steadily fixate or stare at a target, it is difficult for the eyes to maintain steady and accurate fixation on that one point in space (Ditchburn, 1973). The eyes will tend to drift off of the fixation point; however, the visual system does not monitor this movement until it exceeds a critical point. In the autokinetic situation, retinal image movement has been signaled in the absence of commands to initiate voluntary eye movements. This is the situation under which the movement of the retinal image is attributed to an externally moving object (see Table 11-1). There is no information that the eyes have moved, so illusory movement of the dim spot of light is seen.

other interesting examples that illustrate the relationships between eye movements, visual stability, and the perception of motion.

Movement sensitivity

Now that we have discussed some factors that affect the apparent movement of objects, we might next ask, "What is the minimum amount of motion that is necessary before we perceive an object as moving?" To answer this question, we must measure a movement threshold just as we established thresholds for the minimum amount of light or sound needed for perception (see Chapter 2). Our sensitivity to the movement of an external target depends on several variables. In experimental settings, movement thresholds have usually been stud-

ied using a small point of light that moves against a stationary background. For instance, Hermann Aubert (1886) found that observers could detect the movement of a luminous dot in the dark, 50 cm from the eye, when it was moving at about 2.5 mm per second (which is about two-tenths of a degree of visual angle per second).

The appearance of movement, however, depends on more than the target alone. Thus, our ability to detect motion increases when there is a stationary background, such as a square frame surrounding a dot, that is visible to the observer. Under these circumstances, observers are ten times more sensitive. The minimum movement that can be detected is about 0.25 mm per second (or three-hundredths of a degree of visual angle per second). This small displacement per unit of time represents an incredible degree of movement sensitivity. If a snail were to crawl across a desk 1½ m wide at this rate, it would take it an hour and forty minutes to go from end to end. This finding demonstrates that our perception of movement is facilitated by the presence of other stimuli that are stationary or moving at different rates. Recently, Nakayama and Tyler (1981) measured movement sensitivity using moving random dot stimuli in which the target was a group of dots, which made up a group by the perceptual principle of common fate (see Chapter 12), moving over a field of other constantly moving dots. Nakayama and Tyler argued that this display allows for the measurement of the real movement threshold in the absence of stationary context information that could allow the observer to *deduce* that a target had moved on the basis that it changed position relative to some of the fixed targets in the field. Even with this type of control, they found that movement sensitivity was very good, with observers requiring a displacement of only 5 seconds of arc (or 0.001 degree of visual angle) for the detection of motion.

Movement sensitivity will also vary depending on whether the eye is stationary or moving, as shown by the **Aubert-Fleischel paradox** (named for the two researchers who explored the effect). Aubert and Fleischel noted that when we track a target with our eyes while it moves relative to a stationary background, it appears to move more slowly than it would if we were to fixate steadily on the stationary background. This phenomenon was called a paradox because it seemed that pursuit of a moving target should provide a more salient impression of motion, since both the image movement of the background and the signals from the moving eye are present. This phenomenon can lead to several perceptual distortions. An observer will not only underestimate the velocity of a target that is

tracked with the eye but will also tend to underestimate the distance that the target has moved (Mack and Herman, 1972). Overall, these data may simply indicate that the eye-head movement system is not as sensitive as the image-retina system.

Movement sensitivity also varies for different retinal locations. You will recall from Chapter 6 that visual acuity diminishes as we move away from the fovea. In a similar fashion, our ability to detect slow target movements (up to about 1.5 degree per second) decreases with distance from the fovea (Lichtenstein, 1963; McColgin, 1960; Choudhury and Crossey, 1981). For higher target velocities, however, this relationship reverses. At moderate to fast velocities, the peripheral retina is better able to detect movement, even though the decrease in acuity is so great that the observer may not recognize what is moving (Bhatia, 1975; B. Brown, 1972). Also, Choudhury and Crossey (1981) have demonstrated that the temporal peripheral retina may be more efficient at detecting target movement than the nasal peripheral retina.

There are probably anatomical reasons for this difference. As we noted earlier and in Chapter 3, there are two major types of retinal ganglion cells, which differ in their speed of information transmission, their receptive field size, and in the nature of their neural response. These are the X and Y cells. The Y cells, which seem better suited for movement detection (because of their quick response to any moving target in their receptive fields) are abundant in the peripheral retina but scarce in the foveal region (Lennie, 1980). It may be this difference in the retinal distribution of X and Y cells that permits easier detection of a moving target rather than a stationary target in the peripheral retina. You can experience this effect for yourself using Demonstration Box 11-7.

Human visual acuity for stationary targets is

Demonstration Box 11-7. The Troxler effect

The **Troxler effect** can be used to demonstrate the salience of movement stimulation in the peripheral retina. The Troxler effect deals with the fact that stationary targets, which stimulate the peripheral retina, will disappear under conditions of steady, unmoving stimulation. However, it can also be used to illustrate how movement in the periphery can revitalize the percept of a target that has faded.

Take a sheet of blank typing paper. Using the longer side (the 27.5-cm side), place a small fixation dot at one end of the paper and a straight line at the opposite end. The diagram given below can help you to visualize the stimulus conditions. Now hold the paper in front of you at a distance of about 25 cm. Make sure that the fixation dot is directly in front of you so that you can look directly at it. While fixating the dot, try to pay attention to the straight line in your peripheral visual field (but keep your eyes on the dot). After about 10-15 seconds, you should notice that the line in the peripheral field has faded from view (the Troxler effect). Now, gently shake the paper, and the line will reappear. Thus the movement of an image can cause its reappearance in the peripheral retina.

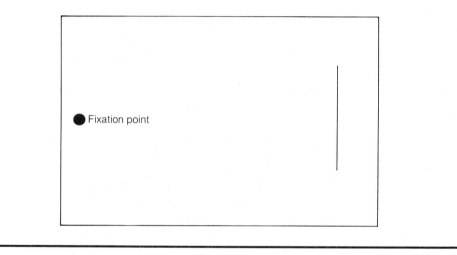

Fixation point

said to be *anisotropic*; that is, it displays varying degrees of sensitivity for targets oriented in different directions. This means that observers have greater sensitivity for the detection of vertical and horizontal line stimuli than they do for stimuli in oblique orientations, as we discussed in Chapter 6. Ball and Sekuler (1980) have shown a similar phenomenon in motion perception. They had observers *fixate* (stare at) a spot in the visual field while target dots were moved in one of two directions in the periphery. Either the targets were moved *toward* the fixation point or they were moved *away* from it. Ball and Sekuler found that observers were more sensitive to movement away from the fixation point or to what they called *centrifugal motion*. They have hypothesized that the importance of the characteristic outward optical flow of information across the retina as we move forward through external space (that is, the motion perspective information we discussed in Chapter 10) for the guidance of our bodies in the environment, could account for the increased sensitivity for this direction of motion.

Context and movement

In the preceding section we saw how the addition of a visual context or background can increase our sensitivity to motion. Actually, under certain conditions a visual context can also distort our perception of movement. For example, Duncker (1929) placed a bright dot in a dark visual field. When the dot was moved very slowly, observers were not certain it was moving. However, when a stationary dot was placed near the moving dot (in effect becoming the visual context), it became quite clear that one of the dots was in motion. Curiously, observers could not identify *which* of the two dots was moving. Duncker then altered the context somewhat. He surrounded the moving dot with a stationary luminous frame that was rectangular. Under these circumstances, the motion ambiguity was removed. Observers were now able to tell that the dot rather than the frame was in motion. Duncker then varied his experiment so that the dot was stationary and the luminous rectangular frame was moving. Under these circumstances the dot still appeared to be moving. In other words, Duncker had produced an illusion of movement of the stationary dot by moving the surrounding visual context. Duncker called this **induced motion** since the perceived movement of the dot was induced by the real movement of the surrounding visual context.

A common example of this same phenomenon occurs in everyday life. On a moonlit night we sometimes perceive the moon as rushing through clouds, when actually the clouds are moving while the moon maintains a stationary position in the sky. The clouds provide a surrounding context that is in motion and, consistent with the principle that Duncker discovered in the laboratory, they induce an apparent motion of the stationary moon. Duncker's **principle of surroundedness**, in which an enclosed or surrounded object is perceived to move relative to an enclosing or surrounding object, summarizes both the laboratory results and the everyday experience.

Another interesting everyday example of this principle exists. Probably most of you have had the experience of sitting in a bus or a train parked next to another vehicle, when all at once the adjacent vehicle starts to move. Instead of correctly attributing the movement to the vehicle next to your own, however, you have a powerful sensation that you are in motion. In this case, the principle of surroundedness has produced an *induced motion of the self*. As the surrounded object, you feel as though you are in motion. It is a powerful sensation that can be difficult to overcome even when you are aware of the source of real movement (Howard, 1982). The demonstration described in Demonstration Box 11-8, will allow you to experience induced motion of the self.

Induced motion seems to depend on certain relationships between the target and the frame. For instance, Wallach (1972a) used an arrangement in which a small target was surrounded by a rectangular frame, which in turn was surrounded by a larger circular frame as shown in Figure 11-5. An interesting thing happens when we move the rectangle in one direction and the circle in another. Suppose the rectangular frame is moved toward the left and the circular frame is moved downward. In both cases, the speed of movement is quite slow. One would expect that since the dot is enclosed by the two frames, the rectangle

---

Demonstration Box 11-8. Induced motion of the self

Induced motion of the self is the basis of an old party game. To play it you need two friends, a narrow board about 1 meter in length, and a blindfold.

Blindfold one of your friends and position the person until he or she is standing in the center of the board (which is lying on the floor). Now you and your other friend position yourselves on either end of the board, kneel, and have the standing, blindfolded person place one hand on each of your heads. Tell your blindfolded friend that you will now lift the board until it is about 30 cm from the floor. At this point, you will ask your friend to remain blindfolded but to jump off the board. Rather than lifting the board, however, you and your other friend lower your bodies (in unison

and in a slow, even motion) until you have moved to a squatting position. Since your blindfolded friend has a hand on each of your heads, and you have told the person that he or she is to be lifted from the ground, your friend should experience your downward motion (since you and your friend are the surrounding context) as an illusory upward motion of the body (since the person on the board is the surrounded object). This should be apparent when you ask the person to jump from the board. He or she should experience great surprise at the fact that the board has remained on the floor and that the experienced upward motion was, in fact, an illusion.

---

and the circle, the induced motion of the dot would be affected by both the direction of the movement of the rectangle and by the direction of the movement of the circle. If the final induced motion is the average of that caused by each frame alone, we might expect it to move along a diagonal path upward and to the right. However, the induced movement of the dot is only affected by the closest frame. Thus, the dot seems to move to the right along a horizontal path in a direction opposite to the real movement of the rectangle. This is the same path that the dot would take (in terms of its induced motion) if only the rectangular frame was present and moving.

Gogel and Koslow (1972) have shown that in order to induce motion, the target and the background must be at the same distance from the observer (that is, apparently near one another). If the frame that supplies the context is too far in front of or behind the target, no motion will be induced. This *principle of spatial adjacency* makes it possible to put two dif-

ferent frames on separate sides of the visual field and, by moving them in opposite directions, to induce motion in two opposite directions for enclosed targets (Gogel, 1977). These results show that our perception of movement does not depend simply on physical motion, but it also involves complex processing of many variables. The background is as important as the moving target.

What causes induced motion? One explanation states that our eyes are caught by the size of the larger surrounding stimuli, and thus tend to track it. Because of this, the image of the stationary object moves across the retina in the opposite direction. According to this explanation, however, the visual system does not adequately monitor the pursuit eye movements and, hence, attributes the change in the stationary target's image to actual movement. Notice that this explanation is similar to the one offered for the autokinetic effect described in Demonstration Box 11-6. Schulman (1979) conducted a study that allowed him

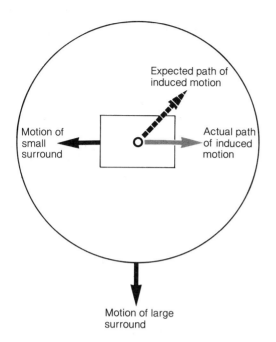

Figure 11-5. The direction of induced motion seems to be affected only by the immediate context or surround. Here, real movement is indicated by the heavy black arrows, induced motion by the gray arrow, and the expected motion by the dotted arrow.

to investigate the relationship between eye movements and induced motion. He had observers track the path of the moving surround while he positioned the stationary surrounded object either close to or far away from the portion of the context being tracked. Schulman found that the observers most frequently reported a direction of induced motion that indicated that the illusion was being controlled by the portion of the surround that was in closest physical proximity to the stationary target. He concluded that eye movements have no effect on induced motion; its control rests in the relative displacement of objects in the visual field, especially if they are close to the stationary object.

Biological motion

Many of the experiments that we have been describing use simple stimuli. However, we could question the relevance of these experimental findings to real-world situations where we experience very complex motion patterns. Can observers detect and identify more complex movement patterns that can be related more directly to our everyday experience? In a series of studies, Johansson (1976a) has investigated what he has called **biological motion**. Although he and his co-workers have done a number of studies that have shown how various perspective transformations can predict the motion of differing objects, perhaps his most interesting work is with movement patterns.

Consider the intricate series of movement patterns accomplished by the human skeletal structure when we walk across the room. Even in this simple act many precise movements are occurring in a coordinated pattern. Would an observer be able to identify these motions as the act of walking in the absence of any other information? To answer this question, Johansson and his co-workers used the following technique. They attached small flashlight bulbs to the shoulders, elbows, wrists, hips, knees, and ankles of a person (see Figure 11-6A). Then they made a film of the person as he moved around in a darkened room. Observers who watched the film saw only a pattern of lights moving in total darkness. Not only were the observers able to tell that it was a person walking, but they were also able to detect abnormalities, such as a simulated small limp. In another experiment, two people with similar arrays of lights were filmed while performing a spirited folk dance. Figure 11-6B shows a series of sequential positions from the folk dance in which the black dots mark the positions of the lights. Once again, even with only a

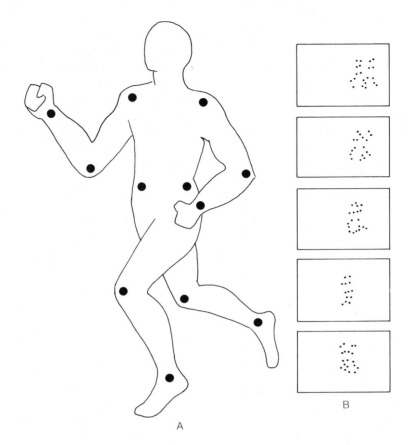

                                                                         B

                                                                         A

Figure 11-6. An example of the type of displays used by investigators to study patterns of humans in motion. (A) Positions of lights af- *fixed to individuals. (B) A sequence of movement positions made by a dancing couple.*

moving pattern of lights, observers had no difficulty recognizing that the motion was actually a dancing couple. Johansson (1976b) also showed that observers needed little time to make these identifications. In fact, 200 msec was sufficient to recognize the pattern of lights as a human body in motion (Johansson, von Hofsten, and Jansson, 1980).

Other investigators (Barclay, Cutting, and Kozlowski, 1978; Cutting and Kozlowski, 1977; Kozlowski and Cutting, 1977) have extended and elaborated on these findings. For

example, in one study they photographed a group of people who were acquainted with one another. The individuals were photographed with only lighted portions of several joints visible. Several months later the same individuals were invited to watch the films and attempt to identify themselves and their friends. The observers were able to identify themselves and others correctly on a fair percentage of trials, although their performance was not perfect. These investigators also asked their observers how they went about making their identifications of various individuals in the film. Observers mentioned a variety of motion components such as the speed, bounciness, and rhythm of the walker, the amount of arm swing, or the length of steps as features that allowed them to make their identification. In other studies, these same investigators found that observers could tell whether a person was a male or a female, despite seeing only a moving pattern of dots. In fact, it was not necessary for all the body joints to be represented in the light display for people to make correct identifications. Even when only the ankles were represented, observers could detect the sex of the walker. They could also make these gender identifications within about 5 seconds of viewing. This indicates that not only are there biological motion patterns that can be readily identified, but there are also motion patterns that become part of one's sex identification as well as part of one's identity. It seems analogous to the uniqueness of a person's facial feature composition.

Cutting, Proffitt, and Kozlowski (1978) attempted to determine the nature of the information used to determine the gender of the walker in the light display. They proposed that the torso of the body acts like a flat spring with the limbs in symmetrical motion around it. This, along with certain individual differences in bodily dimensions (such as the relative widths of the shoulders and hips) provides a *center of movement* that is not necessarily associated with any body part; however, it organizes the coherent motion of the body parts in an individual fashion making identification possible.

This type of research lends support to the notion that motion perception is a primary ability that is integrated into our ability to recognize familiar objects. Regardless of the cues being used, the observer quickly integrates the total pattern into a moving object. There is no con-

scious deduction needed, rather the percept seems to simply "be there." While physical motion seems to require certain successive transformations of static objects over time, the perception of motion seems to utilize many other sources of information.

GLOSSARY

The following definitions are specific to this book.

Afterimage   A visual sensation that continues after an intense or prolonged exposure to a stimulus.

Aubert-Fleischel paradox   The phenomenon of perceived movement being slower when a moving target is fixated than when one fixates a stationary background behind a moving target.

Autokinetic effect   The illusion of movement of a stationary point of light viewed in an otherwise totally dark field.

Biological motion   The concept of the intricate movement patterns accomplished, for example, by the skeletal structure of a human crossing a room.

Circadian rhythm   A rhythmic biological cycle occurring at approximately 24-hour intervals.

Event-processing hypothesis   The theory of time perception suggesting that perceived time is a cognitive process determined by the amount of sensory information processed during a particular interval.

Eye drift   Drifting movement of the eyes away from a target after prolonged fixation.

Eye-head system   A movement perception system that monitors and differentiates observer-generated from object-generated movement.

Filled duration illusion   An interval filled with stimulus events perceived as longer than an identical duration without stimulus events.

Image-retina system   A movement perception system that detects movement within the retinal image.

Indifference interval   A time duration, about 0.7

seconds, that does not give rise to either an overestimation or underestimation of its length.

Induced motion   An illusion of movement of a stationary object caused by the motion of the background or surrounding context.

Inflow theory   The suggestion that eye motion is detected and compensated for through feedback information from the six extraocular muscles controlling eye movement.

Internal timer hypothesis   A theory of time perception suggesting that there is a biological or physiological basis to time perception.

Interstimulus interval   The time span between the end of one stimulus input and the beginning of the next stimulus.

Kappa effect   The phenomenon in which altering the distance between two successively presented stimuli alters the apparent interstimulus interval. *See* Tau effect.

Outflow principle   The suggestion that brain commands initiating eye movements enable the eye-head movement system to differentiate object-generated from observer-generated movement in the retinal image.

Perceptual moment   The hypothetical basic psychological unit of time, estimated to be between 25 and 150 msec.

Phi phenomenon   Apparent movement between two successive presentations of stimuli in different spatial locations.

Principle of surroundedness   The principle that an enclosed or surrounded object appears to move relative to an enclosing or surrounding background.

Selective adaptation   A psychophysical technique in which motion-specific cells in the visual system are fatigued, causing reduced sensitivity to other visual stimuli moving in the same direction and at the same speed as the previously exposed adapting pattern.

Smooth-pursuit movements   The continuous eye movement involved in following a smoothly and steadily moving object.

Spiral aftereffect   An illusion of continued motion after a rotating spiral has stopped moving.

Stabilized retinal image   An image whose retinal position remains constant regardless of eye movements.

Stroboscopic movement   *See* Phi phenomenon.

Tau effect   The phenomenon in which altering the interstimulus interval between two stimulus events alters the perceived distance between them. *See* Kappa effect.

Troxler effect   The effect that stationary targets stimulating the peripheral retina will disappear under conditions of steady, unmoving stimulation.

Voluntary eye movements   Eye movements under voluntary command of the brain, such as smooth pursuit movements.

12

Form

THE INVENTOR SAT MUSING AT HIS workbench. Although he had a robot that could move quickly and that was remarkably strong, he still had problems. Although the eye sockets had been equipped with extremely sensitive television cameras, the inventor still could not decide how to instruct the robot to respond to the patterns that represent objects in the world. The first problem had arisen when he directed the mechanical man to pick up the object in front of him, which was a cup on a table. The robot lifted the entire table instead. Certainly, any child can tell the difference between an object and its background. Why couldn't this marvelous machine do it? He had checked the circuits carefully, and they had picked up every contour and every change in brightness that passed in front of the camera lens. Perhaps there was more to the perception of forms and patterns than simply the perception of the contours defining them. The inventor mused, "I wonder how *I* know where the cup ends and the table begins?"

CONTOUR

The most primitive stimulus element needed for visual form perception is the presence of a **contour**. A contour can be defined as an area within the visual array where an abrupt change in luminance exists. For example, a simple contour, and probably one of the simplest visual forms, would be generated by drawing a black line on a white sheet of paper. The sharp change from black to white defines this line as a visible contour. The normal optic array is filled with contour information, and an area completely enclosed by a contour is usually seen as a distinct and separate form. The presence of a series of contour-bounded "blobs" in the incoming visual stimulation is usually perceived as a group of objects in the external environment.

Visual contour and stimulus change

Actually, virtually all visual perception is dependent on the presence of contours, as can be demonstrated experimentally by eliminating all abrupt luminance changes in the visual field. A field that contains no visible contours is called a **Ganzfeld** (which is German for "whole field"). A series of studies has shown that perception in a Ganzfeld is quite unusual. Observers generally report that all they see is "a shapeless fog that goes on forever." If the field is filled with colored light, any hint of hue fades in a few moments, and gray fog is all that can be seen (Cohen, 1958). After prolonged exposure to the Ganzfeld, many observers experience a perceptual *blank out*, which is the phenomenal impression that all sense of vision has been lost. It is almost as if one has gone blind. Vision, however, returns quickly when a shadow is cast or a change in luminance is introduced in one local region of the field (Avant, 1965; Cohen, 1957). Blank out never occurs when an adequate number of contours are in the field. The very existence of blank out, and the fact that one can recover from it by introducing contours in the field, indicates that areas of abrupt intensity change (in other words, contours) are necessary for any sort of vision. While the Ganzfeld is an artificial stimulus situation, blank outs can also occur in natural environments. For instance, in the Arctic, when the terrain is covered by snow and there is little luminance change within the retinal image, we have a naturally occurring Ganzfeld. *Snow blindness*, where observers report that they unaccountably lose their sense of sight after much time viewing this featureless, snow-covered white expanse, is an occurrence of blank out. You may experience some of the

---

Demonstration Box 12-1. The Ganzfeld

Although Ganzfeld situations have been produced with elaborate laboratory equipment, there are several simple ways to produce a Ganzfeld that will allow you to experience this contourless field for yourself. You can take a table tennis ball and cut it in half, placing one-half over each eye, or you can use two white plastic spoons (like those probably available in any campus cafeteria) to produce a Ganzfeld by placing the bowls of the two spoons over each eye as shown in the accompanying figure. Direct your gaze toward a light source (a fluorescent lamp, say) prior to placing the objects before your eyes, so that your field of view will be flooded with diffuse, contourless light. Stay in this position for a few minutes and monitor any changes or alterations in your conscious perceptual experience. If the light originally had a tint, you will soon notice that the color will fade into a gray. After a while you will suddenly feel that you cannot see. This feeling of blindness is called "blank out." It seems that in the absence of contours in the field, vision ceases. If a friend now casts a shadow over part of the field (say, with a pencil across the spoons), vision will immediately return with the introduction of this contour.

Spoon

---

sensations associated with the Ganzfeld for yourself by using Demonstration Box 12-1.

Other conditions can lead to a disruption of normal contour information and also tend to eliminate form perception. In Chapter 11 we discussed an experimental technique that produces a **stabilized retinal image**. You may remember that a stabilized retinal image is one that stimulates the same group of retinal receptors regardless of how the eye moves. In other words, the image is stopped or immobile and does not move across the retinal surface as we shift our eyes from target to target. When an image is stabilized on the retinal surface, it does not stay visible for long. In fact, a general loss of color and contour information occurs within a few seconds after the image is presented to the eye (Heckenmueller, 1965; Pritchard, Heron, and Hebb, 1960; Riggs, Ratliff, Cornsweet, and Cornsweet, 1953; Yarbus, 1967). Because we normally have little difficulty in keeping nonstabilized targets in view for as long as we wish to look at them, we must ask what causes the stabilized retinal image to fade.

Our eyes are always scanning the visual field. Even when we fixate (stare steadily at) a particular place in the visual field, tiny involuntary eye movements, called *microsaccades*, continue to occur. These small eye movements occur many times per second. Thus, the retinal image is constantly slipping and sliding over different retinal receptors as the eye quivers. For any given retinal receptor, there will be a period of time when it is being stimulated by one part of the visual array, followed by a period of time when that image has moved from this receptor because of a tiny eye movement and another stimulus has taken its place. In other words, there are temporal variations ("on" times followed by "off" times) in the stimulation. When we artificially stabilize the retinal image, we remove these temporal variations. Since the stabilized image fades from view after a brief period, this means that a luminance difference in the visual field is not sufficient for contour perception. Constant change in the stimulation is needed for an image to be seen continuously. This is further supported by the fact that flickering the stabilized image on and off will tend to keep it from fading (Cornsweet, 1956). This was the technique we used in Demonstration Box 3-3 (page 63), where you drew the pattern of the blood vessels that

lie on top of your own retina. Because these are stable and unchanging stimuli regardless of how you may move your eyes, they are completely stabilized images, hence not normally visible. We brought them back to visibility by providing a light source that caused their shadows to move slightly, and this change in the stimulus made them momentarily visible. Of course, the image faded as soon as the stimulus became constant and unchanging again.

We can interpret the information gained from research using the Ganzfeld and the stabilized retinal image technique as indicating that vision requires temporal and spatial change to function normally. When changes or local luminance differences are removed, such as when the visual field contains no contours at all, or when we stop temporal variation across the retinal receptors, consciousness of visual stimulation ceases, and no forms, patterns, or stimulus gradations are seen. The importance of change may explain the function of lateral inhibition (as discussed in Chapter 6) as being a process that tends to emphasize contours by accentuating the spatial change from a bright to a dark area. In any event, contours are one form of local stimulus change to which the visual system seems to be especially attuned.

Emergence of visual contours

An important characteristic of visual contours is that they do not appear immediately to our conscious experience. Some time must elapse between the presentation of a contour to the eye and the perceptual experience of that contour. If we interfere with the visual system's processing of the contour before this time has passed, we may never see it. Werner (1935) first demonstrated this in an ingenious experiment. He briefly flashed a stimulus that was simply a black disk on a white background (the target), and then followed this a short time later with a quick exposure of a black ring (the mask) in the same region of the visual field. The inner circumference of the ring just matched the outer circumference of the disk. He varied the time between the disappearance from view of the disk and the ring's first appearance (this is known as the *interstimulus interval*). When the interstimulus interval was between 100 and 200 msec, observers often reported that they could not see the disk at all, or that it had become less distinct, or dimmer, and that its boundary was hazy. This experiment and its results are diagrammed in Figure 12-1. Werner (1935) interpreted the apparent disappearance of the disk as indicating that the inner contour of the ring had interfered with the formation of the contour of the disk, thus *masking* it by pre-

venting it from being seen. When the interval between the stimuli was too great, the disk contour had already formed, and its perception was impervious to interference. When the interval was too short, the disk and the ring appeared to merge into a single, large disk. This general kind of phenomenon, where one stimulus interferes with the perception of another, has come to be called **backward masking** (backward, because the second stimulus masks a target that has already come and gone). When contours on adjacent parts of the retina interfere with one another, we call this situation **metacontrast** to differentiate it from other forms of visual masking.

We now know that contours can be masked by flashes of light, dots, fields of bars, stripes, and curves of all descriptions, and by a wide

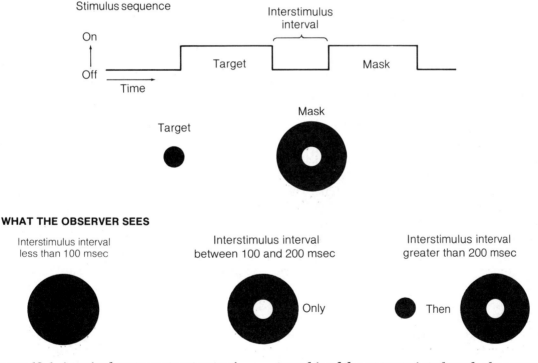

Figure 12-1. A typical metacontrast experiment. Notice that when the interstimulus interval is of the appropriate length, the target is often not seen at all.

variety of more specific visual contours (Kahneman, 1968; Lefton, 1973). Metacontrast is of
most interest to us here, since it deals with the
interaction of adjacent contours. Since Werner's
(1935) study, a number of investigators have
produced the general finding that a particular
interstimulus interval exists between a target
and a mask, varying with type of target and
mask, that results in the greatest contour interference. This time is usually between 30 and
100 msec (Lefton, 1973). Because of this, the
results of masking experiments may be shown
as an inverted U-shaped function, as indicated
by the black line in Figure 12-2. The actual relationship between the temporal separation of
the stimuli and the amount of masking is still a
matter of some controversy. Inverted U relationships are reported when the target and
mask are about equally intense. If the mask is
much brighter than the target, a different relationship is found. The greatest degree of masking is found for the shortest target and mask
separations, and the effect diminishes as the
interval increases, as shown by the white
line in Figure 12-2.

Since visual masking can dramatically affect
our perception of contours, it is probably involved with some of the same mechanisms
that give rise to our perception of contours in
the first place. On the basis of masking data, at
least three major ideas have been offered to
explain how contours interact over time. The
first suggests that the contour interactions result from lateral inhibitory interactions between visual neurons (as we discussed in
Chapter 6). One contour can mask another
when the excitation aroused by the target contour is overcome by the inhibition aroused by
the mask's contours (Weisstein, 1968; Weisstein, Ozog, and Szoc, 1975). The second idea
involves a notion similar to the psychological
moment discussed in Chapter 11. A stimulus
affects a sensory system for a certain period of

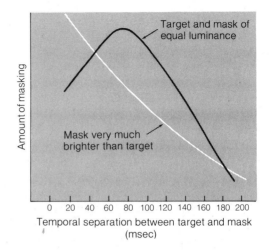

**Figure 12-2. The relationship between the
amount of visual masking and the time interval between target and mask. Notice that different relationships are found depending on
the relative luminances of target and mask.**

time, even *after* the stimulus itself ceases to be
present. This period is usually about 250 msec
in length. If two reasonably similar stimuli enter the visual processing system within this
brief period, they add together, or the processing of the first set of contours may be canceled
or blocked in order to process the most recent
contour information (see Reed, 1973). The
third idea maintains that contour perception
requires more than the simple detection of a
luminance difference between two regions of
the visual field. The visual system may decompose brightness variations into their separate
spatial frequency components in much the
same way that the ear separates the various
frequencies that make up a musical chord (see
Chapter 6). Each of these components may be
processed in separate channels (see Graham,
1981). Contours with similar spatial frequency
components may interfere with each other,
while those with different components will
not (see Weisstein, Harris, Berbaum, Tangney,

Figure   **345**

and Williams, 1977). Thus, we see that the processing of even simple contours is not so simple.

FIGURE

In our discussion of contour, we said that the simplest perceptible form is a line. Most of our visual experience, however, is composed of integrated units that we call **figures**. For instance, a group of straight lines of equal length joined together to form four equal angles of 90 degrees is the figure we call a square. Figures are integrated groups of contours. The perception of figure is basic to our other perceptual experiences. We must be able to differentiate figures as distinct from the backgrounds (or **grounds**) from which they emerge. Therefore, we must be able to distinguish a pen or a coffee cup as a separate entity, different from the desk on which it rests (remember the robot's problem). Although this sounds simple, the perceptual separation of figures, from each other and from the surrounding stimuli that make up their background, involves some complex processes.

Figure-ground separation

Figure 12-3 illustrates one of the complexities of the figure-ground problem. It is an example

Figure 12-3. A reversible figure-ground stimulus in which a pair of black faces or a white vase (or perhaps a bird bath) are seen alternately.

of an ambiguous, or reversible, pattern. By "reversible" we mean our perception of what is seen as figure and ground within this configuration can alternate, or reverse. When you look at this picture, you might see a bird bath or a vase that appears as a white figure standing in front of the black background. Yet, in a few moments of viewing, the percept might change. Now you may see two silhouette faces looking at each other. The black of the faces seems to be in front of the white of the background. Another interesting aspect of this reversal is that the contour (defining the face or the vase) always "belongs" to the figure. It seems to "hold the figure together." Notice also that you cannot "see" both the faces and the vase simultaneously. They seem to alternate in consciousness. This simple demonstration points out that the perception of figures is a psychological act of interpretation, and not necessarily directly predictable from the stimulus array.

We have already noted some of the perceived (or *phenomenal*) differences between figure and ground. In addition to the ones we've already mentioned, Rubin (1915, 1921) pointed out that figures usually appear closer than the ground, they appear to be more "thinglike," and seem to have a shape (as opposed to the background that is relatively formless). Figures usually are seen as more meaningful and are remembered more easily. Coren (1969a) observed that the region perceived as figure shows more brightness contrast than the same area perceived as ground. Finally, Wong and Weisstein (1982) found that our ability to discriminate the angle of tilt of a short, straight line is better when it is flashed on the part of Figure 12-3 seen as figure (either the vase or the faces, depending on which is seen at the moment) than when it is flashed on the portion seen as ground (for example, the black part when the vase is seen as figure).

Although we can list the perceptual attributes of figures and grounds, we are still a long way from fully understanding the stimulus factors and psychological processing that give rise to these attributes. However, a few relevant factors have been isolated. For instance, Figure 12-4A shows a reversible figure that alternately appears as a light *X* or a dark Maltese cross. In Figure 12-4B we have simply altered the size of the sectors, yet it is now much easier to see the dark cross than it is to see the

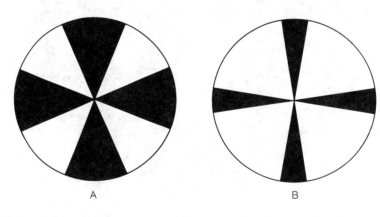

A   B

Figure 12-4. (A) An ambiguous figure-ground stimulus in which a white X and a black Maltese cross are seen alternately. (B) In this stimulus, the smaller figure (the black Maltese cross) is dominant.

Figure   **347**

light *X*. It seems that the smaller the stimulus the more likely it is to be seen as figure.

It may have occurred to you that there is another factor that helps to separate figure from ground in normal viewing situations. Remember that one of the properties mentioned by Rubin in his catalog of figure-ground differences was that the figure appears to be closer than ground. This apparent depth difference is almost invariably found. Perhaps it is the case that, rather than figure-ground separation causing the change in perceived depth, perceived depth differences *cause* the separation of figure and ground. This implies that reversible figure-ground percepts, such as Figure 12-3, only arise in situations where we are dealing with flat stimulus arrays where the usual depth information (see Chapter 10) cannot be employed. An interesting phenomenon illustrates how form can emerge through the use of depth cues in a two-dimensional array. Look at Figure 12-5. Here we have an array that seems to contain a white triangle. Despite the fact that the perception of the white triangular figure is quite compelling, there are actually no real contours (abrupt changes from dark to light) that define the triangular figure. The contours we "see" are not physically present. Figures like this triangle are bounded by **subjective contours**, since the observer perceptually "creates" the contours defining the form.

One explanation offered for subjective contours is relevant to our discussion of the emergence of figure from ground in two-dimensional arrays (see Ware, 1981 for a discussion of other views). Coren (1972) suggested that subjective contours arise when we use depth cues within a configuration to help organize an otherwise meaningless array into a simpler, more meaningful figure. In the case of Figure 12-5, the depth cue present within this array is interposition. As you may remember from our discussion of depth cues in Chapter

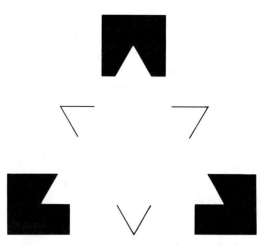

Figure 12-5. A subjective contour figure in which a white central triangle is seen although none is present (from S. Coren, Psychological Review, *1972, 79, copyright 1972 by the American Psychological Association. Reprinted by permission.).*

10, when one object blocks our view of another object, the occluded object is perceived as the more distant one. In the case of subjective contour figures, the presence of interposition cues helps to provide a meaningful figural organization for the gaps in the squares and in the outlined triangle. Figure emerges from ground as a consequence of this process. An imaginary contour arises to separate the figure from the ground, which heightens the perceived depth separation. In support of the idea that implicit depth cues are responsible for the creation of this type of subjectively contoured figure are data that, under special viewing conditions where no other cues for depth are available, these subjective figures do appear to stand well out in front of their backgrounds (Coren and Porac, 1983). We earlier saw another example of this phenomenon, where depth cues can create figures bounded by subjective contours, when we dealt with random dot stereograms (see Demonstration Box 10-4, page 298). Theoretically, it is quite interesting that the figures defined by subjective contours act remarkably like "real" contours, even to the extent that they can mask a real contour (Lehmkuhle and Fox, 1980; Weisstein, Matthews, and Berbaum, 1974), facilitate judgments of the position of a dot (Pomerantz, Goldberg, Golder, and Tetewsky, 1981), and cause motion aftereffects similar to those caused by moving real contours (Smith and Over, 1979). The emergence of subjective contours may indicate that the segregation of figure from ground is related to the separation of our visual world into various depth planes.

Implicit depth cues may carry over to two-dimensional situations and assist us in achieving meaningful figural organization. An outlined square on a piece of white paper may be seen as a figure because it blocks part of our perception of the white surface (via interposition), thus being pushed perceptually forward as a figure. Hochberg (1971b, 1978) has proposed an alternative view, maintaining that we make certain eye and head movements to take in information from real world scenes. These regular movement patterns lead us to expect certain kinds of figures and grounds to appear in certain ways. Such expectations are called **schemas**, which are internal models of objects in the world based on our experiences and habits. Schemas may form the basis of figure-ground separation in perception. An example of such habits in operation can be seen when we consider how stimulus motion can give an array the quality of being an object, thus changing its perceived form. This is the so-called **kinetic depth effect** discussed by Gibson (1966), Rock (1975), and Kaufman (1974). Demonstration Box 12-2 illustrates this effect.

Yet another approach has been proposed by Buffart, Leeuwenberg, and Restle (1981). They argued that our perceptual systems produce a variety of possible interpretations, or codes,

for any particular visual display. Some of these codes will be quite complex, while others will be simple. The theory asserts that whichever figure-ground organization is described by the simplest code will be the one that is seen. Buffart et al. (1981) experimentally confirmed the predictions of this theory for a wide variety of two-dimensional line drawing figures. Further, there is evidence that the ground may actually be playing the primary role in such processing, since codes for possible grounds may be tested for simplicity before codes for possible figures (Calis and Leeuwenberg, 1981).

Laws of figural organization

Most of the visual patterns we perceive are composed of a number of elements. These elements are not seen as a random chaotic array of different hues and brightness levels. Rather, our perception is organized into objects and groupings, including such common things as a desk, a shelf of books, a sheaf of papers, a floor, a wall, and so forth. It is quite easy to discern whether a given contour belongs to a book or the table on which it lies. As we noted in the previous section, this is simply the organization of the field into figure and ground. The more general question of how all aspects of perception come to be organized was central to a group of psychologists (Max Wertheimer, Kurt Koffka, and Wolfgang Kohler were the most influential), who formed the **Gestalt** school of psychology. *Gestalt* is a German word that can be translated to mean "form," "whole," or even "whole form." The Gestaltists were interested in processes that cause certain elements to seem to be part of the same figure or grouping, while others seem to belong to other figures or groups. They formulated several laws of perceptual organization that govern the emergence of a visual figure (Werthei-

Figure 349

Demonstration Box 12-2. Kinetic Depth

In order to see how movement can create the impression of a three-dimensional form in a two-dimensional array, you will need a candle and a piece of stiff wire (a coat hanger or a long pipe cleaner will do). Bend the wire into a random three-dimensional shape. Now light the candle and darken the room. Place the bent wire so that it casts a shadow on a blank wall as shown in the figure. Notice that when the shape is absolutely motionless, the shadow is easily seen as a flat pattern of lines. Now, if you rotate it with your hand, the shadow suddenly changes form, becoming a three-dimensional object that cannot be seen as flat, despite the fact that you are viewing a two-dimensional shadow.

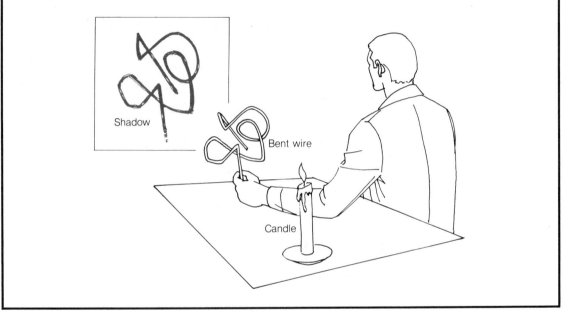

Shadow

Bent wire

Candle

mer, 1958/1923). Their basic observation is that elements within a pattern do not seem to operate independently. At the phenomenal level, there appear to be attractive "forces" among the various elements that cause them to form a meaningful and coherent figure, much as gravity organizes the planets, sun, and moons of our solar system. They described how certain regular properties of elements within a pattern bring about the emergence of stable figures.

Figure 12-6A is usually seen as two clusters of dots. Although the array actually contains 12 individual elements (dots), perceptual processes organize them into two groups. This is an example of the **law of proximity**, which states that elements close to one another tend to be seen as a perceptual unit or figure. Figure 12-6B generally is seen as a triangle composed of black dots on a background of (or surrounded by a swarm of) X's. This is an example of the operation of the **law of similarity** that maintains that similar objects tend

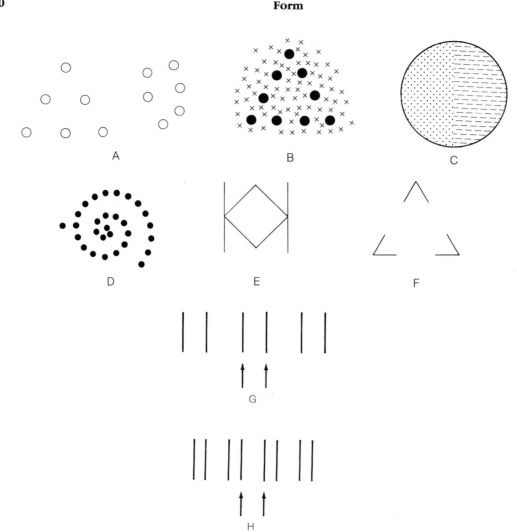

Figure 12-6. Examples of the Gestalt princi- ples of figural organization. (A) grouping by proximity; (B) and (C) grouping by similar- ity; (D) good continuation; (E) an extreme example of closure in which two common fig-

ures are bidden; (F) closure; (G) and (H) ex- amples of the distortion of the distance be- tween elements (the distances delineated by arrows are the same) by the principle of proximity.

to be grouped together. Another example of this law is seen in Figure 12-6C, where the two halves of the circular field appear quite separate because of grouping by similarity (for a more advanced analysis of such effects see Julesz, 1981). Figure 12-6D is viewed usually

as a spiral of dots with one standing outside. This is an example of the principle of **good continuation**, which states that elements that appear to follow in the same direction (as in a straight line or simple curve) tend to be grouped together. Figure 12-6E is an example of the

Figure 351

principle of **closure**, which states that when a space is enclosed by a contour it tends to be perceived as a figure. Most people see a diamond between two vertical lines here. Actually, Figure 12-6*E* also could be seen as a letter *W* stacked on a letter *M*, or a normal *K* and a mirror-image *K* facing each other, were it not for the compelling nature of closure. Closure also allows us to complete broken contours as in Figure 12-6*F*, which is seen as a triangle rather than simply as three separated acute angles.

These organizational mechanisms operate without any conscious effort on our part. The field of view simply appears to be organized, and the possibility that things could appear in any different organization takes some effort on our part. These Gestalt processes are so powerful that they can even cause distortions in our perception of the spatial relationships of the elements they organize into figures. For example, Coren and Girgus (1980) found that when groups of elements are organized by any of the principles, distances between elements belonging to the *same* group are perceptually *underestimated* relative to the same physical distance if it occurs between elements belonging to different perceptual groupings. You can see this in Figures 12-6*G* and 12-6*H*, which show two groupings on the basis of proximity. Despite the fact that the distance between the two middle lines in each figure is physically the same, the distance seems larger when the two lines appear to be parts of different groups. Coren and Girgus (1980) concluded that such distortions work to enhance and support the organization created by the Gestalt principles.

Figural goodness

The Gestalt psychologists felt that the principles of figural organization worked in harmony to bring about perception of the most stable, consistent, and simple forms possible from the visual array. They described this process as the **law of Pragnanz**, which maintains that the psychological organization of the percept will always be as "good" as the prevailing conditions allow. In this definition the term *good* is not fully specified; however, it includes such properties as regularity, symmetry, simplicity, and others we will encounter in the course of our discussion. The German word *Pragnanz* is not easy to translate into English; in general, it refers to "conveying the essence of something." In perception, the essence is sometimes better than the complete reality. In normal viewing, the differentiation of figure from ground and the organization of coherent forms or groups out of discrete elements simplifies the appearance of the perceptual array and reduces perceptual ambiguity. Pragnanz is a statement of this tendency toward simplicity and figural goodness in your conscious percept. Demonstration Box 12-3 gives you a method for further exploring the operation of Pragnanz.

Earlier we showed how depth cues can assist in the separation of figure from ground. In some instances, depth is the result of figural organization rather than an aid to it. For example, Kopfermann (1930) used figures similar to those shown in Figure 12-7 to study circumstances under which people perceive drawings as either two- or three-dimensional. She demonstrated that a two-dimensional percept will dominate when such an organization is figurally good or simple. In other words, when the two-dimensional organization is compact and symmetrical with good continuation between the lines, this organization will dominate. When this is not the case, observers will tend to perceive the drawing as three-dimensional. Therefore, in Figure 12-7 the figures are ordered from *A* through *C* with *C* being the least likely to be perceived as three-dimensional. Hochberg and Brooks (1960)

Demonstration Box 12-3. Pragnanz

Look at the accompanying figures for a moment and (without looking back again) draw them on a separate piece of paper. When you have finished, return to this box.

Now carefully compare the figures you drew to the actual figures. Did you pick up the fact that the "circle" is actually a tilted ellipse? that the "square"

contains no right angles? that the "triangle" has two rounded corners and an open one? that the *X* is actually made up of curved lines? Look back at your reproductions. If you drew (or remembered) just a good circle, square, triangle, and *X*, your percepts have been "cleaned up" by the action of Pragnanz.

---

suggested that this results from the fact that a three-dimensional organization may actually be *simpler* than a two-dimensional one. Thus, Figure 12-7A is seen as a three-dimensional cube because to imagine it as a two-dimensional pattern made up of triangles, trapezoids, and a parallelogram, interlocked like a puzzle, is more complex. Hochberg and Brooks (1960) suggested a quantitative representation of fig-

ural complexity based on the stimulus itself. They used the following expression: *Figural complexity = (number of angles + number of different angles)/2 × number of separate continuous line segments) + (total number of angles)*. They found that the higher this value, the more likely a figure is to be seen as three-dimensional.

One of the interesting aspects of the work

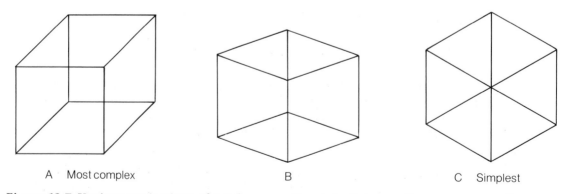

A   Most complex   B   C   Simplest

Figure 12-7. Various projections of a cube. The simpler the figures, the more they are seen as two dimensional; the more complex

they are, the more they are seen as three-dimensional.

Figure 353

by Hochberg and Brooks (1960) is the suggestion that figural organization or "goodness" can be defined in terms of the *amount of information* needed to specify a particular coherent organization. Such aspects of the form as the number of line segments, the number of angles, and the size and differing varieties of lines and angles can be considered to be information needed to evoke the perception of a particular type of figure. Information theory (which was discussed in Chapter 2) has been used to explicitly quantify figural goodness in several studies. To see how information theory applies to patterns, consider Figure 12-8, where we have broken up a square visual field into separate, smaller squares called "cells" (we call the whole array a *matrix*). Notice that we can construct a variety of patterns simply by filling in cells as we have done in Figure 12-8A. Suppose that we asked you to guess the figure present, without actually seeing it, simply by guessing whether each cell was black or white. Because each guess deals with two alternatives, the answer to each contains one bit of information, as we pointed out in Chapter 2. If we filled in the pattern randomly, in order to guess the complete pattern you

would need 64 guesses (one for each cell) or 64 bits of information (one for each guess needed). Suppose we told you that the left side was the mirror image of the right side. This is called a *vertically symmetrical pattern*, since the mirror images are symmetrical around a vertical line. Under this condition, you would only need to guess either the 32 cells on the right or on the left in order to guess the pattern, thus reducing the amount of information to 32 bits. Therefore, a vertically symmetrical figure, such as 12-8B contains less information than an asymmetrical figure such as 12-8A. Figure 12-8C, which is symmetrical around both the vertical and horizontal axes, contains even less information than the other two patterns (16 bits), since only one corner (16 cells) must be known before the entire pattern can be derived.

Attneave (1954) proposed that quantifying patterns in this manner could lead to an understanding of figural goodness. In general, he reasoned that "good" patterns are simpler in that they contain less information. Thus, they are often more symmetrical or predictable. Attneave (1955) argued that observers should be better able to recognize symmetrical patterns

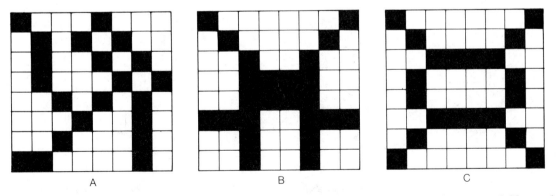

Figure 12-8. Examples of symmetry in patterns: (A) no symmetry; (B) symmetry around vertical axis above the letter B; *(C) symmetry around both vertical and horizontal (through middle) axes.*

than irregular ones, simply because symmetrical patterns require the retention of less information. Using matrices of dot patterns, some of which were symmetrical and some of which were not, Attneave (1955) verified this prediction, and he also showed that it was the amount of information in the pattern rather than symmetry per se that was the important aspect. Thus, an 8 × 8 matrix (containing 64 cells) with horizontal and vertical symmetry is remembered as easily as a 4 × 4 matrix (16 cells) with no symmetry, since both contain 16 bits of information. Recently, Yodogawa (1982) has provided a mathematically rigorous measure of pattern symmetry, based on infor-

mation theory, that nicely predicts judgments of pattern goodness and of pattern complexity.

Garner (1962, 1974) has offered a different information theory approach to the problem of figural goodness. He noted that many figures alter their appearance when they are rotated or when they are presented in mirror-image form. The total number of different patterns that can be produced may be classified as the set of stimuli from which a given example is drawn. Consider the 3 × 3 dot-matrix examples shown in Figure 12-9. Notice that each is shown with all possible unique rotations and reflections. Figure 12-9A is unique, 12-9B produces four unique patterns, and 12-9C pro-

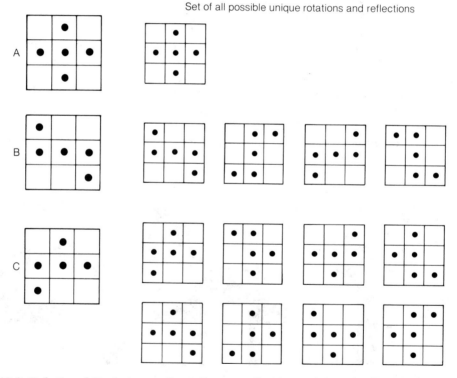

Set of all possible unique rotations and reflections

Figure 12-9. Relationships between figural goodness and the set of possible alternative stimuli that can be created by rotations and *reflections: (A) is the "best" figure and (C) is the "worst" (based on Handel and Garner, 1965).*

duces eight. Garner found that the smaller the set of possible figures, the more likely an observer was to rate the pattern as "good" (Garner and Clement, 1963; Handel and Garner, 1965). Of course, the smaller the number of possible stimulus alternatives, the lower the amount of information, as we saw in Chapter 2. Thus, we are again drawn to the conclusion that the "good" figures are simple and contain less information.

Other approaches to the quantitative descriptions of figural goodness have also been tried. For instance, one system is based on the actual processing steps involved in mentally coding any pattern (Leeuwenberg, 1967, 1971). Several different final codes can be produced for the same pattern because the mental rules or operations may be applied in different orders to different groups of pattern elements. Here, the idea of Pragnanz predicts that the final percept will correspond to the interpretation that has the simplest mental code (Leeuwenberg, 1971; van Tuijl, 1980). Again, the conclusion seems to be that in pattern perception, simpler is better.

VISUAL PATTERN PERCEPTION

The inventor sat beside his robot. He continued to speculate on how he could construct the circuits to allow his mechanical marvel to recognize objects on the basis of the pattern of visual information available in the image. His first thought had been to design a circuit to match each possible stimulus element. Of course, he would need an extremely large collection of elements to recognize all the typical patterns available in the world. Then he remembered the masked ball he had once attended. Everybody had dressed in bizarre costumes and had worn wigs, masks, and

make-up. Yet he was still able to identify almost all his friends by sight—how could that be if each of the individual facial elements was changed? There must be another way to go about recognizing patterns. He looked at the metallic hulk beside him and continued to muse.

When we consider all the processes that underlie the recognition of complex, everyday patterns, we find that they can be conveniently classified into two types. One type, called **data-driven processing**, begins with the arrival of sensory information at the receptors (data). This input is said to *drive* a series of analyses. The analyses begin with the registration of **distinctive features**, such as luminance differences in the image, colors, lines and angles, and other attributes of a pattern that distinguish it from other patterns. This analysis proceeds from the retina up through the various levels of the visual pathways, until it reaches the higher centers of the brain. The other type of processing is termed **conceptually-driven processing**. It operates in quite a different way, using higher level *conceptual* processes, including memories of past experiences, general organizational strategies, and expectations based on knowledge of the world or the surrounding context or situation. These processes guide an active search for certain patterns in the input. Both types of analysis can occur simultaneously, or they may occur one after the other, as features detected by data-driven processing suggest hypotheses about what an input pattern is, while conceptually-driven processing guides the search for specific details necessary to complete the percept. Both are needed, since if processing were only conceptually-driven one would only see what had been expected (or wanted), while if processing were only data-driven, prior knowledge and experience would play no role in what was perceived. Let's look at the evidence for these two basic types of processing separately before we consider how they interact in the recognition of complex patterns.

Data-driven processing

At the physiological level, it is relatively easy to find a number of data-driven mechanisms that seem to respond to (detect) distinctive features of patterns. For instance, in Chapter 6 we spoke of lateral inhibition that accentuates local changes in brightness and perhaps color. In Chapter 3 we indicated that neural units respond to specific features, such as the orientation of a line, its length, whether it forms an angle with another line, and so forth. An interesting source of evidence for data-driven processing of patterns on the basis of features such as these comes from work on stabilized images (a technique we discussed earlier in the chapter). As you recall, we mentioned that when we stop the movement of the image on the retina (keep it stationary on one section of the retinal surface, regardless of how the eye moves) it fades. This fading is not a gradual

uniform disappearance of the whole figure, nor is it a disappearance of little random bits of the figure. Rather, it is a chunk-by-chunk disappearance of whole lines and units (Evans and Wells, 1967; Heckenmueller, 1965; Pritchard et al., 1960). For instance, if we presented an observer with a stabilized outline square, we would expect the fade-out to look something like the sequence shown in Figure 12-10A. It would not appear as shown in 12-10B. Since the disappearance is feature by feature, some researchers have taken this as evidence for an initial feature-by-feature build up of the perceptual experience in the first place. This may occur through data-driven cortical feature analyzers (see Milner, 1974).

We have been using an intuitive definition of "features" in speaking of pattern analysis. There are, however, more objective ways to approach features. One early study that is still suggestive is that of Attneave (1954), who asked observers to represent a figure by means of a series of ten dots. The observers tended to place the dots on points of the form that changed direction most sharply. We can represent common objects or pictures quite easily

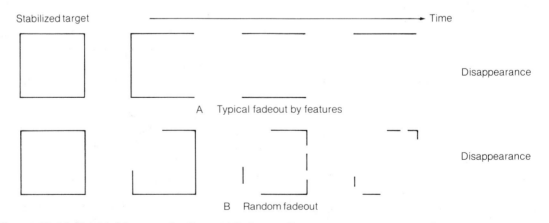

Figure 12-10. Typical feature-by-feature fading of a stabilized retinal image is shown in (A) as opposed to what would be expected if disappearance was random in its time course, shown in (B).

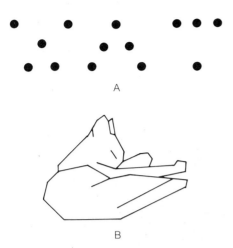

A

B

Figure 12-11. The importance of points of change in the direction of contours for pattern recognition. In (A) the letters are recognizable even though only points of change are indicated by the dots. In (B) the cat is recognizable even though points of change are merely connected by straight lines. (Figure B is from F. Attneave, Psychological Review, *1954, 61, copyright 1954 by the American Psychological Association. Reprinted by permission.)*

by indicating only points where the contours change direction. Thus, in Figure 12-11*A* it is easy to recognize the alphabetic letters even though only dots, representing points where lines end or meet, are indicated. In Figure 12-11*B*, only the points of maximum curvature have been extracted and connected with a straight edge, yet the form of a sleeping cat is seen clearly. Local aspects of a stimulus, related to more intuitively defined features, may provide adequate information about a pattern. In some cases, local information can be so striking that it actually interferes with perception of the whole pattern, as can be seen in Demonstration Box 12-4.

There are several other ways one can go about investigating the relative importance of

local features in pattern recognition. For instance, Cheatham (1952) tried a visual masking situation. He used simple targets (such as triangles and squares) and followed them with a very bright masking stimulus. As we showed in Figure 12-2, under these circumstances the amount of masking decreases as the interval between the target and mask is increased. Cheatham noticed that when the intervals were small, the target was not seen, but when the intervals became longer, his observers began to report seeing something. They did not simply see a dim image of the target but rather reported features in a specific order. Cheatham reasoned that the most important features would be processed first and would be visible after a short masking interval, while less important features would be processed more slowly and could be masked by a stimulus presented even after a substantially greater period of time. Observers reported that the first parts of the figures that were seen were the sides (often only one or two would appear). As the interstimulus interval increased, they could next report the presence of angles. The color of the figure became apparent only after the whole contour was visible. This finding seems to indicate that detection of specific features precedes the combination of the features into a perceptual object.

Another approach to the problem of isolating features used in the recognition of patterns involves looking at the types of confusions that people make when performing a recognition task. For instance, if we use alphabet letters as our target patterns, we find that *R* is most often confused with *P*, while *C* is most often confused with *G* or *O* (Kinney, Marsetta, and Showman, 1966). Gibson, Osser, Schiff, and Smith (1963) suggested a set of local features that could be used to recognize letters. The set included the number of lines, their orientation, curvature, and symmetry, among others. Geyer

Demonstration Box 12-4. The role of local features in pattern recognition

Harmon (1973) and Harmon and Julesz (1973) have presented an interesting set of demonstrations that illustrate how local features can interfere with a more global percept. One of their demonstrations is presented in the figure, a computer-processed block representation of a photograph. The brightness information from this scan is then locally averaged, so that the brightness value in each of the squares is an average of a number of brightness samples taken in that area of the picture. This technique can be used to see if such local brightness information can elicit the percept of the original photograph. To try this, look at the figure at normal reading distance. Do you recognize the person? Try again, viewing from 2 m this time. (It will also help if you squint your eyes.) If you follow these instructions, you should be able to identify this block portrait as a very famous historical person. If not, the name of the individual is printed upside down in the bottom right-hand corner of this page (From Harmon, L. D., & Julesz, B. *Science*, 1973, **180**, 1194–1197. © 19173 by the American Association for the Advancement of Science).

Abraham Lincoln

and DeWald (1973), and more recently Keren
and Baggen (1981) and Townsend and Ashby
(1982), were able to show that letter confusions could be accounted for by a small set
of such local features.

All the evidence we have presented suggests
that the detection and later combination of
distinctive features play an important role in
pattern perception. A conceptual difficulty remains, however. Any of the "features" we have
discussed (a line or an angle) would be called
a figure itself if it were not part of a larger
form. How do we know what is the overall
shape or pattern as opposed to what is merely
a part? Somehow an extraction of the **global**
aspects of the figure must be made to distinguish it from the smaller, **local** details. It is
interesting to consider how these two aspects
of patterns interact in how we perceive a visual form.

Navon (1977) addressed himself to this
problem by using stimuli like those in Figure 12-12. You will notice that Figure 12-12A
contains two large *H* figures. One is composed
of small *H*'s and one of small *S*'s. The large *H*
composed of small *H*'s is *globally-locally consistent* since the overall organization of the figure (a large *H*) agrees with the more local
contour information (the small *H*'s). On the
other hand, the large *H* composed of small *S*'s
is *globally-locally inconsistent* since the overall organization disagrees with the local information. Figure 12-12B shows a similar pair of
large *S*'s. Navon asked his observers to indicate
on each of many trials whether the global character of the letter was an *H* or an *S* regardless of
the small letters that made it up (he called this
the *globally-directed* condition). On other series of trials, observers were to indicate whether
the large letters were composed of small *H*'s or
S's regardless of the global identity of the letter
(he called this the *locally-directed* condition).
He recorded how long it took observers to
make each of these types of identification.

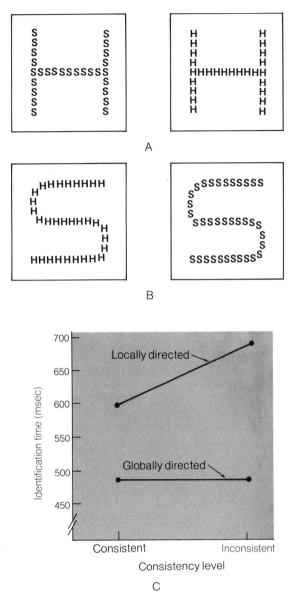

*Figure 12-12. Examples of figures that are
globally and locally consistent or inconsistent are shown in (A) and (B); (C) shows the
effect of task instructions and type of stimulus on identification time (based on Navon,
1977).*

The results of his experiment are shown in Figure 12-12*C*. Global aspects of such patterns are apparently dominant under these conditions. The recognition times for the locally directed trials were longer than for globally directed trials, especially when the identity of the form at the global level was inconsistent with that of the smaller forms. However, the globally directed response times were equally fast regardless of the consistency or inconsistency of local information. Since global judgments were faster and immune to interference from inconsistent local aspects, we would say that global aspects of the figure had **processing dominance** over the local aspects.

Navon's (1977) result stimulated several other researchers to investigate the interaction between global and local aspects of visual patterns. While most studies have found that global processing is generally faster, some others, using stimuli that differ in size or spacing, have reported faster processing of local features (e.g., Martin, 1979). This suggests that several processes may be involved. For instance, Kinchla and Wolfe (1979) found that the global aspects of compound letters such as those in Figure 12-12 were only identified faster if the whole pattern was relatively small, while local features were identified more quickly if the pattern was large. They concluded that features of about 2 degrees visual angle (about the size of a quarter held at arm's length) were processed fastest, with features of other sizes being identified more and more slowly as their size departed from the optimum.

Other experiments indicate that an important aspect of performance in such pattern recognition tasks is where attention is directed. Thus, Hoffman (1980) had observers indicate whether the global or local aspect of a compound letter was the same as that of one of a previously presented set of letters. He found that observers could pay attention to either or both levels of the compound letter, but that paying attention to both slowed responses. Ward (1982b) further demonstrated the importance of attention in determining whether global or local aspects of the pattern are dominant by using a task in which two patterns were presented one after the other. If the observer had to identify the global aspect of the pattern on both presentations, or the local on both presentations, responses were much faster, and more resistant to interference, than if a shift from local to global or the reverse was called for. Thus, it seems that switching attention from one level of processing to another is detrimental to performance. Such data make it clear that either global or local aspects of a form can have perceptual priority or processing dominance, depending on the specific stimuli presented and the attentional state of the observer.

Several other investigators have studied processing dominance from different perspectives (see Julesz, 1981). For example, Pomerantz, Sager, and Stoever (1977) showed that, in groupings of simple linear features, those that form closed, "good" figures are much easier to recognize than those composed of the same features in a different arrangement. These data seem to indicate some kind of direct (faster or earlier) perception of such "good" figures.

What is it about *good* figures that gives them processing dominance over less good figures? Several different explanations have been offered. Perhaps figural goodness is itself treated as if it were a feature or collection of features. If it were a perceptually dominant feature, then it might be extracted earlier than nondominant features and, hence, elicit faster responses. While some investigators have suggested that certain features do have such processing priority (Navon, 1977, 1981) others maintain that nearly all features are extracted from the visual image with roughly the same time course (Boer and Keuss, 1982; Miller, 1981).

One aspect of good figures that always seems to come to mind is that they have a certain unitary wholeness. In other words, they seem coherent and not easily broken into components. One analysis of processing dominance that incorporates this idea introduces the concept of an **integral stimulus**, which is a stimulus that is seen in all its aspects simultaneously. A lightbulb is such a stimulus, since it is seen to have shape and color all at once (Lockhead, 1966). Integral stimuli have many characteristics reminiscent of good figures. In contrast, a **separable stimulus** is one that has features that cannot be easily integrated. An example of a separable stimulus is the letter Q, in which the circle and the "tail" appear to be distinct parts. Notice that the separable portion breaks the "goodness" of the simple symmetrical circle. Lockhead (1972) argued that integral stimuli are processed first as "blobs" at a global level, *before* they are analyzed into their component parts. This seems to be one way to explain how some stimuli are identified more quickly than other stimuli made of the same features that have been combined in a different way (Lockhead, 1979; Lockhead and King, 1977; Monahan and Lockhead, 1977). If integral stimuli are automatically joined into perceptual objects by some principle of perceptual organization, then it may take extra time and effort to decompose them again in order to analyze the subparts. This means that the good, integral whole has processing dominance over its component parts.

When we discussed global versus local processing, we noted that processing dominance may be affected by attentional factors. Attention also seems to interact with figural goodness in determining how well we process certain patterns and pattern components. Many patterns are not really very *good* (and

are certainly not very integral). This includes the compound letter stimuli we illustrated in Figure 12-12 (see Pomerantz, 1983). Such stimuli tend to be synthesized into perceptual objects by attentional factors, as well as by the Gestalt principles. Treisman and Gelade (1980) theorized that we need to pay attention to a particular place in visual space in order to join the separately extracted features of a pattern into a proper perceptual object. This would explain why dividing attention between aspects of a pattern would slow identification at all levels. The less attention paid to features at a given level, the more difficult (and slower) it would be to combine those aspects into a perceptual object. Since there is much evidence that suggests that our attention is usually "caught" by good figures, or the *best* aspects of figures, it would also explain why better features are more easily and quickly joined into perceptual objects. Gestalt processes operating on the entire pattern would produce groups of elements that would be easy to join together into a perceptual unit (Prinzmetal, 1981; Treisman, 1982). The relationship between attention and the Gestalt principals of perceptual organization is thus like that of a train engine to its track. While the force and movement is provided by the engine (attention), the path that it must follow, if it is to go anywhere at all, is determined by the pattern of the track (the principles of organization). Of course, the fuel that powers the engine is data-driven feature extraction.

Conceptually-driven processing

Data-driven processes do not operate in isolation. Many facts about pattern recognition simply cannot be accounted for by any feature extraction process alone. For example, the **context** in which it appears can affect our ability to

A,B,C,D,E,F
10, 11, 12, 13, 14

Figure 12-13. The effect of context on pattern recognition. Notice that the B *and the* 13 *are identical.*

recognize a letter or word symbol (Eisenberg and Becker, 1982; Lawry, 1980; Mason, 1982). The context provides one type of conceptual information relevant to interpreting any stimulus. Look at Figure 12-13. Most people read these two lines as *A, B, C, D, E, F* and *10, 11, 12, 13, 14*, respectively. Notice, however, that the symbol you "saw " as *B* and the one you "saw" as *13* are identical. The context in which the two patterns occur alters our recognition of the figure. This is a conceptually-driven alteration since it depends on knowledge and assumptions. Remember the "data" (the actual stimulus input) are identical for both the perceptual organizations of *B* and *13*.

The use of a general organizing scheme in the recognition and remembrance of complex picture scenes has been demonstrated in a study by Mandler and Parker (1976). These investigators showed drawings, similar to Figure 12-14A, to observers. They then asked them to reconstruct the pictures either immediately after viewing or after a period of one week. In addition, a group of control observers, who had never seen the pictures, was given the array of objects within the pictures (as in Figure 12-14B). They were asked to reconstruct them as if they had seen a picture of them together. These researchers found that all the observers accurately reproduced the position of items on the vertical dimension. This was the case even for observers who had not

previously seen the actual target pictures. Mandler and Parker (1976) argued that this reflects the use of a conceptual framework based on an observer's experience with real world scenes. There are characteristic up-down organizations; for example, some objects usually appear above the horizon line while other objects appear below the horizon line. This type of information, which is part of our expectations about the organization of the world, can also help us to recognize scenes and to place objects within them (Mandler and Johnson, 1976). When "naturally" organized pictures such as Figure 12-14A are viewed for only 10 seconds, observers can correctly recognize whether the objects have been rearranged or are in the same position more than 80 percent of the time when tested four months later. On the other hand, spatial rearrangements in "unorganized" pictures such as Figure 12-14B are remembered fewer than 50 percent of the time (Mandler and Ritchey, 1977).

Palmer (1975a) studied a related problem. He looked at the ability of observers to recognize specific items within a picture when they were placed within an appropriate as opposed to an inappropriate context. He argued that we have expectations about which objects should appear in particular scenes. Looking at Figure 12-15, which is a kitchen scene, the top figure on the right, a loaf of bread, is the one that could be most appropriately inserted into that scene. Palmer presented observers with a set of such scenes. The presentation of each scene was followed by a briefly exposed target object that the observer was asked to identify. The contextual fit between the scene and the target object was either appropriate (such as a kitchen scene and a loaf of bread) or it was inappropriate (a kitchen scene followed by a drum). As you might expect, there was greater recognition of a target object when it was preceded by a scene that provided an appropriate

Figure 12-14. Meaningful objects in (A) natural and (B) scrambled locations.

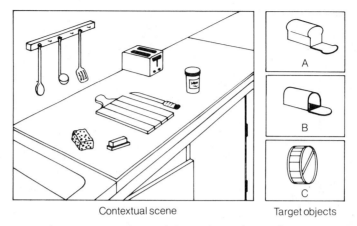

Contextual scene   Target objects

Figure 12-15. Context and target stimuli used by Palmer (1975a).

context. This type of result also reflects the use of prior expectations in the recognition process.

Interaction of data-driven and conceptually-driven processing

How does the data-driven analysis of local or global features interact with memories, expectations, context, and other concepts concerning the meaning of a pattern? Palmer (1975b) and Norman (1976) have argued that the two types of processing must proceed simultaneously and jointly. Our final interpretation of a particular pattern results from a melding together of the individual features and the context in which they occur. Palmer (1975b) demonstrated this notion in relation to face perception. Look at Figure 12-16. Notice that when seen as part of a face, any bump or line will suffice to depict a feature. When we take these features out of context, they do not really portray the objects very well. We actually require a more detailed presentation (such as those in Figure 12-16C) to recognize facial

features unambiguously when presented in isolation.

Meaning and expectation can direct which details within a pattern are chosen for analysis. This is shown in a study by Yarbus (1967). He recorded eye movement patterns while observers scanned pictures. He asked his observers to look at the pictures with different intentions in mind. He found that, when observers were asked to estimate the material wealth of the persons in the picture, they would scan and fixate different feaures than when they were asked to determine the ages of the persons depicted. Figure 12-17A shows a typical picture along with typical eye scan patterns when trying to assess age (12-17B) and wealth (12-17C). Recent studies have shown that unexpected objects in a visual scene (for example, a cow in a living room) attract longer fixations than do expected objects (Antes and Penland, 1981; Friedman, 1979). Even when observers were well motivated to distribute their attention equally, and succeeded to the extent of looking at everything about equally often, they nevertheless fixated longer on the unexpected objects

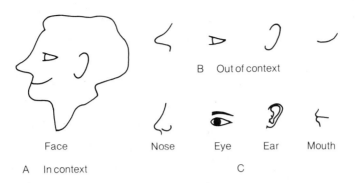

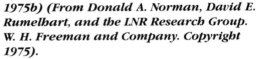

Figure 12-16. Facial components are easily recognized in context (A), but out of context they are much less identifiable (B) unless they are made more detailed (C) (Palmer, *1975b) (From Donald A. Norman, David E. Rumelhart, and the LNR Research Group. W. H. Freeman and Company. Copyright 1975).*

Figure 12-17. Eye movement patterns made when viewing the picture (A) vary depending on whether the viewer was asked the age of the individuals in the picture (scan pattern B *or their wealth (scan pattern C) (From Yarbus, 1967. Copyright Plenum Publishing Co., reprinted by permission).*

(Friedman and Liebelt, 1981). The perceptual consequences that follow from these differences in viewing behavior are that the unexpected objects are remembered and recognized more easily (Friedman, 1979), and exchanges of one unexpected object for another (for example, a cow for a car in a living room) are noticed far more than are exchanges of one expected object for another (for example, a chair for a table in a living room). Local visual details of expected objects in a scene are not usually analysed to a very high level of processing, while those of unexpected objects are.

A particularly striking example of how data-driven and conceptually-driven processing can interact is provided by the *visual-geometric illusions* we considered briefly in Chapter 1 and that we will encounter in other contexts in Chapters 14 and 16. Remember that visual illusions are simple drawings in which our perception of stimulus relationships, such as size, shape, or direction of figural elements, systematically differs from what would be expected on the basis of a knowledge of its physical dimensions. Figure 12-18 shows a version of the **Mueller-Lyer illusion**, which is created with

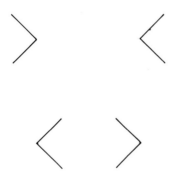

Figure 12-18. The Mueller-Lyer illusion, in which the distance between the vertexes of the upper pair of wings appears larger than that between the lower pair, even though they are equal.

a few simple lines. Here, the separation between the vertexes of the upper pair of outward pointing "wings" appears to be longer than the separation between the vertexes of the lower pair of inward pointing "wings," despite the fact that those distances are equal. This illusion can be quite strong, with a difference in apparent inter-vertex distance of 25 percent or more in some configurations.

Why should we select illusion stimuli to demonstrate how data-driven and conceptually-driven processing interact to form the percept? First, these are physically quite simple stimuli, created from a simple set of lines on paper. They are two-dimensional, hence should not be expected to involve different depth or distance processing of their elements. Only two levels of stimulus intensity are involved, namely, light reflected from the lines and from the background. A second reason for selecting these stimuli for analysis is the fact that the perception differs from what would be expected on the basis of physical measurements. Percepts such as these may provide us with an opportunity to see how perception is shaped and formed within the individual rather than simply representing a snapshot of the environment, transmitted from the eye to the brain. A final reason for considering these figures is that there is a wealth of research knowledge about them; they have been studied for more than a century (see Coren and Girgus, 1978).

How does the final illusory percept arise from the interaction between data-driven and conceptually-driven processes? The analysis begins with more peripheral data-driven events. First, the image of the stimulus is projected onto the retinal surface, thus evoking the photochemical response and triggering the first level of neural processing. However, the image is not transferred in an unmodified form from the retina to the higher centers. Data-driven analyses that will contribute to the appearance of the illusion are occurring at this level. As you probably recall from Chapters 3 and 6, interactions occur between retinal neurons, and they often involve inhibition. Thus, the activity in one cell can decrease the activity in another nearby retinal cell. This process, which we called **lateral inhibition**, was shown to affect our perception of brightness. It can also affect our perception of where a contour is located.

Consider Figure 12-19A. Here we have a cross-sectional picture of the retinal response to a bright spot stimulus. Notice that in the central area the neural response is quite vigorous, well above the base line of neural firing, but on either side the surrounding cells are inhibited. Given this pattern of response, one would simply see the bright spot as shown (perhaps with a darker region immediately around it). If we present two spots that are close together, as in Figure 12-19B, the two active and excited areas will tend to overlap, and we will see only one spot. If, however, the two spots are placed at an appropriate distance from each other, the inhibitory activity set up by one cell will overlap with the excited region set up by the other cell. This will distort the pattern of activity so that the two spots appear to be farther away than they actually are, as shown in Figure 12-19C (Békésy, 1967; Ganz, 1966).

The combination of this pattern of fusion and repulsion, resulting from these lateral inhibitory effects, will cause the neural response to, and thus the perception of, figures made of converging lines to be somewhat distorted. For instance, a simple angle should appear to be slightly flared out at the wide portions and have its vertex pushed into the body of the angle near the point, as shown in Figure 12-20A. This effect should cause a distortion so that the distance between the vertexes of the angles will appear to be more distant in the up-

per figure, and closer in the lower figure, as shown in Figure 12-20B.

We can experimentally verify that part of the illusion is a result of this data-driven neural effect. The neural interactions require the presence of lines that converge or intersect on the retina. Therefore, we can eliminate these effects by removing all the lines from the illusion and replacing the line ends and vertices with dots. When this is done for the Mueller-Lyer illusion (Figure 12-21), the illusion is greatly weakened, as we would expect, although some of it still occurs (Coren, 1970). Such results show that the first, data-driven, neural encoding process can, in fact, affect the final perceptual experience. The fact that some distortion remains after these mechanisms are bypassed suggests that processes at higher levels in the visual system also may be involved. There is some suggestion that interactions between adjacent neural units can occur at the level of the cortex and that these interactions serve to distort size or shape. These interactions are complex and deal with the modification of the responses of adjacent orientation specific units or line detectors (Blakemore, Carpenter, and Georgeson, 1970; Burns and Pritchard, 1971). Such results suggest that both retinal and cortical data-driven processing may alter or modify any visual experience.

Conceptually-driven processing also affects the final perception of the Mueller-Lyer illusion. For instance, the manner in which attention is distributed over the figure can alter the size of the distortion. Look at Figure 12-22. Notice that we have four dots located at the intersections of the white and dark lines. First, try to ignore those lines (wings) and compare the horizontal distance between the upper and the lower pairs of dots. Notice that these distances appear to be equal to each other. Now pay attention to the wings made up of black lines and try to ignore the white wings. By

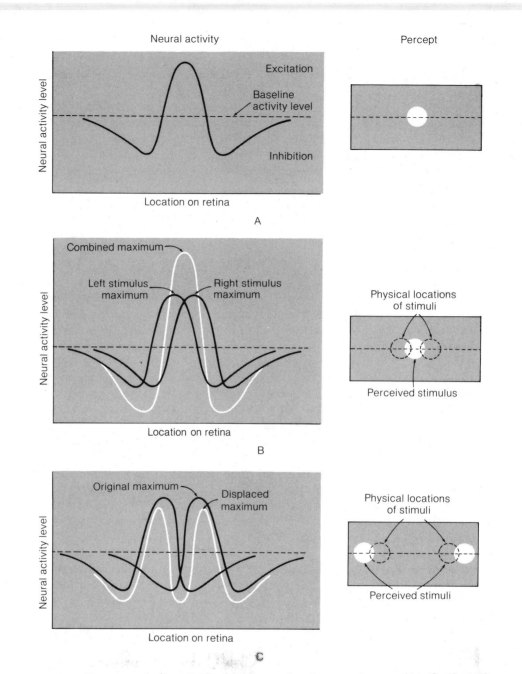

Figure 12-19. (A) *The spread of excitation and inhibition across the retina when stimulated by a single spot of light.* **(B)** *Two spots close together result in a single distribution of neural activity that is seen as one spot.* **(C)** *Two spots at an appropriate distance from* *each other produce a distribution of neural activity in which the regions of maximum excitation are displaced away from each other, causing an apparent displacement of the spots.*

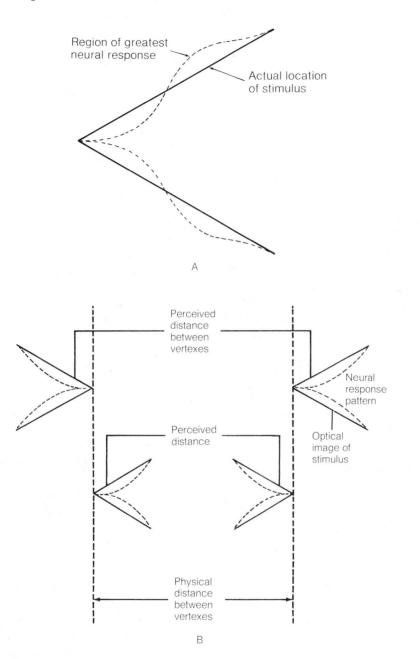

Figure 12-20. (A) The dotted line shows the expected ridge of peak neural activity when the retinal image is the angle shown by the solid line. (B) Illustration of how the neural ac- *tivity pattern in (A) could lead to distorted perceptions of the distances between the vertexes of the wings of the Meuller-Lyer figure (Figure 12-18).*

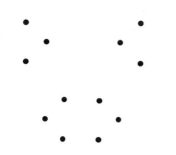

Figure 12-21. The dot form of the Mueller-Lyer illusion figure (based on Coren, 1970).

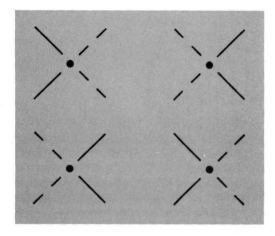

Figure 12-22. When you ignore the wings of the figure and pay attention to the dots only, the inter-dot distances in the upper and lower figures appear equal; paying attention to the black wings makes the inter-dot distance of the upper wings appear larger than that of the lower wings, while paying attention to the white wings reverses the illusion.

keeping your attention on the black elements, you are actually attending to a configuration much like that in Figure 12-18. Just as in that illusion figure, you should now see the horizontal distance between the upper pair of dots as greater than that between the lower pair of dots. The direction of the illusion is reversed if you pay attention to the white wings and try

to ignore the black wings; now the distance between the upper pair of dots seems to be shorter than that between the lower pair of dots. Coren and Porac (in press) showed that such illusions are about half as great as the illusion created by the ordinary Mueller-Lyer figure (Figure 12-18), but since it exists at all it must be created mostly by conceptually-driven processing of the stimulus. We can change the perceptual experience of the figure from no illusion to a reversible illusion of length without making any changes at all in the physical stimulus. All that has been done is to alter the distribution of attention across the figure. The data provided by retina and neural inputs remains the same, only the conceptual organization has changed.

Conceptually-driven processing (including use of depth cues, practice, and culturally affected processing strategies) contributes to the final percept for stimuli such as those in Figure 12-18. Coren and Girgus (1978) estimated that roughly half the distortion in such illusions is caused by factors that we can identify with data-driven processing, and the other half is caused by factors that we can identify with conceptually-driven processing. The two seem to interact in a complex fashion to produce the final perceptual experience (Coren and Ward, 1979). At any rate, it is clear that both types of processing typically contribute to our perceptual experience as well as to how we interpret and identify visual patterns.

Theories of visual pattern recognition

Since pattern recognition is such an important visual phenomenon, it isn't surprising that many investigators have offered theories that attempt to account for the major facts. In general, these theories fall into two major groups. Some emphasize a data-driven, relatively *pas-*

sive, analysis of features and some emphasize conceptually-driven, more *active* processing of input. Neither type has had complete success in explaining pattern recognition, so it is important to examine a major example of each type to see what we can use to formulate a general view that is more useful.

Much of the experimental work that we have discussed seems to be best interpreted when we view pattern recognition as dominated by a data-driven feature analysis. Models based on such an interpretation conceive of the pattern recognition process as one that involves a hierarchial system in which the sensory input is passed from lower to higher levels until it is finally combined at some central site. Let's look at one such model called **Pandemonium** (Selfridge, 1959). Figure 12-23 pictures one kind of of Pandemonium system. This system of pattern recognition, which actually began as a computer program, is based on a series of successive stages of feature analysis and recombination. Each stage has been given the term *demon*, because, descriptively, you can conceive of each stage as a series of little demons shouting out the results of their analyses.

Pandemonium works in the following way. The first stage, or the *image demon*, merely passes on an "image" or copy of the signal that has been registered in the visual system. This image is then analyzed by all the *feature demons* simultaneously (in *parallel*). The feature demons look for particular features within the incoming pattern, such as lines, angles, and curves. The feature demons are monitored by *cognitive demons*, and each cognitive demon is responsible for searching for a particular pattern. So, for example, if we are talking about letters presented to an observer, each cognitive demon might be responsible for recognizing a particular letter. The cognitive demons monitor the feature demons in order to detect the presence of features within the input that are included in the pattern for which they are responsible. Therefore, an *A* cognitive demon would be looking for the presence of certain oblique straight lines, certain acute angles, and a horizontal line. As the information is analyzed by the feature demons, the cognitive demons start "yelling" when they find a feature appropriate to their own pattern, and the more features they find, the louder they yell. A *decision demon* listens to the "pandemonium" caused by the yelling of the various cognitive demons. It chooses the cognitive demon (or pattern) that is making the most noise as the one that is most likely to be the pattern presented to the sensory system.

Programming a computer to act according to the rules that define the Pandemonium model and others like it has demonstrated that in certain cases such models can perform about as well as humans in identifying handwritten letters (Selfridge and Neisser, 1963; Uhr & Vossler, 1963; Wallingford, 1972) and this system can also be extended to the recognition of complex auditory patterns (Tou, 1981). More sophisticated versions of such models also can account for confusions between letters (Keren and Baggen, 1981; Townsend and Ashby, 1982) and some more complicated aspects of visual perception (Marr, 1982). Under certain conditions letter identification can be a completely data-driven process, producing only an abstract representation of a sensory input that contains no information about the physical aspects of the input such as its size or orientation, in much the way that you might talk about a letter *X* abstractly, without any reference to type style, size, and so on (Friedman, 1980). Even when these models do contain some primitive conceptual processes, however, they still have considerable difficulty with problems such as figure-ground separation, context effects, and faster processing of

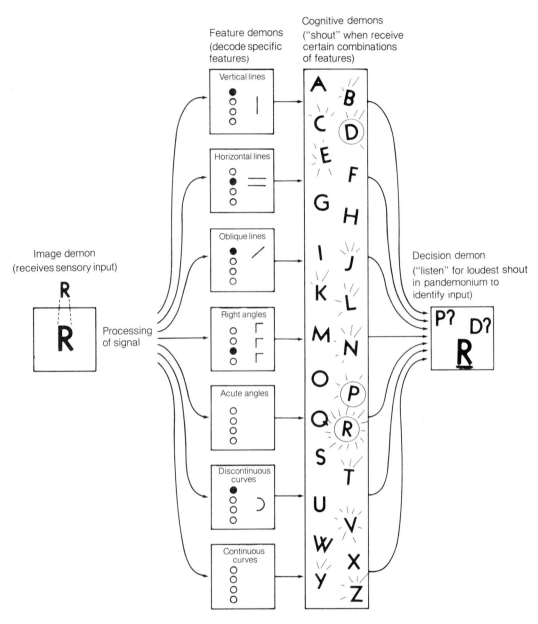

Figure 12-23. The Pandemonium model in action. The number of each type of feature registered by the feature demons is indicated by which circle is blackened in each box and by the number of times the feature is printed in the box.

"good" figures or "blobs." It is apparent that the greatest lack in these models is in the area of conceptually-driven processing.

One of the more important ideas concerning conceptually-driven processes in pattern recognition is probably **analysis-by-synthesis**. This concept appears to have been invented by Halle and Stevens (1962) to describe Stevens' (1960) computer program that attempted to recognize spoken language. It has been popularized by Neisser (1967). Analysis-by-synthesis requires two steps. First, a hypothesis as to the identity of the stimulus is generated by the higher centers on the basis of context and expectations. A first guess might be that the stimulus is, for example, a square. The first guess is then used to guide the second stage, which is a search for the specific features that make up the "guessed" target. This is usually called matching to a prototype or testing a schema (Neisser, 1976; Reed, 1973). The prototype, or schema, here would be a square. If the features actually present do not match those expected, a new prototype (hypothesis) is generated and the process is repeated. Thus, higher level conceptual processes always guide lower level feature extraction processes. This could explain context effects in which features are more easily detected when they are part of a meaningful objectlike whole (Lanze, Weisstein, and Harris, 1982; Weisstein and Harris, 1974; Womersley, 1977). Analysis-by-synthesis requires an active central processor to continually monitor the outputs of feature detectors, give tips to the cognitive demons, remember what has gone on before, and predict what will come next. The second aspect of analysis-by-synthesis, the reanalysis of a pattern when recognition fails, resembles Bruner's (1957) suggestion about perceptual readiness. Bruner argued that under some conditions we have to search for cues as to what a visual pattern is and that we have a hierarchy of possible identities to work with. We go back and forth between the hierarchy of possibilities and the features of the input, looking for a match. We identify the pattern as the highest category in our hierarchy (which represents our motivations and expectations) that sufficiently matches the input features. Reed (1973) suggested that we seldom use this aspect of analysis-by-synthesis, but it is available for use on ambiguous or novel patterns.

A recent theory that makes some progress toward integrating data-driven and conceptually-driven processing is Treisman's **feature integration theory** (Treisman, 1982; Treisman and Gelade, 1980; Treisman and Schmidt, 1982). This theory assumes that the various features of the visual scene are registered early and at the same time without requiring the overt act of paying attention to them. This is clearly a data-driven registration process. However, each of the various types of features of an object, such as its shape, color, and position, are recorded separately, without being joined into a perceptual object. In order to correctly synthesize the various attributes into a perceptual object, attention must be paid to a particular location in visual space. Attention is directed to that location either by the presence of a dominant feature in a particular region, or during a systematic search for a particular object and its features, or even just during an exploratory scan. This resembles the conceptually-driven processing of the analysis-by-synthesis theories, except that attention or search is assumed to have no influence on which features are extracted but rather on how they are conjoined or synthesized into perceptual objects. One interesting consequence of this theory is the unusual prediction that sometimes, if attention is overloaded, various features of objects or patterns may be joined incorrectly, producing percepts that differ from the actual stimulus situation. For example, there may be a red O and a blue X in the visual field, but one will see a nonexistent blue O. This prediction has been verified experimentally (Treisman and Schmidt, 1982).

Clearly some sort of combination of data-driven and conceptually-driven processing is necessary to explain more complex pattern processing. Take for instance the case of a painting by the Dutch painter Pieter Drost, which has hung in the municipal museum of Innsbruck, Austria, since 1889. The painting was titled "The Boy and the Vulture" until a studious art scholar pointed out that the scantily clad "boy" was actually a girl and the "vulture" was a pigeon. The museum now lists the painting as "Maiden with Dove." Imagine the complex interactions between data-driven and conceptually-driven processes in curators, scholars, and thousands of visitors that caused the original erroneous description, allowed it to persist for so many years, and finally "noticed" the error.

GLOSSARY

The following definitions are specific to this book.

Analysis-by-synthesis A theory of conceptually-driven processing based on perceptual readiness and the testing of schemas.

Backward masking The phenomenon whereby exposure to a second stimulus interferes with the perception of an initial stimulus if the second stimulus is presented within a certain critical interval.

Closure A principle of perceptual organization in which spaces enclosed by contours are most easily seen as figures.

Conceptually-driven processing Information processing that is guided by memories and expectations concerning the nature of the incoming stimulation.

Context Stimuli present in the environment that alter the perception of other stimuli.

Contour An area within the visual array where there is an abrupt change in luminance.

Data-driven processing Information processing based on the activation of structures within the sensory system that respond automatically to properties of the incoming array.

Distinctive features Attributes of a pattern that distinguish it from other patterns.

Feature integration theory A theory of how features are integrated to form perceptual objects; it assumes that features are extracted in parallel and automatically but that attention must be paid to a particular spatial locus in order for perceptual objects to be formed from the features.

Figures Integrated visual experience that "stands out" in the center of attention, usually an object as opposed to a background.

Ganzfeld A visual field that contains no visible contours.

Gestalt A concept and school of psychology emphasizing the notion of meaningful and coherent form, or "whole".

Global The overall aspects of a figure as opposed to the local details.

Good continuation The principle that elements that appear to follow in the same direction tend to be grouped together.

Ground The background against which figures appear.

Integral stimulus A stimulus that is experienced in all of its aspects at once and inseparably.

Kinetic depth effect When stimulus motion imparts a perception of depth to a two-dimensional form.

Lateral inhibition The process of adjacent visual units inhibiting one another, e.g., the more a cell is stimulated, the more it responds and inhibits its neighbor cells.

Law of Pragnanz The principle that the psychological organization of the percept will always be as "good" as prevailing conditions allow.

Law of Proximity The principle that elements close to one another tend to be seen as a perceptual figure or unit.

Law of Similarity The principle that similar objects tend to be perceptually grouped together.

Local The detailed aspects of a figure as opposed to the global aspects.

Metacontrast A form of backward masking in which the second stimulus has contours that are adjacent to, but not overlapping, those of the first stimulus.

Mueller-Lyer illusion A visual-geometric illusion of size.

Pandemonium A computer model of pattern recognition based on a series of successive stages of feature analysis and recombination.

Processing dominance When some aspects of a form are processed faster, or are more immune to interference from but interfere more with, other aspects of the same form.

Schemas Patterns of expectations built up through continued exposure and experience with sets of stimuli.

Separable stimulus A stimulus that has single features that cannot be easily integrated.

Stabilized retinal image An image whose retinal position remains constant regardless of eye movements.

Subjective contours Contours that are consciously experienced, but not associated with physical stimulus change.

13

Speech

The Production of Speech Sounds
    The Vocal Organs
    Vowels and Consonants
    Phonemes and Formants
Speech Recognition and Perception
    Feature Detectors and Syllable
        Recognition
    The Perception of Continuous Speech
Theories of Speech Perception
    Analysis-by-Synthesis
    Feature Analysis

376

THE INVENTOR STOOD LOOKING AT the ocean waves lapping over his short-circuited robot. His thoughts ran back over recent events. This was to be the ultimate android, with full abilities to recognize both visual and auditory patterns. It was to be capable of responding to human language, both written and spoken, and to be able to recognize objects in its world. While testing its visual abilities, the inventor had called it over to view a test object by giving it the simple commands "Go! See!" The machine had turned, crashed through the wall, and had run until it finally stopped chest deep in the ocean. "Maybe it thought that I said "Go, sea!" he mused, "Why, even a child. . ." His thoughts were interupted by a hiss, as sea water encountered another electrically active circuit.

For the average observer, of course, recognizing words involves the identification of sequences of sounds produced by the human voice. Thus, the inventor is correct in viewing speech perception as an auditory version of pattern perception. When trying to understand a given sequence of human speech sounds, however, we encounter some difficulties similar to that of the robot. These occur as **homophones**, which are words that sound alike when spoken, such as *see* and *sea* or *so* and *sew*, but actually have different spellings and different meanings. Clearly the recognition of the *meaning* intended by the speaker requires more than simply the accurate recognition of the sound pattern. Such considerations highlight some of the problematic aspects of speech perception and why it is of interest to psychologists. The accurate sensory reception and cognitive comprehension of the speech signal depends on the auditory mechanisms that decode the speech signal, the structures of articulation, such as the vocal chords and the lips, that produce the speech sound, and also on the context in which the words are produced. For example, although *so* and *sew* can be differentiated when printed, their accurate comprehension when spoken depends on the context of the conversation. This type of ambiguity is characteristic of other modes of language presentation as well. For instance, lip readers have difficulty with words such as *married* and *buried*, because these two words are **homophenes**, or words that look alike when they are spoken. To the outside observer, the pattern of lip movements to articulate these two words is almost identical, which makes the comprehension of meaning based on lip reading something of a problem. Similarities in the auditory signal or the articulatory pattern that produces the speech sound do not guarantee that the words are similar in meaning.

The meaningful interpretation of speech is usually taken for granted until we have to learn a foreign language. At that time, we suddenly become aware that speech is just a collection of sound stimuli. The coherent understanding of speech requires us to look at the organization of these "noises" rather than at individual sounds. In other words, we are looking for an auditory pattern, and recognition of the pattern gives us the "meaning" of the utterance.

As we have pointed out, listening to a spoken sentence is not like reading a printed sentence. In written sentences we have letters and words separated by spaces and punctuation marks. You might suppose, as a first guess, that similar groupings, over time, occur in spoken sentences, with a series of sounds alternating with silences, along with longer silences between words and at the end of sentences. If this were the case, it would be easy to identify the individual segments or features of the speech signal. However, there are problems with this model of decoding speech signals (Clark and Clark, 1977). For example, speech is usually continuous, and it is not composed of clearly separated, individual segments of sounds. While to the listener there may appear to be silences between words and sentences, these silences are largely illusory. Speech is better described as a continuously varying auditory signal, much like a siren, with very few breaks in the sound stimulus.

Another problem with the comparison of the printed and spoken word has to do with the fact that each letter of the spoken word does not have constant properties. For example, the letter *l* is printed very much the same way, regardless of the word in which it appears. However, an *l* is pronounced quite differently in different words. The *l*'s in *lip* and *pill*, although printed alike, do not have identical pronunciations. Furthermore, people speak with differing accents and differing voice qualities; sometimes they speak through devices that distort or alter the sound of the voice (such as a telephone) and perhaps even through barriers (such as food in the mouth). The decoding of each speech segment is quite remarkable given the variability in how speech sounds are produced.

A third aspect that makes it difficult to compare speech with printed sequences of words is speed. Although speech normally occurs at about 12 units per second, it can be understood at rates of up to about 50 units per second (Foulke and Sticht, 1969). This rate of processing is much faster than would be expected from experiments involving nonspeech sounds. Such experiments indicate that individuals can only determine the correct order of nonspeech sounds when they are occurring more slowly than about 1 every 1.5 seconds, or 2/3 unit per sec (Warren, Obusek, Farmer, and Warren, 1969). If we are processing speech by listening to each unit and then putting the units together in proper order, we could not possibly be accomplishing this task at the speeds at which human observers have

been shown to comprehend speech. Recognition of speech, therefore, poses some interesting perceptual challenges.

THE PRODUCTION OF SPEECH SOUNDS

As we noted before, in many ways speech perception is best understood as a form of auditory pattern perception. It is, therefore, important to isolate the stimulus features that allow us to recognize speech stimuli. Unfortunately, the specific features that distinguish one passage of speech from another are more difficult to isolate than those that differentiate various visual patterns, owing to the complex nature of spoken word sounds. Quite often it is simpler to characterize uttered sounds on the basis of the way they are produced by the speaker rather than to isolate all the sound frequencies and temporal characteristics of the stimulus. Consider, for instance, the *p* sound in *pill* and *spill*. In terms of how they are pronounced, these two sounds are different. The *p* in *pill* is accompanied by a small puff of air, which would extinguish a lighted match held in front of your mouth, whereas the *p* in *spill* is not. The two *p* sounds are distinct **phonetic**, or sound, segments produced by the physiological structures that determine the qualities of the human voice.

The vocal organs

Figure 13-1 diagrams the entire human vocal apparatus in cross-section. The human vocal apparatus can be divided into two major sections. The **lungs**, **trachea**, and **larynx** compose one segment, while all the structures or air passages above the larynx, called the **vocal tract**, make up the other.

The human respiratory system is the major source of "power" for the production of hu-

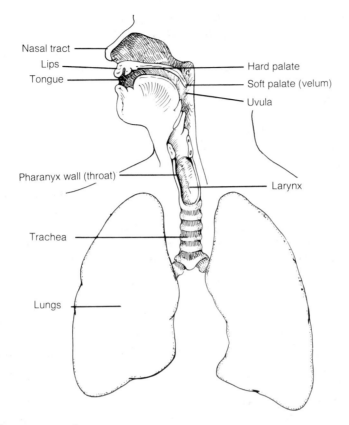

Nasal tract

Lips

Tongue

Hard palate

Soft palate (velum)

Uvula

Pharanyx wall (throat)

Larynx

Trachea

Lungs

Figure 13-1. The human vocal tract.

man speech. Air is expelled from the lungs, goes up the trachea (or *windpipe*, to use a more common name) and into the larynx, where it passes between two small muscular folds called the **vocal folds** (or *vocal cords*). The vocal folds are a pair of thin flaps with a gap, the **glottis**, in between. When the vocal folds are held apart, free breathing is permitted, and air flows freely into the **pharynx** (throat) and mouth. Occasionally, the vocal folds are held tightly together so that air cannot pass, such as when you hold your breath or prepare to cough. The most important position of the vocal folds for speech production, however, is one in which there is a restricted passage of air from the lungs to the mouth.

When the vocal folds have only a narrow passage between them as air flows by, they vibrate as a result of the pressure of the air stream. The air from the lungs forces its way through the vocal folds in a series of short puffs. Before each puff, the air pressure below the folds increases until it is sufficient to force them apart to release the puff of air. After the release the pressure decreases so that the folds are able to close again. This opening and closing action, as a result of changes in air pressure across the vocal folds, contributes to the production of the human voice.

The size of the vocal folds, the tension on them, and the air pressure exerted all affect the sound quality of a human voice. Puff rates (the opening and closing of the vocal folds over time) in the human larynx can vary from as low as 40 puffs per second to as high as 1500 puffs per second. On average, larger vocal folds produce lower puff rates and a lower pitch to the human voice. In a choir, for example, the singers in the bass section have larger vocal folds, lower puff rates, and therefore lower-pitched voices than those who are singing the tenor parts. In addition, variations in the tension of the vocal folds produces variations in the pitch of the voice. The higher the tension of the vocal folds, the higher is the pitch of the emitted sound. The size of the vocal folds determines the range over which variations in tension cause variations in pitch. Since the vocal folds are so important in the variations of pitch in the human voice, you can see why professional opera singers take extreme precautions to protect and rest this part of the sound-producing apparatus.

The air passages above the larynx, which make up the *vocal tract*, are also an important factor in speech production. Part of the vocal tract lies within the mouth and pharynx—the *oral tract*—while the remainder is in the nose—the *nasal tract*. The parts of the oral tract that are used to produce sounds are called **articulators**. In order to produce sounds, the lower articulators (the *lower lip and teeth* and the *tongue*) often move toward those that form the upper surface of the oral tract (the *upper lip and teeth*, the *alveolar ridge*, the *hard and soft palates*, the *uvula*, and the *back wall of the pharynx*). The names and locations of the upper and lower articulators are shown in Figure 13-1. Say a word, such as "capital," while attending to the movements of your lips and tongue and you will experience the continuous movement of these articulators. The tongue touches the roof of your mouth for part of the word while the lips come together and apart.

In the English language, the entire vocal apparatus produces basically two types of speech sounds—*vowels* and *consonants*. Speech sounds are produced by alternating sequences of opening and closing the vocal tract. The closing movements produce consonants while the opening movements produce vowels.

Vowels and consonants

Roughly speaking, vowels are formed when the vocal folds vibrate as air moves through the open mouth. The production of vowel sounds, however, also involves a combination of three factors. The first and second components have to do with the position of the tongue, whether the front, center, or back of the tongue is involved and its relative height in the mouth. Try repeating the words "heed," "hid," "head," and "had" while attending closely to the position of the tongue. You should be able to feel the tongue gradually lower as you move through the sequence from "heed" to "had." The third component in the production of vowel sounds is the degree of lip rounding. Try saying "who," called a *rounded* vowel sound and "he," called an *unrounded* vowel sound. If you watch yourself in a mirror while producing these sounds, it is easy to see the difference in the degree of pursing or rounding of the lips.

Consonant formation is somewhat more complex, but it can also be classified along three basic dimensions. First, consonant sounds are either *voiced* or *voiceless*. A voiced consonant is one whose pronunciation is accompanied by the vibration of the vocal folds, while unvoiced or voiceless consonants are not. If you try Demonstration Box 13-1, you will experience the difference between voiced and voiceless consonants for yourself.

Consonants can also be classified by their

manner and place of production. Consonant sounds can be formed in three ways and, therefore, are often given three different names that describe the way in which they are produced. *Stop consonants* are formed by a sudden, complete stopping of the stream of breath followed by a sudden release. Try saying the sounds of "t," "k," and "b." All of these are stop consonants. Second, we have *fricatives*, which are formed by forcing the breath through a narrow opening that is formed by placing the tongue or lips against the palate or teeth. Generally, fricatives produce a hissing sound, such as "s," "z," or "f." Third, there are *nasal consonants*, where the nose passage is open and the sound is produced through the nose, such as in "m" or "n." Generally, there are two places of production within the oral tract that characterize consonant sounds. Either much of the action has to do with the lips, called *labial* production, or most of the action is within the mouth where the tongue assumes different positions for different sound types. For example, in one type of sound, which is classified as having an *alveolar* method of production, the tongue is brought to the ridge behind the teeth (the alveola). To see the difference between labial consonants and other types of production locales, produce a "b" or a "p" sound (labial) as opposed to a "t" or a "d" sound (alveolar).

Demonstration Box 13-2 uses Tables 13-1 and 13-2, which provide simplified versions of the classifications of vowel and consonant sounds. As you can see, each individual sound is a coordinated effort among the various dimensions that characterize vowel and consonant production. Try saying each of the sounds while attending to the action of your oral tract and you will begin to experience the complexities of speech production.

Phonemes and formants

An alternate way of characterizing speech features depends on the attributes of the sounds themselves, rather than on the way they are produced. In this feature classification system, the basic unit is the **phoneme**, which is defined as the smallest sound unit distinguishing

Table 13-1. Classification of English vowels based on tongue positions (based on Clark and Clark, 1977)

Height of tongue	Part of the tongue involved		
	Front	**Central**	**Back**
High	*ee* (b*ee*t) *i* (b*i*t)	*y* (marr*y*)	*oo* (h*oo*t) *u* (p*u*t)
Middle	*a* (*a*te) *e* (b*e*t)	*a* (sof*a*)	*oa* (b*oa*t) *ou* (b*ou*ght)
Low	*a* (b*a*t)	*u* (b*u*t)	*o* (p*o*t)

one speech sound from another. The English language has about 40 phonemes (although there is some dispute as to the exact number), and these are listed in Table 13-3, which contains the phonemes of general North American English, excluding regional dialect sounds. Some languages use as few as 20 phonemes while others have as many as 60 or more. The list of phonemes may be used as a first catalog of acoustical (sound quality) as opposed to phonetic (sound production) speech features.

Because of the diversity in the articulation of speech sounds, the speech signal that reaches the ear is rather complex. As you learned in

Chapter 4, sounds can be classified according to their frequency, which is usually expressed in terms of cycles per second, or Hertz (Hz). Speech can be studied acoustically as one would study any complex sound by analyzing the different frequencies that compose it. One way to display this information graphically is in the form of **speech spectrograms**, some of which are shown in Figure 13-2. The horizontal axis of the spectrogram shows time in milliseconds from the onset of the speech signal. The vertical axis gives the frequency of the component sounds in Hertz. The variations in the lightness and the darkness of the smudges shown on the spectrogram indicate how intense the sound is at each frequency and at each point in time. For example, in the spectrogram depicted in Figure 13-2, there are very intense sounds from about 300 to 700 Hz for about 200 msec in the pronunciation of the syllable "bab."

The spectrogram shows other interesting aspects of speech. As we have discussed, the human voice starts in the lungs and throat with the vibration of the vocal folds. The vocal folds can vibrate at different rates, with higher vibration rates being associated with higher-pitched voices (Ladefoged, 1975). Therefore, we can

Table 13-2. Classification of consonants of North American English

	Voiced		Voiceless	
Place of Production	Lips	Inside mouth[a]	Lips	Inside mouth
Method of Production				
Stop	b (*b*at)	d (*d*in) g (*g*ot)	p (*p*at)	t (*t*in) k (*c*ot)
Fricative	v (*v*at)	th (*th*y) z (*z*ip) z (a*z*ure) g (*g*yp)	f (*f*at)	th (*th*igh) s (*s*ip) sh (*sh*ip) h (*h*ip) ch (*ch*ip)
Nasal	m (*m*at)	n (g*n*at) ng (si*ng*)		

a. Includes the placement of the tongue against the ridge at the back of the upper teeth and against the soft and the hard palate (technically known as *alveolar, palatal,* and *velar* methods of production)

Table 13-3. The major phonemes of general North American English

Consonants		Vowels
The *p* in pea	The *th* in thigh	The *ee* in beet
The *b* in beet	The *th* in thy	The *i* in bit
The *m* in meet	The *sh* in short	The *ai* in bait
The *t* in toy	The *s* in measure	The *e* in bet
The *d* in dog	The *ch* in chip	The *a* in bat
The *n* in neat	The *g* in gyp	The *oo* in boot
The *k* in kill	The *l* in lap	The *u* in put
The *g* in good	The *r* in rope	The *u* in but
The *f* in foot	The *y* in year	The *oa* in boat
The *s* in sit	The *w* in wet	The *ou* in bought
The *ng* in sing	The *wh* in whet	The *o* in dot
The *v* in vote	The *h* in hot	The *a* in sofa
The *z* in zip		The *y* in marry
		The *i* in bite
		The *ou* in out
		The *oy* in toy

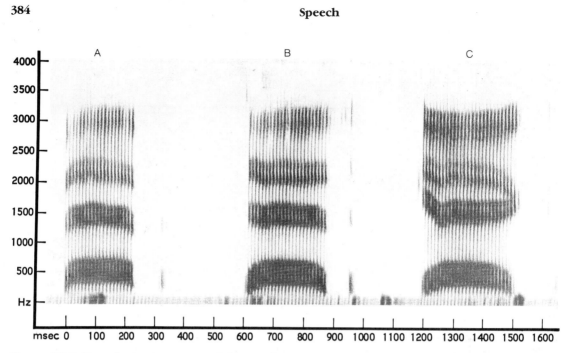

Figure 13-2. Speech spectrograms of the words (A) bab, (B) dad, and (C) gag, spoken with a British accent (from A Course in Phonetics *by Peter Ladefoged. Copyright 1975 by Harcourt Brace Jovanovich and reproduced with their permission).*

relate these differences in pitch to a different fundamental frequency for each voice. As you may remember from Chapter 8, any complex tone has a fundamental frequency; therefore, speech in this way is very much like other complex tones. If the vocal folds are vibrating at 128 times per second, for example, we will have a fundamental frequency of 128 Hz. Simultaneous with the production of this fundamental frequency, the voice also produces harmonics of this frequency. In other words, frequencies that are whole number multiples of the fundamental frequency are also produced. In our example, with a fundamental frequency of 128 Hz, we would also find harmonics of 256, 384, and 512 Hz. As these vibrations pass through the pharynx and the oral tract, some of the harmonics are enhanced while others are diminished. This strengthening and weakening leads to a particular pattern of sound.

If you look once again at Figure 13-2A, the spectrogram for "bab," you will notice that frequency enhancement has occurred in a band around 500 Hz and also in a band around 1450 Hz. This is where the darkest smudges on the spectrogram occur. These bands of enhanced sound are called **formants**. The lowest (at 500 Hz) is the *first formant*, and the next lowest (at 1450 Hz) is the *second formant*. These two formants correspond to two major cavities in the vocal system, the pharynx and the oral tract. The shape of these cavities is responsible for the first and second formants, and any changes in the shapes of these cavities will change the frequency placement of the first and second formant. It is this change in formants that distinguishes one vowel sound from another. For example, the pronunciation of the word "had" might produce average frequencies for the first two formants at 690 Hz and at 1660 Hz (Ladefoged, 1975). It seems that only vowels have this quality. Consonants are distinguished by abrupt changes in the formants. Such changes are sometimes accompanied by wide bands of sound spread over the whole frequency range. For example, the pronunciation of "she" would give a broad smear of energy up and down the spectrogram.

The spectrogram reveals that speech is a very complex sound with frequency and energy differences occurring over time. Each consonant and each vowel sound in the English language seems to consist of a different pattern of differing amounts of energy at the various sound frequencies. It is remarkable that this pattern can be recognized by a listener as quickly as it is, so that speech is intelligible and meaningful.

SPEECH RECOGNITION AND PERCEPTION

A current controversy surrounding perceptual aspects of speech involves two basic positions. One viewpoint states that speech perception is based on a system of special *feature detectors*. These detectors are supposed to be physiologically based mechanisms that detect certain specific properties, such as voiced versus unvoiced, fricatives, stops and so on, in much the same fashion that there are specific feature detectors in the visual cortex (Abbs and Sussman, 1971; Jacobson, Fant, and Halle, 1952, 1961). Thus, investigators usually try to isolate specific aspects of the signal to which these hypothesized "speech detectors" might respond

(Eimas and Corbit, 1973). The other point of view claims that speech signals are like other auditory signals, varying in frequency composition and loudness, and are processed by the same mechanisms that process all auditory input. In other words, speech is not a special stimulus, it is just a different type of sound (Huggins, 1981). These different points of view have been applied to the study of the perception of individual words or syllables and also to the perception of complete phrases and sentences. Both approaches have searched for *invariant properties* in the speech signal, that is, properties that do not change in relation to each other (despite speaker variations in pitch and dialect) and which serve as cues to speech recognition.

Feature detectors and syllable recognition

We have already indicated the complexities of speech production, where voicing and other articulatory differences contribute in unique combinations to the production of each phoneme. In addition, there are formant relationships that differ when different syllables are produced, as you have seen in Figure 13-2. To give you some idea of the details involved, we can look at the articulatory stages in the production of simple stop consonant-vowel syllables, such as "ba" or "da" (Dorman, Studdert-Kennedy, and Raphael, 1977). First, the mouth is closed and then there is a brief explosion (of about 20 msec) when the vocal tract opens. Third, there is a brief period of frication as air is blown through the gradually widening opening. This third stage lasts about 10 msec. Fourth, there is the stage in which the vocal tract and tongue move to the position appropriate for the following vowel, and finally, there is the final tongue position and vocal fold vibration that produces the formant transitions. Thus, within a few milliseconds of syllable production, there are five distinct stages, three related to the stop consonant and two related to the vowel that follows it.

With such a diversity of articulatory characteristics and the resultant myriad of acoustical properties in the speech signal, it is not surprising that some of them have been singled out to be studied separately. Investigators have begun by asking if each of these selected features contributes to the recognition of syllables and words and, if so, how. Eimas and Corbit (1973), in an influential study, investigated whether there might be physiological feature detectors tuned to the various physical properties of the speech sound. They reasoned that if such physiological feature detectors exist for specific speech properties, then one should be able to fatigue these physiological systems by a prolonged exposure to stimulation to which they are particularly sensitive. The idea here is that the fatigued mechanism should then be less sensitive to that particular stimulus, and this should show up as a reduced ability on the part of the observer to recognize stimuli that use that feature. They chose to study the characteristics of voiced versus unvoiced stop consonants in English (*p*, *t*, and *k* are unvoiced; *b*, *d*, and *g* are voiced, as we saw in Demonstration Box 13-2). In producing a stop-consonant sound followed by a vowel sound, there is a period of time after the column of air has been stopped by the lips or tongue before the vocal cords begin to vibrate to produce the voiced sounds or the vowel sound (we have already described these stages in detail). This latency is called the **voice onset time**. Small differences in voice onset time are usually sufficient to distinguish between voiced and unvoiced stop consonants in English. For example, there is a 60 msec time

difference between the onset of the vowel sound in "ba" and "pa" with the voiced "ba" being the faster.

By varying the voice onset time systematically, the point of transition, where observers call a target stimulus "ba" as opposed to "pa," can be determined (Lisker and Abramson, 1970). They called this transition point the **phonemic boundary**, and conceptualized it as a sort of difference threshold, such as those that we discussed in Chapter 2. Eimas and Corbit (1973) adapted observers to one specific category (for example, to "ba") by repeatedly presenting the stimulus sound. Supposedly this adaptation should reduce the sensitivity of the feature analyzers that, hypothetically, respond to faster voice onset. In fact, they did find that after this period of adaption, the boundary between "ba" and "pa" had shifted, and observers would now call certain stimuli "pa" even though they had originally classified them as "ba." The researchers argued that these results implied that the neural detectors for the feature of voiced versus unvoiced had been fatigued. Other investigators have shown that a variety of other characteristics of speech can also be adapted through repeated exposure. Some of these characteristics include features associated with the place of articulation, such as the lips versus the inside of the mouth, while others deal with purely acoustic cues, such as vowel pronunciation (Diehl, 1981).

Another feature that has been studied is the location and composition of the various formants and their role in syllable recognition. For example, Klein, Plomp, and Pols (1970) looked at the importance of formants in the perception of vowel sounds. As we have noted, vowels are characterized by the modulation (changing in a particular way) of sound as it passes through the oral cavity, giving rise to formants, or bands of high energy output positioned at characteristic frequencies in a speech spectrogram. These investigators had individuals pronounce 12 different vowels in a *b-vowel-t* context (such as "bat" or "bit"). They made test vowels by removing 100 msec segments of the steady vowel sound from this pronounced word. They then had observers attempt to identify the 100 msec segments of the vowels. Observers were reasonably good at this and achieved about 74 percent correct identification of the segments. Next, the investigators looked at the confusion errors between vowels. You will notice that this is quite similar to the technique used to study feature detection in letter perception, which we discussed in Chapter 12. They reasoned that if observers tended to confuse vowels it might be because the vowels shared certain features. They found that two vowels were confused with one another to the extent that the first two formants contained frequencies that were similar. Thus, they found that acoustical properties of the vowel sound could predict perceptual confusions, with the first two formants acting as if they were the critical features.

In a more recent study, Jusczyk, Smith, and Murphy (1981) presented observers with a series of consonant-vowel syllables (such as "bi" or "di"). However, they asked the observers to listen to them and classify them based on the identity of the initial consonant after hearing only the first 30 msec of each syllable. In some instances, this 30 msec segment contained full formant information while in other instances the segment contained only the second and third formants. Observers could make accurate classifications of the initial consonant only for the segments containing full formant information. Jusczyk et al. (1981) concluded that there are enough features available in consonant sounds to allow observers to accurately

identify consonants irrespective of the nature of the vowel that follows. Thus, formant information may be important not only in vowel but also in consonant recognition.

The investigation of phoneme production and formant information concentrates on a particular feature that is characteristic of the speech signal specifically. However, speech is also a sound stimulus, although it is a very complex one. It contains different frequencies of sounds that last for different durations, it has variations in loudness, and so forth. It is possible that these simple sound features may also play a role in speech recognition. Perhaps we do not need to resort to hypothesizing that there are special speech features and speech feature detectors. There is some evidence to support this point of view. For example, nonspeech sounds differ in their onset time also. Those with a rapid onset might sound like a plucked string on a violin while those with a gradual onset might sound like a bow moving across a string. Using these types of stimuli, Cutting (1976) was able to show identification boundaries and adaptation effects, such as those that we have discussed for consonant-vowel syllables. In addition, Diehl (1976) was able to move the boundary between phonemes starting with *b* and *w* by using a nonspeech adaptor. Also, Ingram (1975) showed that the classification of sounds based on the identity of the initial consonant was highly correlated with the duration of the initial consonant. In other words, the length of the sound, rather than any special quality of its production, accounted for much of the perceptual similarity between consonants. Studies such as these demonstrate that nonspeech sound stimuli can produce effects similar to those found with speech stimuli and indicate that simple auditory features may play a role in speech recognition (Huggins, 1981).

As in visual pattern perception, we also find that the meaning of speech sounds can affect our perception or recognition of a specific stimulus. **Phonology**, or the meaning attached to the speech signal, seems to be as important as its phonetic or distinguishable sound qualities. This point has been demonstrated by Day (1968, 1970), who presented observers with sequences of sounds, some to the right ear and some to the left ear. The left ear might hear *b-a-n-k-e-t* while the right ear would hear *l-a-n-k-e-t*. Some observers heard the individual sequences of sounds; other observers fused the two sequences of sounds and heard the word *blanket*. However, none of the observers heard *lbanket*, a sequence that is excluded by the phonological rules of English. In English, an *l* is never followed by a *b* at the beginning of a word. Individuals even fused the two sequences of sounds into the word "blanket" when *lanket* was presented a few milliseconds before *banket*. This suggests that meaning or expectation operates against the perception of sound sequences that are not appropriate to the language we are decoding. These expectations seem to form an interpretive context that plays a role in syllable and word recognition.

The perception of continuous speech

Our previous discussion concerned only the perception of syllables and words. What about the perception of longer and meaningful sequences? If we wanted to take a *bottom-up* or *data-driven* approach (as we discussed in Chapter 12), we might say that recognition of continuous speech would start with low level auditory properties that combine into phonemes, which in turn, combine into syllables, words, and sentences. In other words, continuous speech recognition is built from the bottom up, from the simple to the complex. Several problems exist, however, with such a model of continuous speech. For example, observers can detect more readily the consonant *b* if it occurs in a real word as opposed to a pseudoword (a word that follows the phonological constraints of English but has no meaning). So, if observers are asked to respond quickly to words beginning with "b," they are faster in response to a stimulus such as "bit" than to "bip" (Rubin, Turvey, and Van Gelder, 1976). Such results are difficult to explain if we assume that we must recognize speech based on the simple fusion of sounds to make up sentences in a bottom-up fashion.

The continuity of normal speech provides a detailed context that creates expectations or sets for the reception of certain types of stimuli. Thus, if we heard a garbled sentence that ran "the boy hit the ball with a ..at," we might probably discard such candidates for the last word as "cat" and "rat" and opt for the more likely choice "bat." In this way, the meaningful context increases our ability to recognize words. We can say that speech forms a single stream within which the sequence of sound and its meanings are easier to follow. This suggests that speech recognition has a *top-down* or *conceptually-driven* component, with the more complex cognitive structures guiding our perception of the simple acoustical elements (Huggins, 1981). This principle is demonstrated in an experiment by Pollack and Pickett (1964). They secretly recorded people engaged in spontaneous conversation. They then played back single words extracted from these tape recordings to other observers and asked them to identify the words. They found that single words were correctly identified 47 percent of the time. When you listen to an entire stream of continuous speech, however, you do not have the impression that words have to be guessed. The stream of speech

---

Demonstration Box 13-3. Context and speech recognition

The stream of normal speech is fairly continuous; it does not typically have the gaps we perceive between words. Yet, these gaps are connected with our recognition of the words. In fact, it seems that we insert the gaps between words to correspond to our interpretation of their meaning. The context of the speech greatly affects our interpretation of the nearly continuous stream of ordinary speech and thus influences where we perceive gaps—that is, where we perceive the boundaries of the words to be. To do this demonstration, suggested by Goldstein (1980), read the following phrase rapidly and smoothly to a friend: "In mud eels are, in clay none are." Ask your listener to write down the phrase he or she heard. Now, tell your listener that you are going to read a sentence from a book that describes where various types of amphibians can be found. Then read the above sentence, trying to read it at the same speed as you did the first time. After your listener writes down what he or she heard this time, you can compare the sentences (or nonsentences) that were heard both with and without the context. Without context, you might find responses such as "In muddies, sar, in clay nanar" or "In may deals are, en clainanar" (Reddy, 1976). Here the words in the sentence are difficult to recognize when presented rapidly, and a strange and largely meaningless set of segments is generated. When the proper context is supplied, however, the same speech sounds are correctly segmented into words, as you should find when you look at the response from the second presentation.

---

seems intact and quite intelligible. In an interesting addition to their experiment, Pollack and Pickett (1964) continued to present longer and longer strings of words to surround the single words they had presented first. As the amount of speech surrounding the word increased, observers became progressively more accurate in identifying the word. Therefore, the more acoustic, syntactic, and meaningful information available, the better the recognition of words. You can experience the dramatic effect of context on word recognition for yourself by trying Demonstration Box 13-3.

In a similar vein, Warren (1970) discovered that the context of a sentence can actually cause an observer to fill in a gap present in a continuous speech. He called this the **phonemic restoration effect**, and it works in the following way. Warren (1970) presented observers with a taped sentence: "The state governors met with their respective legislatures convening in the capital city." A segment corresponding to the s in "legislatures" was deleted and replaced with a cough. Only one observer out of twenty noticed that any speech sounds were missing. In other words, observers restored the deleted phoneme in the course of processing and recognizing the taped material. It is interesting to compare some of these context effects in the recognition of speech patterns to those observed in visual pattern perception that we saw in Chapter 12. It is particularly instructive to compare the effects in Demonstration Box 13-3 to those in Figure 12-13.

A more recent study by Samuels (1981), however, has indicated that acoustic as well as contextual information may play a role in the phonemic restoration effect (and, therefore, in the perception of continuous speech). He replaced sections of words with segments of white noise (a hiss), or he added white noise to sections of words. In addition, he used words that vary in the frequency with which they appear in the English language (hence their familiarity to the observer), and also that vary in length. He argued that these variables alter the context in which the replaced or added word segment appears, since, for instance, a longer word provides a longer relevant context. In addition, he noted the phonemes that were replaced by the noise, since some of the phonemes would sound more like the hissing sound of the random noise (such fricatives as "z," for example). Notice that this manipulation most directly affects the acoustic information. His results supported the notion that both contextual and acoustic information are active in the phonemic restoration effect. The highest degrees of restoration (or saying that speech was present when the phoneme had been replaced by random noise) occurred in longer words (longer context), but also in words in which a fricative had been replaced by noise (greatest acoustic confusion). When he used sentences that provided a particular context, he found that observers were more likely to restore the phoneme (say that the word was complete) when it was best predicted by the context of the sentence. Samuels's (1981) results support both a *top-down* and a *bottom-up* model of continuous speech perception where both lower and higher level information interact to guide speech recognition.

Another study, however, is more difficult to reconcile with the notion that acoustic information, usually found in the speech signal, plays an important role in continuous speech perception. Remez, Rubin, Pisoni, and Carrell (1981) took the natural utterance of the sentence, "Where were you a year ago?" and reproduced it in such a way that only the frequency and the amplitude variation of the natural speech formants in the orginal utterance were preserved. Thus, their stimulus con-

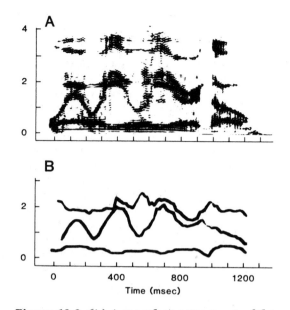

Figure 13-3. (A) A speech spectrogram of the spoken sentence "Where were you a year ago?" compared with (B) a synthetic replica of the sentence based on variations of only three tones (from Remez, Rubin, Pisoni, and Carrell, 1981, Science, 212, p. 947. Copyright 1981 by the American Association for the Advancement of Science. Reprinted by permission.)

sisted of three tones that matched the center frequencies and the amplitudes of the first three formants in the orginal spoken sentence. Figure 13-3 shows the spectrogram of the original spoken sentence and the spectrogram of the synthetic replica. All other acoustic information that is usually present in natural speech was absent in their stimulus. Observers listened to the synthetic signal and attempted to identify it. Only a few observers identified the tones as speech when they were not told what to expect (under these conditions, responses of "science fiction sounds" and "computer bleeps" were common). Even under these conditions, however, a few observers reproduced the natural sentence exactly. More accuracy was found when subjects were informed that they would hear a sentence reproduced by a computer. More responses indicating the perception of the complete sentence or parts of it occurred under these instructional conditions. Despite the fact that the observers recognized the unnatural quality of the speech signal, linguistic information leading to word recognition was processed, especially in the observers who were primed to hear a synthetically produced sentence. Remez et al. (1981) concluded that speech perception can endure the absence of much of the usual acoustic information if the pattern of change over time in the natural signal is preserved. Their results suggest that if acoustic information contributes to the perception of continuous speech, it is not the short term acoustic information available when syllables are spoken, but rather the pattern of acoustic change over time that is the important component. This probably explains why we can still recognize speech when presented to us through sound distorting devices, such as telephones, poor radios, or even when speech emanates from inside a barrel or behind a closed door. The telephone signal loses much of its low frequency components, while speaking through a door cuts out most of the high frequency components. Despite such acoustical distortions, the speech is still generally intelligible.

THEORIES OF SPEECH PERCEPTION

Several types of theories of speech perception are of historical as well as current interest. Each emphasizes the different aspects of speech perception that we have discussed, namely, speech production, contextual and integrative processing, and lastly, phonemic and acoustic feature analysis.

Analysis-by-synthesis

A matching principle forms the basis of the **analysis-by-synthesis** approach to speech perception (Stevens and Halle, 1964). Observers are assumed to have an internal speech production system by which they can generate or "synthesize" speech sounds for themselves. Presumably, when a string of speech sounds is encountered, an attempt is made by the listener to match these sounds in terms of the articulatory movements that she would have to make to produce similar sounds herself. What is, in effect, matched is the auditory input to the motor pattern needed to make the sounds. In other words, the central concept in speech perception becomes *speech production*, with the hearer metaphorically repeating the sounds to herself, in order to decode them. As we shall see, such a theory depends on the movements used in the speech production sequence; hence, it is usually listed as one of the **motor theories** of speech perception (Leiberman, Cooper, Shankweiler, and Studdert-Kennedy, 1967; Stevens and House, 1972).

Evidence for motor theories has been derived from the way in which sounds are classified. For instance the *d* in the composite sound "di" is given the same name as the *d* in the sound "du," despite the fact that they are different acoustically. Their sound structures are certainly no more similar than the *d* in "di" is to the *b* in "bi." Yet why are the *d*'s recognized as being in the same class? The motor theory argument states that both *d*'s are pronounced with the same articulatory movement of the tongue, accompanied by voicing. In effect, listeners conclude that since the same motor sequence is used, the speaker intended to produce the same *d* sound for both utterances. The fact that the sound is not the same is irrelevant, just as the pitch of voice, speed of speech, and speech defects are irrelevant. The local features of the sound are ignored and attempts are made to match speech input to how the listener would reproduce it.

A study by Lehiste and Peterson (1959) gives direct evidence in favor of such an analysis of speech. They looked at the perception of the loudness of vowels. Vowel sounds may differ widely in the amount of sound energy they contain when spoken with the same effort. Thus, the *ee* sound in "beet" contains much more sound energy than the *oa* sound in "boat," when spoken with the same effort. Lehiste and Peterson were able to show that when observers are presented with the *ee* sound and the *oa* sound at exactly the same acoustical energy, the *oa* was judged to be louder. Thus, the judgment of loudness followed the inferences about the amount of effort needed to reproduce the sound, rather than an analysis of the actual stimulus features.

In spite of this evidence, motor theories can only be part of the answer. For instance, there are reported cases of indivduals who, for neurological reasons, could not speak. If a motor theory were taken as the only mechanism involved in speech perception, such individuals should also not be able to understand speech; yet, many can (Fourcin, 1975; Lenneberg, 1962). We can also understand the speech of people with extreme dialects, those who stutter, and many other groups whose speech we could not possibly hope to reproduce. Thus, a motor theory must be taken as an abstract, perceptual strategy used by a hypothesis-generating process that tries to determine how the speaker would have to say what has been said.

Feature analysis

A more recent alternative to analysis-by-synthesis and its motor theory component is the approach that stresses **feature analysis** of the speech signal. Two major viewpoints are subsumed under this general approach. As we mentioned earlier in the chapter, one viewpoint states that the feature components of speech are special units, unique to the speech signal, while the other approach claims that auditory or acoustic feature analysis is sufficient to account for speech perception. We deal with the "speech is special" view first.

Linguists seem to agree that phonemes comprise bundles of *distinctive features*. The presence or absence of a feature defines the minimal meaningful distinction between two spoken words. For example, "bad" and "pad" differ only in that the first consonant is either voiced, *b*, or voiceless, *p* (Diehl, 1981). This agreement among linguists makes a distinctive feature approach to speech perception an attractive alternative from a psychological perspective. However, psychologists cannot agree on the precise nature of the distinctive features that distinguish the perception of speech and whether or not they are physiologically based. In the early 1970s, investigators postulated that we have neural detectors that are sensitive to certain complex speech properties, especially those that are linked to distinctive features, such as voicing (Abbs and Sussman, 1971; Eimas and Corbit, 1973). As discussed in a previous section of this chapter, Eimas and Corbit (1973) postulated that *voice onset time* was such a feature; they then used adaptation experiments to explore the neural basis of this feature. Since that time, a number of lines of evidence have been proposed as support for this type of neurally based feature analysis. The results of adaptation experiments (which were described earlier), along with the manner in which observers categorize speech sounds, were cited as supportive of this viewpoint. In addition, studies of the electrical activity in the auditory pathways of nonhuman species, such as frogs, squirrel monkeys, and birds, have shown selective responses to species-specific significant communicative vocalizations, such as mating calls (see Diehl, 1981, for a review of this literature). It is argued that all these research efforts seem to confirm that biologically based mechanisms selectively respond to the complex distinctive features of human vocal communication.

An alternative to the distinctive feature approach is one that proposes that analysis of the auditory component features of the speech signal contains enough information to allow for the formulation of theories or models that can account for our perception of speech. A system proposed by Klatt (1980), which is a computer model, is an example of such a point of view. Klatt claims that transitions between phonetic segments (speech) can be represented by a small number of types of features.

These features reveal themselves in detailed analyses of speech spectrograms of the type shown in Figure 13-2. For example, look at Figure 13-4 showing a spectrogram of the phrase "to the top of the hill." The other graphs show 10 msec spectral analyses of what is happening to the speech signal as the speaker moves from saying the *t* to the *o* sound in the word "top." You can see that both the level of sound energy (decibels) and the frequency (Hertz) are changing over the brief 10 msec period for each sound feature under analysis. In this segment there are silences, bursts, aspirations (a voiceless period), voicing onset, and vowel midpoint, all of which serve to discriminate this segment from others. Klatt's model of the analysis of the speech

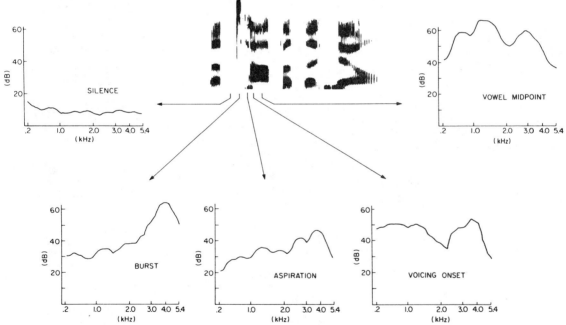

Figure 13-4. A speech spectrogram of the phrase "to the top of the hill," showing a number of different features present in the brief time period that the speaker's voice moves from the t *sound to the* o *sound in the word "top" (from "Speech Perception: A Model of Acoustic Pho-* netic Analysis" by D. Klatt in **Perception and Production of Fluent Speech** *(p. 252), by R. Cole (Ed.), 1980, Hillsdale, NJ: Lawrence Erlbaum Associates. Copyright 1980 by Lawrence Erlbaum Associates. Reprinted by permission.).*

signal proposes 55 such segment types. It is proposed that these brief segments (analyzed, perhaps, in 10 msec chunks) within the speech signal are matched to preexisting templates that decode the signal and bring about speech recognition. Notice that this model of speech perception proposes feature analysis, but it is an analysis of the acoustic properties of the stimulus rather than its phonemic properties. With the hypothesis that we have templates that can match and code these features into recognizable speech, we can account for speech perception without assuming specialized speech feature detectors.

Although feature analysis theories dominate current approaches to speech perception and recognition, there is still vigorous debate over the nature of the features and their analysis. The current hope is that the attempts to produce voice-activated computer systems may provide some useful new leads to how speech signals may be decomposed and then resynthesized into a recognizable, meaningful, and articulate stream of communication. In turn, this may stimulate the creation of new theoretical approaches to speech perception. For the moment, however, we can look at it as a form of auditory pattern perception, but one with a number of added issues due to the fact, perhaps, that these are auditory patterns that we not only hear, but produce for ourselves.

GLOSSARY

The following definitions are specific to this book.

Analysis-by-synthesis   A theory of speech perception that assumes that observers match internally synthesized speech with the incoming speech signal in order to comprehend spoken language.

Articulators   Structures in the oral tract of the vocal apparatus, such as the tongue and lips, that shape the sound of human speech.

Feature analysis   An approach to speech perception that emphasizes the role of speech components (features) in comprehension.

Formants   The bands of enhanced sound, seen as dark smudges on a spectogram.

Glottis   The gap that separates the vocal folds.

Homophenes   Words that are produced by almost identical patterns of lip movements.

Homophones   Words that are pronounced similarly, but spelled differently.

Larynx   The structure in the human vocal apparatus that contains the sound-producing vocal folds.

Lungs   The source of "air power" required for the production of human speech.

Motor theories   Theories of speech perception that emphasize the importance of the muscular movements in the production of speech sounds for its eventual comprehension.

Pharynx   Part of the vocal tract, commonly known as the throat.

Phoneme   The smallest sound unit that distinguishes one speech sound from another.

Phonemic boundary   An experimentally determined point at which different speech sounds can be discriminated.

Phonemic restoration effect   The tendency for observers to perceptually fill in missing sounds in meaningful utterances.

Phonetic   A term referring to speech sound segments and their production.

Phonology   The study of the meaning attached to a speech signal.

Speech spectograms   Graphic representations of the frequency and intensity of speech signals, plotted over time.

Trachea   The "windpipe" that connects the lungs to the larynx and vocal tract.

Vocal folds   A pair of thin flaps in the larynx that vibrate as a result of air pressure. Also known as vocal cords.

Vocal tract   All the structures or air passages above the larynx involved in speech production.

Voice onset time   A latency in producing a vowel sound following a stop-consonant sound.

The constancies

THE RANGE OF STIMULI THAT REACHES our receptors is huge. Many of these different stimuli result in unique sensory experiences, but some of them are totally unnoticed. Let us consider what happens when you leave your chair to step outside for a brief stroll. You are probably quite conscious of the change in your auditory environment, as the sounds shift from the quiet of the interior to the roar of traffic on the street, for example. Tactual sensations also change, from the softness of the carpet to the hard feeling of the concrete. The street smells are different, too, with the exhaust fumes of cars now more salient, or perhaps the smell of newly mown grass. The visual input also undergoes striking changes as you move from a dim interior to a blazing, sunlit street, or from the warm glow of a living room to the darkness of the night.

This diversity and change contributes to the excitement and richness of our sensory world; yet, at the level of perceptual analysis, it is the unnoticed changes that are more mysterious and puzzling. To see this more clearly, imagine that you are looking at the actual image projected on the retina of your eye. What changes are actually taking place in the retinal image as you walk down the street? Human observers execute between two and four eye movements per second. Therefore, as you scan the environment, objects momentarily appear in the visual image and then disappear, as if they are blinking out of existence as you change your direction of gaze. Even if you fixated an object as you approached it, the retinal image would still not be constant; rather, it would grow larger as you came closer and smaller as you moved away. Should you pass under a tree and look at your hand swinging by your side, its retinal image would become much dimmer than it was in the sunlight. You do not experience these changes in the retinal image consciously, however. You are merely walking down the street. Objects remain in a permanent position, despite the fact that their images appear and disappear within your eye. You feel as though you draw closer to objects of a fixed size, and your hand seems to be the same color and brightness regardless of the intensity of the light falling on it.

The discrepancies between retinal image properties and conscious experiences are examples that we "construct" the world from our visual input rather than "seeing" it directly. Since the physical world does not change as the light, our direction of gaze, or our distance from a target changes, we construct a corresponding stable world in consciousness. The way in which this stability is created and maintained is an interesting story, which revolves around a set of visual phenomena known as the **constancies**. There are three varieties of perceptual constancies, each of which defines a class of phenomena. There are constancies related to visual objects, such as their size and shape; constancies related to qualities of those visual objects, such as their brightness and hue; and constancies that deal with relationships between visual objects, such as their position or orientation.

OBJECT CONSTANCIES

Size constancy

To understand size constancy, you must be aware of the relationship between the size of the visual image on the retinal surface and the distance between the observer's eye and the object being observed. As the distance between the eye and the object increases, the size of the retinal image decreases. This relationship is shown in Figure 14-1. As you probably recall from Chapter 6, retinal image size is usually expressed and measured in terms of its

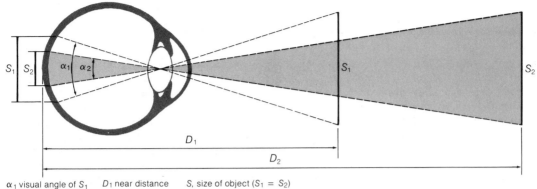

α_1 visual angle of S_1 D_1 near distance S, size of object ($S_1 = S_2$)
α_2 visual angle of S_2 D_2 far distance

Figure 14-1. The visual angle. Although the physical size (S) of the object does not change, changes in distance (D) will result in changes in the size of the visual angle (α, or alpha). Here α_1 (object S_1 close to the eye) is larger than α_2 (object S_2 far from the eye).

visual angle. The visual angle for S1 (stimulus 1) is 1 and for S2 is 2. Like other angles, they are expressed in degrees, minutes, and seconds of arc. Thus, the image size of a quarter (25-cent piece) held at arm's length is about 2 degrees, while at a distance of about 80 meters the quarter would have a visual angle of 1 minute of arc. At a distance of 5 km it would have only the tiny retinal image size of 1 second of arc. Thus, as its distance from an observer increases, its retinal image size decreases.

Let us return to our earlier description of the physical changes in visual stimulation as one walks down the street. Now you may have begun to realize what would be happening if an observer perceived an object's size only in terms of its retinal image size. If such were the case, a man who is 180 cm (about 6 ft) tall would look like a small child when he was at a reasonable distance but would appear to "grow" as we approached him. Of course this does not happen. Instead, we perceive him to be "man size" regardless of his relative distance from us. This stability of perceived size despite changes in objective distance and retinal image size is called **size constancy**. In es-

sence it involves assigning a constant size to an object in consciousness, no matter what its distance or retinal size may be.

A good example of the operation of size constancy in human observers is found in a common experience that may have happened to you. While on vacation you discover a magnificent panoramic scene that overlooks a range of majestic mountains far in the distance. You are overawed. In great excitement, you quickly snap a photograph to share with your friends when you return home. After having gathered your friends together for a slide show of your trip, however, you are greatly disappointed to discover that the photograph does not convey the same impression of the scene as your personal view. In fact, those formerly majestic mountains appear to be puny. In disgust you attempt to explain how "it was really quite awesome." Such occurences can be explained in terms of the operation of size constancy. Although the eye can be compared to a camera in many ways, ultimately a camera does not act like a human observer. It does not compensate for the size changes that are related to distance changes. Since the camera

Demonstration Box 14-1. Distance and retinal image size

Hold out your hand in front of you at arm's length. Keep your eyes fixed on your hand as you move it toward your face and away several times. Although the retinal image size of your hand is smaller when it is seen at arm's length, you probably perceived no difference in size as you moved your hand.

Now hold up the index finger of your left hand in front of your face, as shown in the figure, at a distance of about 20 cm. Fixate it carefully. Now position your right hand at arm's length behind your fixated finger. While maintaining fixation on your fingertip, bring your right hand toward and away from your face. Do not let your fixation waver from your finger, but also try to pay attention to the image of your hand as it moves closer

to and farther away from your face. Under this second set of circumstances, you should suddenly see your hand change in size. You will perceive it as being smaller when it is held at arm's length, and you will see it enlarge as you move it toward your face. This simple demonstration allows you to experience the relationship between retinal image size and distance. Ordinarily, when we are paying attention to an object, the size constancy mechanism is immediately called into operation and the changes in retinal image size with distance are not perceived. When our attention is slightly diverted, we can experience the proximal (retinal) rather than the distal (objective or real) size.

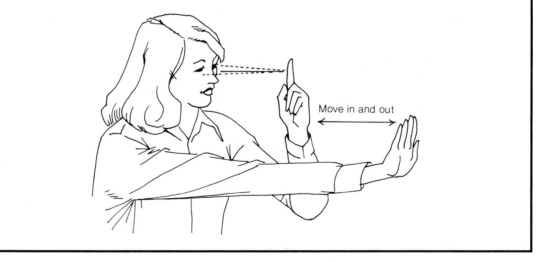

Move in and out

registers only angular size, it does not make the perceptual correction needed to keep those distant objects "mountain size," and our own size constancy mechanism does not work as effectively when we view pictures as when we view the real objects (Coren and Girgus, 1977). Demonstration Box 14-1 can allow you to experience the relationship between retinal

image size, distance, and the size constancy correction for yourself.

Shape constancy

Epstein and Park (1963) have defined shape constancy as the "relative constancy of the perceived shape of an object despite variations in its orientation." You might ask, "Why should an object look any different if its orientation changes?" Figure 14-2 attempts to answer this question. If you take a rectangular card or object and tilt or slant it so that the top is now farther from you than the bottom, you have changed the shape of the retinal image. As we increase the tilt, the retinal image becomes more like a trapezoid with the formerly vertical sides tapering outward. Yet the object still "looks" rectangular. The same happens when we swing a door outward. The large changes in the shape of retinal image are ignored, and the door still appears to be rectangular. In

achieving shape constancy, the perceptual system appears to compensate for changes in slant in a way that is analogous to the compensation for distance changes in size constancy. Follow the instructions in Demonstration Box 14-2 to see this for yourself.

CONSTANCIES OF OBJECT PROPERTIES

After we have identified the presence of any object within the visual field, two of the most salient aspects of its visual existence are its qualities of brightness and color (hue). The

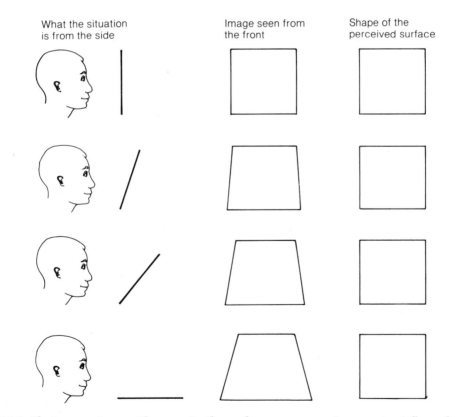

Figure 14-2. Shape constancy. Changes in the tilt or slant of forms will cause changes in the shape of the retinal image; perceived shape, *however, remains constant (based on Lindsay and Norman, 1977).*

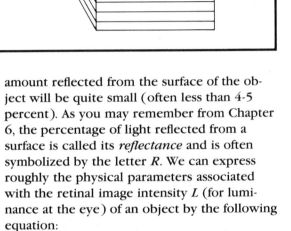
identification of an object and the sensory processing of the qualities of that object are tied very closely. We perceive most visual stimuli as totalities and not as bundles of distinct and discrete sensations. Since the qualities of an object are an integral part of the stability of its perceptual existence, it seems reasonable to expect such qualities to also remain stable despite variations in physical stimulation.

Brightness constancy

In the case of perceived brightness there is a clear analogue to the operation of size constancy. Consider the retinal image first. Its brightness depends on two things. The first is the amount of light from any source, such as the sun or a light bulb, that falls on the object. This is called *illuminance* and is often symbolized by the letter E. Secondly, different object surfaces reflect differing amounts of light to the eye of the observer. For example, a white surface will reflect most (perhaps 80-90 percent) of the light that falls on it back to the eye. On the other hand, a black surface will absorb a great deal of the light, and the

amount reflected from the surface of the object will be quite small (often less than 4-5 percent). As you may remember from Chapter 6, the percentage of light reflected from a surface is called its *reflectance* and is often symbolized by the letter R. We can express roughly the physical parameters associated with the retinal image intensity L (for luminance at the eye) of an object by the following equation:

$$L = E \times R$$

Let us see how this works by putting some numbers into the formula. If we have a light source that has a physical intensity of 100 units falling on a surface that reflects 90 percent of the illuminating light, we would calculate a luminance value of 90 units ($L = 100 \times 0.90 = 90$). One might suppose that this simple example indicates that our perception of how light or dark an object appears should depend on the solution to this equation. Certainly the intensity of the retinal image changes as the values within the equation change. Just as perceived size does not appear to vary as the retinal image size changes, however, perceived brightness remains relatively constant even as the physical intensity of the retinal image changes. A piece of white paper appears to be approximately the same brightness whether it is viewed in the dim light of an artificially lit room or in bright sunlight. This is in spite of the fact that the intensity of the retinal image differs for the two viewing conditions. One can observe the operation of **brightness**, or **lightness**, **constancy** very clearly in experimental situations like the one shown in Figure 14-3.

In Figure 14-3, an observer is sitting in a room with a piece of gray cardboard hanging from the ceiling a few feet in front of the chair. Directly in front of the observer is a box with

a window through which can be seen a series of papers graded in brightness from black through shades of gray to white. This graded or comparison series is independently illuminated, and it is not affected by the illumination in the room that falls on the suspended gray cardboard. With identical illumination in the room and within the box, we ask our subject to choose a comparison gray that appears to be the same as the gray cardboard hanging in front of the chair. Based on our knowledge of the luminance formula, we are not surprised when our observer chooses a comparison gray that is physically identical to the gray of the stimulus hanging in the room. Now we cut the room illumination by one-half but do not

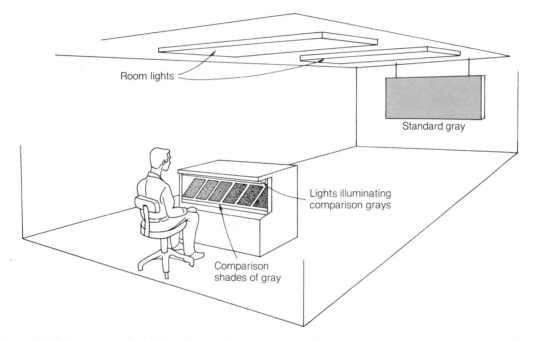

Figure 14-3. An example of the classical experimental setup for the measurement of brightness constancy. The observer sees a standard gray target illuminated by room lights and is asked to choose the matching gray from a comparison series. The comparison series is seen through a box that provides independent illumination and prevents the intrusion of room light (from Cornsweet, 1970).

change the illumination on our comparison series. If our observer were making matches based on the physical intensity of the retinal image, what would he do?

Table 14-1 shows that matches based on the strict solution of the luminance equation would dictate that the observer should choose a comparison gray that has one-half the surface reflectance of the standard. Typically, however, the observer will choose the comparison gray that is physically identical to (of the same reflectance as) the standard, and this pattern will continue, regardless of the illumination changes we may impose on the suspended gray cardboard. Perhaps it is just this type of behavior that prompted Thouless (1931) to talk of the constancies in terms of a "regression to the real object." It is quite clear that, in the experimental situation used to study brightness constancy, it is the relative reflectance of the stimulus hanging in the room and not the $L = ER$ solution that determines which comparison stimulus is chosen as its match. Thus, we can define brightness constancy in terms of the dependence of perceived brightness on the reflectance of a surface rather than on luminance values at the retina.

Color or hue constancy

Based on our discussion of color vision in Chapter 7, you should be aware that our perception of a color is a result of a complex interaction between the reflectance properties of a given pigment and the wavelength composition of the light that falls on that pigment. Since properties of both lights and pigments are in a continual flux as we move about in our environment, one might expect that an object's color would appear to change as we changed the lighting conditions. We can iden-

Table 14-1. L = ER Solutions for observer's behavior in a brightness constancy experiment

Test situation #1: Equal illuminance (100 units) in the room and on the comparison series.

Room	Comparison Series
$L = ER$	$L = ER$
$L = 100 (.50)$	$L = 100 (.50)$
$L = 50$	$L = 100$

The two grays match perceptually and physically.

Test situation #2: Room illuminance (50 units), one-half of that on the comparison series (100 units).

Perceptual Match

Room	Comparison Series
$L = ER$	$L = ER$
$L = 50 (.50)^a$	$L = 100 (.50)^a$
$L = 25$	$L = 50$

Physical Match

Room	Comparison Series
$L = ER$	$L = ER$
$L = 50 (.50)^b$	$L = 100 (.25)^b$
$L = 25$	$L = 25$

a. Identical reflectances chosen although the value of L differs.
b. The reflectance of the comparison gray is one-half that of the stimulus in the room. However, the value of L is equal in the two cases.

tify red as red, however, whether it is viewed under fluorescent lights that have a dominant blue hue or incandescent lights that are basically yellow. Thus, **color constancy** refers to our ability to maintain the perception of a constant hue for a given object, despite variations

---

Demonstration Box 14-3. Color constancy

To carry out this demonstration you will need a reduction screen, which is simply a ½ cm hole cut into the center of a dark piece of cardboard. In addition, you will need a fluorescent and a tungsten light source (such as your desk lamp and your room light, respectively) and a piece of colored paper (green works best). Hold the paper under the tungsten light. Notice its color. Next hold the colored sheet under a fluorescent lamp and notice that it still appears to be the same color under both light sources. Now look at the paper through the reduction screen, making sure that nothing else is visible through the hole except the patch of color. If you have used green paper, it should appear to be yellow-green under the tungsten light but blue-green when under the fluorescent lamp. In a full-cue situation with context information available, the operation of color constancy prevented you from seeing this hue change.

---

in the color quality of the incident light. Of course, such variations will change the color of the retinal image; in consciousness, however, the color remains constant. Although, at some level, we may respond to variations in the illuminant, our ability to state, for instance, "Yes, it is a red of some type," remains intact. You can explore the nature of this perceptual ability using Demonstration Box 14-3.

Color and brightness constancy share common aspects. First, they both relate to the surface qualities of objects in the visual environment. Brightness constancy is associated with **achromatic** (or noncolored) aspects of the objects. In other words, it deals with the perception of things as dark or light. On the other hand, hue constancy lends stability to our perceptual experience of colored objects. Both hue and brightness constancy demonstrate how physical variations relate to, but do not fully account for, our final perceptual experience. Sensory psychologists often use the constancies of size, shape, brightness, and hue to demonstrate how the properties of the object in the visual environment (termed the **distal stimulus**) tend to determine our emerging percepts in spite of variations in the retinal image (or **proximal stimulus**). We have introduced the terms distal and proximal because they are commonly used in discussions and research relating to the visual constancies. It may help you to remember which word describes each stimulus if you keep in mind that distal is derived from the Latin "dist," meaning "to stand apart" or "to be distant." It is easy to see how this term applies to the object standing apart from us in the visual environment. Proximal stems from the Latin "proxima," meaning "nearest." Of the two stimuli, the retinal image is the closest to us, yet our perceptual experience is a reconstruction of the external object in the world.

CONSTANCIES OF OBJECT RELATIONS

The constancies of size, shape, brightness, and color deal with the perceptual stability of static objects within visual space. However, there are additional visual constancies that maintain perceptual regularity throughout movements of either the observer or the object of regard.

Position constancy

When we freely walk about or move our heads, the image of the world stimulating the retinal surface moves in an orderly and systematic fashion. For example, when you move your head to the right, the retinal image of all stationary objects slides across the retinal surface to the left. Despite the fact that the retinal image moves, we do not experience the world as moving (see Chapter 11). Stationary objects seem to remain in a constant position regardless of our own movement. This is known as **position constancy**. Retinal displacement can arise from two sources. First, the observer can move while the world remains stationary (although its retinal image has moved). On the other hand, the world may have moved while the observer has remained in a constant position. Either way, the relationship between the observer and the objects in the external field of view is monitored, and the visual system correctly discriminates between the two origins of retinal displacement or movement.

Direction constancy

In Chapter 10, we discussed the notion of *egocentric localization*—the ability to localize external objects in relationship to our own bodies. When our eyes look straight ahead and the image of an object is stimulating both foveas, we perceive the object we are looking at as lying directly in front of our bodies. However, we can move our eyes and look off to the side, away from the object. Under these circumstances we are still able to localize the object as lying straight ahead of our bodies. Thus, in spite of eye movements, the egocentric direction of objects (where they lie relative to our bodies) remains constant. This is called **direction constancy**.

Position and direction constancy can be distinguished from each other in the following way. Eye movements do not change egocentric direction relative to our bodies. Head and body movements, however, can change egocentric direction. For example, look at an object that is straight ahead of your body. Now shift your head to one side. Since we tend to use the head as the reference point for egocentric direction (see Chapter 10), the object no longer seems to be directly straight ahead. Although the object is now perceived to lie in a different direction, its position in space is the same as it was before the head movement. Position and direction constancy are related but separable phenomena (Shebilske, 1977).

The constancies exemplify how changes in proximal stimulation (the retinal image) are not exactly reproduced in our final perceptual experience. Our visual world remains stable, and the perceived qualities of the distant objects remain constant. Objects in the visual field are often more predictive of our experience than the retinal image, which supposedly provides our contact with the world. Hence, the perceptual constancies also reveal the complex interaction that takes place between the structures of the visual system and the properties of incoming visual stimulation.

MECHANISMS IN THE CONSTANCIES

The constancies demonstrate that the physical realities are interwoven in a complex manner. One must ignore some aspects of the retinal situation if one is to represent the object more accurately in perception. In addition, each constancy seems to represent a coupling of several perceptual abilities. For example, size constancy couples our ability to perceive size with our ability to perceive distance. Epstein (1973, 1977) proposed that the visual system operates according to rules of processing

Demonstration Box 14-4. Size constancy and apparent distance

An easy way to demonstrate how apparent distance affects apparent size requires that you carefully fixate the point marked *X* in the accompanying white square while holding the book under a strong light. After a minute or so, you will form an afterimage (see Chapter 8) of the square. If you now transfer your gaze to a blank piece of paper on your desk, you will see a ghostly dark square floating there. This is the afterimage, which will appear to be several centimeters long on each side. Now shift your gaze so that you are looking at a more distant, light-colored wall. Again you will see the dark square projected against the wall, but now it will appear to be much larger in size. Because of the nature of an afterimage, its visual angle does not change. But as you project it against surfaces at varying distances from you, its apparent size changes. It appears to be larger when it is projected on a distant surface. This is an example of how size and distance perception interact by means of the size constancy mechanism. The quantitative expression of the relationship is often called *Emmert's law*.

whereby certain variables are combined to achieve constancy in perception. In the following discussion, we will attempt to see which variables are involved and what rules of combination are used.

Size and distance information

The first approach to the problem of size constancy must be to ask why the perception of size does not change as retinal image size varies. Somehow the distance of the target is taken into account and the size percept is adjusted. In other words, we estimate distance and size together. This suggests that changes in apparent distance should alter our perception of apparent size. This is not a bad suggestion, as can be seen from Demonstration Box 14-4. Unfortunately, the suggestion that size constancy simply involves "taking distance into account" evades the question. How does one "take distance into account?" And, still unanswered, what is the actual underlying causal mechanism? Let us start by considering the interaction between size and distance information.

When we fixate objects at different distances, the lens of the eye changes shape to accommodate for changes in fixation distance. Simultaneously, the eyes either converge for near objects or diverge for distant objects to produce stable binocular foveal fixation. These two processes, working together, bring about a focused binocular retinal image over a wide range of fixation distances. We know that the retinal image size decreases as the observer-target distance increases; however, we also know that we do not perceive these changes in retinal image size. Why not? One explanation concerns the information available from the physiological changes brought about by convergence and accommodation changes.

In our discussion of position constancy, we mentioned that the visual system can differentiate between internally generated and externally generated movement, both of which cause image displacement across the retinal surface. If the visual system "knows" that the observer has made a head movement, it takes this into account and attributes the retinal displacement to internally generated sources. As a result, the external world remains stable. Such a phenomenon implies that the visual system has the physiological capability of monitoring changes in proximal stimulation. Suppose the same situation holds for accommodation and convergence changes. These changes could "inform" the visual system that distance is changing and, thus, retinal image size is varying. If distance is monitored by the visual system, image changes can be anticipated and a perceptual compensation applied. The essence of this argument is that information from convergence and accommodation changes, which signal distance variation, are taken into account so that alterations in retinal image size are not perceived.

How does one go about testing this theory? First of all, if this reasoning has any validity, we would expect that in the absence of any other information about the distance of the target (such as the pictorial cues to distance cataloged in Chapter 10), changes in accommodation and convergence would result in changes in perceived size. After all, if retinal image size is kept constant, but the visual system receives a signal that the object forming this image is close to the observer, the object should be perceived as smaller. An identically sized target that is indicated to be more distant from the observer should be processed as being larger (remember that size constancy functions to "blow up" or enlarge the size of distant objects in the perceptual view).

In general, then, one has to set up a situation where retinal image size remains constant, but physiological sources signal changes in distance. Such a situation should result in changes in perceived size. This experiment was conducted by Leibowitz and Moore (1966). Their experimental observers viewed a white triangle in an otherwise completely dark field. They matched the size of this stimulus by making size adjustments in a similar triangle. Accommodation and convergence were varied by inserting prisms and lenses before the eyes, forcing the subjects to adjust their convergence and accommodation to closer or farther distances when viewing the target, although the retinal size remained constant. If these depth cues help to stabilize the perception of size, this experimental manipulation should result in changes in perceived size.

The prediction of the investigators was confirmed. The size of the target, judged to be equal to that of the standard triangle, increased as accommodative and convergence changes were manipulated to indicate increasing target distance. Hence, it seems that the state of the oculomotor (eye muscle) system, which varies with the distance of the distal stimulus, conveys information that helps to stabilize size perception. Since the perception of size seems to be linked to the perception of distance in some way, this is one way in which structures within the visual system "take distance into account" in computing the size constancy correction.

Information about the extent of accommodative and convergence movements is not the only mechanism at work in size constancy. Leibowitz (1971) has indicated that these sources of distance information appear to be useful in the preservation of size constancy only for fairly close distances (within arm's length). This makes sense since most of these adjustments take place for targets within 1-2 meters of the observer. In fact, current data indicate that the resting position of the eyes (where the fixation control mechanisms are relaxed) is between 0.5 and 1.0 meters. Thus, when the distance information mechanism breaks down, it is not surprising to find that size constancy also fails. It is easy to demonstrate the disruption of size constancy at very large target-observer distances. One need only to climb to the top of a tall building and note that people appear to be tiny dolls and cars appear to be little toys.

Recently, Ross, Jenkins, and Johnstone (1980) have argued that this breakdown in size constancy with increasing target distance can be related to the disruptive effect of small retinal size on size perception. They claimed that the tendency to maintain a constant retinal size breaks down when the visual angle subtended by the target falls below 0.5 degrees. In a series of experiments to test this notion, however, Day, Stuart, and Dickinson (1980) were unable to find support for such a disruption; rather, they found that size constancy was maintained at all visual angle sizes. Thus, Day et al. (1980) concluded that breakdowns in size constancy in natural viewing situations may be a result of lack of typical distance cues in abnormal viewing situations, such as when viewing targets from a tall building or an airplane.

Size and stimulus relationships

There is a geometric regularity in the visual array that provides us with much information. Thus, the convergence of parallel lines as a function of distance (called linear perspective) and the increasing textural density of more distant fields of elements that we discussed in Chapter 10 are sufficiently regular in their occurrence to serve as reliable cues for distance. Such cues may assist in the maintenence of size constancy. Gibson (1950) and Rock (1975) have pointed out that constant relationships within the visual array may contribute to size constancy.

For example, we can imagine two objects of the same size sitting on a surface at different distances from the observer. As you know from Chapter 10, the fact that textured surfaces show gradations of coarseness as they recede into the distance is a powerful distance cue. If two objects at different distances appear to cover the same number of textured elements (in other words, their relationship to the textured surface remains constant), they will remain perceptually the same size. This principle is exemplified in Figure 14-4. You will notice that here we have three cubes that appear to be about the same size but that appear to vary in distance. Despite the fact that their image size differs, notice that each cube covers just slightly more than one texture element. Thus, the observer could deduce that the cubes are physically equal (which is simply the result of size constancy correction) by comparing the relative size of the objects with the size of the surrounding texture elements.

To be convinced of this argument, however, we need to rely on some experimental evidence

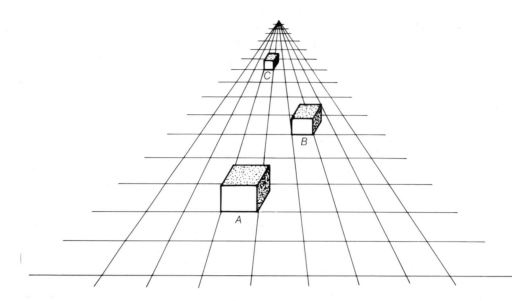

Figure 14-4. Relational determinants of size constancy. Cubes A, B, and C cover the same number of texture elements on the receding *ground. This constant relationship to these figural aspects of the visual environment helps to maintain size constancy.*

that indicates that an observer's ability to make judgments consistent with the preservation of size constancy differs in the presence and absence of context. Many experiments have demonstrated how cues in the visual array contribute to the maintainence of size constancy (for example, the classic experiment was performed by Holway and Boring, 1941). In one such experiment by Harvey and Leibowitz (1967), observers were asked to choose a size match for a standard target that was placed at various distances. There were two viewing conditions. One corresponded to natural situations with many contextual cues, and the second involved the removal of the surrounding context by having the observers view the standard target through a small opening that blocked the view of everything but the target to be observed. The visual angle of the standard target was kept constant at all viewing distances. Hence, if size constancy

were maintained, each observer should continue to choose a larger and larger variable target to match the standard as the viewing distance increased.

Under natural viewing conditions, size matches conformed very well to the predictions based on the efficient operation of the size constancy mechanism. This was the case for all the observer-target distances used in this experiment. When the context was removed, however, size matches conformed to constancy predictions only at viewing distances up to about 120 cm. After that, size matches began to deviate from the predictions based on size constancy. This experiment shows the role of context in the maintenance of size perception. In addition, it demonstrates the operation of several mechanisms in size constancy. Since there is no difference between the two viewing conditions at relatively small observer-target distances, one might argue that accommodation and convergence information about distance is primarily responsible for size perception when the observer is relatively close to the object. On the other hand, when the observer is not in close proximity to the object, contextual cues appear to play a more prominent role in maintaining the stability of perceived size. Hence, both physiological and stimulus variables appear to be involved in this perceptual process.

The ability to use information from the geometric relationships within the stimulus context seems to be affected by experience or maturity or both. This is demonstrated by the fact that children show patterns of size constancy that differ from those of adults. The size matching behavior of children and adults does not differ at close observation distances where information from convergence and accommodation seems to operate. When, however, the target is farther away and contextual information is more important to the maintenance of size constancy, children have greater difficulty making the appropriate size constancy responses. This type of data, reported by Zeigler and Leibowitz (1957), suggests that the effective use of context information is based on some learned components or, at least, on components that must mature in some way. Adult observers show more stable size matching behavior across a wider range of observation distances. Thus, the accuracy of size constancy seems to depend on both the availability of depth information and the observer's ability to use it.

Size constancy and illusion

Size constancy allows our perception of the relative size of objects to differ from what is predicted on the basis of knowledge of the retinal image size. This is quite important in that an accurate picture of the size of objects in the real world should not depend on our distance from such objects. Thus, consider Figure 14-5A, which shows two logs lying in the middle of a road. Notice that the upper log appears to be the same size as the lower one, although it is quite clear that they have been drawn two different sizes on the paper. Since the contextual distance cues in the visual array (perspective, texture, and others) indicate that the upper log is more distant, we see it as being the same size as the closer log in spite of the fact that it is drawn slightly smaller. This is another example of size constancy.

Now consider Figure 14-5B. Here we have two logs that appear to be different in size, with the more distant one appearing to be longer than the closer one. If you measure them with a ruler you will see that they have been drawn exactly the same physical size. Once again, this merely represents the operation of size constancy. To the extent that the picture mimics the conditions in the real world, the upper log appears to be more distant. Hence, it can cause the same-sized retinal image as the lower log only under conditions in which it is physically longer. Since in the picture the logs have been drawn the same size, our perception is corrected appropriately.

Now let us look at Figure 14-5C, where we see two converging lines and two horizontal lines. Notice that the upper line appears to be sightly longer. Like the logs in Figure 14-5B, the two lines are physically equal in length; hence, the percept of unequal size is an illusion. This configuration is usually called the *Ponzo illusion*. It is an illusion, however, only in the sense that no context for depth or distance has been deliberately drawn into the figure. Yet the constancy corrective mechanism has been inappropriately evoked, resulting in this distorted, illusory percept of the relative

Figure 14-5. (A) The two logs lying on the road appear to be at different distances. Therefore their apparent size is the same despite the fact that the apparently more distant log is physically smaller (on the page) than the other one. (B) The logs are identical in size; however, the one that appears to be more dis- tant looks larger. The application of size constancy can lead to illusions of size, as seen in (C), which is the Ponzo illusion and is similar to (B) except that the context indicating distance and depth has been greatly reduced (based on Coren and Girgus, 1978).

length of the two horizontal lines. In some instances, a very fine distinction exists between a picture and a simple array of lines that produces a visual illusion. Thus, one might easily imagine a child producing 14-5C when asked to draw 14-5B.

In some cases, the cues that inappropriately elicit size constancy are more difficult to see. Consider Figure 14-6. The vertical line marked A appears to be shorter than the vertical line marked B although they are equal in length. This distortion, called the *Mueller-Lyer illusion*, has also been explained in terms of size constancy (Eijkman, Jongsma, and Vincent, 1981; Madden and Burt, 1981). For example, the wings turned toward the vertical line might mimic the perspective cues of the outside of a building (shown in dark lines in Figure 14-6C), while the wings turned away from the vertical line might mimic an interior corner of a room (shown in Figure 14-6D). To the extent that the closest point in the array is the plane of the paper, it is easy to see that if the wings imply increases or decreases in distance away from that plane, the vertical shaft in B is more distant than that pictured in A. Hence, the operation of size constancy enlarges the

apparent length of B relative to A. Notice again that this is an illusion of size only in the sense that no depth or distance was intended; therefore, the application of size constancy is inappropriate in this situation. Several other illusion distortions also act as though observers were responding to implied depth cues in the configuration (Coren and Girgus, 1978; Ward, Porac, Coren, and Girgus, 1977).

Shape constancy

An intimate relationship appears to exist between size and shape constancy. Both are related to distance perception. For shape constancy, however, the distance information pertains to the relative distance of different *parts* of the object from the observer—in other words, its orientation in space or its slant. When we ask "how does the observer take slant into account?" the answers are similar to those for size constancy. The amount of available information indicating the slant of the object seems to be critical. In unrestricted viewing, with many contextual cues available, observers tend to perceive the shape

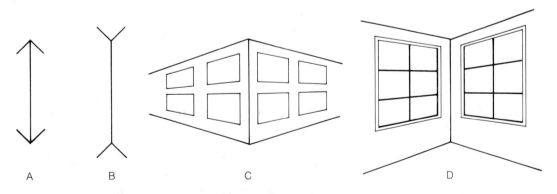

A   B   C   D

Figure 14-6. (A) The underestimated segment of the Mueller-Lyer illusion. (B) The overesti- *mated segment. (C and D) The corresponding perspective configurations.*

and slant of objects with remarkable accuracy (Lappin and Preble, 1975). As in the size constancy situation, when observers are prevented from using contextual or depth information that would indicate the degree of slant, the operation of shape constancy becomes less accurate, and the percept comes to reflect the retinal situation rather than the actual object (Leibowitz and Bourne, 1956).

The degree of shape constancy obtained can be further altered by the type of instructions that the observer is given in the experimental task. Carlson (1977) and Kaess (1980) have analyzed the effects of instructions for both size and shape constancy and found that they affect judgment quite drastically. Essentially, observers can either be asked to report the size and shape of the objects that they are viewing (the **objective instruction**) or be asked to report the size and shape of their retinal image (the **projective instruction**). The objective instruction is closest to normal viewing, where the perceptual task is to derive what is "out there." The projective instruction is similar to what an artist must do in trying to translate a scene being viewed onto a canvas consisting of sizes and shapes of colored regions that will represent objects in space when viewed by an observer. It has been shown (Gilinsky, 1955; Leibowitz and Harvey, 1969) that when observers are asked to adopt the projective viewing set, they show lesser degrees of constancy. These data suggest that the constancies depend on higher level cognitive corrections that may include some learned components.

One especially interesting aspect of the data is that observers, judging the projective shape of objects, cannot completely "turn off" the constancy correction. They continue to make constancy corrections although the judgments become more like the retinal image (Lappin

and Preble, 1975; Lichte and Borresen, 1967). These data, combined with the findings of Epstein, Hatfield, and Muise (1977) (which showed that, much like any cognitive task, the more processing time available, the more shape constancy is found), suggest that shape constancy is an automatic, higher level process. The shape constancy correction probably involves cognitive adjustments of the percept to bring it into closer correspondence with the external reality.

Brightness and color constancy

Of all the constancies, brightness and color have aroused the most heated theoretical debates. While some investigators have attempted to deal with constancies in terms of more cognitive, higher level information processing mechanisms, others have suggested that they can be completely explained in terms of relatively inflexible structural processes, in other words, known physiological mechanisms. To be successful, each theory must explain why the brightness and color of an object remain constant despite changes in the illumination falling on it.

The strucural mechanism that has been offered to explain brightness constancy (and by extension, color constancy) involves some of the same processes of neural interaction proposed to explain brightness contrast and Mach bands in Chapter 6. These involve lateral inhibitory interactions between adjacent regions of the retina. Thus, Cornsweet (1970) suggests that when we uniformly increase the amount of light falling on a region of the visual field containing a number of items of different reflectances, the actual response of the neural units that signal brightness does not change significantly. On the basis of animal experimentation, there is some evidence that the neural response of the earliest levels of processing in the retina changes logarithmically with luminance changes (note, however, that this does not mean that brightness grows logarithmically). Because of this, if we increase the illumination over an area uniformly, all regions of the retina increase their response rate by the same relative amounts. For example, suppose that we have two stimuli in the visual field, one with 30 percent reflectance and the other with 80 percent reflectance. If the light falling on each one is 10 units, we get 3 units of luminance from one and 8 units of luminance from the other, reflecting from the surface to reach the eye. If we double the amount of light falling on the surface, we have increased the illumination intensity to 20 units, and the reflected light becomes 6 and 16 units, respectively. Although it looks as though we should get different amounts of brightness increase for both stimuli (since one has increased by 3 units and the other by 8 units), we have kept a constant ratio between the two stimuli. The ratio of 6/16 is equal to 3/8. When we take the logarithm of each value, we find that we have increased each by the same amount (we have added 0.3 log units of response as we doubled the input). Cornsweet now adds one additional assumption. He assumes that the amount of lateral inhibition increases as we increase the rate of response of any retinal region. Since the amount of stimulation and the amount of inhibition both increase equally, the overall response of the eye to increased illumination remains relatively unchanged.

Several predictions can be made by such a theory. For instance, brightness constancy should depend on having several different levels of reflectance under the same illumination in close proximity in the visual field. This prediction is confirmed in the results of a classic experiment by Gelb (1929). He illuminated an object with a concealed light source. The il-

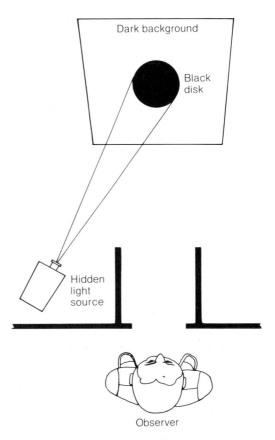

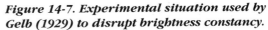

Figure 14-7. Experimental situation used by Gelb (1929) to disrupt brightness constancy.

luminated object was placed in a dimly lit field as shown by the experimental situation in Figure 14-7. The illuminated object was a black disc; however, observers reported seeing a white disc in dim light rather than a black disc that was brightly lit. Of course, this result represents a complete failure of constancy. If constancy were operating, the observers would see the black disc as black even though it was brightly lit. Gelb then tried a second manipulation. He placed a piece of white paper in front of the brightly lit black disc. As soon as this was done, observers reported that the disc was

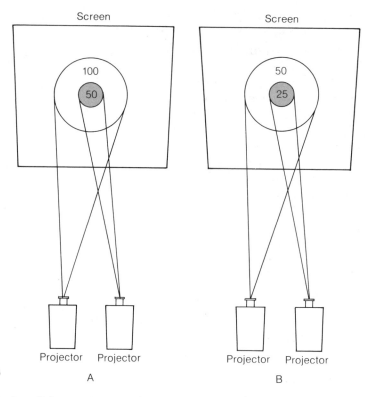

Figure 14-8. Relational determinants of brightness constancy. Wallach (1948, 1972b) found that regardless of absolute physical intensity, equal brightness would be perceived when targets stood in an equal intensity ratio with their surroundings. In this example, *which demonstrates the experimental technique used by Wallach, the central circles will appear to be equally bright because they both stand in a 1/2 intensity ratio with their respective surroundings.*

black. In other words, with the addition of the reference white paper, constancy returned. As soon as the piece of white paper was removed, however, the black disc returned to its former white appearance. Thus, although the observers now had information that the target was a brightly lit black object, the additional information did not help them to maintain constancy in the absence of the additional brightness level in the field (the piece of white paper).

Other evidence supports the constant-ratio notion of brightness constancy. Wallach (1948, 1972b) found that the perceived brightness of a target is a constant ratio of its light intensity compared with that of its surroundings. Look at Figure 14-8. Here you see two central targets, each surrounded by an outer ring that serves as a variable intensity background. The central circles and the outer rings are independently illuminated. The observers are asked to set the two inner circles until they appear equally bright. When this is done, we find the observers have set the intensity so that the ratios of the two sets of stimuli are the same. For example, suppose we set the central circle in Figure 14-8A to be 50 intensity units and the outer ring to be 100 intensity units. In order for the central circle in Figure 14-8B to appear to be equally bright, it must also be in a 2/1 ratio with its outer circle. Therefore, if the outer circle's intensity in Figure 14-8B is 50 units, a central circle of 25 units (another 2/1 ratio) will appear to be as bright as the central circle of 50 intensity units in Figure 14-8A. It is not the absolute intensity levels that matter; rather, it is the brightness ratio between targets and their surroundings or between adjacent objects that seems to maintain brightness constancy.

The equal ratios reported in the preceding studies and the need for more than one object to be in the field appear to support a structural basis for brightness constancy. Several recent investigators have elaborated on this mechanism (Richards, 1977; Marr, 1974). Unfortunately, other data show that this theory works both too well and too poorly. It works too well in terms of experiments that have attempted to directly measure the brightness interactions between adjacent areas. Such work suggests that the inhibitory effects do not reproduce the ratios exactly (Heinemann, 1955; Diamond, 1960). Therefore, brightness constancy is better than the physiology would lead us to predict. A simple structural theory also cannot explain a number of observations. For instance, one does not reproduce Wallach's ratio results if the target is simply suspended on a thread a few centimeters in front of the background rather than placed at the same level as the background (Mershon and Gogel, 1970). Also, Gilchrist (1980) has shown that changes in the spatial position of surfaces of differing brightness and brightness ratios will affect the perceived brightness in ways that are not consistent with a strict interpretation of structural

theories. In general, he found that perceived illumination, reflectance, and spatial position (especially the perceived depth arrangements in the array) interacted to affect brightness constancy. Certainly if the only important factor is adjacent areas of brightness on the retina, such manipulations should make no difference.

Finally, evidence exists that observers do "take into account" the amount of illumination falling on targets, which brings us to a second theoretical position. Since the time of Helmholtz (mid-1800s) investigators have suggested that brightness and color constancy are maintained by mechanisms similar to those involved in shape and size constancy. In the present case, however, the observer adjusts the percept not according to distance cues but according to cues that suggest the amount of illumination and the direction from which it comes. Thus, in the Gelb experiment they would argue that the introduction of the white piece of paper provides a cue indicating that there is an intense, hidden light source. This information evokes the formerly inoperative constancy correction.

Several such cues seem to be important in triggering brightness constancy. For instance, the presence of visible shadows seems to produce a brightness correction (MacLeod, 1947). Another factor is the perceived orientation of the target relative to the light. For example, one set of experiments arranged a situation so that an observer viewed a trapezoidal object. When viewed with one eye the target appeared as if it were a flat rectangle lying on a table. When viewed with both eyes it appeared to be standing upright. Shadows cast by surrounding objects gave observers information about the direction of the light source that was positioned above the object. The orientation of the object relative to the light source determines the amount of light falling on it, and

Demonstration Box 14-5. Brightness constancy

To a certain extent, brightness constancy depends on assumptions that the observer makes about the nature of the world. Consider the gray tube shown below. Notice that the gray of the interior of the tube appears to be lighter than the gray of the exterior. In fact, they are the same gray. Coren and Komoda (1973) suggested that this apparent brightness difference involves a cognitive adjustment based on presumptions that we make about the environment. If the tube were real, its interior would be likely to receive less light than its exterior. In the tube pictured below, however, the same amount of light reaches the eye from both the apparent interior and the apparent exterior surfaces. This could only happen if the interior surface reflects a greater proportion of the light that reaches it; in other words, the internal surface must have a greater reflectance. This demonstration shows one way in which brightness constancy operates. The visual system makes presumptions about the amount of light reaching surfaces and adjusts the perceptual experience so that the apparent brightness corresponds to the assumed relative reflectances rather than to the actual distribution of light reaching the eye. Also, notice one other interesting aspect of the tube shown below, namely, that either the right- or the left-hand portion can be viewed as the interior or the exterior surface. A figure that can assume several different orientations depending on one's point of view is called a *reversible figure*. Notice how the apparent brightness difference between the two sides changes depending on whether you see the right or the left side as the interior surface. The apparent inner surface, regardless of whether it is the right or the left, appears to be the lighter one.

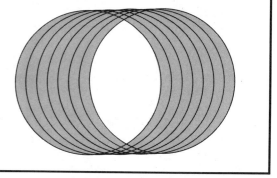

therefore, it also determines the magnitude of brightness constancy needed to maintain an accurate brightness experience. If the perceptual system makes its corrections on the basis of cues to illumination, the apparent brightness of the target should change according to its perceived rather than its physical orientation relative to the light source (Beck, 1965; Flock and Freedberg, 1970; Hochberg and Beck, 1954). Of course, the same amount of light is reaching the eye from the target, regardless of its perceived orientation. When the target appears flat, the perceptual system "presumes" that much light is falling on it from the light directly above it. Because of this, the con-

stancy correction operates to make the target appear darker when it is seen as flat (to correct for the extra light) than when it is seen as upright. Demonstration Box 14-5 shows you how your presumptions about the illumination falling on a surface can affect its apparent brightness.

As with the structural theory, the cognitive-correction approach does not account for all the data. For instance, the change in apparent brightness, as we change the apparent orientation of the object, is smaller than would be expected if the 90 degree difference in slant were taken completely into account. Thus, brightness constancy involves both cognitive and structural mechanism, as do most other perceptual phenomena.

The simplicity of our visual world is derived from a complex interaction of variables. Some of these processes are within the visual system itself, and some appear to be related to how the world is structured and how this structure presents itself to the human observer. At any rate, we must look beyond simple properties of the proximal stimulus to answer our questions concerning how and why things look the way they do. Often the unnoticed changes, such as those associated with the size of the retinal image as we change distances from a target, or its brightness as we change illumination levels, are more important than those that are noticed.

GLOSSARY

The following definitions are specific to this book.

Achromatic   Noncolored.

Brightness constancy   The process by which the apparent brightness of a stimulus remains unchanged, despite changes in physical illumination.

Color constancy   The phenomenon whereby the color of an object does not appear to change despite changes in the hue of the light falling on it.

Constancies   The tendency for perceptual qualities (size, shape, hue, and so on) to remain stable despite variations in the properties of the retinal image.

Direction constancy   The stability of an object's perceived direction despite changes in eye position.

Distal stimulus   Stimulus "out there" in the environment; the visual object.

Emmert's law   The quantitative expression of the relationship between apparent size and apparent distance; afterimages appear larger when projected on a more distant surface.

Lightness constancy   *See* Brightness constancy.

Objective instructions   Instructions directing an observer to report the size and shape of a visual stimulus.

Position constancy   Stable perceived position of objects despite body, eye, or head movements.

Projective instructions   Instructions directing an observer to report the size and shape of his or her retinal image.

Proximal stimulus   Stimulus "up close"; e.g., a retinal image is a proximal stimulus.

Size constancy   The stability of perceived size despite changes in objective distance and retinal image size.

15

Attention and Search

THE POLICEMAN RAN UP TO THE dazed pedestrian, "Did you see the license number of the car that just hit you?"

"Well," came the shaky answer. "Actually I was looking at the dog next to the driver. It was a huge St. Bernard wearing a jewel-studded collar with a gold medallion hanging from it that said 'WHY NOT?' It was wearing sunglasses, a red beret, and a green and yellow paisley scarf. Come to think of it, I guess I just didn't pay much attention to the license plate of the car."

What is the relationship between attention and perception? The notion of attention involves selection. To "pay attention" to something means to process some portion of the incoming sensory information and to let other aspects of the external scene slip away. In our example, the pedestrian's attention was captured by the apparel worn by the dog and not by the license number of the car that struck her. Although the dog, the driver, and the car were all part of the scene the pedestrian observed, only one portion of it was selected for sensory processing. The dog became the only portion of the incident that could be related to the police. Paying attention means to be *perceptually selective*. Not everything that we are exposed to becomes part of our conscious perceptual experience. Also, attention seems to require some type of *mental effort*; in other words, it requires not only appropriate receptor preparation but also a focusing of our cognitive abilities so that we can process the sensory input fully. We might say that we must allocate a certain amount of our perceptual and cognitive resources to an incoming input in order to say that we have paid attention to it.

Because attention seems to determine, at least in part, what a person actually perceives in any given situation, one would think that it would be central to any discussion of percep-

tion. However, such has not always been the case. The concept of attention, as well as investigations into the phenomena associated with it, have had a stormy history. Its importance was recognized quite early by William James (1890), who noted that "what is called our 'experience' is almost entirely determined by our habits of attention. A thing may be presented to a man a hundred times, but if he persistently fails to notice it, it cannot be said to enter into his experience." In the early part of the present century, many psychologists, such as William James and E. B. Titchner, felt that the study and examination of attention was of crucial concern. However, this view was not shared by other researchers, including behaviorists such as J. B. Watson, who opposed the "mentalistic" and "private" appearance of the concept. His arguments were quite convincing and resulted in a virtual cessation of concentrated investigation on this issue until around 1950, when its importance again became apparent because of the rising interest in more cognitive matters. As a result of this pause in the flow of research, contemporary notions of attention have a rather brief history by scientific standards. This fact may account for much of the controversy and lack of agreement about the issue that is characteristic of the current literature. For example, many researchers cannot even agree on the scope of the phenomena to be covered by the word *attention*. Some feel that as many as ten different types of behavioral events can be classified under attention, while others choose to include only seven and still others mention only two types of attention (Boring, 1970; Moray, 1969; Posner and Boies, 1971; Swets and Kristofferson, 1970; Treisman, 1969). In our discussion, we will focus on several distinct areas that have received a great deal of research effort since the 1950s. They concern the mechanisms of orienting attention, divided and selective

419

attention, vigilance (the ability to sustain attention during long, tedious tasks), and processes of visual search. First, however, let's look at the general ways in which the attentive process has been conceptualized by researchers.

MODELS OF ATTENTION

As we noted in the previous section, there is no full agreement as to the precise nature of attention. However, there are several approaches to the problem, which seem to be quite useful and may help us to organize our thinking about attention. Such approaches are often given substance in the form of a **model** of attention. A model of a process is like a hypothesis devised to explain a series of complex events and how they relate to each other. The researchers who have devised these models feel that they describe the process of attention, including its association to other aspects of perception and cognition, such as memory. They have conducted experiments to test the models so they can assess the fit between their idealized versions of the attention process (the model) and actual human behavior during a task that requires attention. We will briefly describe some of these models of attention so that you will have a conceptual framework into which the actual data about attention may be sorted.

Bottleneck models of attention

The term used to describe this class of models has been borrowed from Kahneman (1973). **Bottleneck models** assume that we are limited by our biological constitution to attending to, or thinking about, only one thing at a time. Sensory information coming in from all our senses, containing many different stimuli, or stimulus dimensions that we might attend to, gets delayed at a bottleneck in our information processing system much like droplets of water awaiting their turns to flow through the narrow neck of a bottle. The bottleneck acts like a filter, letting through only certain information. If the processing of any incoming information gets delayed for too long, however, the information is lost, either forgotten or replaced by new information. This happens to much of the information coming in. Only some of it is able to pass through the bottleneck in time for it to obtain complete analysis and processing. The remainder is lost. The fully analyzed portion of the input is that portion that is attended to (for instance the dog in our earlier example), while the information blocked by the filter, and thus never entered into consciousness, is the unattended material (the license plate).

Of course, the theoretically important issue is how the bottleneck develops and what controls the flow of information through it. Often this issue is approached by trying to find out where in the perceptual processing sequence this selection or filtering process takes place. Some types of bottleneck models state that the selection process occurs immediately after sensory registration. We can call these the **early selection models** (Broadbent, 1958; Duncan, 1980a). One of these is graphically shown in Figure 15-1A. Basically, early filtering means that certain stimulus flows are pinched off based on the physically identifiable characteristics of the stimuli, rather than on an interpretation of the content of the stimulus. Thus, although an unlimited amount of information may stimulate the sense receptors, only a limited amount gets through for contact with later processing stages such as memory. For example, you may wish to identify words spoken by only one person in a crowded room filled with talking people. The sensory impres-

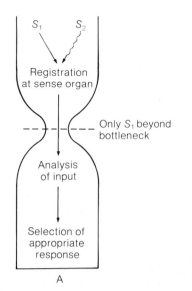 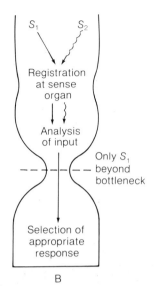

A   B

Figure 15-1. Schematic diagrams of two types of bottleneck models of attention. Both models assume that perceptual selectivity stems from a structural limitation on our capacity to process all the incoming stimulation (stimuli are indicated by S_1 and S_2). (A) The early selection models see the limitation as oc- *curring at the earliest stages; only limited amounts of stimulation are channeled along for further processing. (B) The late selection models conceptualize stimulus selection (attention) as occurring at later stages of information processing.*

sion (frequency composition, loudness, and so forth) of all voices is registered; however, only the words with the particular physical characteristics (that is, voice quality, location, pitch, and so on) associated with the person to whom you are attending are passed on to be processed fully for comprehension. Unfortunately, such a notion may be an overly simple way to conceptualize the attention process. For example, we can voluntarily switch our attention to another conversation. To do this, however, requires that we use some characteristics of the different voices, perhaps the meaning of what they are saying or their timbre or average pitch, to differentiate among the various speakers. How could we do this if such characteristics never get processed because the unattended voices are filtered out at

a very early stage? The ability to account for switches in attention is a major problem for a model that sees selectivity as operating very early in sensory processing.

A second type of bottleneck model answers these objections. This class of models requires, first, learning something about the nature of each stimulus, and then selecting on the basis of the content or information that it contains. This means that selection occurs during the analysis and memory encoding stages and thus it is rather late in the sequence of information processing (see Figure 15-1*B*). These are **late selection models** (Deutsch and Deutsch, 1963; Duncan, 1980a; Norman, 1968; Shiffrin and Schneider, 1977). In late selection models, all channels of incoming information are monitored and processed at least to a limited extent, with the attentional selectivity occurring when it is time to enter the stimulus sequence into a longer lasting memory storage. At the very least, all input makes contact with the appropriate memories so that, unlike the early selection models, processing of unattended material does not stop shortly after sensory registration.

Capacity models of attention

Capacity models do not assume that our brains are structured so that we can only attend to one input at a time. Rather, they assume that attentional limits are imposed by the fact that we have only a limited amount of mental resources that can be applied to any perceptual task (Kahneman, 1973; Moray, 1967). It seems clear that paying attention to any stimulus requires mental effort. Therefore, if we try to attend to several streams of stimuli that are complex, rapid, or difficult to discriminate, we may only be able to attend to a single stream of input, since each requires so much mental effort. Simpler stimuli, requiring little processing, may allow us to attend to more than one channel of input. Thus, it seems as if we have a fixed "budget" containing our mental resources, and on any given task we must allocate (or distribute) our resources as effectively as possible in order to meet our needs.

One important distinction between capacity and bottleneck models is in the source of information processing limitations. Bottleneck models are compatible with the notion of some sort of *structural* limitations within us, which in turn cause the filtering process we call attention. On the other hand, capacity models assume that our apparently limited attentional ability arises from demands for mental effort that exceed the available capacity to

exert that effort. If processing inputs on all sensory channels requires more effort than is available, only some of the input can be processed, the remainder will be lost. The specific stimulus channels lost or processed depend on the allocation of the available reserve of mental effort. Figure 15-2 summarizes this type of model in a schematic diagram.

Let us see how this class of model works.

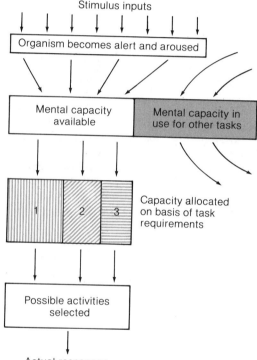

Figure 15-2. A schematic diagram of a capacity model of attention. This type of model assumes that there are limitations on our processing capacities. We have a limited amount of processing capacity that we can allocate between different stimuli, or tasks, that occur simultaneously. The stimulus, or task, that takes the greater amount of processing capacity will be the one engaging most of our attention.

When we are first learning to drive a car, it requires a great deal of effort to attend to the integration of skills needed to perform this complex task. Novice drivers find it quite difficult to do anything but drive the car. As the skill becomes more automatic, however, it begins to require less of the total processing capacity. This reduction in effort leaves us free to pay attention to competing activities, such as carrying on a conversation. Thus, the notion of allocating limited amounts of effort is highly compatible with everyday activities. Highly practiced skills require very little processing capacity once they are learned, allowing us to divide our attention rather effectively when a competing activity arises. This class of model is more fluid in the sense that it does not specify the types of interference that may occur to disrupt attention. Interference depends solely on the types of tasks involved. On the other hand, bottleneck models predict that certain tasks will interfere with each other while others will not. For example, two highly similar prose passages fed into the two ears will tap into the same groups of perceptual analyzers, linguistic expectations, and memories. When this happens it will be very hard to attend to one of the passages and to ignore the other.

Figure 15-2 shows a schematic diagram of the earlier versions of capacity models that argued for a fixed pool or amount of processing capacity available for allocation among processing tasks. Later versions of these models have proposed a multiple resource system in which a limited capacity exists for each distinct type of processing, and portions of these limited types of resources can be allocated among mental operations (Beatty, 1982; Navon and Gopher, 1979, 1980; Sanders, 1979; Wickens, 1979, 1980). As long as the task demands do not exceed the capacity of any one pool, an individual can perform several tasks or mental operations simultaneously without interference. Some researchers have stressed the strategy aspect of capacity models and have claimed that the ability to do several things at once is only constrained by an individual's level of skill at the task and not by capacity limits in a pool of processing resources (Hirst, Spelke, Reaves, Caharack, and Neisser, 1980).

COVERT VERSUS OVERT ATTENTION

Up to now we have been describing some general notions as to how attention may be conceptualized. Now that we have established this framework, let us turn to the actual phenomena associated with attention. Perhaps the phrases "to catch one's attention" and "to pay attention to" provide a good starting point. Usually when we are "paying attention" to something or someone, we have pointed our sense organs (and, therefore, oriented attention) toward the source of the sound or light stimulation. To use the technical term psychologists prefer, we say that an observer has emitted an **orienting response**, in which the sense organs have been positioned so that we can optimally receive the stimuli (Mostofsky, 1970; Posner, 1980).

In Chapters 3 and 6, you learned that the fovea is the very small region in the retina that provides the clearest and most detailed vision. When paying attention to a visual object, we generally "look" at it, meaning that we orient our eyes so that the image of the object of interest falls within the foveal area. Unfortunately, attention as a psychological process is not nearly as simple as receptor orientation alone. Simply noting which target is imaged on the fovea does not guarantee that the target is being attended to. It is well known that people can look without seeing, and it is also possible to see without looking.

Covert orienting

Posner and his associates (Posner, 1978, 1980; Posner, Snyder, and Davidson, 1980) have conducted extensive studies on the relationship between what is termed **covert** and **overt orienting**. Overt orienting is shown in the movement of the head or the eyes toward a source of sensory input. On the other hand, covert orienting is achieved by some internal mechanism that seems to shift the **mental effort** needed for processing input from one stimulus to another, without any observable movement on the part of the person. Posner has studied these two forms of orienting the attention by arranging experimental situations that require individuals to detect targets in various parts of the visual field. He has been able to show that individuals can shift attention to various stimuli even though they do not actually direct their eyes to the area where the target has been presented. The stimulus presentation he used to conduct these studies is diagrammed in Figure 15-3A. There were three types of presentations. The first was a *neutral* trial in which no attempt was made to direct the observer's attention at all. Here, a plus sign appeared in the middle of the field to cue the beginning of a trial, and the observer was simply asked to determine whether a light flash had occurred on the left or the right side of the field. The other two types of trials attempted to shift the observer's attention to one side or another by using an arrow pointing to the side where the target was most likely to be. On *valid* trials (which occurred 80 percent of the time), the stimulus was actually on the side that the arrow pointed to, while on *invalid* trials (the remaining 20 percent of the trials) it was on the opposite side. Observers were not permitted to move their eyes around the visual field. Their only task was to press a button as soon as they detected the target, regardless of which side it appeared on. With

this procedure Posner et al. were able to study whether or not observers could detect the targets in the absence of overt eye movements and also the effect of knowing where in space the target would occur.

The results of this experiment are shown in Figure 15-3B. As you can see, the reaction

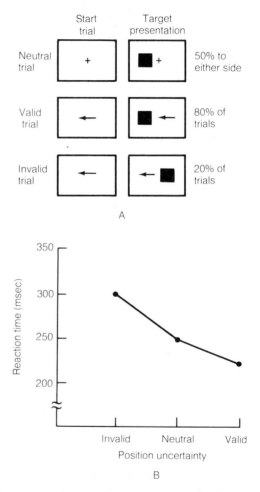

Figure 15-3. (A) Stimulus presentations used to study covert orienting of attention. (B) Results of reaction time studies of covert orienting, showing that knowledge of the stimulus position produces the most rapid detection (based on Posner, 1980).

time (the time between the onset of the peripheral detection target and the observer's response) is approximately 50 milliseconds faster on the valid trials than on the invalid trials. Thus, not only can observers shift attention in the absence of eye movement, but also they seem to benefit from directing their attention toward the region of the field where the stimulus occurs. This covert orientation of attention seems to allow them to respond more rapidly to the target even in the absence of overt orienting. In addition, Posner et al. have been able to show that the advance knowledge of spatial position, which in turn allows the redirection of attention, produces similar beneficial effects when the detection target is presented to the fovea as well as to the peripheral retina. For this reason, they have argued that the fovea is not the center of an attention field; in other words, there is no special neural wiring that ties the fovea to attention. This type of work is important because it demonstrates that attention cannot be tied directly to simple physiological orienting mechanisms. We seem to be able to shift covert attention (as suggested by Helmholtz [1962] long ago) as well as overt attention, at least in the visual modality.

Vigilance

Vigilance refers to the maintenance of overt attention during long, often boring tasks in which an observer tries to detect some type of signal (such as a blip on a radar screen). Research into vigilance began as a result of attentional problems found among radar operators during World War II (Jerison, 1970). After a certain time on duty, the operators tended to become tired, and this resulted in a decrease in their ability to detect signals from incoming planes. As a result of such observations, Mackworth (1950) conducted some experiments to investigate problems associated with sustaining attention over prolonged periods of time. In these original experiments, observers watched a stimulus much like a clock hand moving in steps around a blank clock face. The hand moved in regular steps, but occasionally a double step took place. The observer was asked to detect the occurrence of this double step by pressing a key each time it occurred. Mackworth found that after only one-half hour of watching, detection performance had dropped; the observers were actually missing more than one out of every four events. Physical fatigue seemed to be an unlikely explanation for this poor performance since the workload in this situation was really very light. Was the sensory system (in this case, vision) becoming fatigued and thus losing its original sensitivity? Or was the performance decrease caused by some factor that resulted in the observer just failing to respond, even though the sensory system was able to detect the critical stimulus event? Either factor, or both, would lead to the observed decrease in detection over time.

The questions asked in the study of vigilance are very similar to those associated with Signal Detection Theory (discussed in Chapter 2). If you remember, when a detection problem is couched in signal detection terms, a researcher can calculate d', the measure of the observer's sensitivity, and also *beta*, the measure of the location of the observer's criterion, or response bias. Since either a decrease in sensitivity or a decrease in an observer's overall tendency to respond "yes" to a signal would account for the decrease in vigilance performance, such an analysis is well suited to the present situation. When various investigators analyzed the vigilance problem from this viewpoint, they found that sensitivity (or d') did not change over time. However, observers became more cautious in saying "yes" as their time on watch progressed (Broadbent and

Gregory, 1963, 1965). This seems to indicate that changes in performance during a vigilance task may not be caused by a fatiguing of the sensory system so much as by a change in an observer's willingness to say that the signal has been detected. More recent work has shown that decreases in performance during vigilance tasks can be reduced if the observer is given a good deal of practice and if the vigilance task is one that can occur relatively automatically with little expenditure of effort (Fisk and Schneider, 1981).

Studies of vigilance and sustained attention demonstrate some interesting points. For instance, these tasks illustrate that paying overt attention to an external stimulus is an intense activity that requires mental effort. In general, psychologists agree that effort is not expended unless the observer is aroused in some way. Certain levels of physiological arousal, including maintenance of certain bodily positions, tensing of specific muscle groups, and continual active concentration, are part of sustaining overt attention. You can relate this to any situation in which you have "snapped back" to an alert posture after you have found yourself dozing off during a dull lecture. What happens during vigilance tasks, however, illustrates that ever increasing levels of arousal may not bring about the best performance. As arousal levels increase, attention becomes more narrowly focused on the central target of interest while other information is ignored. In the case of the vigilance task, this may lead to the shift toward an increasingly strict criterion for saying "yes" to the presence of a signal. Performance, as we have seen, suffers when this happens. Alternatively, some tasks require so much effort that redesigning them to make them more effortless (or training the observers to a high degree of proficiency) results in a reduction of arousal and an improvement of performance.

In 1908, Yerkes and Dodson formulated the

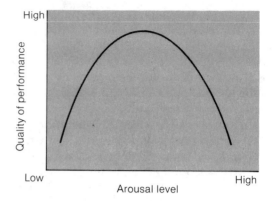

Figure 15-4. The Yerkes-Dodson law. The quality of performance seems to be best at middle levels of arousal.

relationship between arousal and performance in a way now known as the **Yerkes-Dodson law**. This relationship is shown graphically in Figure 15-4. As you can see, it has the shape of an upside-down *U*, which indicates that there is a midrange of arousal that brings about optimum performance on a given task.

The relationship between arousal, or some level of alertness, and performance is not simple. This fact can be demonstrated in another way. When observers are given a warning signal that lets them prepare themselves to take in some sensory information, they seem to do better than if no warning is given before the presentation of a sensory stimulus, as we saw in the Posner et al. experiments described earlier. The best performance seems to occur when the warning signal is presented between 200 and 500 msec before the onset of the target. Once again these data indicate that a certain degree of alertness is optimal, and that it takes a certain period of time for an observer to achieve this level. If the forewarning period is too long, however, the critical arousal period for optimal performance passes and accuracy declines (Posner and Boies, 1971).

DIVIDED ATTENTION

Most of us have little difficulty carrying on two or more activities simultaneously. We can read a book, scratch our heads, and chew on a snack —all at the same time. You might be tempted to say that you are conscious of the words in the book, while the rest of your activities remain unconscious. However, the evidence indicates that you are probably expending some mental effort on all these activities, although reading the book is taking the most effort. One can think of gaining mastery over a skill (such as driving a car) as a gradual withdrawal of mental effort until it can be performed almost automatically and with seemingly little attention. This leaves us free to expend mental effort on other things (such as talking to a friend or singing with the radio as we drive). Hence, the old saying, "Practice makes perfect," can be rephrased, "Practice makes automatic," or even, perhaps, "Practice makes unconscious." Thus, a practiced typist may be totally unconscious of the individual key strokes involved in forming each word.

This does not mean that certain aspects of the situation are no longer perceived at all, but rather that they are perceived in a different way and at a different level. Norman (1976) describes this process in terms of the establishment of *schemas*, or frameworks, that allow us to organize large chunks of information that are then stored in memory for later, and very efficient coding and retrieval. Chess masters, for example, have engaged in extensive study of the combinations of pieces and squares on the board that characterize typical attacks or defenses. These familiar formations are then seen as coherent patterns on the board. Thus, for the chess master, any individual game becomes an expression of, or a deviation from, these well-learned patterns. This automatic

control, gained through extensive practice, allows the chess master to concentrate more effort on more strategic aspects of the game than a novice player is able to, since the novice must spend time and effort on simply encoding where each individual piece is, and what the pieces may do in this given situation. **Automaticity** of such cognitive processes allows us effectively to divide our attention among various mental activities (LaBerge, 1973, 1975; Schneider and Shiffrin, 1977; Shiffrin and Schneider, 1977). Divided attention, in many instances, is highly dependent on memory and the efficient systems that we have developed for grouping in the storage and retrieval of information (Duncan, 1980b).

Recent research has been concerned with processes that affect our ability to divide attention between different tasks and between different sets of stimuli. Typically, it has been based on the capacity models of attention discussed at the beginning of the chapter. We will discuss some of this research when we deal with visual search at the end of this chapter. However, divided attention also deals with the issue of how easy or difficult it is to allocate attentive processes within or among the various sense modalities. You can get an idea of the nature of the problem from Demonstration Box 15-1.

Divided attention in vision

Moray (1969) has commented that one of the most striking differences between hearing and vision is the fact that, without the help of closing one eye, we are not able to tell which eye is receiving the visual stimulation. This is not true in audition, where when only one ear has received a signal, we can easily designate which one was involved. The two eyes appear to operate in a parallel or simultaneous fashion

---

Demonstration Box 15-1. Divided attention and effort

You can perform a simple experiment to demonstrate the ease with which you can divide your attention and how this ability interacts with the amount of effort you are expending on a task. As you read these words, you are probably paying close attention to them, and you are probably not really attending to other things. Now shift your attention to the pressure of your buttocks against the chair on which you are sitting. The activity of sitting is well-practiced, and you need to expend very little effort on its performance. However, you can easily shift your attention to the activity if you are asked to do so. Now concentrate on the act of sitting and try to continue reading the book. Is it easier or more difficult to understand the words in the book while you are concentrating on another activity? Reading new material usually requires large amounts of mental effort. Therefore, it is difficult to divide one's attention when performing such a demanding task.

---

in which the binocular (two-eyed) information is perceived as a unit. Each eye's input seems to lose its particular identity (often lyrically called its *eye signature*). Researchers, interested in whether or not observers could tell if their right or their left eyes had received visual stimulation, tested this by placing observers in a dark room and secretly covering one eye. When a stimulus was presented monocularly (to one eye), observers were asked to guess which eye had seen it. They were unable to do this with any reliability, which seems to indicate that the separate channels from the two eyes are not usually distinguishable (Smith, 1945; Pickersgill, 1961). More recent research has shown, however, that observers have the ability to make these monocular discriminations if the visual stimulus has certain spatial frequency components or if observers have feedback about the accuracy of their guesses (Blake and Cormack, 1979; Porac and Coren, 1981).

There is another condition in which the two eyes seem to compete for conscious attention. This situation involves an experimental procedure known as **binocular rivalry**. As the name suggests, we can set up conditions in which the two eyes will act as rivals for attention. Using a stereoscope, which is an optical instrument that allows us to stimulate the right and left eyes separately (discussed in Chapter 10), we can present an observer with a set of stimuli that will not combine into a single, unified image. In such cases each eye's view tends to alternately appear in consciousness. In other words, the right eye's view will be seen for a short time but then will disappear and the left eye's view will take over. These alternations will continue as long as the observer views the rivaling stimuli.

Binocular rivalry can be effectively produced by presenting an observer with lined stimuli that are grossly different in orientation. For example, we might put a grid of horizontal lines in one eye and a grid of vertical lines in the other. Also, we might present different colors to the two eyes, such as red in one and green in the other. In both instances the stimuli will not combine, or *fuse*, and binocular rivalry will occur. Demonstration Box 15-2 allows you to experience binocular rivalry for yourself. Although binocular rivalry illustrates that the two eyes can operate somewhat independently, it can only be produced under certain laboratory conditions. In everyday viewing, we do not seem to be able to divide our attention between the two eyes, although we sometimes seem able to detect differences between the eyes when asked to do so.

Demonstration Box 15-2. Binocular rivalry

You may demonstrate binocular rivalry by using the accompanying figure and a pocket mirror. Place the mirror on the center line of Figure *B* and hold your head as shown in Figure *A* (this is the same technique that was used in Chapter 12 to demonstrate form in random-dot stereograms).

Adjust it until the figure seen in the mirror appears to be at the same distance as the picture when seen directly. Now view the pictures for a few moments. At first you will see one set of lines; then they will be replaced by the other as they rival each other, alternating in and out of consciousness.

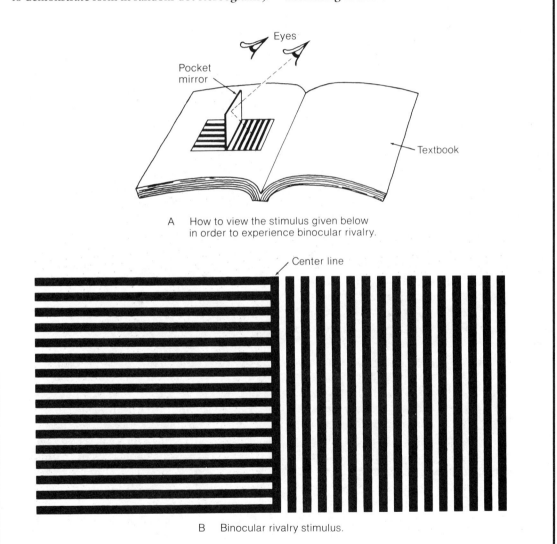

A   How to view the stimulus given below
in order to experience binocular rivalry.

B   Binocular rivalry stimulus.

Divided attention in audition

As mentioned in the previous section, it is well known that observers can distinguish the origin of stimulation (right ear versus left ear) in the auditory modality. In the early 1950s, Donald Broadbent took advantage of this fact to study divided attention with auditory stimulation. He called each ear a *channel* of information and asked a rather straightforward question: Is it easier to respond to input within one channel than to respond to input across different channels? In other words, would observers perform with greater efficiency when they were asked to respond to only one channel at a time, or when they were asked to divide their attention between two channels?

Broadbent (1954) had his observers wear a set of stereophonic headphones through which a different stimulus could be presented to each ear. This is sometimes called **dichotic** presentation. On each trial three different numbers were presented to each ear; for example, the right ear might receive 1, 3, 5 while the left ear simultaneously received 2, 4, 6. Broadbent had already ascertained that observers could recall a string of six numbers with about 96 percent accuracy when all the numbers were presented to both ears in a single sequence. He now wanted to know how they would perform given two types of recall instructions. First, they were asked to recall the three numbers presented to one ear and then the three numbers presented to the other ear. Therefore, a correct response in our example would be 1, 3, 5, 2, 4, 6. In the second condition, observers were asked to repeat the numbers in their order of presentation. Since the numbers had been presented to both ears simultaneously, the correct order of report in this instance would be 1, 2, 3, 4, 5, 6 (or 2, 1, 4, 3, 6, 5). Broadbent found that observers could report the entire string of numbers about 65 percent of the time when they were

responding ear by ear, but only 20 percent of the time when they were repeating the numbers by order of presentation across the two ears. He interpreted this as reflecting a loss of information processing capability when attention was switched between channels several times. Broadbent suggested that the order of auditory processing was determined by the channels of input and that switching between channels brought about a division of attention and poorer performance.

It wasn't long before other researchers took exception to this line of reasoning. In 1960, Gray and Wedderburn published results that led them to question the assumption that the two ears function as separate channels. They used Broadbent's technique but they modified his six stimulus items. They used both numbers and words, three in each ear, with each ear receiving some words and some numbers. However, the words composed a meaningful phrase, so that the simultaneous stimulus presentation went something like "three, aunt, eight" in the left ear and "dear, two, Jane" in the right ear. You will notice that this stimulus series contains the organized and meaningful phrase, "Dear Aunt Jane." Under these conditions, the observers performed with equal efficiency, regardless of whether they reported the items by ear or by order of presentation.

These results contradict the notion that separation of physical channels will determine the order of information processing, and they also indicate the important role of memory in our ability to divide our attention. The expectations built up through our knowledge and experience with language are stored in memory. These expectations can aid us in overcoming physical constraints on information processing. From the moment of input into a sensory system, various expectations, based on our stored memories, are alerted, and these expectations interact in the final production of a perceptual experience. In other words, not only the physical aspects of the stimulus but also our own interpretations and expectations can determine the order of processing and the allocation of attention as we shall see in Chapter 17.

Perhaps a good way to think of the above distinction is to use the distinction between **data-driven** and **conceptually-driven** processes (Lindsay and Norman, 1977; Norman, 1976). Data-driven processes are those based on the limits and actions of physiological structures in direct response to incoming sensory information. For example, a stimulus enters the eye and proceeds through the various structures that process the image and respond to color, shape, and contrast. Such data-driven mechanisms have been discussed earlier in relationship to form and speech perception (Chapters 12 and 13). On the other hand, conceptually-driven processes are those that depend on our prior knowledge or our expectations concerning the nature of the incoming stimulation. Suppose a facelike image enters the eye; our prior experience and knowledge of human faces can guide the efficiency with which we process this sensory input. Gray and Wedderburn's experiment described before demonstrates the operation of conceptually-driven processes very nicely, since the stimuli seem to be coded in terms of meaning (word sequence), as well as in the data-driven manner represented by ear of input. Although some loss of processing efficiency appears to occur when we shift our attention between the two ears (Massaro, 1975), let us point out again that physical characteristics of our receptors alone do not seem to determine how well we can allocate our effort to optimally perceive and code a set of stimuli.

Miller (1982) has studied the ability of observers to divide attention between the visual and auditory modalities. Observers were required to respond as quickly as possible to the onset of a signal in either the visual or the auditory modalities (sometimes a trial consisted of both a visual and an auditory signal and the observer had to respond to both). Miller found response times were slightly faster to the dual presentation of visual and auditory signals than to the presentation of either one alone. Based on these data, he argued that detection is equally good when divided across two channels than when focused on only one. Thus, when considering interactions across sensory modalities, it seems that we are able to divide our attention more effectively than if we are dealing with different channels within one particular sensory system.

SELECTIVE ATTENTION

In many ways a separation between selective and divided attention is artificial. This is because most research on selective attention has dealt not only with how well we can process the information on the channel to which we are attending, but also with the fate of the information on the unattended channel. In other words, if information is coming in to both ears and you are asked to pay close attention to the stimulation in the right ear, it would be of interest to know how well you can do this. This is equivalent to asking how well you can *selectively attend* to one of several channels of information. Also, while you are attending to this set of inputs (in our current example the right ear), what is happening to the unattended information (in the left ear)? Can you respond to any of it (that is, has your attention really been divided?) or is it all lost? While most of the research surrounding selective attention has stemmed from considerations of the bottleneck models described earlier, our everyday experience tells us that what we pay attention to is seen or heard sharply and clearly while everything else is vague, ill-defined, and certainly not remembered. Let us see how research evidence bears out our casual observations.

The cocktail party problem

Although many intriguing diversions occupy your time when you attend a cocktail party, in the interests of science, observe your patterns of attention the next time you find yourself in such a situation. Despite the surrounding noise of many speakers in the same room, it is not difficult to listen to a conversation that has engaged your interest. In effect, you "tune out" the rest of the party in order to selectively attend to the portions of the incoming stimulation that are important to you.

You can demonstrate the restriction of attention under high levels of arousal, which was mentioned in the early part of the chapter, by reflecting on party conversations that you have had with attractive members of the opposite sex. When you had the good fortune to encounter such a person at a party, how much of the rest of the party did you remember? However, you can still switch your attention rather rapidly if something happens across the room. If you are waiting for the arrival of more refreshments, for example, you can monitor events at the doorway while still participating in a conversation. Hence, a cocktail party demonstrates not only selective listening, but also an ability to divide attention in order to pick up elements that are meaningful to your present situation.

At the time that Broadbent was conducting his research in England, Colin Cherry, in the United States, became interested in the problems represented by cocktail party behavior. To study them he introduced a new experimental technique called **shadowing**. In a shadowing experiment, an observer is presented with two messages in different channels. For instance, one may be presented

auditorially and the other visually, or one message may be sent to the right ear while a different one goes into the left ear. The observer is asked to repeat aloud (shadow) one of the messages as it occurs. This technique is used to force observers to pay attention to one of the messages, and it was thought that repeating it aloud would require close attention. Therefore, during a shadowing experiment, an experimenter can discover how well an observer can shadow a message and also determine the amount of information picked up from a competing message that is not shadowed.

First, let us consider a series of variables that a message. Observers can easily shadow a message if it is organized prose, for example, a selection from a novel. They have more difficulty shadowing randomly arranged words and the greatest difficulty with nonsense words (collections of letters that are assumed to have no meaning, such as *glak*). In addition, when shadowing a message, an observer tends to lag behind the words slightly, so that whole phrases are grouped together. This is called *phrase shadowing*. If an observer is asked to shadow syllable by syllable, or to repeat each sound as it is presented (called *phonemic shadowing*), the task is much more difficult. Thus, grammatical structure and our familarity with language help us to attend to a stimulus in the face of competing input. This is another example of conceptually-driven involvement in selective attention. On the other hand, data-driven aspects of the message can help us attend to one of the two competing messages. If the two auditory messages come from spatially separated places, are different in pitch (for instance, a male voice speaking one message and a female voice speaking the other), or are presented at different speeds, this can help direct and maintain attention on one of the inputs. For an example of such a data-driven process, see Demonstration Box 15-3.

Demonstration Box 15-3. Selective attention and the precedence effect

You may remember our discussion of the precedence effect from Chapter 8, where we listed
some variables that affect our ability to localize
the position of sound sources in space. When
sounds are emitted in enclosed spaces, they tend
to cause echoes as they bounce from walls, ceilings, and floors. However, we can still make a correct localization of the sound source because the
sound emanating directly from this source will
reach our ears before its echo. The auditory system is sensitive to these time differences and can
use this information in the localization of sound-
producing sources. The direction of the sound
emanating directly from the sound source takes
precedence over other sounds in localization,
hence the name *precedence effect*.

The precedence effect can also be helpful in selective attention, when we are attempting to process one of many simultaneously occurring stimulus events. A good example of this is found in
cocktail party situations, where you may try to follow one of many competing conversations. This
aspect of selective attention is helped by the spatial and temporal separation of the auditory inputs. You can demonstrate this for yourself with
the aid of two friends (preferably of the same sex)
and a door. First have your friends stand as shown
in Figure *A*, while each reads passages from a
book or newspaper simultaneously. Notice that
even with your eyes closed you can easily separate and locate the two messages. Now have your
friends stand as shown in Figure *B*. Notice that in
this situation each is standing out of your line of
sight, and the messages must travel out through
the open door. This means that they will tend to
reach you at the same time and come from the
same direction. Now, again with your eyes closed,
notice how difficult it is to locate the voices and
to separate their messages.

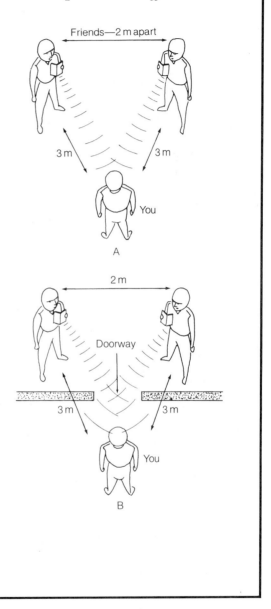

Now let's look at what Cherry found out about the rejected, or unshadowed, message. Essentially, he discovered that his observers could relate relatively little about the rejected message except that they assumed it was prose. Later, Moray (1959) tried to determine exactly how much information from the unshadowed message was processed. He found that although some words were repeatedly presented, and the observers were told that they would be asked about the information in the rejected message, they were unable to report the unshadowed words. There are several possible explanations for this result. Perhaps observers were not processing any information from the unattended channel, and thus they did not hear it. If this were the case, however, we would not be able to perceive anything except that which was the object of our attention, and we could never be diverted from attending to a conversation by an extraneous stimulus. Of course, this is not the case, since at one time or another you have probably heard your name mentioned by someone nearby, even though you were not attending to the conversation.

Another possibility stems from a difficulty with the memory of, rather than the perception of, the rejected message. Both Cherry and Moray had waited a few seconds after the end of the experimental messages before asking their observers about the unshadowed message. Perhaps when you are not paying attention to something, it is processed by your sensory system but is not committed to a long-lasting memory. To test this idea, an experimenter need only interrupt shadowing to ask the observer about what had just occured in the competing message. When this is done, more of the rejected message can be recalled; the recalled material usually includes the last five to seven words, numbers, or whatever units are being shadowed (Glucksberg and Cowen, 1970; Norman, 1969). Once again we encoun-

ter the role of memory, with the data indicating that attending to a stimulus allows it to be more fully and more permanently entered into memory. This seems to be most consistent with the late selection version of the bottleneck models of selective attention. Unattended input, on the other hand, is more fleeting and seems to be quickly lost or never entered into memory. Try the shadowing task in Demonstration Box 15-4 to experience the relationship between selective attention and memory.

VISUAL SEARCH

Unlike the ears, which are stationary organs whose movement depends on head movement, the eyes are always moving, searching, and exploring the visual field with high speed, ballistic movements, called **saccades**. Since the small foveal area in the retina is most highly suited to a detailed analysis of visual information, we must move our eyes to allow targets of interest to stimulate the fovea. Therefore, attentive processes in vision relate both to situations in which the eye is moving and to situations in which the eye remains immobile.

A typical way to study selective attention in vision during eye movements is to engage the observer in a visual search task. For example, we could ask an observer to find a target letter embedded in a long list of other distracting letters. The observer must then move his or her eyes or *scan* the array until the target is found. This technique was used by Neisser and his associates (Neisser, 1967) in a series of experiments. They used 50-line lists of letters, and the observers were asked to look for a target letter that appeared in an unpredictable position. The observers scanned the list from top to bottom, and the experimenter recorded the amount of time it took them to find the target

Demonstration Box 15-4. Selective attention and memory

In the accompanying passage, the relevant message is shaded while the irrelevant message is printed in the normal fashion. You are to read the shaded passage aloud as rapidly as possible, ignoring the irrelevant (unshaded) message. Now without cheating and looking back, write down all the words you remember from the irrelevant message. Go back and read the shaded passage again, but this time stop after each line to write down the words you recall from the irrelevant message (without looking back at it). You should find that the list of remembered words is longer when your reading is interrupted and you are not asked to recall all the irrelevant message at once (from Lindsay and Norman, 1977).

In performing an experiment like this one on man attention car it house is boy critically hat important shoe that candy the old material horse that tree is pen being phone read cow by book the hot subject tape for pin the stand relevant view task sky be read cohesive man and car grammatically house complete boy but hat without shoe either candy being horse so tree easy pen that phone full cow attention book is hot not tape required pin in stand order view to sky read red it not too difficult.

item. As you would expect, when the target was close to the end of the list, observers spent more time searching for it. In general, however, they performed the search task with great speed. Neisser estimated that after some practice his observers could scan at a speed of about ten lines of letters (each containing six letters) per second.

In much the same way that we analyzed the shadowing task, we can look at the search experiments and ask what factors affect the ability to find an embedded target with speed and efficiency. Practicing the task certainly increases one's speed; however, the nature of the lists can also have an effect. It is much more difficult to discriminate the target letter when it is embedded in a list of letters that are visually similar to it. Thus, like the shadowing task, physical similarities and differences can alter our ability to selectively attend to one aspect of the input. You can demonstrate this effect for yourself in Demonstration Box 15-5.

What happens to the unattended channel in visual search tasks? In other words, what hap-

pens to the other letters in the list that are not targets? Neisser states that his observers reported that the other letters were just a blur and that they did not "see" individual letters. This implies that the observers are not searching letter by letter but that they are taking in the information in chunks. As these chunks are processed, only the distinctive features of the target stimulus appear to be noted and stand out. This type of reasoning would explain why physical similarities between targets and nontargets make the visual search somewhat harder.

As we have mentioned, selective processes in vision are closely tied with the movement of the eyes to fixate a target of interest. Neisser's work has indicated that information during visual search is processed in chunks. Therefore, it seems reasonable to ask about the size of these chunks and to investigate just how much visual information can be taken in within one glance. We can describe attention as a beam of light in which the central part represents the point of focus (Hernandez-

---

Demonstration Box 15-5. Stimulus characteristics and search time

For this demonstration you will need a stop watch or a clock with a sweep second hand. Look at the time and then search List A for the letter Z. When you are finished note the time it took you to find it. Now do the same for List B and then return to this text.

You probably found List B much less difficult and your search to be faster (even though the Z's are both at the same line). This is because the letters in List B are quite dissimilar from the target (all the letters except the Z have a round segment), while in List A they are all angular like the target. Thus the characteristics of the target and nontarget items interact in a search task.

(A)	(B)
VWMIEX	GODUCQ
VMWIEX	QCURDO
XVWMEI	DUCOQG
WXVEMI	CGRDQU
XMEWIV	UDRCOQ
MXIVEW	GQCORU
VEWMIX	GOQUCD
EMVXWI	GDQUOC
IVWMEX	URDCGO
IEVMWX	GODRQC
IVMXEW	CGUROQ
EWVMIX	UCGROD
EXWMVI	DQRCGU
IXEMWV	QDOCGU
VXWEMI	ODUGQR
MXVEWI	QCDUGO
XVWMEI	CQOGRD
MWXVIE	QUGCDR
VIMEXW	URDGQO
EXVWIM	GRUQDO
WVZMXE	DUZGRO
XEMIWV	OCDURQ
WXIMEV	UOCGQD
EMWIVX	RGQCOU
IVEMXW	GRUDQO

Peon, 1964; Treisman and Gelade, 1980). If this description is adequate, we are asking how wide this beam of light may be. In other words, how much visual information can we process at once during one fixation, or more technically, we seek to measure the **span of apprehension**.

Perhaps the most well-known contemporary studies on this issue were conducted by Sperling (1960). He used a **tachistoscope**, which is an experimental apparatus that allows the presentation of visual material for very brief periods of time. In tachistoscopic terms 1 second (1000 msec) is a very long time. Sperling used displays containing from 3 to 12 letters, and presented them to his observers for 50 msec each. An observer was given a score sheet that looked like the spatial arrangement of the display. She was asked to mark each letter in its correct position once the display was no longer visible. With displays of three to four letters, Sperling's observers were very accurate; however, when the displays contained more letters, observers were still averaging only about four correct items per display.

Before concluding that the span of apprehension was approximately four items, Sperling felt he had to investigate another possibility. Perhaps his observers actually saw more than they could report, and since the presentation time was so brief, it was difficult to hold the entire display in memory. Even though the observers started writing down their answers as soon as the display had disappeared, perhaps their memory of the remaining items had faded by the time they reached the fourth item. Sperling wanted to separate the limitations of memory from the limitations of perception. To do this he devised an experiment in which he showed his observers three horizontal rows of four letters each as in Figure 15-5. After the display had been flashed for 50 msec, an auditory cue was presented to the observer. This was a short tone that varied in pitch. If the pitch was high, the observer was to repeat the top row, and if it was low or in a midrange, the bottom or middle row was to be reported. The observer never knew which of these tones would be presented after the visual display. This experimental technique has been called **partial report** since the observer is asked to report only part, not all, of the array.

By taking the number of letters correctly identified from each row and multiplying it by three (for the three rows in the display), an

A R P I
X W H Q
Y Z E D

Figure 15-5. Typical experimental stimuli used by Sperling in studying apprehension span.

experimenter can estimate how much information is being processed while the display is visible. Sperling found that with practice his observers could correctly recall about three letters out of each row. Multiplying this figure by three, we can see that the information available from this brief visual display is nine rather than four items.

When the effect of memory decay is taken into account, we find that the span of apprehension is much wider than that shown by the original experiment. Once again we find that memory interacts with attentional processes. When information is entering the visual system very rapidly (for example, during a series of eye movements), much more may be "seen" than can be effectively entered into memory and stored for later use.

Automatic versus controlled search

A more recent approach to the role of attention in target detection during visual search has involved designing experiments to separate **serial** from **parallel processing** in early stages of visual information processing. Serial processing means that stimuli are processed sequentially, one after another, while parallel processing means that a number of stimuli are processed simultaneously. If observers' performances change when the search arrays increase in size (there are more distractor elements to search through for the target), then this might indicate that detection during visual search is a serial process; in other words, the distractor elements must be checked one at a time to see whether they are the target. If this is the case, increases in the number of elements to be searched will bring about increases in the search time. Alternatively, observers may search arrays in a parallel way where the distractor elements are checked all at once for the presence of the target. In this case, search time will not be affected by increases in the size of the visual arrays.

Since there is evidence for both types of processing (see Spoehr and Lehmkuhle, 1982), a series of experiments by Shiffrin and Schneider (Shiffrin and Schneider, 1977; Schneider and Shiffrin, 1977) was designed to attempt to explain these varied results. They used a *multiple-frame detection task* that combines the features of Neisser's and Sperling's experiments. Their stimulus presentation procedure is shown in Figure 15-6A. As can be seen, each observer saw 20 frames (or flashed stimulus arrays) on each trial in which each frame contained four stimulus positions. Each position contained either a digit, a letter, or a dot matrix pattern. At the start of each trial, the observer was given a set of target items to search for in the frame sequence. They knew that only one of the target items could appear on any trial and that it could appear in any frame except the first three and the last two. When the target was detected, the observer pushed a button. Within this basic design, these researchers varied several aspects of the experiment. First, the size of the set of target items varied (either 1 or 4); second, the exposure duration of each frame varied from 40 to 800 msec and, lastly, the frames contained 1, 2, or

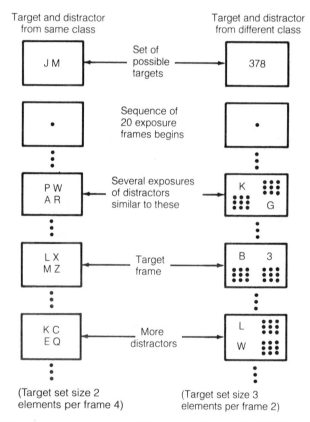

Figure 15-6. Typical stimulus sequences used in a search task by Shiffrin and Schneider (1977)

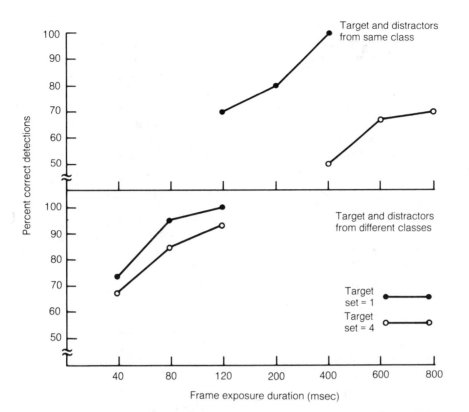

Figure 15-7. Percent correct target detections for stimulus exposures, each of which contained four elements, where distracters came from the same or a different stimulus class, *and the total number of possible targets was 1 or 4 (based on Shiffrin and Schneider, 1977).*

4 elements. An important addition to these manipulations was the relationship between the elements in the target set and those nontargets (distractors) that appeared in the frame sequence. In one condition, target items were from one category (for example, digits), while distractors were from another category (for example, letters). In other conditions distractors and targets were all from the same category (either letters or digits), with targets on one trial being distractors on the following trial and vice versa. Examples of both these types of conditions are shown in Figure 15-6.

Shiffrin and Schneider chose these variables with the following rationale. They reasoned that the time of frame exposure was important because they could observe the amount of time the observers needed to fully process the items. They reasoned further that varying the number of elements in each frame would allow them to study the serial versus parallel nature of the search process. This, in combination with varying the number of targets that the observer was asked to detect, would permit them to assess the limits of the parallel or serial comparison process. Figure 15-7 shows one result of these experiments for a condition where each frame contained four items. As you can see, observers who were tested where target and distractors were from the *same class* were affected by both exposure time for each frame and target set size. Performance (percentage of correct detections) was best for longer exposures when the set of possible targets contained only one item. On the other hand, observers in the conditions where targets and distractors were from *different classes* showed the same type of performance increases with increasing exposure time, regardless of the size of the target set. Although we have shown the results of only one condition where four items were present on each exposure, these results were consistent across stimulus set sizes as well. The number of stimuli present per exposure significantly affected performance in conditions where targets and distractors are drawn from the same class (larger numbers of stimuli per exposure produced poor performance), while it did not affect performance when targets and distractors were drawn from different classes of stimuli.

Based on these results, Schneider and Shiffrin proposed that there are two types of visual search. The first is a **controlled search**, where each item in the target set is compared serially (one after the other) and individually to each item in every exposure frame. A detection decision will only be made after this is done. For this reason, performance will be affected by the number of stimuli per exposure and the size of the set of possible targets. This accounts for observer performance in the conditions where targets and distractors were from the same class of stimuli. Alternatively, if targets are from different classes than the distractors, observers can use an **automatic search**, given the appropriate stimulus conditions. This type of search allows the detection process to operate in parallel so the observers do not have to search item by item. The control of attention is automatic and only aspects of the display that are relevant to the target

detection are processed. This search procedure would not be affected by number of stimuli per frame or target set size. These researchers have argued that this type of search process develops after a great deal of experience with distinguishing certain types of visual stimuli (for example, distinguishing digits from numbers); therefore, less visual attention is demanded in search across several stimulus classes than in one where the distractors and targets are drawn from the same class of stimuli. This argument assumes that differences in attentional control (with the by-product being serial or parallel processing of visual elements) are a result of perceptual learning. One can learn to quickly distinguish the relevant features that differentiate one category of items from another, so that these features "pop out" and the search is automatic. There are instances, however, in which experience and learning can interfere with certain types of tasks. Try the demonstration of the **Stroop effect** described in Demonstration Box 15-6 to explore this for yourself.

Where does this leave us with the notion of attention? We know from our experience that we can control the peceptual flow into consciousness by altering the way we distribute our attention. We can divide and switch our attention with relative ease, and we can selectively attend to only one of several events occurring simultaneously. Research evidence supports each of the models discussed at the beginning of the chapter. In the final "complete" explanation of attention, it will most probably be shown that both structural limitations as well as limitations on processing capacities play a role in perceptual selectivity. Our discussion of attention has demonstrated how perception is dependent on memories, prior expectations, and learning, and also how perception can be altered by such factors. This dependency has already emerged in Chapters 10, 12, and 13, and we will see it again in Chap-

---

Demonstration Box 15-6. The Stroop phenomenon

The **Stroop effect** is an interesting example of how well-learned material can interfere with our ability to attend to the demands of a task. In 1935, Stroop found that observers had difficulty screening out meaningful information even when it was irrelevant to the task. He devised three situations. In the first he recorded how long it took individuals to read a list of color names, such as red and green, printed in black ink. He then took an equal number of color patches and recorded how long it took observers to name each one of the series. Then he took a color name and printed it in a color of ink that did not coincide with the linguistic information (for example, the word *blue* printed in red ink). When he had observers name the ink color in this last series, he found that they often erroneously read the printed color name rather than the ink color name; therefore, it took them much longer to read through this last series.

The Stroop effect demonstrates that meaningful linguistic information is difficult to ignore, and the automatic expectations that have come to be associated with the presence of words often take over, resulting in difficulties in focusing attention.

Color plate 7 is an example of the Stroop Color Word Test so you can try this for yourself. Have a friend time you with either the second hand of a watch or with a stop watch, if you have one, as you read each group. Start timing with the word "go" and read across the lines in exactly the same fashion for each group. When the last response is made in each group, stop timing and note your response time. You should find that reading the color names will take the least amount of time, while naming the colors of the ink when the printed word names a different color will take you the most time. Naming the color patches will fall in between these two.

---

ters 17 and 18. Clearly, such data suggest that we must go beyond the mere registration of sensory input at the sense organ to understand how we construct our perceptual experiences.

GLOSSARY

The following definitions are specific to this book.

Automaticity   When cognitive, perceptual, or motor processes can be accomplished with little conscious awareness and little allocation of mental effort.

Automatic search   A type of visual search in which detection and comparison processes operate in parallel.

Binocular rivalry   A situation in which the unfusable stimulation of the two eyes leads to alternation of the monocular views.

Bottleneck models   Models of attention that assume a structural limitation on the amount of information that can be processed at one time.

Capacity models   Models of attention that assume limits on an observer's ability to allocate mental effort to various stimuli.

Conceptually-driven   processing   Information processing that is guided by memories and expectations concerning the nature of the incoming stimulation.

Controlled search   A type of visual search in which detection and comparison processes operate serially.

Data-driven processing   Information processing based on the activation of structures within the sensory system that respond to individual properties of the incoming array.

Dichotic   Presentation of different stimuli to each of the two ears.

Early selection models   Models of attention in which information selection occurs immediately after sensory registration.

Late selection models Models of attention in which selection occurs rather late in the stages of information processing, for example, in memory.

Mental effort A concept used to describe a state of alertness in attentional tasks. It seems to be accompanied by changes in physiological arousal.

Model A hypothesis that attempts to explain a series of complex events and how they relate to one another.

Orienting response The response where an observer turns toward and orients her receptors toward a novel stimulus.

Parallel processing A pattern of visual search in which critical features are extracted from an array simultaneously.

Partial report An experimental technique used in span of apprehension experiments in which the observer is asked to repeat only part, not all, of the presented material.

Saccades High speed, ballistic eye movements that facilitate exploration of the visual field.

Serial processing A pattern of visual search in which critical features are extracted from an array one after the other.

Shadowing A technique of directing an observer's attention to particular input; the observer repeats as closely as possible the verbal input he is receiving, usually in a particular ear.

Span of apprehension The amount of visual information an observer can pick up during a single fixation.

Stroop effect The difficulty that observers have in eliminating meaningful but conflicting information from a task even when that information is irrelevant to the task.

Tachistoscope An experimental device allowing presentation of visual material for very brief periods of time.

Vigilance A form of attention that emphasizes maintenance of alertness and accuracy of observation during long tasks.

Yerkes-Dodson law The principle that arousal and performance are related, a midrange of arousal yielding optimum performance levels.

16

Development

T HE CAMP COUNSELOR TURNED TO the newest arrival and asked, "And how old are you, son?"

"Well," said the boy, "it all depends. According to my latest set of anatomical tests I'm 7. According to my physical dexterity test I'm 10. I've got a mental age of 11, a moral age of 9, and a social age of 10. If you are referring to my chronological age though, that's 8, but nobody pays any attention to that these days."

This child's comments point out that there are significant changes in many of our physical and psychological characteristics as we age. Each of these changes has its own time course. Some changes simply represent physiological transformations occurring as the body matures (such as a person's anatomical age). Others represent patterns of behavior that are learned as the individual grows older (such as social or moral age). Still others may represent a combination of both learning and maturation (such as mental age). Although no one refers to a *perceptual age*, there are also changes in perceptual characteristics that occur as an individual develops and matures. These changes tend to represent improvements producing perceptual experiences that more accurately represent the physical environment. Some perceptual capacities, however, seem to deteriorate with age.

In considering how an individual's perceptual functioning changes, we can adopt two different perspectives. The first is long term, viewing people over their entire life span. This is the *developmental approach*, which assumes that knowledge of a person's chronological age will allow us to predict many aspects of perceptual behavior. The alternate approach is short term, viewing the changes that occur in perceptual responses as a result of a circumscribed set of experiences. This is the *perceptual learning approach*. It is based on the presumption that our interactions with the world can shape our percepts. These two approaches are not mutually exclusive; understanding the nature of perception often requires us to use both viewpoints. Common to both the learning and developmental viewpoints is the conclusion that, despite our lack of awareness of it, perception is continually undergoing change. Your experience of the world differs from individuals who are 10 years older or 10 years younger than you. Because the two approaches use different techniques and tend to address somewhat different theoretical issues, however, we will deal with these areas in separate chapters, beginning with the developmental approach, and proceeding to the issue of the effects of learning and experience in Chapter 17.

PERCEPTION IN INFANTS

Before discussing how perception changes as we age and develop, we must first know what perceptual capacities we had at the moment of birth. Unfortunately, newborn infants (*neonates*) are difficult to test. They tend to be asleep most of the time, and in addition, they do not respond to instructions nor answer our questions in any direct verbal fashion. Finally, they produce only a limited range of observable behaviors. These problems require experimenters to be rather ingenious in devising measures of the perceptual abilities of the very young. It also often forces researchers to use animal subjects, rather than humans, to obtain direct physiological measures of functioning.

Basic visual functions

Let us begin by looking at the physiology of the infant's visual system. The infant's retina contains rods and cones as does the adult's. Electrical measures seem to indicate that these receptors are functioning from birth, although the responses may not yet exactly match those of older children or adults (Aantaa, 1970; Maurer, 1975). Anatomically, however, the retina still seems immature. For instance, the region of the central fovea is still not well defined in a one-week old infant (Abramov, Gordon, Hendrickson, Hainline, Dobson, and LaBossiere, 1982). Visual development seems to take place first in the central retina, with the peripheral portion maturing several weeks later (Russoff, 1979).

Knowledge of the status of the visual pathways in newborns and infants comes mostly from animal studies, with the cat providing most of the data. If we measure the physiological functions of the various sites in the visual pathways of the cat, at the time when the animal first opens its eyes, we get results like those shown in Table 16-1 (see Norton, 1981a).

Table 16-1 shows that a number of adultlike and immature response patterns coexist in the newborn cat. Thus, in the retinal ganglion cell, we find the expected center-surround arrangement of excitatory and inhibitory responses;

Table 16-1. The functional condition of various sites in the visual pathways of the newborn (based on measures taken on the cat)

Adultlike responses	Immature responses
Retinal Ganglion Cells	
Center-surround organization of receptive fields	Low activity level
	Overly large receptive fields
Adult percentage of on/off center	Slow responses to light and weak inhibition
	X vs. Y responses not clear
Lateral Geniculate Nucleus	
Normal visual field mapping	Low activity and silent areas
Binocular separation of inputs	Large receptive field diameter
	Slow, sluggish, fatiguable responding
Superior Colliculus	
Normal visual field mapping	Slow, sluggish fatiguable responses
Center-surround receptive fields	Large receptive fields
Adult percentage of on/off center	No movement direction sensitivity
Striate Cortex	
Normal visual field mapping	Sluggish, fatigable responses
Adult separation of responses by eye of input	Many silent cells
	Fewer or absent orientaton and direction selective cells with broader tuning
	No binocular disparity cells

however, the receptive fields differ in size from those of the adult, and there is a general sluggishness in the response rate.

In Chapter 3 we discussed two different visual response types which we called X and Y. These responses appear to involve different types of information processing, with the X responses associated principally with detail vision, while the Y responses seem to be specialized for movement and rapid response. These two systems were characterized by both response pattern differences, as well as different pathways to the cortex. In the infant cat, however, these two response types are not as well defined, and the difference between the sustained response (X) and transient response (Y) systems is much reduced (Hamasaki and Sutija, 1979; Mooney, Dubin, and Russoff, 1979).

At the lateral geniculate nucleus, we do find the adult correspondence between retinal response location and geniculate response location, the separation of the inputs from the two eyes into clearly defined layers, and some evidence of the X-like sustained response types. Many of the cells in the geniculate, however, simply don't seem to respond to any sort of visual inputs, responses are generally slow and fatigue easily, and the transient Y-like responses seem to be absent (Daniels, Pettigrew, and Norman, 1978). A somewhat similar pattern emerges for the superior colliculus, with the general topography resembling that of the adult and with center-surround organization of responses. Again, however, receptive field size is too large, responses are slow and weak and not particularly direction sensitive (Norton, 1981).

Finally, at the level of the primary visual cortex, we find that the inputs of the two eyes do separate into the expected columnar arrangement discussed in Chapter 3, and directional and orientation sensitive cells (both simple and complex) are found. However, responses are grudging and easily fatiguable, many fewer of these feature specific cells seem to be present, and binocular disparity sensitive cells seem to be almost absent (Blakemore and Van Sluyters, 1975; Fregnac, 1979; Fregnac and Imbert, 1978). Thus, overall, many of the characteristics of the adult system seem to be present or anticipated in the newborn visual system, but the full adult pattern of response clearly is not present. There appear to be different rates of maturation of many of the characteristics of the visual system. Thus, for instance, there is a suggestion that the X pathways to the cortex may mature more quickly than the Y pathways (Maurer and Lewis, 1979), and it is certainly clear that the responses of the neonate are slower and less vigorous than those of the adult, suggesting that the quality of visual information reaching the newborn cortex may be somewhat diminished (see Movshon and Van Sluyters, 1981).

In humans, we can determine how well the visual cortex of the infant is functioning by measuring what is called the **visually evoked response** (often abbreviated **VER**). This is a change in the electrical activity produced by the brain in response to a visual stimulus. One usually records a VER by fixing electrodes (generally flat pieces of silver) to the scalp and connecting them to very sensitive amplifiers. Almost all newborn infants (including most premature infants) show some VER, although it differs somewhat from the adult response in its pattern, size, and speed (Ellingson, 1968; Umezaki and Morrell, 1970). Over a period of about three months, the infant's electrical responses to visual stimuli come to look more and more like those of adults (Atkinson and Braddick, 1981; Harter and Suitt, 1970; Jensen and Engel, 1971). It is generally agreed that during the first year the actual neural functioning of the visual system may continue to mature, and it may not reach full adult capabilities until the end of the second year (Elling-son, Lathrop, Nelson, and Donahy, 1972; Movshon and Van Sluyters, 1981).

Directional responses

At a behavioral level we can find some responses in newborns to the direction, distance, or movement of stimuli. Many of these responses appear in the form of reflexes. The most common is the *rooting response*, in which a child will reflexively turn its head in the direction of a touch to the cheek. This response helps the child to localize the breast for feeding, and also, since it turns the eyes as well, provides a first opportunity to begin to coordinate sight with touch. Evidence indicates that such *intersensory* or *intermodal* coordination between the senses, such as touch and vision, is not fully developed in the newborn. Thus, neonates neither reach out to touch what they see, nor do they turn to see what is touching them (Abravanel, 1981; Bushnell, 1981). By the age of 3 months, however, infants seem to have extracted the behavioral rule, "What I can see in a particular place I can also touch in exactly the same place," and hence begin reaching for seen objects (White and Held, 1966). From this point on, infants tend to overgeneralize, by persistently trying to touch things that they see, even when it is inappropriate. A striking example of this is the problems provided by glass, a substance that one can see through but can't reach through. Eight-month-old infants will push, pick, or scratch at a transparent surface, trying to get the objects seen behind it. Furthermore, they seem driven by their new found connection between sight and touch, since they persist in this inappropriate reaching, even if they've encountered the obstacle previously or if they have been shown a way to detour around or

under the glass surface (Bushnell, 1979). Similar problems are created by mirrors (Berthenthal and Fischer, 1978).

Newborns seem to be able to localize the direction of a sound source by turning either their head or their eyes (Butterworth, 1981; Muir and Field, 1979). Perhaps the most impressive demonstration comes from Wertheimer (1961), who tested an infant girl's ability to localize stimuli 3 minutes after birth. With the infant lying on her back, a toy "cricket" was sounded next to her right or left ear. Two observers noted whether the eyes moved to the infant's right or to her left—or not at all. On 18 out of the 22 times when the child's eyes moved, they moved in the direction of the click. When the experiment was completed, the child was still only 10 minutes old; hence, these data allow us to conclude that some directional aspects of auditory stimuli are accurately processed and are capable of guiding behavior from birth.

You probably recall from Chapter 8 that there are several binaural cues that help to indicate the direction of a sound relative to the listener. The two most important of these are the time differences in the arrival of the sounds to the two ears (first to the closer ear), and the intensity differences between the two ears since the head acts as a sound shield damping the intensity to the more distant side (see Green, 1976; Moore, 1977). Which of these cues is most effective for the infant? By directly controlling both the time differences between the ears, and intensity of sound reaching the two ears, Clifton, Morrongiello, Kulig, and Dowd (1981) demonstrated that newborn infants, and those up to about 9 weeks of age, respond to intensity differences between the two ears by turning in the direction of the sound. The more complex time discrimination cue, however, is not adequate to induce the child to turn its head in the appropriate direction. By age 5 months, however, both cues are effective and cause the child to look in the direction of the sound source.

Further spatial abilities are shown by the fact that infants are capable of directing their eye movements toward targets. Neonates tend to move their eyes in a conjugate fashion (both eyes together) and seem to have the capacity to make convergent and divergent eye movements. If we present a young infant (about 2 weeks of age) with a target that suddenly appears 15 or 20 degrees from the fovea, he will turn his eyes in the direction of the stimulus (Tronick, 1972). As the infant grows older, he will direct his eyes toward targets that appear even farther away in the periphery (Harris and MacFarlane, 1974). Furthermore, 3-month-old infants seem to be able to recognize targets out in the edge or periphery of their visual field well enough to guide their eyes to selected or preferred stimuli (Maurer and Lewis, 1981).

When newborns are presented with a target, which appears and then moves to one side or another, they will track it (Dayton, Jones, Steele, and Rose, 1964; Schulman, 1973). This is not to say that the infants' eye movements are exactly like those of adults. You may recall from Chapter 15 that there are two types of voluntary eye movements. The first are *saccadic eye movements*, which are fast, sharp movements from one target to another. These are the eye movements used to center the fovea on the target of interest and seem to accompany the direction of attention toward a target. The other form of eye movement has a somewhat less voluntary component. It is the smooth pursuing or tracking of a steadily moving object, such as a ball flying through the air, or a person on a swing, where the eyes track the target with a uniform and even motion. This *smooth pursuit eye movement* does not appear in the newborn, who seems rather to

track smoothly moving objects with short jumpy saccadic eye movements. Thus, rather than keeping pace with the moving target, the infant seems to attempt to grab a fixed glimpse of it, then waits till it drifts from view, and then attempts to look at it again, thus producing a set of little stepwise movements rather than a smooth tracking. The more adultlike pattern of smooth movement begins to emerge at 8 to 10 weeks of age (Aslin, 1981).

The fact that an infant's eye movements respond to moving or dispaced stimuli can be used to measure other capacities in the newborn. For instance, if we show an adult observer a field with a continuously moving pattern (such as a screen full of stripes all moving in one direction), we get a characteristic eye movement pattern. The eye will smoothly track in the direction of the movement for a distance and then snap back in the opposite direction. After this return movement, the observer's eyes lock on to another stripe and follow it, and this process repeats itself continually while the observer views the array. This repetitive eye movement sequence in the presence of a moving pattern is called **optokinetic nystagmus**. A generally similar (albeit not as smooth) pattern of eye movements is found in infants younger than 5 days (Gorman, Cogan, and Gellis, 1957). In fact, its appearance is so reliable that the absence of optokinetic nystagmus is an indication that there may be neurological problems (Brazelton, Scholl, and Robey, 1966). This eye movement pattern seems to be automatic or reflex in nature, rather than under voluntary control, and it seems to be controlled by the tecto-pulvinar system, which we described in Chapter 3 (Atkinson and Braddick, 1981; Hoffmann, 1979). To the perceptual scientist, these reflex movements are important as a tool; thus, we can use the optokinetic response to measure other aspects of visual function. If an infant cannot see a pattern of moving stripes (because visual acuity or brightness responses are insufficient to make them visible), she will not be able to track the moving pattern. This provides a good methodological tool for the study of infant vision. For instance, Doris, Casper, and Poresky (1967) varied the brightness difference between dark and light stripes. They found that when the stripes were very bright, even babies as young as 4 days of age showed the optokinetic response. As the infants became older, they were more likely to respond to dimmer stripes, up to the age of 4 months, when their response level stabilized. This result suggests that the sensitivity to brightness differences improves over the first few months of life.

One can also use the optokinetic response to test the visual acuity of infants. The technique involves finding the narrowest width of stripes that will still produce the tracking response. This method has shown that the visual acuity of neonates is quite poor. It is around 6/120 in Snellen values. This is quite low when we consider that 6/12 is usually given as the legal definition of impaired vision. Such poor acuity is probably a result of the fact that infants younger than 1 month have virtually no accommodative ability. They act as if their lenses were fixed for focusing on stimuli at about 19 cm from the eye (White, 1971). By 3 months, however, the accommodative response is functioning well, and acuity improves steadily until about 6 months of age (Dobson and Teller, 1978).

Brightness and color discrimination

With the limited response repertoire available to a young baby, we can appreciate the methodological breakthrough accomplished by Fantz (1961). His procedure, called **preferential looking**, involves first placing young babies in a special chamber (they either lie on their backs or sit in an infant chair). Visual stimuli are then placed on the walls or the roof of the chamber, and there is a tiny hole through which the experimenter can watch the baby. When the baby views one of a pair of stimulus patterns placed in the chamber, the experimenter can detect this by noting the direction in which the eyes are turned. The experimenter triggers a timer that records how long the infant views each of the two stimuli. If the baby looks at one target longer than the other, this is taken as an indication of a preference for it. The existence of a preference implies that the infant can tell the difference between the patterns. This simple result does not tell us *why* the baby preferred to look at one stimulus rather than the other, nor can we be absolutely sure that the absence of any viewing preference necessarily means that the baby cannot discriminate between the two targets. However, the existence of differences in viewing times does suggest that infants can discriminate between the target stimuli. An apparatus used for such studies is shown as Figure 16-1.

There have been many elaborations of this technique, such as one by Teller (1981). Her procedure allows one to investigate detection of stimuli, as well as discrimination between stimuli. Here, only one stimulus is presented, and the infant's response is monitored by a hidden observer or television camera. If, on the basis of the infant's head and eye movements alone, the *observer* can correctly tell whether the test target was presented to the left or right side of the screen, it is presumed that the information concerning the position of the target has passed from the screen, in through the infant's visual system, and then back out through the infant's behavior. Thus, at the minimum, it suggests that the infant can at least *see* the stimulus.

A further variation of monitoring an infant's

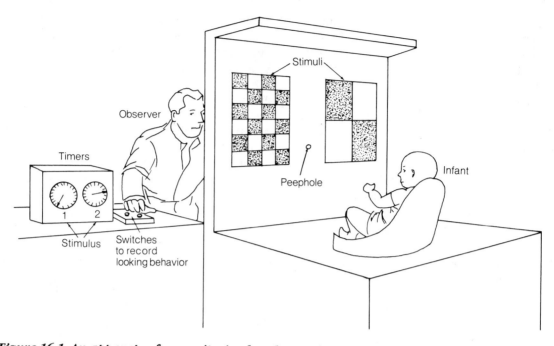

Figure 16-1. An apparatus for monitoring how long infants view particular stimuli.

looking behavior allows one to see if any apparent difference between stimuli is noticeable to an infant. Again, only one stimulus is presented, and the viewing behavior is monitored. At first the infant will spend a good deal of time looking at the stimulus, but as time passes he will cease to pay any attention to it, perhaps because it has lost it's novelty value. This process is called **habituation**. If we now present a novel stimulus, we will, once again, provoke looking behavior. Thus, the presence of renewed looking at the stimulus suggests that the infant can recognize that something has changed and that the present stimulus is different from the former one (Cohen and Salapatek, 1975).

A variety of such techniques has been used to assess the basic sensitivity of infants to brightness and color. In general, it has been found that 3-month-old infants are about ten

times less sensitive to light, both under dark-adapted (scotopic) and light-adapted (photopic) conditions, than are adults, while month-old infants are about 50 times less sensitive (Peeples and Teller, 1978; Powers, Schneck, and Teller, 1981). Despite this difference, however, infants, like adults, are still exquisitely sensitive to small amounts of light. Thus, if an adult can detect an input of only one quantum of light per second hitting anywhere in a patch of 1300 rod receptors, a 3-month-old infant would only need an input of about 6 or 7 quanta of light over the same region, and a 1-month-old infant would still detect an input of about 24 quanta of light (see Teller, 1981).

A number of studies show that despite differences in *absolute* sensitivity, the *relative* sensitivity of infants and adults to different wavelengths of light seems to be about the same. Both are most sensitive to middle wavelengths and exhibit a gradual decrease in sensitivity to longer and shorter wavelengths (Dobson, 1976; Moskowitz-Cook, 1979; Werner, 1979). This does not mean, however, that infants have color vision equivalent to that of the adult. In general, young infants do show the ability to discriminate between colors (Bornstein, 1978; Salapatek and Banks, 1979; Werner, 1979). Color vision matures, however, and discrimination performance improves. Thus Teller (1981) reports that most 1-month-old infants fail to discriminate red or green or both colors from the yellow background on which they are shown when the target and background brightness is made equivalent. More than half of the 2-month-old infants succeeded in this discrimination, while virtually all of the 3-month-old group had no difficulty distinguishing these colors. Overall, the ability to discriminate red from green seems to emerge at about 11 or 12 weeks of age, while 2-month-old infants seem at least to be able to discriminate a broad band blue, blue-green, orange, red, reddish-purple, and bluish purple from white (Schaller, 1975; Teller and Bornstein, 1982). The major problem in the 2-month-old infant seems to be that

the short wavelength (blue) discriminating mechanism seems to be quite immature, and seems to be slow in developing (Pulos, Teller, and Buck, 1980).

Although the young infant does have brightness and color vision, brightness sensitivity lags behind that of the adult, and color perception is still in the process of developing. For those of you who have access to a young infant, Demonstration Box 16-1 presents some simple demonstrations of an infant's perceptual capacity.

Pattern discrimination

The preferential looking technique has been used extensively to explore pattern perception in infants. Using this procedure, it is possible to show that premature infants, born 1 to 2 months before a full term gestation, still often preferentially look at patterned stimuli rather than plain ones of equal average brightness and also sometimes discriminate between different patterns (Fantz and Miranda, 1977). This means that the optical and neural basis of pattern vision does not abruptly become

---

Demonstration Box 16-1. Infant perception

For this demonstration you need one special piece of equipment, namely an infant, preferably under 2 months of age. If you can find one, there are several simple things to try.

(1) To demonstrate auditory localization ability, simply look squarely at the child, and make a sound (use a rattle, or snap your fingers), and watch the infant's head. You should see the eyes flick in the direction of the sound, or the head will turn.

(2) To demonstrate tactual localization ability, stroke the infant's cheek lightly with your finger.

The infant should turn in the direction of the touch.

(3) To demonstrate that the infant's accommodation is limited to close objects, slowly move a pencil from side to side near the infant's face (about 18 cm or 7 inches is best). Notice that the infant will track the pencil. Now repeat this, only varying the distance to 1 or 2 meters away from the child, and notice that little, if any, tracking occurs.

functional after the full term of pregnancy, the age at which they can first be ordinarily observed, but rather have already matured to a reasonable degree of function before the normal birth time.

Preferential looking studies have shown that young infants can discriminate among a variety of different types of patterns. For instance, in one experiment, newborn infants were shown pairs of targets. These neonates showed a clear preference for viewing patterns (stripes) over a plain square, and also preferred patterns with high contrast between the figures and the background. They showed a preference for large over small patterns, indicating that they can discriminate size. They showed an ability to perceive the number of stimuli by preferring stimuli with many rather than few elements. In addition, they showed some ability to discriminate certain aspects defining contours, such as curvature, by preferring curved to straight line elements. Figure 16-2 shows some sample forms, and the star indicates those most preferred by newborns. (Fantz and Yeh, 1979).

Preferences in viewing also show that some more global aspects of pattern perception are possible for the young infant. It has become clear that infants can discriminate the orientation of patterns within the first few weeks (Maurer and Martello, 1980) and perhaps even on the first day of life. Furthermore, they seem to be aware of certain forms of symmetry, or its absence (Bornstein, 1981).

Generally, infants prefer moderately complex stimuli over those that are very simple or very complex, although preferences do change with age (Karmel and Maisel, 1975). There seems to be a clear age progression in pattern preference. Younger infants prefer simple patterns with highly contrasting elements, while infants of around 5 months of age can make more subtle distinctions in contrast and configuration (Fantz and Yeh, 1979).

Some findings have indicated that certain meaningful patterns receive special attention, even from neonates. A number of researchers have studied the response of infants to targets

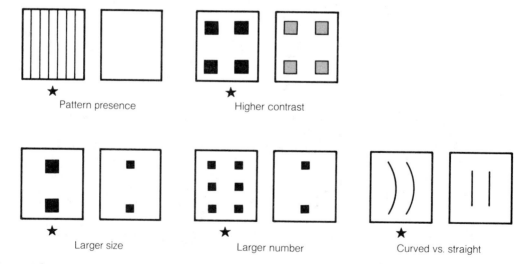

Figure 16-2. Patterns most looked at by newborns are indicated with a star for each pair of stimuli (based on Fantz and Yeh, 1979).

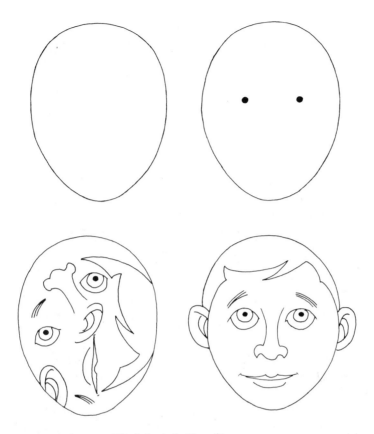

Figure 16-3. Schematic and scrambled facial stimuli.

that approximate the human face. One common procedure is to use some targets that are just head-shaped, others containing only some features, such as a hairline or eyes, some containing scrambled facial features, and others that actually look like faces. Samples of such stimuli are shown in Figure 16-3. In general, newborns seem to have a preference for looking at stimuli that contain facial features over other similar stimuli that do not (Fantz, 1965b; Gorsen, Sarty, and Wu, 1975). Mere preference for faces, however, does not mean that the facelike stimulus is actually seen as a "face." The infant younger than 1 month does not seem to attend to the arrangement of facial fea-

tures, and it is only when the child reaches 15 or 16 weeks of age that he begins to discriminate between scrambled and normally arranged facial features (Carey, 1981; Haaf, 1977). Between 1 month and 4 months, infants begin to take note of certain features in the facial stimulus. By about 10 or 12 weeks, infants will notice and recognize changes in hairline and eyes of facial stimuli; changes in mouth and nose configurations, however, go unnoticed (Caron, Caron, Caldwell, and Weiss, 1973). The configurational and specific features picked up by infants only 1 month of age do seem to be sufficient to permit the child to recognize his own mother's face from that of a stranger (Maurer and Salapatek, 1976), which suggests that young infants can discriminate among certain classes of fairly complex patterns.

PERCEPTUAL CHANGE THROUGH CHILDHOOD

Throughout childhood there is a general improvement in perceptual discrimination, recognition, and information processing. Many of these changes occur fairly rapidly within the first year or two, while others continue over much longer time spans.

The most dramatic changes seem to occur at around the age of 2 months (Atkinson and Braddick, 1981; Maurer and Lewis, 1979). At this age, a sudden spurt in the child's visual abilities takes place. Resolution of spatial frequencies increases markedly (Braddick and Atkinson, 1979), tracking behavior becomes more adultlike (Atkinson, 1979), the ability to recognize individual elements surrounded by an enclosing contour appears (Milewski, 1976), and infants begin to show more adultlike eye movement patterns when viewing figures (Hainline, 1978). By 4 months of age, stereoscopic depth perception appears, and this ability appears to improve over the first 2 years (Fox, Aslin, Shea, and Dumais, 1980; Held, 1981). The ability to discriminate depth based on binocular disparity seems to improve throughout childhood, and on through early adolescence (Romano, Romano, and Puklin, 1975).

Other basic visual processes also seem to improve rapidly over the first 2 years. Thus, visual acuity, which is originally quite poor, improves steadily into early childhood (Gwiazda, Brill, Mohindra, and Held, 1980), and early astigmatic problems (uneven curvature of the cornea), which serve to lower visual resolution in infants, also disappear (Atkinson, Braddick, and French, 1979; Ingram and Barr, 1979). By 5 years of age, children seem to have fully developed scotopic and photopic visual systems, which tend to show adaptation effects and sensitivities equivalent to those of adults.

Eye movements and information processing

In addition to changes in basic sensory processes, changes in the manner in which visual information is acquired and processed appear to take place. One of the most informative ways to monitor these changes is to observe the way in which a child selects information from external stimuli. In Chapter 6 we mentioned that visual acuity is best in the foveal region of the retina; it rapidly deteriorates with increasing distance from the foveal center. Eye movements are used to place the image of a target on the fovea where it can best be seen. There is no guarantee that an observer is paying attention to stimuli imaged on the fovea, but the eyes do tend to fixate stimuli being studied by an observer. Some developmental theorists, such as Piaget (1969), have argued that patterns of eye movements may provide some clues as to which stimuli are being selected and compared by individuals of different ages. For instance, we know that adults display a strong tendency for the eye to be drawn toward targets that the individual finds informative, unusual, or of particular functional value (Antes, 1974; Friedman and Liebelt, 1981; Loftus and Mackworth, 1978). Thus, by monitoring eye movement patterns in children, we may be able to determine the manner in which children are viewing, and hence constructing, their visual world.

Infants from birth to 2 months do make a variety of eye movements, such as fixating stationary stimuli, tracking moving stimuli, or guiding their eyes toward stimuli in the periphery (Lewis, Maurer, and Kay, 1978); however, their eye movements differ from the adult pattern. For instance, they have a tendency to lose the stimulus they are trying to follow when tracking, resulting in overshooting, backtracks, and so forth (Kremenitzer, Vaughan, Kurtzberg, and Dowling, 1979). In addition, they typically do not move their eyes to the most informative parts of the stimulus (at least by adult standards) but rather seem to view only limited parts of the stimulus, usually around a border or corner (Day, 1975; Mackworth and Bruner, 1970). Infants of 1 month tend to direct their eyes toward one distinctive feature of a visual stimulus, such as the corner of a triangle (Haith and Campos, 1977; Salapatek and Kessen, 1973). Their eyes seem to be captured by the feature since they dwell on it for prolonged periods. Since the gaze of a 1-month-old infant is caught by the first contour encountered, most of the viewing time is spent focused on the external contours of a form. If the stimulus has internal features, they seem to be ignored or missed. This picture changes by the age of 2 months. Now the infant scans the contours a little more, and shorter periods are spent on each feature (Hainline, 1978; Salapatek, 1975). In addition, the infant dwells almost exclusively on the internal features of the stimulus, seemingly ignoring the overall pattern. These differences are shown in Figure 16-4.

Changes in eye movement patterns continue beyond infancy. The patterns of 3- and 4-year-olds are similar to those of a 2-month-old infant. Children of this age spend most of their time dwelling on the internal details of a figure, with only an occasional eye movement beyond the contour boundary. This is shown

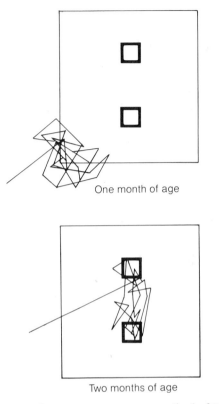

Figure 16-4. Eye movements typical of 1- and 2-month-old infants.

in Figure 16-5A. The 4- or 5-year-old child has begun to make eye movement excursions toward the surrounding contour (Figure 16-5B). At 6 and 7 years of age, there is a systematic scan of the outer portions of the stimulus, with occasional eye movements into the interior. This is shown in Figure 16-5C (Zaporozhets, 1965).

Eye movement patterns have important consequences for certain percepual discrimination tasks. Vurpillot (1968) presented children between the ages of 2 and 9 years with pictures of houses. They were asked to indicate whether or not the houses appeared to be the same. As

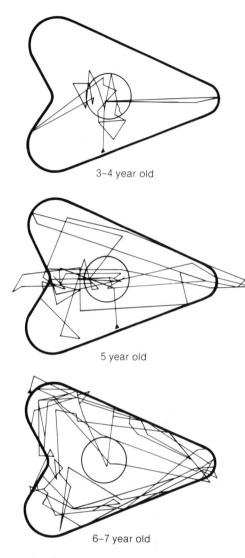

3–4 year old

5 year old

6–7 year old

Figure 16-5. Changes in eye movements from ages 3 to 6. (A) 3- to 4-year-old; (B) 5-year-old; (C) 6- to 7-year-old (from Zaporozhets, 1965, copyright The Society for Research in Child Development, Inc.).

can be seen from Figure 16-6, the pairs of houses differ as a function of the contents of the windows; therefore, the most efficient strategy for determining the similarity (or lack of similarity) between the pairs is to compare the corresponding pairs of windows. In other words, the upper left window of one house would be visually compared with the upper left window of the other. This would continue until a difference was found, thus allowing the observer to make a same-different decision.

Vurpillot (1968) found that the youngest children did not conduct a systematic search. Rather, they often continued searching through the houses even after looking at a pair of windows that were quite different. This lack of systematic viewing was accompanied by a low degree of accuracy in the discrimination judgments of the younger children. Older children, with more regular and systematic viewing patterns, were much more accurate.

In a figure matching task, Cohen (1981) found that 5- and 8-year-old children take longer to decide where to move their eyes than adults in the same task. In addition, they make more eye movements and are less likely than adults to look directly at the matching target in their first eye movements. It is probably likely that these differences reflect differences in strategies of information pick-up, rather than direct differences in visual capacity, since eye movements seem to be strongly affected by task demands, meaning, context, and expectations (Antes and Penland, 1981; Findlay, 1981; Stark and Ellis, 1981).

Pattern perception and discrimination

As a child becomes older, there is a gradual movement toward a consideration of the more global aspects of a pattern and its elements (Elkind,

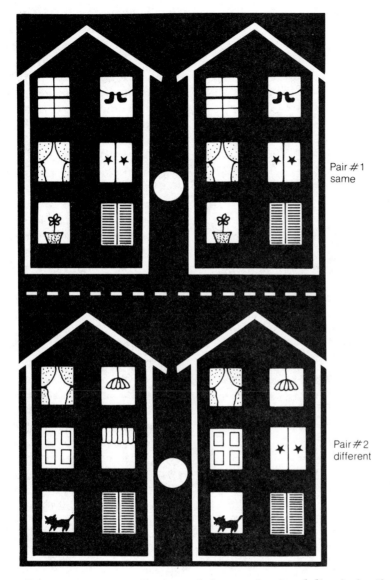

Figure 16-6. Stimuli to measure developmental changes in visual discrimination ability (based on Vurpillot, 1968).

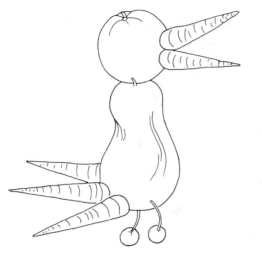

Figure 16-7. A vegetable-fruit bird figure used to measure part versus whole perception in children.

1978). For instance, consider Figure 16-7. It consists of a number of objects (fruits and vegetables) that are organized into a larger figure (a bird); children 4 and 5 years old report seeing only the parts ("carrots and a pear and an orange"). By the age of 7, children report seeing both the parts and the global organization ("fruits and carrots and a bird"). By 8 or 9 years, the majority of children respond in terms of both the parts and the global organization ("a bird made of fruits and vegetables").

A number of other studies have shown that the ability to discriminate between visual patterns improves with age (Cratty, 1979). For instance, a classic study by Gibson, Gibson, Pick, and Osser (1962) shows a steady improvement in a child's ability to discriminate between nonsense patterns and their transformations between the ages of 4 and 8 years. Mickwitz (1973) has demonstrated that older children are more efficient at extracting details that make some targets different from others. Since the discrimination ability of both older and younger children improves with practice, it may be that these age-related improvements are themselves the result of learning.

An interesting example of the improvement of pattern recognition with age involves the recognition of human faces. The very impressive achievements that we noted above for 5- to 7-month-old infants in recognizing face from nonface stimuli should not be misinterpreted. The development of the ability to encode and recognize faces continues for many years (Carey, 1981; Flin, 1980). Thus, we find that a rapid increase in the ability of children to recognize unfamiliar faces occurs between the ages of 6 and 10. To estimate the magnitude of this change we might note that under conditions in which a 6-year-old will only recognize a little more than half the faces shown her (60 percent), a 10-year-old will recognize nearly all of them (95 percent). Furthermore, improvement in ability can be observed even through adolescence to the age of 16 (Carey, Diamond, and Woods, 1980).

One form of pattern discrimination error seems to be characteristic of young children. This involves mirror reversals. Thus, we find that children confuse lateral mirror image pairs, such as *p* and *q*, or *b* and *d*, more frequently than up-down mirror image pairs, such as *p* and *b*, or *q* and *d* (Springer and Deutsch, 1981). These confusions seem to be quite common in young children (around 3 years old) and gradually decrease until the child is about 10 or 11 (Gaddes, 1980; Serpell, 1971). Some of the improvement seems to be associated with educational processes, since between the ages of 5½ and 6½ there is a sudden increase in the ability to make such discriminations. It is likely that the improvement is caused by the formal instruction in reading and writing that usually begins at about that age. With appropriate training, kindergarten-aged children can learn the left-right discrimination quite well, although it still seems to be more difficult than the up-down discrimination (Clark and Whitehurst, 1974).

When a child continues to have difficulties with left-right confusions, he can experience later problems with reading. The specific term used for such reading disabilities (when they are not associated with other disturbances such as mental retardation, sensory impairment, or emotional problems) is **dyslexia**. While estimates of the incidence of dyslexia vary widely, it seems that the problem affects no less than 2 percent of all children in Western countries, with the incidence perhaps reaching as high as 10 percent (Bannatyne, 1971; Gaddes, 1976; Spreen,1976). This is a problem that seems to have a perceptual rather than an intellectual basis. The dyslexic individual may be highly talented in all other respects, except for the reading problems. There are many case histories of exceptional people who have been dyslexic, among them the inventor Thomas A. Edison, the surgeon Harvey Gushing, the sculptor Auguste Rodin, U.S. president Woodrow Wilson, and the author Hans Christian Anderson. One characeristic of all children who have been diagnosed as dyslexic is that they show confusions between the left-right mirror images of targets, although they have no problem with the up-down mirror images (Gaddes, 1980; Newland, 1972; Sidman and Kirk, 1974).

Letter reversals in children suggest that a child is relatively insensitive to the orientation of a stimulus. There is an interesting quirk associated with this issue. Consider a stimulus, such as a human face, that has a familiar orientation. When a face is inverted, it seems to lose much of its facelike quality, and even very familiar individuals are difficult to recognize when their photographs are turned upside down (Rock, 1974). Thus, it is not surprising to find that adult observers, who have had

thousands of exposures to upright faces, show greater accuracy of identification when faces are upright than when they are inverted (Yin, 1970). The facial recognition performance of 6-year-olds, however, is not affected by the orientation of the face. Their ability to recognize faces is the same, regardless of whether the face is presented in a normal or in an inverted position. By the age of 10 years, the child's facial recognition responses begin to look like those of adults; in other words, recognition ability is disrupted when the faces are inverted (Carey and Diamond, 1977). It seems that the adult's sensitivity to orientation differences gives rise to poorer performance in 20-year-olds, whose ability to recognize inverted familiar faces is worse than that of 5-year-olds tested on the same task. You can explore the adult sensitivity to orientation in yourself by using Demonstration Box 16-2.

PERCEPTUAL CHANGE IN ADULTS

Perceptual and sensory functions continue to change throughout the life span, although the rate of change is usually slower than during infancy and childhood. Also, while the earlier changes seem to indicate increasing efficiency in perceptual processing, some diminishing in sensitivity becomes apparent around the age of 40, as sensory receptors age and neural efficiency drops.

If we consider visual processing, for example, we find a number of structural and neural changes that might be expected to reduce visual sensitivity. For instance, the aging eye generally shows a smaller pupil size; hence, less light is admitted into the eye (Weale, 1963). In addition, the crystalline lens continues to grow and darken, again limiting the amount of light actually reaching the retina (Coren and Girgus,

Demonstration Box 16-2. Orientation and stimulus recognition

Adults are more rigid in their reliance on normal orientations than are children. Look at Figures A through D. They are quite difficult to identify, but turn the page and watch them suddenly become recognizable. This effect is especially striking for faces and for handwritten script.

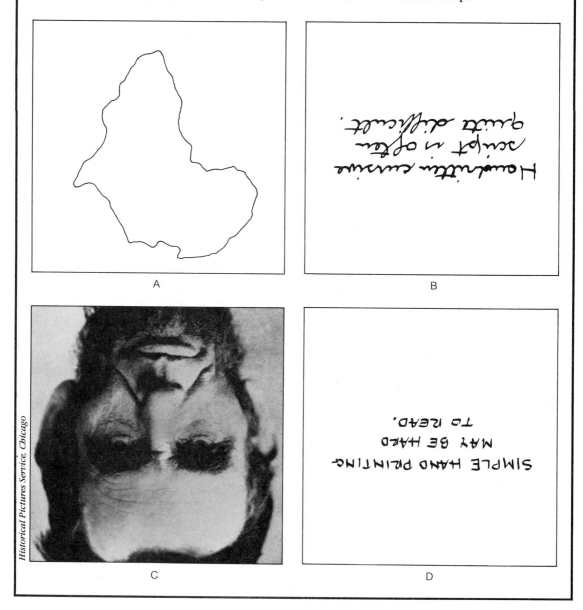

A

B

Historical Pictures Service, Chicago

C

D

1972a). Of course, in the presence of reduced effective light input as a result of such factors, we would expect a decrease in sensitivity. If we look at the period between 20 and 70 years of age, we find a consistent decrease in threshold sensitivities for the detection of spots of light (Fozard, Wolf, Bell, McFarland, and Podolsky, 1977). This is particularly evident in dark adaptation. Although the time to reach minimum threshold remains the same, the maximum sensitivity eventually achieved decreases with age. This is shown in Figure 16-8 (McFarland, Domey, Warren, and Ward, 1960).

A gradual deterioration in color vision also takes place with age. It seems that sensitivity to the shorter wavelengths of light (those in the blue range) continually diminishes from birth until death (Bornstein, 1977; Lakowski, 1962).

Differences such as these seem to be compounded in the central nervous system. For instance, in the primary visual cortex of humans, there is actually neuronal loss with age. This neuron loss is quite extensive. Consider, for instance, the area of the cortex receiving foveal projections. In a 20-year-old this area contains about 46 million neurons per gram of tissue, while in an 80-year-old the neuronal density has been reduced by nearly one-half, coming to only 24 million neurons per gram of tissue (Devaney and Johnson, 1980).

While the number of remaining neurons is adequate for most visual tasks, one might expect this reduction in the number of responding units to show up as a reduction in visual acuity as well as in reduced sensitivity. Such a reduction in visual acuity in the aging eye has been shown (Richards, 1977); the pattern it follows, however, is quite interesting. While older observers are still able to resolve visual details, the light levels necessary for them to do so is greatly increased. In terms of our discussion in Chapter 6, we would say

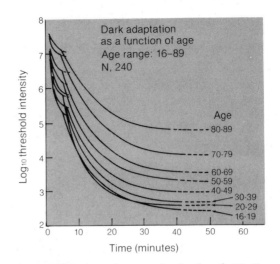

Figure 16-8. Age changes in dark-adaptation (from McFarland et al., 1960).

that the contrast threshold is higher for these older observers (Leibowitz, Post, and Ginsburg, 1980). Furthermore, it appears that the neural system that responds to transient stimulation (remember the Y cells discussed in Chapter 3) shows the greatest degree of diminished sensitivity (Sekuler and Hutman, 1980). These findings suggest that in such tasks as night driving, where good acuity and response to relatively fast moving stimuli are required although illumination conditions are low, older individuals might be quite inefficient and may even be at risk.

The sensitivity in a number of other modalities also decreases with advancing age. The pattern of change, however, is not always consistent. Thus, although older observers show a reduced sensitivity to touch (Thornbury and Mistretta, 1981), they do not show any decrease in their sensitivity to pain (Harkins and Chapman, 1977).

Some of the most noticeable changes with age occur in the realm of taste and smell. Odor sensitivity is greatly diminished, although the reduction is not uniform across all stimuli. For instance, elderly subjects seem best able to discriminate among fruity odors, compared with other classes of scents (Schiffman and Pasternak, 1979). There is also a diminished sensitivity to the primary tastes. For instance, thresholds rise measurably, although not dramatically, for both salt and sugar (Grzegorczyk, Jones, and Mistretta, 1979; Moore, Nielsen, and Mistretta, 1982). The combination of diminishing sensitivity to both odor and taste in the elderly greatly reduces their ability to identify foods, especially when blended or pureed so that they are not recognizable by sight or texture (Schiffman, 1977). Just how large a deficit results can be seen by comparing the performance of a group of 20-year-olds with that of a group of elderly subjects (average age 73) and seeing how poorly the older people do at recognizing foods by taste and smell alone. As can be seen in Table 16-2, in most instances the younger individuals do twice as well, although on some common items, such as coffee, performance is about the same, regardless of age.

Table 16-2. The percentage of 20-year-olds versus the percentage of elderly individuals (mean age of 73 years) who correctly identified some common foods in pureed form (based on Schiffman, 1977)

Food	20-year-olds	Elderly
Apple	81	55
Lemon	52	24
Strawberry	78	33
Broccoli	30	0
Carrot	63	7
Corn	67	38
Beef	41	28
Coffee	89	70
Sugar	63	57

Several types of change seem to affect all the sensory modalities. The most important of these is a general slowing of neural responses, accompanied by an increasing persistence of the stimulus (actually, slower recovery or clearing time). This means that older individuals have more trouble with briefly presented stimuli (Hoyer and Plude, 1980), show slower reaction times to stimulus onsets (Stern, Oster, and Newport, 1980), and cannot readily recognize stimuli arriving in a rapid sequence (Birren, Woods, and Williams, 1980). This slowing of perceptual processing of the elderly individual becomes most apparent when the perceptual tasks increase in complexity (Cerella, Poon, and Williams, 1980; Cunningham, 1980).

Another rather general change seems to involve the distribution of attention to perceptual tasks. Much of this can be traced to Kahneman's (1973) idea that attention represents the dividing or allocating of a fixed amount of attentional resources to various tasks (see Chapter 15). Older individuals seem to have more difficulty dividing their attention between various stimuli or input channels (Craik and Simon, 1980). In addition, they seem to have more difficulty extracting relevant from irrelevant targets in search or recognition tasks (Rabbitt, 1977; Walsh, 1982). The more similar the irrelevant stimuli are to the target stimuli, the greater the difficulty that all observers have in detecting targets in a search task; elderly observers, however, have their performance disrupted at levels of difficulty that do not seem to affect younger observers (Farkas and Hoyer, 1980). One way to summarize these data is to say that older observers seem to be bothered by *perceptual noise*, which unlike the *neurological noise* found in all sensory systems (remember the discussion of this in Chapter 2), is actually *environmental noise*, which the younger observer can successfully filter out, while the elderly individual,

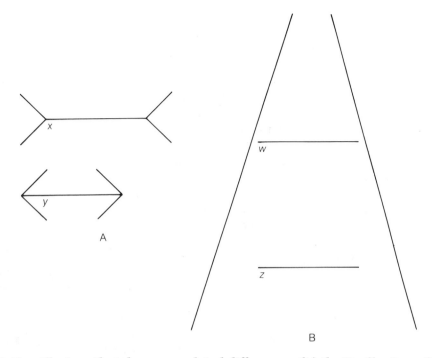

Figure 16-9. Two illusions that show age-related differences. (A) the Mueller-Lyer; (B) the Ponzo.

perhaps because of limited attentional capacity, cannot (Layton, 1975).

Although some perceptual functions tend to diminish with age, responses to one class of complex visual problems become better, or more accurate, with age. This set of phenomena concerns responses to **visual-geometric illusions**. These are simple line drawings in which the *actual* size, shape, or direction of some elements differs from the *perceived* size, shape, or direction (see Coren and Girgus, 1978). We have already encountered some of these illusions in Chapters 1 and 14; two of them are shown in Figure 16-9. Figure 16-9A *shows the* **Mueller-Lyer illusion**, in which the line marked x appears to be longer than the line marked y. Figure 16-9B shows the **Ponzo illusion**, in which the line marked w

appears to be longer than the line marked z. This is the case in spite of the fact that x and y are physically equal in length, and w and z are also physically equal to each other.

Susceptibility to the distortion in visual-geometric illusions varies with age over an individual's life span (Porac and Coren, 1981). For instance, one study measured susceptibility to the Mueller-Lyer illusion (Figure 16-9A) in individuals ranging in age from 8 to 80 years. Illusion magnitude (the degree to which individuals are susceptible to the perceived differences in line length) was found to *decrease* until about the age of 25. After this point, it remained relatively constant even through the oldest groups (Coren, Porac, Green, and Dawson, 1977). In general, adults have been found to be less susceptible to the distortions in visual-geometric illusions (Coren and Girgus, 1978; Pick and Pick, 1970), although there are some exceptions to this rule (Lorden, Atkeson, and Pollack, 1979). Since illusion figures cause complex perceptual errors, these data show that as we grow older our conscious perception becomes more accurate, that is to say, a better reflection of the actual physical properties of objects or stimuli that we are observing. How do these changes come about? It seems unlikely that this type of age trend is related only to the aging process itself. More likely, it is a reflection of our experience and interactions with our environment. How such learning and experience can affect what we perceive is the topic of the next chapter.

GLOSSARY

The following definitions are specific to this book.

Dyslexia   Impaired reading ability, usually involving letter reversals.

Habituation   The process by which an observer ceases to respond to a repeated stimulus.

Mueller-Lyer illusion   An illusion of size in which the perceived length of a line is affected by the direction of its contextual wings.

Optokinetic nystagmus   An eye movement sequence in which there is a smooth movement and a quick return in the presence of a moving pattern.

Ponzo illusion   An illusion of size in which the perceived length of a line is affected by its place in the context of surrounding converging lines.

Preferential looking   A behavioral measure of infant stimulus discrimination in which target fixation time is assumed to be positively related to stimulus preference.

Visual-geometric illusions   Simple line drawings in which the actual physical characteristics of certain elements differ from the perception of those elements.

Visually evoked response (VER)   The change in the electrical activity produced by the brain in response to a visual stimulus.

17

Learning and Experience

AN ARTICLE IN THE NEW YORK *TIMES* spoke of a tea expert who was consulted about the components of a blend of tea that an American company was about to market. A small cup of it was poured for him. He sniffed it gently, sipped a bit, swished it around in his mouth a little, then looked up.

"I detect," he said crisply, "a rather good Assam, a run-of-the-mill Darjeeling, a mediocre Ceylon, and of course, the tea bag." (Root, 1974).

While you and I might be amazed at performances such as these, or similar ones of expert wine tasters, we must recognize that this degree of perceptual discrimination has come about through years of training and experience. In other words, this expert had to *learn* to taste and recognize these flavors.

Although most people are willing to admit that some aspects of perception are affected by learning and experience, they do not recognize how much of our immediate perceptual experience is influenced by our past history. In fact, our past can even influence whether or not we perceive anything at all in some circumstances. For example, suppose we briefly flash a visual stimulus in front of you. If we have chosen the duration and intensity of the stimulus carefully, you may be unaware of any aspect of the stimulus. If we flash the same stimulus again, we would expect that, again, you would see nothing. With repeated presentations, however, something about its appearance will begin to change. Soon you will be able to make out fragments of this stimulus, and after a while these fragments will become more complex. Eventually, the entire stimulus pattern will be recognized on every trial, even though the luminance and exposure durations are the same as for the very first trials when you saw and recognized nothing! (Uhlarik and Johnson, 1978). Your prior experience with this stimulus has changed your perceptual abilities in some manner, and now you can see what was formerly invisible. In other words, during the course of this experiment, you have *learned* to see this pattern.

EXPERIENCE AND DEVELOPMENT

As the organism develops, its nervous system matures, and over the years, many changes in physiology and perceptual ability also come about simply as a result of physiological maturation. Of course, as the months and years roll by, the organism is also accumulating new experiences with the environment and is encountering many chances to learn new perceptual coordinations. It is a particular concern for us to understand how the natural course of development interacts with the individual's particular life history to shape our perception of the world.

Experience can affect the development of the individual's perceptual processes in several different ways. We have outlined the ways in Figure 17-1 (see Aslin, 1981; Gottlieb, 1981).

The strongest form of interaction between experience and development is **induction**. Here, the presence of some sort of relevant experience actually determines both the presence and final level of the ability (Figure 17-1*A*). The weakest form of effect we will call **maturation**. This actually represents no effect at all, and the ability might be expected to develop regardless of the individual's experience or lack of it (17-1*B*). Another possible interaction is **enhancement**. Here the final level of an ability, which is already present or developing, is improved as a result of experiential factors (17-1*C*). **Facilitation**, on the other hand, enhances the rate at which an ability develops, but not its final level. Thus, experience provides earlier acquisition of the skill, not greater

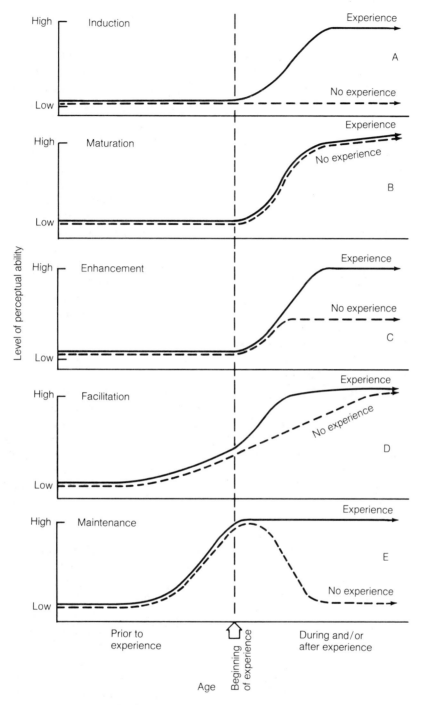

Figure 17-1. Various ways in which experience can interact with the development of perceptual abilities.

proficiency (17-1*D*). Finally, there is **maintenance**, which serves to stabilize, or to keep, an ability that is already present (17-1*E*). Of course, different mechanisms might be expected to produce each of these patterns of interaction between development and experience.

Restricted and selective rearing

The most direct method for assessing the relationship between development and experience is to deprive the observer of the opportunity to use a particular sensory modality from the moment of birth. After the individual has fully matured, we test the perceptual capacities in the deprived modality. If they have developed poorly, we have demonstrated the need for experience in the development of normal functions. This technique is called **restricted rearing**. (We previously encountered this procedure in Chapter 10 when we discussed the development of depth perception). A somewhat more elegant technique involves deliberately altering the pattern of experience that the developing organism is exposed to from birth. For example, an animal may be exposed to only diffuse light, vertical stripes, the color red, and so forth. Such a procedure should selectively *bias* rather than eliminate, certain perceptual abilities, if experience plays a role in their development. This proceedure is known as **selective rearing**.

Neurophysiological effects. Recent research indicates that experience may play a role in the development of sensory physiological structures themselves. For instance, as discussed in Chapter 16, the visual pathways and visual cortex of the newborn differ from those of the adult; there are fewer responsive cells, and these show lesser degrees of directional and orientational sensitivity (see also Blake-

more, 1978; Norton, 1981). Visual experience, in addition to the growth and maturation of the nervous system, seems to be necessary for the development of normal visual functioning. This has been demonstrated though restricted rearing studies.

Let us consider what happens if we completely deprive an animal of visual input by rearing it in the dark from birth. This animal will have a visual cortex that shows reduced overall responsiveness, when tested using the electrode implantation techniques discussed in Chapter 3. Furthermore, those cells that are found will not show the usual degree of orientation and movement selectivity (Blakemore, 1978; Leventhal and Hirsch, 1980). The visual cortex of such animals appears to be quite immature, as a result of the absence of the usual history of visual experience.

Such neurophysiological disruption in the absence of visual experience can be found all along the visual pathways. Some effects are as peripheral as the retina, but they appear as well in the other stations along the visual pathways, such as the superior colliculus, the lateral geniculate nucleus, and the visual cortex (Movshon and Van Sluyters, 1981; Riesen and Zilbert, 1975). Different aspects of the visual pathways seem to be more or less susceptible to damage as a result of total restriction of visual experience. Thus, we find that X and W cells are relatively unaffected by dark rearing, while Y cells are readily lost if no visual experience is available (Hoffman and Sherman, 1975; Rothblat and Schwartz, 1978). Perhaps the most hopeful sign arising out of this myriad of deficits is the fact that even animals that have been raised for a year after birth in total darkness eventually show some recovery after several months of exposure to illuminated surroundings, although recovery is never complete (Cynader, Berman, and Hein, 1976).

Much subtler neurophysiological changes

come about through selective rearing practices. For instance, in Chapter 3 we stated that cells in the visual cortex tend to show *ocular dominance*. This means that, although most cells in the cortex can be activated by stimulation of either eye, they tend to respond more vigorously to one eye. The fact that most cells respond somewhat to each eye's input probably has to do with the use of the depth cue of binocular disparity (see Chapter 10). Suppose that we rear an animal from birth, so that it only views the world through one eye. Later we test the ability of the two eyes separately, to produce a response in the visual cortex. We would probably find that the majority of the cells are activated by the experienced eye, and often less than 10 percent of the cells can be driven by the deprived eye (Hubel, Wiesel, and LeVay, 1977).

The degree of disruption of normal functioning seems to depend on *when* the period of deprivation begins. If the animal is deprived of binocular viewing during the period from 3 weeks to 3 months after birth, large disruptions of the normal pattern of binocular response occur. If the monocular viewing period is instituted after this period, however, even for periods of up to a year, virtually no effect is found (Cynader, Timney, and Mitchell, 1980; Pettigrew, 1978). This means that there is a particular point in time at which the visual experience is most required and most effective. Such an interval is called a **critical period**, and it characterizes many aspects of the interaction between experience and development (Mitchell, 1981). Critical periods may correspond to periods of maximal growth and development in the nervous system (Hickey, 1977). Any disruption of normal visual experience during the critical period, even for periods as short as 3 days, produces measurable changes in the responses of cells in the visual system (Freeman, Mallach, and Hartley, 1981).

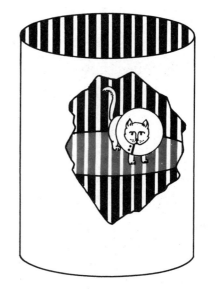

Figure 17-2. An apparatus for selectively rearing a kitten so that its only visual experience will be with vertical contours.

Perhaps the most subtle form of selective visual rearing involves limiting an animal to a world containing only contours oriented in one direction. Thus, an animal might be exposed to only vertically oriented lines from birth. This is accomplished by either affixing the animal with goggles, which contain lines of only one orientation, or giving the animal experience for a few hours each day in an apparatus similar to that shown in Figure 17-2. This is simply a large cylinder containing nothing but vertical stripes and a clear plastic floor on which the animal stands. Notice that the animal is wearing a special collar that prevents it from seeing its own limbs.

What happens in the nervous system after exposure to this kind of selective rearing and stimulation might be called *environmental surgery*. Normally, when we insert an electrode into the visual cortex in order to map receptive fields, we find large numbers of cells that respond most strongly to lines in a particular orientation, as we saw in Chapter 3. However, the particular preferred orientations are rather evenly distributed. Thus, recording the characteristics of a number of cells in the visual cortex of a normal animal, and then depicting each preferred stimulus orientation as a line, normally results in a diagrammatic distribution of cells such as that shown on the left in Figure 17-3. However, recording from an animal that has never seen horizontal stripes produces quite a different result. In this animal, virtually no cells are responsive to horizontally oriented lines, resulting in a distribution of preferred stimulus orientations much like that shown on the right in Figure 17-3 (Hirsch and Spinelli, 1970; Mitchell, 1980). It is as if the absence of horizontally oriented stimuli in the environment has served as an experiential scalpel that has systematically cut off any responding to stimuli, other than the vertical stimuli to which the animal was exposed over its lifetime. Again, there is a critical period between 3 weeks and 3 months during which the effects of this sort of selective stimulation seems to be most effective (Mitchell, 1981; Rothblat and Schwartz, 1978).

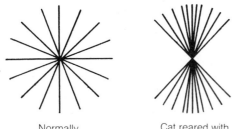

Normally reared cat   Cat reared with vertical stripes

Figure 17-3. The distribution of the preferred orientation of cortical receptive fields in a normally reared cat and a cat reared with selective exposure to vertical contours. Each line indicates the preferred orientation of one cell.

Blake (1981) has summarized the current research evidence, "In effect, the neurophysiologists have compiled a set of recipes for creating animals with specific kinds of neural deficits at sites along the visual pathways." (p. 97). The ingredients that go into these recipes are all experiences or the lack of certain normal experiences with visual stimuli.

Perceptual effects. How do all these neurophysiological changes affect what the organism perceives? There is a slight divergence between the physiological and the behavioral data when we answer this question. Consider a kitten reared in total darkness until the age of 6 months. When we remove this kitten from darkness, it at first appears to be completely blind; within about 48 hours of exposure to illuminated surroundings, however, the kitten begins to show some visual responsiveness. Various forms of sensory-motor coordination begin to appear in a piecemeal fashion and, after a 6-week period of normal experience, a great deal of recovery has occurred. Direct measures of visual acuity show a gradual improvement. If the animal had been dark-reared for only about 4 months, the acuity gradually would return to that of a normally reared cat; however, visual acuity never reaches normal levels for animals that have been dark-reared for longer periods (Timney, Mitchell, and Griffin, 1978). Although many of the physiological changes appear to be permanent, there seems to be enough plasticity in the animal to allow for considerable behavioral recovery of function after the initial period of deprivation. Still, there will be measurable deficits in many visual tasks, including obstacle avoidance, tracking, jumping under visual guidance, and eye blinks to oncoming objects, even after 2 years of normal experience (Mitchell, 1978; Rothblat and Schwartz, 1978).

Restricted rearing studies cannot be conducted with human observers because of the possibility of producing long-lasting perceptual difficulties. Some clinical conditions, however, reproduce the circumstances needed to study the effects of experience on perception. For example, Senden (1960) collected case reports of individuals who had suffered from lifelong blindness as a result of cataracts; such individuals later had vision restored through surgery. After the removal of the cataracts, these adults were unable to recognize familiar objects by sight, although they were capable of recognizing them if they were allowed to touch the objects. For instance, when asked to discriminate between a square and a triangle, they had to undertake the painstaking procedure of seeking out and counting the corners of the figure before the forms could be distinguished from each other.

These newly sighted observers seemed able to detect the presence or absence of an object in the visual field, but this seemed to be the extent of their abilities. For example, one patient was shown a watch and was asked whether it was round or square. When he seemed unable to answer, he was asked whether or not he knew the shape of a square or a circle. He was able to position his hands to form both a square and a circular shape, but he could not visually identify the shape of the watch. When the watch was placed in his hands, he immediately recognized it as being round. Thus his sense of touch, which he had relied on throughout his years of blindness, was able to compensate for his untrained sense of vision.

As in the physiological measures, *selective rearing* produces more subtle effects behaviorally. For instance, the most dramatic behavioral effects of rearing animals with one eye occluded is a reduction in the visual acuity of the deprived eye (Mitchell, 1981). However, there are a number of interesting visual field effects as well. **Visual field** refers to the region of the outside world to which an eye will respond, measured in degrees around the head. For instance Figure 17-4A shows the

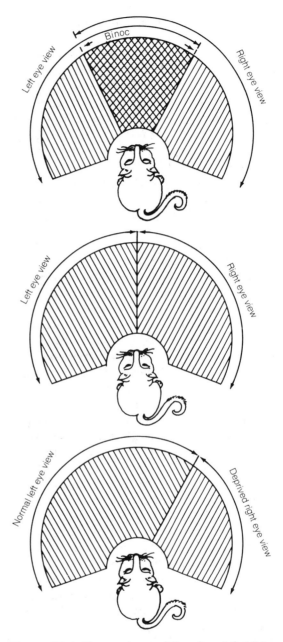

Figure 17-4. The regions of the visual field in which a cat will respond to visual stimuli presented to the right or left eye are altered by depriving one or both eyes of visual experience from birth (based on Sherman, 1973).

visual fields for the right and left eyes of a cat. There is a rather large region of overlap between the two eyes in the frontal part of the field. This is the region of binocular vision, where either or both eyes of the cat should be able to see an object. Generally, if an interesting stimulus appears in the visual field of a cat, it will immediately turn its eyes and head toward it, indicating that it has seen the stimulus. We can use this response to measure the effectiveness of stimuli in the visual field of the cat, and if we cover one eye at a time, we can measure each visual field separately.

Let us first consider an animal that has been completely dark reared. Such an animal shows a severe loss of response in the region of binocular overlap. Each eye seems to respond only to objects on its side of the head as is shown in Figure 17-4B. An animal reared with one eye occluded does not show a binocularly responsive region of the visual field. Instead, the eye that had normal visual experience shows a normal visual field, overlapping well to the opposite side. The eye that did not receive visual experience, however, acts as if it only responds to targets that are far to the side of the head, but it excludes all the binocular visual field that the normal eye covers (Sherman, 1973). A similar effect was reported for a young man who was born with a cataract that prevented any patterned vision in his left eye (his visual experience was similar to the monocularly reared animals we have been discussing). When this cataract was removed at age 19, the normal eye had its usual visual field size, but the patient simply could not detect any stimuli in a large portion of the region where the views of the two eyes overlapped (the binocular region) with the deprived (cataract) eye. Although there was some recovery over the next 10 months, the visual field of the deprived eye never became as large as that of the normal eye (Moran and Gordon, 1982).

The other form of selective rearing, where an animal is reared under conditions of exposure to horizontal or vertical stripes alone, also produces a behavioral deficit in addition to the change in the distribution of cells in the cortex with a specific set of preferred orientations. Here the results are not as dramatic as one might expect. Animals that have been reared only with vertical stripes are not *blind* to horizontal stripes, rather they have measureably lower visual acuity for stripes in an orientation never seen during their rearing (Hirsch, 1972; Muir and Mitchell, 1975).

There is an interesting analogy to this type of selective rearing used with cats. This analogy arises from a common visual problem known as **astigmatism**. Astigmatism usually occurs if the cornea of the eye is a bit too cylindrical in shape along some dimension instead of being completely spherical. This deviation in shape will bring contours of some orientations into sharper focus than those in other orientations. Thus with a vertical astigmatism, horizontal lines will be clear, and vertical lines will be blurry, and so forth. The fact that this condition can mimic selective rearing effects was shown by Freeman and Pettigrew (1973), who reared cats wearing cylindrical lenses that artifically created an astigmatism. They were able to show that such partial selective rearing can also alter the distribution of preferred orientations of visual neurons, with a reduction in the number of cells preferring the blurred orientation. Astigmatism at an early age in humans causes a permanent loss of visual acuity in the direction of the astigmatism. This is an acuity loss due to neural changes, because it remains even after correcting for any optical errors. It is probably the result of selective restriction of exposure to contours in the astigmatic direction (Mitchell, 1980).

A particular variation of this same selective rearing effect is caused by living in an urbanized environment. The nature of our carpentered cities means that we have frequent exposure to vertical lines (defining walls, corners, furniture legs, and so forth) and to horizontal lines (defining floors, ceilings, table edges, and so forth). Proportionally, then, we have very little exposure to oblique lines. Therefore, as inhabitants of such a selectively stimulating environment, one might expect that we would show a reduced acuity for diagonal lines relative to horizontal and vertical lines. In fact, this is confirmed by evidence that the human visual system is *anisotropic*, meaning that it often reacts differently to stimuli depending on their orientation. In general, the normal visual system shows a slight but well defined preference for horizontal or vertical stimuli over diagonal stimuli. This is demonstrated in a number of acuity-related tasks, where resolution acuity and vernier acuity seem to be poorer for stimuli oriented diagonally (Bowker and Mandler, 1981; Corwin, Moskowitz-Cook, and Green, 1977; Leibowitz, 1955). This phenomenon is known as the **oblique effect**, and can

be demonstrated easily using Demonstration Box 17-1.

The role of a selective environment in the oblique effect was studied by Annis and Frost (1973). They compared the variations in acuity as a function of the orientation of lines in a group of students from Queens University in Kingston, Ontario, with that observed in a group of Cree Indians from James Bay, Quebec. The students had all grown up in typical North American buildings. The Cree Indians, on the other hand, were among the last to be raised in traditional housing consisting of a cook tent (or *meechwop*) in summer, and a winter lodge (or *matoocan*) during the rest of the year. Both the insides and outsides of these structures consist of a rich array of contours, with no obvious preponderance of verticals and horizontals. In addition, the natural environment of the Cree shows no excesses of verticals and horizontals, as does the urbanized environment of the students. In line with the selective exposure hypothesis, the students showed the expected reduction in acuity for

---

Demonstration Box 17-1. The oblique effect

To demonstrate that visual acuity is better for horizontal or vertical stimuli than for obliquely oriented stimuli, prop this book up on a table so that you can see the three stimulus patterns. Now slowly walk backward from the book until you can no longer resolve clearly the oblique lines in the center circle. It will appear uniform gray at this point, as your resolution acuity fails. Notice, however, that at this distance you still can see that the left circle contains vertical lines, and the right contains horizontal lines, thus indicating your greater visual acuity for these orientations.

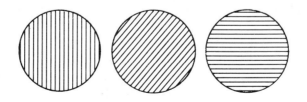

obliquely oriented contours, while the Cree, without this selective exposure, did not.

SENSORY-MOTOR LEARNING

One variable that seems to be essential for the development of normal visual functioning involves not only the eyes but also the entire body. It seems that normal perceptual development depends on active bodily movement under visual guidance. Holst and Mittelsteadt (1950) offered a distinction between stimulus input that simply acts on passive observers, which they called **exafference**, and stimulation that changes as a result of an individual's own movements, called **reafference**.

Reafference has been suggested as necessary for the development of accurate visually guided spatial behavior (Hein, 1980). An experiment by Held and Hein (1963) elegantly demonstrates this notion. They reared kittens in the dark until they were 8-12 weeks of age. From that age on, the kittens received 3 hours of patterned visual exposure in a "carousel" apparatus, shown in Figure 17-5. As you can see from the figure, one of the animals is *active* and can walk around freely. The other animal is *passive* and is carried around in a gondola that moves in exactly the same direction and at exactly the same speed as the movements of the active animal. Thus, the moving animal experiences changing visual stimuli as a result of its own movements (reafference); the passive animal experiences the same stimulation but not as the result of self-generated movements (exafference).

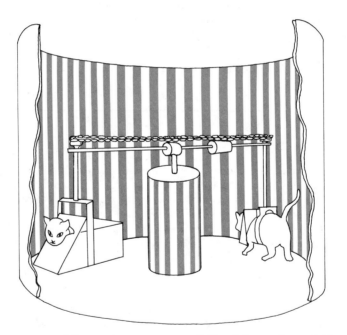

Figure 17-5. A kitten carousel for active or passive exposure to visual stimulation (From R. Held, and A. Hein, **Journal of Comparative** *and Physiological Psychology, 1963, 56. Copyright 1963 by the American Psychological Association. Reprinted by permission).*

The animals were later tested on a series of behaviors involving depth perception. These behaviors included dodging or blinking when presented with a rapidly approaching object and the avoidance of the deep side of the visual cliff (see Chapter 10). They were also tested for the *visual placing response*, a paw extension (as if to avoid collision) when the animal is moved quickly toward a surface. In all three measures, the active animals performed like normal kittens while the passive animals showed little evidence of depth perception.

An interesting extension of this work, which shows the specificity of experiential effects, was done by Hein, Held, and Gower (1970). They repeated the carousel experiment; however, each animal received both active and passive exposure. One eye was used when the visual exposure was active, while the other eye was used when the visual exposure was passive. They reported that when the kittens were tested on the actively exposed eye, they seemed to have normal depth perception, while when tested on the passively exposed eye they acted as if they did not.

How much of the development of our visually guided behavior requires practice and exposure? Consider the simple task of reaching out and picking up an object with one hand. This involves not only the accurate assessment of the distance and the size of the object, but the ability to guide our limb on the basis of the perceptual information. Hein and Held (1967) reared kittens in the dark until they were 4 weeks old. After this period, they were allowed 6 hours of free movement each day in a lighted and patterned environment. During the time when the cats received their exposure to patterned stimuli, however, they wore lightweight opaque collars that prevented them from seeing their bodies or paws while they moved about (see Figure 17-6). The remain-

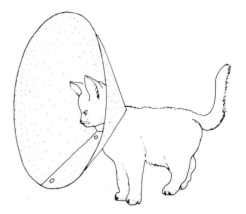

Figure 17-6. A kitten in collar that prevents a view of its paws (From A. Hein and R. Held, Science, 1967, 158, 390-392. Copyright 1967 by the American Association for the Advancement of Science).

der of the time, the kittens were placed in a dark room. After 12 days of such exposure, these animals showed normal depth perception, but their ability to accurately place their paws by visually directing them toward targets was quite poor. Nonetheless, after 18 hours of free movement in a lighted environment, with their paws visible, all directional confusions seemed to have disappeared.

Hein and Diamond (1971) conducted a similar experiment in which each of the cats' front paws were placed in separate cones, rather than using collars. One cone was opaque, while the other one was transparent so that the animal could see its limb. When tested using the exposed limb, cats accurately placed their paws, but the unexposed limb could not be accurately directed toward the targets. In another experiment, Held and Bauer (1967) reared a monkey for 34 days without sight of its limbs. When the animal was first exposed to a view of its arm, it acted startled and spent much time looking at its hand. The animal's behavior was awkward and inaccurate but improved rapidly with practice. When the other hand (which had not been previously exposed) was tested, it also showed inaccurate reaching until some experience had been gained.

There are reports of behaviors in human infants that seem similar to the responses of the deprived monkey. White (1971) reports that after the first month of life (during which infants are alert about 5 percent of the time), infants spent many hours watching their hands. Their reaching is quite inaccurate at first but improves steadily. Actually, practice can speed up this process of perceptual development. If one arranges conditions so that there are many objects to reach for and to play with, infants develop accurate reaching behavior several weeks earlier than children who have not received this type of enriched experience. Experience with the sight of actively moving parts of the body seems to be a necessary condition for the successful development of visually guided behavior (Hein, 1980).

PERCEPTUAL REARRANGEMENT

In 1896 George Stratton reasoned that if some aspects of the perception of space and direction were learned, then it ought to be possible to learn a new set of spatial percepts. To test this idea, Stratton used a technique that altered spatial relations in the visual world (Stratton, 1897a, b). His technique involved wearing a set of goggles that optically rotated the field of view by 180 degrees, so that everything appeared to be upside down. Such a procedure is called optical **rearrangement** (Welch, 1978).

More recently, Kohler (1962, 1964) elaborated on this procedure. Kohler's observers often wore optically distorting devices for several weeks. Observers reported that at first

the world seemed very unstable. The visual field appeared to swing as the observer turned his head. During this stage of the experiment, observers often had difficulty walking and needed help performing very simple tasks. After about 3 days, however, one observer was able to ride a bicycle, and after only a few weeks he was able to ski. The observers reported that they sporadically experienced the world as being upright. If they observed common events that have definite directional components, such as smoke rising from a cigarette or water pouring from a pitcher, they reported that the world appeared to be upright. This seems to suggest that their ability to adapt to the optically rearranged visual input was facilitated by the notion of gravitational direction along with interaction with familiar events and objects. Kohler suggests that a real perceptual change had taken place because, when the inverting lenses were removed, the observers experienced a sense of discomfort. The world suddenly appeared to be inverted again, and they had difficulty moving about. The readaptation to the normal upright world was accomplished within a period of about 1 hour. Demonstration Box 17-2 shows how you can experience this inverted visual stimulation.

Most rearrangement studies involve a less dramatic change of optical input. A common technique is to use a *wedge prism*, which is a wedge-shaped piece of glass that bends, or refracts, light. The locations of objects viewed through the prism seem to be shifted in the direction of the apex (the pointed edge of the wedge). If an observer viewed the world through goggles containing such prisms and reached for an object, she would find herself missing it. After only a few minutes of practice, however, the observer's reaching would become quite accurate. We would say that she had *adapted* to the prismatic distortion; in other words, she has compensated for the opti-

---

Demonstration Box 17-2. Optical inversion

You can experience some of the effects associated with inverted optical stimulation by holding a mirror as shown in the accompanying figure. Walk around and view the world by looking up at the mirror. Notice that the world seems inverted, and also notice how the world swings as you turn. Now pour some water from a glass. Does the water pour up or down? Are you sure?

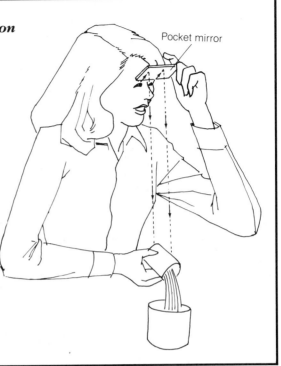

Pocket mirror

---

cal distortion. If the observer is consciously correcting for the distortion (for instance, saying to herself something like "I must reach 10 degrees to the right of where the object appears"), when the goggles are removed she will, of course, know that the distortion is no longer present. Being rational, she should then drop this conscious correction and reach for seen stimuli with her usual accuracy. On the other hand, suppose that some perceptual change has occurred. Under these circumstances, we would expect that the visual world now appears to be shifted several degrees to one side. When reaching for an object, the observer should err in the direction opposite to that of the initial distortion. These errors, which occur after exposure to wedge-prism distortion, are called **aftereffects**. The oc-

currence of aftereffects in prism adaptation provides evidence that some perceptual rearrangement has occurred (Harris, 1980). This process is outlined in Figure 17-7.

A number of investigators have attempted to specify what conditions are necessary for adaptation to rearranged stimulation (Welch, 1978). Held and Hein (1958) have argued that adaptation depends on active movements, as does the development of visually guided behavior discussed earlier. They tested this notion by having observers view their hands through a prism under one of three conditions. One was a no-movement condition in which the observers viewed a stationary hand. The second was a passive movement condition where the observer's arm was swung back and forth by the experimenter. The third was an active

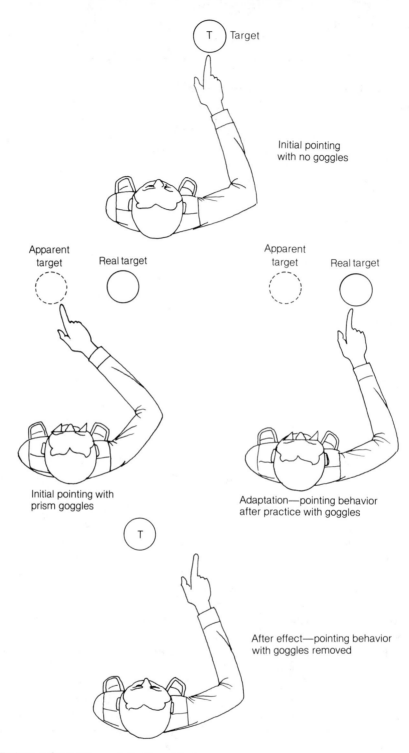

Figure 17-7. Prism adaptation and aftereffect.

movement condition where the observers saw their hands through the prism while they actively moved the hands from side to side. There was considerable adaptation to the distortion produced by the prism under the active movement condition, while in the other conditions there was not. These results have been verified several times (Pick and Hay, 1965).

Another series of experiments used conditions similar to the kitten carousel (which we discussed earlier in the chapter). Observers wearing displacing prism goggles either walked around for about 1 hour (active exposure) or were wheeled around in a wheelchair over the same path for about 1 hour (passive exposure). They were then measured to see if any perceptual change had taken place. Adaptation to the prismatic distortion occurred in the active condition but not during the passive exposure condition (Held and Bossom, 1961; Mikaelian and Held, 1964).

One important aspect of active movement under the optically distorted conditions seems to be that it provides observers with some sort of error feedback, which informs them of the direction and the extent of the distortion. This information provides a basis for learning a new correlation between the incoming stimuli and the conscious percept. The more information we give observers about the nature of their errors, the greater is the adaptation to the distortion (Coren, 1966; Welch, 1969, 1971).

Some investigators suggest that error information in the absence of active movement is sufficient to produce prism adaptation. Howard, Craske, and Templeton (1965) had observers watch a rotating rod through an optical system that displaced it to one side. For some observers the rod appeared to be displaced to the side, and they merely watched it rotate. For another group the rod appeared displaced to the same degree; however, as the rod swung about, it brushed the observer across the lips, indicating that it was directly in front of the

observer rather than off to the side as it appeared. Although both groups were passive, the groups receiving the information that their percept was erroneous (being touched by a stimulus that looked like it would pass them by) showed perceptual adaptation while the other group did not. Thus information indicating how our percepts are in error may be sufficient to produce adaptation (Howard, Anstis, and Lucia, 1974).

What actually changes during the adaptation process? This issue is still being debated. Some researchers believe that adaptation simply alters the *felt position* of various parts of the body. This is based on the observation that after prism adaptation, when observers are asked to point to a straight ahead position (by feel alone), they tend to point off to the side. This indicates some proprioceptive or "felt" component in the aftereffect (Harris, 1980). Other data indicate that this may be only part of the process (Mikaelian, 1974; Redding and Wallace, 1976). For example, animals can still adapt to the visual displacement when the nerves that provide information about the position of the arm are severed (Bossom and Ommaya, 1968; Taub and Berman, 1968). The consensus is that a perceptual shift is actually taking place, which is the result of recalibration of the higher centers used to interpret perceptual input (Welch, 1978). Some evidence for this comes from an interesting experiment by Foley (1970, 1974). She placed wedge prisms in front of the eyes of observers so that the direction of displacement was different for each eye. Either one eye saw an upward displacement and the other a downward displacement, or one eye saw a displacement to the right and the other to the left. After several hours of exposure, the two eyes were tested separately. The results indicated that each eye had adapted to its own particular distortion. This result implies a perceptual recalibration. It seems likely that adaptation to optically rearranged stimuli involves some form of perceptual learning altering the appearance of visual space. However, whether the process of learning to deal with rearranged spatial stimuli involves the same mechanisms that may have gone into the original development of our perception of space is not clear.

Another form of perceptual learning is similar to rearrangement in that it involves learning to compensate for a perceptual error. It differs from the situations we have been discussing in that the error is not optical in nature, and the observer usually is not conscious either of the erroneous perception or of any perceptual change. The situation that we are discussing involves *visual geometric illusions*, which are simple line drawings that evoke percepts differing in size or shape from those that would be expected on the basis of the actual physical measurements of the stimuli. We have encountered several of these already, in Chapters 1, 12, 14, and 16, including the Mueller-Lyer illusion (Figure 16-9) in which the horizontal line with the outwardly turned wings appears longer than the line with the inwardly turned wings, despite the fact that both are physically equal in length. Suppose we present the Mueller-Lyer figure to an observer and measure her susceptibility to the line length distortion. Next we instruct her to begin moving her eyes across the figure, scanning from one end of the horizontal line to the other on both portions of the figure. We ask her to be as accurate as possible with her eye movements. At 1 minute intervals we stop the scanning process and take measurements of illusion magnitude until a total of 5 minutes of viewing time has elapsed. This simple process of inspection leads to a 40 percent reduction in the original illusion magnitude. This decrease, known as **illusion decrement**, has been demonstrated many times (see Coren and Girgus, 1972b, 1978).

What is happening in this situation? How does the observer know that the percept is wrong in the first place, and why does the size of the illusory effect decrease? The answer seems to lie in the pattern of the observer's eye movements. If we measure the actual pattern of eye movements an observer makes over an illusion figure, we find that the eyes are directed to move as if the distorted percept were actually correct. In other words, if the eyes were resting on the end of the line in the perceptually elongated portion of the Mueller-Lyer figure (Figure 17-8A), an attempt to look at the far end of the line would produce an eye movement that is too long. This eye movement error is in agreement with the percept, which tends to overestimate the length of the line. A corrective adjustment in the eye movement must be made if the fovea is to come to rest on the exact end of the line. The opposite happens for the underestimated portion of the Mueller-Lyer figure (Figure 17-8B). Here the eye movements are too short (again in agreement with the perceptual underestimation of the line length), and a corrective adjustment must be made. These two segments of the Mueller-Lyer figure are shown in Figure 17-8A and B while the eye movement patterns over the portions of the figure are shown in 17-8C.

In Chapters 15 and 16 we saw instances where patterns of eye movements could be used to tell us something about the information processing abilities of an observer. The same type of reasoning can be applied to the study of eye movement patterns across illusion configurations. As the observer views the illusory array, eye movements and eye movement errors provide information about the existence (as well as the direction and the strength) of the illusory distortion. This error information can be used by the observer to correct the percept. This point of view is sup-

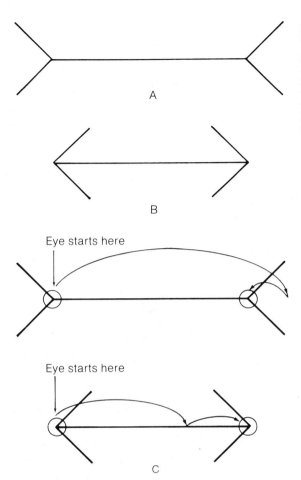

Figure 17-8. *The overestimated (A) and underestimated (B) portions of the Mueller-Lyer illusion, and (C) typical eye movements obtained when viewing them.*

ported by the fact that an illusion decrement does not occur unless the observer is allowed to scan the figure. (Coren and Hoenig, 1972; Festinger, White, and Allyn, 1968).

The phenomenon of illusion decrement implies that perceptual learning is taking place. The information obtained from the eye movements is being used to reduce a perceptual error, and the direction of this change (from

greater to lesser illusion susceptibility) mimics that which is associated with perceptual rearrangement studies. The most interesting aspect of this form of perceptual adjustment, however, is the fact that nothing about it appears to be available to consciousness. Unless provided with a ruler or a direct explanation, the observer does not consciously know that the original perception is in error, nor does he know that that illusory error has been reduced as a result of his active interactions with the illusion figure! The percept simply becomes more accurate with no change in the observer's own awareness.

CONTEXT AND MEANING

All percepts are ambiguous. Consider a target that casts a square image on the retinal surface. The object the image represents could actually be one of an infinite number of different shapes at any distance or inclination relative to the observer, as shown in Figure 17-9. Because any retinal image can be caused by a variety of different physical targets in the world, it is surprising that our normal perceptual experiences are generally so unambiguous. Actually, what we perceive is the result of a decision-making process in which we deduce, on the basis of all available information, what the stimulus object is. This *transactional viewpoint* maintains that any current perceptual experience consists of a complex evaluation of the significance of stimuli reaching our receptors. Through our life experience we learn that certain objects or conditions have a high probability of being related to each other. On this basis we derive our *best bet* as to what we are viewing. In a sense, the world we are experiencing is more the result of perceptual processing than the cause of the perception (Coren,

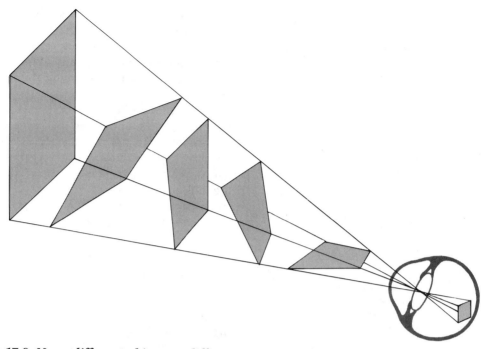

Figure 17-9. Many different objects at different distances and slants, all of which cast the same square retinal image (from Coren and Girgus, 1978).

1983; Ittelson, 1962). The transactional approach implies that if our expectations change, or our analysis of the situation changes, then our perceptual experience will also change (Ames, 1951; Brunswick, 1955). A simple example of the effect of context and expectations can be seen in Demonstration Box 17-3.

Most of our percepts are constructed from incomplete stimuli. Look at Figure 17-10A. It is clear that this represents a dog, yet it should also be clear that there is no dog present. The figure is completely constructed in the *mind's eye* of the observer. The elephant in Figure 17-10B will probably be somewhat more difficult to recognize. The less familar the object, the more difficult is the recognition. Once having seen (or "constructed") the figure, however, the meaningful organization will be apparent immediately when you look at it again. Our ability to perceive these stimuli as objects

depends on our prior experience. This was shown by Steinfield (1967), who found that when observers were told a story about an ocean cruise they recognized Figure 17-10C as a steamship in less than 5 seconds. Observers who were told an irrelevant story took six times longer to recognize the figure.

Some of the experiences that affect perception may take place at a preconscious level. For instance, much earlier in the chapter we spoke of an experiment in which researchers Haber and Hershenson (1965) presented a word for so brief a time period that it could not be recognized. They found that if the word was presented several times, even though the length of time of each presentation was not increased, the word was eventually recognized (Haber and Hershenson, 1965; Uhlarik and Johnson, 1978). If the word was not identified on the first presentation, why should an ob-

---

Demonstration Box 17-3. A context effect on perception

Read the accompanying handwritten message.

You probably read it as "My phone number is area code 604, 876-1569. Please call!" If you did, you were being affected by several contextual influences on perception. Go back to the message and look carefully at the script. You will see that the two pairs of characters you read as the word *is* and the numbers *15* are identical. In addition, the *b* in the word phone and the *b* in the word number are identical, as are the *d* in the word code and the *l* in the word please. You saw each letter or number when you first read the message within a context, and this context determined how you interpreted the script character.

My phone number 15 area
code 604, 876-1569. Please call!

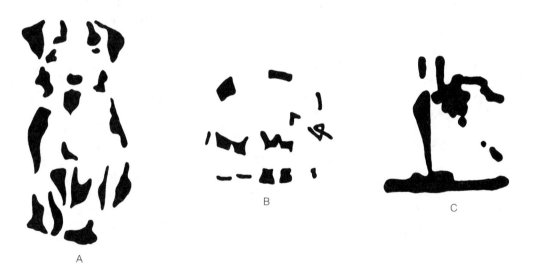

Figure 17-10. Some degraded stimuli that may be seen as objects (based on Street, 1931).

server be able to recognize it after repeated exposures? Dodwell (1971) has suggested that very fast presentations of stimuli do not give the brain sufficient time to do the necessary computations required for recognition. The partially processed stimulus is held in memory, and as the information extraction continues, hypotheses are formed and checked until the stimulus appears to make sense. At this point, the conscious recognition response takes place (Doherty and Keeley, 1972).

The same perceptual hypotheses, allowing

us eventually to formulate a percept from minimal or degraded input, can also be used to modify our perception so that it no longer accurately represents the stimulus. For example, Ross and Schilder (1934) presented observers with a series of briefly flashed line drawings. Some of the drawings were incomplete or distorted, such as three-armed people and faces with a mouth missing. A look at some of their observers' comments is informative. When presented with the side view of a dog with the left hind leg missing, the subject reported, "It's a dog, a wolf, two ears stand upright, a round mouth, a long tail." The experimenter then instructed the observer, "Look at his legs." Observer: "He has five toes on each leg." Experimenter: "Look at the hind legs." Observer: "I saw two; the tail goes up."

Despite ongoing pressure from the experimenter, the observer continued to correct the percept, filling in the missing leg on the hypothesis that dogs have four legs.

These researchers also used a drawing of a woman's head facing downward. She had two large eyes as well as a large third eye on her forehead. One observer described the picture as "a woman with long hair, black, two eyes, one nose, one mouth, two ears." The stimulus was presented again briefly, and the observer was asked if the forehead was in order, to which he replied, "Yes." After several other stimuli were presented again, the observer now reported, "The same woman I saw before. She is funny: big eyes, a big nose, and a big

mouth." Experimenter: "Look at the forehead." Observer: "She has a small curl in the middle."

Even with additional brief presentations, this observer still insisted that all that appeared on the forehead was a curl of hair. Third eyes do not occur normally, so we apparently correct our percept on the basis of our expectations—we see extra hair, not extra eyes. You may see how expectations alter our perception in Demonstration Box 17-4.

Language as well as expectations may modify percepts. This view was advanced by Whorf (1956) and Sapir (1939), who suggested that specific language labels for certain types of stimuli increase the ease of perceptual recognition. They maintain, for example, that the Eskimo, whose language has a wide variety of different names for different kinds of snow, may be able to make better discrimination among types of snow than those of us who speak English and have only the single label "snow."

An example of how language can affect perception is seen in a classic experiment conducted by Gottschaldt (1926, 1929), who gave observers from 3 to 520 presentations of a simple target. He then asked them to find these targets in a more complex figure. Such a target is shown in Figure 17-11, where Figure 17-11A is embedded in Figure 17-11B. He reported that prolonged experience with the simple figure did not make it any easier to find it when it was hidden in the more complex stimulus. Djang (1937) repeated this experiment. Her

---

Demonstration Box 17-4. An expectancy effect on perception

Turn to color plate 8 and *quickly* count the number of aces of spades that you see. Then return to this demonstration box. Although you probably only saw three aces of spades, there are actually five. Two of the aces of spades are printed in red ink, rather than in black. Since you "expect" spades to be black, your recognition process for incongruent or unexpected stimuli is impaired.

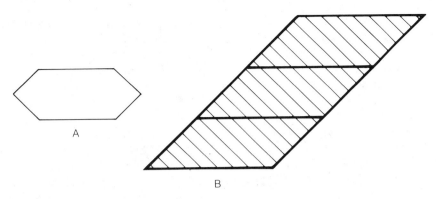

Figure 17-11. Figure **A** *may be found embedded in Figure* **B.**

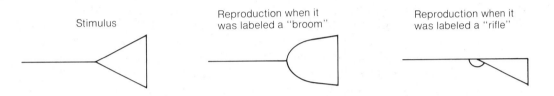

Figure 17-12. The effects of labels on later perceptual recall.

observers, however, did not just look at the simple stimulus; they were required to draw it. She reports that when such active practice is combined with exposure, there was an improvement in later recognition of the simple component embedded in the more complex figure. Schwartz (1961) then added a language component. He had observers learn distinctive verbal labels to attach to each of the simple figures. This modification of the experiment resulted in an improved ability to find and recognize the named stimuli. Verbal labeling, however, can either help or hinder recognition. Ellis and Muller (1964) trained subjects using either a *narrow* labeling system (one label for each shape) or a *wide* labeling system (one label for four shapes). In later tests of recognition for these forms, the group using the narrow labeling approach performed better than the group simply observing the shapes without labeling; the group using the

wide labeling system had the fewest correct recognitions. Thus, the wide labeling seems to emphasize the learning of similarities between the stimuli, which later results in poorer discrimination and recognition.

Language and expectation can also serve to modify the later reports of what we have seen. Carmichael, Hogan, and Walter (1932) presented observers with simple line drawings and associated each with a label. Observers were asked to reproduce these drawings. In general, their reproductions were biased in the direction of the verbal label. When presented with Figure 17-12A and told that it was a broom, observers tended to reproduce patterns similar to 17-12B. When told that it was a rifle, observers tended to reproduce patterns similar to that in 17-12C. In this experiment, the reproductions occurred only a few moments after the stimulus was taken away. Such distortions in our recollections of what we have seen may have important consequences for many behaviors, including such things as scientific observation and eye witness testimony. For example, eye witness reports of events that occurred during a crime tend to be remarkably unreliable, even when obtained immediately after the event. Observers have a tendency to include details that they could not have seen. Such details are often provided on the basis of the observer's expectations or biases (Buckhout, 1976; Loftus, 1979; Yarmey, 1979).

Loftus (1974) demonstrated how words used to question observers about a filmed auto accident could cause them to distort their perceptal memory. When witnesses were asked about what happened when one car *smashed* into another (as opposed to using a more neutral term, such as *made contact* with the other car), they were more likely to report having seen broken glass flying about (even though there was none). One might argue that such distortion is a distortion in memory, rather than in perception. Unfortunately, whenever an observer reports what he has *seen*, he is always dealing with events that occurred in the past. For instance, the description of a picture flashed on a screen in front of an observer for a fraction of second is really obtained from his memory, since the image is no longer present by the time the observer begins his report. Thus, any perceptual report must have some memory component.

It seems that by increasing the degree of memory involved, by increasing the time interval between the perception and the report, one may increase the amount of deviation from what was actually observed. For instance, in another experiment Loftus (1979) showed observers a brief videotape of an automobile accident and then asked them some questions about what they had just observed. For one group of observers, one of the questions was, "How fast was the white sports car going while traveling along the country road?" For the other group the question was, "How fast was the white sports car going when it passed the barn while traveling along the country road?" In fact, no barn was present. Yet when questioned about the incident a week later, more than 17 percent of the group exposed to the false suggestion about a barn answered the question "Did you see a barn?" by saying "Yes," as opposed to only 3 percent of the group that did not get such a suggestion.

Some interesting suggestions emerge from research of this sort. For instance, when one has perceived something, the perceptual memory resists any later change. Thus, in one experiment subjects viewed a series of slides showing the theft of a large, bright red wallet. Virtually none of the observers could be induced later to recall the color of the wallet as brown (Loftus, 1979). In fact, recent evidence indicates that the suggestions or false context that are provided *after* the occurrence of the perceptual event only fill in gaps in the perception, much as the observer's expectation that dogs have four legs caused the missing leg to be added perceptually in the experiment discussed earlier (Yuille, 1983).

ENVIRONMENTAL AND LIFE HISTORY DIFFERENCES

Each of us is surrounded by a particular set of environmental stimuli. We have seen earlier what effect the availability, or nonavailability, of particular stimuli can have on the neural development of certain sensory systems, and hence on the observer's later perceptual abilities. Aspects of our environment and culture, however, may teach us different sets of perceptual strategies and may alter the internal set of expectations and analyses that we bring to each new perceptual situation. Thus, if we live in the desert or on the pampas or the plains, we are exposed to broad vistas of open space that are never experienced by a forest dweller. If we live in a technologically advanced country, we are exposed to sets of visual stimuli (such as photographs and television) that are usually not available to someone dwelling in the African bush or the Australian outback. Such differences, especially when experienced over one's entire lifetime, may have dramatic consequences for the perceptual process.

The effects of culture

In our civilized, urbanized, and media-intensive culture, we are inundated with images—not just the images of our immediate environment, but images representing environments or objects that are not present. These latter images are in the form of patterns of color, or black and white, shown on televisions and in cinemas. There are photographs in magazines and newspapers, where we might "see" a baby elephant peaceably grazing a few feet in front of its gigantic mother, all in a 5 cm square smudge of black ink on a perfectly flat surface. If you have some artistic talent, you may be able to represent such a scene with a few strokes of a pen on a sheet of paper and thus be able to let your friends "see for themselves" what you have seen. This seems like a perfectly natural fact of life.

Pictures, of the sort that we encounter daily, are often viewed as simply "windows" through which we see other worlds (Haber, 1980). Certainly, these images must follow all the same optical laws as the real world. Certainly, every observer must follow these laws to interpret such stimuli in the same way that we do. Unfortunately, neither statement is completely "certain." While pictures do contain much information that mimics the optical patterns encountered in natural viewing (Gibson, 1979;

Sedgwick, 1980), many discrepancies exist between the image and reality. For instance, the actual sizes of the images are usually too large or too small, which in turn ruins the geometric correspondence between the image and the actual scene (Lumsden, 1980). Furthermore, even if one could make the geometry of perspective perfect, it would only be correct for one single viewing angle, and viewing any image from a vantage point other than the viewpoint adopted by the camera or artist who produced the image ought to lead to distorted percepts (Kennedy and Ostry, 1976). Such expected distortions, however, do not appear (Rosinski and Farber, 1980). We could enlarge this list of discrepancies between the real scene and its image endlessly. For instance, the image is flat, while the real world is three dimensional. The image is interpreted correctly even if its colors are all wrong, or even if there are no colors at all, and so forth. Such considerations have led some theorists to the conclusion that pictures may be a sort of visual language that is created and read according to the agreed-upon set of conventions in any given culture. Thus, pictures are not direct representations of reality at all (Gombrich, 1972; Goodman, 1968). At the very least, they must be interpreted as hypotheses that are shared among individuals growing up with a common heritage (Gregory, 1974). By either of these two theories, the perception of pictures must be learned in some manner.

Before we investigate whether we must learn to interpret pictures, it is important for us to specify that we are really talking about two separate skills. The first is the ability to recognize objects depicted in a picture, and the second is the ability to interpret the three-dimensional arrangement implied in the flat image.

Hochberg and Brooks (1962) conducted a heroic experiment, using one of their children as the subject. The child was reared to the age of 19 months, carefully shielded from any sort of pictorial representation. This meant that the television was never used in the child's presence, nor were there magazines or picture books. Even the labels on cans and boxes of food were removed or covered. When the child was tested after this restricted rearing, he had no difficulty identifying pictures of common items. This result implies that one need not learn to recognize patterns or drawings as representations of real world objects.

The unlearned nature of picture identification seems to be supported by the fact that colored photos are recognized immediately when shown to individuals who have lived in cultures where they have never experienced pictures (Hagen and Jones, 1978). When black and white photos or drawings are used, however, individuals reared in isolated cultures sometimes have difficulties that are strange to those who have been reared with the continuous company of graphic images. Deregowski (1980) has collected a number of such reports, including one from a Scottish missionary working in Malawi (a country in southwestern Africa between northern Rhodesia and Mozambique) nearly 75 years ago: "Take a picture in black and white, and the natives cannot see it. You may tell the natives: 'This is a picture of an ox and a dog'; and the people will look at it and look at you, and that look says that they consider you a liar. Perhaps you say again, 'Yes, this is a picture of an ox and a dog. Look at the horn of the ox, and there is his tail!' And the boy will say, 'Oh, yes, and there is the dog's nose and eyes and ears!' Then the old people will look again and clap their hands and say, 'Oh yes, it is a dog. . . .'"

Clearly, such a report indicates that the individuals involved did not respond to the photo with the immediate spontaneous recognition that we find characteristic of viewing pictures. Still, when their attention was directed to the relevant aspects of the pattern, they did have

an "Aha!" experience of recognition, indicating that the ability to recognize the pattern was still there, although they lacked training to direct their attention appropriately.

While there may be a general ability to recognize objects depicted in pictures, recognizing the implied spatial relationships seems to be more subject to cultural and educational influences. Identifying depth in a flat image requires a certain amount of selection among the perceptual cues available. For instance, the photograph might include such cues for depth as **linear perspective**, **interposition**, and **texture gradients**, among others mentioned in Chapter 10. However, there are also cues indicating that the picture is flat. For instance, there is no **binocular disparity** between items in the picture, and all the elements in the photo require the same degree of **accommodation** and **convergence**. Thus, to see a drawing or a photograph as representing an arrangement of objects in three dimensions, rather than as a flat surface with different shadings of dark and light, you must attend to some depth cues and ignore others. An observer's particular perceptual strategy may depend on her life history and the relative frequency with which certain cues are encountered in the immediate environment.

Hudson (1960, 1962) has attempted to separate cultural factors associated with the use of pictorial depth information. His technique consisted of using a series of pictures that depicted certain combinations of pictorial depth cues. Figure 17-13 shows one picture from Hudson's series, and as you can see, it depicts a hunting scene containing two pictorial depth cues. The first is **interposition**, in which objects closer to the observer block our view of portions of more distant objects. Since the hunter and the antelope are covering portions of the rocks, they appear closer to the observer than the rocks.

The second pictorial depth cue contained

Figure 17-13. A figure used to test ability to respond to pictorial depth cues (based on Hudson, 1962).

in this drawing is **familiar size**. We know the relative sizes of familiar objects; therefore, if an object is depicted as relatively small or large, we will judge its distance from us in a way consistent with our expectations based on its known size. For example, an elephant is a very large animal. In Figure 17-13, however, the elephant is one of the smallest objects in the picture. If we are responding to the cue of familiar size, we would tend to see the elephant as the most distant object in this hunting scene. When something as large as an elephant casts a smaller image than an antelope, the elephant must be farther away, since it is physically larger than the antelope.

Hudson used these stimuli because they are uniquely constructed to allow for both **two-dimensional** (no use of pictorial depth) and **three-dimensional** (full use of pictorial depth) types of responses. Suppose that we asked an observer to describe what she saw in this picture. First, we would expect her to identify correctly all the component objects in the picture. Suppose we also asked her to describe the actions taking place. A correct three-dimensional response would indicate that the hunter was attempting to spear the an-

telope (which is, of course, nearer to him than the elephant if you are perceiving pictorial depth). A two-dimensional response would state that the hunter is attempting to spear the elephant, which is actually physically closer to the tip of the spear in the picture. Such a response would indicate that the observer had not responded to either the interposition or the familiar size cues that place the elephant at a greater perceptual distance than the antelope from the hunter.

These stimuli have been used in a number of studies conducted throughout Africa, testing observers from a number of tribal and linguistic groups (Deregowski, 1980). The results indicate that relatively isolated and uneducated African observers have difficulty seeing pictorial depth within these pictures, relative to more urbanized Western observers, a fact that has been verified using other types of pictures (Jahoda and McGurk, 1974). The ability to perceive three dimensionally seems to be improved if more depth cues are added (Kilbride and Leibowitz, 1975; Hagen and Jones, 1978), or if formal education, involving the use of picture books, drawings, and so forth has been experienced (Kilbride and Robbins, 1968; Leibowitz

Demonstration Box 17-5. Cross-cultural differences in perception

The figure accompanying this box is sometimes called the "Devil's tuning fork." Look at the figure for about 30 seconds or so; then close the book and try to draw it from memory. Return to this box when you have done this.

Most of you probably found this task to be quite difficult. The source of your difficulty comes from the fact that your cultural experience with graphic representations has caused you to interpret this two-dimensional stimulus as a three-dimensional object. Unfortunately, such an interpretation leads to problems since the depth cues implied in this figure are ambiguous. It is interesting to note that Africans who have not received formal education have no difficulty reproducing the figure. Since they do not interpret the figure as three-dimensional they merely see a pattern of flat lines, which is easy to reproduce.

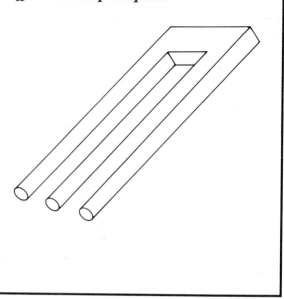

and Pick, 1972). You can explore your own tendencies to use certain depth cues but not others by trying Demonstration Box 17-5.

Culturally determined conventions associated with the interpretation of pictures can be best shown in situations where the flat, stationary picture is not only supposed to depict three dimensionality but also motion. For instance, Figure 17-14 depicts a scene in which there are three different forms of motion. From left to right, we see a speeding car, a boy rapidly whipping his head around, and a dog with a wagging tail. Of course, there is no actual motion, yet we "read" such motion into the picture. Within Western cultures, such interpretation of motion in pictorial arrays may appear as early as 4 years of age (Freidman and Stevenson, 1975). Non-Western cultures, without pictorial experience, however, virtually never "see" movement in such representations. The likelihood that movement will be seen in such an array seems to improve with

Figure 17-14. Figures conventionally recognized as being in motion by Western observers, but not necessarily by non-Western observers.

education, urbanization, and exposure to pictorial materials (Duncan, Gourlay, and Hudson, 1973; Friedman and Stevenson, 1980).

Certain facets of the environment make us more or less responsive to certain patterns of depth cues appearing in pictures. For instance, the **carpentered world hypothesis** begins with the observation that in the urbanized Western world, rooms and buildings are usually rectangular, many objects in the environment have right-angled corners, city streets have straight sides, and so forth. Surrounded by such an environment, we may learn to depend more heavily on depth cues based on linear perspective than would people who live in more primitive rural environments (Coren and Girgus, 1978; Gregory, 1966; Segall, Campbell, and Herskovits, 1966). For example, the Zulus have been described as surrounded by a circular culture. They live in round huts with round doors. They do not plough their land in straight lines but tend to use curved furrows. Individuals living in such a world would not be expected to rely on linear perspective as heavily as those of us living in a more linear environment.

In a classic study, Segall, Campbell, and Herskovits (1966) compared the responsiveness of individuals in carpentered versus noncarpentered environments to certain types of depth cues. Instead of using Hudson-like pictures as stimulus materials, however, they chose a more subtle class of patterns, namely the visual-geometric illusions. Some of these configurations have already been discussed in Chapter 14, where we pointed out how susceptibility to size distortions in some figures, such as the Mueller-Lyer illusion may depend on a three-dimensional interpretation of the pattern (see Figure 14-6). As discussed then, the apparently longer portion of the Mueller-Lyer figure may be interpreted as a corner of a room receding in depth because the wings of

the illusion act as linear perspective cues. The inappropriate application of size constancy based on this interpretation of the wings of the figure as perspective cues results in our overestimation of the size of this segment of the figure relative to the segment with the inwardly turned wings. Since pictorial depth information is thought to play a role in the formation of these illusory percepts, these types of configurations are well-suited to an exploration of the carpentered world hypothesis.

Segall et al. (1966) gathered data from throughout Africa and also from several groups of people living in Evanston, Illinois. Although there are variations within the noncarpentered samples, the average Mueller-Lyer illusion was greater for the more urban groups. Similar results have been reported for other perspective-related illusions (Coren and Girgus, 1978; Deregowski, 1980; Kilbride and Leibowitz, 1975).

Although the observed differences in illusion susceptibility for different cultural groups may be partially caused by factors other than experience with a carpentered world (Berry, 1971; Coren and Porac, 1978; Pollack and Silvar, 1967), there is ample evidence that the absence of experience with certain types of depth cues impairs other perceptual functions (such as size constancy) that depend on depth perception. One of the most striking examples of this was provided by the anthropologist Turnbull (1961). He observed the behavior of the Bambuti Pygmies, who live in the Ituri Forest in the Congo. Because they live in the dense rain forest, their vision is generally limited to short distances, with vistas that extend for, at most, 30 meters. Therefore, their life history seems to lack the visual experience needed to learn to use the depth cues responsible for the maintenance of size constancy at greater viewing distances. Turnbull noted one instance when he had taken his Bambuti guide, Kenge, out of the forest for the first time in his life. They were crossing over a broad plain and happened to spot a herd of buffalo: "Kenge looked over the plains and down to where a herd of about a hundred buffalo were grazing some miles away. He asked me what kind of insects they were, and I told him they were buffalo, twice as big as the forest buffalo known to him. He laughed loudly and told me not to tell such stupid stories. . . . We got into the car and drove down to where the animals were grazing. He watched them getting larger and larger, and though he was as courageous as any pigmy, he moved over and sat close to me and muttered that it was witchcraft. . . . Finally, when he realized that they were real buffalo he was no longer afraid, but what puzzled him still was why they had been so small, and whether they really had been small and suddenly grown larger, or whether it had been some kind of trickery." (From C. Turnbull, *American Journal of Psychology*, 74. Copyright 1961 by The University of Illinois Press.)

Turnbull's description of Kenge's perceptual impressions suggests that our experience with particular stimuli prevalent in our immediate environment can result in differences in how we perceive new stimuli and situations. It seems that we learn to utilize stimulus information to which we are continually exposed and fail to learn to utilize stimuli that are rare. This holds for the auditory as well as the visual environment.

The most dominant feature in our auditory environment is the constant flow of language sounds that surrounds us. As noted in Chapter 13, each language uses a small set of sound features to differentiate the phonemes, which are the functionally characteristic sounds of that language. Different languages use different subsets and combinations of these phonetic, or sound features. This means that some sounds may be treated as distinctively different in some languages, and not in others. For instance, while the sounds /r/ and /l/ are treated as individual phonemes in English, they are not in Japanese. This fact would be expected to bias the auditory experiences of individuals brought up surrounded by these two languages. Thus, in an auditory environment produced by Japanese speakers, these two sounds will be blended and intermixed, while in the context of English speakers, the two sounds will be articulated more clearly and responded to differently. This difference in auditory environment could alter the perception of such sound differences in much the same way that differences in visual environments and experience with certain types of graphic materials alter the perception of visual stimuli.

Numerous studies have shown that adults who have grown up with exposure to only one language often have difficulty discriminating certain nonnative linguistic contrasts (Strange and Jenkins, 1978). This type of difficulty may persist even if the adult has learned the second language and now appears to be fluent in the second language. For example, Goto (1971) recorded pairs of words that contrasted the /r/ and /l/ sounds (such as *lead* vs. *read*, or *play* vs. *pray*). Several native Japanese speakers, who were bilingual, could produce these sounds so that native English-speaking listeners could differentiate them without error. However, this seems to be a learned ability to *produce* rather than to *perceive* the phonemic difference, since, when asked to listen to recordings of pairs of words that contrasted these phonemes, the native Japanese speakers could not do so, even when listening to their own speech productions!

The mechanism responsible for our ability to discriminate some speech sounds but not others is still somewhat ambiguous. Evidence suggests learning through exposure and experience plays a role in the ability to discriminate between various linguistic sounds; thus, some linguistic discriminations seem to be learned during the childhood years (Eilers, Wilson, and Moore, 1979). For example, adults but not infants can make distinctions between certain speech sounds (Eilers, Gavin, and Wilson, 1979). On the other hand, infants seem to be born with the ability to discriminate certain sound pairs not used in their native tongue, and appear to lose this ability as adults (Trehub, 1976). A striking example was provided by Werker, Gilbert, Humphrey, and Tees (1981), who presented English-speaking and Hindi-speaking adults with pairs of sounds that are differentiated as different phonemes in Hindi but not in English. As one might expect, the adult Hindi speakers could make the discrimination, but the adult English speakers could not. The interesting result, however, is that when 6-month-old infants were tested, they *could* make the discrimination. In terms of our earlier discussion about the relationship between experience and development, these results suggest that different aspects of the perception of speechlike sounds follow different courses. While some auditory discriminations are *facilitated* through contact with particular sounds in the linguistic environment, others are lost through their absence or rarity, thus showing that experience is neccessary for their *maintenance* (see Walley, Pisoni, and Aslin, 1981). Much of what we perceive and many of the perceptual distinctions we make are a product of the culture and environment in which we were reared.

The effects of occupation

Even within a given culture, there is selective exposure to different sets of environmental stimuli. You are exposed to your occupational setting for about one-half your adult working life, and specific sets of occupational experiences can affect your perceptual abilities, both at the physiological level and at the higher cognitive levels. One aspect of an occupation that may have physiological effects on a sensory system is the magnitude of sound, light, or chemical stimulation to which one is exposed.

Consider, for example, the amount of auditory input that bombards you in your occupational setting. While some work environments are relatively quiet (such as offices and small stores), others are associated with continuous, high intensity noise (for example, factories and mills). Figure 17-15 illustrates the effects of noise on hearing for different occupations. The horizontal axis represents the frequencies at which hearing was tested in a sample of male office, farm, and factory workers. The 0 decibel point on the vertical axis represents the average minimum threshold for an auditory experience. The three curves on the graph plot the average threshold sound intensity at each of the frequencies used in the test. As you can

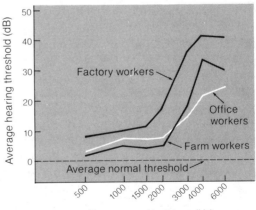

Figure 17-15. The effect of occupation on hearing (based on Glorig, Wheeler, Quiggle, Grings, and Summerfield, 1954).

see, the group of factory workers has a lower sensitivity (higher average thresholds). Fortunately, many factory workers have begun to wear earphones, which help protect them from the ill effects of continual noise exposure.

According to Kryter (1970), factory workers are not the only group that should be concerned about continual exposure to very loud sounds. For instance, soldiers exposed to the sound of gunfire and airline pilots exposed to engine noises have been shown to have hearing deficits. The loss tends to be greatest in the higher frequency ranges and seems to increase in severity as the length of the exposure increases. Thus, airline pilots who have from 1000 to 2000 hours flying time have an average audibility threshold of approximately 0 dB at a sound frequency of 4000 Hz. More experienced pilots, however, with 10,000-16,000 hours flying time, have an average audibility threshold of 10 dB at the same sound frequency.

Rice, Hyley, Bartlett, Bedford, Gregory, and Hallum (1968) have shown that performers of rock music may also suffer hearing losses. In Figure 17-16 we once again have plotted average audibility thresholds in decibels on the vertical axis and test frequencies along the horizontal axis. The lowest curve represents the thresholds of the control group of nonperformers. Notice that relative to nonperformers of the same age, the rock performers have elevated audibility thresholds (lower sensitivity). At 4000 Hz there is approximately a 20 dB difference between the thresholds of the performers and the controls. To give you a reference point, a 20 dB difference would be roughly equivalent to being able to hear a normal conversational tone as opposed to a shout. Figure 17-16 also shows the immediate effects of prolonged exposure to very loud sounds. The white curve on this graph plots the measured thresholds immediately after 85 minutes

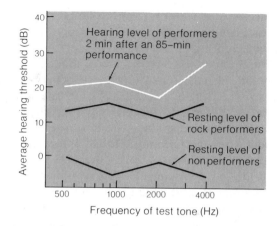

Figure 17-16. A comparison of the hearing of rock musicians to that of nonperformers (based on Rice, Hyley, Bartlett, Bedford, Gregory, and Hallum, 1968).

of exposure to very loud music, and as you can see, the threshold at 4000 Hz has risen to 27 dB.

In a similar vein, some occupations expose the eyes to high intensity lights (such as welding arcs and furnace blazes). In the same manner that prolonged high intensity sound can impair hearing, prolonged high intensity light can permanently impair vision (Noell, 1980).

Some occupations tend to involve specific experiences or training programs that attempt to alter perceptual abilities. Thus, pilots, especially those in the military, are often given training to improve the basic visual capacities associated with binocular depth perception, visual acuity, and so forth. There is a strong conviction among both the students and instructors who participate in such programs that such visual training is quite effective. Optometric measurements, however, do not show any beneficial changes (Goodson and Rahe, 1981). Similarly, the police believe that because of their training and practical experiences, they develop a superior ability to observe details. Actually, this does not seem to be the case (see Loftus, 1979; Yarmey, 1979), although some recently developed training programs offer some improvement (Yuille, 1983).

An interesting aspect of police as observers or eyewitnesses is that they seem somewhat more prone to making certain types of interpretive errors in their perceptions of people and activities. This appears to result from the fact that specific past experiences produce a sensitization or predisposition to "see" a situation in a certain way, especially when alternative perceptual experiences are possible (as when the stimulus is ambiguous or degraded because of poor viewing conditions). Technically, this is known as a **perceptual set**, and it refers specifically to the expectancies or predispositions an observer brings to the perceptual situation. In many respects, set can be thought of as another example of selective attention (as we discussed in Chapter 15), in which the observer is set to process some but not all portions of the incoming information. An example of the operation of this perceptual set appears in a study in which police officers and civilians were shown films of a street scene over a period of several hours. Their task was to watch for various people (whose photos were on display below the screen) and for certain types of actions (normal exchanges of goods versus theft, and so forth). Although the police tended to report more *alleged* thefts than the nonpolice, there was no significant difference between the police and civilians in their actual detection of people and actions.

A more subtle demonstration of this effect of set was provided by Toch and Schulte (1961), who studied perception of violence and crime in visual scenes requiring the resolution of some ambiguity. They simultaneously presented different pictures to each eye in a stereoscope. One eye was shown a violent scene and the other a nonviolent one, as in the pair of stimuli

Figure 17-17. A stereogram used to test for occupational influences on the perception of violence (from H. H. Toch and R. Schulte, British Journal of Psychology, *1961, 52, 389-393).*

in Figure 17-17. If these two views were seen simultaneously by the two eyes, perceptual confusion should result. Observers tend to resolve this ambiguous situation in favor of one scene or the other; this scene then dominates the percept. Toch and Schulte were interested in exploring the notion that police students would be predisposed to interpret this particular ambiguous situation in terms of the violent as opposed to the nonviolent scene. They compared the performance of advanced police administration students with two control groups (beginning police students and university students). In general, they found that the advanced police students interpreted the stereograms as depicting violence approximately twice as many times as the other two groups. Thus, their data provide some evidence that certain occupations, especially those requiring intensive training, may set an individual to interpret ambiguous stimulation in a particular way.

Do not think that we are singling out the police for particular scrutiny. Perceptual set associated with occupational training and experience can affect all groups of individuals. Scientists, who pride themselves on their observational abilities, also are swayed by their expectations, especially in ambiguous observational situations such as provided by certain X-ray patterns and telescopic or microscopic views. The psychologist Boring (1953) recounted an experience in which a biologist friend once showed him a set of drawings of the *same* microscopic specimen made before and after the discovery of chromosomes. While none of the "before" drawings showed or suggested any chromosomes at all, there were certainly plenty of chromosomes to be seen afterward! Thus, it seems clear that our percepts are shaped by much more than the simple pattern of stimulation reaching our eyes.

GLOSSARY

The following definitions are specific to this book.

Accommodation The process by which the lens of the eye varies its focus.

Aftereffects Errors in hand-eye coordination that follow adaptation to wedge-prism distortion.

Astigmatism Deviation of part of the cornea from a perfectly spherical shape.

Binocular disparity The difference between the images seen by the two eyes as a result of their separation in space.

Carpentered world hypothesis A hypothesis that states that individuals living in urban environments characterized by straight lines and angles will tend to depend more on depth cues based on linear perspective than would people living in more primitive rural environments.

Convergence The rotation of both eyes toward the nose as fixated objects become closer.

Critical period A period during which sensory experience is essential if perceptual development is to proceed normally.

Enhancement An improvement in the final level of a developing ability caused by relevant experience.

Exafference Stimulus input that acts on a passive observer.

Facilitation Enhancement of the rate at which an ability develops.

Familiar size The known or remembered size of objects.

Illusion decrement The decrease in the magnitude of a visual illusion with prolonged free viewing.

Induction A process in development whereby experience determines the presence and final level of a related ability.

Interposition The depth cue based on the visual blocking of an object or part of an object from view by another closer object.

Linear perspective The convergence of parallel lines as they recede into the distance.

Maintenance Preservation of a developed ability by relevant experience.

Maturation Development of an ability independently of experience.

Oblique effect The phenomenon whereby acuity for diagonally oriented stimuli is poorer than for horizontally or vertically oriented stimuli.

Perceptual set The expectancies or predispositions that an observer brings to a perceptual situation.

Reafference Stimulus input that results from an observer's own movements.

Rearrangement An experimental technique that alters spatial relations in the visual world.

Restricted rearing An experimental technique in which an animal is reared without the opportunity to use a designated form of sensory input.

Selective rearing An experimental technique in which an animal is reared under conditions of selective exposure to external stimuli.

Texture gradient A distance cue based on variations in surface texture as a function of distance from the observer.

Three-dimensional response Possessing pictorial depth.

Two-dimensional response Lacking pictorial depth.

Visual field The portion of the visual environment to which an eye will respond, measured in degrees around the head.

18

Individual Differences

SHE WAVED THE PATCH OF CLOTH AND raised her voice to say, "It's dark blue, why do you insist on calling it dark green?"

"It looks green to me."

"You mean you've chosen to call it green. My eyes are perfect and it looks blue to me; therefore it is blue."

"Listen, it looks green to me. I know what looks green and what looks blue. You know, this isn't the first time we've disagreed on things like this. After all, you are always saying that I make coffee too strong and too bitter, while I think your coffee tastes too weak. I think we just see the world differently."

Let us step back from this argument for a moment to recall that perception is not simply a process by which the qualities of the world get transferred from "out there" to "in here." Remember that perception involves many levels of processing. Not only must the peripheral sensory receptors be stimulated, but stimuli must be interpreted and encoded. As one ancient philosopher said, "The eyes are blind; only the mind sees." If this premise is true, it is possible that individuals can differ in the way that they perceive their worlds, since it is certainly true that no two minds seem to work in the same way.

There are many factors that can cause individuals to have different perceptions even when encountering identical stimuli. For instance, in Chapter 16 we saw that individuals of different ages often perceived certain stimuli differently, while in Chapter 17 we discovered that an individual's past experience or expectations can alter perception. Actually, there are many mechanisms that operate to make each person's perceptual experiences unique. These mechanisms include physiological factors that can alter the sensory receptors themselves or the neural apparatus that decodes the sensory information. There is also a contribution from an individual's cognitive or perceptual *style*, which is actually a reflection of personality differences and different approaches to gathering information from the environment. Even an individual's gender seems to cause differences in the way in which sensory information is processed. All these factors lead to individual differences in perception. One of the most interesting aspects of perception is the consideration of why the world you perceive may not necessarily be the same as the world perceived by others.

PHYSIOLOGICAL DIFFERENCES

We are complex physiological machines. We certainly have seen how factors that alter the structure and function of our sensory apparatus will alter what we perceive. For example, nonfunctional retinal cones will cause color vision deficits. Calcium deposits on the bones of the inner ear will lessen the intensity of sounds in the environment, while it will make your own voice seem very loud to you. In addition to such specific factors, some physiological variables affect the body generally and tend also to affect perception as a sort of side effect.

The effects of drugs

A number of drugs can cause marked changes in sensory capacities. For instance, smokers continually ingest a number of active chemicals. The most important of these is the poison nicotine; next in importance is the gas carbon monoxide. Because these chemicals enter the body predominantly through the mouth, it is not surprising that the major sensory effects of smoking tobacco focus on the sense of taste. Evidence indicates that absolute taste thresholds are higher for smokers than for nonsmokers, with smokers being especially insensitive to such bitter tastes as quinine (Kaplan and Glanville, 1964; Sinnot and Rauth, 1937). Smoking also affects vision; most of these effects are probably caused by the inhalation of carbon monoxide. Carbon monoxide has been shown to produce alterations in performance on some visual tasks, particularly those involving sustained visual attention (Roche, Horvath, Gliner, Wagner, and Borgia, 1981). In addition, smoking tends to reduce one's ability to make brightness intensity discriminations, especially under scotopic illumination conditions (Rhee, Kim, and Kim, 1965). This might explain why smokers tend to have more nighttime driving accidents than nonsmokers. Evidence also exists that ingestion of nicotine will affect the rate of decay observed in certain visual aftereffects (such as the afterimages associated with viewing bright targets, or the fatigue effects of prolonged staring at certain types of patterns, as we discussed in Chapters 6 and 7, for instance). Specifically, it has been hypothesized that these perceptual effects occur because the action of nicotine includes a tendency to increase neural inhibition within the visual system (Amure, 1978).

One general theme that seems to be characteristic of the data describing the effects of drugs on perception is that drugs that depress neural activity, such as sedatives, barbiturates, tranquilizers, and alcohol, also decrease sensory acuity. For example, Hellekant (1965) measured the effect of alcohol on taste sensitivity by recording directly from the chorda tympani nerve of a cat. This nerve conveys taste sensations from most of the tongue. Alcohol reduced responsiveness to sweet (sucrose), acid (acetic acid), salt (sodium chloride), and bitter (quinine) stimuli. The strongest reduction of taste response was for the bitter stimuli. Alcohol may also affect other sensory systems, and recent studies suggest that these effects may be cumulative. A case in point is a study that tested the auditory system and found that chronic alcoholics show delays in the neural electrical response to auditory signals when compared with nonalcoholics (Begleiter, Porjesz, and Chou, 1981). Studies of the effect of alcohol on visual abilities have produced similar findings. Research with chronic alcoholics has demonstrated differences in color vision, with alcoholics displaying a higher incidence of color vision deficiencies than nonalcoholic observers (Granger and Ikeda, 1968; Reynolds, 1979). In addition, one does not have to be an alcoholic or a habitual drinker to show the effects of alcohol on visual perception. In some studies, where observers have been given differing amounts of alcohol to drink and the effect on sensory response has been monitored for each successive amount, there are indications that higher doses of alcohol affect an individual's ability to follow a moving target with the eyes (Flom, Brown, Adams, and Jones, 1977; Levy, Lipton, and Holtzman, 1981). The amounts involved do not have to be very high, since MacArthur and Sekuler (1982) have shown that even small amounts of alcohol can decrease an observer's ability to detect the onset of a moving stimulus.

The overall sensitivity of the visual and auditory systems is also affected by many depressant drugs. A very popular technique for measuring visual responsiveness is the **critical flicker fusion frequency** (usually abbreviated CFF). This task requires an observer to view a flickering light. As the flicker rate is increased, the observer will eventually no longer see the successive on and off cycles, but rather will see the stimulus sequence fused into a steady, continuous light. The flicker speed that results in the perceptual shift from an apparently flickering to an apparently steady light is the CFF. The more sensitive the eye is to changes in illumination level, the greater the flicker frequency that will be needed to cause the perception of flicker to disappear. A similar task is used in hearing. This is called the **auditory flutter fusion** task (AFF). It is defined as the interval at which the listener first reports that a series of sequentially presented tones has merged into a continuous sound. Depressant drugs, such as alcohol and tranquilizers, tend to lower both the CFF and the AFF, thus indicating that the visual and auditory systems are acting sluggishly and with less sensitivity under the influence of such drugs (Besser, 1966; Holland, 1960).

Drugs that increase the arousal level of the observer, such as stimulants like caffeine and amphetamines (and even some of the B vitamins), may in some instances improve the sensitivity of the observer. These effects, however, do not seem to be as widespread or as reproducible as those obtained with depressant drugs. We do find that amphetamines and caffeine tend to increase the responsiveness of both the visual and auditory systems when sensitivity is measured using the CFF and the AFF. Such drugs seem also to increase the sensitivity of the olfactory system (Turner, 1968). Demonstration Box 18-1 provides a relatively simple perceptual task that can show you the effects of a stimulant on perception.

The hallucinogenic and psychoactive drugs, including LSD, mescaline, psilocybin, and marijuana, are often reported to have profound perceptual effects. For instance, Aldous Huxley (1963) described his visual experiences after taking mescaline saying: "First and most important is the experience of light. . . . All colors are intensified to a pitch far beyond anything seen in the normal state, and at the same time

---

Demonstration Box 18-1. The effects of stimulants on figure reversals

Look at the accompanying figure (which is called the *Necker Cube*) and notice that it tends to reverse its apparent orientation as you view it steadily. Sometimes the face with the corner labeled *A* seems closer than the face with the corner labeled *B*, and at other times *B* appears closer. Most people show a fairly constant rate of reversal for this figure. Have a friend monitor you for 1 minute as you look at the figure. Call out each time the figure reverses its apparent orientation, while your friend counts the number of reversals.

Now drink a cup of coffee. Don't use decaffeinated coffee since we want you to receive a dose of caffeine. Caffeine is a stimulant, and it should increase your visual responsiveness (as well as keeping you awake for the rest of the chapter). The effects take about 10-15 minutes to appear. After this interval, repeat the viewing process.

Look at the figure for 1 minute while a friend records the number of reversals. You should find that the stimulant has increased the number of perceptual shifts you experience.

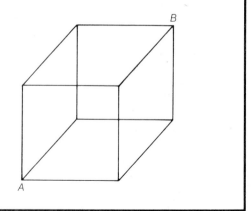

the mind's capacity for recognizing fine distinctions of tone and hue is notably heightened." Unfortunately, although some aspects of the subjective experience seem to be heightened, actual measurements do not always indicate increased sensitivity. For instance, Hartman and Hollister (1963) found that LSD, mescaline, and psilocybin all reduced the accuracy of color discriminations. Carlson (1958) showed that LSD reduced visual sensitivity in a threshold task. Furthermore, there are reports of blurred vision (Hoffer and Osmond, 1967) and slower than normal adaptation to darkness for observers under the influence of LSD (Ostfeld, 1961). Susceptibility to at least one visual geometric illusion, the Mueller-Lyer, increases under the influence of LSD (Edwards and Cohen, 1961). On the other hand, LSD does seem to improve auditory acuity and seems to enhance the CFF (Hoffer and Osmond, 1967; Williams, 1979).

Similarly, when observers are asked to describe their experiences, they often report that moderate doses of marijuana (cannabis) seem to improve visual clarity and acuity. Unfortunately, the experimental results indicate that actually, as with LSD, the perceptual effects involve losses in sensitivity. For instance, in a vigilance task where observers were asked to fixate a target and report stimuli appearing in the periphery of vision, smoking marijuana produced fewer accurate reports. Such an effect could be a result of a narrowing of attention induced by the drug. It also might occur because the observers could not be bothered to press the switch. This second explanation probably does not account for the results, since on those trials when the stimuli were reported, the reaction times were as quick as when observers were not under the influence of the drug (Moskowitz, Sharma, and McGlothlin, 1972). Intake of marijuana has also been shown to increase the time interval needed to

mask a visual stimulus (visual masking is discussed in Chapter 12), indicating that it acts somewhat like a sedative and decreases the speed of visual information processing (Braff, Silverton, Saccuzzo, and Janowsky, 1981). As with alcohol, prolonged use of marijuana seems to have a cumulative effect. This shows up particularly in color discrimination, which has been shown to be poorer in habitual marijuana users. These effects are particularly marked in the blue region (Adams, Brown, Haegerstrom-Portnoy, and Flom, 1976). Some more complex sensory effects have been reported after the smoking of cannabis. Some observers experience changes in depth perception and distortions in the perception of size (Tart, 1971). In addition, there is a report that the autokinetic effect, which is the illusory movement of a stationary light viewed in total darkness (illustrated in Demonstration Box 11-6) may become exaggerated. This last observation has led one group of experimenters to caution against night driving while under the influence of marijuana (Sharma and Moskowitz, 1972). On the other hand, marijuana, even at relatively high intake levels, does not seem to impair eye movement facility, since neither saccadic eye movements nor the ability to pursue a moving visual stimulus with the eyes is affected by its ingestion (Flom, Brown, Adams, and Jones, 1977).

Although contact with hallucinogenic drugs involves a departure from everyday behavior for most people, many of the stimulants (such as caffeine) and depressants (such as tobacco and alcohol) that alter perception are used commonly. Everyday drugs, including antihistamines and aspirin, can cause the perceptual responses of individuals to differ. For instance, aspirin may cause dimness of vision or ringing in the ears (Goodman and Gilman, 1965). Thus, an individual who has just had a cup of coffee or a martini, or who has tried to tend to a headache, may differ from other individuals in perceptual responses because of the actions of the ingested drugs.

The effects of physical pathology

Many pathological conditions affect perception. The most obvious of these are maladies that directly damage a particular receptor organ. Thus, *glaucoma*, which causes a pressure increase inside the eye, can produce blindness if left untreated, and *otosclerosis*, which causes the bones of the middle ear to become immobile, will impair hearing. There are, however, some pathological conditions that cause disturbances in very special and complex aspects of perception, rather than simply causing a loss of sensitivity to a given stimulus dimension. Such effects are often caused by severe toxic conditions, such as carbon monoxide poisoning, as well as by diseases or injuries that damage or reduce the functioning in some parts of the brain (Critchley, 1964; Davidoff, 1975; Luria, 1973). These can affect such complex functions as the ability to recognize objects or to place them in space, and they may also affect the ability to distribute attention. In general, these problems are called **agnosias**, from the Greek *a* meaning "not" and *gnosis* meaning "intuitive knowledge." People suffering from agnosias seem to perceive but do not seem to be capable of understanding the information presented to them.

Freud (1953) noticed a form of perceptual disturbance that he called **visual object agnosia**. Some of his patients were unable to recognize familiar objects, although there seemed to be no psychopathological disturbance or readily detectable elementary damage to the visual apparatus. More recent work (Luria, 1973) has suggested that agnosias

might arise from lesions in the secondary visual areas of the cortex. These lesions do not cause blindness nor do they seem to diminish visual acuity. Rather, they make it difficult for a person to combine parts of an object and to recognize them. For example, Luria describes a patient who was given a picture of a pair of eyeglasses. The patient examined the picture carefully in a manner indicating that he was confused and did not know exactly what it represented. He then started to guess. "There is a circle . . . and another circle . . . a cross bar . . . why it must be a bicycle?"

Such patients seem to have problems separating the parts of the figure from the overall context. Thus, if the patient is shown a drawing of a clock, such as is shown in Figure 18-1*A*, the patient can usually identify it correctly. However, if one simply crosses out the clock with a couple of lines, as in Figure 18-1*B*, the patient can no longer recognize what the picture represents. Such a patient may identify a telephone, with a dial, as a clock, or perceive a sofa, upholstered in brown fabric, as a trunk. Recognition difficulties seem to be even more pronounced when the stimuli are presented for less than 500 msec.

What sort of underlying mechanisms are involved in these perceptual disturbances? As long ago as 1909, the Hungarian neurologist Balint made some observations that suggest an attentional mechanism. He found that his patients had a definite decrease in attention span, being able to see only one object at a time, regardless of its size. For instance, such a person could not place a dot in the center of a circle since this would require paying attention to both the circle and the dot simultaneously. This type of patient is said to be suffering from **simultagnosia**. Thus, if the patient were shown a series of overlapping objects, such as those in Figure 18-2, she might report a single object, for example, the hammer, and deny

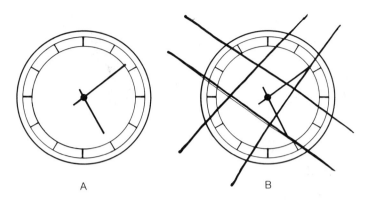

Figure 18-1. (A) A figure recognized as a clock. (B) A figure no longer recognizable to a visual agnosic.

that she can see any of the others (Williams, 1970). If such individuals are asked to copy a simple drawing, such as the one shown as Figure 18-3A, they would depict only its individual parts. Essentially, they would give a visual list of most of the details, as opposed to an overall integration of the parts into a whole figure. A drawing typical of such a patient is shown in Figure 18-3B.

A number of physiological experiments tend to show that this defect is caused by disturbances in the temporal region of the cortex. It also seems to be specific to the way in which attention is distributed to the visual targets (Butters, Barton, and Brody, 1970; Gerbrandt, Spinelli, and Pribram, 1970). Luria (1973) claims that injections of caffeine (to stimulate the appropriate region of the cortex) can reduce some of the symptoms, thus allowing the patient to be able to attend to two or three objects in the visual field simultaneously. Unfortunately, this improvement lasts only as long as the drug is active.

Some of the agnosia effects are quite general and may involve more than one sensory modality. Patients with diseases of the parietal lobe of the brain may show a **spatial agnosia**. They have difficulty negotiating their way around

the world. They make wrong turns even in familiar surroundings and do not easily recognize landmarks. They can become lost in their own homes. This problem does not appear to be caused by a defect in a single, specific sensory modality. These patients seem to be just as impaired using their tactile or kinesthetic senses as their visual (Heaton, 1968; Weinstein, Cole, Mitchell, and Lyerly, 1964). Such patients often show a unilateral neglect of

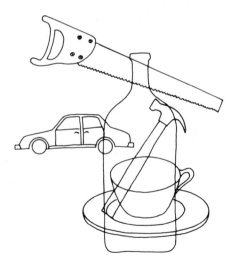

Figure 18-2. A test figure for simultagnosia.

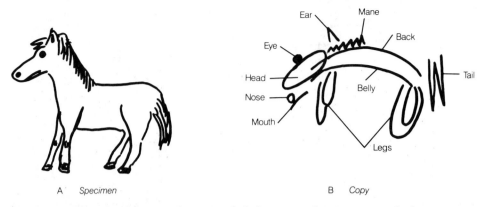

A   *Specimen* B   *Copy*

Figure 18-3. (A) The target figure to be copied. (B) A reproduction typical of a person suffering from visual object agnosia.

space. For example, if asked to draw symmetrical objects, they will usually produce some sort of imperfection on one side. Thus, an individual with left-sided spatial agnosia would reproduce Figure 18-4*A* as 18-4*B*.

While some of these perceptual effects are quite general, others are very specific. For instance, there is a rare disorder called **prosopagnosia**. In this type of agnosia the patient has difficulty recognizing human faces. In extreme cases, the patient may not even recognize his or her own face in a mirror. Prosopagnosia is

of interest because the human face is a very important stimulus. Your mother's face was probably one of the first visual forms to which you attended as an infant. When children draw, the face is usually the first part of the body to be depicted. Thus, we find that facial perception is one of the aspects of form recognition that is lost only in cases of serious brain injury, and often returns much earlier than other cognitive functions when recovery from brain damage occurs (Heaton, 1968).

A related disorder is called **autotopagnosia**,

A   *Specimen* B   *Copy*

Figure 18-4. (A) A target figure to be copied. (B) A reproduction typical of a person with unilateral spatial agnosia.

which is the distorted perception of body image and body parts. For example, one patient, when asked to point to her ear, looked around for it and replied that she must have lost it. Finger agnosias and finger naming difficulties are the most widely known forms of specific autotopagnosias, and these are thought to be associated with lesions in the left parietal portion of the brain (Pirozzolo, 1978).

Although we have concentrated on the visual sense in this discussion, similar difficulties are found in speech and sound recognition. These difficulties are usually grouped under the overall heading **aphasia** (from *a* meaning "not" and *phasis* meaning "utterance"). Such individuals suffer from an inability to name common objects and often fail to recognize the meanings of words designating common objects (Luria, 1972; Tsvetkova, 1972). These problems indicate that, when the integrity of the nervous system is disrupted, severe perceptual consequences can result. In addition, there are specific auditory agnosias, resulting from damage in the auditory pathways, that lead to the selective loss of the perception of words, called "pure word deafness"; the perception of nonlinguistic sounds, called *sound agnosia*; and the perception of music, called *sensory amusia* (Pirozzolo, 1978). There are

great numbers of different forms of agnosia or higher perceptual disruption. A number of these are listed and named in Table 18-1.

Most perceptual agnosias seem to have been caused by physiological damage, usually of the higher brain centers involved in the interpretation of stimuli. Thus, when we find agnosias, we tend often to find damage of particular brain sites. These sites are, however, usually not the *primary* receiving areas of the cortex for that particular sensory modality. Thus, visual agnosias often are associated with damage to the forward portions of the occipital cortex, generally areas 18 and 19, which are the secondary visual areas and in the temporal lobes, which are tertiary visual processing areas and seem to be associated with complex visual analysis, as we saw in Chapter 3. The same pattern is associated with the other sensory modalities, with the various forms of agnosia associated with secondary and tertiary areas of the cortex, rather than the primary recieving areas. A map of areas typically found to be damaged when an individual demonstrates various perceptual agnosias is shown as Figure 18-5.

All individual differences in perception are not a result of specific forms of physiological differences, however. In the next sections, we will consider factors that affect perception that may or may not have a physiological basis; or

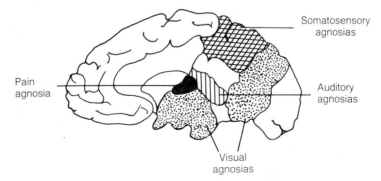

Figure 18-5. Damage to particular portions of the brain is often associated with the indicated agnosias.

Table 18-1. Some of the more common forms of agnosia that manifest themselves as complex perceptual deficits

Type of agnosia	Sensory modality	Perceptual deficit
Object agnosia	Visual	Inability to name, recognize, or to use objects
Color agnosia	Visual	Inability to associate colors with objects
Drawing agnosia	Visual	Inability to recognize drawn stimuli
Spatial agnosia	Visual	Deficits in stereoscopic vision and ability to relate objects in space
Simultagnosia	Visual	Inability to attend to more than one visual object at a time
Prosopagnosia	Visual	Inability to recognize faces
Unilateral neglect	Visual	Apparent deficit in processing stimuli on one side
Amusia	Auditory	Inability to recognize melodies, often accompanied by inability to reproduce rhythm or tempo
Sound agnosia	Auditory	Inability to identify the meaning of nonverbal sounds (i.e. bells, dog bark)
Sensory aphasia (Wernicke's aphasia)	Auditory	Inability to comprehend speech, although verbal production unimpaired (as opposed to motor or Broca's aphasia, which affects production but not comprehension)
Astereagnosia	Somatosensory	Inability to recognize objects by touch
Autotopagnosia	Somatosensory	Inability to name or localize body parts
Asomatagnosia	Somatosensory	Inability to recognize bodily states
Asymbolia for pain	Somatosensory	Inability to localize or properly react to pain

alternatively, the perceptual effects may be the result of a combination of physiological and experiential processes. Unlike drug and specific sensory damage, the causes of gender and personality differences are harder to specify, although both appear to exist.

GENDER DIFFERENCES

The sex of an individual may partially determine what is perceived in any given stimulus situation. Gender, of course, carries with it many physiological implications. One of the most important involves the chemical differences in the bodies of men and women resulting from the presence of specific male or female hormones. These chemicals are carried in the blood, which infuses and supplies all our sensory receptors, and they even reach many of our most vital neural centers. Thus, it would not be surprising to find that men and women might differ in certain sensory and perceptual capacities.

Examples of sex differences in perceptual effects are found in both taste and olfaction. For instance, women, on average, have more acute senses of smell than men (Money, 1965). This difference seems to be directly attributable to hormonal influences, since the acuity of a female's sense of smell varies within the menstrual cycle, reaching its peak at midcycle when estrogen (one of the major female hormones) levels are at their highest (Mair, Bouffard, Engen, and Morton, 1978). Women whose ovaries are less active than normal have impaired smell sensitivity, but this defect can be remedied by the administration of estrogen. On the other hand, doses of androgen (the male hormone) make the sense of smell less sensitive (Schneider, Costiloe, Howard, and Wolf, 1958).

Some hormonal effects on perception are quite subtle. There is a sex difference in taste preference, with females showing a stronger preference for the sweet taste than males. This is true for rats as well as humans. When the ovaries of female rats are removed, their preference for the sweet taste diminishes, while therapeutic doses of estrogen can restore the taste preference (Zucker, Wade, and Ziegler, 1972). Indirectly, this may also explain reports that women using contraceptive pills (which often contain estrogen) tend to complain that they have a tendency to gain weight and to overeat sweets.

Male-female differences are found in other sensory modalities as well (McGuinness, 1976a). For example, women usually show greater touch sensitivity than do men (Weinstein and Sersen, 1961; Ippolitov, 1972). Measurements of auditory thresholds have demonstrated that, on the average, females show superior sensitivity. This sex difference increases when higher frequencies are used to measure the threshold; it also increases with age (Corso, 1959; McGuinness, 1972; Royster, Royster, and Thomas, 1980). Responses to pain produced by electric shock show that women generally are more sensitive than men. These pain thresholds also seem to vary over the menstrual cycle (Tedford, Warren, and Flynn, 1977).

Sex differences in vision seem to be more complex. Males generally appear to have much better visual acuity under photopic conditions (Burg, 1966; Roberts, 1964), while females have lower thresholds (measurements of the minimum amount of light that can be detected) under scotopic conditions (McGuinness and Lewis, 1976). This sex difference seems to be present from childhood (see McGuinness and Pribram, 1979). Some evidence exists that the visual acuity of women varies with their menstrual cycle (Parlee, 1983). It seems to be poorest just prior to and during menstruation.

The hormone progesterone (another predominantly female hormone) is often prescribed for women who suffer from severe anxiety or depression during menstruation. This hormone relieves these symptoms and also restores visual acuity to its normal level in most patients (Dalton, 1964). When acuity is measured at different spatial frequencies (known as measurements of contrast sensitivity—see Chapter 6), females show greater sensitivity in the low spatial frequency ranges, while males are more sensitive at the high spatial frequencies (McGuinness and Pribram, 1979). Also, there is some suggestion that females tend to dark-adapt more rapidly than males (McGuinness, 1976b).

An interesting and complex sex difference concerns *visual-spatial* abilities, or tasks that involve nonverbal cognitive manipulations. Such tasks seem to produce consistent sex differences favoring males. For example, one of these tasks involves **disembedding**, or the ability to disentangle a target object from a surrounding, and often confusing, context. For example, in Figure 18-6A, you see a figure marked "target" that is hidden, or embedded, in the more complex figure beside it. The observer's task is to find the simple shape as quickly as possible. Such tasks are usually called the **embedded figures test** or the **hidden figures test**. A different spatial task involves the ability to recognize targets when they have been rotated, An example of this task is shown in Figure 18-6B. The observer has to recognize the shape marked "target" from among the three figures next to it. It is often difficult to recognize which shape is exactly the same as the target, since the correct shape has been rotated into a different spatial orientation.

Both these types of tasks produce performance differences favoring males (Maccoby and Jacklin, 1974; Wilson, DeFries, McClearn,

Vandenberg, Johnson, and Rashad, 1975). Males are either more accurate in their responses or show greater speed when completing such tasks (see Harris, 1981). In addition, McGlone (1981) has shown that females approach these tasks differently than do males. Females appear to make more rotational hand movements while completing cognitive rotations than males; in other words, they more frequently need concrete aids for task completion than do males. Demonstration Box 18-2 provides an opportunity for you to test this sex related difference in spatial ability for yourself.

Disembedding a figure, or recognizing it, when it has been rotated in space is a complex task that would seem to involve many learned skills, and would seem to be affected by one's familiarity with such things as maps and blueprints, which might involve the use of similar skills. Thus, it is surprising to find that there is a body of evidence suggesting that some of the same physiological factors distinguishing males from females might be responsible for some portion of these effects. Dawson (1967) used a series of these tests on a number of West African males who suffered from a disease that results in estrogen levels higher than those usually found in males. When tested on a series of spatial tasks, these males showed reduced spatial ability relative to a sample of nonaffected males. Similar effects were found in certain South American tribes, where the males habitually chew the leaves of the coca shrub, thus releasing cocaine, which in turn, tends to decrease the secretion of the male hormone testosterone. Such males tend to show typical signs of feminization (including enlarged breasts, widened hips, softened skin texture, and so on), and also show reduced spatial abilities, similar to those of females. The male hormones seem to have a direct influence on these spatial abilities. Thus, males who

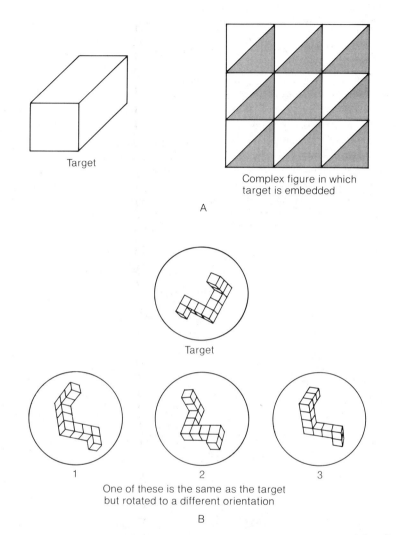

Target

Complex figure in which
target is embedded

A

Target

1   2   3

One of these is the same as the target
but rotated to a different orientation

B

Figure 18-6. (A) An embedded figures test in which the target is found in the more complex array. (B) A mental rotation test in which the *target is found as one of the three test figures but is in a different orientation.*

are insensitive to androgen also show reduced spatial abilities, while females with high androgen levels show greater spatial ability (Masica, Money, Ehrhardt, and Lewis, 1969; Peterson, 1976).

Other physiological factors also have been proposed to account for the performance dif-

ferences on such spatial tasks. One suggestion is that spatial abilities may be influenced by a sex-linked gene (Bock and Kolakowski, 1973; Yen, 1975). In addition, the rate at which individuals mature seems to play a role. In this case "maturing" means showing their secondary sexual characteristics. Typically, late

Demonstration Box 18-2. Gender differences in mental rotation

For this demonstration you will need a stopwatch or a wristwatch that allows you to read seconds (either with a sweep hand or digitally). You will also need a couple of male and female friends. Test them one at a time. First show them what is meant by a mental rotation task by using Figure 18-6A. If they have difficulty, point out that only stimulus 3 can be rotated to be identical to the target, while the other two are differently shaped figures. Next, tell your observers that they will see another target figure and a set of 12 test figures. Five of the test figures are identical in shape to the target figures, and their task is to pick out those 5 as quickly as possible. Start your watch, show them the figure, and time how long it takes for them to find the five correct ones. If they get any wrong, tell them, but keep the time going until all 5 are found. The correct answers are on the bottom of page 512.

You should notice that on average females will take longer at this task than do males. Another interesting observation should be that females are more likely to perceive the task as being difficult, as indicated by comments like "I can never do this sort of thing" or "I'm terrible at this" and so forth.

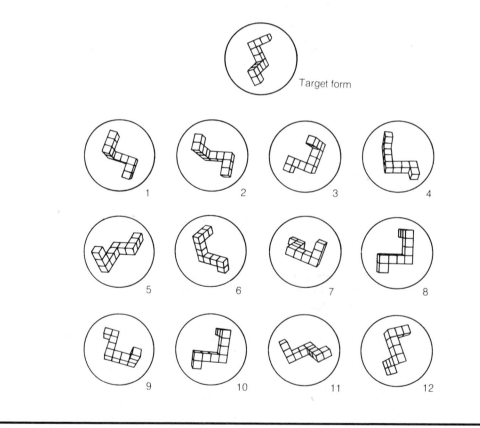

maturing individuals are better on such spatial tasks than early maturing individuals (Waber, 1976, 1977).

We have been dealing only with some of the physical variables that seem to produce different patterns of perceptual abilities in males and females. Of course, there will be many factors relating to experience, life history, and cultural influences that will also affect perceptual behaviors. As we discussed in Chapter 17, many aspects of perception are subject to learning influences. Research has shown that even at an early age males and females may differ in the types of tasks and activities in which they engage and also in the tools, implements, and utensils that they use in their everyday activities (see Harris, 1981). These factors can also influence some aspects of perception. The learning approach to gender differences in information processing has been studied by Bem (1981). She had observers fill out a questionnaire that measured the degree to which males and females consider themselves to be "a typical male or female" or "androgynous" (a mixture of typical male and female behaviors). She then had these same observers attempt to recognize and recall words. These words were classified as either characteristically female (for example "blushing"), male (such as "hurling"), or neutral (like "stepping"). Those individuals who had the strongest identification with male or female behaviors tended to group the items together according to these gender classifications at the time of recall much more than the individuals who were apparently more androgynous. Bem (1981) argues that we learn to identify ourselves strongly with one of the genders, or we learn to identify ourselves as a mixture (androgynous), perhaps because of parental and societal attitudes and actions. We, then, process information through this *gender schema* which which in turn, leads to cognitive differences related to gender differ-

ences. Demonstration Box 18-3 provides a perceptual recognition task that occasionally produces different responses from males and females. The task in the demonstration shows differences that are likely to have an experiential rather than a physiological basis.

PERSONALITY AND COGNITIVE STYLE DIFFERENCES

There are a myriad of nonperceptual ways in which individuals differ from one another. Some people are outgoing and sociable; others are withdrawn and prefer to be alone. Some are careful and methodical in everything; others are haphazard and unsystematic. The total of all these behavior traits composes the individual's personality. People with different personalities tend to behave differently in many social situations and tend to respond differently to information of various sorts. Do they also perceive the world differently?

There have been many attempts to link individual differences in personality to individual differences in perception. Often the perceptual responses themselves are used to classify individuals as belonging to one personality type or another. For instance, some evidence indicates that *embedded figure tasks* (such as the one that we discussed above, and illustrated in Figure 18-6A) not only separate individuals according to their spatial abilities, but also separate individuals according to underlying personality type. Observers who have difficulty with this task are called **field dependent**. They have been classified by personality tests as being socially dependent, eager to make a good impression, conforming, and sensitive to their social surroundings (Konstadt and Forman, 1965; Linton and Graham, 1959; Ruble and Nakamura, 1972). Individuals who have

Demonstration Box 18-3. Sex differences and object identification

Look at the three accompanying figures and decide what each looks like. Do this before reading any further.

Responses to patterns similar to these show differences depending on the sex of the observer. Most males view Figure (A) as a brush or a centipede, while females tend to view it as a comb or teeth. Most men view (B) as a target, while women tend to view it as a dinner plate (but both respond equally with ring and tire). Most men see Figure (C) as a head, while women tend to view it as a cup.

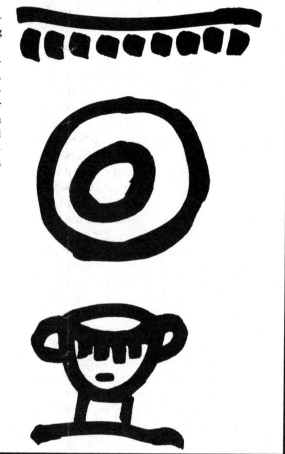

little difficulty with such perceptual disembedding tasks are called **field independent** people. They have been characterized by the same tests as being self-reliant, inner-directed, and individualistic (Alexander and Gudeman, 1965; Crutchfield, Woodworth, and Albrecht, 1958; Klein, 1970). Witkin has been one of the major proponents of this approach. He and his associates look upon both the personality and perceptual effects as examples of an individual's

cognitive style (Witkin and Berry, 1975). They maintain that perceptual, cognitive, personality, and social interactions are affected by the same set of processes that determine how a person approaches the world. In effect, cognitive style is part of what we call in everyday language "lifestyle," affecting not only our habitual interpersonal and task oriented behaviors, but also the way in which we process information and, in effect, the way in which

Answers to Demonstration Box 18-2: 3, 6, 7, 9, 11

we perceive the world. Thus, by measuring how you normally respond in complex perceptual situations, we can predict how you will approach many other, nonperceptual, aspects of your life.

While some investigators use perception as the starting point to make predictions about personality, others have attempted to go in the opposite direction, predicting individual differences in perception from prior considerations of personality theory. Characteristic of this approach is the work first started by Eysenck (1967). He divided individuals into two groups on the basis of whether they were outgoing and sociable (**extroverts**) or more withdrawn and self-contained (**introverts**). Eysenck found that he could classify individuals along this dimension on the basis of a simple questionnaire, and he speculated on some physiological differences that might account for the differences in personality traits. He suggested that extroverts have a neural system that is slower to respond and more weakly aroused by stimuli than that of introverts. In addition, they generate neural inhibition more quickly. If this physiological speculation is correct, then we can expect introverts to be more perceptually sensitive than extroverts.

Several studies have investigated the effect of introversion-extroversion on perception. Introverts seem to have more sensitive perceptual systems as predicted by the theory. They show lower average thresholds for vision (Siddle, Morrish, White, and Mangen, 1969), hearing (Stelmack and Campbell, 1974), touch (Coles, Gale, and Kline, 1971), and pain (Halsam, 1967). In addition, introverts have been shown to be better at tasks requiring sustained attention or vigilance (Harkins and Geen, 1975).

When studying the effects of personality factors on perception, it is important to be sure that we are measuring perceptual sensitivity rather than simply detecting differences in how observers respond. It could be the case that introverts simply say "Yes, I detected the stimulus" more often than extroverts. Signal Detection Theory (discussed in Chapter 2) allows us to separate these possibilities. When Stelmack and Campbell (1974) analyzed their data from this viewpoint, they found that introverts have more sensitive hearing than extroverts, even though extroverts are more biased toward saying "yes."

Another way to ascertain sensitivity independent of the observer's response bias is to use direct physiological measurements. One technique is called **evoked response recording**. An electrode is placed on an observer's head over the region of the cortex receiving the primary sensory information for the sense modality being tested. Another electrode, elsewhere on the body, serves as a reference electrode. Any changes in the electrical activity of this brain region can be picked up by sensitive recording devices, and such activity presumably means that the sensory information has, at least, been registered in the brain. In this way, Stelmack, Achorn, and Michaud (1977) demonstrated that introverts seem to have greater auditory sensitivity than extroverts. Unfortunately, not all researchers have been able to verify these findings (Campbell, Baribeau-Braun, and Braun, 1981). This may mean that nonsensory factors, such as motivation or distribution of attention, or even the sort of cognitive style that we discussed above, may account for the differences between introverts and extroverts on sensory tasks, rather than direct neurological differences.

It is surprising nonetheless that the answers to a few questions about how a person interacts with other individuals can predict how one person's perceptual responses may differ from those of another. Demonstration Box 18-4 allows you to estimate your own degree

---

Demonstration Box 18-4. Introversion-extroversion and taste perception

It is easy to determine your own standing on introversion versus extroversion by answering the following questions with a "yes" or a "no."

(1) Do you often wish for more excitement in life?

(2) Do you often say things without stopping to think?

(3) Do you like going out a lot?

(4) Do other people think of you as being lively?

(5) Do you like interacting with people?

If you answered all the questions "yes," you are rather extroverted, while if you answered them all "no," you are rather introverted.

Have some friends and/or relatives answer these questions, but add one additional item to the list.

(6) Do you like spicy foods?

What answer do you expect extroverts versus introverts to give? What *sensory data* would lead you to expect that answer?

---

of introversion and extroversion, and to test a typical perceptual preference for yourself.

Since personality factors found in the general population can affect the processing of sensory information, it is not surprising that there are dramatic perceptual effects associated with certain severe personality disorders. The perceptual responses that differentiate schizophrenic from nonschizophrenic observers is one area that has received a great amount of research attention. **Schizophrenia** (from the Greek for "split mind") is the most frequent diagnosis of a severe or *psychotic* personality disorder. It is usually characterized by a withdrawal from the environment, reduced levels of emotional response, a reduction in abstract thinking, and a general diminishing of daily activity. In other words, schizophrenia is a disorder that affects all aspects of one's social and cognitive life. Studies of the perceptual responses of schizophrenics have shown that they differ from control groups in their performance on time estimation (Wahl and Sieg, 1980), attentional tasks (Cegalis and Deptula, 1981), and even on the

perception of visual aftereffects (Tress and Kugler, 1979). Several studies have shown also that schizophrenics display eye movement patterns that differ from control groups; they perform poorly when they are asked to track a moving target with their eyes (Iacono, Peloquin, Lumry, Valentine, and Tuason, 1982; Levin, Lipton, and Holzman, 1981). Since poor eye tracking behavior is also found in the close relatives of schizophrenics (those who are not affected with the disorder), it has been suggested that eye movement behavior may be a genetic marker for the disorder (Iacono et al., 1982). This suggests that perceptual behavior can be used as an indicator of the presence of underlying processes that could promote personality disorders.

Overall, who you are, the kind of person that you are, and your life history all affect what you perceive in any stimulus situation. Since you differ along these dimensions from those around you, your perception of the world has a unique flavor. What you percieve in any situation is not neccessarily the same as that perceived by the person next to you.

GLOSSARY

The following definitions are specific to this book.

Agnosia A pathological condition where an individual can no longer attach meaning to a sensory impression.

Aphasia A perceptual disorder usually resulting in difficulties involving speech and sound recognition.

Auditory flutter fusion The rate of interruption of a continuous tone at which an observer first hears a continuous sound.

Autotopagnosia Distorted perception of body image and body parts.

Cognitive style The overall personality and perceptual predispositions that are characteristics of a particular individual.

Critical flicker fusion frequency The minimum cyclic rate of a flickering light that is perceived as continuous.

Disembedding The ability to disentangle a target object from a surrounding, and often confusing, context.

Embedded figures test A task used to determine spatial abilities, in which a subject is asked to find a simple shape hidden in a more complex figure.

Evoked response An electrical response in the brain brought on by presentation of a stimulus.

Extrovert An outgoing and sociable person.

Field dependent Individuals exhibiting difficulty with embedded figures tasks.

Field independent Individuals exhibiting little difficulty with embedded figures tasks.

Hidden figures test *See* Embedded figures test.

Introvert A withdrawn and self-contained person.

Prosopagnosia A perceptual disorder in which an individual cannot recognize human faces.

Schizophrenia A psychotic disorder characterized by withdrawal from the environment, reduced levels of emotional response, a reduction in abstract thinking, and a general diminishing in daily activity.

Simultagnosia An attentional disorder in which an individual cannot pay attention to more than one stimulus at a time.

Spatial agnosia A perceptual disorder in which individuals cannot accurately localize objects or themselves.

Visual object agnosia An inability to recognize familiar objects in the absence of organic or psychopathological damage to the visual apparatus.

Epilog

"Am I real?" she asked.

The soft sound of her voice caused his head to turn.

"I hear you," he said.

"Am I really here?" she asked.

He turned his eyes in her direction.

"I see you," he said.

"Am I still alive?" she asked.

He reached out and touched the soft surface of her lips.

"You feel warm," he said.

"Am I truly beautiful to you?" she asked.

He inhaled the soft fragrance of her familiar perfume.

"You are real," he said, and knew it was true.

Poets and scientists alike recognize that the only way that we learn about any of the realities in our environment is through our senses. We have no other windows to the world, no other means of assessing truth or falsity than the evidence of sight, hearing, touch, taste, and smell. We have tried to escort you on an intellectual and scientific survey of the capabilities and limitations of your sensory and perceptual systems and have shown that there are many steps involved in the process of translating a physical stimulus in your environment into a perceptual event in your consciousness. You now know that the senses do not merely "take snapshots" of the outside world and present them to your waiting consciousness. Sometimes the "reality" in consciousness is not the same as the "reality" in the physical world.

We hope that we have shaken you out of the "common sense" belief in the nature of sensory information so eloquently stated by Thomas Reid in 1785, when he wrote:

By all the laws of all nations, in the most solemn judicial trials, wherein men's fortunes and lives are at stake, the sentence passes according to the testimony of eye and ear, witnesses of good credit. An upright judge will give a fair hearing to every objection that can be made to the integrity of a witness, and allow it to be possible that he may be corrupted; but no judge will ever suppose that witnesses may be imposed upon by trusting to their eyes and ears. And if a skeptical counsel should ever plead against the testimony of the witnesses, that they had no other evidence for what

517

they declared than the testimony of their eyes and ears, and that we ought not to put so much faith in our senses as to deprive men of life or fortune upon their testimony, surely no upright judge would admit a plea of this kind. I believe that no counsel, however skeptical, ever dared to offer such an argument; and, if it were offered, it would be rejected with disdain (Essay 2, Chapter 5).

By now you should know that a percept and an object are two different things. We do not perceive what is "out there," rather we perceive what is "in here." Our senses can only inform us of their own status. They can inform us of the electrical status of neurons or the physical or the chemical status of receptors. The outside world is never taken into our consciousness. The outside world is rather our own creation, psychologically synthesized from the mass of sensations that envelop us.

In many respects, the ultimate question that perception must ask was stated by John Stuart Mill in 1865. He asked, "What is it we mean, or what is it which leads us to say, that the objects we perceive are external to us, and not a part of our own thoughts?" That remains, perhaps, the ultimate, unresolved perceptual puzzle.

References

Aantaa, E. (1970). Light-induced and spontaneous variations in the amplitude of the electro-oculogram. *Acta Otolaryngologica, Supplementum,* 267.

Abbs, J. H., & Sussman, H. M. (1971). Neurophysiological feature detectors and speech perception: Discussion of theoretical implications. *Journal of Speech and Hearing Research, 14,* 23–36.

Abramov, I., Gordon, J., Hendrickson, A., Hainline, L., Dobson, V., & LaBossiere, E. (1982). The retina of the newborn human infant. *Science, 217,* 265–267.

Abravanel, E. (1981). Integrating the information from eyes and hands: A developmental account. In R. D. Walk & H. L. Pick, Jr. (Eds.), *Intersensory perception and sensory integration.* New York: Plenum.

Adam, N., Rosner, B. S., Hosick, E. C., & Clark, D. L. (1971). Effect of anesthetic drugs on time production and alpha rhythm. *Perception & Psychophysics, 10,* 133–136.

Adams, A. S., Brown, B., Haegerstrom-Portnoy, G., & Flom, M. C. (1976). Evidence for acute effects of alcohol and marijuana on color discrimination. *Perception & Psychophysics, 20,* 119–124.

Adams, J. A. (1977). Feedback theory of how joint receptors regulate the timing and positioning of a limb. *Psychological Review, 84,* 503–523.

Akil, H., & Watson, S. J. (1980). The role of endogenous opiates in pain control. In H. W. Kosterlitz & L. Y. Terenius (Eds.), *Pain and society* (pp. 201–222). Weinheim: Verlag Chemie Gmblt.

Alexander, J. B., & Gudeman, H. E. (1965). Personal and interpersonal measures of field dependence. *Perceptual and Motor Skills, 20,* 70–86.

Alexander, K. R., & Shansky, M. S. (1976). Influence of hue, value, and chroma on the perceived heaviness of colours. *Perception & Psychophysics, 19,* 72–74.

Allan, L. G. (1979). The perception of time. *Perception & Psychophysics, 26,* 340–354.

Allison, A. C. (1953). The structure of the olfactory bulb and its relation to the olfactory pathways in the rabbit and the rat. *Journal of Comparative Neurology, 98,* 309–348.

Ames, A., Jr. (1951). Visual perception and the rotating trapezoid window. *Psychological Monographs, 65,* (14, Whole No. 324).

Amoore, J. E. (1969). A plan to identify most of the primary odors. In C. Pfaffman (Ed.), *Olfaction and taste III* (pp. 158–171). New York: The Rockefeller University Press.

Amoore, J. E. (1970). *Molecular basis of odor.* Springfield, IL: Thomas.

Amoore, J. E. (1975). Four primary odor modalities of man: Experimental evidence and possible significance. In D. A. Denton & J. P. Coghlan (Eds.), *Olfaction and taste V* (pp. 283–289). New York: Academic Press.

Amoore, J. E., Johnston, J. W., Jr., & Rubin, M. (1964). The stereochemical theory of odor. *Scientific American, 210,* 42–49.

Amoore, J. E., Pelosi, P., & Forrester, L. J. (1977). Specific anosmias to 5α-androst-16 en-3 one and w-pentadecaloctone: The urinous and musky odors. *Chemical Senses and Flavor, 5,* 401–425.

Amure, B. O. (1978). Nicotine and decay of the McCollough effect. *Vision Research, 18,* 1449–1451.

Anderson, N. H. (1970a). Averaging model applied to the size-weight illusion. *Perception & Psychophysics, 77,* 153–170.

Anderson, N. H. (1970b). Functional measurement and psychophysical judgment. *Psychological Review, 77,* 153–170.

Anderson, N. H. (1975). On the role of context effects in psychophysical judgment. *Psychological Review, 82,* 462–482.

Anderson, N. S., & Fitts, P. M. (1958). Amount of information gained during brief exposures of numerals and colors. *Journal of Experimental Psychology, 56,* 362–369.

Andrews, B. W., & Pollen, D. A. (1979). Relationship between spatial frequency selectivity and receptive field profile of simple cells. *Journal of Physiology, 287,* 163–176.

Annis, R. C., & Frost, B. (1973). Human visual ecology and orientation anisotropies in acuity. *Science, 182,* 729–731.

Anstis, S., Rogers, B., & Henry, J. (1978). Interactions between simultaneous contrast and colored afterimages. *Vision Research, 18,* 899–911.

Antes, J. R. (1974). The time course of picture viewing. *Journal of Experimental Psychology, 103,* 62–70.

Antes, J., & Penland, J. (1981). Picture context effects on eye movement patterns. In D. Fisher, R. Monty, & J. Senders (Eds.), *Eye movements: Cognition and visual perception* (pp. 157–170). Hillsdale, NJ: Lawrence Erlbaum Associates.

Arvidson, K., & Friberg, U. (1980). Human taste response and taste bud number in fungiform papillae. *Science, 209,* 807–808.

Aslin, R. N. (1981). Development of smooth pursuit in human infants. In D. Fisher, R. Monty, & J. Senders (Eds.), *Eye movements: Cognition and visual perception* (pp. 31–51). Hillsdale, NJ: Lawrence Erlbaum Associates.

Aslin, R. N. (1981). Experiential influences and sensitive periods in perceptual development: A unified model. In R. N. Aslin, J. R. Alberts, & M. R. Petersen (Eds.), *Development of perception: Psychobiological perspectives: Vol. 2. The visual system* (pp. 45–93). New York: Academic Press.

Aslin, R. N., & Dumais, S. (1980). Binocular vision in infants: A review and a theoretical framework. In H. Reese and L. Lipsett (Eds.), *Advances in child development and behavior* (Vol. 15). New York: Academic Press.

Atkinson, J. (1979). Development of optokinetic nystagmus in the human infant and monkey infant: An analogue to development in kittens. In R. D. Freeman (Ed.), *Developmental neurobiology of vision.* New York: Plenum.

Atkinson, J., & Braddick, O. (1981). Acuity, contrast sensitivity and accommodation in infancy. In R. N. Aslin, J. R. Alberts, & M. R. Petersen (Eds.), *Development of perception: Psychobiological perspectives: Vol. 2. The visual system* (pp. 243–278). New York: Academic Press.

Atkinson, J., Braddick, O., & French, J. (1979). Contrast sensitivity of the human neonate measured by the visual evoked potential. *Investigative Ophthalmology and Visual Sciences, 18,* 210–213.

Atkinson, W. H. (1976). Electrophysiological evidence for Stevens' power law at the medial geniculate of the cat. *Brain Research, 19,* 175–178.

Atkinson, W. H. (1978). Click-evoked response at the superior colliculus of the cat. *Experimental Neurology, 62,* 501–509.

Atkinson, W. H. (1982). A general equation for sensory magnitude. *Perception & Psychophysics, 31,* 26–40.

Attneave, F. (1954). Some informational aspects of visual perception. *Psychological Review, 61,* 183–193.

Attneave, F. (1955). Symmetry, information and memory for patterns. *American Journal of Psychology, 68,* 209–222.

Aubert, H. (1886). Die Bewegungsempfindung. *Archiv fuer die Gesamte Physiologie des Menschen and der Tiere, 39,* 347–370.

Augenstine, L. G. (1962). A model of how humans process information. *Biometrics, 18,* 420–421.

Avant, L. L. (1965). Vision in the Ganzfeld. *Psychological Bulletin, 64,* 246–258.

Avant, L. L., & Lyman, P. J. (1975). Stimulus familiarity modifies perceived duration in prerecognition visual processing. *Journal of Experimental Psychology: Human Perception and Performance, 1,* 205–213.

Avant, L. L., Lyman, P. J., & Antes, J. R. (1975). Effects of stimulus familiarity upon judged visual duration. *Perception & Psychophysics, 17,* 253–262.

Baddeley, A. D. (1966). Time estimation at reduced body temperature. *American Journal of Psychology, 79,* 475–479.

Baird, J. C., Green, D. M., & Luce, R. D. (1980). Variability and sequential effects in cross modality matching of area and loudness. *Journal of Experimental Psychology: Human Perception and Performance, 6,* 277–289.

Baird, J. C., Lewis, C., & Romer, D. (1970). Relative frequencies of numerical responses in ratio estimation. *Perception & Psychophysics, 8,* 358–362.

Baird, J. C., & Noma, E. (1978). *Fundamentals of scaling and psychophysics.* New York: Wiley.

Ball, K., & Sekuler, R. (1980). Human vision favors centrifugal motion. *Perception, 9,* 317–325.

Ball, W., & Vurpillot, E. (1976). La perception du mouvement en profondur chez le nourrisson. *L'Annee Psychologique, 67,* 393–400.

Bannatyne, A. (1971). *Language, reading and learning disabilities.* Springfield, IL: Thomas.

Barbeito, R. (1981). Sighting dominance: An explanation based on the processing of visual direction in tests of sighting dominance. *Vision Research, 21,* 855–860.

Barclay, C. D., Cutting, J. E., & Kozlowski, L. T. (1978). Temporal and spatial factors in gait perception that influence gender recognition. *Perception & Psychophysics, 23,* 145–152.

Bartleson, C. J. (1960). Memory colors of familiar objects. *Journal of the Optical Society of America, 50,* 73–77.

Bartoshuk, L. M. (1974). Taste illusions: Some demonstrations. *Annals of the New York Academy of Sciences, 237,* 279–285.

Bartoshuk, L. M. (1978). Gustatory system. In R. B. Masterton (Ed.), *Handbook of behavioral neurobiology: Vol. I. Sensory integration.* New York: Plenum.

Bartoshuk, L. M. (1979). Bitter taste of saccharine related to the genetic ability to taste the bitter substance 6-n-propythiouracil, *Science, 205,* 934–935.

Batteau, D. W. (1967). The role of the pinna in human localization. *Proceedings of the Royal Society of London, Series B, 168,* 158–180.

Beatty, J. (1982). Task-evoked pupillary responses, processing load, and the structure of processing resources. *Psychological Bulletin, 91,* 276–292.

Beck, J. (1965). Apparent spatial position and the perception of lightness. *Journal of Experimental Psychology, 69,* 170–179.

Beck, J., & Schwartz, T. (1979). Verner acuity with dot test objects. *Vision Research, 19,* 313–319.

Beck, N. C., & Siegel, L. J. (1980). Preparation for childbirth and contemporary research on pain, anxiety, and stress reduction: A review and critique. *Psychosomatic Medicine, 42,* 429–447.

Begg, I. S., & Lakowski, R. (1980). A comparison of color vision with other methods of clinical assessment in diabetics with macular oedema. In *Colour vision deficiencies V* (pp. 295–298). Bristol: Adam Hilger.

Begleiter, H., Porjesz, B., & Chou, C. L. (1981). Auditory brain-stem potentials in chronic alcoholics. *Science, 211,* 1064–1066.

Beidler, L.M., & Smallman, R.L. (1965). Renewal of cells within taste buds. *Journal of Cell Biology, 27,* 263–272.

Békésy, G. von. (1947). A new audiometer. *Acta Otolaryngologica, 35,* 411–422.

Békésy, G. von. (1959). Synchronism of neural discharges and their demultiplication in pitch perception on the skin and in learning. *Journal of the Acoustical Society of America, 31,* 338–349.

Békésy, G. von. (1960). *Experiments in hearing.* New York: McGraw-Hill.

Békésy, G. von. (1967). *Sensory inhibition.* Princeton, NJ: Princeton University Press.

Bem, S. L. (1981). Gender schema theory: A cognitive account of sex typing. *Psychological Review, 88,* 354–364.

Berkley, M. A. (1982). Neural substrates of the visual perception of movement. In A. H. Wertheim, W. A. Wagenaar, & H. W. Leibowitz (Eds.), *Tutorials on motion perception* (pp. 201–229). New York: Plenum.

Berlin, B., & Kay, P. (1969). *Basic color terms.* Berkeley: University of California Press.

Berry, J. W. (1971). Mueller-Lyer susceptibility: Culture, ecology, race? *International Journal of Psychology, 6,* 193–197.

Berthenthal, B., & Fischer, K. (1978). Development of self-recognition in the infant. *Developmental Psychology, 14,* 44–50.

Besser, G. (1966). Centrally acting drugs and auditory flutter. In A. Herxheimer (Ed.), *Proceedings of the Symposium on Drugs and Sensory Functions* (pp. 199–200). London: S. S. Churchill.

Bhatia, B. (1975). Minimum separable as function of speed of a moving object. *Vision Research, 15,* 23–33.

Billings, B. L., & Stokinger, T. E. (1977). Investigation of several aspects of low-frequency (200 Hz) central masking. *Journal of the Acoustical Society of America, 61,* 1260–1263.

Birren, J., Woods, A., & Williams, M. (1980). Behavioral slowing with age: Causes, organization, and consequences. In L. Poon (Ed.), *Aging in the 1980s* (pp. 293–308). Washington, DC: American Psychological Association.

Blake, R. (1981). Strategies for assessing visual deficits in animals with selective neural deficits. In. R. N. Aslin, J. R. Alberts, & M. R. Petersen (Eds.), *Development of perception: Vol. 2. The visual system.* New York: Academic Press.

Blake, R., & Cormack, R. (1979). On utrocular discrimination. *Perception & Psychophysics, 26,* 53–68.

Blakemore, C. (1975). Central visual processing. In M. S. Gazzaniga & C. Blakemore (Eds.), *Handbook of psychobiology* (pp. 241–268). New York: Academic Press.

Blakemore, C. (1978). Maturation and modification in the developing visual system. In R. Held, M. W. Leibowitz, & H. L. Teuber (Eds.), *Handbook of sensory physiology: Vol. VIII. Perception* (pp. 377–436). New York: Springer-Verlag.

Blakemore, C., Carpenter, R. H. S., & Georgeson, M. A. (1970). Lateral inhibition between orientation detectors in the human visual system. *Nature (London), 228,* 37–39.

Blakemore, C., & Van Sluyters, R. C. (1975). Innate and environmental factors in the development of the kitten's visual cortex. *Journal of Physiology, 248,* 633–716.

Blakeslee, A. F., & Salmon, T. H. (1935). Genetics of sensory thresholds: Individual taste reactions for different substances. *Proceedings of the National Academy of Sciences of the U.S.A., 21,* 84–90.

Blazynski, C., & Ostroy, S. E. (1981). Dual pathways in the photolysis of rhodopsin: Studies using a direct chemical method. *Vision Research, 21,* 833–841.

Bliss, J. C., Katcher, M. H., Rogers, C.H., & Shepard, R. P. (1970). Optical-to-tactile image conversion for the blind. *IEEE Transactions on Man-Machine Systems, 11,* 58–65.

Block, R. A., George, E.J., & Reed, M. A. (1980). A watched pot sometimes boils: A study of duration experience. *Acta Psychologica, 46,* 81–94.

Bock, R. D., & Kolakowski, D. (1973). Further evidence of sex-linked major gene influence on human spatial visualizing ability. *American Journal of Human Genetics, 25,* 1–14.

Boer, L., & Keuss, P. (1982). Global precedence as a post perceptual effect: An analysis of speed accuracy trade-off functions. *Perception & Psychophysics, 31,* 358–366.

Bolton, T. L. (1894). Rhythm. *American Journal of Psychology, 6,* 145–238.

Borg, G., Diamant, H., Oakley, B., Strom, L., & Zotterman, Y. (1967). A comparative study of neural and psychophysical responses to gustatory stimuli. In T. Hayashi (Ed.), *Olfaction and taste II* (pp. 253–264). Oxford: Pergamon Press.

Boring, E. G. (1953). The role of theory in experimental psychology. *American Journal of Psychology, 66,* 169–184.

Boring, E. G. (1970). Attention: Research beliefs concerning the conception in scientific psychology before 1930. In D. I. Mostofsky (Ed.), *Attention: Contemporary theory and analysis* (pp. 5–8). New York: Appleton-Century-Crofts.

Bornstein, M. H. (1973). Color vision and color naming: A psychophysiological hypothesis of cultural difference. *Psychological Bulletin, 80,* 257–285.

Bornstein, M. H. (1975). The influence of visual perception on culture. *American Anthropologist, 77,* 774–798.

Bornstein, M. H. (1976). Infants are trichomats. *Journal of Experimental Child Psychology, 21,* 425–445.

Bornstein, M. H. (1977). Developmental pseudocyanapsia: Ontogenetic change in human color vision. *American Journal of Optometry and Physiological Optics, 54,* 464–469.

Bornstein, M. H. (1978). Chromatic vision in infancy. In H. Reese & L. Lipsitt (Eds.), *Advances in child development and behavior* (Vol. 12). New York: Academic Press.

Bornstein, M. H. (1981). Two kinds of perceptual organization near the beginning of life. In W. Collins (Ed.), *Aspects of the development of competence.* Hillsdale, NJ: Lawrence Erlbaum Associates.

Bornstein, M. H., Kessen, W., & Weiskopf, S. (1976). Color vision and hue categorization in young human infants. *Journal of Experimental Psychology: Human Perception and Performance, 2,* 115–129.

Bornstein, M. H., & Monroe, M. D. (1978). Color-naming evidence for tritan vision in the fovea. *American Journal of Optometry and Physiological Optics, 55,* 627–630.

Bossom, J., & Ommaya, A. K. (1968). Visuo-motor adaptation (to prismatic transformation of the retinal image) in monkeys with bilateral dorsal rhizotomy. *Brain, 91,* 161–172.

Bowen, R. W. (1981). Latencies for chromatic and achromatic visual mechanisms. *Vision Research, 2,* 1457–1466.

Bowker, D. O., & Mandler, M. B. (1981). Apparent contrast of suprathreshold gratings varies with stimulus orientation. *Perception & Psychophysics, 29,* 585–588.

Bowmaker, J. K., & Dartnall, H. M. A. (1980). Visual pigments of rods and cones in a human retina. *Journal of Physiology, 298,* 501–511.

Boyd, I. A., & Roberts, T. D. M. (1953). Proprioceptive discharges from the stretch receptors in the knee-joint of the cat. *Journal of Physiology (London), 122,* 38–58.

Boynton, R. M. (1971). Color vision. In J. W. Kling, & L. A. Riggs (Eds.), *Woodworth and Schlossberg's experimental psychology* (3rd ed., pp. 315–368). New York: Holt, Rinehart & Winston.

Boynton, R. M. (1978). Ten years of research with the minimally distinct border. In J. C. Armington, J. Krauskopf, & B. R. Wooten (Eds.), *Visual psychophysics and physiology: A volume dedicated to Lorrin Riggs* (pp. 193–207). New York: Academic Press.

Boynton, R. M. (1979). *Human color vision.* New York: Holt, Rinehart & Winston.

Boynton, R. M., & Gordon, J. (1965). Bezold-Brucke hue shift measured by color-naming technique. *Journal of the Optical Society of America, 55,* 78–86.

Braddick, O., & Atkinson, J. (1979). Accommodation and acuity in the human infant. In R. D. Freeman (Ed.), *Developmental neurobiology of vision* (pp. 289–300). New York: Plenum.

Braddick, O., Atkinson, J., Julesz, B., Kropfl, W., Bodis-Wollner, I., & Raab, E. (1980). Cortical binocularity in infants. *Nature, 288,* 363–365.

Braff, D. L., Silverton, L., Saccuzzo, & Janowski, D. S. (1981). Impaired speed of visual information processing in marihuana intoxication. *American Journal of Psychiatry, 138,* 1051–1056.

Brazelton, T., Scholl, M., & Robey, J. (1966). Visual responses in the newborn. *Pediatrics, 37,* 284–290.

Brillat-Savarin, J. A. (1971). *The physiology of taste: Or meditations on transcendental gastronomy* (M. K. F. Fisher, Trans.). New York: Knopf. (Original work published 1825)

Broadbent, D. E. (1954). The role of auditory localization and attention in memory span. *Journal of Experimental Psychology, 47,* 191–196.

Broadbent, D. E. (1958). *Perception and communication.* London: Pergamon Press.

Broadbent, D. E., & Gregory, M. (1963). Vigilance considered as a statistical decision. *British Journal of Psychology, 54,* 309–323.

Broadbent, D. E., & Gregory, M. (1965). Effects of noise and of signal rate upon vigilance analyzed by means of decision theory. *Human Factors, 7,* 155–162.

Brodmann, K. (1914). Physiologie des gehirng. In F. Krause (Ed.), *Allsemaie chirurgie der gehirnkankheiten*. Stuttgart: F. Enke.

Brown, B. (1972). Resolution thresholds for moving targets at the fovea and in the peripheral retina. *Vision Research, 12*, 293–304.

Brown, E. L., & Deffenbacher, K. (1979). *Perception and the senses*. New York: Oxford University Press.

Brown, P. E. (1972). Use of acupuncture in major surgery. *Lancet, 1*, 1328–1330.

Brown, P. K., & Wald, G. (1964). Visual pigments in single rods and cones of the human retina. *Science, 144*, 45–52.

Brown, R. E. (1979). Mammalian social odors: A critical review. *Advances in the Study of Behavior, 10*, 103–162.

Brown, T. S. (1975). General biology of sensory systems. In B. Scharf (Ed.), *Experimental sensory psychology* (pp. 69–111). Glenview, IL: Scott, Foresman.

Brown, W. (1910). The judgment of difference. *University of California, Berkeley, Publications in Psychology, 1*, 1–71.

Bruce, C., Desimone, R., & Gross, C. G. (1981). Visual properties of neurons in a polysensory area in superior temporal sulcus of the macaque. *Journal of Neurophysiology, 46*, 369–384.

Bruner, J. S. (1957). Going beyond the information given. In J. S. Bruner et al., (Eds.), *Contemporary approaches to cognition: The Colorado symposium*. Cambridge, MA: Harvard University Press.

Bruner, J. S., Postman, L., & Rodrigues, J. (1951). Expectations and the perception of color. *American Journal of Psychology, 64*, 216–227.

Brunswick, E. (1952). The conceptual framework of psychology. *International Encyclopedia of Unified Science, 1*, No. 10.

Brunswick, E. (1955). Representative design and probabilistic theory in a functional psychology. *Psychological Review, 62*, 193–217.

Brunswick, E. (1956). *Perception as a representative design of psychological experiments*. Berkeley: University of California Press.

Buckhout, R. (1976). Eyewitness testimony. In R. Held & W. Richards (Eds.), *Recent progress in perception* (pp. 205–213). San Francisco: Freeman.

Buffardi, L. (1971). Factors affecting the filled-duration illusion in the auditory, tactual, and visual modalities. *Perception & Psychophysics, 10*, 292–294.

Buffart, H., Leeuwenberg, E., & Restle, F. (1981). Coding theory of visual pattern completion. *Journal of Experimental Psychology: Human Perception and Performance, 7*, 241–274.

Burg, A. (1966). Visual acuity as measured by dynamic and static tests: A comparative evaluation. *Journal of Applied Psychology, 50*, 460–466.

Burns, B. D., & Pritchard, R. (1971). Geometrical illusions and the response of neurones in the cat's visual cortex to angle patterns. *Journal of Physiology (London), 213*, 599–616.

Burns, E. M. (1981). Circularity in relative pitch judgments for inharmonic complex tones: The shepard demonstrations revisited, again. *Perception & Psychophysics, 30*, 467–472.

Burnside, W. (1971). Judgment of short-time-intervals while performing mathematical tasks. *Perception & Psychophysics, 9*, 404–406.

Bushnell, E. (1979). *Visual-tactual knowledge in infancy*. Unpublished dissertation, University of Minnesota.

Bushnell, E. (1981). The ontogeny of intermodal relations: Vision and touch in infancy. In R. Walk & H. Pick (Eds.), *Intersensory perception and sensory integration* (pp. 5–36). New York: Plenum.

Butler, R. A., Levy, E. T., & Neff, W. D. (1980). Apparent distance of sounds recorded in echoic and anechoic chambers. *Journal of Experimental Psychology: Human Perception and Performance, 6*, 745–750.

Butters, N., Barton, M., & Brody, B. A. (1970). Right parietal lobe and cross-model associations. *Cortex, 6*, 19–46.

Butterworth, G. (1981). The origins of auditory-visual perception and visual proprioception in human development. In R. D. Walk & H. L. Pick, Jr. (Eds.), *Sensory perception and sensory integration*. New York: Plenum.

Caelli, T. (1982). On discriminating visual textures and images. *Perception & Psychophysics, 31*, 149–159.

Cagan, R. H., & Rein, L. D. (1980). Biochemical basis of recognition of taste and olfactory stimuli. In H. van der Starre (Ed.), *Olfaction and taste VII*. London: IRL Press.

Cahoon, D. & Edmonds, E. M. (1980). The watched pot still won't boil: Expectancy as a variable in estimating the passage of time. *Bulletin of the Psychonomic Society, 16*, 115–116.

Cain, D. P., & Bindra, D. (1972). Response of amygdala single units to odors in the rat. *Experimental Neurology, 35*, 98–110.

Cain, W. S. (1969). Odor intensity: Differences in the exponent of the psychophysical function. *Perception & Psychophysics, 6*, 349–354.

Cain, W. S. (1977). Differential sensitivity for smell: "Noise" at the nose. *Science, 195*, 796–798.

Cain, W. S. (1979). To know with the nose: Keys to odor identification. *Science, 203*, 467–470.

Cain, W. S., & Engen, T. (1969). Olfactory adaptation and the scaling of odor intensity. In C. Pfaffman (Ed.), *Olfaction and taste III* (pp. 127–141). New York: The Rockefeller University Press.

Cain, W. S., & Johnson, F., Jr. (1978). Lability of odor pleasantness: Influence of mere exposure. *Perception, 7*, 459–465.

Calis, G., & Leeuwenberg, E. (1981). Grounding the figure. *Journal of Experimental Psychology: Human Perception and Performance, 7*, 1386–1397.

Campbell, F. W., & Maffei, L. (1974). Contrast and spatial frequency. *Scientific American, 231*, 106–114.

Campbell, K. B., Baribeau-Braun, J., & Braun, C. (1981). Neuroanatomical and physiological foundations of extraversion. *Psychophysiology, 18*, 263–267.

Campos, J. J., Hiatt, S., Ramsay, D., Henderson, C. & Svejda, M. (1978). The emergence of fear on the visual cliff. In M. Lewis & L. Rosenblum (Eds.), *The origins of affect* (pp. 149–182). New York: Plenum.

Campos, J. J., Langer, A., & Krowitz, A. (1970). Cardiac responses on the visual-cliff in pre-locomotor human infants. *Science, 170*, 196–197.

Carey, S. (1981). The development of face perception. In G. Davies, H. Ellis, & J. Shepherd (Eds.), *Perceiving and remembering faces* (pp. 9–38). London: Academic Press.

Carey, S., & Diamond, R. (1977). From piecemeal to configurational representation of faces. *Science, 195*, 312–314.

Carey, S., Diamond, R., & Woods, B. (1980). The development of face recognition. A maturational component. *Developmental Psychology, 16*, 257–269.

Carlson, V. (1958). Effect of lysergic acid diethylamide (LSD-25) on the absolute visual threshold. *Journal of Comparative and Physiological Psychology, 51*, 528–531.

Carlson, V. R. (1977). Instructions and perceptual constancy judgments. In W. Epstein (Ed.), *Stability and constancy in visual perception: Mechanisms and processes* (pp. 217–254). New York: Wiley.

Carmichael, L., Hogan, H. P., & Walter, A. A. (1932). An experimental study of the effect of language on the reproduction of visually perceived forms. *Journal of Experimental Psychology, 15*, 73–86.

Caron, A., Caron, R., Caldwell, R., & Weiss, S. (1973). Infant perception of the structural properties of the face. *Developmental Psychology, 9*, 385–399.

Carter, R. R., & Hirsch, J. (1955). An experimental comparison of several psychological scales of weight. *American Journal of Psychology, 68*, 645–49.

Casey, K. L. (1978). Neural mechanisms of pain. In E. C. Carterette & M. P. Friedman (Eds.), *Handbook of perception: Vol. VIB. Feeling and hurting* (pp. 183–230). New York: Academic Press.

Casey, K. L. & Morrow, T. J. (1983). Ventral posterior thalamic neurons differentially responsive to noxious stimulation of the awake monkey. *Science, 221*, 675–677.

Cattell, J. M. (1886). The influence of the intensity of the stimulus on the length of the reaction time. *Brain, 9*, 512–514.

Cegalis, J. A., & Deptula, D. (1981). Attention in schizophrenia: Signal detection in the visual periphery. *Journal of Nervous and Mental Health Diseases, 169*, 751–760.

Cerella, J., Poon, L., & Williams, D. (1980). Age and

the complexity hypothesis. In L. Poon (Ed.), *Aging in the 1980s* (pp. 332–345). Washington, DC: American Psychological Association.

Chapman, C. R. (1978). The hurtful world: Pathological pain and its control. In E. C. Carterette & M. P. Friedman (Eds.), *Handbook of perception: Vol. VIB. Feeling and hurting*, (pp. 264–301). New York: Academic Press.

Cheatham, P. G. (1952). Visual latency as a function of stimulus brightness and contour shape. *Journal of Experimental Psychology, 43*, 369–380.

Cheng, T. O. (1973). Acupuncture anesthesia. *Science, 179*, 521.

Cherry, E. C. (1953). Some experiments on the recognition of speech, with one and with two ears. *Journal of the Acoustical Society of America, 25*, 975–979.

Chocolle, R. (1940). Variations des temps de réaction auditifs en fonction de l'intensité à diverses fréquences. *Annee Psychologique, 41*, 65–124.

Chocolle, R. (1943). Relation de la latence d'une sensation auditive différentielle avec l'amplitude d'une variation brusque de fréquence . . . d'intensité. *Bulletin de Biologie, 137*, 643–644, 751–752.

Chocolle, R. (1962). Les effets des interactions interaurales dans l'audition. *Journale de Psychologie, 3*, 255, 282.

Choudhury, B. P., & Crossey, A. D. (1981). Slow-movement sensitivity in the human field of vision. *Physiology and Behavior, 26*, 125–128.

Clark, H. H., & Clark, E. V. (1977). *Psychology and language: An introduction to psycholinguistics*. New York: Harcourt Brace Jovanovich.

Clark, J. C., & Whitehurst, G. S. (1974). Asymmetrical stimulus control and the mirror-image problem. *Journal of Experimental Child Psychology, 17*, 147–166.

Clark, W. C., & Yang, J. C. (1974). Acupunctural analgesia? Evaluation by signal detection theory. *Science, 184*, 1096–1098.

Clifton, R., Morrongiello, B., Kulig, J., & Dowd, J. (1981). Developmental changes in auditory localization in infancy. In R. Aslin, J. Alberts, & M. Petersen, (Eds.), *Development of perception: Psychobiological perspectives: Vol. 1. Audition,*

somatic perception, and the chemical senses (pp. 141–160). London: Academic Press.

Cohen, K. (1981). The development of strategies of visual search. In D. Fisher, R. Monty, & J. Senders (Eds.), *Eye movements: Cognition and visual perception* (pp. 271–288). Hillsdale, NJ: Lawrence Erlbaum Associates.

Cohen, L. B., & Salapatek, P. (1975). *Infant perception: From sensation to cognition* (Vols. 1 & 2). New York: Academic Press.

Cohen, W. (1957). Spatial and textural characteristics of the Ganzfeld. *American Journal of Psychology, 70*, 403–410.

Cohen, W. (1958). Color-perception in the chromatic Ganzfeld. *American Journal of Psychology, 71*, 390–394.

Coles, M. G., Gale, A., & Kline, P. (1971). Personality and habituation of the orienting reaction: Tonic and response measures of electrodermal activity. *Psychophysiology, 8*, 54–63.

Collings, V. B. (1974). Human taste response as a function of locus of stimulation on the tongue and soft palate. *Perception & Psychophysics, 16*, 169–174.

Comfort, A. (1971). Likelihood of human pheromones. *Nature, 230*, 432–433.

Coren, S. (1966). Adaptation to prismatic displacement as a function of the amount of available information. *Psychonomic Science, 4*, 407–408.

Coren, S. (1969a). Brightness contrast as a function of figure-ground relations. *Journal of Experimental Psychology, 80*, 517–524.

Coren, S. (1969b). The influence of optical aberrations on the magnitude of the Poggendorff illusion. *Perception & Psychophysics, 6*, 185–186.

Coren, S. (1970). Lateral inhibition and geometric illusions. *Quarterly Journal of Experimental Psychology, 22*, 274–278.

Coren, S. (1972). Subjective contours and apparent depth. *Psychological Review, 79*, 359–367.

Coren, S. (1981). The interaction between eye movements and visual illusions. In D. F. Fisher, R. A. Monty, & J. W. Senders (Eds.), *Eye movements: Cognition and visual perception*. Hillsdale, NJ: Lawrence Erlbaum Associates.

Coren, S. (1983). Set. In R. J. Corsini (Ed.), *The encyclopedia of psychology*. New York: Wiley.

Coren, S., Bradley, D. R., Hoenig, P., & Girgus, J. S. (1975). The effect of smooth tracking and saccadic eye movements on the perception of size: The shrinking circle illusion. *Vision Research, 15,* 49–55.

Coren, S., & Girgus, J. S. (1972a). Density of human lens pigmentation: In vivo measures over an extended age range. *Vision Research, 12,* 343–346.

Coren, S., & Girgus, J. S. (1972b). Illusion decrement in intersecting line figures. *Psychonomic Science, 26,* 108–110.

Coren, S., & Girgus, J. S. (1972c). Differentiation and decrement in the Mueller-Lyer illusion. *Perception & Psychophysics, 12,* 466–470.

Coren, S., & Girgus, J. S. (1977). Illusions and constancies. In W. Epstein (Ed.), *Stability and constancy in visual perception: Mechanisms and processes* (pp. 255–284). New York: Wiley.

Coren, S., & Girgus, J. S. (1978). *Seeing is deceiving: The psychology of visual illusions.* Hillsdale, NJ: Lawrence Erlbaum Associates.

Coren, S., & Girgus, J. S. (1980). Principles of perceptual organization and spatial distortion: The gestalt illusions. *Journal of Experimental Psychology: Human Perception and Performance, 6,* 404–412.

Coren, S., & Hoenig, P. (1972). Eye movements and decrement in the Oppel-Kundt illusion. *Perception & Psychophysics, 12,* 224–225.

Coren, S., & Keith, B. (1970). Bezold-Brucke effect: Pigment or neural locus? *Journal of the Optical Society of America, 60,* 559–562.

Coren, S., & Komoda, M. K. (1973). Apparent lightness as a function of perceived direction of incident illumination. *American Journal of Psychology, 86,* 345–349.

Coren, S., & Porac, C. (1978). Iris pigmentation and visual-geometric illusions. *Perception, 7,* 473–478.

Coren, S., & Porac, C. (1983). Subjective contours and apparent depth: A direct test. *Perception & Psychophysics, 33,* 197–200.

Coren, S., & Porac, C. (in press). The creation and reversal of the Mueller-Lyer illusion through attentional manipulation. *Perception.*

Coren, S., Porac, C., & Duncan, P. (1981). Lateral preference in pre-school children and young adults. *Child Development, 52,* 443–450.

Coren, S., Porac, C., Green, S., & Dawson, I. (1977, November). The Mueller-Lyer illusion from age 8 to 80. Paper delivered at the meeting of The Psychonomic Society, Washington, DC.

Coren, S. & Ward, L. M. (1979). Levels of processing in visual illusions: The combination and interaction of distortion-producing mechanisms. *Journal of Experimental Psychology: Human Perception and Performance, 5,* 324–335.

Cornsweet, T. N. (1956). Determination of the stimuli for involuntary drifts and saccadic eye movements. *Journal of the Optical Society of America, 46,* 987–993.

Cornsweet, T. N. (1962). The staircase-method in psychophysics. *American Journal of Psychology, 75,* 485–491.

Cornsweet, T. N. (1970). *Visual perception.* New York: Academic Press.

Correia, M. J., & Guedry, F. E. (1978). The vestibular system: Basic biophysical and physiological mechanisms. In R. B. Masterton (Ed.), *Handbook of behavioral neurobiology: Vol. I. Sensory integration* (pp. 311–351). New York: Plenum.

Corso, J. F. (1959). Age and sex differences in thresholds. *Journal of the Acoustical Society of America, 31,* 498–509.

Corwin, T. R., Moskowitz-Cook, A., & Green, M. A. (1977). The oblique effect in a vernier acuity situation. *Perception & Psychophysics, 21,* 445–449.

Costanzo, R. M., & Gardner, E. B. (1981). Multiple-joint neurons in somatosensory cortex of awake monkeys. *Brain Research, 24,* 321–333.

Cowley, J. J., Johnson, A. L., & Brooksbank, B. W. L. (1977). The effect of two odorous compounds on performance in an assessment-of-people test. *Psychoneuroendocrinology, 2,* 159–172.

Craig, J. C. (1977). Vibrotactile pattern perception: Extraordinary observers. *Science, 196,* 450–452.

Craig, J. C. (1981). Tactile letter recognition: Pattern duration and modes of pattern generation. *Perception & Psychophysics, 30,* 540–546.

Craig, K. D. (1978). Social modeling influences on

pain. In R. A. Sternbach (Ed.), *The psychology of pain* (pp. 73–109). New York: Raven Press.

Craig, K. D., Best, H., & Ward, L. M. (1975). Social modeling influences on psychophysical judgments of electrical stimulation. *Journal of Abnormal Psychology, 84,* 366–373.

Craig, K. D., & Coren, S. (1975). Signal detection analysis of social modeling influences on pain expressions. *Journal of Psychosomatic Research, 19,* 105–112.

Craig, K. D., & Prkachin, K. M. (1978). Social modeling influences on sensory decision theory and psychophysiological indexes of pain. *Journal of Personality and Social Psychology, 36,* 805–815.

Craik, F., & Simon, E. (1980). The roles of attention and depth of processing in understanding age differences in memory. In L. Poon, J. Fozard, L. Cermak, and L. Thompson (Eds.), *New directions in memory and aging: Proceedings of the George A. Talland Memorial Conference* (pp. 95–112). Hillsdale, NJ: Lawrence Erlbaum Associates.

Crane, H. D. (1982). IHC-TM connect-disconnect in relation to sensitization and masking of an HF-tone burst by an LF tone. IV. *Journal of the Acoustical Society of America, 71,* 1183–1193.

Cratty, B. (1979). *Perceptual and motor development in infants and children.* Englewood Cliffs, NJ: Prentice-Hall.

Creed, R. S., Denny-Brown, D., Eccles, J. C., Liddell, E. G. T., & Sherrington, C. S. (1932). *Reflex activity of the spinal cord.* Reprint. London & New York: Oxford University Press, Clarendon, 1972.

Critchley, M. (1964). The problem of visual agnosia. *Journal of Neurological Science, 1,* 274.

Critchley, M. (1970). *The dyslexic child.* London: Heinemann.

Crossman, E. R. F. W. (1953). Entropy and choice time: The effect of frequency unbalance on choice response. *Quarterly Journal of Experimental Psychology, 5,* 41–51.

Crutchfield, R. S., Woodworth, D. G., & Albrecht, R. E. (1958). *Perceptual performance and the effective person.* (WADC-TN-58-60). Lackland Air Force Base, Texas: Wright Air Development Center. (NTIS No. AD-151-039)

Cuddy, L. L., Cohen, A. J. & Mewhort, D. J. K. (1981). Perception of structure in short melodic sequences. *Journal of Experimental Psychology: Human Perception and Performance, 7,* 869–883.

Cunningham, W. (1980). Speed, age and qualitative differences in cognitive functioning. In L. Poon (Ed.), *Aging in the 1980s* (pp. 327–331). Washington, DC: American Psychological Association.

Cutting, J. E. (1976). Auditory and linguistic processes in speech perception: Inferences from six fusions in dichotic listening. *Psychological Review, 83,* 114–140.

Cutting, J. E., & Kozlowski, L. T. (1977). Recognizing friends by their walk: Gait perception without familiarity cues. *Bulletin of the Psychonomic Society, 9,* 353–356.

Cutting, J. E., Proffitt, D. R., & Kozlowski, L. T. (1978). A biomechanical invariant for gait perception. *Journal of Experimental Psychology: Human Perception and Performance, 4,* 357–372.

Cynader, M., Berman, N., & Hein, A. (1976). Recovery of function in cat visual cortex following prolonged deprivation. *Experimental Brain Research, 25,* 139–156.

Cynader, M., Timney, B. N., & Mitchell, D. E. (1980). Period of susceptibility of kitten visual cortex to the effects of monocular deprivation extends beyond 6 months of age. *Brain Research, 191,* 545–550.

Dallenbach, K. M. (1927). The temperature spots and end-organs. *American Journal of Psychology, 39,* 402–427.

Dallenbach, K. M. (1939). Pain: History and present status. *American Journal of Psychology, 52,* 331–347.

Dallos, P. (1978). Biophysics of the cochlea. In E. C. Carterette & M. P. Friedman (Eds.), *Handbook of perception: Vol. IV. Hearing* (pp. 125–162). New York: Academic Press.

Dallos, P. (1981). Cochlear physiology. *Annual Review of Psychology, 32,* 153–190.

Dallos, P., Santos-Sacchi, J., & Flock, A. (1982). Intracellular recordings from cochlear outer hair cells. *Science, 18,* 582–584.

Dalton, K. (1964). *The premenstrual syndrome.* Springfield, IL: Thomas.

Dalziel, C. C., & Egan, D. J. (1982). Crystalline lens thickness changes as observed by pachometry. *American Journal of Optometry and Physiological Optics, 59,* 442–447.

Daniels, J. D., Pettigrew, J. D., & Norman, J. L. (1978). Development of single-neuron responses in kitten's lateral geniculate nucleus. *Journal of Neurophysiology, 41,* 1373–1393.

Darian-Smith, I., Sugitani, M., Heywood, J., Karita, K., & Goodwin, A. (1982). Touching textured surfaces: Cells in somatosensory cortex respond both to finger movement and to surface features. *Science, 218,* 906–909.

Dartnall, H. M. A. (1957). *The visual pigments.* London: Methuen.

Davidoff, J. B. (1975). *Differences in visual perception: The individual eye.* New York: Academic Press.

Davidson, H. P. (1935). A study of the confusing letters b, d, p, q. *Journal of Genetic Psychology, 47,* 458–468.

Dawson, J. L. (1967). Cultural and physiological influences upon spatial processes in West Africa. I. *International Journal of Psychology, 2,* 115–128.

Day, M. (1975). Developmental trends in visual scanning. In H. W. Reese (Ed.), *Advances in child development and behavior* (Vol. 10, pp. 154–193). New York: Academic Press.

Day, R. H. (1961). On the stereoscopic observation of geometric illusion. *Perceptual and Motor Skills, 13,* 247–258.

Day, R. H., Stuart, G. W., & Dickinson, R. G. (1980). Size constancy does not fail below half a degree. *Perception & Psychophysics, 28,* 263–265.

Day, R. H., Stuart, G. W., & Post, R. B. (1978). The effect of refractive error on size constancy and shape constancy. *Perception, 7,* 557–588.

Day, R. S. (1968). Fusion in dichotic listening. Unpublished doctoral dissertation, Stanford University.

Day, R. S. (1970). Temporal order judgments in speech: Are individuals language-bound or stimulus-bound? *Haskins Laboratories Status Report.* (SR-21/22, pp. 71–87).

Dayton, G., Jones, M., Steele, B., & Rose, M. (1964).

Developmental study of coordinated eye movements in the human infant: II. An electrooculographic study of the fixation reflex in the newborn. *Archives of Ophthalmology, 71,* 871–875.

Delk, J. L., & Fillenbaum, S. (1965). Differences in perceived color as a function of characteristic color. *American Journal of Psychology, 78,* 290–293.

De Monasterio, F. M. (1978). Center and surround mechanisms of opponent-color X and Y ganglion cells of retina of macaques. *Journal of Neurophysiology, 41,* 1418–1434.

Deregowski, J. B. (1973). Illusion and culture. In R. L. Gregory & G. H. Gombrich (Eds.), *Illusion in nature and art* (pp. 161–192). New York: Scribner.

Deregowski, J. B. (1980). *Illusions, patterns and pictures: A cross-cultural perspective.* London: Academic Press.

Derrington, A. M., & Fuchs, A. F. (1981). The development of spatial-frequency selectivity in kitten striate cortex. *Journal of Physiology, 316,* 1–10.

Desimone, R., Albright, T. D., Gross, C. G., & Bruce, C. (1980). Responses of inferior temporal neurons to complex visual stimuli. *Society of Neurosciences: Abstracts, 6,* 581.

Desimone, R., & Gross, C. G. (1979). Visual areas in the temporal cortex of the macaque. *Brain Research, 178,* 363–380.

Deutsch, D. (1978). The psychology of music. In E. C. Carterette & M. P. Friedman (Eds.), *Handbook of perception: Vol. X. Perceptual ecology.* New York: Academic Press.

Deutsch, D. (Ed.). (1982). *The psychology of music.* New York: Academic Press.

Deutsch, D., & Feroe, J. (1981). The internal representation of pitch sequences in tonal music. *Psychological Review, 88,* 503–522.

Deutsch, J. A., & Deutsch, D. (1963). Attention: Some theoretical considerations. *Psychological Review, 70,* 80–90.

DeValois, R. L. (1971). Contributions of different lateral geniculate cell types to visual behavior. *Vision Research, 11,* 383–396.

DeValois, R. L., Albrecht, D. G., & Thorell, L. G.

(1982). Spatial frequency selectivity of cells in macaque visual cortex. *Vision Research*, *22*, 545–559.

DeValois, R. L., & DeValois, K. K. (1975). Neural coding of color. In E. C. Carterette & M. P. Friedman (Eds.), *Handbook of perception: Vol. V. Seeing* (pp. 117–168). New York: Academic Press.

DeValois, R. L. & DeValois, K. K. (1980). Spatial vision. *Annual Review of Psychology*, *31*, 309–341.

DeValois, R. L., Yund, E. W., & Hepler, N. (1982). The orientation and direction selectivity of cells in macaque visual cortex. *Vision Research*, *22*, 531–544.

Devaney, K. O., & Johnson, H. A. (1980). Neuron loss in the aging visual cortex of man. *Journal of Gerontology*, *35*, 836–841.

De Vries, H., & Stuiver, M. (1961). The absolute sensitivity of the human sense of smell. In W. A. Rosenblith (Ed.), *Communication processes* (pp. 159–167). New York: Wiley.

Diamant, H., Funakoshi, M., Strom, L., & Zotterman, Y. (1963). Electrophysiological studies on human taste nerves. In Y. Zotterman (Ed.), *Olfaction and taste* (pp. 191–203). Oxford: Pergamon Press.

Diamant, H., & Zotterman, Y. (1969). A comparative study on the neural and psychophysical response to taste stimuli. In C. Pfaffman (Ed.), *Olfaction and taste III* (pp. 428–435). New York: The Rockefeller University Press.

Diamond, A. L. (1960). A theory of depression and enhancement in the brightness response. *Psychological Review*, *67*, 168–199.

Diehl, R. L. (1976). Feature analyzers for the phonetic dimension stop vs continuant. *Perception & Psychophysics*, *19*, 267–272.

Diehl, R. L. (1981). Feature detectors for speech: A critical reappraisal. *Psychological Bulletin*, *89*, 1–18.

Ditchburn, R. W. (1973). *Eye movements and perception*. Oxford: Clarendon Press.

Djang, S. (1937). The role of past experience in the visual apprehension of masked forms. *Journal of Experimental Psychology*, *20*, 29–59.

Dobson, V. (1976). Spectral sensitivity of the 2-month-old infant as measured by the visual evoked cortical potential. *Vision Research*, *16*, 367–374.

Dobson, V., & Teller, D. Y. (1978). Visual acuity in human infants: A review and comparison of behavioral and electrophysiological studies. *Vision Research*, *18*, 1469–1483.

Dodwell, P. C. (1971). On perceptual clarity. *Psychological Review*, *78*, 275–279.

Doetsch, G. S., Ganchrow, J. J., Nelson, L. M., & Erickson, R. P. (1969). Information processing in the taste system of the rat. In C. Pfaffman (Ed.), *Olfaction and taste III* (pp. 492–511). New York: The Rockefeller University Press.

Doherty, M. E., & Keeley, S. M. (1972). On the identification of repeatedly presented visual stimuli. *Psychological Bulletin*, *78*, 142–154.

Donaldson, I. M. L., & Long, A. C. (1980). Interactions between extraocular proprioceptive and visual signals in the superior colliculus of the cat. *Journal of Physiology*, *298*, 85–110.

Doris, J., Casper, M., & Poresky, R. (1967). Differential brightness thresholds in infancy. *Journal of Experimental Child Psychology*, *5*, 522–535.

Dorman, M. F., Studdart-Kennedy, M., & Raphael, I. J. (1977). Stop-consonant recognition: Release bursts and formant transitions as functionally equivalent, context-dependent cues. *Perception & Psychophysics*, *22*, 109–122.

Doty, R. L., Orndorff, M. M., Leyden, J., & Kligman, A. (1978). Communication of gender from human axillary odors: Relationship to perceived intensity and hedonicity. *Behavioral Biology*, *23*, 373–380.

Droscher, V. B. (1971). *The magic of the senses: New discoveries in animal perception*. New York: Harper & Row.

Drum, B. (1980). Relation of brightness to threshold for light-adapted and dark-adapted rods and cones: Effects of retinal eccentricity on target size. *Perception*, *9*, 633–650.

Drum, B. (1981). Brightness interactions between rods and cones. *Perception & Psychophysics*, *29*, 505–510.

Duncan, H. F., Gourlay, N., & Hudson, W. (1973). *A study of pictorial perception among the Bantu and white primary school children in South Af-*

rica. Johannesberg: Witwatersrand University Press.

Duncan, J. (1980a). The demonstration of capacity limitation. *Cognitive Psychology, 12*, 75–96.

Duncan, J. (1980b). The locus of interference in the perception of simultaneous stimuli. *Psychological Review, 87*, 272–300.

Duncker, K. (1929). Uber induzierte Bewegung (ein Beitrag zur Theorie optisch warigenommener Bewegung). *Psychologishe Forschung, 2*, 180–259.

Duncker, K. (1939). The influence of past experience upon perceptual properties. *American Journal of Psychology, 52*, 255–265.

Edwards, A., & Cohen, S. (1961). Visual illusions, tactile sensibility and reaction time under LSD-25. *Psychopharmacologia, 2*, 297–303.

Efron, R. (1967). The duration of the present. *Annals of the New York Academy of Sciences, 138*, 713–729.

Egan, J. P. (1975). *Signal detection theory and ROC-analysis*. New York: Academic Press.

Eijkman, E. G. J., Jongsma, H. J., & Vincent, J. (1981). Two-dimensional filtering oriented line detectors and figural aspects as determinants of visual illusions. *Perception & Psychophysics, 29*, 352–358.

Eilers, R., Gavin, W., & Wilson, W. (1979). Linguistic experience and phonemic perception in infancy: A cross linguistic study. *Child Development, 50*, 14–18.

Eilers, R., Wilson, W., & Moore, T. (1979). Speech perception in the language innocent and the language wise: A study in the perception of voice onset time. *Journal of Child Language, 6*, 1–18.

Eimas, P. D., & Corbit, J. D. (1973). Selective adaptation of linguistic feature detectors. *Cognitive Psychology, 4*, 99–109.

Eisenberg, P., & Becker, C. (1982). Semantic context effects in visual word recognition sentence processing and reading: Evidence for semantic strategies. *Journal of Experimental Psychology: Human Perception and Performance, 8*, 739–756.

Elkind, D. (1978). *The child's reality: Three developmental themes*. Hillsdale, NJ: Lawrence Erlbaum Associates.

Ellingson, R. (1968). Clinical applications of evoked potential techniques in infants and children. *Electroencephalography and Clinical Neurophysiology, 24*, 293.

Ellingson, R., Lathrop, G., Nelson, G., & Donahy, T. (1972). Visual evoked potentials of infants. *Reveue d'Electroencephalographie et de Neurophysiologie Clinique, 2*, 395–400.

Ellis, H. (1905). *Sexual selection in man*. New York: Davis.

Ellis, H. C., & Muller, D. G. (1964). Transfer in perceptual learning following stimulus predifferentiation. *Journal of Experimental Psychology, 68*, 388–395.

Engen, T. (1982). *The perception of odors*. New York: Academic Press.

Engen, T., & Tulunary, U. (1956). Some sources of error in half-heaviness judgments. *Journal of Experimental Psychology, 54*, 208–212.

Epstein, W. (1973). The process of taking into account in visual perception. *Perception, 2*, 267–285.

Epstein, W. (1977). Observations concerning the contemporary analysis of constancies. In W. Epstein (Ed.), *Stability and constancy in visual perception: Mechanisms and processes* (pp. 437–448). New York: Wiley.

Epstein, W., & Baratz, S. S. (1964). Relative size in isolation as a stimulus for relative perceived distance. *Journal of Experimental Psychology, 67*, 507–513.

Epstein, W., & Hanson, S. (1977). Discrimination of unique motion-path length. *Perception & Psychophysics, 22*, 152–158.

Epstein, W., Hatfield, G., & Muise, G. (1977). Perceived shape at a slant as a function of processing time and processing load. *Journal of Experimental Psychology: Human Perception and Performance, 3*, 473–483.

Epstein, W., & Park, J. N. (1963). Shape constancy: Functional relationships and theoretical formulations. *Psychological Bulletin, 62*, 180–196.

Erickson, R. P. (1963). Sensory neural patterns and gustation. In Y. Zotterman (Ed.), *Olfaction and taste* (pp. 205–213). Oxford: Pergamon Press.

Erickson, R. P. & Covey, E. (1980). On the singularity of taste sensations: What is a taste primary? *Physiology and Behavior, 25,* 527–533.

Erickson, R. P., & Schiffman, S. S. (1975). The chemical senses: A systematic approach. In M. S. Gazzaniga & C. Blakemore (Eds.), *Handbook of psychobiology.* New York: Academic Press.

Eriksen, C. W., & Collins, J. F. (1968). Sensory traces versus the psychological movement in the temporal organization of form. *Journal of Experimental Psychology, 77,* 376–382.

Eriksen, C. W., & Hake, H. W. (1955). Absolute judgments as a function of stimulus range and number of stimulus and responses categories. *Journal of Experimental Psychology, 49,* 323–332.

Erulkar, S. C. (1972). Comparative aspects of spatial localization of sound. *Physiological Review, 52,* 237–360.

Evans, C. R., & Wells, A. M. (1967). Fragmentation phenomena associated with binocular stabilization. *British Journal of Physiological Optics, 24,* 45–50.

Evans, E. F. (1975). Cochlear nerve and cochlear nucleus. In W. D. Keidel & W. D. Neff (Eds.), *Handbook of sensory physiology: Vol. V/2 Auditory system: Physiology (CNS). Behavioral Studies. Psychoacoustics.* New York: Springer-Verlag.

Eysenck, H. J. (1967). *The biological basis of personality.* Springfield, IL: Thomas.

Falk, J., & Bindra, D. (1954). Judgment of time as a function of serial position and stress. *Journal of Experimental Psychology, 47,* 279–282.

Falmagne, J. C. (1974). Foundations of Fechnerian psychophysics. In D. Krantz, R. C. Atkinson, R. D. Luce, & P. Suppes (Eds.), *Contemporary developments in mathematical psychology.* (Vol. II, pp. 121–159). San Francisco: Freeman.

Fantz, R. L. (1961). The origin of form perception. *Scientific American, 204,* 66–72.

Fantz, R. L. (1964). Visual experience in infants: Decreased attention to familiar patterns relative to novel ones. *Science, 146,* 668–670.

Fantz, R. L. (1965a). Visual perception from birth as shown by pattern selectivity. *Annals of the New York Academy of Sciences, 118,* 793–814.

Fantz, R. L. (1965b). Ontogeny of perception. In A. M. Schrier, H. F. Harlow, & F. Stonllnitz (Eds.), *Behavior of nonhuman primates.* (Vol. 2, pp. 365–403). New York: Academic Press.

Fantz, R. L., & Miranda, S. B. (1977). Visual processing in the newborn preterm, and mentally high-risk infant. In L. Gluck (Ed.), *Intrauterine asphyxia and the developing fetal brain* (pp. 453–471). Chicago: Year Book Medical Publishers.

Fantz, R. L., & Yeh, J. (1979). Configurational selectives: Critical for development of visual perception and attention. *Canadian Journal of Psychology, 33,* 277–287.

Farkas, M., & Hoyer, W. (1980). Processing consequences of perceptual grouping in selective attention. *Journal of Gerontology, 35,* 207–216.

Farrell, J. E. (1983). Visual transformations underlying apparent movement. *Perception & Psychophysics, 33,* 85–92.

Faurion, A., Saito, S., & MacLeod, P. (1980). Sweet taste involves several distinct receptor mechanisms. *Chemical Senses, 5,* 107–121.

Favreau, O. E., & Cavanagh, P. (1981). Color and luminance: Independent frequency shifts. *Science, 212,* 831–832.

Fechner, G. T. (1966). *Elements of psychophysics.* (H. E. Alder, Trans.). New York: Holt, Rinehart & Winston. (Original work published 1860)

Fender, D. H. (1971). Time delays in the human eye-tracking system. In P. Bach-y-Rita, C. C. Collins, & J. E. Hyde (Eds.), *The control of eye movements* (pp. 539–543). New York: Academic Press.

Festinger, L., Allyn, M. R., & White, C. W. (1971). The perception of color with achromatic stimulation. *Vision Research, 11,* 591–612.

Festinger, L., Coren, S., & Rivers, G. (1970). The effect of attention on brightness contrast and assimilation. *American Journal of Psychology, 83,* 189–207.

Festinger, L., & Easton, M. (1974). Inference about the efferent system based on a perceptual illusion produced by eye movements. *Psychological Review, 81,* 44–58.

Festinger, L., White, C. W., & Allyn, M. R. (1968). Eye movements and decrement in the Mueller-Lyer illusion. *Perception & Psychophysics, 3,* 376–382.

Filer, R., & Meals, D. (1949). The effect of motivating

conditions on the estimation of time. *Journal of Experimental Psychology, 39,* 327–331.

Findlay, J. (1981). Local and global influences on saccadic eye movements. In D. Fisher, R. Monty, & J. Senders (Eds.), *Eye movements: Cognition and visual perception* (pp. 171–179). Hillsdale, NJ: Lawrence Erlbaum Associates.

Fisher, R. (1967). The biological fabric of time. In Interdisciplinary perspectives of time. *Annals of the New York Academy of Sciences, 138,* 451–465.

Fisk, A. D., & Schneider, W. (1981). Control and automatic processing during tasks requiring sustained attention: A new approach to vigilance. *Human Factors, 23,* 737–750.

Flandrin, J. M., & Jeannerod, M. (1981). Effects of unilateral superior colliculus ablation on oculomotor and vestibulo-ocular responses in the cat. *Experimental Brain Research, 42,* 73–80.

Flannery, R., & Butler, R. A. (1981). Spectral cues provided in the pinna for monaural localization in the horizontal plane. *Perception & Psychophysics, 29,* 438–444.

Flin, R. H. (1980). Age effects in children's memory for unfamiliar faces. *Developmental Psychology, 16,* 373–374.

Flock, H., & Freedberg, E. (1970). Perceived angle of incidence and achromatic surface color. *Perception & Psychophysics, 8,* 251–256.

Flom, M. C., Brown, B., Adams, A. J., & Jones, R. T. (1976). Alcohol and marihuana effects on ocular tracking. *American Journal of Optometry and Physiological Optics, 53,* 764–773.

Foley, J. E. (1970). Prism adaptation with opposed base orientation: The weighting of direction information from the two eyes. *Perception & Psychophysics, 8,* 23–25.

Foley, J. E. (1974). Factors governing interocular transfer of prism adaptation. *Psychological Review, 81,* 183–186.

Foulke, E., & Sticht, T. (1969). Review of research on the intelligibility and comprehension of accelerated speech. *Psychological Bulletin, 72,* 50–62.

Fourcin, A. J. (1975). Speech perception in the absence of speech productive ability. In N. O'Connor (Ed.), *Language, cognitive deficits, and retardation* (pp. 33–43). London: Butterworth.

Fox, R. (1981). Stereopsis in animals and human infants: A review of behavioral investigations. In R. Aslin, J. Alberts, & M. Petersen (Eds.), *Development of perception: Psychobiological perspectives: Vol. 2. The visual system* (pp. 335–381). New York: Academic Press.

Fox, R., Aslin, R. N., Shea, S. L., & Dumais, S. T. (1980). Stereopsis in infants. *Science, 207,* 323–324.

Fozard, J., Wolf, E., Bell, B., McFarland, R., & Podolsky, S. (1977). Visual perception and communication. In J. Birren & K. Schaie (Eds.), *Handbook of the psychology of aging.* New York: Van Nostrand Reinhold.

Fraisse, P. (1963). *The psychology of time.* New York: Harper & Row.

Frank, M. (1975). Response patterns of rat glossopharyngeal taste neurons. In D. A. Denton and P. Coghlan (Eds.), *Olfaction and taste V.* New York: Academic Press.

Frankenhauser, M. (1959). *Estimation of time.* Stockholm: Almqvist & Wiksell.

Freeman, R., Mallach, R., & Hartley, S. (1981). Responsivity of normal kitten striate cortex deteriorates after brief binocular deprivation. *Journal of Neurophysiology, 45,* 1074–1084.

Freeman, R., & Pettigrew, J. (1973). Alteration of visual cortex from environmental asymmetries. *Nature, 246,* 359–360.

Fregnac, V. (1979). Development of orientation selectivity in the primary visual cortex of normally dark reared kittens. *Biological Cybernetics, 34,* 187–193.

Fregnac, V., & Imbert, M. (1978). Early development of visual cortical cells in normal and dark reared kittens: Relationships between orientation selectivity and ocular dominance. *Journal of Physiology, 278,* 27–44.

Freud, S. (1953). *An aphasia.* London: Imago.

Frey, M. von, & Goldman, A. (1915). Der zeitliche Verlauf det Einstellung bei den Druckempfindungen. *Zeitschrift feur Biologie, 65,* 183–202.

Frey, M. von, & Kiesow, F. (1899). Uber die Function der Tastkorperchen. *Zeitschrift feur Psychologie, 20,* 126–163.

Friedman, A. (1979). Framing pictures: The role of knowledge in automatized encoding and memory for gist. *Journal of Experimental Psychology: General, 108,* 316–355.

Friedman, A., & Liebelt, L. (1981). On the time course of viewing pictures with a view towards remembering. In D. Fisher, R. Monty, & J. Senders (Eds.), *Eye movements: Cognition and visual perception* (pp. 137–155). Hillsdale, NJ: Lawrence Erlbaum Associates.

Friedman, R. B. (1980). Identity without form: Abstract representations of letters. *Perception & Psychophysics, 28,* 53–60.

Friedman, S. L., & Stevenson, M. B. (1975). Developmental changes in the understanding of implied motion in two-dimensional pictures. *Child Development, 46,* 773–778.

Friedman, S., & Stevenson, M. (1980). Perception of movements in pictures. In M. Hagen (Ed.), *Perception of pictures: Vol. I. Alberti's window: The projective model of pictorial information* (pp. 225–255). New York: Academic Press.

Frisby, J. P. (1980). *Seeing: Illusion, brain and mind.* Oxford: Oxford University Press.

Funakoshi, M., Kasahara, Y., Yamamoto, T., & Kawamura, Y. (1972). Taste coding and central perception. In D. Schneider (Ed.), *Olfaction and taste IV* (pp. 336–342). Stuttgart: Wissenshaftliche Verlagsgesellschaft MBH.

Funkenstein, H. H., Nelson, P. G., Winter, P., Wolberg, Z., & Newman, J. D. (1971). Unit responses in auditory cortex of awake squirrel monkeys to vocal stimulation. In M. B. Sachs (Ed.), *Physiology of the auditory system* (pp. 307–326). Baltimore: National Educational Consultants, Inc.

Gaddes, W. H. (1976). Prevalence estimates and the need for definition of learning disabilities. In R. M. Knights & D. J. Bakker (Eds.), *The neuropsychology of learning disorders,* Baltimore: University Park Press.

Gaddes, W. H. (1980) *Learning disabilities and brain function: A neuropsychological approach.* New York: Springer-Verlag.

Galanter, E. (1962). Contemporary psychophysics. In R. Brown, E. Galanter, E. Hess, & G. Mandler (Eds.), *New directions in psychology* (pp. 87–157). New York: Holt, Rinehart & Winston.

Ganz, L. (1966). Mechanism of the figural after-effects. *Psychological Review, 73,* 128–150.

Gardner, E. B., & Costanzo, R. H. (1981). Properties of kinesthetic neurons in somatosensory cortex of awake monkeys. *Brain Research, 214,* 301–319.

Gardner, R. J. (1979). Lipophilicity and the perception of bitterness. *Chemical Senses and Flavor, 4,* 275–286.

Garner, W. R. (1953). An informational analysis of absolute judgments of loudness. *Journal of Experimental Psychology, 46,* 373–380.

Garner, W. R. (1962). *Uncertainty and structure as psychological concepts.* New York: Wiley.

Garner, W. R. (1974). *The processing of information and structure.* Potomac, MD: Lawrence Erlbaum Associates.

Garner, W. R., & Clement, D. E. (1963). Goodness of pattern and pattern uncertainty. *Journal of Verbal Learning and Verbal Behavior, 2,* 446–452.

Garner, W. R., & Hake, H. W. (1951). The amount of information in absolute judgments. *Psychological Review, 58,* 446–459.

Gelb, A. (1929). Die "Farbenkonstanz" der Sehdinge. *Handbuch der normalen und pathologische Physiologie, 12,* 549–678.

Geldard, F. A. (1972). *The human senses* (2nd ed.). New York: Wiley.

Gent, J. F. (1979). An exponential model for adaptation in taste. *Sensory Processes, 3,* 303–316.

Gerbrandt, L. K., Spinelli, D. N., & Pribram, K. H. (1970). Interaction of visual attention and temporal cortex stimulation on electrical activity evoked in striate cortex. *Electroencephalography and Clinical Neurology, 29,* 146.

Gescheider, G. A., & Verrillo, R. T. (1982). Contralateral enhancement and suppression of vibrotactile sensation. *Perception & Psychophysics, 32,* 69–74.

Gesteland, R. C., Lettvin, J. Y., Pitts, W. H., & Rojas, A. (1963). Odor specificities of the frog's olfactory receptors. In Y. Zotterman (Ed.), *Olfaction and taste* (pp. 19–34). Oxford: Pergamon Press.

Geyer, L. H., & DeWald, C. G. (1973). Feature lists and confusion matrices. *Perception & Psychophysics, 14,* 471–482.

Giachetti, I., & MacLeod, P. (1975). Cortical neuron responses to odours in the rat. In D. A. Denton

& J. P. Coghlan (Eds.), *Olfaction and taste V* (pp. 303–307). New York: Academic Press.

Gibson, E. J. (1969). *Principles of perceptual learning and development*. New York: Appleton-Century-Crofts.

Gibson, E. J., Gibson, J. J., Pick, A. D., & Osser, H. (1962). A developmental study of the discrimination of letterlike forms. *Journal of Comparative and Physiological Psychology, 55*, 897–906.

Gibson, E. J., Osser, H., Schiff, W., & Smith, J. (1963). An analysis of critical features of letters, tested by a confusion matrix. In *A basic research program on reading* (Cooperative Research Project No. 639). Washington, DC: U.S. Office of Education.

Gibson, E. J. & Walk, R. (1960). The "visual cliff". *Scientific American, 202*, 64–71.

Gibson, J. J. (1950). *Perception of the visual world*. Boston: Houghton Mifflin.

Gibson, J. J. (1966). *The senses considered as perceptual systems*. Boston: Houghton Mifflin.

Gibson, J. J. (1979). *The ecological approach to visual perception*. Boston: Houghton Mifflin.

Gibson, J. J., Kaplan, G. A., Reynolds, H. V., & Wheeler, K. (1969). The change from visible to invisible: A study of optical transitions. *Perception & Psychophysics, 5*, 113–116.

Gibson, R. H., and Tomko, D. L. (1972). The relation between category and magnitude estimates of tactile intensity. *Perception & Psychophysics, 12*, 135–138.

Gilchrist, A. L. (1980). When does perceived lightness depend on perceived spatial arrangement? *Perception & Psychophysics, 28*, 527–538.

Gilinsky, A. S. (1955). The effect of attitude upon the perception of size. *American Journal of Psychology, 68*, 173–192.

Giraldez, F., Geijo, E., & Belmonte, C. (1979). Response characteristics of corneal sensory fibers to mechanical and thermal stimulation. *Brain Research, 177*, 571–576.

Glorig, A., Wheeler, D., Quigle, R., Grings, W., & Summerfield, A. (1970). 1954 Wisconsin State Fair hearing survey: Statistical treatment of clinical and audiometric data. Cited in D. D. Kryter, *The*

effects of noise on man (p. 116). New York: Academic Press.

Glucksberg, S., & Cowen, G. N., Jr. (1970). Memory for nonattended auditory material. *Cognitive Psychology, 1*, 149–156.

Gogel, W. C. (1977). Independent motion induction in separated portions of the visual field. *Bulletin of the Psychonomic Society, 10*, 408–410.

Gogel, W. C., Gregg, J. M., & Wainwright, A. (1961). Convergence as a cue to absolute distance (Report No. 467, pp. 1–16). Fort Knox, KY: U.S. Army Medical Research Laboratory.

Gogel, W. C., & Koslow, M. (1972). The adjacency principle and induced movement. *Perception & Psychophysics, 11*, 309–324.

Goldfoot, D. A., Kravetz, M. A., Goy, R. W., & Freeman, S. K. (1976). Lack of effect of vaginal lavages and aliphatic acids on ejaculatory responses in Rhesus monkeys: Behavioral and chemical analyses. *Hormones and Behavior, 7*, 1–27.

Goldstein, E. B. (1980). *Sensation and perception*. Belmont, CA: Wadsworth.

Goldstone, S., Boardman, W. K., & Lhamon, W. T. (1958). Effect of quinal barbitone dextroamphetamine, and placebo on apparent time. *British Journal of Psychology, 49*, 324–328.

Gombrich, E. H. (1972). The mask and the face: The perception of physiognomic likeness in life and art. In E. H. Gombrich, J. Hochberg, & M. Black (Eds.), *Art perception and reality*. Baltimore: Johns Hopkins Press.

Goodman, L., & Gilman, A. (Eds.), (1965). *The pharmacological basis of therapeutics*. New York: Macmillan.

Goodman, N. (1968). *Languages of art*. New York: Bobbs-Merrill.

Goodson, R., & Rahe, A. (1981). Visual training effects on normal vision. *American Journal of Optometry and Physiological Optics, 58*, 787–791.

Gordon, B. (1976). The superior colliculus of the brain. In R. Held & W. Richards (Eds.), *Recent progress in perception* (pp. 85–95). San Francisco: Freeman.

Gorman, J., Cogan, D., & Gellis, S. (1957). An apparatus for grading the visual acuity of infants on the basis of opticokinetic nystagmus. *Pediatrics, 19*, 1088–1092.

Gorsen, C., Sarty, M., & Wu, R. (1975). Visual following and pattern discrimination of face-like stimuli by newborn infants. *Pediatrics, 56,* 544–549.

Goto, H. (1971). Auditory perception by normal Japanese adults of the sounds "L" or "R". *Neuropsychologia, 9,* 317–323.

Gottlieb, G. (1981). Roles of early experience in species-specific perceptual development. In R. Aslin, J. Alberts, & M. Petersen (Eds.), *Development of perception: Psychobiological perspectives: Vol. 1. Audition, somatic perception and the chemical senses* (pp. 5–44). New York: Academic Press.

Gottschaldt, K. (1926). Uber den Einfluss der Erfahrung auf die Wahrnehmung von Figuren. I. *Psychologische Forschung, 8,* 261–317.

Gottschaldt, K. (1929). Uber den Einfluss der Erfahrung auf die Wahrenhmung von Figuren. II. *Psychologische Forschung, 12,* 1–87.

Gottschaldt, K. M., & Vahle-Hinz, C. (1981). Merkle cell receptors: Structure and transducer function. *Science, 214,* 183–185.

Gouras, P., & Kruger, J. (1979). Responses of cells in foveal visual cortex of the monkey to pure color contrast. *Journal of Neurophysiology, 42,* 850–860.

Graham, C. H. (1965). Visual space perception. In C. H. Graham (Ed.), *Vision and visual perception* (pp. 504–547). New York: Wiley.

Graham, C. H., & Hsia, Y. (1958). Color defect and color theory. *Science, 127,* 657–682.

Graham, F. K., & Clifton, R. K. (1966). Heart-rate change as a component of the orienting response. *Psychological Bulletin, 65,* 305–320.

Graham, F. K., & Jackson, J. C. (1970). Arousal systems and infant heart-rate responses. In H. W. Reese & L. P. Lipsitt (Eds.), *Advances in child development and behavior* (Vol. 5, pp. 60–117). New York: Academic Press.

Graham, N. (1980). Spatial-frequency channels in human vision: Detecting edges without edge detectors. In C. S. Harris (Ed.), *Visual coding and adaptability* (pp. 215–262). New York: Lawrence Erlbaum Associates.

Graham, N. (1981). Psychophysics of spatial-frequency channels. In M. Kuboby & J. Pomerantz (Eds.), *Perceptual organization.* Hillsdale, NJ.: Lawrence Erlbaum Associates.

Granger, G. W., & Ikeda, H. (1968). Drugs and visual thresholds. In A. Herxheimer (Ed.), *Drugs and sensory functions* (pp. 299–344). London: Churchill.

Gray, J., & Wedderburn, A. (1960). Grouping strategies with simultaneous stimuli. *Quarterly Journal of Experimental Psychology, 12,* 180–194.

Green, D. G., & Powers, M. K. (1982). Mechanisms of light adaptation in rat retina. *Vision Research, 22,* 209–216.

Green, D. M. (1976). *An introduction to hearing.* Hillsdale, NJ: Lawrence Erlbaum Associates.

Green, D. M., Nachmias, J., Kearny, J. K. & Jeffress, L. A. (1979). Intensity discrimination with gated and continuous sinusoids. *Journal of the Acoustical Society of America, 66,* 1051–1056.

Green, D. M., & Swets, J. A. (1966). *Signal detection theory and psychophysics.* Reprint. New York: Krieger, 1974.

Greenberg, M. J. (1981). The dependence of odor intensity on the hydrophobic properties of molecules. In H. R. Moskowitz & C. B. Warren (Eds.), *Odor quality and chemical structure* (pp. 177–194). Washington, DC: American Chemical Society.

Gregory, R. L. (1966). *Eye and brain.* New York: World University Library.

Gregory, R. L. (1974). *Concepts and mechanisms of perception.* London: Duckworth.

Grice, G. R., Nullmeyer, R., & Schnizlein, J. M. (1979). Variable criterion analysis of brightness effects in simple reaction time. *Journal of Experimental Psychology: Human Perception and Performance, 5,* 303–314.

Grier, J. B. (1971). Nonparametric indexes for sensitivity and bias: Computing formulas. *Psychological Bulletin, 75,* 424–429.

Gross, C. G., Rocha-Miranda, E. C., & Bender, D. B. (1972). Visual properties of neurons in inferotemporal cortex of the macaque. *Journal of Neurophysiology, 35,* 96–111.

Grossberg, J. M., & Grant, B. F. (1978). Clinical psychophysics. *Psychological Bulletin, 85,* 1154–1176.

Grzegorczyk, P. B., Jones, S. W., & Mistretta, C. M.

(1979). Age-related differences in salt taste acuity. *Journal of Gerontology, 34,* 834–940.

Guitton, D., Crommelink, M., & Roucoux, A. (1980). Stimulation of the superior colliculus in the alert cat: I. Eye movement and neck EMG activity evoked when the head is restrained. *Experimental Brain Research, 39,* 63–74.

Gulick, W. L. (1971). *Hearing: Physiology and psychophysics.* London & New York: Oxford University Press.

Gwiazda, J., Brill, S., Mohindra, I., & Held, R. (1980). Preferential looking acuity in infants from 2 to 58 weeks of age. *American Journal of Optometry and Physiological Optics, 57,* 428–432.

Haaf, R. (1977). Visual responses to complex facelike patterns by 15 and 20 week old infants. *Developmental Psychology, 38,* 893–899.

Haber, R. (1980). Perceiving space from pictures: A theoretical analysis. In M. Hagen (Ed.), *Perception of pictures: Vol. 1. Alberti's window: The projective model of pictorial information* (pp. 3–31). New York: Academic Press.

Haber, R.N., & Hershenson, M. (1965). The effects of repeated brief exposures on the growth of a percept. *Journal of Experimental Psychology, 69,* 40–46.

Hagen, M., & Jones, R. (1978). Cultural effects on pictorial perception: How many words is one picture really worth? In R. Walk and H. Pick (Eds.), *Perception and experience* (pp. 171–212). New York: Plenum.

Hahn, H. (1934). Die Adaptation des Geschmackssinnes. *Zeitschrift fuer Sinnesphysiologie, 65,* 105–145.

Hainline, L. (1978). Developmental changes in the scanning of face and nonface patterns by infants. *Journal of Experimental Child Psychology, 25,* 90–115.

Haith, M. M., & Campos, J. J. (1977). Human infancy. *Annual Review of Psychology, 28,* 251–293.

Hall, J. W., III, & Peters, R. W. (1982). Change in the pitch of a complex tone following its association with a second complex tone. *Journal of the Acoustical Society of America, 71,* 142–146.

Hall, M. J., Bartoshuk, L. M., Cain, W. S., & Stevens, J. C. (1975). PTC taste blindness and the taste of caffeine. *Nature (London), 253,* 442–443.

Halle, M., & Stevens, K. (1962). Speech recognition: A model and a program for research. *IRE Transactions on Information Theory, IT-8,* 155–159.

Halpern, B. P., & Meiselman, H. L. (1980). Taste psychophysics based on a simulation of human drinking. *Chemical Senses, 5,* 279–294.

Halsam, D. (1967). Individual differences in pain threshold and level of arousal. *British Journal of Psychology, 58,* 139–142.

Hamalainen, H., & Jarvilehto, T. (1981). Peripheral neural basis of tactile sensations in man: I. Effect of frequency and probe area on sensations elicited by single mechanical pulses on hairy and glabrous skin of the hand. *Brain Research, 219,* 1–12.

Hamasaki, D. J., & Sutija, V. G. (1979). Development of X- and Y-cells in kittens. *Experimental Brain Research, 35,* 9–23.

Handel, S., & Garner, W. R. (1965). The structure of visual pattern associates and pattern goodness. *Perception & Psychophysics, 1,* 33–38.

Handel, S., & Oshinsky, J. S. (1981). The meter of syncopated auditory polyrhythms. *Perception & Psychophysics, 30,* 1–9.

Hardy, J. D. Stolwijk, J. A. J., & Hoffman, D. (1968). Pain following step increase in skin temperature. In D. R. Kenshalo (Ed.), *The skin senses* (pp. 444–457). Springfield, IL: Thomas.

Hardy, J. D., Wolff, H. G., & Goodell, H. (1943). The pain threshold in man. *Research Publications, Association for Research in Nervous and Mental Disease, 23,* 1–15.

Hardy, J. D., Wolff, H. G., & Goodell, H. (1947). Studies on pain: Discrimination of differences in intensity of a pain stimulus as a basis of a scale of pain intensity. *Journal of Clinical Investigation, 26,* 1152–1158.

Harkins, S. W., & Chapman, C. R. (1977). The perception of induced dental pain in young and elderly women. *Journal of Gerontology, 32,* 428–435.

Harkins S., & Geen, R. G. (1975). Discriminability and criterion differences between extraverts and introverts during vigilance. *Journal of Research in Personality, 9,* 335–340.

Harmon, L. D. (1973). The recognition of faces. *Scientific American, 229,* 70–82.

Harmon, L. D., & Julesz, B. (1973). Masking in visual recognition: Effects of two dimensional filtered noise. *Science, 180,* 1194–1197.

Harper, R. S. (1953). The perceptual modification of coloured figures. *American Journal of Psychology, 66,* 86–89.

Harrington, T. L., Harrington, M. K., Wilkins, C. A., & Koh, Y. O. (1980). Visual orientation by motion-produced blur patterns: Detection of divergence. *Perception & Psychophysics, 28,* 293–305.

Harris, C. S. (1965). Perceptual adaptation to inverted, reversed and displaced vision. *Psychological Review, 72,* 419–444.

Harris, C. S. (1980). Insight or out of sight?: Two examples of perceptual plasticity in the human adult. In C. S. Harris (Ed.), *Visual coding and adaptability* (pp. 95–149). Hillsdale, NJ: Lawrence Erlbaum Associates.

Harris, L. J. (1981). Sex related variations in spatial skills. In L. S. Liben, A. H. Patterson, & N. Newcombe (Eds.), *Spatial representation and behavior: Theory and application.* New York: Academic Press.

Harris, P., & MacFarlane, A. (1974). The growth of the effective visual field from birth to seven weeks. *Journal of Experimental Child Psychology, 18,* 340–348.

Harter, M., & Suitt, C. (1970). Visually-evoked cortical responses and pattern vision in the infant: A longitudinal study. *Psychonomic Science, 18,* 235–237.

Hartline, H. K. (1940). The receptive fields of optic nerve fibers. *American Journal of Physiology, 130,* 690–699.

Hartline, H. K., & Ratliff, F. (1957). Inhibitory interaction of receptor units in the eye of Limulus. *Journal of General Physiology, 40,* 357–376.

Hartman, A., & Hollister, L. (1963). Effect of mescaline, lysergic and diethylamide and psilocybin on color perception. *Psychopharmacologia, 4,* 441–451.

Harvey, L. O., Jr., & Leibowitz, H. (1967). Effects of exposure duration, cue reduction, and temporary monocularity on size matching at short distances. *Journal of the Optical Society of America, 57,* 249–253.

Head, H. (1920). *Studies in neurology.* London & New York: Oxford University Press.

Heaton, J. M. (1968). *The eye: Phenomenology and psychology of function and disorder.* London: Tavistock.

Hecht, S., & Mandelbaum, M. (1938). Rod-cone dark adaptation and vitamin A. *Science, 88,* 219–221.

Hecht, S., Shlaer, S., & Pirenne, M. H. (1942). Energy, quanta, and vision. *Journal of General Physiology, 25,* 819–840.

Heckenmueller, E. G. (1965). Stabilization of the retinal image: A review of method, effects, and theory. *Psychological Bulletin, 63,* 157–169.

Heggelund, P. (1981a). Receptive field organization of simple cells in cat striate cortex. *Experimental Brain Research, 42,* 89–98.

Heggelund, P. (1981b). Receptive field organization of complex cells in cat striate cortex. *Experimental Brain Research, 42,* 99–107.

Hein, A. (1980). The development of visually guided behaviour. In C. Harris (Ed.), *Visual coding and adaptability* (pp. 51–68). Hillsdale, NJ: Lawrence Erlbaum Associates.

Hein, A., & Held, R. (1967). Dissociation of the visual placing response into elicited and guided components. *Science, 158,* 390–392.

Hein, A., Held, R., & Gower, E. C. (1970). Development and segmentation of visually controlled movement by selective exposure during rearing. *Journal of Comparative and Physiological Psychology, 73,* 181–187.

Hein, S., & Diamond, R. M. (1971). Contrasting development of visually triggered and guided movements in kittens with respect to interocular and interline equivalence. *Journal of Comparative and Physiological Psychology, 76,* 219–224.

Heinemann, E. G. (1955). Simultaneous brightness induction as a function of inducing and test field luminance. *Journal of Experimental Psychology, 50,* 89–96.

Held, R. (1981). Development of acuity in infants with normal and anomalous visual experience. In R. Aslin, J. Alberts, & M. Petersen (Eds.), *Development of perception: Psychobiological perspectives: Vol. 2. The visual system* (pp. 279–297). New York: Academic Press.

Held, R., & Bauer, J. A. (1967). Visually guided reaching in infant monkeys after restricted rearing. *Science, 155,* 718–720.

Held, R., & Bossom, J. (1961). Neonatal deprivation and adult rearrangement: Complementary techniques for analyzing plastic sensory-motor coordinations. *Journal of Comparative and Physiological Psychology, 54,* 33–37.

Held, R., & Hein, A. (1958). Adaptation of disarranged hand-eye coordination contingent upon re-afferent stimulation. *Perceptual and Motor Skills, 8,* 87–90.

Held, R., & Hein, A. (1963). Movement-produced stimulation in the development of visually guided behavior. *Journal of Comparative and Physiological Psychology, 56,* 872–876.

Held, R., & Hein, A. (1967). On the modifiability of form perception. In W. Wathen-Dunn (Ed.), *Models for the perception of speech and visual form* (pp. 296–304). Cambridge, MA: MIT Press.

Hellekant, G. (1965). Electrophysiological investigation of the gustatory effect of ethyl alcohol: The summated response of the chorda tympani in the cat, dog and rat. *Acta Physiologica Scandinavica, 64,* 392–397.

Hellstrom, A. (1979). Time errors and differential sensation weighting. *Journal of Experimental Psychology: Human Perception and Performance, 5,* 460–477.

Helmholtz, H. E. F. von. (1930). *The sensations of tone* (A. J. Ellis, Trans.). New York: Longmans, Green. (Original work published 1863)

Helmholtz, H. E. F. von. (1962). *Treatise on Physiological Optics* J. P. C. Southall (Ed. and Trans.). New York: Dover. (Original work published 1909)

Helson, H. (1959). Adaptation level theory. In S. Koch (Ed.), *Psychology: A study of a science* (Vol. 1, pp. 565–621). New York: McGraw-Hill.

Helson, H. (1964). *Adaptation level theory: An experimental and systematic approach to behavior.* New York: Harper & Row.

Henmon, V. A. C. (1906). The time of perception as a measure of differences in sensations. *Archives of Philosophy, Psychology and Scientific Methods,* No. 8.

Henning, H. (1915). Der Geruch. I. *Zietschrift fuer Psychologie, 73,* 161–257.

Henning, H. (1916). Die Qualitatenreihe des Geschmaks. *Zeitschrift fuer Psychologie, 74,* 203–219.

Hensel, H. (1966). Classes of receptor units predominantly related to thermal stimuli. In A. V. S. de Ruech & J. Knight (Eds.), *Touch, heat and pain* (pp. 275–288). Boston: Little, Brown.

Hensel, H. (1968). Electrophysiology of cutaneous thermoreceptors. In D. R. Kenshalo (Ed.), *The skin senses* (pp. 384–399). Springfield, IL: Thomas.

Hensel, H. (1981). *Thermoreception and temperature regulation.* New York: Academic Press.

Hering, E. (1964). *Outlines of a theory of the light sense* (L. M. Hurvich & D. Jameson, Trans.). Cambridge, MA: Harvard University Press. (Original work published 1878)

Hernandez-Peon, R. (1964). Psychiatric implications of neurophysiological research. *Bulletin of the Meninger Clinic, 28,* 165–185.

Hershenson, M. (1969). Perception of letter arrays as a function of absolute retinal locus. *Journal of Experimental Psychology, 80,* 201–202.

Hess, E. H. (1950). Development of the chick's response to light and shade cues of depth. *Journal of Comparative and Physiological Psychology, 43,* 112–122.

Hess, E. H. (1965). Attitude and pupil size. *Scientific American, 212,* 46–54.

Hick, W. E. (1952). On the rate of gain of information. *Quarterly Journal of Experimental Psychology, 4,* 11–26.

Hickey, T. L. (1977). Postnatal development of the human lateral geniculate nucleus: Relationship to a critical period for the visual system. *Science, 198,* 836–838.

Hicks, R. E. & Allen, D. A. (1979). The repetition effect in judgments of temporal duration across minutes, days and months. *American Journal of Psychology, 92,* 323–333.

Hicks, R. E., Miller, G. W., & Kinsbourne, M. (1976). Prospective and retrospective judgments of time as a function of amount of information processed. *American Journal of Psychology, 89,* 719–730.

Hirsch, H. (1972). Visual perception in cats after environmental surgery. *Experimental Brain Research*, 15, 405–423.

Hirsch, H. V. B., & Jacobson, N. (1975). The perfectible brain: Principles of neuronal development. In M. S. Gazzaniga & C. Blakemore (Eds.), *Handbook of psychobiology* (pp. 107–137). New York: Academic Press.

Hirsch, H. V., & Spinelli, D. N. (1970). Visual experience modifies distribution of horizontally and vertically oriented receptive fields in cats. *Science*, 168, 869–871.

Hirsh, I. J. (1948). The influence of interaural phase on interaural summation and inhibition. *Journal of the Acoustical Society of America*, 20, 536–544.

Hirst, W., Spelke, E., Reaves, C. C., Caharack, G., & Neisser, U. (1980). Dividing attention without alternation or automaticity. *Journal of Experimental Psychology: General*, 109, 98–117.

Hoagland, H. (1933). The physiological control of judgment of duration: Evidence for a chemical clock. *Journal of General Psychology*, 9, 267–287.

Hochberg, J. (1971a). Perception: II. Space and movement. In J. W. Kling & L. A. Riggs (Eds.), *Woodworth and Schlossberg's experimental psychology* (3rd ed., pp. 475–550). New York: Holt, Rinehart & Winston.

Hochberg, J. (1971b). Perception: I. Color and shape. In J. W. Kling & L. A. Riggs (Eds.), *Woodworth and Schlossberg's experimental psychology* (3rd ed., pp. 395–474). New York: Holt, Rinehart & Winston.

Hochberg, J. (1972). Nativism and empiricism in perception. In L. Postman (Ed.), *Psychology in the making* (pp. 255–330). New York: Knopf.

Hochberg, J. (1978). *Perception* (2nd ed.). Englewood Cliffs, NJ: Prentice-Hall.

Hochberg, J., & Beck, J. (1954). Apparent spatial arrangement and perceived brightness. *Journal of Experimental Psychology*, 47, 263–266.

Hochberg, J., & Brooks, V. (1960). The psychophysics of form: Reversible-perspective drawings of spatial objects. *American Journal of Psychology*, 73, 337–354.

Hochberg, J., & Brooks, U. (1962). Pictorial recognition as an unlearned ability: A study of one child's performance. *American Journal of Psychology*, 75, 624–628.

Hodos, W. (1970). A nonparametric index of response bias for use in detection and recognition experiments. *Psychological Bulletin*, 74, 351–354.

Hoffer, A., & Osmond, H. (1967). *The hallucinogens*. New York: Academic Press.

Hoffman, J. E. (1980). Interaction between global and local levels of form. *Journal of Experimental Psychology: Human Perception and Performance*, 6, 222–234.

Hoffmann, K. P. (1973). Conduction velocity in pathways from retina to superior colliculus in the cat: A correlation with receptive-field properties. *Journal of Neurophysiology*, 36, 409–424.

Hoffmann, K. P. (1979). Optokinetic nystagmus and single cell responses in the nucleus tractus opticus after early monocular deprivation in the cat. In R. D. Freeman (Ed.), *Developmental neurobiology of vision*, (pp. 63–72). New York: Plenum.

Hoffmann, K. P., & Sherman, S. (1975). Effects of early binocular deprivation on visual input to cat superior colliculus. *Journal of Neurophysiology*, 38, 1049–1059.

Holland, H. (1960). Drugs and personality: XII. A comparison of several drugs by the flicker-fusion method. *Journal of Mental Science*, 106, 858–861.

Holst, E. von, & Mittelstaedt, H. (1950). Das Reafenzprinzip (wechselwirkungen zeischen zentral Nervensystem und Peripherie). *Naturwissenschaften*, 37, 464–476.

Holway, A. F., & Boring, E. G. (1941). Determinants of apparent visual size with distance variant. *American Journal of Psychology*, 54, 21–37.

Houtsma, A. J. M., & Goldstein, J. L. (1972). The central origin of the pitch of complex tones: Evidence from musical interval recognition. *Journal of the Acoustical Society of America*, 51, 520–529.

Howard, I. P. (1982). *Human visual orientation*. Chichester: Wiley.

Howard, I. P., Anstis, S., & Lucia, H. C. (1974). The relative lability of mobile and stationary components in a visual-motor adaptation task. *Quar-*

terly Journal of Experimental Psychology, 26, 293–300.

Howard, I. P., Craske, B., & Templeton, W. B. (1965). Visuomotor adaptation to discordant exafferent stimulation. *Journal of Experimental Psychology, 70,* 189–191.

Hoyer, W., & Plude, D. (1980). Attentional and perceptual processes in the study of cognitive aging. In L. Poon (Ed.), *Aging in the 1980s* (pp. 227–238). Washington, DC: American Psychological Association.

Hubbell, W. L., & Bownds, M. D. (1979). Visual transduction in vertebrate photoreceptors. *Annual Review of Neurosciences, 2,* 17–34.

Hubel, D. H., & Wiesel, T. N. (1962). Receptive fields, binocular interaction and functional architecture in the cat's visual cortex. *Journal of Physiology (London), 160,* 106–154.

Hubel, D. H., & Wiesel, T. N. (1968). Receptive fields and functional architecture of monkey striate cortex. *Journal of Physiology (London), 195,* 215–243.

Hubel, D., & Wiesel, T. (1979). Brain mechanisms of vision. *Scientific American, 82,* 84–97.

Hubel, D., Weisel, T., & LeVay, S. (1977). Plasticity of ocular dominance columns in monkey striate cortex. *Philosophical Transactions of the Royal Society of London B, 278,* 377–409.

Hudson, W. (1960). Pictorial depth perception in subcultural groups in Africa. *Journal of Social Psychology, 52,* 183–208.

Hudson, W. (1962). Pictorial perception and educational adaptation in Africa. *Psychologia, Africana, 9,* 226–239.

Huggins, A. W. F. (1981). Speech perception and auditory processing. In D. J. Getty & J. H. Howard (Eds.), *Auditory and visual pattern recognition.* Hillsdale, NJ: Lawrence Erlbaum Associates.

Hughes, G. W., & Hemdal, J. F. (1965). *Speech analysis.* Lafayette, IN: Purdue Research Foundation.

Hurvich, L. M. (1981). *Color vision.* Sunderland, MA: Sinauer Associates.

Hurvich, L. M., & Jameson, D. (1974). Opponent processes as a model of neural organization. *American Psychologist, 29,* 88–102.

Hutman, L. P., & Sekuler, R. (1980). Spatial vision and aging: II. Criterion effects. *Journal of Gerontology, 35,* 700–706.

Hutz, C. S., & Bechtoldt, H. P. (1980). The development of binocular discrimination in infants. *Bulletin of the Psychonomic Society, 16,* 83–86.

Huxley, A. (1963). *The doors of perception and heaven and hell.* New York: Harper & Row.

Hyman, A., Mentyer, T., & Calderone, L. (1979). The contribution of olfaction to taste discrimination. *Bulletin of the Psychonomic Society, 13,* 359–362.

Iacono, W. G., Peloquin, L. J., Lumry, A. E., Valentine, R. H., & Tuason, V. B. (1982). Eye tracking in patients with unipolar and bipolar affective disorders in remission. *Journal of Abnormal Psychology, 91,* 35–44.

Ingram, J. C. (1975). *Perceptual dimensions of phonemic recognition.* Doctoral dissertation, University of Alberta, Edmonton, Alberta.

Ingram, R. M., & Barr, A. (1979). Changes in refraction between the ages of 1 and 3½ years. *British Journal of Ophthalmology, 63,* 39–42.

Ippolitov, F. W. (1973). Interanalyser differences in the sensitivity-strength parameter for vision, hearing and cutaneous modalities. In V. D. Nebylitsyn & J. A. Gray (Eds.), *Biological bases of individual behavior* (pp. 43–61). New York: Academic Press.

Ittelson, W. H. (1951). Size as a cue to distance: Static localization. *American Journal of Psychology, 64,* 54–67.

Ittelson, W. H. (1960). Visual space perception. Berlin & New York: Springer-Verlag.

Ittelson, W. H. (1962). Perception and transactional psychology. In S. Koch (Ed.), *Psychology: A study of a science* (Vol. 4, pp. 660–704). New York: MacGraw-Hill.

Jacobs, G. H. (1976). Color vision. *Annual Review of Psychology, 27,* 63–89.

Jacobson, R., Fant, G. G. M., & Halle, M. (1952). Preliminaries to speech analysis (Acoustical Lab Technical Lab Report No. 13). Massachusetts Institute of Technology.

Jacobson, R., Fant, G. G. M., & Halle, M. (1961). *Preliminaries to speech analysis: The distinctive features and their correlates.* Cambridge, MA: MIT Press.

Jahoda, G., & McGurk, H. (1974). Pictorial depth perception: A developmental study. *British Journal of Psychology, 65,* 141–149.

James, W. (1890). *The principles of psychology.* New York: Holt, Rinehart & Winston.

Jameson, D., & Hurvich, L. M. (1959). Note on factors influencing the relation between stereoscopic acuity and observation distance. *Journal of the Optical Society of America, 49,* 639.

Jameson, D., & Hurvich, L. M. (1964). Theory of brightness and color contrast in human vision. *Vision Research, 4,* 135–154.

Jarvis, J. R. (1977). On Fechner-Benham subjective colour. *Vision Research, 17,* 445–451.

Javel, E. (1981). Suppression of auditory nerve responses: I. Temporal analysis, intensity effects and suppression contours. *Journal of the Acoustical Society of America, 69,* 1735–1745.

Jennings, J. A. M., & Charman, W. N. (1981). Off-axis image quality in the human eye. *Vision Research, 21,* 445–455.

Jensen, D., & Engel, R. (1971). Statistical procedures for relating dichotomous responses to maturation and EEG measurements. *Electroencephalography and Clinical Neurophysiology, 30,* 437–443.

Jerison, H. J. (1970). Vigilance, discrimination and attention. In D. I. Mostofsky (Ed.), *Attention: Contemporary theory and analysis* (pp. 127–148). New York: Appleton-Century-Crofts.

Jesteadt, W. (1980). An adaptive procedure for subjective judgments. *Perception & Psychophysics, 28,* 85–88.

Jesteadt, W., Bacon, S. P., & Lehman, J. R. (1982). Forward masking as a function of frequency, masker level, and signal delay. *Journal of the Acoustical Society of America, 71,* 950–962.

Jesteadt, W., & Wier, C. C. (1977). Comparison of monaural and binaural discrimination of intensity and frequency. *Journal of the Acoustical Society of America, 61,* 1599–1603.

Jesteadt, W., Wier, C. C., & Green, D. M. (1977). Intensity discrimination as a function of frequency and sensation level. *Journal of the Acoustical Society of America, 61,* 169–177.

Johansson, G. (1976a). Visual motion perception. In R. Held & W. Richards (Eds.), *Recent progress in perception: Readings from Scientific American* (pp. 67–75). San Francisco: Freeman. (Reprinted from *Scientific American,* 1975)

Johansson, G. (1976b). Spatio-temporal differentiation and integration in visual motion perception. *Psychological Research, 38,* 379–393.

Johansson, G., von Hofsten, C., & Jansson, G. (1980). Event perception. *Annual Review of Psychology, 31,* 27–63.

Johnson, D. H. (1980). The relationship between spike rate and synchrony in responses of auditory-nerve fibers to single tones. *Journal of the Acoustical Society of America, 68,* 1115–1122.

Jones, B., & Huang, Y. L. (1982). Space-time dependencies in psychophysical judgment of extent and duration: Algebraic models of the Tau and Kappa effects. *Psychological Bulletin, 91,* 128–142.

Julesz, B. (1971). *Foundations of cyclopean perception.* Chicago: University of Chicago Press.

Julesz, B. (1981). Textons, the elements of texture perception and their interactions. *Nature, 290,* 91–97.

Julesz, B., & Schumer, R. A. (1981). Early visual perception. *Annual Review of Psychology, 32,* 575–627.

Jusczyk, P. W., Smith, L. B., & Murphy, C. (1981). The perceptual classification of speech. *Perception & Psychophysics, 30,* 10–23.

Kaess, D. W. (1980). Instructions and decision times of size-constancy responses. *Perception & Psychophysics, 27,* 477–482.

Kahneman, D. (1966). Time-intensity reciprocity in acuity as a function of luminance and figure-ground contrast. *Vision Research, 6,* 207–215.

Kahneman, D. (1968). Method, findings, and theory in studies of visual masking. *Psychological Bulletin, 70,* 404–425.

Kahneman, D. (1973). *Attention and effort.* Englewood Cliffs, NJ: Prentice-Hall.

Kahneman, D., Norman, J., & Kubovy, M. (1967). Critical duration for the resolution of form: Centrally or peripherally determined? *Journal of Experimental Psychology, 73,* 323–327.

Kaneko, A., Nishimura, Y., Tachibana, M., Tauchi, M., & Shimai, K. (1981). Physiological and morphological studies of signal pathways in the carp retina. *Vision Research, 21*, 1519–1526.

Kaplan, A., & Glanville, E. (1964). Taste thresholds for bitterness and cigarette smoking. *Nature (London), 202*, 1366.

Karmel, B. Z., & Maisel, E. B. (1975). A neuronal activity model for infant visual attention. In L. B. Cohen & P. Salapatek (Eds.), *Infant perception: From sensation to cognition: Vol. 1. Basic visual processes* (pp. 78–133). New York: Academic Press.

Karvellas, P. C., Pokorny, J., Smith, V. C., & Tanczos, Z. (1979). Hue reversal in the Fechner-Benham color effect following white light adaption. *Vision Research, 19*, 1277–1279.

Kasamatsu, T. (1976). Visual cortical neurons influenced by the oculomotor input: Characterization of their receptive field properties. *Brain Research, 113*, 271–292.

Kauer, J. S. (1980). Some spatial characteristics of central information processing in the vertebrate olfactory pathway. In H. vander Starre (Ed.), *Olfaction and taste VII*. London: IRL Press.

Kaufman, L. (1974). *Sight and mind: An introduction to visual perception*. London & New York: Oxford University Press.

Kaufmann, R., Maland, J., & Yonas, A. (1981). Sensitivity of 5 and 7-month-old infants to pictorial depth information. *Journal of Experimental Child Psychology, 32*, 162–168.

Keller, H. (1931). *The story of my life*. New York: Doubleday.

Kennedy, J., & Ostry, D. (1976). Approaches to picture perception: Perceptual experience and ecological optics. *Canadian Journal of Psychology, 30*, 90–98.

Kennedy, L. M., & Halpern, B. P. (1980). A biphasic model for the action of the gymnemic acids and ziziphins on taste receptor cell membranes. *Chemical Senses, 5*, 149–158.

Kenshalo, D. R. (Ed.). (1980). *Sensory functions of the skin of humans*. New York: Plenum.

Kenshalo, D. R., & Nafe, J. P. (1962). A quantitative theory of feeling: 1960. *Psychological Review, 69*, 17–33.

Kenshalo, D. R., Nafe, J. P., & Brooks, B. (1961). Variations in thermal sensitivity. *Science, 134*, 104–105.

Kenshalo, D. R., & Scott, H. A., Jr. (1966). Temporal course of thermal adaptation. *Science, 151*, 1095–1096.

Keren, G., & Baggen, S. (1981). Recognition models of alphanumeric characters. *Perception & Psychophysics, 29*, 234–245.

Keverne, E. B. (1976). Olfactory cues in mammalian sexual behavior. In J. B. Hutchison (Ed.), *Biological determinants of sexual behavior*. New York: Wiley.

Khanna, S. M., & Leonard, D. G. B. (1982). Basilar membrane tuning in the cat cochlea. *Science, 215*, 305–306.

Kiang, N. Y. S., Rho, J. M., Northrop, C. C., Liberman, M. C., & Ryugo, D. K. (1982). Hair-cell innervation by spiral ganglion cells in adult cats. *Science, 217*, 175–177.

Kilbride, P. L., & Leibowitz, H. W. (1975). Factors affecting the magnitude of the Ponzo illusion among the Baganda. *Perception & Psychophysics, 17*, 543–548.

Kilbride, P., & Robbins, M. (1968). Linear perspective pictorial depth perception and education among the Baganda. *Perceptual and Motor Skills, 27*, 601–602.

Kimura, D. (1963). Right temporal-lobe damage. *Archives of Neurology, 8*, 264–271.

Kimura, K., & Beidler, L. M. (1961). Microelectrode study of taste receptors of rat and hamster. *Journal of Cellular and Comparative Physiology, 58*, 131–140.

Kinchla, R., & Wolfe, J. (1979). The order of visual processing: "Top-down," "bottom-up," or "middle-out." *Perception & Psychophysics, 25*, 225–231.

Kinnear, P. R. (1979). The effects of coloured surrounds on colour naming and luminosity. *Vision Research, 19*, 1381–1387.

Kinney, G. C., Marsetta, M., & Showman, D. J. (1966, November). Studies in display symbol legibility: Part XII. The legibility of alphanumeric symbols for digitalized television. Bedford, MA: The Mitre Corporation. (ESD-TR-66-117) Cited in P. H. Lindsay & D. A. Norman. *Human information processing: An introduction to psychology* (2nd ed., pp. 267–268). New York: Academic Press, 1977.

Kirk-Smith, M., Booth, D. A., Carroll, D., & Davies, P. (1978). Human social attitudes affected by androstenol. *Research Communications in Psychology, Psychiatry and Behavior, 3,* 379–384.

Kitzes, L. M., Gibson, M. M., Rose, J. E., & Hind, J. E. (1978). Initial discharge latency and threshold considerations for some neurons in cochlear nucleus complex of the cat. *Journal of Neurophysiology, 41,* 1165–1182.

Klatt, D. H. (1980). Speech perception: A model for acoustic-phonetic analysis and lexical access. In R. Cole (Ed.), *Perception and production of fluent speech.* Hillsdale, NJ: Lawrence Erlbaum Associates.

Klein, G. S. (1970). *Perception, motives and personality.* New York: Knopf.

Klein, W., Plomp, R., & Pols, L. C. W. (1970). Vowel spectra, vowel spaces and vowel identification. *Journal of the Acoustical Society of America, 48,* 999.

Kluver, H., & Bucy, P. C. (1937). "Psychic blindness" and other symptoms following bilateral temporal lobectomy in Rhesus monkeys. *American Journal of Physiology, 119,* 352–353.

Knudsen, E. I., & Konishi, M. (1978a). A neural map of auditory space in the owl. *Science, 200,* 795–797.

Knudsen, E. I., & Konishi, M. (1978b). Center-surround organization of auditory receptive fields in the owl. *Science, 202,* 778–780.

Kohler, I. (1962). Experiments with goggles. *Scientific American, 206,* 62–86.

Kohler, I. (1964). The formation and transformation of the perceptual world. *Psychological Issues, 3* (Whole No. 4).

Kohler, W. (1923). Zur Theories des Sukzessivvergleichs und der Zeitfehler. *Psychologische Forschung, 4,* 115–175.

Kolb, B., & Whishaw, I. Q. (1980). *Fundamentals of human neuropsychology.* San Francisco: Freeman.

Kolb, H., Nelson, R., & Mariani, A. (1981). Amacrine cells, bipolar cells and ganglion cells of the cat retina: A Golgi study. *Vision Research, 21,* 1081–1114.

Konstadt, N., & Forman, E. (1965). Field dependence and external directedness. *Journal of Personality and Social Psychology, 1,* 490–493.

Kopfermann, H. (1930). Psychologische Untersuchungen uber die Wirkung Zweickmen sconalar Darstellungen Korperlicher Gebilde. *Psychologische Forschung, 13,* 293–364. Cited in K. Koffka, *Principles of Gestalt psychology* (pp. 159–160). New York: Harcourt Brace Jovanovich.

Kosterlitz, H. W., & McKnight, A. T. (1981). Opioid peptides and sensory function. In D. Ottoson, (Ed.), *Progress in sensory physiology* (Vol. 1, pp. 31–95). Heidelberg: Springer-Verlag.

Kozlowski, L. T., & Cutting, J. E. (1977). Recognizing the sex of a walker from a dynamic point-light display. *Perception & Psychophysics, 21,* 575–580.

Krauskopf, J., & Reeves, A. (1980). Measurement of the effect of photon noise on detection. *Vision Research, 20,* 193–196.

Kremenitzer, J. P., Vaughan, H. G., Kurtzberg, D., & Dowling, K. (1979). Smooth-pursuit eye movements in the newborn infant. *Child Development, 50,* 442–448.

Krueger, L. E. (1982). A word-superiority effect with print and braille characters. *Perception & Psychophysics, 31,* 345–352.

Kruger, J. (1981). The difference between x- and y-type responses in ganglion cells of the cat's retina. *Vision Research, 21,* 1685–1687.

Kruger, J., & Gouras, P. (1980). Spectral selectivity of cells and its dependence on slit length in monkeys' visual cortex. *Journal of Neurophysiology, 43,* 1055–1069.

Krumhansl, C. L., Bharucha, J. J., & Kessler, E. J. (1982). Perceived harmonic structure of chords in three related musical keys. *Journal of Experimental Psychology: Human Perception and Performance, 8,* 24–36.

Krumhansl, C. L., & Kessler, E. J. (1982). Tracing the dynamic changes in perceived tonal organization in a spatial representation of musical keys. *Psychological Review, 89,* 334–368.

Krumhansl, C. L., & Shepard, R. N. (1979). Quantification of the hierarchy of tonal functions within a diatonic context. *Journal of Experimental Psychology: Human Perception and Performance, 5,* 579–594.

Krutz, D., & Butter, C. M. (1980). Impairments in visual discrimination performance and gaze shifts in monkeys with superior collicular lesions. *Brain Research, 196,* 109–124.

Kryter, K. D. (1970). *The effects of noise on man.* New York: Academic Press.

Kuffler, S. W. (1953). Discharge patterns and functional organization of mammalian retina. *Journal of Neurophysiology, 16,* 37–68.

Kupchella, C. (1976). *Sights and sounds.* Indianapolis: Bobbs-Merrill.

LaBerge, D. (1973). Attention and the measurement of perceptual learning. *Memory and Cognition, 1,* 268–276.

LaBerge, D. (1975). Acquisition of automatic processing in perceptual associative learning. In P. M. A. Rabbit & S. Dornic (Eds.), *Attention and performance* (Vol. 5, pp. 50–64). New York: Academic Press.

Ladefoged, P. (1975). *A course in phonetics.* New York: Harcourt Brace Jovanovich.

Lakowski, R. (1962). Is the deterioration of colour discrimination with age due to lens or retinal changes? *Farbe, 11,* 69–86.

Lakowski, R. (1972). The Pickford-Nicolson anomaloscope as a test for acquired dyschromatopsias. *Modern Problems in Ophthalmology, 11,* 25–33.

Lakowski, R., Aspinall, P. A., & Kinnear, P. R. (1972). Association between colour vision losses and diabetes mellitus. *Ophthalmic Research, 4,* 145–159.

Lakowski, R., & Morton, B. A. (1977). The effect of oral contraceptives on colour vision in diabetic women. *Canadian Journal of Ophthalmology, 12,* 89–97.

Lakowski, R., & Morton, B. A. (1978). Acquired color losses and oral contraceptives. *Modern Problems in Ophthalmology, 19,* 314–318.

Landolt, E. (1889). Tableau d'optotypes pour la determination de l'acuite visuelle. *Societe Francais d'Ophthalmologie. 1,* 385ff.

Lanze, M., Weisstein, N., & Harris, C. (1982). Perceived depth vs. structural relevance in the object-superiority effect. *Perception & Psychophysics, 31,* 376–382.

Lappin, J. S., & Preble, L. D. (1975). A demonstration of shape constancy. *Perception & Psychophysics, 17,* 439–444.

Lashley, K. S. (1931). The mechanism: IV. The cerebral areas necessary for pattern vision in the rat. *Journal of Comparative Neurology, 53,* 419–478.

Lawry, J. A. (1980). The interfering effect of word perception on letter identification. *Perception & Psychophysics, 28,* 577–588.

Layton, B. (1975). Perceptual noise and aging. *Psychological Bulletin, 82,* 875–883.

Leeuwenberg, E. L. J. (1967). *Structural information of visual patterns: An efficient coding system in perception.* The Hague, The Netherlands: Mouton.

Leeuwenberg, E. L. J. (1971). A general coding system, simulating the human classification of visual and auditory patterns. *De Ingenieur, 8,* 134–142.

Lefton, L. A. (1973). Metacontrast: A review. *Perception & Psychophysics, 13,* 161–171.

Lehiste, I., & Peterson, G. (1959). Vowel amplitude and phonemic stress in American English. *Journal of the Acoustical Society of America, 31,* 428–435.

Lehmkuhle, S., & Fox, R. (1980). Effect of depth separation of metacontrast masking. *Journal of Experimental Psychology: Human Perception and Performance, 6,* 605–621.

Lehmkuhle, S., Kratz, K. E., Mangel, S. C., & Sherman, S. M. (1980). Spatial and temporal sensitivity of x- and y-cells in dorsal lateral geniculate nucleus of the cat. *Journal of Neurophysiology, 43,* 520–541.

Leiberman, A. M., Cooper, F. S., Shankweiler, D. P., & Studdert-Kennedy, M. (1967). Perception of the speech code. *Psychological Review, 74,* 431–461.

Leibowitz, H. W. (1955). Some factors influencing the variability of vernier judgments. *American Journal of Psychology, 68,* 266–273.

Leibowitz, H. W. (1971). Sensory, learned, and cognitive mechanisms of size perception. *Annals of the New York Academy of Sciences, 188*, 47–62.

Leibowitz, H. W. (1974). Multiple mechanisms of size perception and size constancy. *Hiroshima Forum for Psychology, 1*, 47–53.

Leibowitz, H. W., & Bourne, L. E. (1956). Time and intensity as determiners of perceived shape. *Journal of Experimental Psychology, 51*, 277–281.

Leibowitz, H. W., & Harvey, L. O., Jr. (1969). Effect of instructions, environment, and type of test object on matched size. *Journal of Experimental Psychology, 81*, 36–43.

Leibowitz, H. W., & Moore, D. (1966). Role of changes in accommodations and convergence in the perception of size. *Journal of the Optical Society of America, 56*, 1120–1123.

Leibowitz, H. W., & Owens, D. A. (1977). Nighttime accidents and selective visual degradation. *Science, 197*, 422–423.

Leibowitz, H., & Pick, H. (1972). Cross-cultural and educational aspects of the Ponzo perspective illusion. *Perception & Psychophysics, 12*, 430–432.

Leibowitz, H. W., Post, R. B., Brandt, T., & Dichgans, J. (1982). Implications of recent developments in dynamic spatial orientation and visual resolution for vehicle guidance. In A. H. Wertheim, W. A. Wagenaar, & H. W. Leibowitz (Eds.), *Tutorials on motion perception*, (pp. 231–260). New York: Plenum.

Leibowitz, H. W., Post, R. B., & Ginsburg, A. (1980). The role of fine detail in visually controlled behavior. *Investigative Ophthalmology and Visual Science, 19*, 846–848.

Lenneberg, E. H. (1962). Understanding language without ability to speak: A case report. *Journal of Abnormal and Social Psychology, 65*, 419–425.

Lennie, P. (1980). Parallel visual pathways: A review. *Vision Research, 20*, 561–594.

Leventhal, A., & Hirsch, H. (1980). Receptive-field properties of different classes of neurons in visual cortex of normal and dark-reared cats. *Journal of Neurophysiology, 43*, 1111–1132.

Levin, S., Lipton, R. B., & Holtzman, P. S. (1981). Pursuit eye movements in psychopathology: Effects of target characteristics. *Biological Psychiatry, 16*, 255–267.

Levine, M. W., & Shefner, J. M. (1981). *Fundamentals of sensation and perception*. Reading, MA: Addison-Wesley.

Levine, P. (1980). Parallel visual pathways: A review. *Vision Research, 20*, 561–594.

Levy, D. L., Lipton, R. B., & Holtzman, P. S. (1981). Smooth pursuit eye movements: Effects of alcohol and chloral hydrate. *Journal of Psychiatric Research, 16*, 1–11.

Lewis, T. L., Maurer, D., & Kay, D. (1978). Newborns' central vision: Whole or hole? *Journal of Experimental Child Psychology, 26*, 193–203.

Liberman, M. C. (1982). Single-neuron labeling in the cat auditory nerve. *Science, 216*, 1239–1241.

Lichte, W. H., & Borresen, C. R. (1967). Influence of instructions on degree of shape constancy. *Journal of Experimental Psychology, 74*, 538–542.

Lichtenstein, M. (1963). Spatio-temporal factors in cessation of smooth apparent motion. *Journal of the Optical Society of America, 53*, 302–306.

Lie, I. (1980). Visual detection and resolution as a function of retinal locus. *Vision Research, 20*, 967–974.

Lim, D. J. (1980). Cochlear anatomy related to cochlear micromechanics: A review. *Journal of the Acoustical Society of America, 67*, 1686–1695.

Lindsay, P. H., & Norman, D. A. (1977). *Human information processing* (2nd ed.). New York: Academic Press.

Linton, H., & Graham, E. (1959). Personality correlates of persuasibility. In I. Janis (Ed.), *Personality and persuasibility*. New Haven, CT: Yale University Press.

Lisker, L., & Abramson, A. (1970). The voicing dimension: Some experiments in comparative phonetics. *Proceedings of the 6th International Congress of Phonetic Sciences*, 563–567.

Lockhead, G. R. (1966). Effects of dimensional redundancy on visual discrimination. *Journal of Experimental Psychology, 72*, 95–104.

Lockhead, G. R. (1970). Identification and the form of multidimensional discrimination space. *Journal of Experimental Psychology, 85*, 1–10.

Lockhead, G. R. (1972). Processing dimensional

stimuli: A note. *Psychological Review, 79*, 410–419.

Lockhead, G. R. (1979). Holistic versus analytic process models: A reply. *Journal of Experimental Psychology: Human Perception and Performance, 5*, 746–755.

Lockhead, G. R., & Byrd, R. (1981). Practically perfect pitch. *Journal of the Acoustical Society of America, 70*, 387–389.

Lockhead, G. R., & King, M. C. (1977). Classifying integral stimuli. *Journal of Experimental Psychology: Human Perception and Performance, 3*, 436–443.

Loewenstein, W. R. (1960). Biological transducers. *Scientific American, 203*, 98–108.

Loftus, E. (1974). Reconstructing memory: The incredible eye witness. *Psychology Today, 8*, 116–119.

Loftus, E. (1979). *Eyewitness testimony*. Cambridge, MA: Harvard University Press.

Loftus, G., & Mackworth, N. (1978). Cognitive determinants of fixation location during picture viewing. *Journal of Experimental Psychology: Human Perception and Performance, 4*, 565–572.

Loomis, J. M. (1981). Tactile pattern perception. *Perception, 10*, 5–27.

Lorden, R., Atkeson, B. M., & Pollack, R. H. (1979). Differences in the magnitude of the Delboeuf illusion and Usnadze effect during adulthood. *Journal of Gerontology, 34*, 229–233.

Lowenstein, O., & Sand, A. (1940). The mechanism of the semicircular canal: A study of the responses of single-fibre preparations to angular accelerations and to rotation at constant speed. *Proceedings of the Royal Society of London, Series B, 129*, 256–275.

Lumsden, E. (1980). Problems of magnification and minification: An explanation of the distortions of distance, slant, shape, and velocity. In M. Hagen (Ed.), *Perception of pictures: Vol. I. Alberti's window: The projective model of pictorial information* (pp. 91–135). New York: Academic Press.

Luria, A. R. (1972). Memory disturbances in local brain lesions. *Neuropsychologia, 9*, 367–375.

Luria, A. R. (1973). *The working brain*. London: Penguin Books.

Lynn, P. A., & Sayers, B. M. A. (1970). Cochlear innervation, signal processing, and their relation to auditory time—intensity effects. *Journal of the Acoustical Society of America, 47*, 523–533.

MacArthur, R. D., & Sekular, R. (1982). Alcohol and motion perception. *Perception & Psychophysics, 31*, 502–505.

Maccoby, E. E., & Jacklin, C. N. (1974). *The psychology of sex differences*. Stanford, CA: Stanford University Press.

Mack, A., & Herman, E. (1972). A new illusion: The under-estimation of distance during pursuit eye movements. *Perception & Psychophysics, 12*, 471–473.

Mackworth, N. H. (1950). Researches on the measurements of human performance. *Medical Research Council (Great Britain), Special Report Series*, (SRS-268).

Mackworth, N. H., & Bruner, J. S. (1970). How adults and children search and recognize pictures. *Human Development, 13*, 149–177.

MacLeod, D. I. A. (1978). Visual sensitivity. *Annual Review of Psychology, 29*, 613–645.

MacLeod, P. (1971). An experimental approach to the peripheral mechanisms of olfactory discrimination. In G. Ohloff, & A. F. Thomas (Eds.), *Gustation and olfaction* (pp. 28–44). New York: Academic Press.

MacLeod, R. (1947). The effects of "artificial penumbra" on the brightness of included areas. In A. Michotte (Ed.), *Miscellanea psychologica* (pp. 1–22). Paris: Librairie Philosophique.

Madden, T. M., & Burt, G. S. (1981). Inappropriate constancy scaling theory and the Mueller-Lyer illusion. *Perceptual and Motor Skills, 52*, 211–218.

Mair, R. G., Bouffard, J. A., Engen, T., & Morton, T. (1978). Olfactory sensitivity during the menstrual cycle. *Sensory Process, 2*, 90–98.

Mandler, J. M., & Johnson, N. S. (1976). Some of the thousand words a picture is worth. *Journal of Experimental Psychology: Human Learning and Memory, 2*, 529–540.

Mandler, J. M., & Parker, R. E. (1976). Memory for descriptive and spatial information in complex figures. *Journal of Experimental Psychology: Human Learning and Memory, 2,* 38–48.

Mandler, J. M., & Ritchey, G. H. (1977). Long-term memory for pictures. *Journal of Experimental Psychology: Human Learning and Memory, 3,* 386–396.

Marks, L. E. (1968). Stimulus range, number of categories, and form of the category scale. *American Journal of Psychology, 81,* 467–479.

Marks, L. E. (1974). On scales of sensation: Prolegomena to any future psychophysics that will be able to come forth as science. *Perception & Psychophysics, 16,* 358–376.

Marks, L. E. (1979a). Summation of vibrotactile intensity: An analogy to auditory critical bands? *Sensory Processes, 3,* 188–203.

Marks, L. E. (1979b). A theory of loudness and loudness judgments. *Psychological Review, 86,* 256–285.

Marks, W. B., Dobelle, W. H., & MacNichol, E. F. (1964). Visual pigments of single primate cones. *Science, 143,* 1181–1183.

Marr, D. (1974). The computation of lightness by the primate retina. *Vision Research, 14,* 1377–1388.

Marr, D. (1982). *Vision: A computational investigation into the human representation and processing of visual information.* San Francisco: Freeman.

Marshall, D. A., & Moulton, D. G. (1981). Olfactory sensitivity to α-ionine in humans and dogs. *Chemical Senses, 6,* 53–61.

Martin, D. K., & Holden, B. A. (1982). A new method for measuring the diameter of the in vivo human cornea. *American Journal of Optometry and Physiological Optics, 59,* 436–441.

Martin, M. (1979). Local and global processing: The role of sparsity. *Memory and Cognition, 7,* 476–484.

Masica, D. N., Money, J., Ehrhardt, A. A., & Lewis, V. G. (1969). IQ, fetal sex hormones and cognitive patterns: Studies in testicular feminizing syndrome of androgen insensitivity. *Johns Hopkins Medical Journal, 124,* 34.

Mason, M. (1982). Recognition time for letters and nonletters: Effects of serial position, array size

and processing order. *Journal of Experimental Psychology: Human Perception and Performance, 8,* 724–738.

Massaro, D. W. (1975). *Experimental psychology and information processing.* Chicago: Rand McNally.

Matin, L. (1982). Visual localization and eye movements. In A. H. Wertheim, W. A. Wagenaar, & H. A. Leibowitz (Eds.), *Tutorials on motion perception.* New York: Plenum.

Matin, L., & MacKinnon, G. E. (1964). Autokinetic movement: Selective manipulation of directional components by image stabilization. *Science, 143,* 147–148.

Matthews, B. H. C. (1933). Nerve endings in mammalian muscle. *Journal of Physiology (London), 78,* 1–53.

Maurer, D. (1975). Infant visual perception: Methods of study. In L. B. Cohen & P. Salapatek (Eds.), *Infant perception: From sensation to cognition: Vol. 1. Basic visual processes.* (pp. 1–77). New York: Academic Press.

Maurer, D., & Lewis, T. L. (1979). A physiological explanation of infants' early visual development. *Canadian Journal of Psychology, 33,* 232–251.

Maurer, D., & Lewis, T. (1981). The influence of peripheral stimuli on infant's eye movements. In D. Fisher, R. Monty, & J. Senders (Eds.), *Eye movements: Cognition and visual perception* (pp. 21–29). Hillsdale, NJ: Lawrence Erlbaum Associates.

Maurer, D., & Martello, M. (1980). The discrimination of orientation by young infants. *Vision Research, 20,* 201–204.

Maurer, D., & Salapatek, P. (1976). Development changes in the scanning of faces by young infants. *Child Development, 47,* 523–527.

Maxwell, J. C. (1873). *Treatise on electricity and magnetism.* Oxford: Clarendon Press.

McBurney, D. H. (1969). Effects of adaptation on human taste function. In C. Pfaffman (Ed.), *Olfaction and taste III* (pp. 407–419). New York: The Rockefeller University Press.

McBurney, D. H., & Bartoshuk, L. M. (1972). Water taste in mammals. In D. Schneider (Ed.), *Olfaction and taste IV* (pp. 329–335). Wissenschaftliche Verlagsgesellschaft MBH.

McBurney, D. H., & Gent, J. F. (1979). On the nature of taste qualities. *Psychological Bulletin, 86,* 151–167.

McBurney, D. H., Levine, J. M., & Cavanaugh, P. H. (1977). Psychophysical and social ratings of human body odor. *Personality and Social Psychology Bulletin, 3,* 135–138.

McColgin, F. H. (1960). Movement threshold in peripheral vision. *Journal of the Optical Society of America, 50,* 774-779.

McCollough, C. (1965). Color adaptation of edge detectors in the human visual system. *Science, 149,* 1115–1116.

McFarland, R. A., Domey, R. G., Warren, A. B., & Ward, D. C. (1960). Dark-adaptation as a function of age: I. A statistical analysis. *Journal of Gerontology, 15,* 149–154.

McGlone, J. (1981). Sexual variations in behavior during spatial and verbal tasks. *Canadian Journal of Psychology, 35,* 277–282.

McGuinness, D. (1972). Hearing: Individual differences in perceiving. *Perception, 1,* 465–473.

McGuinness, D. (1976a). Away from a unisex psychology: Individual differences in visual sensory and perceptual processes. *Perception, 5,* 279–294.

McGuinness, D. (1976b). Sex differences in the organization of perception and cognition. In B. Lloyd & U. Archer (Eds.), *Exploring sex differences* (pp. 123–156). New York: Academic Press.

McGuinness, D., & Lewis, I. (1976). Sex differences in visual persistence: Experiments on the Ganzfeld and the after-image. *Perception, 5,* 295–301.

McGuinness, D., & Pribram, K. (1979). The origins of sensory bias in the development of gender differences in perception and cognition. In M. Bortner (Ed.), *Cognitive growth and development.* New York: Bruner/Mazel.

Melzack, R. (1973a). *The puzzle of pain.* London: Penguin Books.

Melzack, R. (1973b). How acupuncture can block pain. *Impact of Science on Society, 23,* 65–75.

Melzack, R., & Casey, K. L. (1968). Sensory, motivational, and central control determinants of pain. In D. R. Kenshalo (Ed.), *The skin senses* (pp. 423–443). Springfield, IL: Thomas.

Melzack, R., & Wall, P. D. (1965). Pain mechanisms: A new theory. *Science, 150,* 971–979.

Melzack, R., Wall, P. D., & Ty, T. C. (1982). Acute pain in an emergency clinic: Latency of onset and descriptor patterns related to different injuries. *Pain, 14,* 33–43.

Mergner, T., Anastosopoulos, D., Becker, W., & Deecke, L. (1981). Discrimination between trunk and head rotation: A study comparing neuronal data from the cat with human psychophysics. *Acta Psychologica, 48,* 291–302.

Merkel, J. (1885). Die zeitlichen Verhaltnisse der Willensthatigkeit. *Philosophische Studien* (Wundt), *2,* 73–127.

Mershon, D. H., & Bowers, J. N. (1976, November). Reverberation and the specific distance tendency as factors in the auditory perception of egocentric distance. Paper presented at the meeting of the Psychonomic Society.

Mershon, D. H., & Bowers, J. N. (1979). Absolute and relative cues for the auditory perception of egocentric distance. *Perception, 8,* 311–322.

Mershon, D. H., Desaulniers, D. H., & Amerson, T. L., Jr. (1980). Visual capture in auditory distance perception: Proximity image effect reconsidered. *Journal of Auditory Research, 20,* 129–136.

Mershon, D. H., Desaulniers, D. H., Kiefer, S. A., & Amerson, T. L., Jr. (1981). Perceived loudness and visually determined auditory distance. *Perception, 10,* 531–543.

Mershon, D. H., & Gogel, W. C. (1970). Effect of stereoscopic cues on perceived whiteness. *American Journal of Psychology, 83,* 55–67.

Mershon, D. H., & King, L. E. (1975). Intensity and reverberation as factors in the auditory perception of egocentric distance. *Perception & Psychophysics, 18,* 409–415.

Mescavage, A. A., Heimer, W. I., Tatz, S. J., & Runyon, R. P. (1971, April). Time estimation as a function of rate of stimulus change. Paper presented at the annual meeting of the Eastern Psychological Association, New York.

Metzler, D. E., & Harris, C. M. (1978). Shapes of spectral bands of visual pigments. *Vision Research, 18,* 1417–1420.

Meyer, G. E. (1981). Latency differences in monoptic and dichoptic shape and color decision making. *Journal of Experimental Psychology: Human Perception and Performance, 7,* 968–971.

Michael, C. R. (1978a). Color-sensitive complex cells in monkey striate cortex. *Journal of Neurophysiology, 41,* 1250–1266.

Michael, C. R. (1978b). Color vision mechanisms in monkey striate cortex: Dual-opponent cells with concentric receptive fields. *Journal of Neurophysiology, 41,* 572–588.

Michael, C. R. (1981). Columnar organization of color cells in monkey's striate cortex. *Journal of Neurophysiology, 46,* 587–604.

Michael, R. P., & Keverne, E. B. (1968). Pheromones in the communication of sexual status in primates. *Nature, 218,* 746–749.

Michael, R. P., Keverne, E. B., & Bousall, R. W. (1971). Pheromones: Isolation of male sex attractouts from a female primate. *Science, 172,* 964–966.

Mickwitz, M. von (1973). The effect of type and amount of familiarization training on pattern recognition. Doctoral dissertation, University of Pittsburgh.

Mikaelian, H. (1974). Adaptation to displaced hearing: A nonproprioceptive change. *Journal of Experimental Psychology, 103,* 326–330.

Mikaelian, H., & Held, R. (1964). Two types of adaptation to an optically-rotated visual field. *American Journal of Psychology, 77,* 257–263.

Miles, F. A., & Fuller, J. E. (1975). Visual tracking and the primate flocculus. *Science, 189,* 1000–1002.

Milewski, A. E. (1976). Infant's discrimination of internal and external pattern elements. *Journal of Experimental Child Psychology, 22,* 229–246.

Miller, G.A. (1947). Sensitivity to changes in the intensity of white noise and its relation to masking and loudness. *Journal of the Acoustical Society of America, 19,* 609–619.

Miller, G. A. (1956). The magical number seven, plus or minus two: Some limits on our capacity for processing information. *Psychological Review, 63,* 81–97.

Miller, J. (1981). Global precedence in attention and decision. *Journal of Experimental Psychology: Human Perception and Performance, 7,* 1161–1174.

Miller, J. (1982). Divided attention: Evidence for coactivation with redundant signals. *Cognitive Psychology, 14,* 247–279.

Miller, J. M., Beaton, R. D., O'Connor, T., & Pfingst, B. E. (1974). Response pattern complexity of auditory cells in the cortex of unanesthetized monkeys. *Brain Research, 69,* 101–113.

Miller, N. D. (1965). Visual recovery from brief exposures to high luminance. *Journal of the Optical Society of America, 55,* 1661–1669.

Mills, A. W. (1958). On the minimum audible angle. *Journal of the Acoustical Society of America, 30,* 127–246.

Mills, A. W. (1960). Lateralization of high-frequency tones. *Journal of the Acoustical Society of America, 32,* 132–134.

Milne, J., & Milne, M. (1967). *The senses of animals and men.* New York: Atheneum.

Milner, B. (1954). Intellectual function of the temporal lobes. *Psychological Bulletin, 51,* 42–62.

Milner, B. (1958). Psychological defects produced by temporal lobe excision. *Research Publications, Association for Research in Nervous and Mental Disease, 36,* 244–257.

Milner, P. M. (1970). *Physiological psychology.* New York: Holt, Rinehart & Winston.

Milner, P. M. (1974). A model for visual shape recognition. *Psychological Review, 81,* 521–535.

Mitchell, D. (1978). Effect of early visual experience on the development of certain perceptual abilities in animals and man. In R. Walk & H. Pick (Eds.), *Perception and experience* (pp. 37–75). New York: Plenum.

Mitchell, D. (1980). The influence of early visual experience on visual perception. In C. Harris (Ed.), *Visual coding and adaptability* (pp. 1–50). Hillsdale, NJ: Lawrence Erlbaum Associates.

Mitchell, D. (1981). Sensitive periods in visual development. In R. Aslin, J. Alberts, & M. Petersen (Eds.), *Development of perception: Vol. 2. The visual system,* (pp. 1–43). New York: Academic Press.

Monahan, J. S., & Lockhead, G. R. (1977). Identification of integral stimuli. *Journal of Experimental Psychology: General, 106,* 94–110.

Moncrieff, R. W. (1956). Olfactory adaptation and colour likeness. *Journal of Physiology (London), 133,* 301–316.

Money, J. (1965). Psychosexual differentiation. In J. Money (Ed.), *Sex research: New developments* (pp. 3–23). New York: Holt, Rinehart & Winston.

Montellese, S., Sharpe, L. T., & Brown, J. L. (1979). Changes in critical duration during dark-adaptation. *Vision Research, 19,* 1147–1153.

Mooney, R. D., Dubin, M. W., & Rusoff, A. C. (1979). Interneuron circuits in the lateral geniculate nucleus of monocularly deprived cats. *Journal of Comparative Neurology, 187(3),* 533–544.

Moore, B. (1977). *Introduction to the psychology of hearing.* Baltimore: University Park Press.

Moore, L. M., Nielsen, C. R., & Mistretta, C. M. (1982). Sucrose taste thresholds: Age-related differences. *Journal of Gerontology, 37,* 64–69.

Moran, J., & Gordon, B. (1982). Long term visual deprivation in a human. *Vision Research, 22,* 27–36.

Moray, N. (1959). Attention in dichotic listening: Affective cues and the influence of instructions. *Quarterly Journal of Experimental Psychology, 11,* 56–60.

Moray, N. (1967). Where is capacity limited? A survey and a model. *Acta Psychologica, 27,* 84–92.

Moray, N. (1969). *Attention: Selective processes in vision and hearing.* London: Hutchinson Educational.

Moskowitz, H., Sharma, S., & McGlothlin, W. (1972). Effect of marijuana upon peripheral vision as a function of the information processing demands in central vision. *Perceptual and Motor Skills, 35,* 875–882.

Moskowitz, H. R. (1970). Ratio scales of sugar sweetness. *Perception & Psychophysics, 7,* 315–320.

Moskowitz-Cook, A. (1979). The development of photopic spectral sensitivity in human infants. *Vision Research, 9,* 113–114.

Mostofsky, D. I. (1970). The semantics of attention. In D. I. Mostofsky (Ed.), *Attention: Contemporary theory and analysis* (pp. 9–24). New York: Appleton-Century-Crofts.

Mountcastle, V. B., Poggio, G. F., & Werner, G. (1963). The relation of thalamic cell response to peripheral stimuli varied over an intensive continuum. *Journal of Neurophysiology, 26,* 807–834.

Mountcastle, V. B., & Powell, T. P. S. (1959). Central nervous mechanisms subserving position sense and kinesthesis. *Bulletin of the Johns Hopkins Hospital, 105,* 173–200.

Movshon, J. A., & Van Sluyters, R. C. (1981). Visual neural development. *Annual Review of Psychology, 32,* 477–522.

Muir, D., & Field, J. (1979). Newborn infants orient to sounds. *Child Development, 50,* 431–436.

Muir, D., & Mitchell, D. (1975). Behavioral deficits in cats following early selected visual exposure to contours of a single orientation. *Brain Research, 85,* 459–477.

Munsell, A. H. (1915). *Atlas of the Munsell color system.* Maldin, MA: Wadsworth, Howland.

Murphy, C., & Cain, W. S. (1980). Taste and olfaction: Independence vs. intraction. *Physiology and Behavior, 24,* 601–605.

Nafe, J. P., & Wagoner, K. S. (1937). The insensitivity of the cornea to heat and pain derived from high temperatures. *American Journal of Psychology, 49,* 631–635.

Nagy, A. L. (1980). Short-flash Bezold-Brucke hue shifts. *Vision Research, 20,* 361–368.

Naka Ken-Ichi. (1982). The cells horizontal cells talk to. *Vision Research, 22,* 653–660.

Nakayama, K., & Tyler, C. N. (1981). Psychophysical isolation of movement sensitivity by removal of familiar position cues. *Vision Research, 21,* 427–433.

Navon, D. (1977). Forest before trees: The precedence of global features in visual perception. *Cognitive Psychology, 9,* 353–383.

Navon, D. (1981). The forest revisited: More on global precedence. *Psychological Research, 43,* 1–32.

Navon, D., & Gopher, D. (1979). On the economy of the human processing system. *Psychological Review, 86,* 214–255.

Navon, D., & Gopher, D. (1980). Task difficulty, resources, and dual-task performance. In R. S. Nickerson (Ed.), *Attention and performance VIII.* Hillsdale, NJ: Lawrence Erlbaum Associates.

Neisser, U. (1967). *Cognitive psychology.* New York: Appleton-Century-Crofts.

Neisser, U. (1976). *Cognition and reality: Principles and implications of cognitive psychology*. San Francisco: Freeman.

Nelson, R., Kolb, H., Robinson, M. M., & Mariani, A. P. (1981). Neural circuitry of the cat retina: Cone pathways to ganglion cells. *Vision Research, 21*, 1527–1537.

Neuweiler, G., Bruns, V., Schuller, G. (1980). Ears adapted for the detection of motion; or how echolocating bats have exploited the capacities of the mammalian auditory system. *Journal of the Acoustical Society of America, 68*, 741–753.

Newhall, S. M., Burnham, R. W., & Clark, J. R. (1957). Comparison of successive with simultaneous color matching. *Journal of the Optical Society of America, 47*, 43–56.

Newhall, S. M., Nickerson, D., & Judd, D. B. (1943). Final report of the O.S.A. subcommittee on spacing of the Munsell colors. *Journal of the Optical Society of America, 33*, 385–418.

Newland, J. (1972). Children's knowledge of left and right. Unpublished master's thesis, University of Auckland. Cited in M. C. Corballis & J. L. Beale, *The psychology of left and right* (p. 167). Hillsdale, NJ: Lawrence Erlbaum Associates, 1976.

Newman, J. D., & Wolberg, Z. (1973). Responses of single neurons in the auditory cortex of squirrel monkeys to variants of a single call type. *Experimental Neurology, 40*, 821–824.

Noda, H., Freeman, R. B., & Creutzfeldt, O. D. (1972). Neuronal correlates of eye movements in the cat visual cortex. *Science, 175*, 661–664.

Noell, W. (1980). Possible mechanisms of photoreceptor damage by light in mammalian eyes. *Vision Research, 20*, 1163–1172.

Norman, D. A. (1968). Toward a theory of memory and attention. *Psychological Review, 75*, 522–536.

Norman, D. A. (1969). Memory while shadowing. *Quarterly Journal of Experimental Psychology, 21*, 85–93.

Norman, D. A. (1976). *Memory and attention* (2nd ed.). New York: Wiley.

Norton, T. T. (1981a). Development of the visual system and visually guided behavior. In R. Aslin, J. Alberts, & M. Petersen (Eds.), *Development of perception: Psychobiological perspectives: Vol. 2. The visual system* (pp. 113–156). New York: Academic Press.

Norton, T. T. (1981b). Geniculate and extrageniculate visual systems in the tree shrew. In A. R. Morrison & P. L. Strick (Eds.), *Changing concepts of the nervous system* (pp. 377–410). New York: Academic Press.

Norwich, K. H. (1981). The magical number seven: Making a "bit" of "sense." *Perception & Psychophysics, 29*, 409–422.

O'Connell, R. J., & Mozell, M. M. (1969). Quantitative stimulation of frog olfactory receptors. *Journal of Neurophysiology, 32*, 51–63.

O'Mahony, M. (1979). Salt taste adaptation: The psychophysical effects of adapting solutions and residual stimuli from prior tastings on the taste of sodium chloride. *Perception, 8*, 441–476.

O'Mahony, M., & Heintz, C. (1981). Direct magnitude estimation of salt taste intensity with continuous correction for salivary adaptation. *Chemical Senses, 6*, 101–112.

Ono, H., & Weber, E. U. (1981). Nonveridical visual direction produced by monocular viewing. *Journal of Experimental Psychology: Human Perception and Performance, 7*, 937–947.

Orban, G. A., Kennedy, H., & Maes, H. (1981a). Response to movement of neurons in areas 17 and 18 of the cat: Velocity sensitivity. *Journal of Neurophysiology, 45*, 1043–1058.

Orban, G. A., Kennedy, H., & Maes, H. (1981b). Response to movement of neurons in areas 17 and 18 of the cat: Direction sensitivity. *Journal of Neurophysiology, 45*, 1059–1073.

Ornstein, A., & Rotter, G. (1969). Research methodology in temporal perception. *Journal of Experimental Psychology, 79*, 561–564.

Ornstein, R. E. (1969). *On the experience of time*. London: Penguin Books.

Osaka, N. (1980). Luminance range effect on brightness exponent in the fovea and periphery. *Perceptual and Motor Skills, 50*, 1231–1234.

Osaka, N. (1981). Brightness exponent as a function of flash duration and retinal eccentricity. *Perception & Psychophysics, 30*, 144–148.

Osterberg, G. (1935). Topography of the layer of

rods and cones in the human retina. *Acta Ophthalmologica, Supplementum, 6.*

Ostfeld, A. (1961). Effects of LSD-25 and JB318 on tests of visual and perceptual functions in man. *Federation Proceedings, Federation of American Societies for Experimental Biology, 20,* 876–883.

Ottoson, D. (1956). Analysis of the electrical activity of the olfactory epithelium. *Acta Physiologica Scandinavica, 35* (Suppl. 122), 1–83.

Oyama, T. (1968). A behavioristic analysis of Stevens' magnitude estimation method. *Perception & Psychophysics, 3,* 317–320.

Palmer, S. E. (1975a). The effects of contextual scenes on the identification of objects. *Memory and Cognition, 3,* 519–526.

Palmer, S. E. (1975b). Visual perception and world knowledge: Notes on a model of sensory-cognitive interaction. In D. A. Norman & D. E. Rumelhart (Eds.), *Explorations in cognition* (pp. 279–307). San Francisco: Freeman.

Parducci, A. (1965). Category judgment: A range-frequency model. *Psychological Review, 72,* 407–418.

Parker, D. E. (1980). The vestibular apparatus. *Scientific American, 243,* 118–135.

Parlee, M. B. (1983). Menstrual rhythms in sensory processes: A review of fluctuations in vision, olfaction, audition, taste, and touch. *Psychological Bulletin, 93,* 539–548.

Patterson, R. D. (1969). Noise masking of a change in residue pitch. *Journal of the Acoustical Society of America, 45,* 1520–1524.

Patterson, R. D., & Green, D. M. (1978). Auditory masking. In E. C. Carterette & M. P. Friedman (Eds.), *Handbook of Perception: Vol. IV. Hearing.* New York: Academic Press.

Paulus, K., & Haas, E. M. (1980). The influence of solvent viscosity on the threshold values of primary tastes. *Chemical Senses, 5,* 23–32.

Paulus, K., & Reisch, A. M. (1980). The influence of temperature on the threshold values of primary tastes. *Chemical Senses, 5,* 11–21.

Peeples, D., & Teller, D. Y. (1978). White-adapted photopic spectral sensitivity in human infants. *Vision Research, 18,* 49–53.

Peichl, L., & Wassle, H. (1979). Size, scatter and coverage of ganglion-cell receptive-field centers in the cat retina. *Journal of Physiology (London), 291,* 117.

Pelosi, P., & Pisanelli, A. M. (1981). Specific anosmia to 1,8-cineole: The camphor primary odor. *Chemical Senses, 6,* 87–93.

Penfield, W., & Rasmussen, T. (1950). *The cerebral cortex of man.* New York: Macmillan.

Peterson, A. C. (1976). Physical androgyny and cognitive functioning in adolescence. *Developmental Psychology, 12,* 524–533.

Petrig, B., Julesz, B., Kropfl, W., Baumgartner, G., & Anliker, M. (1981). Development of stereopsis and cortical binocularity in human infants: Electrophysiological evidence. *Science, 213,* 1402–1405.

Pettigrew, J. (1978). Stereoscopic visual processing. *Nature, 273,* 9–11.

Pettigrew, J. (1978). The paradox of the critical period for striate cortex. In C. W. Cotman (Ed.), *Neuronal plasticity* (pp. 311–330). New York: Raven.

Pfaff, D. (1968). Effects of temperature and time of day on judgment. *Journal of Experimental Psychology, 76,* 419–422.

Pfaffman, C. (1955). Gustatory nerve impulses in rat, cat, and rabbit. *Journal of Neurophysiology, 18,* 429–440.

Pfaffman, C. (1974). Specificity of the sweet receptors of the squirrel monkey. *Chemical Senses and Flavor, 1,* 61–67.

Pfaffman, C., Bartoshuk, L., & McBurney, D. H. (1971). Taste psychophysics. *Handbook of Sensory Physiology, 1,* 75–101.

Pfaffman, C., Frank, M., & Norgren, R. (1979). Neural mechanisms and behavioral aspects of taste. *Annual Review of Psychology, 30,* 283–325.

Pfeiffer, R. R. (1966). Classification of response patterns of spike discharges for units in the cochlear nucleus: Tone-burst stimulation. *Experimental Brain Research, 1,* 220–235.

Piaget, J. (1969). *The mechanisms of perception.* (G. N. Seagrine, Trans.). New York: Oxford University Press.

Pick, H. L., Jr., & Hay, J. C. (1965). A passive test of the Held reafference hypothesis. *Perceptual and Motor Skills, 20,* 1070–1072.

Pick, H. L., Jr., & Pick, A. D. (1970). Sensory and perceptual development. In P. H. Mussen (Ed.), *Carmichael's manual of child development* (pp. 773–848). New York: Wiley.

Pickersgill, M. J. (1961). On knowing with which eye one is seeing. *Quarterly Journal of Experimental Psychology, 13*, 168–172.

Piggins, D. J., Kingham, J. R., & Holmes, S. M. (1972). Colour, colour saturation and pattern induced by intermittent illumination: An initial study. *British Journal of Physiological Optics, 27*, 120–125.

Pirozzolo, F. J. (1978). *The neuropsychology of developmental reading disorders.* New York: Praeger.

Plateau, M. H. (1872). Sur la mesure des sensations physiques, et sur la loi qui lie l'intensite de la cause excitante. *Bulletin de l'Academie Royale de Belgique, 33*, 376–388.

Poggio, G. F. (1972). Spatial properties of neurons in striate cortex of unanesthetized macaque monkey. *Investigative Ophthalmology, 11*, 368–376.

Poggio, G. F., & Mountcastle, V. B. (1960). A study of the functional contributions of the lemniscal and spinothalamic systems to somatic sensibility: Central nervous mechanisms in pain. *Bulletin of the Johns Hopkins Hospital, 106*, 266–316.

Pollack, I. (1952). The information of elementary auditory displays. *Journal of the Acoustical Society of America, 24*, 745–749.

Pollack, I. (1953). The information of elementary auditory displays: II. *Journal of the Acoustical Society of America, 25*, 765–769.

Pollack, I. (1965). Iterative techniques for unbiased rating scales. *Quarterly Journal of Experimental Psychology, 17*, 139–148.

Pollack, I. (1978). Decoupling of auditory pitch and stimulus frequency: The shepard demonstration revisited. *Journal of the Acoustical Society of America, 63*, 202–206.

Pollack, I., & Norman, D. A. (1964). A nonparametric analysis of recognition experiments. *Psychonomic Science, 1*, 125–126.

Pollack, I., & Pickett, J. M. (1964). Intelligibility of excerpts from fluent speech: Auditory vs. structural context. *Journal of Verbal Learning and Verbal Behavior, 3*, 79–84.

Pollack, R. H., & Silvar, S. D. (1967). Magnitude of the Mueller-Lyer illusion in children as a function of pigmentation of the Fundus oculi. *Psychonomic Science, 8*, 83–84.

Polzella, D. J., Dapolito, F., & Hinsman, M. C. (1977). Cerebral asymmetry in time perception. *Perception & Psychophysics, 21*, 187–192.

Pomerantz, J., Goldberg, D., Golder, P., & Tetewsky, S. (1981). Subjective contours can facilitate performance in a reaction-time task. *Perception & Psychophysics, 29*, 605–611.

Pomerantz, J. R. (1983). Global and local precedence: Selective attention in form and motion perception. *Journal of Experimental Psychology: General, 112*, 000–000.

Pomerantz, J. R., Sager, L. C., & Stoever, R. J. (1977). Perception of wholes of their component parts: Some configural superiority effects. *Journal of Experimental Psychology: Human Perception and Performance, 3*, 422–435.

Poppel, E. (1978). Time perception. In R. Held, H. W. Leibowitz, & H. L. Teuber (Eds.), *Handbook of sensory physiology: Vol. VIII. Perception* (pp. 713–729). New York: Springer-Verlag.

Porac, C., & Coren, S. (1976). The dominant eye. *Psychological Bulletin, 83*, 880–897.

Porac, C. & Coren, S. (1981a). Lateral preference and human behavior. New York: Springer-Verlag.

Porac, C., & Coren, S. (1981b). Life-span age trends in the perception of the Mueller-Lyer: An additional evidence for the existence of two illusions. *Canadian Journal of Psychology, 35*, 58–62.

Porter, R. H., & Moore, J. D. (1981). Human kin recognition by olfactory cues. *Physiology and Behavior, 27*, 493–495.

Posner, M. I. (1978). *Chronometric explorations of mind.* Hillsdale, NJ: Lawrence Erlbaum Associates.

Posner, M. I. (1980). Orienting of attention. *Quarterly Journal of Experimental Psychology, 32*, 3–25.

Posner, M. I., & Boies, S. J. (1971). Components of attention. *Psychological Review, 78*, 391–408.

Posner, M. I., Snyder, C. R. R., & Davidson, B. J.

(1980). Attention and the detection of signals. *Journal of Experimental Psychology: General, 109,* 160–174.

Postman, L., & Egan, J. P. (1949). *Experimental psychology.* New York: Harper & Row.

Poulton, E. C. (1968). The new psychophysics: Six models for magnitude estimation. *Psychological Bulletin, 69,* 1–119.

Poulton, E. C. (1979). Models for biases in judging sensory magnitudes. *Psychological Bulletin, 86,* 777–803.

Poulton, E. C., Edwards, R. S., & Fowler, T. J. (1980). Eliminating subjective biases in judging the loudness of a 1-KHz tone. *Perception & Psychophysics, 27,* 93–103.

Powers, M. K., Schneck, M., & Teller, D. Y. (1981). Spectral sensitivity of human infants at absolute visual threshold. *Vision Research, 21,* 1005–1016.

Prazdny, K. (1982). Blur patterns: A comment. *Perception & Psychophysics, 31,* 190–191.

Prinzmetal, W. (1981). Principles of feature integration in visual perception. *Perception & Psychophysics, 30,* 330–340.

Pritchard, R. M., Heron, W., & Hebb, D. O. (1960). Visual perception approached by the method of stabilized images. *Canadian Journal of Psychology, 14,* 67–77.

Puckett, J. deW., & Steinman, R. M. (1969). Tracking eye movements with and without saccadic correction. *Vision Research, 9,* 295–303.

Pulos, E., Teller, D. Y., & Buck, S. L. (1980). Infant color vision: A search for short-wave length-sensitive mechanisms by means of chromatic adaptation. *Vision Research, 20,* 485–493.

Rabbitt, P. (1977). Changes in problem solving ability in old age. In J. Birren & K. Schaie (Eds.), *Handbook of the psychology of aging.* New York: Van Nostrand Reinhold.

Rader, N., Bausano, M., & Richards, J. E. (1980). On the nature of the visual-cliff-avoidance response in human infants. *Child Development, 51,* 61–68.

Randsom-Hogg, A., & Spillman, L. (1980). Perceptive field size in fovea of the light and dark adapted. *Vision Research, 20,* 221–228.

Ratliff, F. (1965). *Mach bands: Quantitative studies on neural networks in the retina.* San Francisco: Holden-Day.

Rayleigh, Lord. (1907). On our perception of sound direction. *Philosophical Magazine, (6), 13,* 214–232.

Redding, G., & Wallace, B. (1976). Components of displacement adaptation in acquisition and decay as a function of hard and hall exposure. *Perception & Psychophysics, 20,* 453–459.

Reddy, D. R. (1976). Speech recognition by machine: A review. *Proceedings of the IEEE, 64,* 501–531.

Reed, S. K. (1973). *Psychological processes in pattern recognition.* New York: Academic Press.

Regan, D., Beverley, K., & Cynader, M. (1979). The visual perception of motion in depth. *Scientific American, 241,* 136–151.

Reid, T. (1785). *Essays on the intellectual powers of man.* Edinburgh.

Remez, R. E., Rubin, P. E., Pisoni, D. B., & Carrell, T. D. (1981). Speech perception without traditional speech cues. *Science, 212,* 947–950.

Restle, F. (1971). Visual illusions. In M. H. Appley (Ed.), *Adaptation-level theory* (pp. 55–69). New York: Academic Press.

Restle, F. (1978). Assimilation produced by contrast. In J. S. Castellan & F. Restle (Eds.), *Cognitive theory (Vol. 3).* Hillsdale, NJ: Lawrence Erlbaum Associates.

Reynolds, D. C. (1979). A visual profile of the alcoholic driver. *American Journal of Optometry and Physiological Optics, 56,* 241–251.

Rhee, K., Kim, D., & Kim, Y. (1965). The effects of smoking on night vision. 14th Pacific Medical Conference (Professional papers).

Rice, C. G., Hyley, J. B., Bartlett, B., Bedford, W., Gregory, W., & Hallum, G. (1968). A pilot study on the effects of pop group music on hearing. Cited in K. D. Kryter (Ed.). (1970). *The effects of noise on man* (p. 203). New York: Academic Press.

Richards, J. E., & Rader, N. (1981). Crawling-onset age predicts visual cliff avoidance in infants. *Journal of Experimental Psychology: Human Perception and Performance, 7,* 382–387.

Richards, W. (1977). Lessons in constancy from neurophysiology. In W. W. Epstein (Ed.), *Stability and constancy in visual perception: Mecha-*

nisms and processes (pp. 421–436). New York: Wiley.

Riesen, A. H. (1947). The development of visual perception in man and chimpanzee. *Science, 106,* 107–108.

Riesen, A. H., & Aarons, L. (1959). Visual movement and intensity discrimination in cats after early deprivation of pattern-vision. *Journal of Comparative and Physiological Psychology, 52,* 142–149.

Riesen, A., & Zilbert, D. (1975). Behavioral consequences of variations in early sensory environments. In A. Riesen (Ed.), *The developmental neuropsychology of sensory deprivation.* (pp. 211–252). New York: Academic Press.

Riesz, R. R. (1928). Differential intensity sensitivity of the ear for pure tones. *Physical Review, 31,* 867–875.

Riggs, L. A., Ratliff, F., Cornsweet, J. C., & Cornsweet, T. N. (1953). The disappearance of steadily fixated visual test objects. *Journal of the Optical Society of America, 43,* 495–501.

Riggs, L. A., Volkmann, F. C., & Moore, R. K. (1981). Suppression of the blackout due to blinks. *Vision Research, 21,* 1075–1079.

Roberts, J. (1964). *Binocular visual acuity of adults.* Washington, DC: U.S. Department of Health, Education and Welfare.

Robertson, P. W. (1967). Color words and colour vision. *Biology and Human Affairs, 33,* 28–33.

Robinson, D. W., & Dadson, R. S. (1956). A redetermination of the equal-loudness relations for pure tones. *British Journal of Applied Physics, 7,* 166–181.

Robson, J. G. (1975). Receptive fields: Neural representation of the spatial and intensive attributes of the visual image. In E. C. Carterette & M. P. Friedman (Eds.), *Handbook of perception: Vol. 5. Seeing* (pp. 82–116). New York: Academic Press.

Robson, J. G. (1980). Neural images: The physiological basis of spatial vision. In C. S. Harris (Ed.), *Visual coding and adaptability.* (pp. 177–214). Hillsdale, NJ: Lawrence Erlbaum Associates.

Roche, S., Horvath, S., Gliner, J., Wagner, J., & Borgia, J. (1981). Sustained visual attention and carbon monoxide: Estimation of adaptation effects. *Human Factors, 23,* 175–184.

Rock, I. (1974). *Orientation and form.* New York: Academic Press.

Rock, I. (1975). *An introduction to perception.* New York: Macmillan.

Rock, I., & Halper, F. (1969). Form perception without a retinal image. *American Journal of Psychology, 82,* 425–440.

Rockland, K. S., & Pandya, P. N. (1981). Cortical connections of the occipital lobe in the rhesus monkey: Interconnections between areas 17, 18, 19 and the superior temporal sulcus. *Brain Research, 212,* 249–270.

Rodieck, R. W. (1967). Receptive fields in the cat retina: A new type. *Science, 157,* 90–92.

Rodieck, R. W. (1973). *The vertebrate retina: Principles of structure and function.* San Francisco: Freeman.

Rodieck, R. W. (1979). Visual pathways. *Annual Review of Neurosciences, 2,* 193–225.

Rodieck, R. W., & Stone, J. (1965). Analysis of receptive fields of cat retinal ganglion cells. *Journal of Neurophysiology, 28,* 833–849.

Roelofs, C. O. (1935). Optische Lokalisation, *Archiv fuer Augenheilkunde, 109,* 395–415.

Rogel, M. J. (1978). A critical evaluation of the possibility of higher primate reproductive and sexual pheromones. *Psychological Bulletin, 85,* 810–830.

Romani, G. L., Williamson, S. J., & Kaufman, L. (1982). Tonotopic organization of the human auditory cortex. *Science, 216,* 1339–1340.

Romano, P. E., Romano, J. A., & Puklin, J. E. (1975). Stereoactivity development in children with normal single vision. *American Journal of Ophthalmology, 79,* 966–971.

Root, W. (1974, December 22). Of wine and noses. *New York Times Magazine,* pp. 14 et seq.

Rose, J. E., Brugge, J. F., Anderson, D. J., & Hind, J. E. (1967). Phase-locked response to low frequency tones in single auditory nerve fibers of the squirrel monkey. *Journal of Neurophysiology, 30,* 769–793.

Rose, J. E., Galambos, R., & Hughes, J. (1959). Microelectrode studies of the cochlear nuclei of the cat. *Johns Hopkins Hospital Bulletin, 104,* 211–251.

Rose, J. E., Galambos, R., & Hughes, J. (1960) Organization of frequency sensitive neurons in the cochlear nuclear complex of the cat. In G. L. Rasmussen & W. F. Windle (Eds.), *Neural mechanisms of the auditory and vestibular systems* (pp. 116–136). Springfield, IL: Thomas.

Rosinski, R., & Farber, J. (1980). Compensation for viewing point in the perception of pictured space. In M. Hagen (Ed.), *Perception of pictures: Vol. 1. Alberti's window: The projective model of pictorial information* (pp. 137–176). New York: Academic Press.

Ross, J., Jenkins, B., and Johnstone, J. R. (1980). Size constancy fails below half a degree. *Nature, 283,* 473–474.

Ross, N., & Schilder, P. (1934). Tachistoscopic experiments on the perception of the human figure. *Journal of General Psychology, 10,* 152–172.

Rothblat, L., & Schwartz, M. (1978). Altered early environment: Effects on the brain and visual behavior. In R. Walk & H. Pick (Eds.), *Perception and experience* (pp. 7–36). New York: Plenum.

Royster, L. H., Royster, J. D., & Thomas, W. G. (1980). Representative hearing levels by race and sex in North Carolina industry. *Journal of the Acoustical Society of America, 68,* 551–566.

Rubin, E. (1915). *Synoplevede Figuren.* Copenhagen: Gyldendalske.

Rubin, E. (1921). *Visuell wahrgenommene Figuren.* Copenhagen: Gyldendalske.

Rubin, P., Turvey, M. T., & Van Gelder, P. (1976). Initial phonemes are detected faster in spoken words than in nonspoken words. *Perception & Psychophysics, 19,* 394–398.

Ruble, D. N., & Nakamura, C. Y. (1972). Task orientation versus social orientation in young children and their attention to relevant social cues. *Child Development, 43,* 471–480.

Ruggieri, V., Cei, A., Ceridono, D., & Bergerone, C. (1980). Dimensional approach to the study of sighting dominance. *Perceptual and Motor Skills, 51,* 247–251.

Rushton, W. A. H. (1962). Visual pigments in man. *Scientific American, 205,* 120–132.

Rushton, W. A. H. (1965). Cone pigment dynamics in the deuteranope. *Journal of Physiology (London), 176,* 38–45.

Russell, M. J. (1976). Human olfactory communication. *Nature (London), 260,* 520–522.

Russoff, A. C. (1979). Development of ganglion cells in the retina of the cat. In R. D. Freeman (Ed.), *Developmental neurobiology of vision* (pp. 19–30). New York: Plenum.

Sachs, M. B., & Kiang, N. Y. S. (1968). Two-tone inhibition in auditory nerve fibers. *Journal of the Acoustical Society of America, 43,* 1120–1128.

Salapatek, P. (1975). Pattern perception in early infancy. In L. B. Cohen & P. Salapatek (Eds.), *Infant perception: From sensation to cognition* (Vol. 1, pp. 133–248). New York: Academic Press.

Salapatek, P., & Banks, M. (1978). Infant sensory assessment: Vision. In F. D. Minifie & L. X. J. Lloyd (Eds.), *Communicative and cognitive abilities: Early behavioral assessment.* Baltimore: University Park Press.

Salapatek, P., & Kessen, W. (1973). Prolonged investigation of a plane geometric triangle by the human newborn. *Journal of Experimental Child Psychology, 15,* 22–29.

Samuels, A. B. (1981). Phonemic restoration: Insights from a new methodology. *Journal of Experimental Psychology: General, 110,* 474–494.

Sanders, A. F. (1979). Some remarks on mental load. In N. Moray (Ed.), *Mental workload: Theory and measurement.* New York: Plenum.

Sapir, E. (1939). *Language.* New York: Harcourt, Brace & World.

Schaller, M. J. (1975). Chromatic vision in human infants: Conditioned operant fixation to "hues" of varying intensity. *Bulletin of the Psychonomic Society, 6,* 39–42.

Scharf, B. (1964). Partial masking. *Acustica, 14,* 16–23.

Scharf, B. (1975). Audition. In B. Scharf (Ed.), *Experimental sensory psychology* (pp. 112–149). Glenview, IL: Scott, Foresman.

Scharf, B. (1978). Loudness. In E. C. Carterette & M. P. Friedman (Eds.), *Handbook of Perception: Vol. IV. Hearing* (pp. 187–242). New York: Academic Press.

Schenkel, K. D. (1967). Die beidohrigen Mithorschoellen von Impulsen. *Acustica, 18,* 38–46.

Schiffman, S. S. (1974). Physiochemical correlates of olfactory quality. *Science, 185,* 112–117.

Schiffman, S. S. (1977). Food recognition by the elderly. *Journal of Gerontology, 32,* 586–592.

Schiffman, S. S., & Dackis, C. (1975). Taste of nutrients: Amino acids, vitamins, and fatty acids. *Perception & Psychophysics, 17,* 140–146.

Schiffman, S. S., & Erickson, R. P. (1971). A theoretical review: A psychophysical model for gustatory quality. *Physiology and Behavior, 7,* 617–633.

Schiffman, S. S., McElroy, A. E., & Erikson, R. F. (1980). The range of taste quality of sodium salts. *Physiology and Behavior, 24,* 217–224.

Schiffman, S. S., & Pasternak, M. (1979). Decreased discrimination of food odors in the elderly. *Journal of Gerontology, 84,* 73–79.

Schiffman, S. S., Reilly, D. A., & Clark, T. B., III. (1979). Qualitative differences among sweeteners. *Physiology and Behavior, 23,* 1–9.

Schiller, P., & Weiner, M. (1962). Binocular and stereoscopic viewing of geometric illusions. *Perceptual and Motor Skills, 13,* 739–747.

Schmiedt, R. A., Zwislocki, J. J., & Hamerik, R. P. (1980). Effects of hair cell lesions on responses of cochlear nerve fibers: I. Lesions, tuning curves, two-tone inhibition, and responses to trapezoidal-wave patterns. *Journal of Neurophysiology, 43,* 1367–1389.

Schneider, B. A., & Bissett, R. J. (1981). The dimensions of tonal experience: A nometric scaling approach. *Perception & Psychophysics, 30,* 39–48.

Schneider, D. (1969). Insect olfaction: Deciphering system for chemical messages. *Science, 163,* 1031–1037.

Schneider, G. E. (1969). Two visual systems. *Science, 163,* 895–902.

Schneider, R., Costiloe, J., Howard, R., & Wolf, S. (1958). Olfactory perception thresholds in hypogonadal women: Changes accompanying administration of androgen and estrogen. *Journal of Clinical Endocrinology, 18,* 379–390.

Schneider, W., & Shiffrin, R. M. (1977). Controlled and automatic human information processing: I. Detection, search and attention. *Psychological Review, 84,* 1–66.

Schriever, W. (1925). Experimentelle Studien uber stereokopische Sehen. *Zeitschrift fuer Psychologie, 96,* 113–170.

Schubert, E. D. (1978). History of research on hearing. In E. C. Carterette & M. P. Friedman (Eds.), *Handbook of Perception: Vol. IV. Hearing* (pp. 41–80). New York: Academic Press.

Schull, J., Kaplan, H., & O'Brien, C. P. (1981). Naloxone can alter experimental pain and mood in humans. *Physiological Psychology, 9,* 245–250.

Schulman, C. (1973). Eye movements in infants using dc recording. *Neuropaediatrie, 4,* 76–87.

Schulman, P. H. (1979). Eye movements do not cause induced motion. *Perception & Psychophysics, 26,* 381–383.

Schwartz, A. N., Campos, J. J., & Baisel, E. J. (1972, April). The visual cliff: Cardiac and behavioral responses on the deep and shallow sides at five and nine months of age. Paper presented at the meetings of the Eastern Psychological Association.

Schwartz, C. B. (1961). Visual discrimination of camouflaged figures. Unpublished doctoral dissertation, University of California at Berkeley.

Scott, T. R., & Erickson, R. P. (1971). Synaptic processing of taste-quality information in the thalamus of the rat. *Journal of Neurophysiology, 34,* 868–884.

Sedgwick, H. (1980). The geometry of spatial layout in pictorial representation. In M. Hagen (Ed.), *Perception of pictures: Vol. I. Alberti's window: The projective model of pictorial information* (pp. 33–90). New York: Academic Press.

Segall, M. H., Campbell, D. T., & Herskovits, M. J. (1966). *The influence of culture on visual perception.* Indianapolis: Bobbs-Merrill.

Sekuler, R. (1975). Visual motion perception. In E. C. Carterette & M. P. Friedman (Eds.), *Handbook of perception: Vol. V. Seeing* (pp. 387–433). New York: Academic Press.

Sekuler, R., Ball, K., Tynan, P., & Machmer, J. (1982). Psychophysics of motion perception. In A. H. Wertheim, W. A. Wagenaar, & H. W. Leibowitz, (Eds.), *Tutorials on motion perception* (pp. 81–100). New York: Plenum.

Sekuler, R., & Ganz, L. (1963). A new aftereffect of

seen movement with a stabilized retinal image. *Science, 139,* 419–420.

Sekuler, R., & Hutman, L. P. (1980). Spatial vision and aging: I. Contrast sensitivity. *Journal of Gerontology, 35,* 692–699.

Selfridge, O. G. (1959). Pandemonium: A paradigm for learning. In D. V. Blake & A. W. Uttley (Eds.), *Proceedings of the Symposium on the Mechanisation of Thought Processes* (pp. 511–529). London: HM Stationery Office.

Selfridge, O. G., & Neisser, U. (1963). Pattern recognition by machine. In E. A. Feigenbaum & J. Feldman (Eds.), *Computers and thought* (pp. 237–250). New York: McGraw-Hill.

Senden, M. von. (1960). *Space and sight: The perception of space and shape in congenitally blind patients before and after operation.* London: Methuen.

Serpell, R. (1971). Discrimination of orientation by Zambian children. *Journal of Comparative Physiology, 75,* 312.

Shallice, T., & Vickers, D. (1964). Theories and experiments on discrimination times. *Ergonomics, 7,* 37–49.

Shannon, C. E., & Weaver, W. (1949). *The mathematical theory of communication.* Urbana: University of Illinois Press.

Sharma, S., & Moskowitz, H. (1972). Effect of marijuana on the visual autokinetic phenomenon. *Perceptual and Motor Skills, 35,* 891.

Shea, S. L., Fox, R., Aslin, R. N., & Dumais, S. T. (1980). Assessment of stereopsis in human infants. *Investigative Ophthalmology, 19,* 1400–1404.

Shebilske, W. (1977). Visuomotor coordination in visual direction and position constancies. In W. Epstein (Ed.), *Stability and constancy in visual perception: Mechanisms and processes* (pp. 23–70). New York: Wiley.

Shepard, R. N. (1964). Circularity in judgments of relative pitch. *Journal of the Acoustical Society of America, 36,* 2346–2353.

Shepard, R. N. (1982). Geometrical approximations to the structure of musical pitch. *Psychological Review, 89,* 305–333.

Sherman, S. M. (1973). Visual field defects in monocularly and binocularly deprived cats. *Brain Research, 49,* 25–45.

Sherman, S. M. (1979). The functional significance of x and y cells in normal and visually deprived cats. *Trends in Neuroscience, 2,* 192–195.

Sherrington, C. S. (1906). *Integrative action of the nervous system.* New Haven, CT: Yale University Press.

Shiffrin, R. M., & Grantham, D. W. (1974). Can attention be allocated to sensory modalities? *Perception & Psychophysics, 15,* 460–474.

Shiffrin, R. M., Pisoni, D. B., & Castaneda-Mendez, K. (1974). Is attention shared between the ears? *Cognitive Psychology, 6,* 190–215.

Shiffrin, R. M., & Schneider, W. (1977). Controlled and automatic human information processing: II. Perceptual learning, automatic attending and a general theory. *Psychological Review, 84,* 127–190.

Shower, E. G., & Biddulph, R. (1931). Differential pitch sensitivity of the ear. *Journal of the Acoustical Society of America, 3,* 275–287.

Siddle, D. A., Morrish, R. B., White, K. D., & Mangan, G. L. (1969). Relation of visual sensitivity to extraversion. *Journal of Experimental Research in Personality, 3,* 264–267.

Sidman, M., & Kirk, B. (1974). Letter reversals in naming, writing, and matching to sample. *Child Development, 45,* 616–625.

Simmons, F. B., Epley, J. M., Lummis, R. C., Guttman, N., Frishkopf, L. S., Harmon, L. D., & Zwicker, E. (1965). Auditory nerve: Electrical stimulation in man. *Science, 148,* 104–106.

Sinclair, D. C., & Stokes, B. A. R. (1964). The production and characteristics of "second pain." *Brain, 87,* 609–618.

Sinnot, J., & Rauth, J. (1937). Effect of smoking on taste thresholds. *Journal of General Psychology, 17,* 155–162.

Sivian, L. S., & White, S. D. (1933). On minimum audible sound fields. *Journal of the Acoustical Society of America, 4,* 288–321.

Smith, A., & Over, R. (1979). Motor aftereffect with subjective contours. *Perception & Psychophysics, 25,* 95–98.

Smith, S. (1945). Utrocular, or "which eye" discrimination. *Journal of Experimental Psychology, 35,* 1–14.

Smythe, E., & Goldstone, S. (1957). The time sense: A

normative, genetic study of the development of time perception. *Perceptual and Motor Skills*, 7, 49–59.

Snellen, H. (1862). *Probebuchstaben zur Bestimmung der Sehscharfe*. Utrecht: Weijer.

Snyder, S. H. (1977). Opiate receptors and internal opiates. *Scientific American*, 236, 44–56.

So, Y. T., & Shapley, R. (1981). Spatial tuning of cells in and around lateral geniculate nucleus of the cat: X and y cells and perigeniculate interneurons. *Journal of Neurophysiology*, 45, 107–120.

Sokolov, E. N. (1960). *Perception and the conditioned reflex*. New York: Macmillan.

Southwick, E., & Schiffman, S. S. (1980). Odor quality of pyridyl ketones. *Chemical Senses*, 5, 343–357.

Sperling, G. (1960). The information available in brief visual presentation. *Psychological Monographs*, 74, (11, Whole No. 498).

Sperling, H. G., Johnson, C., & Harwerth, R. S. (1980). Differential spectral photic damage to primate cones. *Vision Research*, 20, 1117–1125.

Sperry, R. W. (1943). Effect of 180 degree rotation of the retinal field on visuomotor coordination. *Journal of Experimental Zoology*, 92, 263–277.

Spoehr, K. T., & Lehmkuhle, S. W. (1982). *Visual information processing*. San Francisco: Freeman.

Spoendlin, H. H. (1978). The afferent innervation of the cochlea. In R. F. Naunton & C. Fernandey (Eds.), *Evoked electrical activity in the auditory nervous system*, (pp. 21–42). New York: Academic Press.

Spreen, O. (1976). Neuropsychology of learning disorders: Post conference review. In R. M. Knights & D. J. Bakker (Eds.), *The neuropsychology of learning disorders*. Baltimore: University Park Press.

Springer, S. P., & Deutsch, G. (1981). *Left brain, right brain*. San Francisco: Freeman.

Stark, L., & Ellis, S. (1981). Scanpaths revisited: Cognitive models direct active looking. In D. Fisher, R. Monty, & J. Senders (Eds.), *Eye movements: Cognition and visual perception* (pp. 193–226). Hillsdale, NJ: Lawrence Erlbaum Associates.

Stebbins, W. C. (1980). The evolution of hearing in the mammals. In A. N. Popper & R. R. Fay (Eds.), *Comparative studies of hearing in vertebrates* (pp. 421–436). New York: Springer-Verlag.

Steinberg, A. (1955). Changes in time perception induced by an anaesthetic drug. *British Journal of Psychology*, 46, 273–279.

Steinfield, G. J. (1967). Concepts of set and availability and their relation to the reorganization of ambiguous pictorial stimuli. *Psychological Review*, 74, 505–525.

Steinmack, A. (1944). Reaction time to change, compared with other psychophysical methods. *Archives of Psychology, New York* (No. 292).

Stelmack, R. M., Achorn, E., & Michaud, A. (1977). Extraversion and individual differences in auditory evoked response. *Psychophysiology*, 14, 368–374.

Stelmack, R. M., & Campbell, K. B. (1974). Extraversion and auditory sensitivity to high and low frequency. *Perceptual and Motor Skills*, 38, 875–879.

Stephens, P. R., & Young, J. Z. (1982). The stacocyst of the squid Loligo. *Journal of Zoology, London*, 197, 241–266.

Stern, J., Oster, P. J., & Newport, K. (1980). Reaction time measures, hemispheric specialization, and age. In L. Poon (Ed.), *Aging in the 1980s*. Washington, DC: American Psychological Association.

Sternbach, R. A. (1963). Congenital insensitivity to pain: A review. *Psychological Bulletin*, 60, 252–264.

Sternbach, R. A., & Tursky, B. (1964). On the psychophysical power function in electric shock. *Psychonomic Science*, 1, 247–248.

Sternberg, S. (1975). Memory scanning: New findings and current controversies. *Quarterly Journal of Experimental Psychology*, 27, 1–32.

Stevens, J. C. (1979). Variation of cold sensitivity over the body surface. *Sensory Processes*, 3, 317–326.

Stevens, J. C., & Marks, L. E. (1980). Cross-modality matching functions generated by magnitude estimation. *Perception & Psychophysics*, 27, 379–389.

Stevens, J. C., & Stevens, S. S. (1960). Warmth and

cold: Dynamics of sensory intensity. *Journal of Experimental Psychology, 60*, 183–192.

Stevens, K. N. (1960). Towards a model for speech recognition. *Journal of the Acoustical Society of America, 32*, 47–55.

Stevens, K. N., & Halle, M. (1964). Remarks on analysis by synthesis and distinctive features. In W. Wathen-Dunn (Ed.), *Models for the perception of speech and visual form* (pp. 88–102). Cambridge, MA: MIT Press.

Stevens, K. N. & House, A. S. (1972). Speech perception. In J. V. Tobias (Ed.), *Foundation of modern auditory theory* (Vol. 2, pp. 3–62). New York: Academic Press.

Stevens, S. S. (1934). The attributes of tones. *Proceedings of the National Academy of Sciences of the U.S.A., 20*, 457–459.

Stevens, S. S. (1935). The relation of pitch to intensity. *Journal of the Acoustical Society of America, 6*, 150–154.

Stevens, S. S. (1946). On the theory of scales of measurement. *Science, 103*, 677–680.

Stevens, S. S. (1956). The direct estimation of sensory magnitudes—loudness. *American Journal of Psychology, 69*, 1–25.

Stevens, S. S. (1959). Tactile vibration: Dynamics of sensory intensity. *Journal of Experimental Psychology, 57*, 210–218.

Stevens, S. S. (1961). The psychophysics of sensory function. In W. A. Rosenlith (Ed.), *Sensory communication* (pp. 1–33). Cambridge, MA: MIT Press.

Stevens, S. S. (1969). Sensory scales of taste intensity. *Perception & Psychophysics, 6*, 302–308.

Stevens, S. S. (1975). *Psychophysics: Introduction to its perceptual, neural, and social prospects.* New York: Wiley.

Stevens, S. S., & Galanter, E. (1957). Ratio scales and category scales for a dozen perceptual continua. *Journal of Experimental Psychology, 54*, 377–411.

Stevens, S. S., & Newman, E. B. (1934). The localization of pure tones. *Proceedings of the National Academy of Sciences of the U.S.A., 20*, 593–596.

Stevens, S. S., Volkman, J., & Newman, E. B. (1937). A scale for the measurement of the psychological magnitude of pitch. *Journal of the Acoustical Society of America, 8*, 185–190.

Stevens, S. S., & Warshovsky, F. (1965). *Sound and hearing.* New York: Time-Life Books.

Stone, J., & Dreher, B. (1973). Projection of X- and Y-cells of the cat's lateral geniculate nucleus to areas 17 and 18 of the visual cortex. *Journal of Neurophysiology, 36*, 551–567.

Stone, J., & Hoffman, K. P. (1972). Very slow conduction ganglion cells in the cat's retina: A major new functional type? *Brain Research, 43*, 610–616.

Stone, L. S. (1960). Polarization of the retina and development of vision. *Journal of Experimental Zoology, 145*, 85–93.

Strange, W., & Jenkins, J. (1978). Role of linguistic experience in the perception of speech. In R. Walk & H. Pick (Eds.), *Perception and experience* (pp. 125–169). New York: Plenum.

Stratton, G. M. (1896). Some preliminary experiments on vision without inversion of the retinal image. *Psychological Review, 3*, 611–617.

Stratton, G. M. (1897a). Upright vision and the retinal image. *Psychological Review, 4*, 182–187.

Stratton, G. M. (1897b). Vision without inversion of the retinal image. *Psychological Review, 4*, 341–360.

Street, R. F. (1931). *A gestalt completion test: A study of a cross-section of intellect.* New York: Bureau of Publication, Teachers College, Columbia University.

Stromeyer, C. F., III. (1978). Form-color aftereffects in human vision. In R. Held, H. Leibowitz, & H. L. Teuber, (Eds.), *Handbook of sensory physiology: Vol. VIII. Perception* (pp. 97–142). New York: Springer-Verlag.

Stroop, J. (1935). Studies of interference in serial verbal reactions. *Journal of Experimental Psychology, 18*, 624–643.

Stroud, J. M. (1955). The fine structure of psychological time. In H. Quastler (Ed.), *Information theory in psychology: Problems and methods* (pp. 174–207). Glencoe, IL: Free Press.

Supra, M., Cotzin, M. E., & Dallenbach, K. M. (1944). "Facial vision": The perception of obstacles by the blind. *American Journal of Psychology, 57*, 133–183.

Svaetichin, G. (1956). Spectral response curves of single cones. *Acta Physiologica Scandinavica, 1*, 93–101.

Svaetichin, G., & MacNichol, E. F., Jr. (1958). Retinal mechanisms for achromatic vision. *Annals of the New York Academy of Sciences, 74*, 385–404.

Swarbrick, L., & Whitfield, I. C. (1972). Auditory cortical units selectively responsive to stimulus "shape." *Journal of Physiology (London), 224*, 68–69.

Swartz, P. (1953). A new method for scaling pain. *Journal of Experimental Psychology, 45*, 288–293.

Swensson, R. G. (1980). A two-stage detection model applied to skilled visual search by radiologists. *Perception & Psychophysics, 27*, 11–16.

Swets, J. A., & Kristofferson, A. B. (1970). Attention. *Annual Review of Psychology, 21*, 339–366.

Szentagothai, J. (1950). The elementary vestibulo-ocular reflex arc. *Journal of Neurophysiology, 13*, 395–407.

Tancredi, L., Lelj, F., & Temussi, P. A. (1979). Three-dimensional mapping of the bitter taste receptor site. *Chemical Senses and Flavor, 4*, 259–265.

Tart, C. (1971). *On being stoned.* Palo Alto: Science and Behavior Books.

Taub, A. (1972). Acupuncture. *Science, 178*, 9.

Taub, E., & Berman, A. J. (1968). Movement and learning in the absence of sensory feedback. In S. J. Freeman (Ed.), *The neuropsychology of spatially oriented behavior.* Homewood, IL: Dorsey.

Tedford, W. H., Warren, D. E., & Flynn, W. E. (1977). Alternation of shock aversion thresholds during menstrual cycle. *Perception & Psychophysics, 21*, 193–196.

Tees, R. C. (1974). Effect of visual deprivation on development of depth perception in the rat. *Journal of Comparative and Physiological Psychology, 86*, 300–308.

Tees, R. C. & Midgley, G. (1978). Extent of recovery of function after early sensory deprivation in the rat. *Journal of Comparative and Physiological Psychology, 92*, 768–777.

Teghtsoonian, R. (1971). On the exponents in Ste-

vens' Law and the constant in Ekman's Law. *Psychological Review, 78*, 71–80.

Teghtsoonian, R. (1975). Review of Psychophysics by S. S. Stevens. *American Journal of Psychology, 88*, 677–684.

Teller, D. Y. (1981). Color vision in infants. In R. Aslin, J. Alberts, & M. Petersen (Eds.), *Development of perception: Psychobiological perspectives: Vol. 2. The visual system* (pp. 298–312). New York: Academic Press.

Teller, D. Y., & Bornstein, M. H. (1982). Color perception. In L. Cohen & P. Salapatek (Eds.), *Handbook of infant perception.* New York: Academic Press.

Terenius, L., & Wahlstrom, A. (1975). Morphine-like ligand for opiate receptors in human CSF. *Life Sciences, 16*, 1759–1764.

Terhardt, E. (1974). Pitch, consonance and harmony. *Journal of the Acoustical Society of America, 55*, 1061–1069.

Terhardt, E. (1978). Psychoacoustic evaluation of musical sounds. *Perception & Psychophysics, 23*, 483–492.

Thomas, E., & Brown, I. (1974). Time perception and the filled duration illusion. *Perception & Psychophysics, 16*, 449–458.

Thomas, E. A. C., & Weaver, W. B. (1975). Cognitive processing and time perception. *Perception & Psychophysics, 17*, 363–367.

Thornbury, J. M., & Mistretta, C. M. (1981). Tactile sensitivity as a function of age. *Journal of Gerontology, 36*, 34–39.

Thouless, R. H. (1931). Phenomenal regression to the real object. *British Journal of Psychology, 21*, 339–359.

Timney, B., Mitchell, D. E., & Griffin, F. (1978). The development of vision in cats after extended periods of dark rearing. *Experimental Brain Research, 31*, 547–560.

Toch, H. H., & Schulte, R. (1961). Readiness to perceive violence as a result of police training. *British Journal of Psychology, 52*, 389–393.

Torgerson, W. S. (1961). Distances and ratios in psychophysical scaling. *Acta Psychologica, 19*, 201–205.

Tou, J. (1981). Feature-extraction approach to auditory pattern recognition. In D. Getty & J. Howard (Eds.), *Auditory and visual pattern recognition.* Hillsdale, NJ: Lawrence Erlbaum Associates.

Tower, S. S. (1943). Pain: Definition and properties of the unit for sensory reception. *Research Publications, Association for Research in Nervous and Mental Disease, 23,* 16–43.

Townsend, J., & Ashby, G. (1982). Experimental test of contemporary mathematical models of visual letter recognition. *Journal of Experimental Psychology: Human Perception and Performance, 8,* 834–864.

Trehub, S. (1976). The discrimination of foreign speech contrasts by infants and adults. *Child Development, 47,* 466–472.

Treisman, A. (1969). Strategies and models of selective attention. *Psychological Review, 76,* 282–299.

Treisman, A. (1982). Perceptual graphing and attention in visual search for features and for objects. *Journal of Experimental Psychology: Human Perception and Performance, 8,* 194–214.

Treisman, A., & Schmidt, H. (1982). Illusory conjunctions in the perception of objects. *Cognitive Psychology, 14,* 107–141.

Treisman, A. M., & Gelade, G. (1980). A feature-integration theory of attention. *Cognitive Psychology, 12,* 97–136.

Treisman, M. (1963). Temporal discrimination and the indifference interval: Implications for the model of an internal clock. *Psychological Monographs, 77,* 1–31 (Whole No. 576).

Treisman, M. (1976). On the use and misuse of psychophysical terms. *Psychological Review, 83,* 246–256.

Treisman, M., & Watts, T. R. (1966). Relation between signal detectability theory and the traditional procedures for measuring sensory thresholds: Estimating d' from results given by the method of constant stimuli. *Psychological Bulletin, 66,* 438–454.

Tress, K. H., & Kugler, B. T. (1979). Interocular transfer of movement after-effects in schizophrenia. *British Journal of Psychology, 70,* 389–392.

Troland, L. T. (1921). The enigma of color vision. *American Journal of Physiological Optics, 2,* 23–48.

Tronick, E. (1972). Stimulus control and the growth of the infant's effective visual field. *Perception & Psychophysics, 11,* 373–376.

Tsvetkova, L. S. (1972). *Rehabilitative training in local brain lesions.* Moscow: Pedagogika Publishing House.

Turnbull, C. (1961). Some observations regarding the experiences and behavior of the Bambuti pygmies. *American Journal of Psychology, 74,* 304–308.

Turner, P. (1968). Amphetamines and smell threshold in man. In A. Herxheimer (Ed.), *Drugs and sensory functions* (pp. 91–100). Boston: Little, Brown.

Uhlarik, J., & Johnson, R. (1978). Development of form perception in repeated brief exposures to visual stimuli. In R. Walk & L. Pick, Jr. (Eds.), *Perception and experience.* New York: Plenum.

Uhr, L., & Vossler, C. (1963). A pattern recognition program that generates, evaluates and adjusts its own operators. In E. A. Feigenbaum & J. Feldman (Eds.), *Computers and thought* (pp. 251–268). New York: McGraw-Hill.

Umezaki, H., & Morrell, F. (1970). Developmental study of photic evoked responses in premature infants. *Electroencephalography and Clinical Neurophysiology, 28,* 55–63.

Uttal, W. (1981). *A taxonomy of visual processes.* Hillsdale, NJ: Lawrence Erlbaum Associates.

Vallbo, A. B. (1981). Sensations evoked from the glabrous skin of the human hand by electrical stimulation of unitary mechano-sensitive afferents. *Brain Research, 215,* 359–363.

van Bergeijk, W. A. (1967). The evolution of vertebrate hearing. In W. D. Neff (Ed.), *Contributions to sensory physiology* (Vol. 2, pp. 1–49). New York: Academic Press.

van der Meer, H. C. (1979). Interrelation of the effects of binocular disparity and perspective cues on judgments of depth and height. *Perception & Psychophysics, 26,* 481–488.

Van Essen, D. C. (1979). Visual areas of the mammalian cerebral cortex. *Annual Review of Neurosciences, 2,* 227–263.

van Tuijl, H. (1980). Perceptual interpretation of complex line patterns. *Journal of Experimen-*

tal Psychology: Human Perception and Performance, 6, 197–221.

Verriest, G. (1974). Recent advances in the study of the acquired deficiencies of color vision. *Fondazione "Gorgio Ranchi," 24,* 1–80.

Verillo, R. T. (1975). Cutaneous sensation. In B. Scharf (Ed.), *Experimental sensory psychology* (pp. 150–184). Glenview, IL: Scott, Foresman.

Verrillo, R. T., Fraioli, A. J., & Smith, R. L. (1969). Sensation magnitude of vibrotactile stimuli. *Perception & Psychophysics, 6,* 366–372.

Vierck, C. (1978). Somatosensory system. In R. B. Masterton (Ed.), *Handbook of sensory neurobiology: Vol. I. Sensory integration* (pp. 249–310). New York: Plenum.

Vurpillot, E. (1957). L'influence de la signification du material sur l'illusion de Poggendorff. *Annee Psychologie, 57,* 339–357.

Vurpillot, E. (1968). The development of scanning strategies and their relation to visual differentiation. *Journal of Experimental Child Psychology, 6,* 632–650.

Waber, D. P. (1976). Sex differences in cognition: A function of maturation rate? *Science, 192,* 572–574.

Waber, D. P. (1977). Sex differences in mental abilities, hemispheric lateralization and rate of physical growth at adolescence. *Developmental Psychology, 13,* 29–38.

Wahl, O. F., & Sieg, D. (1980). Time estimation among schizophrenics. *Perceptual and Motor Skills, 50,* 535–541.

Wald, G. (1968). The molecular basis of visual excitation. *Nature (London), 219,* 800–807.

Wald, G., Brown, P. K., & Gibbons, I. R. (1963). The problem of visual excitation. *Journal of the Optical Society of America, 53,* 20–35.

Walk, R. D. (1962, April). Can the duckling respond adequately to depth? Paper presented at the 33rd meeting of the Eastern Psychological Association, Atlantic City.

Walk, R. D. (1964). Class demonstration of visual depth perception with the albino rabbit. *Perceptual and Motor Skills, 18,* 219–224.

Walk, R. D. (1978). Depth perception and experience. In R. Walk & H. Pick (Eds.), *Perception and Experience,* (pp. 77–103). New York: Plenum.

Walk, R. D., & Gibson, E. J. (1961). A comparative and analytic study of visual depth perception. *Psychological Monographs, 75,* 1–44.

Wall, P. D. (1979). On the relation of injury to pain. *Pain, 6,* 253–264.

Wallach, H. (1939). On sound localization. *Journal of the Acoustical Society of America, 10,* 270–274.

Wallach, H. (1948). Brightness constancy and the nature of achromatic colors. *Journal of Experimental Psychology, 38,* 310–324.

Wallach, H. (1972a). The perception of motion. In R. Held & W. Richards (Eds.) *Perception: Mechanisms and models: Readings from Scientific American* (pp. 310–315). San Francisco: Freeman. (Originally published in *Scientific American,* 1959)

Wallach, H. (1972b). The perception of neutral colors. In R. Held & W. Richards (Eds.), *Perception: Mechanisms and models: Readings from Scientific American* (pp. 278–285). San Francisco: Freeman. (Originally published in *Scientific American,* 1963)

Wallach, H., Newman, E. B., & Rosenzweig, M. R. (1949). The precedence effect in sound localization. *American Journal of Psychology, 62,* 315–336.

Wallingford, E. G., Jr. (1972). A visual pattern recognizing computer program based on neurophysiological data. *Behavioral Science, 17,* 241–248.

Walls, G. L. (1951). A theory of ocular dominance. *AMA Archives of Ophthalmology, 45,* 387–412.

Walls, G. L. (1963). *The vertebrate eye and its adaptive radiation.* New York: Hafner.

Walley, A., Pisoni, D., & Aslin, R. (1981). The role of early experience in the development of speech perception. In R. Aslin, J. Alberts, & M. Petersen (Eds.), *Development of perception: Psychobiological perspectives: Vol. 1. Audition, somatic perceptions, and the chemical senses* (pp. 219–256). New York: Academic Press.

Walsh, D. A. (1982). The development of visual information processes in adulthood. In R. Sekuler, D. Kline, & K. Dismukes (Eds.), *Aging and human visual function.* New York: Alan R. Liss.

Ward, L. M. (1971). Some psychophysical properties

of category judgments and magnitude estimations. Doctoral dissertation, Duke University.

Ward, L. M. (1972). Category judgments of loudness in the absence of an experimenter-induced identification function: Sequential effects and power function fit. *Journal of Experimental Psychology, 94,* 179–184.

Ward, L. M. (1973). Repeated magnitude estimations with a variable standard: Sequential effects and other properties. *Perception & Psychophysics, 13,* 193–200.

Ward, L. M. (1974). Power functions for category judgments of duration and line length. *Perceptual and Motor Skills, 38,* 1182.

Ward, L. M. (1975). Sequential dependencies and response range in cross-modality matches of duration to loudness. *Perception & Psychophysics, 18,* 217–223.

Ward, L. M. (1979). Stimulus information and sequential dependencies in magnitude estimation and cross-modality matching. *Journal of Experimental Psychology: Human Perception and Performance, 5,* 444–459.

Ward, L. M. (1982a). Mixed-modality psychophysical scaling: Sequential dependencies and other properties. *Perception & Psychophysics, 31,* 53–62.

Ward, L. M. (1982b). Determinants of attention to local and global features of visual forms. *Journal of Experimental Psychology: Human Perception and Performance, 8,* 562–581.

Ward, L. M., & Coren, S. (1976). The effect of optically-induced blur on the magnitude of the Mueller-Lyer illusion. *Bulletin of the Psychonomic Society, 7,* 483–484.

Ward, L. M., Porac, C., Coren, S., & Girgus, J. S. (1977). The case for misapplied constancy scaling: Depth associations elicited by illusion configurations. *American Journal of Psychology, 90,* 609–620.

Ward, W. D. (1970). Musical perception. In J. V. Tobias (Ed.), *Foundations of modern auditory theory* (Vol. 1, pp. 407–447). New York: Academic Press.

Ware, C. (1981). Subjective contours independent of subjective brightness. *Perception & Psychophysics, 29,* 500–504.

Warren, R. M. (1970). Perceptual restoration of missing speech sounds. *Science, 167,* 392–393.

Warren, R. M., Obusek, C. J., Farmer, R. M., & Warren, R. P. (1969). Auditory sequence: Confusion of patterns other than speech or music. *Science, 164,* 586–587.

Watanabe, T., & Katsuki, Y. (1974). Response patterns of single auditory neurons of the cat to species-specific vocalization. *Japanese Journal of Physiology, 24,* 135–155.

Watkins, L. R., & Mayer, D. J. (1982). Organization of endogenous opiate and nonopiate pain control systems. *Science, 216,* 1185–1192.

Weale, R. A. (1963). *The aging eye.* London: Lewis.

Weale, R. A. (1979). Discoverers of Mach-bands. *Investigative Ophthalmology, and Visual Sciences, 18,* 652–654.

Weber, E. H. (1834). *De pulsu, resorptione, auditu et tactu: Annotationes anatomicae et physiologicae.* Leipzig: Koehler.

Webster, W. R., & Atkin, L. M. (1975). Central auditory processing. In M. S. Gazzaniga & C. Blakemore (Eds.), *Handbook of psychobiology* (pp. 325–364). New York: Academic Press.

Weil, A. T., Zinberg, E., & Nelson, J. N. (1968). Clinical and psychological effects of marijuana in man. *Science, 162,* 1234–1242.

Weinstein, A. D., Goldstone, S., & Boardman, W. K. (1958). The effects of recent and remote frames of reference on temporal judgments of schizophrenic patients. *Journal of Abnormal Psychology, 57,* 241–244.

Weinstein, E. A., Cole, M., Mitchell, M. S., & Lyerly, O. G. (1964). Anosognosia and aphasia. *Archives of Neurology, 10,* 376–386.

Weinstein, S. (1968). Intensive and extensive aspects of tactile sensitivity as a function of body part, sex, and laterality. In D. R. Kenshalo (Ed.), *The skin senses* (pp. 195–218). Springfield, IL: Thomas.

Weinstein, S., & Sersen, E. A. (1961). Tactual sensitivity as a function of handedness and laterality. *Journal of Comparative and Physiological Psychology, 54,* 665–669.

Weisstein, N. A. (1968). Rashevsky-Landahl neural net: Simulation of metacontrast. *Psychological Review, 75,* 494–521.

Weisstein, N. A. (1980). Tutorial: The joy of Fourier analysis. In C. S. Harris (Ed.), *Visual coding and adaptability* (pp. 365–380). Hillsdale, NJ: Lawrence Erlbaum Associates.

Weisstein, N., & Harris, C. (1974). Visual detection of line segments: An object superiority effect. *Science, 186,* 752–755.

Weisstein, N., Harris, C., Berbaum, K., Tangney, J., & Williams, A. (1977). Contrast reduction by small localized stimuli: Extensive spatial spread of above-threshold orientation-selective masking. *Vision Research, 17,* 341–350.

Weisstein, N., Matthews, M., & Berbaum, K. (1974, November). Illusory contours can mask real contours. Paper presented at the meetings of the Psychonomic Society, Boston.

Weisstein, N., Ozog, G., & Szoc, R. (1975). A comparison and elaboration of two models of metacontrast. *Psychological Review, 82,* 325–343.

Welch, R. B. (1969). Adaptation to prism-displaced vision: The importance of target pointing. *Perception & Psychophysics, 5,* 305–309.

Welch, R. B. (1971). Prism adaptation: The "target pointing effect" as a function of exposure trials. *Perception & Psychophysics, 5,* 102–104.

Welch, R. (1978). *Perceptual modification, adapting to altered sensory environments.* New York: Academic Press.

Welford, A. T. (1980). *Reaction times.* London: Academic Press.

Werker, J., Gilbert, J., Humphrey, K., & Tees, R. (1981). Developmental aspects of cross-language speech perception. *Child Development, 52,* 349–355.

Werner, H. (1935). Studies on contour. *American Journal of Psychology, 47,* 40–64.

Werner, J. S. (1979). Developmental change in scotopic sensitivity and the absorption spectrum of the human ocular media. Doctoral dissertation, Brown University.

Wertheimer, M. (1912). Experimentelle Studien uber das Sehen von Bewegung. *Zeitschrift fur Psychologie, 61,* 161–265.

Wertheimer, M. (1958). Principles of perceptual organization. Abridged translation by M. Wertheimer. In D. S. Beardslee & M. Wertheimer (Eds.), *Readings in perception* (pp. 115–137). Princeton, NJ: Van Nostrand-Reinhold. Original work published 1923, *Psychologishe Forschung, 41,* 301–350.

Wertheimer, M. (1961). Psychomotor coordination of auditory and visual space at birth. *Science, 134,* 1692.

Wever, E. G. (1970). *Theory of hearing.* New York: Wiley.

White, B. L. (1971). *Human infants.* Englewood Cliffs, NJ: Prentice-Hall.

White, B. L. & Held, R. (1966). Plasticity of sensorimotor development in the human infant. In J. Rosenblith and W. Allinsmith (Eds.), *The causes of behavior.* Boston: Allyn and Bacon.

White, B. W., Saunders, F. A., Scadden, L., Bach-y-Rita, P., & Collins, C. C. (1970). Seeing with the skin. *Perception & Psychophysics, 7,* 23–27.

White, C. (1963). Temporal numerosity and the psychological unit of duration. *Psychological Monographs, 77,* 1–37 (Whole No. 575).

White, C. W., Lockhead, G. R., & Evans, N. J. (1977). Multidimensional scaling of subjective colors by color-blind observers. *Perception & Psychophysics, 21,* 522–526.

White, C. W., & Montgomery, D. A. (1976). Memory colours in afterimages: A bicentennial demonstration. *Perception & Psychophysics, 19,* 371–374.

Whitfield, I. C. (1968). The organization of the auditory pathways. *Journal of Sound and Vibration Research, 8,* 108–117.

Whitfield, I. C. (1978). The neural code. In E. C. Carterette & M. P. Friedman, (Eds.), *Handbook of perception: Vol. IV. Hearing* (pp. 163–183). New York: Academic Press.

Whitfield, I. C. (1980). Auditory cortex and the pitch of complex tones. *Journal of the Acoustical Society of America, 67,* 644–647.

Whitfield, I. C., & Evans, E. F. (1965). Responses of auditory cortical neurons to stimuli of changing frequency. *Journal of Neurophysiology, 28,* 655–672.

Whitsel, B. L., Dreyer, D. A., Hollins, M., & Young, M. G. (1979). The coding of direction of tactile stimulus movement: Correlative psychophysical and electrophysiological data. In D. R. Kenshalo (Ed.), *Sensory functions of the skin of humans* (pp. 79–108). New York: Plenum.

Whorf, B. L. (1956). Science and linguistics. In J. B. Carroll (Ed.), *Language, thought and reality:*

Selected writings of Benjamin Lee Whorf. Cambridge, MA: MIT Press.

Whytt, R. (1751). *An essay on the vital and other involuntary motions of animals*. Edinburgh: Balfour & Neill.

Wickens, C. D. (1979). Measures of workload, stress and secondary tasks. In N. Moray (Ed.), *Mental workload: Theory and measurement* (pp. 79–100). New York: Plenum.

Wickens, C. D. (1980). The structure of attentional resources. In R. S. Nickerson (Ed.), *Attention and performance VIII*, (pp. 239–257). Hillsdale, NJ: Lawrence Erlbaum Associates.

Wiener, N. (1961). *Cybernetics*. (2nd ed.). Cambridge, MA: MIT Press.

Wier, C. C., Jesteadt, W., & Green, D. M. (1977). Frequency discrimination as a function of frequency and sensation level. *Journal of the Acoustical Society of America, 61,* 178–184.

Wiesel, T. N., & Hubel, D. H. (1966). Spatial and chromatic interactions in the lateral geniculate body of the rhesus monkey. *Journal of Neurophysiology, 29,* 1115–1156.

Willer, J. C., Dehen, H., & Cambier, J. (1981). Stress-induced analgesia in humans: Endogenous opioids and naloxone-reversible depression of pain reflexes. *Science, 212,* 689–690.

Williams, D. R., MacLeod, D. I. A., & Hayhoe, M. M. (1981). Foveal tritanopia. *Vision Research, 21,* 1341–1356.

Williams, J. M. (1979). Distortions of vision and pain: Two functional facets of D-Lysergic diethylamide. *Perceptual and Motor Skills, 49,* 499–528.

Williams, M. (1970). *Brain damage and the mind*. London: Penguin Books.

Wilson, E. O. (1971). *The insect societies*. Cambridge, MA: Harvard University Press.

Wilson, J. R., DeFries, J. C., McClearn, G. C., Vandenberg, S. G., Johnson, R. C., & Rashad, M. N. (1975). Cognitive abilities: Use of family data as a control to assess sex and age differences in two ethnic groups. *International Journal of Aging and Human Development, 6,* 261–275.

Wilson, K. G., & Stelmack, R. M. (1982). Power functions of loudness magnitude estimations and auditory brainstem evoked responses. *Perception & Psychophysics, 31,* 561–565.

Wilson, M. (1957). Effects of circumscribed cortical lesions upon somesthetic and visual discrimination in the monkey. *Journal of Comparative and Physiological Psychology, 50,* 630–635.

Witkin, H. A., & Berry, J. W. (1975). Psychological differentiation in cross-cultural perspective. *Journal of Cross-Cultural Psychology, 6,* 4–87.

Wolff, H. G., & Goodell, B. S. (1943). The relation of attitude and suggestion to the perception of and reaction to pain. *Research Publications, Association for Research in Nervous and Mental Disease, 23,* 434–448.

Womersley, M. (1977). A context effect in feature detection with application of signal detection methodology. *Perception & Psychophysics, 21,* 88–92.

Wong, C., & Weisstein, N. (1982). A new perceptual context-superiority effect: Line segments are more visible against a figure than against a ground. *Science, 218,* 587–589.

Woodrow, H. (1951). Time perception. In S. S. Stevens (Ed.), *Handbook of experimental psychology* (pp. 1224–1236). New York: Wiley.

Woolard, H. H., Weddell, G., & Harpman, J. A. (1940). Observations of the neuro-historical basis of cutaneous pain. *Journal of Anatomy, 74,* 413–440.

Worchel, P., & Dallenbach, K. M. (1947). "Facial vision": Perception of obstacles by the deaf-blind. *American Journal of Psychology, 60,* 502–553.

Wright, N. H. (1964). Temporal summation and backward masking. *Journal of the Acoustical Society of America, 36,* 927–932.

Wright, R. H. (1977). Odor and molecular vibration: Neural coding of olfactory information. *Journal of Theoretical Biology, 64,* 473–502.

Wright, R. H. (1978a). Specific anosmia: A clue to the olfactory code or to something much more important? *Chemical Senses and Flavor, 3,* 235–239.

Wright, R. H. (1978b). The perception of odor intensity: Physics or psychophysics? *Chemical Senses and Flavor, 3,* 73–79.

Wright, R. H. (1978c). The perception of odor intensity: Physics or psychophysics II. *Chemical Senses and Flavor, 3*, 241–245.

Wright, R. H. (1982). *The sense of smell.* Boca Raton, FL: CRC Press.

Wright, R. H., & Burgess, R. E. (1975). Molecular coding of olfactory specificity. *Canadian Journal of Zoology, 53*, 1247–1253.

Wright, W. D. A re-determination of the trichromatic mixture data. *Medical Research Council (Great Britain), Special Report Series*, (SRS-139), 1–38.

Wurtz, R. H. (1969). Comparison of eye movements and stimulus movements on striate cortex neurones of the monkey. *Journal of Neurophysiology, 32*, 987–994.

Wurtz, R. H. (1976). Extra retinal influences on the primitive visual system. In R. A. Monty & J. W. Senders (Eds.), *Eye movements and psychological processes* (pp. 231–244). Hillsdale, NJ: Lawrence Erlbaum Associates.

Wurtz, R. H., & Goldberg, M. E. (1971). Superior colliculus cell responses related to eye movements in awake monkeys. *Science, 171*, 82–84.

Wyburn, G. M., Pickford, R. W., & Hirst, R. J. (1964). *Human senses and perception.* Toronto: University of Toronto Press.

Wyszecki, G., & Stiles, W. S. (1967). *Color science: Concepts and methods, quantitative data and formulas.* New York: Wiley.

Yamamoto, T., Yayama, N., & Kawamura, Y. (1981). Central processing of taste perception. In Y. Katsuki, R. Norgren, & M. Sato (Eds.), *Brain mechanisms of sensation* (pp. 197–208). New York: Wiley.

Yarbus, A. L. (1967). *Eye movements and vision.* New York: Plenum.

Yarmey, A. (1979). *The psychology of eyewitness testimony.* New York: The Free Press.

Yen, W. (1975). Sex-linked major gene influence on selected types of spatial performance. *Behavior Genetics, 5*, 281–298.

Yerkes, R. M., & Dodson, J. D. (1908). The relation of strength of stimulus to rapidity of habit formation. *Journal of Comparative Neurology and Psychology, 18*, 459–482.

Yin, R. K. (1970). Face recognition by brain injured patients—a dissociable ability. *Neuropsychologia, 8*, 395.

Yodogawa, E. (1982). Symmetropy, an entropy-like measure of visual symmetry. *Perception & Psychophysics, 32*, 230–240.

Yonas, A. (1981). Infants' response to optical information for collision. In R. N. Aslin, J. R. Alberts, & M. R. Peterson (Eds.), *Development of perception* (pp. 313–334). New York: Academic Press.

Yonas, A., Cleaves, W., & Pettersen, L. (1978). Development of sensitivity to pictorial depth. *Science, 200*, 77–79.

Yonas, A., Goldsmith, L. T., & Hallstrom, J. (1978). Development of sensitivity to information provided by cast shadows in pictures. *Perception, 7*, 333–341.

Yonas, A., & Pick, H. L. (1975). An approach to the study of infant perception. In L. B. Cohen & P. Salapatek (Eds.), *Infant perception: From sensation to cognition: Vol. 2. Perception of space and sound* (pp. 3–31). New York: Academic Press.

Young, L. R. (1971). Pursuit eye tracking movements. In P. Bach-y-Rita, C. C. Collins, & J. E. Hyde, (Eds.), *The control of eye movements* (pp. 429–443). New York: Academic Press.

Young, R. A. (1977). Some observations on temporal coding of color vision: Psychophysical results. *Vision Research, 17*, 957–965.

Young, R. S. L., Fishman, G. A., & Chen, F. (1980, May). Traumatically acquired color vision defect. *Investigative Ophthalmology and Visual Sciences, 19*, 545–549.

Yuille, J. (1983). Research and teaching with police: A Canadian example. *International Review of Applied Psychology.*

Zaporozhets, A. V. (1965). The development of perception in the preschool child. *Monographs of the Society for Research in Child Development, 30*, 82–101.

Zeigler, H. P., & Leibowitz, H. (1957). Apparent visual size as a function of distance for children and adults. *American Journal of Psychology, 70*, 106–109.

Zigler, M. J. (1932). Pressure adaptation time: A function of intensity and extensity. *American Journal of Psychology, 44*, 709–720.

Zotterman, Y. (1959). Thermal sensations. In J. Fields,

H. W. Magoun, & V. E. Hall (Eds.), *Handbook of Physiology: Section 1: Neurophysiology, 1*, 431–458.

Zucker, I., Wade, G., & Ziegler, R. (1972). Sexual and hormonal influences on eating, taste preferences, and body weight of hamsters. *Physiology and Behavior, 8*, 101–111.

Zuidema, P., Gresnigt, A. M., Bouman, M. A., & Koenderink, J. J. (1978). A quanta coincidence model for absolute threshold vision incorporating deviations from Ricco's Law. *Vision Research, 18*, 1685–1689.

Zurek, P. M. (1980). The precedence effect and its possible role in the avoidance of interaural ambiguities. *Journal of the Acoustical Society of America, 67*, 952–964.

Zwicker, E. (1958). Uber psychologische und methodosche Grundlagen der Lautheit. *Acustica, 8*, 237–258.

Zwislocki, J. J. (1978). Masking: Experimental and theoretical aspects of simultaneous, forward, backward, and central masking. In E. C. Carterette & M. P. Friedman (Eds.), *Handbook of Perception: Vol. IV. Hearing* (pp. 283–336). New York: Academic Press.

Zwislocki, J. J., Damianopoulos, E. N., Buining, E., & Glantz, J. (1967). Central masking: Some steady-state and transient effects. *Perception & Psychophysics, 2*, 59–64.

Zwislocki, J. J., & Goodman, D. A. (1980). Absolute scaling of sensory magnitudes: A validation. *Perception & Psychophysics, 28*, 28–38.

Author index

Subject index